Paul: Apostle to the Gentiles

——— Paul ———
Apostle to the Gentiles

Jürgen Becker

Translated by O. C. Dean, Jr.

Westminster/John Knox Press
Louisville, Kentucky

English translation © 1993 Westminster/John Knox Press

Translated from the German *Paulus: Der Apostel der Völker,* © 1989 J. C. B. Mohr (Paul Siebeck), Tübingen.

Book design by Drew Stevens

First edition

Published by Westminster/John Knox Press
Louisville, Kentucky

This book is printed on acid-free paper that meets the American National Standards Institute Z39.48 standard. ∞

PRINTED IN THE UNITED STATES OF AMERICA
9 8 7 6 5 4 3 2 1

Library of Congress Cataloging-in-Publication Data

Becker, Jürgen, 1934–
  [Paulus. English]
  Paul : apostle to the Gentiles / Jürgen Becker ; translated by
O. C. Dean, Jr. — 1st ed.
       p.   cm.
  Translation of: Paulus.
  Includes bibliographical references and index.
  ISBN 0-664-21930-6 (hb. : acid-free)

  1. Paul, the Apostle, Saint. 2. Christian Saints—Turkey—Tarsus—
Biography. 3. Tarsus (Turkey)—Biography. 4. Bible. N.T.
Epistles of Paul—Criticism, interpretation, etc. I. Title.
BS2506.B4213   1993
225.9'2—dc20
[B]   92-28776

Contents

Foreword to the English Edition

This magisterial work by Jürgen Becker is destined to become a standard work on the apostle Paul, perhaps dislodging the classic treatment of Paul by Günther Bornkamm. The magnitude, depth, and precision of this study will come as a pleasant surprise to many English-language students of Paul who are perhaps unaware of Becker's extensive, but untranslated, works in New Testament studies. Therefore a few words about the author are in order before more specific remarks about this book.

In an academic environment well known for its intensity and productiveness, Becker stands among the most prolific and most respected of German New Testament scholars. Born in 1934, Becker undertook theological studies in Hamburg and Heidelberg, eventually doing research that led to an inaugural dissertation in 1961 on the concepts of salvation and sin in the Dead Sea Scrolls and the New Testament. From 1961 to 1963 he served as a curate and assistant minister in Hamburg before returning to full-time academic work. Becker held his first academic posts from 1963 to 1968 in Heidelberg and Bochum, and during this period he completed a dissertation on the origins of the *Testaments of the Twelve Patriarchs* which qualified him for a university professorship. In 1969 Becker took a chair in New Testament and Judaic studies at Christian-Albrechts University in Kiel, which he occupies today. In addition to the books already identified, Becker has produced numerous scholarly articles, and he has published book-length studies on such diverse topics as the resurrection of the dead in early Christianity, hermeneutics, exegesis and theology, John the Baptist and Jesus of Nazareth, Luther's interpretation of scripture, the future and hope, and commentaries on Galatians and the Gospel According to John. This book on Paul is Becker's most recent major work.

Paul: Apostle to the Gentiles is a study that takes Paul seriously as a human being and as a person of profound religious conviction. This interpretation follows Paul through the course of his life as it views him in the concrete context of his own first-century world. The treatment, as will be evident to all who read it, is comprehensive, thorough, and without pedantry. The best of traditional and contemporary

Pauline studies informs this work, but Becker's study is no mere synthesis of the opinions of others. He adds his own fresh approach to all that he has learned from others and draws conclusions that are original without being idiosyncratic. From beginning to end, this work is careful and imaginative; yet at a glance the detailed nature of the study may belie its boldness. Becker is aware of the problems of interpretation, he goes to all lengths to assemble the evidence necessary for drawing sound conclusions, and he resists both twisting the evidence and stretching it to fit his theory. Indeed, this study is both critical and conservative in the best sense of both words, and it is astonishingly free from the tendency of much of Pauline studies, namely, distorting abstraction.

Gone from this study is an earlier tendency in scholarship to give an exacting reconstruction of the problems and opponents that Paul faced on the mission field in order to interpret the texts in relation to those reconstructions. Yet Becker has not abandoned diligent examination of the information available concerning the situations that Paul confronted. Instead, he recognizes that in the letters Paul views both difficulties and adversaries through lenses that filter, color, and even deliberately distort in order to serve the apostle's arguments. Paul's rhetoric was far from neutral, as Becker points out: "[Paul] is never led by the general, comprehensive question, How can we get all Christian movements to a dialogue at the conference table? Rather, he asks the limited and special question, How do I keep the churches I founded under the gospel as I understand it?" Becker knows and shows that one can comprehend the content of the letters only through recognizing the shape and the function of Paul's statements.

Thus Becker moves carefully to study the person, world, work, letters, and thought of Paul. After a detailed consideration of the chronology of Paul's life, this study works diligently through the evidence available concerning the Hellenistic world in which Paul, Judaism, and early Christianity existed. With the course of Paul's life sketched in all possible detail, and with a clear comprehension of Paul's world, Becker examines the letters sequentially in the context of Paul's life and world. Typically, the reader learns of the city to which Paul wrote, of the situation Paul faced there, of the literary integrity of the letter, of its structure and line of argument; and then one follows Becker through a detailed interpretation of the letter that seeks to answer all necessary historical and theological questions. Moreover, through his work Becker strives to read each letter for itself. For example, the church in Thessalonica was not the church in Rome, and the members of the Macedonian congregation did not know the later, larger letter to Rome;

so, an initial attempt to understand 1 Thessalonians should read that letter only in relation to the position of its writing in Paul's life and the position of the particular church both in the world and in the context of Paul's ministry. Quick recourse to Romans for the interpretation of 1 Thessalonians may distort understanding; yet, to Becker's credit, the comparison of the letters is put on hold, not totally abandoned.

Becker argues that Paul's theology was far from static, so that the letters show that through the course of his life there were significant developments in his thinking. Yet there were also basic convictions that remained steadily from beginning to end. Becker brings to life a Paul who was rich in ideas, conceptually lively, and able to change because he persistently maintained his theological starting point. As Becker describes this process:

> Paul speaks out of the experience of his call and especially out of the experience gained by him and the churches through the effect of the gospel on the worldwide mission field. Thus the apostle expresses himself on the basis of the new being effected by the Spirit, the common experience of all Christians with the gospel that changes people. . . . In this sense the theology of Paul is the theology of experience under the influence of the gospel and of the Spirit connected with it, . . . [so that] if Paul designs his theological statements on the basis of his experience of the gospel, then the content of the gospel must consequently be the measure and criterion of everything—in short, for the interpretation of all reality.

As Becker traces Paul's work and writings one finds three prominent periods in the apostle's thought. These periods may be thought of as levels or stages of comprehension and presentation. First, the earliest period from which we have Paul's letters is the time of his initial residence in Corinth. Here Paul demonstrates the influence of both his background in Hellenistic Judaism and his earlier life and work in the church at Antioch. Paul presents a *theology of election*, God's eschatological election of grace accomplished by the calling of the gospel. First Thessalonians exemplifies this stage. Second, the next period is that of Paul's time in Ephesus. From this era come the Corinthian correspondence, Philemon, and a portion of canonical Philippians (1:1–3:1; 4:1–7, 10–23), all of which articulate a *theology of the cross* concerned with God's election of the church in the gospel and God's relationship with the world. Paul argues that, contrary to human expectation, God chooses what is weak and destroys what is strong, and God makes this known through the crucified One. In this theology is a new perception of God and a new evaluation of humanity and the world. Third, in the final period of Paul's theological development and presentation Becker focuses on Galatians, the remainder of Philippians (3:2–21; 4:8–9), and Romans. Here one finds Paul's *theology of justifica-tion*. In distinction to the previously examined letters, now Paul's writ-ings are characterized by an intense focus on "righteousness" and "being right-wised (or, justified)." Statements about election and the cross are still present, but they occur in relation to more prominent declarations concerning God's sovereign gracious eschatological judg-ment of creation. Paul argues that God's election and work in Christ mean the transformation of life in the power of the Spirit into an exis-tence characterized by faith, hope, and love.

In the German original, only after 394 pages of careful historical and exegetical work does Becker offer a 113-page treatment of the main features of Pauline theology. Thus, close scrutiny of the letters in their original contexts and a hard-won perception of the growth of the apos-tle's theology lead to a fresh statement of the main lines of Paul's thinking and teaching. All who work behind and alongside Becker through the course of this excellent study will emerge with a profound sense of gratitude for his guidance, and they will certainly have a greater understanding of the person, life, work, and thought of Paul, the apostle to the Gentiles, than was previously available to them.

Marion L. Soards

Professor of New Testament Studies
Louisville Presbyterian Theological Seminary

Foreword

The following presentation of Paul is the result of many years of Pauline research, which has had three foci: the study of the literature, discussions with university students, and my own reflection on the problems of the Pauline letters. Thus the book cannot deny its scholarly heritage. Yet it is not written in such a way that only New Testament exegetes will reach for it. Rather, its aim is to build bridges from the guild of exegetes to persons who have a general interest in Paul. There are two reasons for this: It will do exegesis no good if it persists as an internal technical dialogue, and it will do our world no good if Paul falls into oblivion.

To achieve this goal, the presentation has been designed so as to stress broad areas as much as possible, while the highly specialized realm of secondary literature is much less emphasized. Further, in order to keep the vast literature on Paul from flowing into a boundless footnote apparatus that would scare readers away and probably be of full advantage to only a few readers, it was finally decided, after lengthy consideration, to leave out the scholarly apparatus altogether. Since I trust my fellow scholars to observe where I have learned from others, and from them in particular, or where I am of a different opinion, I have forgone annotations of this sort. It was more important to me to present the reader with an overall picture of Paul that can be read as a generally understandable scholarly treatment.

Therefore, after long hesitation I have also forgone a special bibliography. Since, however, the book seeks critical readers who will make comparisons with other presentations, let me point out that there are good bibliographies of the literature on Paul. Among them I would like to mention the following:

Bornkamm, G. "Paulus." In *Die Religion in Geschichte und Gegenwart.* 3rd ed. (1961), 5:166ff.
Bultmann, R. "Zur Geschichte der Paulus-Forschung." In *Das Paulusbild in der neueren Forschung,* Wege der Forschung 24 (1964), 304ff.

————. *Theologie des Neuen Testaments.* 9th ed., revised and expanded by O. Merk (1984).

Hübner, H. "Paulusforschung seit 1945: Ein kritischer Literaturbericht." In *Aufstieg und Niedergang der römischen Welt* II 25.4 (1987), 2649ff.

Lüdemann, G. *Paulus, der Heidenapostel,* vol. 1: Studien zur Chronologie (1980).

Merk, O. "Paulus–Forschung 1936–1985." In *Theologische Rundschau* 53 (1988): 1ff.

Naturally the book seeks not only readers who will refer to other presentations of Paul but, above all, those who will read the Pauline letters themselves. Therefore there are repeated references to the letters of the apostle, along with indications of other sources. All references are made according to the usual abbreviations. Regarding their use, the list of abbreviations at the end of the work will be helpful.

In closing I would like to express my thanks to those who have helped in the completion of this work. With my assistant, Dr. U. Mell, I have had repeated discussions of individual problems. Ms. H. Meyer has, as often before, been of great service in the production of the manuscript. My wife, Ms. Meyer, and Ms. L. Müller-Busse have had a large part in the tedious work of proofreading. Finally, I am grateful to the publishers for their willing cooperation.

Jürgen Becker

Kiel
Spring 1989

Introduction

It is a good sign when interest in Paul leads to a blossoming of Pauline literature, as it has recently. For Paul belongs to Christianity's fundamental beginnings. Here he must be regarded as the very symbol of the Gentile Christianity of the first early Christian generation. At the same time he is, without doubt, the most significant theologian in all of early Christianity. Thus it is no wonder that he has left deep and lasting impressions in the history of Christianity even to the present time. His influence can scarcely be overestimated.

What constitutes the historical significance of the apostle? In answer to that question we will point to four things. First is the turning point in his personal life that forced him to "take every thought captive to obey Christ" (2 Cor. 10:5; cf. Phil. 3:8). Second, he understood how to take the missionary-ecclesiastical experience in the polarity of gospel and Spirit on the one hand and faith, love, and hope on the other and work it up in such a fundamental theological way that his communications to the churches were obviously regarded as exemplary. Moreover, in the great opposition of Jewish and Gentile Christianity that shaped the first early Christian generation, Paul—with all his unbending creative power and the worldwide perspective in which he felt at home—represented so consistently the side of Gentile Christianity that he became the unrivaled "apostle to the Gentiles" (Rom. 11:13), which, by the way, is the last of his self-designations (besides Rom. 15:16) to come down to us. This third point is related to the last one: Paul worked at a crossroads in the history of Christianity. At stake was the question whether Christianity was to understand itself as before, as a part of Judaism, or whether in a new way, under the influence of and in opposition to Judaism, it had to show its independence. With his theology and mission Paul adopted the latter standpoint so thoroughly—even though he was born a Jew—that this way prevailed. In other words, the future of Christianity took shape in his person, without his consciously knowing where what he had begun would come out.

This place of the apostle in history has meant that he has occasionally been regarded as the actual founder of Christianity. Such an evaluation, however, does justice neither to Paul's self-understanding nor to the story of Jesus in the Gentile-Christian churches. Paul always understood himself as a servant of Jesus Christ and an apostle of his Lord, as we learn right away just from a look at the epistolary openings of his correspondence. Moreover, all of those at the Apostolic Council in Jerusalem (Gal. 2:1ff.; Acts 15) agreed that the Antiochene-Pauline way was a legitimate historical expression of the one faith going back to Jesus of Nazareth. The church was established at Easter. It already existed when Paul found it and at first became its persecutor.

With quite a variety of motives, others today want to bind Paul more closely to Judaism than is traditionally done, above all in Protestant exegesis. There are the theologians who look at Paul from the standpoint of the holocaust and find, especially in Romans 9–11, a Pauline position that shows Israel its own way to God. Naturally this then thoroughly colors one's interpretation of Paul's understanding of salvation. But it does not make sense that he should provide for unbelieving Israel a special way of salvation, while at the beginning of the same letter he includes all Jews as sinners in the godlessness of the nations and can recommend only one thing to all sinners without exception: justification by faith in Jesus Christ. There are others who would like to see Paul's categories for interpreting tradition-historical relationships and reality in (almost) unbroken continuity with Judaism. Particular foci here are the apostle's understanding of the law and his doctrine of salvation oriented toward the Jewish concept of atonement. One asks: Can Paul have so misrepresented the Judaism he knew that he imputed to it a "works righteousness" oriented toward the law? However one might trace the Jewish and Pauline understandings of the law, one thing is certain: Paul does not ask what he could expect of Judaism and how he might do justice to its self-understanding; rather, he requalifies everything from the standpoint of Christ and intends to develop accordingly the knowledge that lies in Christ. The primary test question in the Pauline doctrine of salvation must be analogous to this, namely, How does the apostle describe the salvation in Christ offered in the gospel and its life-changing effect on people? How appropriate or central here is, for example, a concept of atonement?

It is quite natural that Paul should be brought to bear in contemporary Christianity in many actualized and systematized ways. That in itself is a good sign and a way of dealing with the apostle that should be encouraged. But the appropriated Paul and the historical Paul cannot be mutually exclusive. The latter must always correct the former. Because it is so uncommonly difficult to do justice to historical reality, and everything historical is all too quickly picked over and instrumentalized, the following work on Paul seeks to emphasize the Paul of history long past. No age escapes partiality and egocentricity, but it may not find its measure and goal in such self-reflection. It must again and again learn to orient itself toward and rub up against what is historically distant and foreign.

Naturally there is no royal pathway for such an access to history. Yet there are aids for the perception of another way and for the avoidance of premature acceptance. Today, of course, these include the social sciences, which help to describe concrete historical relationships. Restricting oneself to issues in the history of ideas is no longer responsible today. Therefore it is now only a question of how to employ the social sciences and how to regard their connection with the dimension of intellectual history. Nonetheless we shall not discuss that now. Rather, it is a question of another aid of a specifically historical kind to which we will give our attention: we mean the only objective way of ordering history, namely, the chronological way.

In my opinion, respect for the historical sequence of events favors a presentation that lets the historical order come into play. That means concretely that Paul should be presented in thoroughgoing developmental-historical fashion, to the extent that it is at all permitted by the sources. That means, among other things, that a Pauline letter will be interpreted for itself in its historical location. The Letter to the Romans is not a tacitly predetermined coordinate system into which all other utterances of the apostle are to be placed. The Christian community in Thessalonica did not know the Letter to the Romans but in 1 Thessalonians had received a letter that—presupposing a basically successful dialogue on the level of author and addressee—could be understood by that community fully and totally. Also, Paul did not have Romans completed in his mind when he wrote 1 Thessalonians.

If we consistently keep the chronological and dialogical position of a letter in view, we will make observations indicating that from his calling until his entry into Rome as a prisoner Paul did not present the same unchanged theology. Rather, with all constancy in a few crucial basic issues, he went through a development that was influenced by his own experiences, by interaction with his churches, and by early Christian history in general. This is what it means to understand Paul; looking into the beginnings of his theology and into its development means to recognize that the apostle thinks through and understands anew, that he changes theological emphasis, and that he expands and carries to new horizons basic decisions and solutions to problems. At his calling the apostle did not simply receive the content of Romans as knowledge to take with him on his way, however surely basic assertions of his theology are rooted in his conversion experience. Anyone who observes the extent to which Paul changes will regain a truly historical person and say farewell to a doctrinal formation that was final and already finished in the beginning. Paul the Christian worked as an apostle about thirty years after his call. In the context of the dynamic of early Christian history, that is a long and substantial time. One should assume all the more that even Paul himself, within certain limits, learned to understand himself and the Christian message anew.

Anyone who places the accent on a historical mode of presentation will awaken expectations that are harbored in connection with the description of the apostle's opponents. Is it not precisely the detective-like snooping out of the opponents' positions that aids in comprehending the historical dialogue? In fact, for this reason the time after the Second World War was also the time of the great, rather detailed sketches of the apostle's opponents, and in this it was again and again primarily—if not exclusively—Paul's Corinthian correspondence that stood at the center of interest. One often had the impression—if an exaggeration is permitted—that one could, for example, reconstruct the Corinthian theology in a more detailed way and understand it better than Paul had himself. Yet there were and are only the limited information from Paul himself and his rather selective and biased arguments with his opponents. Recently therefore, and with justification, there are increasingly more voices that are setting boundaries here to reconstructive reasoning. Anyone who, on the basis of the meaningful principle of hearing the other side, also places some value on historical reconstruction and sees that such a demand is almost impossible to meet in view of the source material for Paul will, out of this insight, practice restraint in the presentation of the opponents. How different our view of Catholicism in the Reformation period would be if we knew only Luther's polemic, or if we knew of Luther only from the Catholic argumentation against him!

Anyone who sees Paul historically in the way indicated faces yet another problem that is again much discussed today: Is the message of justification the view of the apostle that defines his whole theological concept from the beginning, or does it belong in the late phase of Pauline thought? The answer to this question is not a clear yes or no. For, on the one hand, there is a sequence that we can describe with the catch phrases *election theology* (1 Thessalonians), *theology of the cross* (1 and 2 Corinthians), and *justification theology* (Galatians; Philippians 3; Romans). On the other hand, the language of justification in Paul has old and various roots, and in the letters with justification language Paul also does not simply always speak in the same way but makes different emphases.

At the close of this introduction we repeat an often quoted judgment of Rudolf Bultmann, namely, that an understanding of Paul is crucial to an understanding of early Christianity. To this we must add: To the extent that this period of the origins of Christianity has fundamental significance for Christianity in general, an understanding of Paul is also in a certain sense crucial to an understanding of Christianity as a whole.

1
The Early Christian Testimonies
of Paul

1.1 The Pauline Correspondence

Paul is the only figure in early Christianity about whom, because of direct self-testimonies, we can learn biographical and theological details. We owe this to the letters he wrote to his churches. Even though they have been in the New Testament canon since the early church and have thus come to us as the personal testimony of the apostle, Paul himself would not have believed them capable of an influence on the whole of Christendom lasting over the centuries. This legacy was unintentional; he wrote his letters for particular churches because of concrete problems and usually as a substitute for his presence with his congregations. Thus they are designed, first of all and above all, to be community specific and relevant to topics of their day. They are topical, occasional writings. Paul never took pen in hand or dictated to a scribe in order to establish matters of theological orientation that in his view should have validity for all times and all churches.

Even as the author of such topical correspondence Paul stands out quite clearly above the Christendom of his time. Jesus is a prophet in the genre of oratory. He left us not even a signature or a short letter, as did, for example, Bar Kokhba, the ringleader of Judaism's second anti-Roman insurrection. Nor have the other persons known by name in the first early Christian generation—such as the twelve disciples, the Lord's brother James, Stephen and his circle, Barnabas, and Paul's many fellow workers—left behind any literature in the broadest and most general sense of the word. The beginnings of Christianity are "unliterary." Exceptions such as the letter of the Corinthian community to Paul, known from 1 Cor. 7:1, confirm the overall impression. The same is true of the letters of recommendation that the "superlative apostles" may have been able to produce according to 2 Cor. 3:1. In general, one comes to the judgment that in this early period of Christianity there is no need to put the Christian message into literature.

The gospel is, as Luther termed it, an oral "shouting" of the message of salvation.

Thus Jesus' words, deeds, and fate were not written down until after the end of the first early Christian generation. That is, not until after the death of the apostles (above all, Peter, James, Paul) did the written form join the oral tradition, which up to that time had ruled practically alone. On the other hand, the sayings source Q that is reconstructable from Matthew and Luke, the signs source used in John, and the Gospel of Mark are for us the oldest still recognizable testimonies connected with the Jesus tradition. Besides the early Gospel production, however, there is also the composition of letters, pedagogical writings, and apocalypses, as demonstrated by the non-Pauline literature in the latter part of the New Testament canon and the Apostolic Fathers. Thus, in contrast to the first early Christian generation (with the exception of Paul), in the second and third generations we find in conspicuous abundance a high level of production of Christian literature.

These observations on a type of first unliterary, then literarily productive phase of a community and its history, have structural analogies in other community formations. In temporal proximity to early Christianity one can point, for example, to the beginning of Gnosticism. At this point we must warn against a misunderstanding. These comments do not allow us to make individual conclusions, such as that Barnabas or Peter, for example, could not write. They allow only the conclusion that, apart from Paul, no one in the first early Christian generation felt the need to choose the written form of proclamation. In this, Paul is the conspicuous exception.

Thus, thanks to this exceptional position of the apostle, we possess in his letters the oldest written testimonies of Christianity. Perhaps Paul was aware of the special position they gave him. Yet that is not directly apparent from his letters. It would be completely misguided—as already indicated—to suppose of him that he in the remotest way suspected the later importance of his correspondence for the origin of the New Testament canon, for turning points in church history, and in general for theological reflection in Christendom. Such an assumption would be misguided not only because Paul stood with his fellow Christians in the expectation of the imminent end of all things but also because he was not at all interested in achieving lasting fame through literary works, as Cicero and Seneca did. In this he thought neither as a culture-bearing Roman nor as an artist of antiquity. For him the letters, along with the sending of coworkers, were means of caring for his churches, as one can detect especially well, for example, in the Corinthian correspondence, or of helping to open new mission areas, for which the Letter to the Romans offers the best example. As his real work, with which he expected to step before God in the approaching final judgment, he always designated only his churches themselves (1 Thess. 2:1, 9–12, 19–20; 1 Cor. 3:5–17; 9:15–23; 15:10; Gal. 1:16; 3:1–5; Rom. 1:13–14; 15:14–29; etc.). His apostolic work stood or fell with them, not with his letters. For God had commissioned him to missionize the Gentiles with the gospel, not to write letters. It would have amazed him and perhaps even embarrassed him that after his death his churches would largely fall back into the darkness of history and his letters would unexpectedly become the heart of the canon and over the centuries exhibit an almost inestimable history of influence.

Nevertheless it can be no accident that such a history of influence was and still is ordained for the Pauline letters. No one, for example, deemed the superlative apostles' letters of recommendation mentioned in 2 Corinthians worthy of preservation. Without prejudice to the special and limited purpose in the writing of the Pauline letters, it is obvious that with them the apostle succeeded so well in dealing with the particular historically limited situation that since that time and even today other churches have also found themselves in those letters and have read and heard what could be guidance for them too. In short, they obviously encountered an understanding of Christianity that in their opinion possessed general validity and could persevere with lasting convincing power. This inner enlightening power of his letters doubtless proved to be quite decisive in the collection and preservation of his correspondence.

The details of how the collection of the Pauline letters was accomplished have almost completely escaped our knowledge. In the New Testament canon there are now two times seven letters that are ascribed to the apostle:

7 large letters: Romans; 1 and 2 Corinthians; Galatians; Ephesians; Philippians; Colossians
7 small letters: 1 and 2 Thessalonians; 1 and 2 Timothy; Titus; Philemon; Hebrews

Neither the number nor the order is original. This collection is, rather, the end product of many smaller collections and the Pauline as well as the post-Pauline production of these letters.

The beginning stage of the collection of Pauline letters can perhaps be imagined as follows: The crystallization points of a collection were in each case communities to whom Paul had written one or more letters or in which he had long worked. They gathered these letters and added to them the apostolic correspondence they could get from neighbors or which they had acquired through personal or occupational contacts. Also, Paul's coworkers could have made it their business to circulate the letters. In any case, at various places, such as Rome, Corinth, and Ephesus, there arose in this way different small collections, the number of whose letters varied, whose partial amounts did not always coincide, and whose order was different. They were not considered closed collections; rather, efforts were made to expand them when the opportunity presented itself. At the same time, there were surely also churches that possessed only one Pauline letter. Then with passing time whole collections were also exchanged and brought together. In this way the collections became ever more comprehensive and unified, so that the initial multiplicity was reduced to a few types. The present Pauline corpus in the canon is then the last stage of such collecting activity.

There are good reasons to assume that the gathering communities not only arranged the copies of the Pauline letters available to them and in the process perhaps also placed the letter addressed to them at the beginning or end but also reached into the text of the letters. Thus it has always been apparent that the doxology at the end of the Letter to the Romans (Rom. 16:25–27) does not belong to the original letter. It reveals a language dependent on Paul, but typically modified, and contains a theology that is close to the deutero-Pauline Ephesians and Colossians. Can it not be understood very well as the redactional conclusion of a collection of letters? Likewise, the ecumenical portion of the salutation in 1 Cor. 1:2b has always awakened the suspicions of the interpreter, when here after the Corinthian church—and somewhat as an afterthought—all Christians in general are named as addressees. Since Paul otherwise speaks concretely to only one or several churches, but not to the whole of Christianity, it makes better sense to see 1 Cor. 1:2b as the addition of an editor who placed 1 Corinthians at the beginning of a larger collection of Pauline letters. The intention was to say that this collection concerns all of Christendom. At least two other passages with important content are open to the suspicion of being non-Pauline supplements, namely, 1 Cor. 14:33–36 and 2 Cor. 6:14–7:1. Both passages destroy the continuity of their context, and neither is theologically in harmony with Paul. They are no doubt evidence of early Christianity's post-Pauline adaptation of the apostle's letters.

More serious than these redactional questions is the uncertainty of whether all the letters handed down under the apostle's name also originate from the apostle himself. Antiquity offers abundant examples of how, under the authority of great individuals, writings circulated that were written by their students. Thus in principle one must also reckon with pseudepigraphy in the letters of Paul. As a rule, only Romans, 1 and 2 Corinthians, Galatians, Philippians, 1 Thessalonians, and Philemon are today regarded as genuine letters of the apostle. In the case of Colossians and 2 Thessalonians, opinions are divided. Our presentation is based on the more certain core and only now and then draws additional help from the disputed letters. In any case, Ephesians, Colossians, 2 Thessalonians, 1 and 2 Timothy, Titus, and Hebrews are, on the whole, so theologically distant from the other Pauline letters that their pseudonymity is very probable or even certain. The assumption that they are (in part) genuine leads to greater problems than their exclusion from the testimonies directly ascribable to Paul.

For several decades, furthermore, there has been a vigorous discussion of whether at least some letters in their present form are to be understood as the redactional product of combining various Pauline letters. It is certain that Paul wrote more letters than we know today (cf. 1 Cor. 5:9). In addition, hypothetically one can imagine, for example, that a collection could not have room for an unlimited number of letters to a single church, lest it dominate the other churches. Also, short letters with little theological content are certainly not as well suited to regular reading in worship as are long ones with more substance. Such reading aloud, however, was no doubt planned from the beginning, as already indicated in the oldest letter (1 Thess. 5:27). Are these possible reasons for combining several letters into one? Possible reasons are admittedly still not proof. Thus only an analysis of the letters themselves will offer further help.

Here too there are problems. How many weak transitions can one attribute to Paul? How strictly did he hold, say, to a fixed epistolary format? Does a longer letter tolerate small discrepancies better than a shorter one? When he dictated, did he have in mind from the beginning the finished structure of a longer letter? Did he dictate without interruptions? In any case, it must be true that the more stratified and complicated one imagines the interweaving of previous letters and letter fragments into a new letter, the less likely becomes such a thesis, because it is marked by too much hypothesizing that is hard to verify. Conversely, it seems more conceivable if, for example, 2 Corinthians is supposed to be composed of the following once independent sections: (*a*) 2 Cor. 1:1–2:13; 7:5–16; chs. 8–9; (*b*) 2:14–7:4; and (*c*) chs. 10–13 (cf. 8.3 below). In such a case the processing of several letters into a single one would consist essentially of an insertion and arrangement of pieces that formerly did not belong together. In any case, one must be warned against the inflationary reconstruction of many letters. Best substantiated now as before is the division of 2 Corinthians and Philippians. In all other cases one does better on the whole without literary criticism. On the other hand, however, there is no sufficient or compelling reason to ban literary criticism in principle as a methodological question in dealing with the letters. This statement is based in the letters themselves: a break like that between Phil. 3:1 and 3:2 or an isolated special section with self-contained structure and theme as in the case of 2 Corinthians 10–13 must be explained. Thus the literary-critical dissection of Pauline letters remains an auxiliary tool (but admittedly no more) that one cannot dispense with from the beginning because of global considerations.

On the whole, we can conclude that the critically assured literature of the apostle gives us good possibilities for describing him, his work, and his theology. There are a great many better-known figures of antiquity—such as Socrates or Hannibal, Solon or Aeschylus—of whom we can only paint a poorer picture. Also, there is no figure in early Christianity about whom we come even close to being as well informed about as the apostle to the Gentiles.

1.2 The Other Sources

As surely as the letters composed by Paul himself are of primary and inestimable value for knowledge of the apostle, every interpreter of Paul is glad to have further source material available. Here we must point in the first place and above all to the Acts of the Apostles, a good half of which reports only on Paul. In addition, the *First Letter of Clement* and Ignatius of Antioch mention the martyrdoms of Peter and Paul (cf. 15.3 below). Yet both sources are comparatively meager. That is also true of the deutero-Pauline letters (Ephesians; Colossians; 2 Thessalonians; 1 and 2 Timothy; Titus), which are testimonies of how Paulinism developed further after the death of the apostle. But only in a very limited way can they shed historical light on Paul (cf., e.g., 2 Tim. 3:11 in 5.2 below). This judgment applies all the more to writings among the New Testament Apocrypha, especially, for example, the *Acts of Paul* and the correspondence between Seneca and Paul. The *Acts of Paul* are already attested by Tertullian, Hippolytus, and Origen and thus were probably circulated from about. A.D. 150 in the church at large. Not until about one hundred and fifty years later do we find the first traces of the correspondence between the philosopher Seneca and the apostle. Jerome mentions it for the first time in A.D. 392. Both of these writings linked with the name of Paul are so distant from Pauline theology and clearly so far from a historical knowledge of Pauline times that they have no significance for a presentation of Paul. Quite similar judgments are to be made about other apocryphal Pauline literature, for example, the Laodicean letter and the novel-like *Acts of Paul.* Also the Jewish-Christian *Pseudo-Clementines,* which are hostile to Paul, can be completely set aside. Extra-Christian references to Paul are, naturally, totally lacking in the early period of Christianity, and late rabbinic writings scarcely have historical value. Thus it is evident that if we want to describe the life of Paul, the Acts of the Apostles is unrivaled in second place after the Pauline letters.

This position has given great significance and influence to Acts; even today its presentation of the conversion and travels of Paul is still deeply imprinted in the consciousness of Christendom. It usually gave, and today in part still gives, the framework for a biography of Paul, and into it was inserted, in harmonizing fashion, the sporadic information from the apostle on his life story. Such a procedure was felt to be authorized, since reliance was put on the Muratorian canon, which was the first to name Luke, the physician and Paul's coworker in Asia Minor and Greece, as the author of the Third Gospel and Acts (Philemon 24; Col. 4:14; 2 Tim. 4:11). Does this not best explain the extensive passages on Paul and the "we" sections of Acts? Between the composition of Acts and the Muratorian canon, however, lie about one hundred years: ecclesiastical tradition around A.D. 200 does not necessarily reflect correctly the historical details of the first century, especially since neither the Third Gospel nor Acts itself names an author, and during the lengthy period of time since the early years, the authorship could have been combined after the fact. Thus this issue can be decided only by the internal evidence in Acts.

The Acts of the Apostles understands itself as a continuation of the Third Gospel (Acts 1:1). Since the latter can hardly have been composed before A.D. 80 (Luke 21:20, 24 assume some distance from the destruction of Jerusalem), no earlier date can be reached for Acts. Thus at the earliest it originated a generation after Paul. It also presupposes an ecclesiastical situation that already looks back from some distance at the first early Christian generation and, for example, describes presbyterial church organization, which is not attested until the post-Pauline period (Acts 20:17ff.). Above all, however, there are contradictions, large and small, between Acts and Paul, which give clear evidence that Luke, the traveling companion of the apostle, could not have been their author.

Certainly Galatians 1–2, the chief witness for Pauline biography, reproduces the life of Paul neither completely nor without structuring based on the Galatian situation (cf. ch. 2 below). But four observations in this decisive test case work to the disadvantage of Acts. The Antiochene quarrel (5.3 below) is ignored by Acts. Conversely, it knows of a compromise at the Apostolic Council that Paul neither knows about nor would have approved (5.2 below). It reports, further, a second stay of Paul in Jerusalem prior to the council (Acts 11:29–30), which, according to Gal. 1:18–24, could not have taken place. Also, the calling/conversion of the apostle in Acts 9 is understood, in terms of content and conception, considerably differently from Paul himself (cf. 4.1 below).

Further observations reveal the same picture. Acts knows practically nothing about the bustling and by no means problem-free relations between Paul and the Corinthian church (Acts 18). Conversely, Paul's speech in the Athenian Areopagus (Acts 17), as well as his stay in that city, has left no trace in Paul's writing. In addition, at many points the Lukan speech contradicts Pauline theology. It is also especially grave that Acts withholds for the missionary to the Gentiles the title of apostle, which is at the heart of his self-understanding, and at the same time makes him a law-abiding Jewish Christian (Acts 16:1–3; 18:18; 21:26–27; 26:2ff.), whereas it was precisely Paul who, although of Jewish descent, lived and represented thoroughgoing Gentile Christianity. And it must have been especially painful for Paul that he was credited with the circumcision of Timothy (Acts 16:3; cf. Gal. 2:3; 5:11; 6:12, 16; Phil. 3:4, 7).

These indications should suffice to support the judgment that the author of Acts, who lived at least a generation after Paul, did not know Paul himself. Quite apart from the significant differences between Pauline and Lukan theology, which are almost totally ignored here, the book of Acts is so seriously, unharmonizably different from Paul in its information, as just demonstrated above, that the author cannot have been a student of Paul or a traveling companion of the apostle to the Gentiles. Indeed, he did not even use any of Paul's letters; he was probably not even aware of this correspondence. His knowledge rests on general church tradition ("Paul legends"), which was already developing during the apostle's lifetime and had its oldest witness in Gal. 1:23–24. From that tradition—in addition to biographical statements (e.g., Acts 13:9; 16:37–39; 18:3; 22:3; 23:6), the persecution tradition (e.g., 9:1–2; 22:4–5), place-related circumstances in legend style (e.g., 18:1ff.), and itinerary descriptions (e.g., in Acts 16–18)—the author of Acts took, above all, legends of Paul's miraculous activity (e.g., 13:8ff.; 14:8–9) and individual anecdotes (e.g., 19:13ff.). To a great degree he constructed and combined these traditions, without being a historian in the modern sense. Thus, in their present untested form his contributions cannot be smoothly inserted into a modern presentation of Paul and Paul's work, for it is a matter of first separating the Lukan contribution to the presentation from the general knowledge of the church about Paul and then examining this knowledge for its historical faithfulness.

The contribution of the author of Acts to the picture of Paul certainly does not consist only in the collection of individual traditions, in the linguistic reshaping of the same, and in connecting them to one another. Rather, the book of Acts (along with the Third Gospel) has its own theological agenda, which is rooted in the church situation of the last part of the first century and seeks to serve that church. The presentation of Paul in Acts is adapted to this concern. Therefore Paul is not described as a biographically significant person in the early period of the church or as an outstanding theologian of the first early Christian generation; he is characterized, rather, as one who played a decisive role in the development of Christianity from the early Jerusalem community to the worldwide church. Therefore we learn of Paul's death as a martyr, for example, only quite incidentally (Acts 20:25, 38; 21:13), and conversely the stay of the apostle in the capital of the Roman Empire is the crowning conclusion of Acts. Therefore, also, no Pauline speech in Acts brings the theology of the great missionary into play; rather, Paul is given speeches that indicate the sense of direction of church history from the standpoint of Acts.

Under dispute is the question whether ecclesiastical tradition developed around the person of the apostle only as individual bits of oral tradition, or if it was perhaps available in particular cases also in written form and as already organized narrative. Probably this issue will never yield to final clarification, since the writer of Acts in any case greatly reworked his sources. It would indeed also be an impossible undertaking if one wanted, for example, to reconstruct the sayings source from Luke, without being able to draw on Matthew for help. Thus a source separation in Acts repeatedly runs up against considerable obstacles. Nevertheless there are enough clear observations in the text to suggest the possibility of an Antiochene source (basically from Acts 6:1–8:4; 11:19–30; 12:25–15:35) and to construct an itinerary of Paul's journeys (basically from Acts 13ff.). At any rate, the analysis in particular cases then becomes more stringent. Yet it must be clearly said that it is no longer possible to determine the exact extent of the sources. If we nonetheless notice here and there more solidly joined connections, then this leads to the judgment that Luke also possesses a deeper level, which in any case reaches farther back historically than Acts itself.

It is obvious that in view of this state of affairs the self-testimony of the apostle has to receive clear preference. Of course, this statement cannot stand without comment. First, analogies such as the autobiographical information on Luther, Bismarck, or Barth show that even they are not always so free of problems and errors that they can be accepted uncritically. We must seriously take into consideration that in later years, for example, Paul also interpreted his calling in the light of his previous life. Between his calling and the presentation in Philippians 3, after all, lies around a quarter century of turbulent living! Thus we should also make clear which biographical information on Paul we know just from Acts and thus not from Paul himself. In what follows we have compiled only information that can offer a certain degree of probability that it is faithful to history, even if in individual cases its historical worth may be debated.

According to Acts, Paul was born in Tarsus (Acts 9:11; etc.), received the double name Saul/Paul (13:9), and through his family possessed Tarsian and Roman citizenship (22:25–29). He was instructed by Gamaliel I in Jerusalem (22:3) and trained in the linen or leather-working trade (18:3). Even his vision of Christ outside Damascus (Acts 9) can only be inferred from the place-name in Gal. 1:17. The so-called first missionary journey from Antioch (Acts 13–14) is likewise not mentioned in Galatians 1–2. Many places of the Pauline mission in Acts 13–21 are not named in the Pauline correspondence. The apostle's encounter with Gallio, the proconsul of Achaia, before the court in Corinth (Acts 18:12ff.)—so important for the link with absolute chronology—is nowhere mentioned by Paul. Naturally the unquestionably genuine letters of Paul lack any references to the arrest in Jerusalem, the trial, the transfer to Rome, the stay there (Acts 21–28), and the death of Paul (cf. Acts 20:25, 38; 21:13).

Thus, in spite of the admitted priority of Paul's self-testimonies, one would still not want to do without the Acts of the Apostles. Its dramatic and legendary episodic style may place the historian inexorably at the boundaries of the search for historical truth. Yet who wants, for example, to maintain that the trial before Gallio is plainly pious invention? It may have been the presentational design of Acts to assemble all its known traditions at Paul's first stay in a city (thus, e.g., Acts 18), but are such individual traditions therefore already "timeless" and without worth for chronology, for example (cf. ch. 2 below)? In short, only the laborious way of the differentiated evaluation of arguments in each individual case can offer further help. Neither the wholesale condemnation nor the postulated high esteem of Acts helps greatly in the search for historical truth.

2
Chronological Questions
on the Life of the Apostle

The decisive framework for the chronology of Paul's life is indisputably given in Galatians 1–2. As fundamental and valuable as this text is in this matter, it also contains some unpleasant problems. Namely, it deals only with the time from the calling until the end of the Antiochene phase and thus gives absolutely no information on the independent phase of Paul's mission. Moreover, Paul argues throughout in a highly polemical fashion vis-à-vis the Galatians and therefore mentions only what is helpful to that purpose. Thus Paul is not making available to his later biographers a neutral résumé of his career and dates but rather is party to a quarrel that he would like to win: he would like to demonstrate his self-reliance and independence from Jerusalem and has this confirmed by the Jerusalemites through their historical part in the life of the apostle.

Paul places his emphases according to this main idea and leaves out what is not appropriate. Thus on his long stay in Antioch he reports neither when and how he went there and left nor what happened during the long years through the Apostolic Council (Gal. 2:1ff.), the Antiochene incident (2:11ff.), and beyond. Conversely, he mentions his fourteen-day visit with Peter in Jerusalem (1:18–19) no doubt because he must clarify his relationship with Jerusalem. With different aims in his presentation, that would surely not have been so important to him, for he never speaks of it otherwise. He also uses the quarrel with Peter (2:14ff.) to shape the thematic entrance into his main argumentation with the Galatians. Thus he jumps immediately into the present Galatian situation. In 2 Corinthians 11–12, Paul himself gives us the opportunity to know how much he left unmentioned in Galatians 2–3, while, naturally, 2 Corinthians 11–12 also assembles (completely?) in thematic orientation only the sufferings of the apostle and his gifts through revelation. Of his mission independent of Antioch, Paul reports absolutely nothing in Galatians (except on the Galatian mission), although at the time he wrote Galatians he could look back on an astonishing work.

Nothing is said of this essential activity of the apostle to the peoples, because here independence from Jerusalem is completely taken for granted.

For the period after the departure from Antioch we have at our disposal only scattered information on the apostle in his letters, but here statements about the collection for the poor in Jerusalem play a special role. In each case we must decide whether Paul is looking back at events or sharing his travel plans. That he also demonstrably changed his plans, or had to change them, is repeatedly attested: illness (Gal. 4:12ff.), persecutions, arrests, and executions (cf. only 1 Cor. 4:9–13; 15:32; 2 Cor. 1:5–10; 4:7–12; 11:23ff.; Phil. 1:7; 1 Thess. 2:2) also played a role here, as well as unplanned trips, for example, to Corinth (cf. 7.1 below). The individual data cannot always be brought into agreement. Also, they are so episodic that arranging them is often hypothetical and leaves open their interpretation in individual questions. On the whole, it is true for this information even much more than for Galatians 1–2 that Paul was, naturally, not thinking about his later biographers. Finally, with the biographical information in the Letter to the Romans, the self-testimony of the apostle ends altogether.

Thus anyone who wants to take a closer look at Paul's self-testimony will first and foremost turn to Galatians 1–2. The decisive section for the chronological framework of Paul's life begins with Gal. 1:13–14 ("you have heard . . ."). The passage speaks of Paul's Jewish period. Except for the general indication of time ("once"), we learn nothing of chronology—also no immediate information about the geographical surroundings of the only roughly sketched Pharisaic period of his life. A single sentence (Gal. 1:15–17), beginning with an indication of time defined by God's action ("when"), then speaks of the call, an unplanned trip to Jerusalem, the journey into Arabia, that is, the kingdom of Aretas IV lying southeast of Damascus with the cities of Petra, Gerasa, and Philadelphia (now Amman), and the return to Damascus. From this return one can infer that the call occurred in Damascus, which we know Acts confirms. The apostle's aim in this statement is clear: during his early period as a Christian, shaped by the geographic center Damascus/Arabia, Paul had no contact with Jerusalem. How he otherwise occupied his time lies beyond the purpose of his presentation. The easy assumption is missionary activity, but any possible success was not reflected in the sources. Yet that does not mean that we have to assume a mission failure. Without Galatians we would know, for example, of the Pauline churches there only through 1 Cor. 16:1. Also, Paul became conspicuous to the authorities; Aretas, the Nabatean king, had him persecuted (2 Cor. 11:32).

The next section (Gal. 1:18–20) begins with the first of three "then" statements (cf. 1:21; 2:1). To the "then" is added an indication of time ("after three years"), a verb of motion, and a geographic goal ("I went up to Jerusalem"). It is the apostle's first visit to Jerusalem, a private visit of around two weeks with Peter. On the same occasion Paul also saw James, the Lord's brother. All exegetes agree with good reason that the time indication "then" refers to the apostle's call and thus depends on the "when" statement in v. 15. With this the time from the call, geographically defined by Damascus and Arabia, is set at around three years—more exactly, at two plus or minus one, because at that time the beginning year and the ending year were always included.

Now, in v. 21 follows an astonishingly short indication: "Then [the second "then"] I went into the regions of Syria and Cilicia." Without doubt, this time indication refers to the stay in Jerusalem, which Paul ends not by returning to Damascus but by going to Syria and Cilicia, that is, into his homeland. It is crucial for the apostle vis-à-vis the Galatians that he has lived far away from Jerusalem. It is likewise clear that this geographic information separates itself from the events in Galatians 2 to the extent that here Paul is expressly active in another place, namely, in Antioch. Thus we assume that (northern) Syria and Cilicia mean the region around Paul's native city of Tarsus and not the Syrian area around Antioch. Later on, Acts accommodates itself to this information (cf. Acts 11:25–26; 9:30). Galatians 1:21 picks up with the new geographical distance to Jerusalem but says nothing about the temporal span of this period following the Jerusalem visit. Also, nothing is said as to whether Paul undertook another change of location. Of course, the description of the Apostolic Council in Gal. 2:1ff. then presupposes that Paul is living in Antioch, so that a further move must have occurred. This change of location must have happened at some considerable time before the Apostolic Council, for surely Paul only gradually became spokesperson for Antioch, as presupposed in Galatians 2, especially since Barnabas had prior claim to a leading role in Antioch and had to be dislodged from first place.

Apparently in Gal. 1:21 Paul also does not intend at all to describe a whole time span, but only the beginning of one, because in vs. 22–24 he continues his presentation with a description of a situation that is supposed to be true of the whole period from his calling until immediately before the Apostolic Council, at which Paul then for the first time personally encountered the early Jerusalem church. During this whole period, asserts the apostle, there were no personal contacts between him and the Jerusalem church; rather, he was known to the Jerusalemites only by hearsay. Because of this circumstance Paul can skip over any other details about the period between his first, private Jerusalem visit and his second, official one as representative of the church in Antioch. They are outside his theme. This time is, above all, the time he spent in Antioch. Yet from this Antiochene period he is interested in only the two events that have as their theme contact between Jerusalem and him. Everything else is omitted because of the purpose of the whole section.

Here Paul is intentionally silent in Gal. 2:11ff. about the outcome of the quarrel with Peter in connection with the Antiochene incident. This is no doubt an indication that the dispute came out negatively for him. Hence, Paul has scant interest in reporting more about Antioch and Barnabas than is necessary in the context. One may ponder whether it was already a part of the general Pauline legends arising during the apostle's lifetime (Gal. 1:22–24 itself gives evidence) that many churches knew about Paul's long activity in Antioch, especially since surely the Apostolic Council quickly became the topic of conversation in young Christendom and thus Paul became known as an Antiochene and protagonist of the Gentile mission. With this presupposed, Paul did not need to describe to the Galatians in detail when and how he came to Antioch and worked there.

The next indication of time in this whole section introduces the presentation of the Apostolic Council: "Then [the third "then"] after fourteen years I went up again to Jerusalem." This introduction to the event not only corresponds in form and in individual elements precisely to the beginning of the description of the first, private visit in Jerusalem (Gal. 1:18) but through the word "again" also makes express reference to it. Therefore we will reckon the fourteen years (again, thirteen plus or minus one) from this visit, especially since a reference back to the call in vs. 15–16 would reach back too far and is nowhere indicated. Paul wants to say: Between my call and the generally known Apostolic Council I was first privately in Jerusalem, namely, three years after my call, and then not again until fourteen years later at the council. There were no further trips to Jerusalem.

It would also be theoretically possible to make Gal. 2:1 dependent on 1:21, that is, on the immediately previous "then"; but that does not commend itself: 2:1 and 1:18 are too clearly parallel, and 1:21 gives no length of time to which 2:1 could relate. Galatians 1:21 does not say, "Then I went for x years into the regions of North Syria and Cilicia." Since 1:21 only marks the new beginning of a period of time, "then" is also only two weeks (plus travel time) later than the visit with Peter. Thus this recommendation would give practically the same time as in Gal. 1:18.

Frequently overlooked is the fact that the Petrine visit in Antioch, like the call in Gal. 1:15, begins with a "when" that starts something new. It introduces the first of three "when" clauses (also 2:12b, 14), which initially divide the presentation in regard to the Antiochene conflict. Thus a temporal connection between council and visit is missing. It is no longer time periods that are at stake for Paul but rather preserving the essence of his independent gospel in a difficult situation vis-à-vis Peter. It would thus be entirely conceivable that Paul would abandon the chronological order in 2:11ff. and for reasons of content place the crucial case at the end, outside the historical order—especially since in the whole passage he relies on classical rhetoric (cf. 11.2 below); that is, he follows the *narratio* of a judicial speech. Even in the *narratio* the usual sequence in antiquity was the historical order, and abandoning it was the exception. Yet it is in any case crucial that there are strong reasons, based on content, that support leaving the Antiochene incident after the Jerusalem council (cf. 5.3 below).

Thus the observations up to this point yield the following outline for a relative chronology.

Duration	Activity	Galatians
x years	Paul as Pharisee	1:13–14
	Calling, presence in Damascus and Arabia	1:15–17
	First visit in Jerusalem	1:18–20
2 ± 1 years	After 14 days, on to Syria, Cilicia	1:21
13 ± 1 years	Move to Antioch, clearly before the council	
	Second visit in Jerusalem: Apostolic Council	2:1–10
x years	Peter's visit in Antioch	2:11–21

On this basis it will pay us to take an initial look at Acts. When Luke describes the apostle as the former enemy of Christians who was present at the stoning of Stephen and in sympathy with the persecution, this contradicts Paul's statements about his stays in Jerusalem and the assertion that he was "not known by sight" to the Jerusalem Christians prior to the council. We first gain solid historical ground with the calling of Paul at Damascus. This is confirmed as fact by Acts, which gives us the location (Acts 9). Luke describes the move from Cilicia to Antioch with more biographical detail (cf. 5.1 below), yet he does not help in fixing the time more exactly. Luke then describes in a typifying and episodic manner a missionary trip of Barnabas and Paul in Acts 13–14 (the so-called first missionary journey), which falls in the Antiochene period. Paul reports nothing of this in Galatians 1. Nor, because of his presentation principle, does he have to. There are indications (cf. 5.1 below) that suggest a questioning of the often expressed skepticism toward the historical ordering of this missionary activity. It seems better to leave this journey in its historical place than to give it a new, historically later position. Then Luke helps in filling up Paul's Antiochene period before the council. From Gal. 2:11ff. one could infer that Paul left Antioch after the argument with Peter. Even though Acts provides different motivation for the separation between Barnabas and Paul (Acts 15:36ff.), it still places the split soon after the council and has Paul immediately begin his independent mission (the so-called second missionary journey), which leads him for the first time to Europe and has its center in the lengthy stay in Corinth (Acts 15:36–18:17). The itinerary of this trip can be easily checked with the help of 1 Thessalonians (cf. 6.1 below).

At this point, however, we have left the framework provided by Galatians 1–2. Now the task is to find other Pauline ordering factors that enable us to recognize temporal sequences in the further career of the apostle. Foremost among these are the statements in 1 and 2 Corinthians, Galatians, and Romans that speak of the so-called collection journey. They reveal a progression of collection activity and, together with information from their contexts about places and times, make it possible to reconstruct an Ephesian stay for the apostle and a subsequent trip through Macedonia to Corinth.

The oldest literary evidence of the collection is in 1 Cor. 16:1–4. From it we can infer that in Corinth a collection was already basically under way, but the church had asked how it should be carried out in detail. Paul answered from Ephesus (1 Cor. 16:8): they are to proceed in Corinth in the same way that he had (recently) arranged in Galatia, namely, for a lengthy period of time to set some money aside on the first day of the week, so that the beginning of the collection would not be delayed until his arrival. If the overall result is generous, Paul wants to deliver the gift himself in Jerusalem with the representatives of the community; otherwise the funds are to be taken without him to the recipient. From this information we can conclude that since Paul must later direct how Corinth is supposed to gather the offering, he apparently did not introduce it personally in Corinth. Thus the carrier of the lost letter of 1 Cor. 5:9, which was no doubt also written in Ephesus, may have taken the first steps as commissioned by the apostle. Since the Corinthians agreed that they wanted to collect but requested advice as to how they should proceed, only a moderate amount of time passed between their declaration of readiness and the inquiry (1 Cor. 16:1). Paul receives the inquiry shortly before writing 1 Corinthians in Ephesus (1 Cor. 16:7–8), where he wants to remain over winter, because his mission work there is currently flourishing.

The fact that things had not always gone well earlier for him in Ephesus is evidenced in 1 Cor. 15:32, an already somewhat dispassionate statement that at the risk of his life he "fought with beasts at Ephesus." Now, normally a man with the rights of Roman citizenship cannot be condemned. Also, a battle with beasts is missing from the list in 2 Cor. 11:23–29; Paul would hardly have left it out of a summary of his persecutions. Thus the figurative meaning of the statement is the most likely understanding. Consequently Paul was in serious mortal danger because of his opponents (cf. Ignatius, *Rom.* 5.1).

Regarding 1 Cor. 16:1ff., it is also important that Paul plans no extensive collection journey. He leaves open the question of whether he himself will go along to Jerusalem at all, accompanied by envoys from the Corinthian church, or will leave this journey up to the church alone. The mention of this latter possibility first in v. 3 indicates that it would apparently be the usual way; for Paul to want to accompany them is the exception. In any case, Corinth is supposed to gather the collection until his next coming. He will come via Macedonia—perhaps passing the winter there—to Corinth and spend a lengthy period there (16:5–7).

Also, 1 Cor. 16:1 tells us something about the Galatian church: there Paul has already made arrangements that Corinth is to adopt. Why does Paul report nothing of the Ephesian example? Would he not be more likely to point to his current place of residence or to the nearby Macedonians (2 Corinthians 8–9) as an example of how one is to do things, instead of the rather distant Galatians? Does the list of Paul's fellow travelers to Jerusalem in Acts 20:4 not also include two Asians and thus one or two Ephesians? Why does Paul say nothing at all of the collection in Ephesus and Asia?

These questions can be adequately answered only if we first take a closer look at Gal. 2:10. This mention of the collection—the only reference to it in Galatians—is kept rather general. According to this verse, the efforts on behalf of the collection go back to a particular agreement of the Jerusalemites with the Antiochenes (Paul and Barnabas). At the time of the Apostolic Council these two Antiochenes committed themselves in their Gentile-Christian mission field—that is, in Antioch and its area of influence—to the contribution of material support for the poor in the Jerusalem church. Paul also felt himself still bound to this pledge even after he left Antioch, although his worldwide mission, independent of Antioch, could not have been considered in the Jerusalem agreement. His dispute with Peter and James's people (Gal. 2:11ff.) cannot cause him to give it up, either. All his life he felt personally obligated to keep his word. The Letter to the Romans confirms this attitude fully (Rom. 15:27b).

The combination of 1 Cor. 16:1 and Gal. 2:10 reveals that the gathering of the offering in Galatia began more smoothly and with fewer problems than in Corinth and took shape before the Corinthian collection. Did Paul himself introduce it in Galatia? If we take 1 Cor. 16:1 literally ("as I directed"), this is very possible. Did Paul otherwise give no direction on how funds were to be gathered? That is probable. Apparently Paul merely promoted a collection everywhere but left its execution to the churches, who decided independently how they wanted to do it and then, province by province, sent the gifts to Jerusalem with their own envoys. Only in Galatia, where Paul himself had also determined the how, was this different before the Corinthian inquiry. Therefore he can offer to the Corinthians only the Galatians as an analogy, but he cannot report, for example, on the Ephesians.

Yet the Corinthians and the Galatians no doubt have something else in common, which is even capable of generalization. Paul could hardly have introduced the collection in Corinth on his founding visit, for then there would be no uncertainty there as to how the Corinthians should gather it. Similarly, the course of events in Galatia may have been that Paul was in Galatia a second time after the founding visit of the first independent missionary journey (cf. 6.1 below). This may be indicated by Gal. 4:13 and confirmed by Acts 18:23; 19:1. Such a possible second visit can only be accommodated after the apostle's return from his first European journey and thus lies at the beginning of his Ephesian period.

According to 1 Cor. 16:1 the completion of the Galatian collection is still to come. The highly polemical situation in Galatians stands in clear contrast to the unproblematic, casual general reference to the collection in Gal. 2:10. Thus in Galatians, written later than 1 Corinthians, Paul sees no reason to be quiet about the collection in spite of the precarious Galatian situation. If a disruption of the collection had taken place in Galatia, Paul would surely have preferred not to mention the offering in Gal. 2:10. Thus it is more likely that before the entry of the Judaizers (cf. 10.2 and 11.1 below) the Galatians had finished their collection and independently—as expected—taken it to Jerusalem. That happened before the writing of Galatians, while Paul was still in Ephesus. Therefore, in 2 Corinthians 8–9 and Rom. 15:26 Paul says nothing more about this offering. Paul apparently directed the collection in Galatia entirely as stated in 1 Cor. 16:1.

Next, 2 Corinthians 8–9 enables us to recognize a still more advanced stage of the collection in the churches. The often proposed literary-critical separation of the two chapters is unaffected here (cf. 8.3 below), since the situation in regard to the collection is the same in both chapters. Paul, in the meantime, is in Macedonia and has told the churches there that Corinth has been gathering a collection for about a year, and it is supposed to be brought to Jerusalem (2 Cor. 9:2–3). This spurred the Macedonians, without Paul's urging, to follow the Corinthian example (2 Cor. 8:3–4). Now, Titus is sent with two brothers from Macedonia to Corinth to bring about the successful conclusion of the Corinthian collection, because Paul would otherwise have been in a bad position with the Macedonians if he had bragged too much in praise of Corinthian zeal (2 Cor. 8:6, 11, 16–22; 9:4).

From Paul's improvised extra visit to Corinth from Ephesus (2 Cor. 2:3–4, 9; 7:8–12) and from "the letter of tears" (2 Cor. 2:1–4), which Titus brings (2 Cor. 12:18), we can learn that the collection in Corinth was delayed or indeed had perhaps in the meantime come to a standstill. This not only changed the shape of the apostle's plans as first announced in 1 Corinthians 16 but also explains why apparently for about a year already the collection had progressed badly (2 Cor. 8:10; 9:2) and needed special encouragement from Paul (2 Corinthians 8–9!). Yet Paul must also write in such detail in 2 Corinthians 8–9 because his situation vis-à-vis the Corinthians has been made more difficult, since the Macedonians have spontaneously decided to deliver a collection together with Achaia; until now each province naturally did that for itself. Paul has thus come to Macedonia not at all in order to gather the offering there also. Rather, he has come there to visit, in order to travel via Macedonia to Corinth, to bring the collection there to a close, and possibly to go on to Jerusalem (1 Cor. 16:4). That Paul originally did not want to take a collection with him to Macedonia can be learned from 2 Cor. 1:16, where Paul indicates travel plans that have changed since 1 Corinthians 16, but nothing came from these: only the Corinthians were supposed to accompany Paul to Judea. Now, however, the described new situation has come about in his stay in Macedonia. Now Paul can decide all the more surely even before his arrival in Corinth that he will go along to Jerusalem (2 Cor. 8:18–24), which he already had more firmly in mind in 2 Cor. 1:16 than in 1 Cor. 16:4. Therefore also, the Corinthians must make a special effort to be cheerful givers (2 Cor. 9:5ff.). Romans 15:26 indicates that the Corinthians did not leave Paul in the lurch, and thus Paul—now in Corinth himself—can inform the Roman church that he will come to Rome after the delivery of the collection of the Macedonians and Achaians (no other provinces are named!).

This collection from all of Greece, but not from the Pauline missionary territory in general, is not in harmony with the list of fellow travelers in Acts 20:4: the accompaniment of two church members from Asia is hardly understandable in this list if Ephesus and the surrounding area did not take part in the collection. On the other hand, would Paul not have had to say in 2 Corinthians 8–9 that he had Asia's collected offering with him if that were the case? Would he not also have had to mention the two fellow travelers from Asia as he did the Macedonian messengers? Finally, in Rom. 15:26 could he have remained silent with regard to the Roman church, especially if Aquila and Priscilla, the married couple from Ephesus who have now returned to Rome, are now reading the letter (Rom. 16:3) and a man such as the first baptized Asian is among the readers (Rom. 16:5b)? If we consider further that in the list in Acts 20:4 even Philippi and Corinth, for example, are completely missing, and Gaius of Derbe does not fit the Pauline information at all, we must regard with skepticism the list from Acts and not harmonize it with the Pauline data but rather regard the latter alone as reliable. Luke, on the other hand, mentions the delivery of the collection in Jerusalem only incidentally (Acts 24:17). That is surely a (purposefully?) false estimation. But Luke is right to the extent that there was no long, organized, comprehensive collection journey, even according to the Pauline evidence.

Now it is a question of gathering from the letters bits of information that can better define the trip from Ephesus through Macedonia to Corinth. In principle, this route corresponds to the announcement in 1 Cor. 16:5–7, but Paul could not keep to this plan because of an unforeseen, life-threatening persecution in Asia (2 Cor. 1:8–10). Since this danger has just been overcome and is communicated to the Corinthians as very recent news, it cannot be identical with that of 1 Cor. 15:32, for the latter lies farther in the past and is known in Corinth. On the other hand, the imprisonment described in Philippians may be the event that is still going on in Philippians 1 and is overcome in 2 Corinthians 1. Thus Philippians 1 was written before 2 Corinthians 1, and the predicament at the end of Paul's Ephesian stay is doubly attested. We may note in passing that, on the whole, Philippians is silent about the collection. The reason can be deduced from the history of the offering. While staying in Ephesus, Paul has no intention of collecting Macedonian money for Jerusalem. We can probably safely assume that Paul had to give up his travel plans (2 Cor. 1:8–9)—modified in the meantime vis-à-vis 1 Corinthians 16—because of his imprisonment (with almost deadly results) in Ephesus, and after his release traveled rather hastily and in full flight (?) toward Troas (2 Cor. 2:12), remained there for a while, but then departed for Macedonia (2 Cor. 2:13). Here Titus brought Paul good news from Corinth, leading Paul to write the so-called letter of reconciliation (2 Cor. 1:1–2:13; 7:5–16) and thus not to set out himself immediately for Corinth but rather to remain for a while in Macedonia. This situation, on the whole, fits in well with the situation in 2 Corinthians 8–9, so that on this basis—no matter what we decide in terms of literary criticism—both chapters can belong to the letter of reconciliation. It is equally astonishing that the actual journey is practically in harmony with the old plan from 1 Corinthians 16.

These data gained from Paul and their consequences agree to a large extent with the Acts of the Apostles. Right away, of course, time causes problems here at the beginning of the Ephesian period. Acts 18:18–23 describes an itinerary, departing from Corinth and heading toward Syria (i.e., Jerusalem, which lies in the Roman province of Syria; cf. 20:3; 21:3). Paul travels, bound by a vow, from Corinth's eastern harbor of Cenchreae with Aquila and Priscilla to Ephesus, preaches in the synagogue there, and, despite the petitions of the Ephesians to stay, sails to Caesarea and goes from there to Jerusalem. The return trip via Antioch, Galatia, and Phrygia ends in Ephesus (Acts 19:1). Three things in this presentation are confirmed by Paul: the moving of the married couple to Ephesus (1 Cor. 16:19), Paul's stay in Ephesus (1 Cor. 16:8; etc.), and (rather probably) the visit in Galatia (Gal. 4:13).

Beyond this, however, considerable problems remain in this little passage. The itinerary is as extensive as it is empty of content. Through the vow (Acts 18:18ff.), which is supposed to be fulfilled in Jerusalem (cf. chs. 21; 23ff.), Luke apparently wants to present Paul one more time as a true Jewish Christian and provide general motivation for the Jerusalem trip. That Paul, in spite of the petitions, does not remain in Ephesus is no doubt also tacitly determined by the vow, which requires a speedy path to Jerusalem. Moreover, this makes Paul the first missionary in Ephesus, which, however, according to better Lukan knowledge (Acts 19:1ff.), he was not. Yet this Jerusalem trip collides with the information in Galatians 1–2, according to which Paul, at the time of writing Galatians, had been in Jerusalem only twice (visit with Peter, Apostolic Council). Also, neither Luke nor Paul permits the Jerusalem visit in Acts 18:22 to be identified with any other, whether with one of the two in Galatians 1–2 or with the later visit to deliver the collection. Thus this Jerusalem trip shows itself to be a Lukan construct. With this, however, Caesarea on the journey there and Antioch on the journey back are also eliminated as stops on the way. Geographically the two places are obvious constructs that follow from the journey to Jerusalem. Also, Paul himself nowhere suggests that he sought out Antioch again after his departure from there (Gal. 2:11ff.). The opposite is no doubt true: after Gal. 2:11ff. he avoids the city on the Orontes. For the rest, the route Antioch-Galatia-Phrygia (Acts 18:23)–Ephesus (Asia) has to be compared with the information in Acts 16:6. Also, in 19:1 the "upper country" is essentially identical with 18:23, only more general. This produces the following thesis: the Lukan model apparently spoke of a change from Corinth to Ephesus, which Paul and the married couple Aquila and Priscilla undertook together. Right at the beginning of his Ephesian stay Paul visited churches founded earlier in Phrygia and Galatia. This is in agreement with the information taken from Paul if we see two visits indicated in Gal. 4:13.

Unfortunately, according to Acts 18:18–19:40 Paul's stay in Ephesus also gives little hint of what we know from Paul himself. For the events in Acts 19, nonetheless, 19:10 and 22 confirm a longer stay in Ephesus of probably a good two years, to which we must add time for Acts 18:18ff., so that, in all, we come to about three years. The forced departure (also according to Acts) from Ephesus leads Paul through Troas to Macedonia and Achaia (Acts 20:1). Such a trip was already planned by Paul earlier (Acts 19:21–22). A three-month stay in Corinth follows (Acts 20:3). Then begins the journey to Jerusalem, which we can no longer verify with the Pauline letters.

Hence we have received, in all, two frameworks for the relative chronology of Paul's life, one based on Galatians 1–2 and another through observations on the collection theme and accompanying information. With extensions offered by 1 Thessalonians, the first framework stretches from the calling to the founding stay in Corinth. The second began with the move from Corinth to Ephesus and goes to the departure from Corinth (third visit) to Jerusalem. With the help of Acts 18:11 the two frameworks can be provisionally connected. According to this passage, Paul remained in Corinth eighteen months on his founding visit and then sailed along the Asiatic coast (Acts 18:18–19). This length of stay can be tested only rather inexactly against the Pauline evidence. Nonetheless the apostle says that in order not to become a burden to the church, he had difficulties assuring his support (2 Cor. 11:7–9; 1 Cor. 9:15–18). This eliminates the possibility of a very short stay. Also the size of the church at the end of the first visit speaks for a longer residence in Corinth (cf. 6.4 below).

Now we can attempt to mesh this relative chronology with the absolute. Here, unfortunately, Paul is of no further help. In contrast to the Lukan historical works (Luke and Acts) he is uninterested in the dates of world history. His only mention of this kind, made incidentally in 2 Cor. 11:32, is unusable for our purposes. Here Paul mentions the governor of King Aretas, who persecuted him in Damascus. Aretas IV, whose governor was after Paul, ruled from 9 B.C. to A.D. 40, but the fact that Paul's stay in Damascus lies before A.D. 40 can be taken for granted.

First, it is clear that the earliest time for the calling of the apostle is the beginning of the church in Damascus, which in turn must come sometime after Jesus' death, the Easter experience, and the death of Stephen. Today Jesus' date of death is usually placed in the spring of A.D. 30 (less likely, in A.D. 27). The latest fixed point in the life of the apostle is given by the circumstances of his Roman martyrdom (*1 Clement* 5), which, without fear of contradiction, we can probably place in the Neronian period. Nero ruled from A.D. 54 to A.D. 68. His persecution of Christians in A.D. 64 is a point of contact here, for Paul could hardly have died later and probably died earlier. With these two dates we have reached what, by the standards of antiquity, is a rather high level of accuracy.

Nevertheless this still rather approximate dating of Paul's life can be improved through Acts. As surely as Luke was in the habit of emphasizing Christianity's world-historical horizon, some of his synchronisms are totally wrong, and others are not very useful because they cannot be connected with history. Yet his particular service to the chronology of the apostle to the peoples consists in the fact that with the help of Paul's trial before Gallio in Acts 18, we can with relative certainty make the connection to absolute chronology.

In any case, for initial work in absolute chronology we should disregard the other points of contact that Luke makes between Paul's life and world history, though later we may come back to them to fill out the chronological framework. Among the synchronisms unsuited for absolute dating is the famine under Claudius (Acts 11:28). It is often attested as a local event, not as "over all the world." Also the persecution of the Jerusalem church under Herod Agrippa (Acts 12:1ff.; 12:20ff.) and the change in the office of procurator from Felix to Festus (Acts 24:27) cannot be dated independently from Luke and with sufficient certainty. Finally, the edict of Claudius, because of which Aquila and Priscilla, according to Acts 18:2, had "lately" left Rome and met with Paul in Corinth, is not completely free of problems, either. Without Luke the ancient sources cannot be interpreted so surely that the date of A.D. 49, normally rightly assumed with Lukan help, could stand firm and free of doubt even independent of Acts. Also the vague indication "lately" is naturally not especially conducive to a precise chronological connection (cf. 13.1 below).

Lucius Junius Gallio, older brother of the philosopher Seneca and, like him, born in Spanish Cordova, was proconsul in Achaia under Claudius. After that he completed his career as a political official and, like his brother Seneca, had to choose suicide under Nero. His time as proconsul in Achaia is attested by a fragmentarily extant imperial decree, chiseled into stone and addressed to the city of Delphi (the so-called Gallio inscription). Because of the decree his time in office can also be determined quite certainly, namely, from spring A.D. 51 until spring A.D. 52 (possible error: one year earlier).

Now we must note that Luke likes to concentrate the local traditions on the first stay in a place and then arrange them in such a way that an entrance event and a striking final incident become the framework into which everything else is inserted. This presentation concept is found, for example, in Acts 16–19 with the cities of Philippi, Thessalonica, Corinth, and Ephesus. Thus we must establish which stay Acts 18:12–17 should be accorded to and, if possible, when within the visit the event took place. For the trial before Gallio, only the founding stay deserves serious consideration. The visit related to the gathering of the collection lies so late in the relative chronology that coincidence with the Gallio trial can certainly be excluded. And the brief impro-vised visit with its hasty departure had other content in Pauline sources and is ill-suited to be related to the trial. The founding visit, on the other hand, is in terms of time and substance eminently predestined to burden Paul with this event. For the separation of a Gentile-Christian-oriented church from the synagogue would naturally take place very early. If indeed this process of separation is to be connected with the actions of the Corinthian synagogue before Gallio and against Paul, we will have to place Paul's trial before Gallio at the latest toward the end of the apostle's first stay in Corinth, possibly even somewhat earlier, for Paul remains unmolested and does not have to leave the city.

Presupposing from Acts 18:11 an eighteen-month Pauline stay, this yields for the earliest time for Paul's visit fall A.D. 49 to spring A.D. 51 and as the latest fall A.D. 52 to spring A.D. 53. It seems obvious to aver-age these times and reckon with a margin of error of about plus or minus one year, so that we can begin with a calculated date of fall A.D. 50 to spring A.D. 52 for the first Corinthian visit and fit around it the two frameworks of relative chronology. In this process the calculat-ed margin of error naturally becomes somewhat larger because in the relative chronology also the temporal relationship between events can-not always be determined with complete precision. Nevertheless we must maintain that at the end of our considerations it is astonishing how exactly we are now oriented regarding the dates of Paul's life in comparison with those of other ancient figures. The following table gives an overview of these dates.

Dates of Paul's Life

Birth in Tarsus	?
Paul as persecutor of Christians	32
Calling, first mission to Arabia	32
First Jerusalem visit (private, with Peter: 14 days)	34/35
Beginning of work in (northern) Syria/Cilicia	34/35
Paul in Antioch	from 36/37 (?)
Vision according to 2 Cor. 12:1–5	41/43
Mission with Barnabas (Acts 13–14)	before 48
Second visit in Jerusalem: Apostolic Council	48/49
Peter's visit in Antioch	49
Paul leaves Antioch	49
First independent missionary journey toward Corinth,	
including Galatia, Philippi, Thessalonica	49–50
Founding stay in Corinth (first visit)	50–52
First Letter to the Thessalonians	50/51
Paul before Gallio	50/51
Stay in Ephesus and Asia	52–55/56
Second visit in Galatia	52
Danger according to 1 Cor. 15:32	52/53
First Letter to the Corinthians	54
Second visit in Corinth (extra visit)	54
"Letter of tears" from 2 Corinthians	54
Imprisonment/mortal danger	54/55
Letter to Philemon	54/55
"Letter of imprisonment" from Philippians	54/55
Journey from Ephesus to Corinth via Troas, Macedonia	
(the so-called collection journey)	55/56
Letter to the Galatians	56
"Letter of reconciliation" from 2 Corinthians	56
Third visit in Corinth (ca. 3 months)	56
Letter to the Romans	56
Journey from Corinth to Jerusalem with the collection	56/57
Third visit in Jerusalem (collection visit)	57/58
Journey of the prisoner Paul to Rome	58–60 (?)
Stay in Rome and martyrdom	60–62 (?)

On the beginning and the end of the tabular overview two special comments are necessary. First, a word must be said about Paul's age. If we take into consideration the exertions of travel that Paul took upon himself in the last thirty years of his life and the physical burdens he endured through punishment and persecution (cf. only 2 Cor. 11:23–29), and if we also keep in mind his illness (2 Cor. 12:7; Gal. 4:12ff.) and the relatively low average life expectancy in antiquity, then he must have been—even for the conditions of the time—still of a very vigorous age to have been able to endure all of that. Moreover, at the time of his calling Paul had finished his professional training and apparently also completed his Pharisaic education. Hence a calling at the age between twenty and twenty-five is certainly a possible and reasonable assumption. That leads to a birth date of around A.D. 10, with a few years tolerance in either direction, and thus in the last years of the reign of Augustus (d. A.D. 14). This assumption is perhaps supported by Philemon 9. Paul designates himself here as an "old man" (Lat.: *senex*). In antiquity that was from about fifty years on. Yet Philemon 9 may also be merely the subjective judgment of the apostle about his diminishing vitality. The indication in Acts 7:58 that Paul witnessed the stoning of Stephen as a "young man" is entirely worthless. It is only Lukan redaction and too inexact.

The second supplementary remark concerns the last chapter of Paul's life, for which only Acts offers the following, unconfirmable orientation: it mentions two years' imprisonment in Caesarea and again the same length of time in Rome (Acts 24:27; 28:30; on the Spanish trip, cf. 15.3 below). The suspicion is great that we have here approximate, round numbers, but no one can provide more reliable information. Thus we are left with an irreducible chronological inexactitude.

3
Paul as Pharisee from Tarsus

3.1 Biographical Data

Paul shares with many figures of antiquity the fate that only his most significant and most fruitful period is still well known. We can understand this period broadly, namely, from his calling to his death, and thus have the Christian Paul in view. Or we can define it somewhat more narrowly and concentrate on the independent missionary journeys, that is, the time from which the genuine Pauline letters come. However we decide, there is no question that we will be able to learn only a very few things about the Jewish Paul before his calling as an apostle.

That is due above all to Paul himself, for he divides his life into two halves on the basis of his calling, and the Christian Paul has almost entirely disposed of the Jewish period of his life. He experienced his calling as such a profound reorientation and identity crisis that the previous part of his life becomes almost totally inessential and the time after his calling comprises his real life. Therefore in Paul's letters the Jewish portion of his life is not presented at all for its own sake. It only serves here and there, sporadically and typified by a few narrowly limited statements, as dark background and as harshly drawn contrast to the beginning of his second, real life. The most important autobiographical information at this point is found in 1 Cor. 15:9; 2 Cor. 11:22; Gal. 1:13–14; Phil. 3:5–6; and Rom. 9:3–4. With this, Paul sets a self-imposed boundary of knowledge, which we must observe.

Apparently even Paul's contemporaries did not know much more than we about his Jewish life. For beyond Paul himself the few bits of information that Acts places at our disposal—and that Acts no doubt drew from the general Paul legend—are likewise quickly summarized.

These indications are so scant that while they increase somewhat the number of biographical mosaic stones, they do not allow us to construct a satisfactory overall picture of Paul's life. Is it then worth the effort at all to write a special section on Paul as a Jew? Certainly it is hardly justified by the few biographical details as such. Beyond this, however, we should attempt to describe the religious and cultural environment in which the Jew Paul lived. For after such an examination we can expect to understand better the utterances of the Christian Paul.

The scant biographical data can be easily gathered. Through his family Paul belongs to the Hellenistic synagogue in Cilician Tarsus. His parents must have resided in this "no mean city" (Acts 21:39) for a lengthy period of time. This much, in any case, we can infer from Acts (21:39; 22:3), and we can no doubt trust this information. At any rate, there is no other competing or elaborating tradition, except perhaps the news in Jerome (*De viris illustribus* 5) that the family once emigrated from Galilean Gishala. Observations on the Pauline letters, which will be discussed later, can attest indirectly to this Hellenistic-Jewish milieu. Three points may suffice for the time being. The Greek language of Paul is not only free of harsh Semitisms (and thus was hardly learned later as a foreign language, for example, in Jerusalem) but also follows independent Greek style. This Greek style is so smooth that it seems impossible to prove from the linguistic side of his correspondence whether he could speak Hebrew or Aramaic. The Acts of the Apostles assumes that he could (Acts 21:40; 22:2; 26:14), but in any case this cannot be proved by the few foreign, Aramaic words in Paul himself (*abba,* Rom. 8:15; Gal. 4:6; and *marana tha,* 1 Cor. 16:22), since they were common property in early Christianity. Thus it is obvious that from childhood on he was accustomed to speaking as lingua franca the Greek vernacular of the diaspora Jews. Second, we must also mention that Paul's education is, on the one hand, concentrated on the Greek version of the Jewish Bible (Paul uses the Septuagint) and, on the other, defined not insignificantly by common Hellenistic culture (cf. 3.3 below). Finally, as a Christian, Paul almost always sought out Hellenistic-Roman cities, no doubt likewise a reflection of his socialization in a Hellenistic, urban atmosphere. This again fits the Hellenistic city of Tarsus as the place of his youth.

It is more difficult to explain whether Paul's family, and thus by inheritance the apostle himself, possessed Tarsian and imperial Roman citizenship. If Tarsian citizenship was, in practice, of subordinate significance in Paul's life because at least after his calling he never again spent any time in his native city, then a distinct importance is given to his imperial Roman citizenship. Of course, the two citizenships are attested only by Acts, and indeed in texts that are greatly shaped by Luke himself (Acts 16:37–38; 22:25ff.; 23:27; cf. also indirectly 25:10–11; 21:25–26; 28:19). Yet even if these passages contain no pre-Lukan tradition, the assertions formulated by Luke do not therefore necessarily have to be false: Luke may have taken his knowledge from the general Christian knowledge about the apostle to the Gentiles.

Then again, however, it is striking that in the course of a trial or a punishment the Lukan Paul always appeals too late to his Roman citizenship. By such an appeal Paul could have escaped, for example, even the punishments listed in 2 Cor. 11:24ff. Naturally it is conceivable—indeed probable—that Paul did not as a rule make such an appeal, because he consciously understood these persecutions as equivalent to the cross of Christ (cf., e.g., Gal. 6:17). Incidentally, antiquity knows cases where Roman citizenship did not preserve Jews from scourging and crucifixion (cf. Josephus, *Bellum* 2.308). Also, we do not get much farther with the question of how often in the Augustan age and immediately afterward residents of Asia Minor in general were granted Roman citizenship: it rarely happened and was even more rare for Jews in this province. Certainly, Jews in particular also fell into conflict with the duties of a Roman citizen, which included participation in the state cult. Josephus himself, however, is a known example of the fact that here too arrangements could be made without giving up one's Judaism.

Thus the question remains whether a Roman proconsul, instead of making his own judicial decision, would have sent a prisoner like Paul to Rome for judicial disposal if he had not felt required to by the Roman citizenship of the accused. Paul was, after all, a comparatively "small fish," an insignificant case for the Roman administration. Without such a background the shifting of the decision could all too easily be interpreted as weakness in the execution of one's own power. In any case, it is something different when important persons or anti-Roman agitators who are wanted under warrant are transported to Rome, even without Roman citizenship, in order to receive their trial there. Thus it is no doubt historically more probable that in his trial before Festus, Paul did appeal to his Roman citizenship than that Luke inferred this from the transportation of prisoners from Caesarea to Rome with which he was familiar. Thus in distinction to his origin in the city of Tarsus, Paul's Roman citizenship is not fully assured but is still a likely possession of the apostle.

Tarsus lies on the lower course of the Cydnus, which is navigable from there downstream; it was a trade center on the road that led from Antioch to the Asia Minor coast and thus to the Greek cities, and in addition it was a point of departure for the road to the Black Sea, thus a typical city of the world commerce of the day. When Cilicia became a Roman province in 66 B.C., Tarsus became the residence of Roman proconsuls, including at one time Cicero. Here Antony apparently met Cleopatra for the first time. Caesar and Augustus were special benefactors of the city. Augustus had his Stoic teacher Athenodorus reorganize the city. He, like Nestor from the Platonic academy and Lysias, the Epicurean, was among the city's regents. Culturally, the city had a shining past. Many renowned philosophers, grammarians, and poets taught there. Most were representatives of Hellenistic education, in part with an oriental covering. Strabo (*Geographica* 14.5.13) praised the zeal of the residents "in philosophy and general education" and compared them flatteringly with Athens and Alexandria. The city was lauded as "great and fortunate" (Xenophon, *Anabasis* 1.2.23) and placed in a favorable light. In particular it was among places known for Stoic education. Around 140 B.C., Antipater of Tarsus was even the head of the Stoic school. His pupil was the well-known Panaetius. This indicates the intellectual climate of the city: it is a microcosm of the Hellenistic Mediterranean region. Since Paul's parents had integrated themselves (citizenship!) into the city as much as was possible for diaspora Jews, Paul probably breathed this Hellenistic city air. Probably related to this is the fact that Paul was never oriented very far toward the east: Arabia and Mesopotamia did not lie in his field of vision. As a Jew he thought no farther southward than Jerusalem; as a Hellenist he concentrated on Asia Minor, Syria, and Greece; as a citizen of the Roman Empire he knew Rome as the political center of the world. At the end of his life he wants to go to Spain as the western "end of the world."

It was natural for the offspring of better-situated diaspora Jews, like themselves, to grow up multilingual. As already indicated, Luke attests that Paul was versed in Aramaic. Paul designates himself as a "Hebrew born of Hebrews" (Phil. 3:5; cf. 2 Cor. 11:22) and thereby stresses above all the faithful observation of Jewish customs in his family. This no doubt also included the care and preservation of the Aramaic language, so that based on this consideration and in spite of Paul's good Greek, we can infer a knowledge of Aramaic. It is uncertain whether one can deduce from these words that Paul also knew Hebrew. Because of his Pharisaic training this may be likely, in that he probably could read and understand the text of the Hebrew Bible. Nowhere, of course, is it certain that Paul as a Christian translated directly from the Hebrew Bible into Greek. Naturally his churches used the Septuagint throughout. In writing his letters, Paul, as a rule, probably quoted from a memory trained in the Septuagint or here and there even used the Septuagint. It is not at all advisable to conclude from the phrase "Hebrew born of Hebrews" that Paul was born in Palestine or even Jerusalem. In antiquity such a designation was used with much broader meaning.

The family was counted among the descendants of the tribe of Benjamin (Rom. 11:1; Phil. 3:5). The Jewish given name Saul, mentioned only by Acts (9:4, 17; 22:7; 26:14; etc.), may refer to the Benjamite first

king of Israel. In addition to their Semitic name, diaspora Jews normally bore a second, similar-sounding Roman-Hellenistic given name. Similar onomastic pairs included, for example, Joshua and Jason, Silas and
Silvanus. In the Hellenistic world Paul used this second name exclusively. Paul may have had a married sister in Jerusalem (Acts 23:16),
but this information is not at all assured, because the whole section of
Acts from the Pauline stay in Jerusalem to the mission in Rome contains very little reliable information (cf. 15.3 below). He himself did not
marry (cf. 1 Cor. 9:5). His occupation for earning his bread is given in
Acts 18:3 as "tentmaker"; this occurs in connection with the married
couple Priscilla and Aquila, who practiced the same occupation. Paul
does not confirm this directly but gives indications (1 Thess. 2:9;
1 Cor. 9:15, 18; 2 Cor. 11:9) that allow us to credit Luke with historical
truth in this case. Of course, we must not take this occupational designation too narrowly; such things were quite general in antiquity. Thus
we will not go astray if we assume for Paul's occupation a linen or,
less likely, leather-working trade; tents and coverings of all kinds (e.g.,
for protection against the sun or for market stalls and cisterns) were
made out of linen or animal skins. Tarsus was especially well known
for the production of linen and its further processing.

Paul himself says that he belongs to the party of Pharisees (Phil. 3:5)
and that his zeal for the law exceeded that of many of his peers
(Gal. 1:14). In this Paul compares himself very generally with those his
own age, without mentioning a group of fellow students under a rabbi.
That puts us on notice that he probably wants his Pharisaism to be
understood not as an occupational designation but only as a religious
attachment to this Jewish movement. That is also suggested by both
Phil. 3:5–6 and Acts 22:3 (cf. 26:4), which speak of his Pharisaic orientation. The typical triadic series (family background, childhood, and
education) is not intended to speak of his study as a professional education in the institutional sense; rather, according to Hellenistic custom,
it tells how in his reputation in regard to heritage and training Paul as
an adult citizen is to be evaluated according to family, childhood, and
education (for a Hellenistic-Jewish parallel, cf., e.g., Philo, *De vita
Mosis* 1.2). Thus, by all appearances Paul was not instructed in the
Pharisaic interpretation of the law as a regular student of a rabbi, in
order later to assume the occupation of a rabbi himself; rather, he was
educated in the Pharisaic spirit for his view of life. He lived according
to the doctrine of Pharisaism, which was largely a lay movement. So
did his parents, no doubt, before him (Acts 23:6). Furthermore,
nowhere does it mention that Paul was formerly an ordained rabbi.
This would also hardly be possible from the standpoint of his age.

Even if only an approximate date is given by the information in _Sota_ 22a, according to which ordination is not possible before age forty, Paul would have been too young (cf. ch. 2 above).

According to Acts 22:3; 26:5, Paul received part of his Pharisaic education in Jerusalem under Gamaliel I, one of the great contemporary rabbis of the Hillel school. That cannot be verified from Pauline information. Luke welcomes these assertions because he needs Paul's residence in Jerusalem, since he has him present at the persecution of Stephen and has him first persecute Stephen's followers in Jerusalem (Acts 7:58; 8:1, 3; 22:4–5; 26:10–11). Also, it fits his presentation concept not only to have the church begin in Jerusalem but also to place the first group persecution here. Was it not also a sonorous and exciting report to have the future great apostle sit at the feet of the great rabbi? Did this connection not fit in with the Lukan effort to intertwine Christian history with the dates of "world history"? Finally, is the Lukan picture of Paul not on the whole Jewish in orientation, and does this part of Paul's history not belong in that picture? Whatever we decide here, it is significant that because of his Pharisaic training—however received—Paul certainly belonged later to the few early Christians who had a "higher" level of education. These did not include Jesus' disciples but probably did include such Hellenistic townspeople as the "city treasurer" Erastus (Rom. 16:23).

Regardless of this last observation, Paul himself suggests a view of things regarding the stay in Jerusalem that is at least partially different from that of the Acts of the Apostles. At the time of his calling he was residing in Damascus (inference from Gal. 1:17). Also in the years before and after he was not in Jerusalem (Gal. 1:17–18) and indeed unknown by sight to the churches in Jerusalem until well into the years after his calling (Gal. 1:22–24). This last bit of information has been interpreted to mean that Paul only persecuted Stephen's group, not the church around the original apostles, and therefore he could have remained personally unknown to this community. Indeed, it alone remained in the Jewish capital after the persecution. In view of the small scale of things in Jerusalem, however, a persecution of Stephen's group and those participating in it would have to have been known to Peter's group too; Paul cannot have persecuted Stephen's circle without becoming known also to the circle of apostles and their followers. The still small group of Jerusalem Christians and the first post-Easter martyrdom, which certainly caused a stir among all Christians, permit no other thesis. Then, however, we must hold to the clear words of Gal. 1:22–24: at the time of the persecution of Stephen, Paul was not in Jerusalem. No one would understand Galatians 1 differently without the pressure of wanting to harmonize it with Acts 7–8. From Gal. 1:21 we can perhaps infer indirectly that before settling in Damascus, Paul lived in Cilicia. If we assume, namely, that after his calling the apostle chose Cilicia as one of his first mission fields because it was his ancestral homeland, then this has an analogy in the missionary activity of Stephen's people (cf. Acts 11:19–21). They apparently escaped the Jerusalem persecution by seeking out their hometowns in the Jewish Diaspora and missionizing there.

With these observations, however, we have still not at the same time made a final, negative decision about Paul's education with Gamaliel I. Yet this Lukan information has now become not surer but more suspect. Nevertheless Paul could have been with Gamaliel I and received at least a part of his Pharisaic education in the religious center of Pharisaism. This could have happened before Jesus appeared and before there was a Christian church. Therefore this assumption would also preserve the statement in Gal. 1:22 that Paul was personally unknown to the Jerusalem church (until the Apostolic Council). Thus in this case no surer decision can be made. If we leave the situation open or lean more toward a vote against Luke, then we cannot present Paul as a Hillelite. Such beautiful concretization is too hypothetical from the outset. Paul could also have easily received an education in the Pharisaic sense at any larger diaspora synagogue, even in Tarsus. Jerusalem would only have added, so to speak, the "Oxford level."

Some have still wanted to mark Paul as a Hillelite by assuming his familiarity with Hillel's so-called seven rules of interpretation. These, however, are not attested with certainty for Hillel himself, and thus even less clearly for Paul. Indeed, insistence on the legal strictness of the pre-Christian Paul (cf. Gal. 1:14; Phil. 3:6) would sooner lead us to discuss whether Paul once belonged to the other, stricter school of contemporary Judaism, namely, that of Shammai. Even with this hypothesis, however, we are on weak ground historically: in the passages mentioned, Paul is not trying to describe his position within Judaism but to mark the contrast with his present Christian theology. Thus this is where we are: we know that Paul was formerly a strict, law-abiding Pharisee. Beyond that, more specialized conjectures are and remain more than questionable.

We can perhaps extract one more final biographical detail from Gal. 5:11: "If I . . . still preach circumcision, why am I still persecuted?" Specifically, if we relate the opening conditional clause historically to the apostle's Jewish period and note the proselyte solicitation attested in Matt. 23:15, we can turn the Jewish Paul into a synagogal missionary for the law. But this conclusion is neither compelling nor relatively

assured nor supported by other observations. Paul's struggle against
the baptized fringe participants of the synagogue in Damascus (4.2 and
4.3 below) suggests, rather, that he makes a clear separation between
the people of salvation and the Gentiles.

Thus we may hold fast to the conclusion that Paul was a Pharisee
strict in the law but at the same time a resident of a Hellenistic city that
was a center of Hellenistic education. Also, the fact that the Pharisaically oriented family had its own Roman citizenship attests to an access to
the Roman Empire that was certainly typical for a part of diaspora
Judaism. Thus Paul integrates two worlds in his person: Judaism and
Hellenism. Both of these will now receive our attention.

3.2 Paul as Pharisee of the Diaspora

In order to determine Paul's theological position as a Jew, it makes
sense to use as a guide the only information the apostle gives about
himself on this theme. For there is no reason to doubt his self-designation as a former Pharisee or to make him instead Paul the apocalyptist,
for instance, although his Jewish worldview certainly bears apocalyptic
traits, as we will show.

If we examine the Jewish sources on the Pharisaism contemporaneous with Paul, that is, Pharisaism of the Herodian period before the
conquest of Jerusalem by Titus in A.D. 70/71, our thirst for historical
knowledge is more disappointed than satisfied. The later rabbinate not
only greatly limited the tradition but also decisively reworked it from
the standpoint of the victorious faction. Thus the rabbinate later understood itself as the sole Jewish orthodoxy and therefore discredited
other streams in Judaism and suppressed large parts of those traditions.
It also, however, presented its own Pharisaic early history in such a
way that it subsequently flowed directly into orthodoxy, so that the
variety recognizable here and there in early Pharisaism was largely lev-
eled out. Finally, the rabbinate did not comprehend this history at all
as continuity and development but only preserved older episodes and
controversies that seemed important for its interpretation of the law.
How important and typical for their time, however, were these traditions, if we grant historical reliability? If we consider all of this, we will
not be amazed by the variety and disputes in the newer presentations
of the history of Pharisaism.

Nonetheless we can perceive some basic outlines. Like the Essenes,
the Pharisees developed from the Hasidean movement of the second

century B.C. In Paul's time they had long since joined together in close fellowships with the goal of placing the entire people under the sanctifying effects of the Torah through obedience of the law. As surely as their numbers also included priests and scribes, most of the members were laypeople who were more or less dependent on scribal interpretation of the Torah.

Evidence shows that the unification of Pharisaic mentality is a late development in the history. There are various indications of this. In the Herodian period Shammai, Hillel, and their schools stand in conflict on their interpretations of the law. Shammai's school is basically nomistically oriented, while Hillel's is oriented toward the historical situation. Further, a radical, nationalistic, politically oriented segment of the Pharisees between Herod and Titus seems to have acted like zealots against everything foreign, but the majority seems to have withdrawn to only a religious observance of the law. In the Diaspora again, some Pharisees may, among other things, have increased the proselytes and fringe participants of the synagogue, that is, the so-called God-fearers who adhered to Jewish monotheism yet shied away from circumcision. All of these variations are nonetheless reconciled in a fundamental orientation toward the law as the sole life norm for all Israel.

Even the understanding of the law itself, however, underwent varied development in the overall history of Pharisaism. This concerned the fundamental understanding of the law, the interpretation of the Torah's promise of life, and finally the weighting within the law.

In regard to the first point, the law was identified particularly in Pharisaism with the preexistent wisdom through the triumphal procession of wisdom thinking in early Judaism (Sirach). The Torah was thus "the instrument . . . through which the world was created" (*'Abot* 3:14); as such, it is the inner law of all creation and history and the life norm of every human life: the law understood through wisdom led to fear of God (1:3), which was to be realized as doing the law (1:17); the law was a unified entity in which all commandments were equally ranked expressions of the will of the one divine Majesty (2:1). In concealed form this conception can be recognized in Paul, for example, behind Rom. 1:18–3:20.

The law promised life to the doer. In early Christian times Sadduceeism and Essenism still thought of this life in orthodox fashion as the one, earthly life of a person; Pharisaism, on the other hand, taught—probably since the first century B.C.—that this life would receive a continuation in the coming world, and at its beginning would come the handing out of reward and punishment for the behavior of all people in this world vis-à-vis the Torah (Mark 12:18–27 par.;

Acts 23:6–8; *'Abot* 2:1, 7, 16; 3:1, 14–16). With this, a basic view of early Jewish apocalypticism became also a Pharisaic view. Since then not only Pharisaism and wisdom theology but also Pharisaism and apocalypticism have been connected. Paul also shows that he lives in an understanding of reality in which the present reality will be dissolved by a coming eternal one, and the gate into ultimate final salvation is divine judgment (see below).

In both of these decisive turns of Pharisaism we can see how from the standpoint of its fundamental orientation toward the law it could be open to the historical change of the time. Thus it apparently also showed in many cases an intellectual openness to Hellenism and consciously developed the diaspora situation of Judaism along these lines. A beautiful example of this is the Jewish historian Josephus (ca. 37/38 to the end of the first century A.D.). Descended from the Sadducee priestly nobility, he attached himself to Pharisaism in his youth, took part in the Jewish war in Galilee, and fell into Roman imprisonment, in order henceforth to experience the end of the war from Titus's side and then, having acquired Roman citizenship and an annual salary, to live in Rome. His literary work is devoted to the attempt to combine on a Jewish basis Judaism and Hellenistic-Roman culture.

The law contains manifold commandments that in practice must be weighted. The newer research here has shown that the Pharisees held with special intensity the position that the purity laws should be observed in everyday life by the people as a whole and not play a role only as Torah for the priests. This made the sanctification of everyday life a program for the whole people of Israel. To the extent that this goal was also realized in the Hellenistic Diaspora, the separation from all non-Jews was marked with particular clarity. If ritual sanctification in particular, as preservation of their own identity as people of the covenant, was the engine of Pharisaic activity, then we can understand why Paul proceeded so aggressively against Jewish Christians in Damascus, if they regarded this particular boundary as porous (cf. 4.2 below).

These general observations on Pharisaism characterize the consciousness of the Jew Paul only in its overall boundaries. Can we make special statements here about Paul? That will be the case if for this purpose we utilize more consistently than usual the Pauline letters themselves. That means that whoever looks for traditional Jewish material and views in Paul must not simply understand them only as general Christian knowledge of Judaism. Instead, we must ask to what extent such statements describe Paul himself in relation to his former Jewish position. It seems unlikely that Paul formed a view of Judaism only after his conversion. Rather, it is probable that his Christian judgment of Judaism, his Christian description of it, and his adoption of Jewish material have their roots in the apostle's Jewish period. It is hardly imaginable that Paul did not have to become oriented in Judaism until he became a Christian. Rather, it must be true that when Paul characterizes Judaism, his own former Jewishness is fundamentally involved. Here we see an essential difference in the analysis of the Pauline letters and the synoptic tradition. In the latter case, the history of the tradition takes place in the medium of anonymous growth; in the former, an individual bearer of tradition can be identified. From this perspective we recognize in Paul some clear aspects of his Pharisaic teaching. The better they can be checked against Jewish sources, the more reasonably they can be ascribed to the Jewish Paul.

Before any individual discussion we must also note that indications from Paul's writings come to us clothed in the Greek language. In no passage can we, through a smooth reverse translation into Aramaic, make clear that Paul only later—say, as a Christian—undertook a Greek transformation. That leads to the assumption that even as a Jew, Paul probably formulated such assertions in Greek. This is one more indication that Paul was a Hellenistic diaspora Pharisee.

This is also confirmed by the fundamental, polemical theme that the diaspora synagogue disputed with Hellenism: uncompromising monotheism that stood alone in a world of Roman-Hellenistic religion with its tolerant, syncretistic basic attitude. The only true God, as creator and judge, is confronted with the gods (Rom. 1:18–19; 1 Thess. 1:9). The gods are not ontically nothing, but in their positive significance they are irrelevant. They are classified as powerless powers, for example, as demons who are divinely worshiped but for whom worship is not appropriate (1 Cor. 8:4–5; 10:18–22). Their worship is precisely the sin of the pagans as an expression of disobedience of the one God. It leads all the more into human sinful perversion, which shows that the world of pagan gods is not wholesome for human beings and in the Jewish view stands under the judgment of God (Rom. 1:18ff.). Therefore a compromise between Judaism and Hellenism on this topic is impossible. On the contrary, everything of a pagan, sinful nature, as seen in religion and ethics, must be consistently avoided. "Have no fellowship with a godless person," reads a fundamental Pharisaic imperative in *'Abot* 1:7. Thus the usual Pharisee—the above-mentioned Josephus is rather an exception—lives according to a model of confrontational disqualification according to which Israel represents the true religion and all paganism is considered sinful falling away from that religion. If we correctly estimate the Damascene *casus belli* between Paul and the Christians (cf. 4.2 and 4.3 below), he will have consistently represented the Pharisaic purity ideal and the tabooing of all pagan worship. Even Paul prays with the third of the Eighteen Benedictions, "Holy are you and fearful your name, and there is no god but you."

This prayer begins, "Praised are you, . . . God of Abraham, God of Isaac, and God of Jacob, . . . highest God, creator of heaven and the earth, our shield and shield of our fathers." This says two things: the worldwide beginning with the Creator-God, to whom the world and humankind are in debt, is always at the same time soteriologically defined by faith in election, as initiated with the patriarchs of Israel; indeed, it is not by chance that the prayer begins with this soteriological predication of God. According to Gal. 2:15, Paul quite naturally characterizes the different initial situations of Jews and Gentiles as they cross over to Christianity, so that he separates born Jews and Gentile sinners. The thematization of Israel's future destiny in Romans 9–11 is understandable only on the basis of such a distinction between the people of salvation and the other peoples. Because of this fundamental principle of Jewish faith (cf. also 'Abot 1:7; 3:14; 4 Ezra 6:55–56), Paul feels compelled to show by Israel's first bearer of election—that is, by Abraham—the extent to which, from the Christian standpoint, Abraham is now the father of all believers (Galatians 3; Romans 4). First Thessalonians witnesses to how Paul takes this tenet of election, so fundamental for Israel's self-understanding, and revises and reshapes it according to Christian faith (cf. 6.2 below).

This necessarily leads to the disqualification of the Gentiles as unelected, guilty idolaters (cf. Rom. 1:18ff.; Gal. 4:8). Even Paul—now in order to characterize the distinction from Christianity—can, in continuity with the Jewish verdict, call the Gentiles "a crooked and perverse generation" (Phil. 2:15), quoting from Deut. 32:5 (obviously an old Pharisaic custom). Paul's pre-Christian standpoint also seems to shine through when he forbids Christians to go to court "before the unrighteous," that is, before Gentiles (1 Cor. 6:1ff.). The synagogue had already set up its own court system precisely so as not to be delivered up (only) to Gentile justice. Paul carried this over to the relationship between Christians and pagans.

On the other hand, the privileges of Israel can be set forth as Israel's election through the covenant with the fathers, so that Israel now possesses the sonship; the giving of the law as gift for knowing the will of the covenant God, in order by following it to achieve life; worship pleasing to God alone as atonement for Israel's transgressions; and finally the promises, above all that Israel will participate in the final salvation and God will not revoke his promises (Rom. 3:1–2; 11:2, 28–29). In Rom. 9:4

Paul formulates a handy arrangement of Israel's privileges in two groups of three, including

sonship	the giving of the law
glory	cult
the covenants	the promises

The two columns interpret each other: sonship and Torah also belong together in *'Abot* 3:14. The (earthly) glory (of God) dwells in the temple in which Israel established the cult. The covenants (patriarch, Moses) are aimed primarily toward Israel's future. In knowing how to characterize the Jew correctly, Paul as the former Pharisee addresses him in Rom. 2:17ff. in this way:

1. (*a*) He calls himself a Jew,
   (*b*) relies upon the law,
   (*c*) boasts of his relation to God,
   (*d*) knows the will (of God), and,
   (*e*) instructed in the law, approves what is excellent.

This self-evaluation in his relationship to God is matched in the continuation, which draws out the comparison with the Gentiles:

2. (*a*) You are sure that you are a guide to the blind,
   (*b*) a light to those who are in darkness,
   (*c*) a corrector of the foolish,
   (*d*) a teacher of children,
   (*e*) having in the law the embodiment of knowledge and truth.

It is not by chance that the two texts support the prominent position of the Torah, its observance, and its generally being carried out.

That precisely this is Judaism in the Pharisaic interpretation is generally known. That Paul understood himself thus as a Pharisaic Jew is a reasonable deduction. Another look at Phil. 2:15–16 is instructive in ascertaining this conclusion. In this passage Paul transfers Jewish claims and Jewish consciousness to the Christian church. Thus he expects the Christians to "be blameless and innocent." Is that not also what the true Jew is supposed to be (Rom. 2:10, 13; Phil. 3:6)? Further, they are to be "children of God without blemish" (cf. the Jewish sonship in Rom. 9:4), "in the midst of a crooked and perverse generation" (cf. Rom. 2:19–20), "among whom you shine as lights in the world" (cf. Rom. 2:19), "holding fast the word of life" (cf. Rom. 9:4). To this transfer from one communion to the other we add the observation that Paul places himself in the framework of these Jewish privileges when he describes himself as a former Pharisee (Phil. 3:4–6).

The basic concern of Pharisaism was to be equal to this situation of election, that is, to obey the Torah as the revelation of divine will and create for it appropriate validity in the life of each individual Israelite (cf., e.g., *'Abot* 1:12; 2:7, 12): a life for the law to the glory of God. Paul judges his own life-style as a Jew by the all-controlling law and considers himself faultless and righteous (Phil. 3:6; Gal. 1:14). We must not judge this statement right away as self-righteousness according to the parable of the Pharisee and the tax collector (Luke 18:11ff.); rather, we must see first of all that Paul binds human destiny not to his self-estimation but to the judgment of God (1 Cor. 4:3–5), and that this was the typical Pharisaic attitude (*'Abot* 2:1, 14–15; 3:1). "Righteous" means faithful to the Torah in God's judgment. It should be no question that from this basic statement there was then the further possibility of, among other things, seeking eternal life on one's own by patiently accomplishing good works (cf. Rom. 2:7) or even of presenting one's good works to the Judge (Luke 18:11–12).

Being faithful to the Torah includes holding to the law as a lifelong task and being penitent for committed sins, as the law itself includes obedience and atonement:

> The reliance of the righteous is on God their savior.
> Sin upon sin does not dwell in the house of the righteous.
> The righteous man always guards his house,
> so that he can blot out unrighteousness
> when it happens through his trespass.
> He atones for sins of ignorance by fasting
> and humiliation of his soul.
> The Lord purifies every godly man and his house.
>
> (*Pss. Sol.* 3:6–8)

In this way, *Psalms of Solomon* describes the righteous man and contrasts him with the sinner who piles up sin upon sin in his life (*Pss. Sol.* 3:9–10). It is precisely the man faithful to the law who knows that he lives from the divine mercy, which is valid for him, the righteous one, and that until death he must be ready for repentance and reform (*'Abot* 2:2, 8, 12; 3:1, 15; 4:11). We will also have to understand the Pauline assertions in Phil. 3:6; Gal. 1:14 in this sense. Paul would probably also deny to no Jew that he can be righteous in this sense. Paul, of course, would hold this to be no longer of any worth for the sake of the knowledge of Jesus Christ (Phil. 3:7ff.; 12.4 below).

For the Pharisee Paul, living for the law means obedience to the creator and judge. All people owe this obedience to God because of their creatureliness, but Israel has the privilege of knowing the divine will through the law. This human obligation finds its clearest expression in the concept of the last judgment. Paul not only maintained the idea of judgment as a Christian (e.g., 1 Cor. 3:5–17; 2 Cor. 5:10; Rom. 14:10–12); in Rom. 2:2ff. he also treats discursively a Jewish-Hellenistic view of the concept of judgment, which today is correctly considered part of the "pre-Pauline" conceptual content. Of course, in this section the Christian Paul turns these assertions against the Jewish concept in a way that is unbearable to a Jew. But this is done by beginning with common ground shared by him and the Jewish side (v. 2: "We know that . . ."), and on the basis of such a consensus, he holds that it is impossible for the Jew in particular to be found innocent in the divine court. Thus this means that if this polemical pointedness is overlooked, we must see the basic traits of the traditional view of judgment. Indeed, Paul did not merely employ a rootless Hellenistic-Jewish word here and there in this text (e.g., the term for "righteous judgment" in v. 5); rather, such linguistic observations signal an overall view that forms the basis of Paul's thinking and in which he still feels at one with the Jew. Thus it must be true that the overall view of judgment, in which Paul and Judaism are united, is typical for Paul as a former diaspora Jew, if indeed he did not have to form a view of Judaism later, when he became a Christian.

What is this view of judgment like? We will answer this question in such a way as to follow the Pauline text, and at each point a Jewish analogy will be presented. All creatures live in the face of the coming judgment. No one can escape it (Rom. 2:2–3; 9:18–24; cf. 'Abot 2:1; 3:1). Neither a time of judgment nor the temporal imminence of judgment is mentioned. When judgment day will be seems not to be of current interest, but it is crucial that following or rejecting the Torah has judicial consequences (cf. 'Abot 2:1, 15; 3:1). Judgment is made serviceable to the theology of the Torah. It stresses that God's will cannot be disregarded with impunity. God will not be mocked (Gal. 6:7); therefore be doers of the Torah (cf. 'Abot 1:16; 2:8). Until the judgment we have the period of the "riches of his kindness and forbearance and patience," which is meant to drive the individual "to repentance." Whoever does not use this time is stiff-necked and will incur the divine wrath (Rom. 2:4–5; cf. 'Abot 2:1, 8, 10, 12). History is understood as God's making it possible to lead a life for the Torah, and at the same time it is understood consistently with a view toward the last judgment.

Even the Gentiles who are not familiar with the written Torah receive no dispensation from doing the will of God, for—and here a Stoic idea takes on Hellenistic-Jewish form—the requirements of the law are known to them "by nature," because the law "is written on their hearts," as "their conscience" bears witness (Rom. 2:14–15).

The last judgment is conceived as something eschatologically forensic. It proceeds "according to truth" (Rom. 2:2; cf. 'Abot 3:16), that is,
without partiality (Rom. 2:11; cf. 'Abot 4:22; Pss. Sol. 2:18; etc.) as the
revelation of "God's righteous judgment" (Rom. 2:5; T. Levi 3:2; 15:2);
here Paul employs a Hellenistic coinage that he otherwise does not use.
All three assertions mean the incorruptibility of the judge, who favors
no one and rules strictly and unremittingly according to the deeds of
each person (Rom. 2:6) and also judges the "secrets of men" (Rom.
2:16). Since God hands to each person his or her eschatological destiny,
his judgment is righteous (iustitia distributiva), for it corresponds to
"the truth," that is, to the actuality of the person. Thus in Rom. 2:6 Paul
can quote Ps. 62:13 (cf. Prov. 24:12): God "will render to every man
according to his works." Originally this assertion once meant a close
connection between deed and condition, according to which the consequence of a deed immediately strikes back at the doer, and God keeps
this connection in force. Now, however, the statement must be read in
its present context of three judicial principles and thereby receive the
meaning of eschatological "recompense": God establishes righteousness
in an act of judgment by rewarding the doers of good, that is, reckoning
their reward according to their due (Rom. 4:2, 4); but he makes "wrath
and fury" come to the doers of evil (Rom. 2:8ff.). 'Abot also speaks in
this way of the divine "recompense" ('Abot 1:7) and means by that the
eschatological "division of wage," in which God, like an employer,
hands out wages for work accomplished ('Abot 2:16). This reward is
based on the fact that all the deeds of human beings are recorded in a
"book" ('Abot 2:1), and they must render an "account and calculation"
('Abot 3:1); conversely, God "credits" everything to them ('Abot 2:2; 3:8).
Such industrial and commercial language can be painted clearly in the
image of the shifty tradesman and the money lender ('Abot 3:16). The
"storing up" of wrath (Rom. 2:5) is doubtless to be understood against
this background. Thus the idea is that in the last judgment God ratifies
the terminated history of humankind through his settlement of accounts.
He reacts to the deeds of human beings through his judgment. In this
respect, regarded from the standpoint of judgment, deeds have a fundamental significance for salvation or damnation.

It is fundamental to Romans 2, moreover, that reward and punishment are not quantified: as there are only the righteous and the sinners,
there is also only eschatological life or torment. "Glory and honor and
immortality" (again a typically Hellenistic concept!) or "glory and honor
and peace" (Rom. 2:7, 10) tell what "eternal life" is (in 1 Thess. 4:17;
5:10 Paul gives this a new, Christian definition). Conversely, "wrath and
fury" (Rom. 2:8) are qualities of the final state of damnation. For this

reason we must remember Paul's comments on judgment regarding his being righteous under the law: righteous means faithful to the Torah. These statements clearly describe the two outcomes of life in parallel fashion. The Christian Paul, in 1 Thess. 4:13–5:11, for example, will show no more interest in the fate of all unbelievers; he pursues only the salvation of the eschatological church. The Jewish interest in compensating justice at the end of the world, of course, requires this double aspect (e.g., *Pss. Sol.* 3:6–12; etc.). As a Christian, Paul can agree with this Pharisaic view to the extent that he too knows only the fundamental qualification in the last judgment and correspondingly only the one uniform state of salvation.

Between the lines the concept of judgment also contains an anthropological assertion: Pharisaism presupposes that the imperative "you shall" addresses a person whose nature includes "you can." The sin is failure due to the lack of a possible initiative of the individual, not the reflection of a negative qualification of the doer himself or herself. In other words, the freedom of the will is Pharisaic doctrine (cf., e.g., *'Abot* 3:15). Because human beings are in principle free to do good or evil and thus are not ruled by sin (Rom. 7:14–15), we need only to look at their works; they themselves need no fundamental renewal before they can be doers of good. Here Paul will think differently after his calling, as he reshapes his judgment of human beings (cf. 14.3 below).

If, after these comments on the last judgment as sketched by Paul, we turn to Hellenistic Judaism, we will see that it analogously—not throughout, yet certainly in some cases—adopted assertions about the last judgment borrowed from apocalypticism. This is attested, for example, by the *Testaments of the Twelve Patriarchs,* the *Sibylline Oracles,* and *1 Enoch.* Above all, however, *Liber Antiquitatum Biblicarum*—written by an author who at least was close to Pharisaic thinking—shows how apocalyptic thinking could be made serviceable for the Pharisaic understanding of the law, as this new recounting of the history of Israel expands the story of the flood, so that the great flood was one sign among other historical wrathful actions of God (cf. Rom. 1:18ff. before 2:1ff.); then, when the years of the world are fulfilled, God will make all the dead alive and "reward each one according to his works" (cf. Rom. 2:5–6). Here the saved count as the "justified," who will live in another "eternal dwelling" (*Lib. Ant.* 3:9–10).

Although Pharisaism could approach apocalypticism's concept of the last judgment by comprehending it as an integral component of its understanding of the law and thus interpret the Torah's promise of life as eschatological life after judgment, this does not make the Pharisees apocalyptists. The Pharisee Paul was no apocalyptist either, any more than the author of *Liber Antiquitatum Biblicarum* or the one who prays in the *Psalms of Solomon* or the teachers of Israel who speak in *'Abot*. For apocalypticism wants to achieve recognition precisely through the extraordinary revelatory processes associated with the great figures of history, not with truths contained in the Jewish law. What it wants is to establish authority for supplementary truth beside and beyond Moses (cf., e.g., *4 Ezra* 14:37–48). A Pharisee knows only the authority of Moses: the law alone is enough to gain life. Thus the answer that the rich man receives in Luke 16:27–31 to his request that his brothers be given a special revelation is typically Pharisaic: "They have Moses and the prophets; let them hear them. . . . If they do not hear Moses and the prophets, neither will they be convinced if some one should rise from the dead." Therefore the Pharisee also does not speak pseudonymously or anonymously; rather, he teaches with the authority of Moses. With him no forefather appeals, as did Enoch or Ezra, to special revelations that are actually hidden and only disclosed to the seer; he knows only God's revelation of the law on Sinai and its interpretation through oral tradition (*'Abot* 1:1).

The special revelation to which apocalypticism appeals is mostly an expression of a crisis feeling that comprehends earthly history as the history of damnation, in which the view of God's meaning-creating activity is generally hidden or lost. Apocalypticism, with its world experience in the global-historical and cosmic sense, tries to overcome helplessness and despair through such special revelation, in that the latter teaches how world and history are subject to an order and periodicity that are hidden—though now already revealed to selected ones—and how the present time and the cosmic, historical end time are joined. The Pharisee, on the other hand, describes history as the continuous and constant period of God's patience, in which every individual has the opportunity and duty to fulfill the Torah, in order to render an accounting to God one day. He needs no secret historical timetable or cosmic special knowledge about the world and eschatological events. For him, the last judgment is concentrated in the anthropological meaning of the reward and punishment of each human being vis-à-vis the commandments of the Torah. Thus it is also still retained formally by Paul even as a Christian (Rom. 14:10; 2 Cor. 5:10; etc.). There is a tradition originating in the time when Paul was a Pharisee (*'Abot* 3:1): "Pay close attention to three things, and you will not come under the power of sin. Know where you have come from and where you are going and before whom you will have to render an account and calculation. Where did you come from? From a foul-smelling drop. Where are you going? To maggots and worms. Before whom do you have to render an account and calculation? Before the King of all kings." For the Pharisee, the individual can always depend on the reliability of life, because the expectation of divine recompense is constant and unshakable. It all depends on individuals and their obedience to the Torah. They must each endure the coming judgment all alone and for themselves. More than this they do not need to know in life. This basic knowledge, however, is guaranteed certain by Moses.

3.3 Paul and Hellenism

We have just taken an initial look at the fact that the diaspora Pharisee Paul advocates a Judaism shaped by Hellenism (cf. 3.1 and 3.2 above). This fact will now be discussed in a little more detail. Of course, one can settle this as a special issue through a wholesale designation of Judaism in general as Hellenistic in the early Christian period. There is even a certain degree of justification for this. After the kingdoms of the Diadochi had entered the inheritance of Alexander the Great in the eastern Mediterranean basin, this whole region fell under the influence of Greek-Hellenistic language and culture. Even Judaism as a whole did not remain free of it. It still made a difference, however, whether a Jew joined the Maccabeans and fought against acute hellenization, whether an Essene was oriented toward the Hasidean priesthood, whether a resident of Galilean villages—perhaps in spite of many bits and pieces of Greek language—adhered to the traditional religion of the fathers, or whether a Josephus studied the Torah and Greek rhetoric, an Aristobulus or Philo went into Greek philosophy in order to unite it with the Jewish faith, or a Demetrius, Eupolemus, or Artapanus built up a Jewish apologetic vis-à-vis Greek religion and culture. As to the question to what extent an individual person or group was hellenized in language, religion, education, and culture, there were naturally great differences. The question is the same whether one grew up in Judea or Alexandria and whether one dealt with the Greek language only for making oneself more or less understood in everyday life or through knowledge of the language also became a Greek "with the soul" (cf. Josephus, *Contra Apionem* 1.180). Where, then, is Paul of Tarsus to be placed in this spectrum?

Without doubt we can credit Tarsus very generally with the institutional possibilities of receiving an overall Hellenistic education with the ideal of a representative universal education (cf. 3.1 above). In Paul's time we can generally assume the following educational path. First, there was instruction in the elementary area (gymnastics, music, reading, and writing). This was done by private teachers and slaves. On this was built the higher general education, which was the task of the rhetoricians and their schools. They taught grammar, reading the classic writers, rhetoric (knowledge of speaking and composition), dialectic (fundamentals of philosophizing), mathematics, and music theory. Following this came the crowning instruction at the philosopher schools, where they also taught the most important specialized knowledge of all kinds from the whole of antiquity.

We would hardly assume that a Jewish family whose religious attitude was Pharisaic and strict concerning the law (cf. 3.2 above) would send its son to a Gentile school, as surely as Paul could naturally have heard a Gentile rhetorician or philosopher here and there. He himself also betrays no knowledge of Greek philosophy or the old classics. At this point he is clearly different from Philo. Thus it is more likely that he traveled the path of a Jewish education in the Hellenistic Diaspora. Because of the competition factor, this consisted of quite analogous areas of study in regard to the first and second educational levels. Of course, some modifications could and indeed had to be made. The Torah was naturally the main object of instruction. Gymnastics was not highly regarded by the Jews and thus could be neglected. For languages, Aramaic and Greek no doubt dominated the schedule. The introduction to Greek philosophy could be taught with reserve or not at all. It is very unlikely, though, that the Jews would have dispensed with rhetoric: as surely as Jews built up their own judicial system where they could, it still must have been necessary, for example, to defend themselves before Gentile courts when a non-Jew accused them. Surely many Hellenistic Jews also found themselves obliged to give a speech that was acceptable to Hellenistic ears or even praiseworthy at a meeting or a private celebration. Thus we can indeed imagine the Jewish educational institutions in the Diaspora as analogous to Hellenistic education.

Let us assume that Paul received such a Jewish higher general education, which in the quality of the second level corresponded to a Hellenistic education. To substantiate this thesis we will best begin with the apostle's language. For Paul, there is a common linguistic ruling: all non-Jews are "Greeks" (e.g., Rom. 1:16; 2:9–10; etc.). Naturally this distinction, first of all, has soteriological and theological significance: being Greek means being pagan. But the distinction also means that for non-Jews the lingua franca, as a rule, is Greek. Thus Paul writes not only to Philippi and Corinth in the Greek language but likewise to distant Galatia, as well as to the most Roman of all cities: Rome itself. In spite of the naturally polyglot nature of the Gentile-Christian mission field (cf. Acts 2:8–11), it is no serious problem for Paul to missionize in the provincial cities, because he himself learned Greek in Tarsus from childhood on, and everywhere in an analogous urban milieu he ran into Greek as the everyday language.

Paul's knowledge of Greek can be more closely described: he speaks the so-called Koine quite fluently and without any real translated Semitisms. He thinks in this language, and his style is neither linguistically uneven nor harsh, as measured against other documents of his time. He has good control of Greek grammar. From time to time he achieves complex sentences like those in classical Greek literature. He also quotes the Holy Scripture—mostly by heart—according to the Septuagint, which he had apparently read and studied from childhood on; otherwise he could hardly quote from it so extensively. Thus Greek for Paul is not only a marginal assimilation to his readers and hearers but an aspect of his own education. It is therefore quite reasonable here to presuppose formal education from his earliest years.

Further areas of observation for our inquiry are the general means of framing a letter and special means of presentation and argumentation within letters. From the beginning Paul was a master of epistolary style when, following the Greek formula, he divided the opening of a letter into *superscriptio* (statement of sender), *adscriptio* (statement of addressee), and *salutatio* (formulaic greeting) and in doing so formed the *salutatio* into its own sentence according to oriental-Jewish fashion. For the closing of the letters we can also recognize a common typology. Within the letters he succeeds, even in such complex problem areas as that presented, for example, in Romans 1–8, in ordering his train of thought well, in making its sequence transparent, in sensibly handling text signals for the divisions, and in using good formulations to get to the point. Even with every talent and ability to teach oneself, this must as a rule be appropriated through formal education. In addition, Paul does not avail himself of any and all stylistic means but uses Hellenistic models of argumentation as well as the style of the so-called diatribe (if this imprecise expression is permitted as a collective concept). Thus the Hellenistic influence of higher schooling is again apparent.

Moreover, a look at rhetoric is illuminating. Paul and Greek rhetoric is a topic currently receiving a good deal of attention. If we know how much all of public life in Hellenism was defined by the knowledge of rhetoric—as everyone on the *agora,* in the *gerousia,* in the associations, and so forth, could experience how orators appeared, including itinerant preachers of all kinds and those colorful people, the Sophists—then we must in any case grant Paul a certain basic knowledge in this area. Admittedly, at first glance he seems not to think much of rhetoric. He draws the line between himself and his various opponents in Corinth in that he has not missionized "in plausible words of wisdom" (1 Cor. 2:4; cf. also 1 Cor. 1:17, 20; 2:1, 13) and considers himself "unskilled in speaking" (2 Cor. 11:6). The Corinthians seem to have the impression that he is weak in personal appearance and not an especially eloquent speaker (2 Cor. 10:10). This impression, of course, becomes the opposite in his letters! Already to the Thessalonians the apostle writes that he spoke to them neither with flattery nor with the intention of earning money through his speaking (1 Thess. 2:5).

At least here it becomes clear that Paul sets himself off from concrete competitors, who obviously appeared very self-conscious and eloquent, while Paul in this context points in his speech to the sole effectiveness of God and therefore downgrades his own eloquence. He does not simply set himself fundamentally apart from all rhetoric but wants to awaken faith through the content of his speaking: the gospel and its power.

Now we can also understand this as a religious variant of a particular kind in the rhetorical discussion of the period. Cicero's increasing influence on the rhetorical education of the epoch had ensured that the Athenian way of rhetoric, with its love of rhetorical formulation that valued the form of speech more than the content, was permeated with the insight that the starting point of all rhetorical achievement has to be the speaker's knowledge of the subject: speech should primarily convince through its content, not through rhetorical form. Thus it is not at all beside the point to examine whether Paul shows rhetorical ability. This is all the more true when Paul argues downright passionately with his opponents over the kind of "persuasion" through oratory (cf. 1 Cor. 2:4; 2 Cor. 5:11; to the point, 2 Corinthians 10–13). With this he thematizes one of the classical functions of ancient oratory. For example, Gorgias, with respectable long-term effect, defines rhetoric as the "mistress of persuasion" (Plato, *Gorgias* 453A). In antiquity they knew that this art of persuasion is of prominent significance in politics and in court, but how it can also enslave the truth.

In Paul's time rhetoric had long been an element of education. Three typical speeches were distinguished: the judicial speech, the political speech, and the occasional speech. The first type had a kind of guiding function in this threesome. Certainly the Greeks' joy in court trials played a role here. Yet one could also earn good money with such speeches. Everyone, including Paul in Tarsus, could almost regularly hear a judicial defense speech and be exposed to its impression as well as, of course, its technical ingenuity. Thus it is no wonder that recently it has been increasingly observed that Paul relies on the judicial speech precisely where he must defend himself and where he gets into polemics. Especially 1 Corinthians 1–4; chs. 9; 15; 2 Corinthians 10–13; and Galatians are places where the apostle avails himself of various elements of the judicial speech. Even though Paul no doubt hardly proceeds in a regular textbook fashion, and also the genre of the letter brings with it an interruption in the use of such rhetoric, it can hardly be doubted that his way of presentation depends on the rhetoric of antiquity. Here too we are close to the assumption that he owes this knowledge to his time in Tarsus. We can ask again how he acquired such schooling. It is scarcely possible only through listening in the marketplace. Hence this is not a sufficient explanation. Did Paul perhaps become acquainted with the ancient textbooks of rhetoric through a Jewish rhetorician? This assumption is in any case possible. Then did he perhaps even read Pseudo-Cicero's *Rhetorica ad Herennium* or even Cicero's *De inventione* or one of the Stoic works? These questions can only be posed, not answered.

We can pause here and ascertain a preliminary result: there are several indications that together reinforce the impression that Paul enjoyed the higher general education that was available in Hellenism. Thus we must not be too quick to use the questionable connection with Gamaliel I to bind Paul as tightly as possible to Palestine-oriented Judaism without any Hellenistic influence worth mentioning. In the mirror of his letters Paul himself demonstrates how he also received a goodly portion of Hellenistic education. Only thus can we also explain how he, as a former Jew, consistently entered into the founding of Gentile-Christian churches and could interact quite well with the Hellenistic socialization and heritage of his church members. The crucial test case in this regard was and is Corinth. No one can say that Paul did not pass this test. That he could actually have learned this ability from the interpreter of the law Gamaliel I is yet to be proved.

There is education that one must normally acquire through schooling, and education that everyday life can convey. Anyone growing up in Tarsus also takes part in Hellenistic culture by being integrated into the life of the city, even if limited as a Jew. Naturally all of this can and will reemerge as school material. Nevertheless such indications are not sufficiently certain observations in favor of a special school education. Yet a few such phenomena can be cited for Paul.

There is evidence in the Pauline correspondence that the apostle in formerly traditional Jewish contexts presents Hellenistic views that are already closely interwoven with the Jewish context. Examples of this are not hard to find. It is the Hellenistic synagogue that communicated to Paul how the ideas of natural revelation of the Stoics could be linked with typical Jewish polemic against the pagan world (cf. Rom. 1:18ff.;

2:12ff.). His knowledge and judgment of pagan divinities likewise originated in his pre-Christian period (cf. 1 Thess. 1:9; 1 Cor. 8:1–6;
10:14–22). As a Hellenistic Jew, Paul had already become acquainted
with Hellenistic-Jewish paraenetic writing, which he then reshaped as a
Christian (cf., e.g., the catalog of vices in Romans 1; Galatians 5). The
same Hellenistic synagogue, which cultivated a Jewish arrangement
with the Gentile state and thereby adopted the Hellenistic-Roman language of political administration, conveyed to Paul position and language that come to light in Rom. 13:1–7. Even the allegorical method
filled with the Greek spirit, as applied by Paul (although seldom—cf. 1
Cor. 10:1–13; Gal. 4:21–31), was already known to the synagogal interpretation of the Septuagint, as attested by not only, but especially,
Philo, the somewhat older contemporary of Paul from Egyptian Alexandria. These examples, which could be multiplied, make clear that Paul
as a Jew is also sympathetic toward Hellenistic culture.

Pauline Hellenism, however, is not limited to such phenomena as
they appear in the typically Jewish framework. Also in Christian contexts Paul shows that he is still a Hellenist. When Paul describes his
apostolic existence with the aid of a competition in a Greek stadium
(1 Cor. 9:24–27), this reflects his Hellenistic, urban socialization, which
made the traditions of popular philosophy familiar to him. In his statements on baptism Paul is obviously dependent on the popularized
views and language of the Hellenistic mystery religions (cf., e.g.,
Rom. 6:1ff.), naturally, without, as a Jew or a Christian, knowing such a
cult directly. His concept of the church as the "body of Christ"
(Rom. 12:4ff.; 1 Cor. 12:12ff.) is hardly comprehensible without the
background in Greek philosophy. Anyone who wants to eliminate the
connections with Hellenistic tradition, in terms of form and content, in
the hymn to love in 1 Corinthians 13 will scarcely be able to describe
appropriately the intellectual history of its background. The Stoic
omnipotence formulas (Rom. 11:36; 1 Cor. 8:6) also belong in this context. Again, these examples can be multiplied. One who so naturally
speaks and thinks hellenistically must in the crucial years of his early
socialization have dealt with such phenomena, for Paul could hardly
have learned such things first in Antioch. It is typical that actually even
in these cases similar adaptation processes for the Hellenistic synagogues can in general be demonstrated (e.g., competition: 4 Maccabees; mystery language: Philo; on 1 Corinthians 13: cf., above all,
3 Ezra 4:34–40). Thus we can also ascertain for these cases that it was
probably the young Paul's life in a Hellenistic city and his Hellenistic-
Jewish education that conveyed to him the competence later as a
Christian to employ the spirit and tradition of Hellenism as his own.

4

Paul's Calling as Apostle to the Gentiles

4.1 The Sources and the Problems of Their Interpretation

Soon after the turning point in the apostle's life, through which the persecutor of Christians became a preacher of the law-free gospel, there arose a legend about Paul that captured what was special about the character of the apostle and his position in the Christian church; that is, it told from the viewpoint of the church what distinguished him from all other Christians of this period. Because Paul assumes here an exceptional position—not only in his self-understanding but also in the consciousness of early Christendom—such generally circulated tradition developed around his character. Paul refers to it intentionally in Gal. 1:23–24 when he writes: "They [the Jewish Christians] only heard it said, 'He who once persecuted us is now preaching the faith he once tried to destroy.' And they glorified God because of me."

At this point the apostle presupposes that people in Judea and Galatia, and thus no doubt in Christendom as a whole, had knowledge of this tradition. A comparison with a similar text in Acts 9:20–21 shows that here in typical fashion the life of Paul is divided into two parts (persecutor and preacher) in regard to his position with the Christian church, and these two relationships are ordered by the time-oriented contrast "once—now" borrowed from baptismal language (cf. 1 Cor. 6:9–11; Rom. 5:8–11; Col. 2:13; etc.). Most striking here is the use of the rare verb "destroy," which Paul himself otherwise uses only in Gal. 1:13 in order likewise to characterize his persecutory activity. This occurs in Galatians 1 apparently in dependence on the Christian legend of Paul, as it becomes visible in Acts 9. Also, the absolute use of preaching "the faith" and destroying points to extra-Pauline speech (cf. Gal. 6:10).

The creation and recounting of such legends can be placed in the larger context of analogous legend formations, as they soon arose concerning other great figures of early Christianity. The interest was not in the biography of such figures in general but in their association with the church or their significance for the new faith. Thus Peter was the first witness of Easter (Luke 24:34; 1 Cor. 15:5), Stephen was the first martyr of Christendom (Acts 6–7), and Epaenetus became known as the first baptized person in Asia (Rom. 16:5). Paul was added to these as the former persecutor and present preacher of the faith. This Paul legend can claim great age: it was formulated from the viewpoint of the oldest post-Easter center of Christendom and presupposes that Paul is still personally unknown there, that is, among the Judean Christians. Therefore it must have arisen very soon after Paul's calling and in any case before the Apostolic Council (cf. 5.2 below).

From the context of Paul's reception in the postapostolic period two other texts are known that, independently of the genuine Pauline letters, are defined by the Paul legend and reflect the turning point in the apostle's life: Acts 9:1–22 (22:3–21; 26:9–20) and 1 Tim. 1:12–16.

The latter text, and also its tradition, is of a relatively late date and need be mentioned only briefly here. It reads:

> I thank him who has given me strength for this, Christ Jesus our Lord, because he judged me faithful by appointing me to his service, though I formerly blasphemed and persecuted and insulted him; but I received mercy because I had acted ignorantly in unbelief, and the grace of our Lord overflowed for me with the faith and love that are in Christ Jesus. The saying is sure and worthy of full acceptance, that Christ Jesus came into the world to save sinners. And I am the foremost of sinners; but I received mercy for this reason, that in me, as the foremost, Jesus Christ might display his perfect patience for an example to those who were to believe in him for eternal life. (1 Tim. 1:12–16)

The text turns the break in Paul's life into a paradigm as the exemplary case of God's love in Christ for sinners, which is valid for all people. Paul was a blasphemer of God and a persecutor and opponent of the church. But this falls under ignorance, as does the pagans' cult of idols, according to the speech in the Areopagus (Acts 17:30). Thus it can be subsumed under the "patience" of God (cf. Rom. 2:2) and therefore be forgiven graciously.

On the one hand, Paul judges his persecutory activity differently (see below); on the other, the language of the text fits a certain missionary conversion sermon that is contrary to Paul: in place of forgivable ignorance, we find in Paul the inexcusability of humanity (Rom. 1:32; 2:1; 3:9ff.). Although Paul can also turn his calling into a paradigm (Philippians 3), his calling is the model case for the justification of the sinner who considers even the positive things of his old life to be worthless, but not for the conversion of the unknowing sinner. Since in this typification the concrete-historical aspect of the Pauline turning point was at the same time reduced to indications of a quite general kind (once persecutor and opponent, now placed in service), the text offers no further help in the historical judgment of the apostle's calling. It belongs in the history of the later Pauline image.

The other text—namely, Acts 9; 22; 26—was so deeply inscribed into the general Christian consciousness that it has prominently defined the knowledge of Paul up to the present day. Of course, on closer examination this text is also far from the Pauline understanding of his calling. In order to show this, it is sufficient to point especially to Acts 9 and to refer only now and then to the variations in Acts 22 and 26. Today scholars are, with justification, largely in agreement that the latter are Luke's own narrative variants and the pre-Lukan tradition from the general Paul legend is essentially to be found in Acts 9.

Even on an initial examination of the text, Lukan presentational aims become clear. Luke emphatically withholds from Paul the title of apostle in the sense of Acts 1:21 (an apostle is one who moved around with Jesus and witnessed Easter; in Acts 14:4, 14 the concept is used for Paul only in the sense of a church missionary). And he consciously distinguishes between the fundamental Easter events and Paul's vision: the resurrected One appears bodily to the circle of the apostles (Luke 24); with Christ's ascension, this time of appearances comes finally to an end; with Pentecost, the fundamental pneumatic event that defines the path of the gospel has long since become history. Only now is Paul called, and indeed only through a vision from heaven and through an event with very limited value. It is, namely, incomplete, in that first Ananias—on behalf of the Christian community and on his part led by direct divine instruction—makes Paul a Christian, that is, baptizes him (in distinction to the apostles; Acts 9:18–19) and inducts him into his service for the Lord (9:15ff.). Is this supposed to be the Paul who, independently of human authority, knows himself to be called directly by God (Gal. 1:10–17), classifies his vision of the Lord with the Easter appearances (1 Cor. 15:1–11), and claims for himself the same apostolic title as that borne by Peter and the others (1 Corinthians 9; ch. 15; Galatians 1)?

Furthermore, from the traditional persecutor motif Luke has made a qualitatively and quantitatively extensive persecution by Paul: he becomes—completely in the sense of the Paul legend in 1 Timothy 1—as blasphemer, persecutor, and opponent (1 Tim. 1:13) simply the exemplary sinner, who encounters grace through conversion and thus in his person becomes the epitome of the Christian doctrine of salvation by God's mercy. This is also the reason for the conspicuous, thrice-repeated, comprehensive presentation of the Pauline conversion in the

Acts of the Apostles. For this reason also Luke can place the extensive persecution by Paul, ended because of the conversion, over against Paul's great missionary success as a result of this divine grace. Again, 1 Tim. 1:14 is the analogy for this (yet cf. as early as 1 Cor. 15:10).

In particular, Luke shapes the persecution in the following way. A "great persecution" arose against the church in Judea, and in it Saul entered private homes and dragged men and women off to prison (Acts 8:1–3). Paul wants to lay waste to the Christian church, to achieve renunciation of Christianity through scourging, and even aims at the death of the Christians (8:3; 26:9–11; 22:4). The initial flight of the oppressed (8:1) leads to Paul's taking up their persecution practically everywhere, no matter where they may flee to (26:11); in particular, however, he made preparations, supplied with written authorization from the high priest (9:1, 13–14, 21), to realize in the synagogues of Damascus "threats and murder against the disciples of the Lord" and to bring men and women bound to Jerusalem (9:1–2). Thus Paul is carrying out an organized, geographically extensive, and deadly persecution, authorized by the Sanhedrin, with the aim of extinguishing the special Christian group in the synagogue. The pious zeal with which the dark shadow of the apostle here is painted black and larger than life is striking. In its style it belongs to texts from the Hellenistic synagogues, which often loudly called attention to the persecutions directed against it (cf., e.g., 3 and 4 Maccabees).

What remains for the eyes of the historian is the Damascene persecution as background of the calling. We saw already that at the time of the Hellenists Paul was not in Jerusalem at all (cf. ch. 2 above). Thus the mention of the letters of the high priest is also exposed as a construct. They are supposed to smooth the way from Jerusalem to Damascus. Let it be noted, moreover, that such letters cause legal-historical problems. The persecution in cities outside Jerusalem (Acts 26:11) remains vague and abstract, so that only one thing can be maintained: the local tradition of "Damascus" is apparently an old and solid component of the traditional conversion story in Acts 9. There Paul was the persecutor of Christians. But to draw additional historical information from Luke would be problematic.

Naturally Luke himself did not simply make a total revision of Acts 9. Even if here and there the Lukan additions within Acts 9 remain disputed in detail, it is still clear that Luke is narrating a solid tradition. Its structure probably corresponds to the old Paul legend that we encountered in Gal. 1:23–24: the church recounts that "he who once persecuted us is now preaching the faith he once tried to destroy." Acts 9 also deals with the double aspect of the first negative, then positive attitude of Paul toward the church: the persecutor becomes the converted preacher. The church that tells such a personal legend, a conversion story of a man well known in Christendom, is not interested in Paul's apostolic self-understanding, in his theology or his great missionary work among the Gentiles, in the placing of his conversion among the Easter events, and so forth; rather, it turns a famous person—quite analogous to 1 Timothy 1—into the exemplary case of conversion with which the church can be built up and the undecided convinced of Christianity.

The edifying legend thus has two parts: (1) The persecutor who intends to destroy the church is himself almost "destroyed" by the Lord of the church (core of Acts 9:1–9), and (2) through Ananias the Lord takes care that the leading persecutor is healed again and can preach Jesus as the Son of God (core of 9:10–22). Here the decisive structural traits and many individual motifs are marked by a hyperindividualized narrative style. This applies not only to the (probably Lukan) vision dialogue in 9:4b–6 (cf. Gen. 46:2–3; Ex. 3:4–10; etc.) and the topic of the little miracle story in 9:17–19 but in a profound way to the structure and presentation of the whole story. In particular we can study this in the Heliodorus legend of 2 Maccabees 3, in the conversion novel *Joseph and Aseneth*, and, among others, in manifold repetition in 3 Maccabees. All these texts belong to the Hellenistic synagogue, which thus apparently furnished the means by which Christians could tell something similar about Paul. It was, no doubt, Hellenistic Jewish Christians who retold the heritage of the synagogue and turned it against the synagogue (cf. Acts 9:20, 22). Perhaps this also explains why the opposition—so basic for Paul—between persecution out of zeal for the law and devotion to the Gentiles while ignoring the law is missing here. Paul is not called as apostle to the Gentiles; rather, he is a converted Jewish Christian, who represents the truth of Christianity at the synagogue.

From all these reflections on Acts 9 we can draw the following conclusion: Acts does not help us understand the calling of the apostle historically, for the conversion legend is a narrative development of the extra-Pauline tradition whose origins are indicated in Gal. 1:23–24. Its kernel of historical truth consists in the tradition of Damascus as the location, in the evidence of persecution as such, and in the fact of Paul's conversion. All of this we know also and better from Paul. Perhaps, however, with the figure of Ananias—hardly a total invention—Acts 9 has established something beyond Paul to the extent that this man was possibly the first Damascene Christian who took care of Paul after his conversion.

Hence we are entirely dependent on the self-testimony of the apostle. Yet even this poses considerable problems. To begin with, the scripture that may be drawn upon is in dispute. No one argues about the three decisive texts: 1 Cor. 15:1–11; Gal. 1:13–17; Phil. 3:2–14. But still open is the matter of which shorter notations should gain significance and above all how we are to proceed in the case of Rom. 7:7–25 or 2 Cor. 4:6. Then between the calling and the oldest important text, 1 Corinthians 15, there is a temporal distance of more than twenty years: in the light of such a distance, to what extent are original and later viewpoints interwoven in the texts? Paul never describes his Damascus experience per se but speaks of it when his mind is on the consequences that have lasting validity for him. Finally we must consider how even Paul's texts on his calling are extensively shaped by typological language. We can plainly establish that it is his aim to draw on common linguistic models in order to speak about his calling in a way that is as generally valid as possible. Where, then, can we grasp what is particular and individual? In any case, without a careful treatment of the texts in regard to these three points—scripture to be considered, historical distance, and typical language—we will very quickly fall away from history and into speculation.

This danger is not only great when texts in general answer questions only reluctantly but is also especially to be observed in the history of the interpretation of Paul's calling. How frequently has Paul already been employed to reflect the interpreter's theology! Some have discovered in the Pauline texts the pietistic conversion event; others have interpreted it as a decision vis-à-vis the early Christian kerygma, which typically opened a new self-understanding. Some have stressed the underivably contingent, that is, the revelatory character of the unconditional grace of God; others have interpreted psychologically in order to be better able to understand historically. For some, the calling was worth only one or two marginal sentences in the presentation of Paul; for others, it became the key to the whole theology of the apostle in general. Again, others have sought the religious-historical continuum that yielded constants in the radically changing situation and found, for example, apocalypticism, under whose framing conditions Paul replaced law with Christ. It has not been long since biographical information on Paul was completely suppressed. Currently there is more inclination to consider the unity of biography and theology.

Naturally we can never entirely exclude the possibility that interpreters will put themselves into the texts, but we can try to keep transference mechanisms under control! We call attention especially to two aids. First, we should not remove the Pauline experience from the fabric of concrete historical conditions in which the calling took place. That is, the interpretation must be defined as concretely as possible by the struggle between the Pharisee Paul and the Christians at the Damascus synagogue, a conflict that experienced in Paul's calling a resolution that then affected him for his whole life. Therefore we must in three steps speak of the Christian church in Damascus, of Paul's zeal for the law, and of the calling that turned the Pharisee into the apostle to the Gentiles. Second, we will examine the Pauline texts more exactly than before in regard to their typology and contextual peculiarity, in order thus to be able as precisely as possible to differentiate the particular from the typical.

4.2 The Christian Church in the Damascus Synagogue

How the Christian church in Damascus began can be inferred only indirectly. It shares with other early Christian churches (e.g., Rome!) the fate that its beginnings lie in darkness. Had Paul not experienced his calling here, we would know nothing at all of it, for it appears in Acts, in Galatians 1–2, and in 2 Cor. 11:32 only in direct connection with the stay of the apostle in Damascus. The unquestioned assumption is that at the Damascus synagogue a Christian community was formed based on refugees from the circle of Stephen, who, after his martyrdom, left Jerusalem and, among other things, did mission work in the coastal cities as far as Phoenicia, on Cyprus, and in Antioch (Acts 11:19).

Stephen came into deadly collision with Judaism (Acts 6–7). At the time of this event the Christian community around the apostles in the same city, Jerusalem, remained unmolested. Therefore Stephen and his circle, in contrast to the Aramaic-speaking original church, must have been distinguished from other Christians in Jerusalem not only by their Greek speech (whence their name, "Hellenists") but also in their theology. One falls into serious conflict with the Jewish religion, however, only if one publicly transgresses against the law. Hence there must in principle be something correct in the Lukan information in Acts 6:11, 13: the Hellenists are suspect because they "speak blasphemous words against Moses and God" and because they "speak words against this holy place and the law." Thus Stephen, similar to Jesus, to whose intra-Jewish critique of the law he may have referred (cf. Mark 2:1–3:6; 7:15), probably met death because he in his own way stressed the Torah-critical attitude of Jesus more ostentatiously than, for example, Peter.

Unfortunately the accusation against Stephen in Luke is as general as it is distressingly formal. Yet certain things can still be known. It is not by accident that these Greek-speaking Jews around Stephen (almost all) bear Greek names that are uncommon in Palestinian Judaism (Acts 6:5). This allows us to conclude that they come from the Jewish Diaspora, which is expressly stated in the case of the proselyte Nicolaus of Antioch. Thus, in contrast to the Jerusalemites, they think from the standpoint of a Jewish minority situated in a Hellenistic environment. For them, contact with the fringe element of Judaism—for example, with the "God-fearers," the non-Jews who accepted the monotheism of the synagogue but avoided the transition to Judaism through circumcision because of social consequences—was less of a problem than for Jews in an (almost) purely Jewish environment. Did not Jesus' message also quite generally encourage exceptional steps of boundary-crossing acceptance (cf. Mark 5:1–20 par.; 7:24–30 par.)? Could anyone forget that Jesus was considered "a friend of tax collectors and sinners" (Matt. 11:19 = Luke 7:34)? Had he not placed before the Jews a Samaritan as a model (Luke 10:30–37)? In any case, even with all of Jesus' intra-Jewish basic orientation, his open attitude in regard to those who had to suffer the discriminating consequences of strict adherence to the law could not be overlooked. Had not Jesus also used the law to question the law (Mark 10:2–9 par.) and even commanded the Sabbath to be broken for the sake of a neighbor's welfare (Mark 2:27; 3:4)? Had not Jesus, like John the Baptist, placed all Israelites under the wrath of God (Luke 13:1–5) and expected salvation from the dawning dominion of a gracious God instead of from a newfound observance of the law? Was not the preeminence of Israel thus made relative by the permanent sinner status of this people, at least vis-à-vis all others who worshiped the same God? God had exalted this Jesus and thus sanctioned his understanding of God! Should one say this only to Israel and not also to those associated with the synagogue, that is, to those who worshiped the same God? Indeed, they, like Israel, have only their lostness before God as the mark of their present condition!

In any case, after the martyrdom of Stephen we meet one of them, Philip, in typical circumstances (Acts 8:4ff.): He is missionizing among the Samaritans, who, to be sure, esteemed Moses but did not worship in the Jerusalem temple. Afterward, as told in Acts 8:26–40, he converts a eunuch from Ethiopia, who had worshiped the God of the Jews in the temple but as a eunuch could never cross over to Judaism (Deut. 23:1). Both situations quickly result in an exemplary test case: Philip baptizes in Samaria and baptizes the minister of the Candace. Through baptism he turns believers in Christ unrestrictedly into full members of the Christian eschatological church, though the one baptized man was not circumcised at all and the others could be regarded by the Jews only as stepchildren of salvation. Thus Philip oversteps the boundaries of the intra-Jewish consensus by a little, but fundamental, bit: baptism does not have circumcision and recognition by the Jewish congregation as its natural presupposition; rather, baptism is granted— no doubt at first as an exception—also to those who confess the same God yet are only relatively close to Judaism. If the Jewish Christians in general were already a problem for the Jews—it was not for nothing that Jesus of Nazareth ended up on the cross—now, in the form of the Hellenists, they become all the more a case in which the law must be applied.

Acts, incidentally, has such overstepping of the boundaries programmatically carried out also and precisely by Peter by justifying the conversion and baptism of the God-fearing centurion Cornelius through a special intervention of God. Even if the Lukan historical image may have left deep tracks here, a Peter who (at first) even in Antioch, without observing the purity laws, has table fellowship with Gentile Christians (Gal. 2:12) cannot in Antioch have thought much differently from the Hellenists. According to Luke, Peter justifies the baptism of Cornelius with a typical rationale, of which Paul will later also make analogous use at the Apostolic Council (Gal. 2:8–9): If because of the preaching of the gospel Cornelius receives the Holy Spirit and God thus gives him, as "only" a God-fearer, the same gift as the Jewish Christians, why should Peter resist this work of God (Acts 10:15, 17)? He can only confirm the election of God through baptism!

If we understand the Christian church in Damascus as a creation of these Hellenists and let it live in their spirit, then it is also true that they are within the synagogal organization and thus are a special group in the diaspora synagogue of Damascus. Within the Jewish community they are distinguished from the same by faith in the resurrected Jesus, whose imminent arrival is expected for the salvation of the church. In such near expectation it understands itself as the eschatological church, which is held together by the bond of baptism and Spirit. Beyond this, it is also concerned especially about the group of God-fearers, some of whom come to faith. They receive the Spirit (cf. as analogy Acts 8:16–17; 10:44–46; 15:4, 7–8 [= Gal. 2:7–8]); in the mission to them miracles may perhaps have occurred (cf. as analogy Acts 8:5–7, 13; Rom. 15:15; 2 Cor. 12:12). All this, in any case, is understood as a sign from God not to withhold from these believers baptism and full membership in the church of Jesus Christ (Acts 10:28; Gal. 2:7–8). Had not Joel 2:28–32 (3:1–5 in Hebrew; cf. Acts 2:17–21) already promised for the end time the pouring out of "my spirit on all flesh" and announced experiences of the spirit and miracles before the day of the Lord? According to him, should not all who call on the Lord be saved?

If this reconstruction more or less describes the nature of the situation in the Damascus synagogue, then it becomes clear what a strict legalist like Paul (cf. 3.2 above) would have to say about it: in this way they will sneak past the law into salvation. They erase the unsurrenderable boundaries between the people of salvation Israel and the other nations. Anyone who even in a few cases overestimates baptism as a substitute, as it were, for circumcision is a despiser of the law, because he revokes the demands of the law such as circumcision. Yet the God of Israel, among whose worshipers even these troublesome Christians are numbered, has bound his salvation to the law and does not want the holiness of Israel to fall into danger through the baptized Gentiles; not an iota or a dot will be disregarded in the law. Thus, for the sake of the law, it is a question of bringing the Christians into line. God and the law stood against the message of Jesus Christ.

4.3 The Persecutor of the Damascus Church

To the end of his life Paul knew that he was known to Christendom as the former persecutor of the church. This was taught by the early church's Paul legend, which was familiar to Paul himself (cf. 4.1 above). The apostle also had never himself suppressed or kept quiet about this circumstance. Of his letters still available to us, which in all are directed to five churches, he reported on his past to three, namely, to the Corinthians, the Galatians, and the Philippians, knowing that it would also be read aloud publicly in the worship services. From this we can hardly draw the often heard conclusion that Paul only rarely speaks of himself as the onetime persecutor. We must conclude, rather, that there was nothing here to hide, and with this the apostle would have agreed. He could live with the knowledge that this blot was known and even speak of it himself, because forgiveness had come to him from his Lord; his churches understood this also.

To the three mentioned churches he reports in stereotypical language that he "persecuted the church of God" (1 Cor. 15:9; Gal. 1:13) or "the church" (Phil. 3:6). An initial look at the extra-Pauline tradition in Gal. 1:23 and at Acts 9:4–5; 22:4, 7–8; 26:11, 14–15 shows that Paul is not the only one to use the verb "persecute." According to 1 Tim. 1:13, Paul is a "persecutor." Of course, it is more than uncertain whether not only the description of the activity but also the designation of the object in its fundamental generalization comes from typical language: also in Acts 8:3 the object of Paul's aggression is, indeed, quite generally "the church," but other extra-Pauline evidence is lacking (Gal. 1:23: "us"). Otherwise Paul himself speaks still in a general and fundamental way in 1 Cor. 10:32; 11:22 of "the church of God." This expression of his must be compared with other usage of the word "church." Such comparison (cf. 14.6 below) shows that a historically earlier usage in the tradition cannot be successfully distinguished from later statements. For our evaluation we must also note that the three texts on persecution of the church occur in polemical contexts, but they are not themselves the theme in these disputes. Rather, they are used without exception to characterize Paul immediately before his calling. In this way they picture the former time in contrast to the calling. Only in this function do we find the persecution statements in Paul.

Paul likewise uses a set phrase to give the aim of the persecution: he strove "to destroy the church of God" (Gal. 1:13; cf. 4.1 above). If, for the reasons mentioned above in 4.1, we disregard the depiction of the persecution in Acts, we can deduce from Paul only that he was seriously determined to dissolve the synagogal groups of Jewish Christians. Thus there was to be no more Christian movement at the synagogue in Damascus. In order to achieve this primary institutional goal, he persecuted the followers of the resurrected Jesus. Whether this also produced scourgings or stonings must remain an open question. On the basis of analogies in Acts 7; 2 Cor. 11:24–25; John 16:2, however, we should not exclude that possibility from the outset, for neither are human rights a concern for Paul and his immediate environment, nor would Paul have, for the rest of his life, felt his earlier persecuting activity as such an aggravating blot if he had merely discussed it with the Christians.

The reasons for such activity can be deduced from the immediately following description of the persecution: "and I advanced in Judaism beyond many of my own age among my people, so extremely zealous was I for the traditions of my fathers" (Gal. 1:14). Similarly, Phil. 3:6 reads: "as to zeal a persecutor of the church, as to righteousness under the law blameless." In contrast to the description of the persecution, these sentences are in no way indebted to typical language. Thus they must be credited as the direct reflection of Paul's view. With relative clarity the content of these statements is also brought to bear in Acts 22:3–4; 26:5, 9–11. Hence the persecution results from an uncompromising position in regard to the law. Seeing in the law the all-defining norm of life means, among other things, distinguishing between the chosen people of God and the sinful nations, and erecting immovable boundaries (cf. Rom. 2:17–19; 3:1–2; 9:4–5; 11:28; Gal. 2:15). According to Acts 15:1, 5, it is precisely the Pharisees who demand: "Unless you are circumcised according to the custom of Moses, you cannot be saved." The Pharisee Paul probably represented the same understanding of the law. Anyone with such an understanding of the law, especially anyone who through its clear consequences raised himself above his contemporaries, would necessarily fall into conflict with the Damascus Christians. For they, as an establishment of the Hellenists, were about the very business of erasing boundaries (4.2 above). Such beginnings had to be resisted.

Unfortunately we can no longer determine to what extent Paul at the time connected the zeal of his persecution (cf. here also Acts 22:3–4) with the zeal of Phinehas (Numbers 25), which was repeatedly present from the Maccabean revolt to the Jewish rebellion with its excruciating end under Titus. We know that Phinehas devoted himself to the God of Israel for the sake of keeping Israel pure from everything foreign—even to the extent of killing Israelites and foreigners. In order not to deviate from the patriarchal religion "to the right or to the left," Mattathias, according to 1 Maccabees 2, falls "into zeal" like Phinehas, "gives his anger free reign," and kills the king's envoy, who wants to compel the forbidden sacrifice, and the Israelites who want to sacrifice. The same zeal for the law leads the Essenes to hatred against the Gentiles and the disloyal Israelite (1QS 4:5–6, 17–18). The Zealots are known to have sworn themselves to the zeal of Phinehas: the Romans are their archenemies, and the Jews who have a relationship with them are traitors deserving death. We can see that this zeal is characterized by the same clear drawing of boundaries between the patriarchal religion and everything foreign. Can anyone in Paul's time speak at all of so similar a zeal without evoking the spirit of Phinehas? Also, the very rare word for "destroy," whose use in Paul has already been discussed, appears in any case once in Josephus as a characteristic of zealot outrages (Josephus, *Bellum* 4.405). In content, the "extermination" of the "abomination" in Israel is the natural consequence of the zealot spirit. Is it not also appropriate here to observe that as consistently as Paul founded law-free Gentile-Christian churches after his calling, so consistently had he earlier served the law "like a zealot." This he could do especially as a Pharisee, without being a direct follower of a zealot group.

If we understand the Pauline persecution as a consequence of legal strictness, we need not discuss hypothetically whether and in what way Paul took offense at the Christology of the Damascene Christians. He himself says absolutely nothing about it. Besides, it would be completely hypothetical to reconstruct the Christology of these Christians in Damascus. Yet this much can be said: Expecting in Jesus the imminently coming Son of man and judge may have irritated many Jews, but this, like all messianism, is no reason for Jews to undertake such a total conflict as that carried out by Paul. Even the disciples of the Baptist, who after

John's death presumably formed communities, could remain in Judaism in spite of a few difficulties. The followers of the many prophets and messianic pretenders, of whom Josephus reports, were eliminated whenever possible by the Romans for political reasons, but Judaism did not throw them out of the synagogue. Thus the real conflict must have consisted in the Pauline diagnosis that Christians called the law into question. Since they surely substantiated this with their Christology, to this extent and in this sense Jesus Christ (however he may have been christologically titled in Damascus) was naturally also a vexation to Paul.

If we ask about the duration, the kind, and the circumstances of the persecution, the sources provide as good as no information. From Gal. 1:17, 22 it can be concluded that what took place was locally limited to one synagogue in Damascus. Whether Paul was an individual opponent, as his presentation suggests, can be doubted simply for the reason that he elsewhere describes only his own activity when there were demonstrably others likewise involved, too (Gal. 2:11ff.). Thus Paul was probably the spokesman for anti-Christian Jews. We do not know how long the persecution lasted or what means and methods played a role in it. Paul only qualifies his basic activity but does not go into a more detailed description.

The double assertion that Paul was a zealot for the law and a persecutor of Christians is reported for the sake of the essential contrast to the new life defined by his calling: The zealot for the law becomes an apostle who, more consistently than any other, champions the cause of law-free Gentile Christianity. Nowhere in this connection does Paul allow the presumption that already as a Jew he had doubts about the law or felt the law as an unbearable burden. Therefore the details in Romans 7 cannot be drawn on to suggest that Paul had a lengthy struggle with conversion. Even an unconscious and subliminal crisis in the pre-Christian Paul's attitude toward the law can be derived from this text at best with a multilayered hypothesis. This is as far as we can go: for Paul, the "preparation" for his Damascus is his opposition to Christianity. The transition to the other side remains a process that took shape spontaneously in his calling and thereby took place for him with the character of evidence.

4.4 The Calling of the Pharisee as Apostle to the Gentiles

Just as Paul describes his persecuting activities only in typical language without biographical details, in principle he also proceeds the same way with his calling. On closer examination, this will be the case even in the passages in which he has something more discursive to say about this event, such as 1 Cor. 15:8–11; Gal. 1:15–17; Phil. 3:7–11. Nowhere does Paul show interest in a biographical assessment of the process; much less a psychological interpretation. When we see, moreover, that at least in the just-named classical texts Paul speaks of his calling only out of polemical necessity, then the conclusion is quickly reached that the apostle is less interested in his calling than above all— or even only—in the early Christian message and its interpretation. Yet here, however, we are no doubt too quick to systematize and to set up as alternatives things that in Paul are placed in a coordinate relationship. On closer examination, it is also not at all true that Paul speaks of his Damascus only in polemical contexts. In general, the other passages, divided among the letters, are more numerous than these three classical core texts seem to indicate. We only need to see under which viewpoint Paul talks of his turning point. He always speaks as if he has in mind the results, that is, what was thereby communicated to him personally and materially as the new order of things. He does not ask historically: What happened and under which conditions and circumstances? He wants, rather, to discover the present significance: What is true since then for me and the churches? By thus describing the present with the past and connecting the two, he also comes in a limited way to speak about that long-past event.

The first typical context in which Paul mentions his calling is the epistolary opening of Romans, 1 and 2 Corinthians, and Galatians. Only three Pauline letters form the exception here, namely, Philippians, 1 Thessalonians, and Philemon. Because of its more personal character, Philemon is, of course, easily explainable as a special case. Conversely, through passages in Philippians 3 and 1 Thessalonians 2, these two letters have clear text signals that Paul in no way ignores his calling. As a result, Paul always approaches his churches as a called apostle.

The statements in connection with the beginnings of the letters are typical: "a servant of Jesus Christ, called to be an apostle" (Rom. 1:1); "Jesus Christ our Lord, through whom we have received grace and apostleship" (Rom. 1:4–5); "called by the will of God to be an apostle of Christ Jesus" (1 Cor. 1:1); "an apostle of Christ Jesus by the will of God" (2 Cor. 1:1); and "an apostle—not from men nor through man, but through Jesus Christ and God the Father" (Gal. 1:1). Then the purpose of the calling is often named: "set apart for the gospel of God" (Rom. 1:1); "to bring about the obedience of faith . . . among all the nations" (Rom. 1:5). The same idea is expressed in 1 and 2 Corinthians and Galatians through the naming of the Gentile-Christian addressees. Whether in the naming of the gospel (Rom. 1:2–4) or in the mention of

God as the one who is calling (Gal. 1:1), the resurrection of Jesus Christ is mentioned with confessional formulations.

Thus we can ascertain that in this context a typical linguistic field can be recognized, and it contains the following components: calling (election), apostleship (grace), gospel for the Gentiles, and resurrection of Jesus Christ (as the sign of the God who acts or as the content of the gospel). This program for the churches leads through the proclamation of the gospel to the calling of Christians and the establishment of churches (cf. the letter openings). If indeed Paul intentionally placed this context at the beginning of the letters, this has fundamental significance for the letters—that is, for Pauline theology. Certainly the apostle also legitimates himself in this way precisely as the author of the letters; certainly he then develops his theology in the letters not simply as the result of his calling experience but through separately constructed, substantial arguments; yet these letter openings also do not simply assure formally the authority of the apostle. The connection—called as apostle, gospel for the nations, church of Jesus Christ—is at the same time a structural principle and material foundation of his theology. In Romans, Paul does not develop his message of justification as the immediate consequence of his calling. Rather, "by grace alone" and "without the law," which resound in the commission to the nations, are contained in his understanding of his calling in the letter openings, as is the election of the nations through the gospel (on this, cf. 6.2 below).

It is noteworthy that even in the letter openings (Rom. 1:3–4; Gal. 1:1, 4) Paul describes the gospel through traditional confessional formulations. This observation should not be played against the Pauline calling experience with its influence on his theology. Personal calling and pregiven kerygma are not mutually exclusive. Why and to what extent the apostle agrees with the confession and how he integrates it into his theology are determined by his interpretation of his calling.

A second context for a typical interpretation of the calling is given in the passages Rom. 12:3; 15:15; 1 Cor. 3:10; 7:25, 40; 2 Cor. 4:1; 1 Thess. 1:4, 7; Philemon 8. Paul exerts his authority, based on his calling as an apostle, in cases where he would like to add emphasis to his paraenesis (admonition to walk as a Christian), his decisions, and his requests. As an important spiritual authority, however, the apostle can also from case to case withdraw this authority, without in principle giving up his appeal to it. Of course, in these many cases Paul's language is much richer in variation than in the letter openings, yet here too fixed formulations are not lacking: indications of this are the apostolic grace and the right to command and be able to expect obedience. In comparison with the first context we will ascertain that while the first context is typically Pauline, especially through the text signal of the accent on Gentile Christianity, the second corresponds largely to the behavior of prophets and spiritual teachers in the churches. The apostle's calling allows him to make use here of an also otherwise similarly represented authority. What unites the two described contexts is the circumstance that Paul, unforced and on his own initiative, speaks thus not only in passing but emphatically and intentionally. His calling is not only a topic forced upon him but, rather, his self-chosen declaration.

The situation is different in the third context. Here Paul speaks by setting his apostolic life-style apart from non-Christian opponents (1 Thess. 2:1–12); vis-à-vis other Christian ways of life he substantiates his different apostolic way of life on the basis of apostolic rights (1 Corinthians 9); in intrachurch party strife he develops polemically his understanding of apostolate and church (1 Cor. 1:10–4:21); he defends himself before the churches against the "superlative apostles" (2 Corinthians 10–13); or he describes his contested apostolic gospel (1 Cor. 15:1–11; Gal. 1:11–24; 2:1–10; Rom. 15:14–21). In short, speaking here in each case is the besieged, competing apostle who is compelled to substantiate and in a contested situation to define himself or his gospel or both. He does this in such a way that at least with a few typical sayings or even in more detail, he discusses his calling, or mission. Here the chain of key words from the first context play an equally decisive role, even if they are modified in many ways by the apostle's lively use of language.

In three of the named passages Paul gives an overall interpretation of his calling to apostolic service, which exceeds the assertion that he is the apostle immediately called by God to the proclamation of the gospel to the Gentiles. In 1 Cor. 15:1–11 he includes himself as the last in the group of Easter witnesses, as he also in 1 Cor. 9:1–2 claims to count as an Easter witness. Paul also knows about the calling of many missionaries to mission service in distinction to the fundamental Easter experience of Peter, the Twelve, and, for example, the Lord's brother James (1 Cor. 15:5–7). In addition, he knows of his own spiritual experiences of another kind (2 Corinthians 12), which are not interpreted as Easter experiences. Nevertheless he claims to be a witness of Easter; he is, of course, aware of the problems of this claim: he can assert this only for himself as "one untimely born" (1 Cor. 15:8). No other early Christian testimony seconds the apostle in this. His opponents, at least in Galatia, may have questioned it (Gal. 1:1, 20–21). Luke also, without actual polemics, removes Paul from the Easter witnesses (cf. 4.1 above). Because Paul apparently did not always find support for this claim outside his followers, we can see here Paul's own ancient and crucial basic assertion of his understanding of his calling (cf. further 4.5 above).

A short time after the composition of 1 Corinthians, Paul describes to the Galatians his turning point, employing the typology of prophetic calling. First, he follows Isa. 49:1 (cf. Isa. 49:5; Jer. 1:5) when he says of the One calling him that God set him apart in his mother's body (Gal. 1:15; cf. Rom. 1:1). Second, passages such as Rev. 1:1; Matt. 16:17–19 show that for Paul the elements that in Gal. 1:16 define the process of the calling (revelation with God as source and Christ as content, along with the obligation to service) are characteristic of early Christian prophecy in general. Thus Paul substantiates his direct authority from God by emphasizing the prophetic side of his apostolate.

Finally, in Rom. 15:14ff. Paul characterizes the grace given to him by God by saying that he knows he is called "to be a minister of Christ Jesus to the Gentiles in the priestly service of the gospel of God." Otherwise this interpretation has little support in Paul: he understands himself as apostle and prophet, but not as priest. Thus in the first and second overall interpretations as Easter witness and prophet we may find his typical apostolic understanding.

Even the statements on the process of the calling are taken from interpretive contexts already available to the apostle. The conspicuous dimension of the perception is described with three different verbs: he has *seen* the Lord (1 Cor. 9:1; cf. John 20:18, 25; Acts 9:27); Christ *appeared* to him (1 Cor. 15:8; cf. 15:5–7; Luke 24:34; Acts 9:17; 13:31; 26:16); and God *revealed* to him God's Son (Gal. 1:16; cf. 2 Cor. 12:1, 7; Gal. 1:12; 2:2; Rev. 1:1; Matt. 16:17). The first two verbs are taken from the general Easter tradition; the third, from prophetic language. Thus in each case the linguistic usage coincides with the overall interpretation in the context.

The object designations of what is perceived are described with majestic christological titles familiar to Paul and early Christianity. In 1 Cor. 9:1 it is the *Lord* who is seen. In 1 Cor. 15:8 the antecedent is presumably *Christ* in v. 3. And in Gal. 1:15 God reveals *his Son.* All three majestic titles were originally centered in independent christological understandings. The variation in Paul does not indicate that the apostle would like us to understand that one of them was immediately decisive for his calling experience. He apparently wants only to say more generally that outside Damascus he experienced the resurrected One as Savior. This he describes with majestic christological titles that were familiar to him at the time he was writing.

Paul does not intend the "optical" side of his calling to be pushed aside, but for him the crucial assertions are those which describe his induction and commissioning, that is, his installation as an apostle. This includes the fact that from now on Paul sees himself possessed and guided by the Spirit; that is, he understands himself as a charismatic (1 Cor. 2:6ff.; 2 Cor. 12:1ff.). Consequently his proclamation rests on the power of the Spirit (1 Cor. 2:4–5) and is accompanied by signs and wonders (Rom. 15:18–19; 2 Cor. 12:12). He was given the grace of the apostolic office (Rom. 15:15; 1 Cor. 3:10; Gal. 2:9; cf. 1 Cor. 15:10). Through this he has special authority that he can exercise with regard to the church, even if he makes only reluctant use of it (1 Corinthians 9; cf. 1 Thess. 2:7). It serves for the building up of the church (2 Cor. 10:8; 13:10), as he in general understands his commission to Gentile missions (Gal. 1:15–16) as entrusted with the gospel (1 Thess. 2:4) in the sense of a stewardship for which he can expect no wage (1 Cor. 9:17–18) and in which he is completely subject to the law of Christ (1 Cor. 9:21). Indeed, this task holds him like a compulsion (1 Cor. 9:16). He is thus free from all human judgment (1 Cor. 2:15; 4:3ff.) and at the same time servant of Christ and steward of the mysteries of God (4:1), that is, called to preach the gospel (1 Cor. 1:17; 9:12, 18, 23; 1 Thess. 2:2, 4, 9).

Still another, fourth special context can be discerned in Paul. He can generalize his own transformation of life and use it as a paradigm for becoming a Christian. His special calling as the apostle to the Gentiles becomes transparent as a general conversion, which in the mission situation of the first generation stands at the beginning of every Christian life. In this process what is special about the Pauline transformation—above all, becoming Easter witness and apostle to the Gentiles—receives less attention, and what can be accomplished for all people in their own experience is emphasized. Just as the apostle stresses that he received the gospel directly from God and at the same time knows that it is identical with the general early Christian confession, so also, for him, are the two ways of understanding his transformation to be interpreted: the interpretation as special calling and the understanding as general conversion are not antitheses. Naturally we will most easily see the historical particularity of the Pauline experience at the point where the two special statements meet, namely, in the first and third contexts.

The two texts to be named for this fourth context are Phil. 3:2–16 and 2 Cor. 4:6. The second text describes the preaching of all early Christian apostles as follows: with the help of traditional illumination language, Paul interprets "the light of the gospel of the glory of Christ, who is the likeness of God" (2 Cor. 4:4) in such a way that by this means God himself lights up the hearts of people and they receive "the knowledge of the glory of God in the face of Christ." This is what the apostles as preachers have experienced. Through their proclamation this is what happens to all who come to faith (cf. 2 Cor. 3:18): all Christians experience the effect of the gospel in this way, namely, through illumination (4:6), and thus at the same time as transformation (3:18). Since the description of the illumination is generally supposed to be true for all Christians under the gospel, we cannot infer directly from the typical language to the particular experience of Paul. Therefore many exegetes also do not want to see this text brought in at all for the interpretation of the Pauline transformation. We can, however, probably still do it if we begin with the fact that in this context Paul includes himself with all others under the same experience; thus he will also incorporate his special Damascus experience into this generalizing assertion.

In Phil. 3:2ff. as well, the knowledge of Christ creates the crucial transformation, now as revaluation and devaluation of what has been and redefinition of Christian existence under justification by God. Paul achieves the exemplary, paradigmatic interpretation of his conversion by employing typical baptismal and justification language (cf. 12.4 below) to describe his transformation and making this comprehensible to all Christians as analogous to their experience. In this way Christian existence in general is revealed in Paul's conversion (Phil. 3:15). In anti-Jewish polemics, his conversion becomes a means of maintaining the church in the justification that comes through faith. When Paul brings in as an essential idea his identification with the destiny of Jesus (Phil. 3:10–11), he echoes the Gentile-Christian conception of baptism, as he worked it out in Rom. 6:1ff. Such an understanding of baptism was hardly familiar to him during the time in Damascus. That is, among other things, a clear indication of how Paul in Philippians 3 mixes the earlier happening and the present interpretation of his transformation. Thus he reinterprets his experience, among other things, with means that were not at his command until later.

With this we have described the contexts in which Paul reflects the crucial upheaval of his life. What do they say happened to Paul? It is striking that the apostle, in contrast to Acts, nowhere even alludes to hearing. He describes a visionary happening. In this process he receives a new assignment and thereby a new understanding of himself, but neither Christ (thus Acts 9:4–6; cf. 2 Cor. 12:8) nor God talks to him. Naturally we can postulate hearing, because it is otherwise typical in such visionary experiences. Such a hypothesis, however, runs into a text like Gal. 1:15–16, where even the mission and commission significance of the vision is inferred only from the seeing of the Son. Thus the question arises whether Paul could not deduce everything else from the Lord's appearance alone, so that in this case no words were needed at all.

We can answer yes to this question if we consider the life situation in which this happened to Paul. He himself also points to this repeatedly when as background to his calling he brings in his zeal for the law and persecution of Christians and transforms this into the insight that he is now sent as apostle to the Gentiles. Christians in Damascus allowed themselves freedom with regard to the law and based this freedom on Jesus, who for them was resurrected. When Paul persecuted these Christians for the sake of the God of Israel and maintenance of his law, Paul himself experienced the resurrected One. From the preaching and practice of Christians and from discussions with them, he knew their christologically defined teaching. Now this Jesus appeared to him as the resurrected One. This must have made one thing clear to him: Paul was not to change or persecute Christians for the sake of the law; rather, he himself, against his legalistic stance, had to learn a new understanding of God and to change himself, because the Jesus on whom Christians based their illegalities was alive and impressed this fact on him in a special way. Hence he felt himself sent as an apostle who was supposed to missionize especially the Gentiles without regard to the law. Thus the vision of the resurrected One could receive its language and its meaning from the immediate life situation in which it happened: it came to the zealot for the law who attacked the teaching and practice of the Damascus Christians.

It is helpful to note at least in passing how the new Christian Paul must have subsequently been regarded by the synagogue. For pious Jews holding on to the faith of their fathers, the one who had announced the battle against the paganization promoted by Jewish Christians was naturally a good figure with whom to identify. When this same man, however, now became a Jewish apostate himself, it could scarcely have happened without great tension. His assimilation to the Gentiles soon manifested itself as the beginning of a trend. Seldom in Judaism had there been so great a number of departures as in the first early Christian generation. We only need to think, for example, of such well-known names as Barnabas, Apollos, Aquila and Priscilla, and the missionaries from 2 Corinthians, and of the churches that, after their Jewish-Christian beginnings, became Gentile Christian in orientation, such as Antioch and Rome. The many synagogal punishments that Paul suffered (2 Cor. 11:24) are an indication that he was henceforth regarded as a dangerous detractor who was treated with anger and aggression.

4.5 Paul's Self-Designations and Self-Understanding

The comments in the previous section were aimed at perceiving the typology and variety of the texts and at overcoming the temporal and material distance between narration and earlier event. This met with only limited success. For the historian, there are clear restrictions in answering the question, What happened? Yet we have also seen that instead of this historical initiative unknown to him, Paul adopts a different perspective: he describes the ongoing presence of his calling. What was and what is have thus become one unified mural, so that one hardly still suspects that it owes itself to two folios. Naturally, at that time Paul could not have formulated Philippians 3, but that does not matter to him. Naturally Galatians 3–4 was not finished in a flash in Damascus, although in the opening of the letter Paul now places everything under his apostolic calling. This mixture of times is quite all right with him.

Paul knew—namely, in an eternally valid now—that with his calling everything had changed for him from now on and for all time (1 Cor. 9:16; Gal. 1:16). He himself had become someone else, and with him his entire experience of reality and his interpretation of world and history. It is not by chance that we see in all the texts how Paul discards the old and grasps the new as his true future. Thus the calling experience is the repetition of the beginning of creation (2 Cor. 4:6), and this is also essentially true for his transformation: "If any one is in Christ, he is a new creation [and only that is important]; the old has passed away, behold, the new has come" (2 Cor. 5:17). Paul has "died to the law, that I might live to God" (Gal. 2:19); indeed, he no longer lives himself, but Christ in him (Gal. 2:20). According to Gal. 6:14, the world has died to him, and he to the world. For the sake of the towering worth of Jesus Christ, he devaluates everything, even his spotless and blameless observance of the law (Phil. 3:6–9). He struggles only over how he can subject all his thinking to obedience to Christ (2 Cor. 10:5). These easily multiplied statements, whenever individually formulated, are all true for the beginning of his becoming a Christian; they are the reflection of the one basic experience of irrevocably seeing from the inside that he previously did all things wrong and should begin anew under completely different conditions. This refers not only to his individual person; rather, all reality appears in a new light. There are good reasons why this "all things" with its total demand is so typical of Paul (cf., e.g., 1 Cor. 3:21–22; 2 Cor. 5:14–15, 18; 10:5; Phil. 3:8).

This comprehensive perspective can be seen in the concrete contents that have meaning in the Damascus situation. Several aspects can be named. First and fundamentally, for Paul also, the crucified Jesus, whom the Christians in Damascus preached as resurrected and in whose Spirit-effected present they fell into conflict with the law, must have risen. If the God who raises the dead (cf. Rom. 4:17) has exalted

Jesus to himself, then the Father-God of the law has become the Father of Jesus Christ. If God has interpreted himself in this way, then in the Damascene context the law, the Jewish norm for world and history in general, must be understood anew. The Christians who without regard to the law were spreading the salvation of Christ through baptism were right: the faith that involves Christ is sufficient for salvation. One does not have to become (fully) a Jew and be faithful to the law, in order to become also a Christian. Rather, one is in the state of salvation as a Christian even without the law, for Christ alone represents divine salvation.

At the same time, naturally, Paul had to interpret his experience as the gracious acceptance of the persecutor. This understanding contains not only the core of Paul's later judgment on his old life (Philippians 3) but runs tendentially toward the later view, which the apostle summed up in the idea of the justification of the godless (Romans 3–4).

Also for the status of the Christian church we have the beginnings of new aspects: if non-Jews can now become baptized Christians without having themselves circumcised, then God's aim is no longer the continuity of Jewish salvation and the incorporation of proselytes into the people of God but the gathering of nations at the end of days as the new people of salvation, that is, the Christian church. Instead of typical Jewish boundary drawing and separation, God's will is now Christian openness and the spreading of the gospel. In the long run this will lead to the separation of church and synagogue.

Finally, the event had a special character of commitment for the life of Paul himself. Through the Damascus experience, he who was the strictly legalistic Pharisee and persecutor of God's church becomes an apostle of Jesus Christ and the apostle to the Gentiles, in order to expand the church of God under the gospel of Jesus Christ. He could not remain a Pharisaically oriented tentmaker (cf. 3.1 above), nor could he become merely a Christian tentmaker living a Christian life and perhaps also starting a Christian family. The commission to mission was inescapable, a mission that from the very beginning, because of the baptized non-Jews in Damascus, at least tendentially received an entirely new horizon, which spilled over the Jewish boundaries and in which Paul himself would become the representative of the crucified Christ (Gal. 6:17; 2 Cor. 11:23ff.).

In his letters Paul again and again knows how to make concrete events, positions, and decisions transparent to fundamental relationships. Therefore we can assume that he also immediately looked into his Damascus for fundamental implications. Here lie the beginnings of his theological existence.

Paul never gave a name to the fundamental reorientation that he experienced and obediently carried out. What we call his turning point, transformation, calling, or conversion has no immediate counterpart in Pauline language. Yet terminologically he did give a precise name to the newly won relationship between person and lifelong task for himself and for his time, when he designated himself an *apostle* (of Jesus Christ). The term was not a new one he coined. He knows that there were already apostles before him in the early Jerusalem church (1 Cor. 15:8–11; Gal. 1:17, 19), and in his later Christian environment he knows many persons who claim for themselves the title of apostle (cf. Phil. 2:25; 2 Cor. 11:5, 13; 12:11; etc.).

Early Christianity used the term in an especially qualified and conspicuously frequent way, so that it can be considered a key word of early Christianity. An origin of this early Christian term in Hellenism is hardly likely; also, roots in the Jewish concepts of mission and commission are relatively loose, however probable this is indicated by the oldest early Christian use in the Jerusalem early church.

Because of 1 Cor. 15:8–11; Gal. 1:17, 19, there is little question that the oldest Easter witnesses—certainly not all (cf. the five hundred in 1 Cor. 15:6), but up to a certain number that is no longer exactly definable—called themselves apostles of the Lord on the basis of their experience of the resurrected One and the concomitant commission. These include, among others, Peter (Gal. 1:18), probably also James (1 Cor. 15:7), the Twelve (1 Cor. 15:5; cf. Matt. 10:5ff. par.), and Andronicus and Junia (a feminine name!—cf. Rom. 16:7). Indirectly, Paul attests to the closed nature of this Jerusalem circle of apostles and to the fundamental reference to the Easter experience for him (1 Cor. 15:8; 9:1). As clearly as Paul independently fills his apostleship with content, according to type he adds himself to this understanding. For him also, the Easter experience is fundamental (1 Cor. 15:8ff.), and the connection between appearance and commission is clearly demonstrated (Gal. 1:16). Thus he knows that he, as the last called apostle, belongs to this group, which was actually already closed (1 Cor. 15:8ff.).

Whether Paul understood his Damascus experience in this way from the beginning can no longer be determined. The basic text at this point is 1 Corinthians 15, yet it comes about twenty years after Paul's calling. Nonetheless the description of the Apostolic Council in Gal. 2:1ff. (especially vs. 7–8; cf. 5.2 below) indicates that Paul already thought this way at the conference and also that this was expressly accepted by the Jerusalemites. When Acts, which actually withholds from Paul the title of apostle, makes an exception—no doubt conditioned by sources—and calls the dispatched missionary "apostle" (Acts 14:4, 14;

cf. 13:1–3), thus employing a more general use of the word, this does not have to point to an older, different Pauline self-understanding. In spite of his conception of his apostleship as immediately related to Christ, Paul could have missionized with Barnabas: a basic commission by Christ does not necessarily exclude a limited assignment by a congregation. Therefore, since 1 Cor. 9:1; 15:8ff. stand there unchallenged, it is a good working hypothesis that Paul very early defined the connection between (Easter) vision of Christ and apostleship (mission).

Beside this apostleship defined by Easter, there was, above all, a large and certainly not fully unified group of charismatic, itinerant preachers in early Christianity, of whom at least a portion, and perhaps many, also called themselves apostles (cf., e.g., Matt. 9:37–10:16 par.; *Did.* 10–15; 2 Corinthians 10–13). Their typical characteristics are independence from the church, missionary wandering, the claim of special spiritual gifts, and calling by the Spirit as commissioning power and authority. If we put in last place the Easter vision of Christ, we will in principle be able to find everything else in the circle of the twelve apostles with their Easter calling, for charismatic itinerant preacherdom and apostolate directly from Christ in general largely belong to the same type. Also, the latter apparently nowhere disputed the former's use of the apostle title, although there are battles over the question of how an apostle is supposed to appear and to teach (2 Corinthians 10–13; *Did.* 10–15).

When a term such as that of apostle has become only partially fixed in use—as is typical for a dynamic movement such as early Christianity—then a great deal depends on how someone like Paul himself understands his apostleship. For this there are clear statements by the apostle. The claim of apostleship presupposes, first, immediate dependence on God and Christ alone. The apostolic office does not come out of the church and also has no succession in the church, because that would do away with the immediate link between the person and God or Christ as sender. This unquestionable special position is matched by independence vis-à-vis the church. Thus Paul polemically hurls against the Galatians that he is an apostle "not from men nor through man" (Gal. 1:1; cf. 1:11). He tells the Corinthians that with him it is a small matter to be judged by a human court, but he rejects such an intention, as he does not even judge himself; for "it is the Lord [alone] who judges me" (1 Cor. 4:3–5).

With this special position immediately comes an assignment, described in the connection between apostleship and gospel for the Gentiles (cf. 4.4 above). This refers to the law-free gospel of Jesus Christ and the worldwide horizon of the mission (Rom. 1:14–15; 10:14–17). This includes Paul as the symbolic figure of the worldwide

Gentile mission, who represents the one gospel, beside which there is no other (Gal. 1:6–9), and knows that those in Jerusalem agree with him in this estimation (Gal. 2:7ff.). He can describe this gospel through confessional formulas (e.g., Rom. 1:1ff.; 1 Cor. 15:1ff.) but also reduce it to a common denominator such as 2 Cor. 5:20: "So we are ambassadors for Christ, God making his appeal through us. We beseech you on behalf of Christ, be reconciled to God."

With all the prominence of the apostle title, Paul can also describe his special position and assignment with the help of prophetic traditions through the designation of servanthood and priestly task (cf. 4.4 above). Similarly he can characterize his relationship as church founder and cultivator with metaphors from house building (1 Cor. 3:9–17), planting (1 Cor. 3:7), and parental duties (1 Cor. 4:15; Gal. 4:12–20; 1 Thess. 2:7, 11). In all these cases special position (distance) and special nearness are placed in a characteristic relationship. As apostle of Jesus Christ, Paul is dependent on the church: without these fruits of his efforts he would—unimaginably—one day stand before his employer with empty hands (Phil. 2:16; 1 Thess. 2:19; conversely, Gal. 4:11).

Paul's own conduct of life is assimilated to the apostolic task, for he cannot preach to others and not conform to that preaching himself (1 Cor. 9:27). Therefore he disciplines himself as a competitor (1 Cor. 9:24–27), is free, yet makes himself a servant to everyone (1 Cor. 9:19), even forgoing his apostolic rights, in order not to burden the church and have a certain credit before God (1 Cor. 9:1ff.). Above all, the Corinthian itinerant charismatics challenge him as the representative of the gospel also to describe its content as an aspect of his conduct of life. Thus the sufferings and weaknesses of the apostle, as signs of the cross of Christ, become open hands into which God pours his grace, and the presence of the cross becomes at the same time the presence of the power of Christ (2 Cor. 11:16–12:10).

5
Paul as Antiochene Missionary and Theologian

5.1 General Screening of the Statements

Between Paul's calling in Damascus and the following first mission in (northern) Syria and Cilicia, on the one hand, and the beginning of the independent mission of the apostle to the Gentiles, on the other, lie about twelve years of activity in Antioch. It is the longest section in the life of the Christian Paul that is accessible to us. For from his leaving Antioch until his imprisonment in Jerusalem, we can count only about nine years, and the imprisoned Paul was given only about four years until his death in Rome. Thus Paul's missionary activity in Antioch is in fact the most extensive period that comes to us as a unit in the Christian portion of the life of the apostle to the Gentiles.

From this period we still have no letter of Paul. The apostle only begins to write when he becomes an independent missionary and greater geographical distances develop between his travel stops and the newly founded churches. Some things from the Antiochene period, however, are reported by the apostle to other churches, so that we are not completely without testimonies from those years. Among these events are, above all, the Apostolic Council and Peter's visit in Antioch (Gal. 2:1–21) but also, for example, the ecstasy of his being transported into the third heaven (2 Cor. 12:1–5), as well as, apparently, some of his persecutions, which he mentions in catalog fashion in 2 Cor. 11:23–33. Also, for the theological views of the Antiochenes and the apostle we can draw inferences from the traditional materials of the Pauline letters. Thus, on the whole, we are not at all poorly informed about this Pauline period.

Added to these testimonies, now, are the details from the Acts of the Apostles. Acts reports first how Barnabas brings Paul to Antioch (Acts 11:25–26), that the community members in Antioch are called "Christians" (11:26b), that the prophet Agabus appears in Antioch (11:27ff.), and how Paul and Barnabas do mission work together out from Antioch (the so-called first missionary journey: Acts 13–14); it then tells of the Apostolic Council (15:1–35) and, finally, how a quarrel arises between Barnabas and Paul over John Mark, which leads to the separation of the two (15:36ff.). There are considerable tensions between Paul's self-testimony and Acts, and they are discussed in detail in the following sections. Even at first glance, however, we see that not even the events themselves are unanimously attested. A perusal of the following overview makes this clear.

Event	Paul	Acts
Antiochene mission among the Greeks of the city	——	11:20–21
Barnabas brings Paul to Antioch	——	11:25
New designation "Christians"	——	11:26b
Paul's vision	2 Cor.12:1–5	——
Prophecy of Agabus and the gathering from Jerusalem	——	11:27–30 12:24–25
So-called first missionary journey	——	chs. 13–14
Persecutions; in particular, a stoning	2 Cor. 11:25	14:19
Apostolic Council	Gal. 2:1–10	15:1–35
Petrine visit in Antioch	Gal. 2:11–21	——
Quarrel and separation of Paul and Barnabas	——	15:36–41

It is immediately clear that on the basis of position and significance for the whole of early Christian history, the Apostolic Council receives unrivaled priority in this time period. Of the events that precede it, we can look especially at Paul's missionary activity as preparation for this council. For Paul and for the history of Antioch, the quarrel with Peter, naturally, has particular significance: it, and not the situation in Acts 15:36–41, is the probable cause of Paul's departure from Antioch. It remains striking that Acts provides almost no information on the theology of Antioch. Nevertheless the Gentile mission on the so-called first missionary journey (13:46–49; 14:1–7, 8–20, 27) and the quarrel over the law, together with the recognition of Gentile-Christian churches at the Apostolic Council, lead us to suspect what Antioch's great service is, namely, to have embarked on the road to non-Jews. The description of the work of the Spirit in the church (11:27ff.; 13:1–4) is probably basically correct, too, as attested in Gal. 2:2; 2 Cor. 13:1–4. The speech put into Paul's mouth in Antioch of Pisidia, naturally, can be understood neither as a reproduction of Paul's theology nor as a characterization of Antiochene missionary preaching. For Luke, it characterizes the general meaning and direction of the so-called first missionary journey and is his interpretation for his readers.

5.2 The Jerusalem Agreement on a Law-free Gentile Mission

In early Christian times Antioch was the third largest city in the Roman Empire after Rome and Alexandria. It appears in early Christian history for the first time in connection with the proselyte Nicolaus, who is the last to be counted among the circle of seven around Stephen (Acts 6:5). Nicolaus probably became a Christian in Jerusalem. Hence his naming is not in itself the first indication of a Christian church in the capital on the Orontes. It is certain, nonetheless, that there was a large Jewish community in Antioch—no doubt approaching fifty thousand people in Roman times, plus a larger group of God-fearers (Josephus, *Bellum* 7.46)—and that there was good contact with Jerusalem. Therefore it is no wonder that after the death of Stephen, Hellenistic Jewish Christians also founded a small Christian church in Antioch (Acts 11:19).

The beginnings of this church are connected with the name of Barnabas. He stood at the head of the list of five who, according to Acts 13:1, are considered prophets and teachers in Antioch and upon whom—along with the full assembly (Gal. 2:14)—leadership of the church came to rest. Barnabas and Paul (still named second in Acts 13:2, 7; 14:14) are sent out by the church to missionize. But how did Paul come to Antioch? Acts (11:25–26) claims that Barnabas himself went to Tarsus and fetched Paul to the Orontes. Yet Luke could have combined that from Acts 9:30 and 13:1. Naturally Paul would hardly have gained a foothold in this city against the will of the leader of the Antiochene church; to this extent, there is historical truth in Acts 11:25–26. Paul himself confirms that he and Barnabas led the delegation to Jerusalem (Gal. 2:1) and that Peter and Barnabas held back the Antiochene church from Paul's consistent Gentile-Christian course (Gal. 2:11ff.). Hence it remains at least very possible that Barnabas—with the Damascene events in mind—fetched Paul to Antioch precisely in order with his help also to lead the further progress of Antioch toward a more liberal position on the law.

In this respect Barnabas was surely not disappointed by Paul. On the contrary, Paul so decisively promoted a law-free position for the church that in the end he went too far even for them (Gal. 2:11ff.). It appears that in the Apostolic Council and in the Antiochene quarrel with Peter, Paul was the most decisive fighter for a law-free mission, so that we may assume that he soon played the leading role in determining the events in Antioch, and Barnabas, as well as the church, followed him until the visit of Peter in Antioch. In this way the Antiochene church became the pioneer of the law-free Gentile mission.

How things developed in particular within the Christian church in Antioch has largely escaped our knowledge. Paul is completely silent about it, but Acts can offer some answers to our question.

1. The Antiochene Christians missionized parts of the Greek population who had previously had nothing at all to do with the synagogue. They were very successful (Acts 11:20–21).
2. In Antioch the "disciples" were first called "Christians" (Acts 11:26).
3. The church sent Barnabas and Paul out on the so-called first missionary journey (Acts 13–14). It is exemplary for the law-free (13:38–39) Gentile mission (14:27) and the founding of Gentile-Christian churches (13:44–52; 14:21–23).

All this information makes good sense, corresponds to the probable course of history, and forms a good basis for clarifying the situation before the Apostolic Council.

In particular we may conclude the following from these three points. Since the boundary between the God-fearers and those outside the synagogue was fluid, it happened in Antioch—no doubt for the first time in early Christianity—that members of the Christian church, who until then were always a group within the synagogal fellowship, introduced the Christian faith to residents of the city who previously had not had even a loose relationship with Judaism. Thus God-fearers who had become Christians could have approached their relatives about their new faith or perhaps exploited occupational contacts. If God-fearers could be baptized without being first circumcised, then the uncircumcised in general could also be baptized, especially if they also accepted the part of the Christian message that Jews did not need to accept anew, that is, if they abandoned the pagan cult and adopted Jewish-Christian monotheism (1 Thess. 1:9) and thus assimilated themselves to the God-fearers known to the synagogue.

Such additions to the synagogal Christian church naturally led to problems, which had long been growing but now reached an acute stage. Since a Jew could not, for example, eat with Gentiles, or even in a Gentile house, without becoming cultically unclean (Acts 11:2–3; cf. *Acts of John* 8; *Letter of Aristeas* 139–142; 182–183), the synagogue had to understand such a mission as a declaration of war, for it increasingly erased the boundaries between Judaism and paganism. This innovation was an even more blatant break with the law than the one persecuted by the Pharisee Paul in the Damascus church. Now the cultic purity of the synagogue was in fundamental and continual danger. Conversely, the Christians evidently had such good success with this mission that there were a considerable number of Christians who were native "Greeks," that is, non-Jewish residents of the city who used Greek as their everyday language. Also, this mission was apparently more successful than that among the Jews, who now retreated all the more. In short, the Christian church decided to withdraw from the synagogal fellowship. In this way they got rid of the problems of the law and the synagogue and could now continue to missionize unhindered where they had had success.

This separation was publicly attested by the name that the young church received: *Christians*. It is a name that points to the independence of the group and was no doubt bestowed upon the church by outsiders. It means "followers of Christ." Among themselves the Christians called each other "brethren" (1 Thess. 2:1, 17; 4:1, 13; etc.), "beloved by God" (1 Thess. 1:4), or "saints" (1 Cor. 1:2; 6:2; etc.). Jews may have called them the "sect of the Nazarenes" (Acts 24:5). Thus it seems likely that Gentiles gave Christians this new designation when attention was called to them as an already independent group.

Antioch was not just any city but a center of administration, trade, and travel with a relatively large area of influence, which included at least the whole Roman province of Syria. To have an urban perspective meant also to have the whole region in mind. Moreover, Christianity and forward-thinking mission were twin sisters beginning at the latest with the circle of Stephen. The Christians in Antioch also owed their faith to this mission. What was more logical than that they themselves become active in missions? Thus the church sent out Barnabas and Paul. They went to Cyprus and then via Perga, Antioch of Pisidia, Iconium, and Lystra to Derbe, and then followed the same route back to Antioch on the Orontes. In Galatians 1, Paul reports nothing about this missionary undertaking. This has led to a mistrust of Acts. Yet 2 Tim. 3:11 and 2 Cor. 11:24–26 make reference to the itinerary and persecutions (the stoning of Paul!) on the journey, which does not support all the details but in general indicates the historical reliability of Acts for the trip. Also, the Apostolic Council (Acts 15:12; Gal. 2:2, 7–9) presupposes such missionary activity by the Antiochenes. In this way it was precisely the growing Gentile mission and the creation of Gentile-Christian churches that became a problem for Jewish Christians in their Jerusalem center! Because in Antioch there developed a small center of Gentile-Christian missions with the founding of the first law-free churches, this had to lead to discussions at the center of Jewish-Christian, synagogue-related missions, that is, in Jerusalem.

Perhaps in Gal. 2:2 there is yet another reference to an Antiochene mission: Paul fears that with a failure of the trip to Jerusalem he will have run "in vain." That is a statement which in other cases refers to his own missionary foundings, which either are his boast before God (1 Thess. 2:19; Phil. 4:1; 1 Cor. 9:15–18) or—if they fall from faith—determine that Paul has run "in vain" (Phil. 2:16; cf. 1 Thess. 2:1; also 1 Cor. 15:10, 14). Thus Gal. 2:2 probably refers to the apostle's missionary activity outside Antioch, because Antioch itself is not a church he founded. Finally, it should be mentioned that in Galatians 1–2 Paul limits his approximately twelve years of activity in Antioch to only two crucial references, namely, the Apostolic Council and the Antiochene quarrel with Peter. Paul is not trying to present a complete autobiography in Galatians 1–2; rather, he is searching his own life story for the crucial points that he can employ argumentatively against the Judaizers. Since his Gentile mission was a thorn in the side of his Galatian opponents, it made sense for Paul in Galatians 1–2 to go immediately to the event that led to recognition of his mission.

Under discussion at the council is the fundamental issue of whether Christianity can also be founded on faith in Christ alone outside the synagogue and without the prerequisite of the law, and whether such a church can be recognized in the same way as the Jewish-Christian churches within the synagogue. The issue was probably first raised in Antioch when strict Jewish-Christian legalists from Judea appeared in Antioch (cf. Acts 15:1, 5; Gal. 2:4). Luke connects them with Pharisaism but names no big names of early Christianity (not even James!). The innovators in this quarrel are the Antiochenes, who, incidentally, are summoned to Jerusalem neither according to Gal. 2:1 nor Acts 15:2. Rather, the Antiochene church itself decides to clarify the issue with those in Jerusalem. If we imagine that such a decision came about formally in a way analogous to Acts 13:1–3, then this is not different from Paul's position, which he departed on the basis of a revelation, even if such an expression of the Spirit was given only to him personally (cf. Gal. 1:12). Thus the Antiochenes go to Jerusalem, led by Barnabas and Paul. They know what they want: the delegation is headed by the very two missionaries who have programmatically carried out Gentile missions. Other members of the delegation are also involved (Acts 15:2), among them an uncircumcised Christian, Titus (Gal. 2:3). It is a respectable delegation that is firmly in the new Antiochene camp and makes this public through the person of Titus.

The opposing viewpoint is represented by the "false brethren secretly brought in" (Gal. 2:4), as Paul states it in a polemically depreciating way. They look distrustfully at "freedom . . . in Christ Jesus" (Gal. 2:4)—to use an Antiochene slogan of this period—and want to bring the Antiochenes "into bondage," that is, to subject them to the

Jewish law (Gal. 2:4–5). For Paul, this placed at risk the "truth of the gospel" (again a situation-conditioned slogan). As already indicated, according to Acts 15:1, 5, former Pharisees (like Paul!) represent the strict Jewish-Christian standpoint with the principle that one must be circumcised and hold to the law in order to be saved. Thus it is a question of the fundamental meaning of the law for salvation (on the form of the statement, cf. John 3:3, 5).

Paul and Luke agree in their assertions on the issue: ultimate salvation is at risk. According to strict Jewish Christians, the Jewish people alone are chosen. Therefore a Gentile can hope for salvation only if he becomes a Jew through circumcision. Even for Christians there can be no salvation apart from the law. Christians are something like the true Israel within Israel. They cannot establish a Christianity outside the holy people, which overthrows the law by faith (Rom. 3:31) and makes Christ the agent of sin (Gal. 2:17). Christ does not abolish the distinction between the people of salvation and sinners—that is, Gentiles (versus Paul in Gal. 2:17)—but rather is God's last offer to his people of salvation. Therefore Christ and law cannot be separated. They are closely related. Hence baptism cannot replace circumcision but only follow it.

Against this Paul states that the working of God on the mission field is obvious. And God works without partiality (Gal. 2:6). Through the gospel he himself creates faith and gives his Spirit, without Gentiles being circumcised beforehand (cf. 1 Thessalonians 1–2). In this way God himself attests the law-free nature of the gospel. It is not necessary to become a Jew in order to be a Christian. One can be baptized without taking upon oneself circumcision; where the Spirit works without circumcision, there is such freedom. If God in Christ chose the lowly and the lost (cf. 1 Cor. 1:26–30), then the Gentiles are especially meaningful targets of mission.

The foregoing describes the two opposing viewpoints in the discussion. The Jewish-Christian position is the traditional one and the one most understandable from the historical situation. It was the general rule and until then almost the only valid one. The Antiochenes are the exception ideologically and numerically, for previously all other church foundings by the circle of Stephen had remained within the synagogue. The mission in the synagogal fringe group was, of course, a serious problem for (strict) Jews, but the mission of Stephen's people was always linked to the synagogue. Antioch was the first to take a decisive next step.

Concerning the course of the council, Galatians 2 and Acts 15 show sharp differences, which cannot be evened out. The question whether Luke intends to distinguish between a consultation of "the apostles and the elders" (Acts 15:6) and a gathering of the whole church (Acts 15:12, 22) is probably to be answered negatively, for Luke is apparently describing an overall assembly. In Paul, however, the situation seems different: according to Gal. 2:2, he lays the Gentile-Christian gospel before the apostles Peter, John, and James (Gal. 2:9; on the order, cf. below) "privately," so that the previous statement in Gal. 2:2a must refer to the whole church. Moreover, since after an initial description of results in Gal. 2:3–5, v. 6 expressly begins with a further result now related to an understanding with the "pillars," vs. 3–10 can easily refer to two discussions: in vs. 3–5 Paul reports on the full assembly; in vs. 6–10, on the separate discussion with the apostles. If we give priority to Paul, as seems reasonable, then we can consider whether Luke did not redactionally unite in Acts 15 a similar traditional course of events.

More important, though, is the evaluation of the results of the full assembly. Paul provides the crucial information. Through the glorification of God for his transformation—which is expressed by the Judean churches according to Gal. 1:22–24 and which Paul intentionally names immediately before the description of the council as an important circumstance to go with the events in Gal. 1:12ff.—Paul leaves no doubt that the original community in Jerusalem did not simply stand against him in general. Of course, if Paul now wants the Galatians to believe that his law-free gospel is included in this praise (cf. Gal. 1:16 with 1:23), then the tradition still recognizable in Gal. 1:23 (on this point, cf. 4.1 above) sounds more restrained. It does not at all contain this pointedness on the law-free nature of the gospel. Also, the fear that with a negative outcome in Jerusalem the apostle could in general "be running or had run in vain" (Gal. 2:2) indicates that Paul could not expect ahead of time a smooth agreement with his way. Furthermore, it is striking that in Gal. 2:3–5 Paul communicates no clear decision of the whole church, but only tells what they did not demand, namely, the circumcision of Titus (Gal. 2:3), and how he himself withstood the "false brethren" (Gal. 2:4–5). Of course, Paul takes back nothing of the fundamentally positive attitude toward him in Gal. 1:22–24. Yet apparently the anti-Antiochene, strict Jewish Christians in the Jerusalem church had a larger base than Paul would have liked. Even Luke speaks of "much debate" (Acts 15:7), when he otherwise wants to describe particularly the original community as the embodiment of unity and harmony. This church did not reject the Gentile mission (Gal. 2:3!), but they had apparently also not been able to convince the "false brethren" of the correctness of Paul's way.

In this situation everything depended on the apostle. The decision had to come in the separate discussion between the Jerusalem pillars and the Antiochene delegation with Paul as its spokesman. Could the pillars settle this quarrel without the Christian communion breaking apart? Paul describes this discussion and its outcome in his way in a long sentence. The Petrine apostolate is accepted as the norm. Peter unquestionably was the premier Easter witness, apostle, and original missionary (1 Cor. 15:5; Luke 24:34). Even if at the time of the Apostolic Council he had perhaps already turned over to James the leadership of the Jerusalem church (cf. the initial position of James in Gal. 2:9), he remained the symbolic head of post-Easter Jewish Christianity. Such an early change of leadership in Jerusalem is, however, not certain: James stands in the forefront only in the contractual handshaking, as it were; in the essential argumentation only Peter is seen. Since immediately afterward (Gal. 2:12) James's people make trouble in Antioch in violation of the Jerusalem agreement, Paul could have placed James first in the consensus in order to emphasize that James's people are now deviating from the agreement. At any rate, it is also clear that for Acts, Peter more than anyone else has the decisive word (Acts 15:6–12).

According to Paul, the discussion can be summarized as follows. It was generally recognized that God "worked" on the Pauline mission field just as he did for the Petrine mission. There also God "worked" through the gospel, granted the Spirit, and did signs and miracles (cf. Rom. 15:19; 2 Cor. 12:12; Acts 10:44–47; 11:1–18; 14:27; 15:12). Thus the Pauline apostolate is analogous to the Petrine. The conclusion, which Acts elsewhere puts in Peter's mouth (Acts 11:17), becomes visible: "If then God gave the same gift to them [the Christian non-Jews] as he gave to us [the Jewish Christians], . . . who was I that I could withstand God?" Luke sketches a similar theological position in Peter's speech at the council (Acts 15:7–11). It is apparent, incidentally, that this speech contains decisive key words of the election theology of 1 Thessalonians (cf. 6.2 below): through the gospel God chooses the Gentiles and gives them his Spirit and purity of heart because of their faith. Therefore, as Luke has Peter conclude, the law is no longer needed, for "we believe that we shall be saved through the grace of the Lord Jesus." In this way Peter plainly becomes the representative of Gentile-Christian theology.

In any case, if the Lukan Peter grants the uncircumcised baptism and the Spirit, and thus full Christian salvation and full ecclesiastical communion, then according to Galatians 2 the same thing happens at the Apostolic Council. The "grace" (i.e., the apostolate; cf. Rom. 1:5; 15:15; 1 Cor. 3:10), which is given to Paul and generally recognized through comparison with Peter, is interpreted in such a way that from now on there will be, on an equally valid basis, a mission to Jews, with the aim of founding Jewish-Christian churches, and a mission to Gentiles, with the aim of founding Gentile-Christian churches. Baptism is supposed to ratify the work of the gospel even where there is no circumcision.

Circumcision and observance of the law are not to be required retroactively: "For the kingdom of God is not food and drink"—for example, in the purity regulations of the Torah—"but righteousness and peace and joy in the Holy Spirit" (Rom. 14:17), as aptly formulated in an old guiding principle. In this sense it was agreed with a hand-shake that Paul and Barnabas could continue to carry on their Antioch-ene—that is, Gentile-Christian and law-free—mission, whereas the Jerusalemites would continue to devote themselves, as previously, to missions among Jews. Naturally the Antiochenes could also aim at win-ning over Jews, and the Jerusalemites, at winning God-fearers, for example. Crucial are the goal and the church reality that grows out of it. To the Jewish-Christian churches within the synagogue are now added Gentile-Christian churches independent from the synagogue, without circumcision and the law.

Thus on the basis of this separate dialogue, the Antiochenes received for their position the full recognition that was not so clear in the church assembly. This is why Paul gives this consensus so much praise in his letter to the Galatians. No one had even an inkling that Paul would soon leave Antioch and do missions on a global scale. Gentile-Christian churches were still the exception. Jewish Christianity could still under-stand itself as the norm for Christian existence. Had not even the Hel-lenists around Stephen in Jerusalem lived relatively to themselves beside the Christian community of Peter and James? Were there not often in the large cities of the Roman Empire several synagogues beside each other? Could not synagogal and law-free Christianity now also live beside each other here and there? Naturally it would be hard for the Jerusalemites to accept that even Jewish Christians, as in Antioch, stayed away from the synagogue and—like Paul and Barnabas themselves—fit-ted themselves into law-free Christianity. At the Apostolic Council, how-ever, they were apparently willing to tolerate even this as an exception. On the basis of Jewish history one could rest assured that on the whole Jews had only rarely become Gentiles voluntarily. Thus in the future also it would be exceptional for Jewish Christians to want to join Gentile-Christian churches. Totally out of the question for Palestine, this would happen at most here and there in the Diaspora. The fact that this exceptional practice would soon become the rule that Paul took for granted was, as mentioned, still in the future.

Up to this point the presentation of the Apostolic Council follows Paul and Acts 15:1–12. Yet at the Apostolic Council, Luke not only has

Peter give a speech that, prepared by Acts 10, essentially represents the Antiochene standpoint. Later in Acts comes James, who demands from the Gentile Christians a minimum of purity regulations in terms of Leviticus 17–18, so that the Jewish Christians may have contact with them without ritual uncleanness (Acts 15:13–21). This was decided by the church in Jerusalem, who had it presented to the church on the Orontes in writing by envoys from Jerusalem together with the returning Antiochenes. Thus Paul and Barnabas agree with this, and according to Luke they continue to missionize in Antioch under this presupposition (Acts 15:22–35). This is in direct contradiction to the Pauline report in two ways. Paul emphasizes that no conditions were demanded of him; rather, he and Barnabas as envoys of the church had concluded the agreement without such additions. Paul also states that James shared Peter's view without restriction. From this we may conclude that Acts 15:13–35 does not reproduce the reality of the council. The source of James's stipulations can only be surmised. The best hypothesis is that they played a role when James's people appeared in Antioch, and in Acts 15 Luke combines the council and this incident in Antioch. That will become clearer in the next section (5.3 below). That would mean, however, that soon after the council James and his followers chose a compromise between the quite strict anti-Gentile-Christian Jewish Christians and the Pauline mission: he recognized Gentile Christianity but wanted to see the particular problem of relations between Jewish and Gentile Christians regulated along the lines of Leviticus 17–18; in other words, in this way the law would remain the norm.

The Apostolic Council, incidentally, had aftereffects that concerned not only the Antiochene mission. As surely as we know no details about missions running concurrently, we can still perceive at points how outside Palestine the council decision produced positive fruits. Thus without Paul's help the Roman church became Gentile-Christian, apparently after an initial Jewish-Christian phase (cf. 13.1 below). The Alexandrian Apollos appears in Corinth as a Gentile-Christian missionary (cf., e.g., 1 Cor. 3:4ff.): does this mean that a Gentile-Christian church independent of that in Antioch had also arisen in Alexandria? What was the state of the mission of the Hellenists after the council? Paul was, in any case, apparently a welcome guest among them (cf. Acts 15:3; 21:1ff.). How, then, does Peter have followers in Corinth, a Gentile-Christian church (1 Cor. 1:12), and become a martyr of the Gentile-Christian church in Rome (*1 Clem.* 5.4)? Even the itinerant missionaries who appear in Corinth according to 2 Corinthians are former Jews (2 Cor. 11:22) but have a Gentile-Christian orientation during their visit in Corinth, for they teach neither circumcision nor observance of the law. Hence we can say that there are sufficient indications that churches and missionaries outside Palestine soon used the council as a signal also to go the way of Antioch. We are tempted to say that many were waiting precisely for the chance to go the way of Gentile Christianity now secured by the council. Though Paul may have become the most consistent and successful representative of Gentile Christianity, he did not play a purely solo part in its development. For others, too, the council's decision was opportune and advantageous.

5.3 Peter in Antioch

Sometime after the council Peter may have visited the Christian church in Antioch (Gal. 2:11–21). His appearance naturally presupposed the council decision in the Pauline version: during the time of his visit Peter at first lived without qualms or discussion in a Gentile-Christian fashion, that is, in unrestrained living fellowship with the law-free and synagogue-independent church in Antioch, composed of Jewish and Gentile Christians. He thereby defiled himself as a Jewish Christian—who until then had certainly lived as one faithful to the law in Jerusalem—because he apparently valued the unity of the church in Christ higher than the law. His behavior was evidently also natural for all others in Antioch. The visit would have continued in this way very harmoniously had not James's people also journeyed to Peter after a while. On the one hand, they stood by the council, for they demanded neither circumcision nor the keeping of the whole law by the Gentile Christians. Thus Acts 15:1, 5 was not their theme! On the other hand, they followed an even harder legalistic line than James did recently at the council: they demanded, namely, that all Jewish Christians in the church—above all, Peter—live with them an unrestricted synagogal life faithful to the law. Could they not expect this from Peter, since he was the first apostle and symbolic figure of Jewish Christianity (Gal. 2:8–9!)? According to this separation, the Gentile Christians were supposed to form their own church for themselves.

The council had conceded that Jewish Christians in Antioch could also live outside the synagogue and thus free from the law; Paul and Barnabas exemplified this in person, just as Titus as a Gentile Christian exemplified law-free Gentile Christianity. But now James's people demand that Jewish Christians live in a Jewish-Christian way and thus within the synagogue. Since we may assume that standing behind James's people was the Lord's brother, James himself, he must have hardened his stand after the council. Now the Jewish Christians within the synagogue are considered more authentic Christians; for them, continuity with Israel's history of salvation is not negotiable, and the law has fundamental significance for salvation; otherwise they would not have to insist on it. Christianity is to be understood theologically mainly as an intra-Jewish group, just as Jesus and his band of disciples worked within the people of salvation. Gentile Christians are, to be sure, a tolerated exception, but they must be restricted to the exceptional situation. For reasons that lie in the law, they must be considerate of Jewish Christians, and not vice versa. Paul must have felt this, justifiably, as discrimination against the Gentile Christians and as a step backward from the council.

Everything would still have gone well in Antioch if James's people had not made such an impression on Peter with this demand that he gave in to them. Had James in the meantime become number one in Jerusalem? Had Peter perhaps withdrawn from Jerusalem because of James's harder course? In view of this harder pace of the Jerusalem Christians, did Peter fear he would be pressured to justify himself because of a lax attitude on the law? That can no longer be clarified, but one thing is clear: Peter withdrew from the Gentile Christians and thus from the ecclesiastical unity he had so recently promoted by his example.

In his report on the withdrawal of fellowship, Paul elaborates above all on the meal. That is typical, for at that time fellowship was culturally realized especially through table fellowship (cf. Luke 15:1–2; Acts 10:41; 1 Cor. 5:11). In a community not living according to the law, a Jewish Christian like Peter would necessarily have to defile himself, especially since he was no doubt received in a Christian house where the law was not lived (cf. Dan. 1:8–16). Even sharing a meal as a guest would have confronted one with these problems (cf. Acts 11:3). It is to be assumed, however, that Paul is not looking simply at these everyday living situations alone when he mentions the common meal. He is thinking of the Lord's Supper as the common bond of the church. Should the church now celebrate two different Lord's Suppers? For Paul, "the truth of the gospel," that is, the "freedom in Christ" that the council had confirmed, was at stake here (Gal. 2:14; cf. 2:4): If God accepted "sinners," that is, Gentiles, without precondition, then life faithful to the law could not receive priority again through the back door. If God elected Jews and Gentiles to the one eschatological church, which will be saved by him as a whole (1 Thess. 1:10; 4:17; 5:10), then the waiting condition of this church cannot now be redefined by a separation! Thus the result for the Gentile Christians is that they must somehow accommodate themselves to the Jewish Christians faithful to the law. Had this situation not been clarified long ago in Antioch when all Christians together said goodbye to the synagogue? Had the council not recognized this way?

The defection of Peter, however, had consequences. The Jewish Christians left the fellowship. Even Barnabas, who at the council had still argued with Paul on Antioch's side, gave in. He had an Antiochene, Gentile-Christian orientation only as long as Peter stood on his side. That is the way it was at the council, and now he remains Petrine and follows his model back to the synagogue. Paul and the Gentile Christians are isolated. Now that the peace of the church had received a deep split, there was a church assembly. Unfortunately Paul reports only that "before them all"—that is, in a gathering of everybody (cf. 1 Tim. 5:20 and Gal. 1:2)—he attacked Peter (Gal. 2:14). Again (cf. Gal. 2:8) Peter becomes the normative figure by whom they decide what will have ecclesiastical validity. Yet the unambiguous position of the first apostle at the council has, through his behavior, now fallen into doubt.

Paul's speech is surely formulated with the Galatians in mind; in particular, it is intended to serve as preparation for the topics that are to follow (cf. 11.2 below). Thus it is not a record of the Antiochene assembly but the course of an argument for the Galatians. Nevertheless it doubtless contains elements of the Antiochene situation. Presumably, for example, the monstrous sentence in Gal. 2:16 includes as unquestioned church knowledge the assertion that a person is not justified by works of the law but only through faith in Jesus Christ, a consensus statement of Antiochene theology that also appears in Rom. 3:28 (cf. 11.3 below). We only need to remember that justification statements are encountered in traditional early texts, for example, in connection with baptism (documentation in 11.3 below). Then this sentence can be understood as follows: God accepts people through baptism because of their belief in Jesus Christ, not because of legalistic lifestyle, that is, on the basis of circumcision and observance of the law. And precisely this was the basic agreement in the church of Antioch.

We can likewise well imagine that the objection "Is Christ then an agent of sin?" in Gal. 2:17 is a typical Jewish-Christian interjection that Paul also responds to in a different form in Rom. 6:15 when he discusses the question of whether we should sin because we are no longer under the law but under grace. Behind the way of Gentile Christianity, Jewish Christians must have sensed the unconditional grace that wanted to do away with the strict, everlasting will of God announced in the Torah. What else, in their eyes, could have made the Gentiles want to live outside the law?

Through the syntactically analogous sentence structure in Gal. 2:17 and 21b Paul would have the readers understand that he can express his counterposition with equal clarity: "If justification were [to be achieved] through the law, then Christ died to no purpose." This means that Christ's death was not needed at all if justification is to be achieved on the basis of the way of the law. Thus the significance of Jesus' death for salvation is played out against the salvation to be achieved by the way of the law. "Christ alone" is employed as argument against the law. Yet did the Antiochene church not in exactly this way consider the new reality to be defined by Christ's redeeming work? Was it not true particularly for them that "in Christ Jesus neither circumcision nor uncircumcision is of any avail, but faith working through love" (Gal. 5:6)? The church's basis for salvation was, precisely in the Antiochene view, no longer the law but Christ, the gospel about him, faith, and baptism. Hence in 2:17 Paul may very well have employed Antiochene language.

Thus we can no doubt understand elements of the speech as the factual reproduction of the Pauline standpoint vis-à-vis the defector Peter. They make clear what principles the Antiochene Gentile Christians, speaking through Paul, saw at risk: it was a question of whether Christ alone is supposed to be the basis of salvation or whether the law was also fundamentally involved.

The outcome of the quarrel is unknown. If Paul had prevailed, and the Jewish Christians with Peter at the head had given in, Paul could have used this very well in his disagreement with the Galatians and would surely have noted it. Hence the matter probably did not come out well for him. Therefore after this Paul became independent of Barnabas and Antioch, and doubtless at first had a more distant relationship with Peter. Nevertheless he seems to have taken a like-minded Antiochene with him: Silas/Silvanus (cf. 6.1 below). The die was cast for his independent missionary work. From now on he would missionize as envoy of Jesus Christ where Christ had not yet been proclaimed (Rom. 15:20). Thus, as he had stood up for the Gentile Christians of Antioch, from now on he would establish Gentile-Christian churches that were founded on faith, love, and hope (1 Thess. 1:3; 5:8), not on the law as a basic prerequisite.

What became of Antioch? We know nothing definitive on the topic, but there is an appealing hypothesis. Given their previous history, the Antiochenes could not seriously allow their church to break apart. Thus, as so often in history, they had to strike a compromise. They could not return to the days before the Apostolic Council. This was also not demanded openly by James's people or Peter and Barnabas. But they wanted to bring the Jewish-Christian part of the church back under the domination of the law. Jewish Christianity must remain Jewish Christianity! In order to make this possible while maintaining the unity of the church, the Gentile Christians would have to give a little. They should neither be circumcised nor generally placed under the law, but were to ensure the Levitical purity of the Jewish Christians, as, so to speak, a service of love for their brothers and sisters. Therefore they undertook the obligation of James's stipulations according to Leviticus 17–18 (Acts 15:29), namely, to consume no meat sacrificed to idols, abstain from blood, only eat meat slaughtered in a kosher manner, and enter no marriages forbidden in Judaism (i.e., with close relatives). Thus the so-called apostolic decree may have first gained significance in connection with this quarrel. Could it also be hidden behind Paul's reproach of Peter (Gal. 2:14) that he compelled the Gentile Christians to live like Jews? Be that as it may, because the so-called apostolic decree belongs in the same context with the Apostolic Council and concerns the same churches, Luke could have looked at the decree and the council together. That may be the origin of Luke's present view in Acts 15.

Paul does not subject himself to these demands (cf. Gal. 2:6): Acts 15:19–20 is a cultic ritual catalog. For Paul, however, it goes without saying that all ritual laws are irrelevant (Rom. 14:14, 17; 1 Cor. 8:1–6; 10:26). Also, in regard to meat sacrificed to idols, he will recommend to the Gentile-Christian church in Corinth a law-free solution (1 Corinthians 8). According to Paul, at the Gentile market Christians may buy anything as it is—even meat not slaughtered in a kosher manner (1 Cor. 10:25). Of course, marriage with a near relative will be rejected by Paul a few years later (1 Cor. 5:1ff.), but in no small measure, because this is also forbidden according to Roman law (1 Cor. 5:1); the Christian church in general is supposed to live inoffensively toward outsiders (1 Cor. 6:5; 10:31–33; 1 Thess. 4:12). For Paul, these Levitical prohibitions are not simply a service of love by the Gentile Christians for the Jewish Christians but an indication of the priority of Jewish Christianity and thus of the law. The compromise does not rest on reciprocity and equality. It consolidates the observance of the law and makes Gentile Christianity permanently inferior to Jewish Christianity, which now loses something fundamental if it does not do what it should, namely, leave the way of the law. With this, in Paul's view, freedom and the truth of the gospel were ultimately betrayed, for they now had to orient themselves toward the law, not the law toward them.

Incidentally, the new Antiochene way, effected by James's people, found little support in the Christianity of the time. The consistently law-free solution, as once initiated by Antioch, remained the common solution in the Gentile-Christian mission field. It even appears that a man like Barnabas later also found his way back to this position; in any case, Paul can mention him in 1 Cor. 9:6 without rancor. The same may be true for Peter (cf. 5.4 below). Conversely, the Jewish-Christian apocalyptist who wrote the Revelation to John represents at least a part of James's position (Rev. 2:14–15, 24–25) and struggles with churches who transgress against these requirements. The widespread, post-Pauline hesitation to eat meat sacrificed to idols does not immediately have anything to do with James's stipulations; rather, it comes from a general reserve of Christians in dealing with the pagan cult (cf. *Did.* 6:3). Thus James's restrictions presumably remained active requirements for Gentile Christians in some Jewish-Christian circles. In general, however, Gentile Christianity went the Pauline way.

5.4 Paul and Peter

Peter, the Galilean and onetime fisherman (Mark 1:16, 21, 29), is the first Easter witness and thereby becomes the first apostle of the Jewish-Christian church after Easter (1 Cor. 15:5; Luke 24:34). He became neither of these by chance, for even before Jesus' death he was doubtless already group spokesman for the circle of the twelve disciples (cf. Mark 3:16; 8:27ff.; etc.; Acts 1:13). He is considered Jesus' close confidant (Mark 5:37; 9:2; 13:3; 14:33). Paul is a Pharisaic diaspora Jew, does not know Jesus of Nazareth personally, becomes the zealous persecutor of the Christian church in Damascus, and, called as an apostle through a vision, becomes the missionary to the Gentiles par excellence. Two rather different men who, nonetheless, in this early period of Christianity were considered the outstanding apostles (Gal. 2:7–9)! Therefore the question of their relationship with each other has had a special significance from the very beginning.

Given the nature of the sources, we can describe this relationship in only a limited way. After Easter we meet Peter in Jerusalem (Acts 1–5), where he must have at least tolerated Stephen's group, whose later missionary activity was a precondition of Paul's effectiveness (Acts 6–7). In any case, it is not imaginable that this group could have arisen and taken its freer position on the law if the original apostles had been against it at the time. Paul meets Peter for the first time on his private visit in Jerusalem, which he expressly undertakes because he wants to get to know the first apostle personally (Gal. 1:18). He spends about two weeks with Peter and is his guest. We do not know any more about this meeting: Paul explains this visit neither as a time of instruction for his (meager) Jesus tradition nor as a catechetical makeup lesson on the tradition of the earliest confessional formation. Nor does he describe it in any way as problematic. The two of them seem to have granted each other mutual acceptance.

According to Acts, before the time of the Apostolic Council Peter goes out from Jerusalem to visit the Christian churches in the Jewish cities of Lydda and Joppa (Acts 9:32–43); then in Caesarea he baptizes the God-fearer Cornelius, who was highly respected among the Jews (Acts 10:1–2, 22), and this brings him problems with the original church in Jerusalem (Acts 10:1–11:18). It is persecuted by Herod Agrippa I (ca. A.D. 43/44), and Peter escapes an imprisonment by changing locations again to Caesarea (Acts 12:1–25). He is again in Jerusalem for the Apostolic Council (Acts 15). The extent to which we can place confidence in the details of this information is much in dispute. Yet two things can perhaps be established. First, during this period Peter seems to feel responsible for Jewish-Christian churches; therefore he visits them. He is also actively involved in seeing that by way of exception a God-fearer receives baptism without circumcision. This places him close to the mission of Stephen's circle (Acts 8; 11:19–30). The Jerusalem church, in any case, seems in part to be more strictly legalistic, for Peter seems to feel the compulsion to justify what he did. Since Luke, with his program of a harmonious original church, describes things thus, it deserves our attention. We must, however, seriously consider whether Acts 10 is not now placed prior to the Apostolic Council only because of Lukan interest, namely, in order to make the first apostle also in principle responsible for the beginnings of the Gentile mission. Possibly this exceptional baptism without circumcision is a Petrine deed after the council. It fits a Peter who in Antioch at first practices full table fellowship with baptized Gentile Christians. Is this Petrine attitude, with the corresponding consequent deeds, the deeper reason why Peter is no longer to be found in strictly legalistic Jewish Christianity in Jerusalem under James?

Acts 15 and Gal. 2:1–10 agree in regard to Peter's behavior at the council: Peter recognizes, with no ifs, ands, or buts, Paul's law-free mission, yet he himself remains the symbol of Jewish Christianity. Not until Peter's visit in the church at Antioch, which lives in a Gentile-Christian way, is there a break between Peter and Paul, because Peter, on the basis of the actions of James's people, restores the priority of Jewish Christianity to the extent that the Gentile Christians of Antioch are supposed to hold to the minimal demands of Leviticus 17–18. Paul leaves Antioch. Peter remains there perhaps a little longer, but reliable traces of Peter are now erased. The information that is still to be seen shows him from now on in the context of the typically Gentile-Christian missionary region.

According to 1 Cor. 1:12; 3:22, a group in Corinth seems to appeal to Peter. Yet this does not necessarily mean that he himself was in Corinth, although it seems certain that he visited churches together with his wife, and the Corinthians also had knowledge of this (1 Cor. 9:5). In the Pauline mission fields also he was considered the undisputed first Easter witness (1 Cor. 15:5). Yet with his Antiochene stance, could he live at all in the Gentile-Christian churches without creating problems for himself or these churches? It is nowhere indicated and quite improbable that the Petrine groups in Corinth lived as Jewish Christians, that is, committed to Leviticus 17–18. Or had Peter changed his standpoint again after the events in Gal. 2:11ff.? Did he, therefore, necessarily stay only and finally outside Palestine? It is also conspicuous that in 1 Corinthians 1–4 Paul does not continue to write about his disagreement with Peter in the same way as in Gal. 2:11ff., as he would have had to do if Peter or Christians in his name had continued the Antiochene quarrel in Corinth. Also in 1 Cor. 9:1ff. Peter is mentioned completely neutrally. Thus, if soon after the Antiochene incident Peter oriented himself toward Gentile Christianity, like Paul himself, then we may perhaps remember that at Jesus' arrest and during the trial of his Lord, Peter apparently also did not play a very admirable role but rather one defined by vacillation (cf. Mark 14:50 par.; 14:66ff. par.). Was the Antiochene quarrel for Peter perhaps only an interlude?

There is yet another indication that Peter is to be found in Gentile-Christian territory: the tradition of his Roman stay and martyrdom in that city. In any case, it is still best to interpret *1 Clement* 5 in such a way that this letter, written around A.D. 96 from Rome to Corinth, has Peter and Paul executed in Rome under Nero. Around A.D. 110 Ignatius (Ignatius, *Rom.* 4:3) supports this assertion. John 21:15–19 also knows of Peter's martyrdom, without naming the location. Again, a stay of Peter's in Rome is to be inferred from 1 Peter 5:13. Thus around the turn of the century there is a broad tradition, without contradiction, that can be interpreted to indicate that Peter, like Paul, died as a martyr in Rome. Probably we may infer that Peter came to Rome after Paul. If, in writing the Letter to the Romans, Paul had reckoned with a Petrine presence in Rome, it would not have been permissible to omit a greeting to Peter—if for no other reason, because he would not want to offend the church that was giving hospitality to the first apostle. Thus, if the two hardly saw each other again after the Antiochene incident, they still both—in the same place, though separated from each other—became victims of Roman persecution under Nero.

Thus we can say in summary that, until the event in Antioch, Peter and Paul probably had a good relationship with each other. Peter gave decisive help in working for recognition of the Pauline missionary concept. In Antioch this relationship was seriously disrupted because Peter swung toward the stricter Jewish-Christian pace of James's people. Afterward the two apostles probably met no more. Yet it is very possible that Peter reconsidered his Antiochene decision in favor of a more open position toward the Gentile Christians in the sense of the Jerusalem council decision. In 1 Corinthians, Paul no longer reveals any personal reserve in regard to Peter.

5.5 The Significance of the Antiochene Church for Christendom

The Apostolic Council and the Petrine visit in Antioch attest that in the first twenty years after Easter there is, after Jerusalem, no city as prominent in Christianity as Antioch. Thus Antioch entered church history because this community separated itself from the synagogue and formed a law-free fellowship based on Christ alone. That is, it surrendered the previously undisputed, natural conception of the Christian faith as an intra-Jewish group and understood Christianity as a new kind of phenomenon defining itself solely on its own terms. This happened because the law, which within Judaism was the undisputed norm of all group-specific qualification, was no longer recognized as the precondition of Christian baptism and thus of salvation and ecclesiastical self-understanding; therefore it was logical to engage in mission work among the Gentiles and to define the faith and baptism of all people solely on the basis of belonging to Christ and his church. Indeed, a Gentile-Christian life-style was even demanded of Jewish Christians in order thus to even out any possible Jewish superiority, so that no pre-Christian life-style—whether under circumcision or uncircumcision—was accorded a greater nearness to the Christian faith (5.2 above). This was Antioch's hour in church history, for it meant the groundbreaking first step from a Jewish faction to a "world religion," even if at the time Antioch still could not fully recognize this result.

Antioch provided yet a second, related service, namely, that Paul worked about twelve years in this church, matured as the greatest theologian of the first early Christian generation, and certainly energetically helped shape and continued to shape the Antiochene development. Of course, to some extent Antioch probably reversed this bold step toward a Gentile-Christian-oriented church and again placed Gentile Christianity under the law of Leviticus 17–18 (5.3 above). With this they also lost Paul, who consistently continued to fight for the original Antiochene decision. He is the Antiochene who demonstrated the courage to hold fast to the Gentile-Christian course against Peter and the people of

James. This is doubtless related not least of all to his apostolic independence, which was based on his calling.

In many places the Pauline correspondence contains traditional formulations that incorporate the spirit of this Antiochene Gentile Christianity. Indeed, we must generally ask to what extent the traditions treated by Paul were not in essence known to him from Antioch. For the most part, it has been considered sufficient to characterize such material quite generally as "pre-Pauline" or "extra-Pauline." If, however, we take a closer look at Christianity between A.D. 30 and 50, we can easily see that this is an imprecise classification. In the first place, there is the Jewish Christianity at the synagogues in Judea and Galilee (cf. Acts 1–5; 15; 1 Thess. 2:14; Matt. 10:5). Second, we can name the Jewish-Christian churches of the Hellenists. This mission looked back on successes in Samaria (Acts 8:1, 5, 25), in the coastal cities on the Mediterranean from Gaza (8:26) through Azotus (8:40), Lydda (9:32), Joppa (9:36), and Caesarea (8:40) to Phoenicia (11:19) and—not to forget—Damascus, Antioch, and Cyprus (9:2–3, 19; 11:19). Finally, we can point to the Gentile-Christian-oriented mission of Antioch (Syria, southern Asia Minor, and Cyprus—Acts 13–14). Geographically and theologically, this is, on the whole, quite an extensive terrain for the spread of Christianity. Apart from all necessary critique of the conceptual design of Acts, we can doubtless regard this geographical situation roughly as an appropriate description. This means, however, that Paul could have received the traditions of that time only from those three embodiments and expansion territories of Christianity. For we would not want to assume that churches on the coast of Egypt (Acts 18:24) or a Christian house church in Rome (indicated in Acts 18:2–3; Rom. 16:3) already had active contact with Antioch or Paul, especially since these churches were hardly founded much before the independent missionary journeys of the apostle. If we think of their missionization as work achieved by the Hellenists or their sympathizers, which would be the most plausible hypothesis, they contribute no new theological line.

We must further consider the relations of the churches with each other. Peter, as a Palestinian, visits the mission areas of the Hellenists (Acts 9:32ff.; 10:1ff.) and also Antioch (Gal. 2:11ff.). Between Antioch and Jerusalem there was probably a general correspondence (Acts 15; Gal. 2:1ff.). Paul became a Christian in a church of the Hellenists and also later traveled with friendly reception to the churches of the Hellenists (Acts 15:3; 21:3, 8; 27:3). Going out from Antioch, he missionized in their mission field (Acts 13–14). Some foundings of the Hellenists probably became Antiochene. This means that all three streams were apparently in regular contact with each other. In addition, Paul visited Peter privately in Jerusalem (Gal. 1:18). From this we can draw conclusions. If Gentile Christianity is represented only by Antioch and its vicinity as Antiochene missionary area, then in Paul, Gentile-Christian tradition from such an early time must come from Antioch. Naturally Paul could have learned Palestinian Jewish-Christian tradition in Jerusalem, for example. But the essentials were also known in Antioch. The Hellenistic Jewish-Christian tradition is familiar to him since Damascus, yet it also stands at the beginning of the Antiochene church. Thus on the whole we can say that what Paul used later from the old tradition essentially came from the knowledge of the Antiochene community. That is especially true of those traditions which are found in the two oldest Pauline letters (1 Thessalonians and 1 Corinthians) and, most of all, of the Gentile-Christian-oriented pieces here.

If we are to define the designation "pre-Pauline" more closely as (for the most part) Antiochene, we must go a step further. The Gentile-Christian thinking in Antioch is to a considerable extent determined by Paul himself. His leading role in the church is beyond question. In the end he is more consistently Gentile Christian than Antioch itself. Thus "pre-Pauline" is in part also to be defined as "early Pauline": Antiochene church tradition and Pauline thinking in this period cannot be simply separated.

With these presuppositions, of course, we still cannot with certainty design a comprehensive panorama of Antiochene theology, but we can indicate some of its emphases and thereby sketch the beginnings of an overall understanding, without having to put too much trust in reconstructive reasoning. To catch sight of such emphases, we must remember Antioch's new basic experience. It consists in the fact that the Spirit was also at work among non-Jews outside the initially Jewish-Christian church and that they came to faith in Jesus Christ and had themselves baptized. This experience with the Spirit of the gospel and the consequences of faith and baptism for non-Jews had to shine through in Antioch's essential theological utterances. Further, we must remember the typical slogans from Gal. 2:4; 2:5, 14: "freedom . . . in Christ" and the "truth of the gospel" (cf. 5.1 above). This freedom and truth consisted in the fact that the soteriological importance of the law was negated. Thus in a fundamental way Antioch worked up this experience, which took the previous synoptic view of law and faith—normal for Jewish Christians—and reshaped it into a critical relationship, which resulted in antithetical statements in the relation of the two entities.

The "canon" contained therein (Gal. 6:15) is brought to bear in Paul in a traditional group of statements, as found, say, in 1 Cor. 7:19; 12:13; 2 Cor. 5:17; Gal. 3:26–28; 5:5–6; 6:15. These passages, each in its way, attempt, while abolishing the soteriological principle of the synagogue, to describe the new Gentile-Christian consensus or, more exactly, to capture it in a formulaic expression capable of consensus. They are oriented toward the baptismal context. Baptism means two things: receiving the creative Spirit of the end time and being put "in Christ," that is, belonging to the eschatological church. That alone now constitutes the new being; circumcision is rejected as a precondition. This new condition of salvation can be described with the symbolism of clothing (Gal. 3:27; cf. Rom. 13:14), with the metaphor of drinking the Spirit (1 Cor. 12:13), or with the set expression of the "new creation" (2 Cor. 5:17; Gal. 6:15). Christians are "in Christ," as Christ's Spirit also works in them, so that the inner and outer relationships of Christians are so reordered that they belong to a new creation.

This first description can be characterized more exactly in many ways. First, in terms of the history of religions, the new fundamental viewpoint speaks syncretistically, corresponding to the makeup of the church. Thus we observe central expressions that are of Jewish-apocalyptic origin (e.g., "new creation") or that come from Hellenistic mystery language (e.g., the clothing symbolism); yet there are also creative neologisms (e.g., "in Christ"). Theologically conspicuous is the stark prominence of the transformation of one's entire existence. The break with everything past is thus stressed in various ways, and the new life in Christ is fixed in its qualitative and comprehensive newness. Finally, Antioch's special problem situation comes to expression through the theme of the law. In many ways Paul emphasizes that the law, represented by the crucial key words "circumcision" (1 Cor. 7:19; Gal. 5:6; 6:15) and "Jew" (1 Cor. 12:13; Gal. 3:28), no longer has validity. This refers most certainly and without exception to the ritual and ceremonial law. When the Antiochene Christians leave the synagogue with the aim of building an independent Gentile-Christian church life, they give up entirely this part of the observance of the law that separates Jews from Gentiles. Paul takes this decision for granted for the rest of his life. On the other hand, the Antiochenes are not libertines: the new creation is not constituted beyond the divine will. Rather, faith works through love (Gal. 5:6). The lifting of the antithesis of circumcision and uncircumcision does not abolish the requirement of "keeping the [ethical] commandments of God" (1 Cor. 7:19). Of course, the kingdom of God does not consist in "food and drink," that is, in the observance of dietary laws, "but righteousness and peace and joy in the Holy Spirit" (Rom. 14:17). Thus the Spirit, who in baptism has selected the body of the believer as a temple (1 Cor. 6:19), drives us to deeds of love. The Spirit also makes the legal requirement coming from the outside superfluous, but he drives from within toward sanctification in brotherly love, because he is that divine Spirit which the prophets had promised as the Spirit of the end time for the transformation of the inner constitution of humanity (1 Thess. 4:7–9; cf. Ezek. 36:26–27).

If the independence of the Antiochene church from the synagogal fellowship leads to this new description of Christian existence and church reality, and if this characterization is centered on the baptismal gift of the Spirit and the embodiment "in Christ," then it should no longer surprise us that in his oldest letter Paul quite naturally makes existential ontological statements about Christians: "You are all sons of light and sons of the day" (1 Thess. 5:5). This is explained again with clothing symbolism: "Since we belong to the day, let us be sober, and put on the breastplate of faith and love, and for a helmet the hope of salvation" (1 Thess. 5:8). Naturally that recalls, for example, Gal. 3:26–28, where in the baptismal context we find the new being as sonship ("In Christ Jesus you are all sons of God") and the clothing symbolism as a description of the closest relationship to Christ. We should likewise compare 2 Cor. 5:17, where the new being in Christ is described as new creation, so that for Christians the old has passed away and the new has come; a little later (2 Cor. 5:21) this new reality is expressed: "He made him to be sin who knew no sin, so that in him we might become the righteousness of God." This last ontological statement stands at the point where 1 Thess. 5:8; Gal. 3:27 make statements with the help of clothing symbolism. Within the sphere of salvation "in Christ," the "righteousness of God" describes the new Christian reality as it comes about through baptism. Similarly, in 1 Cor. 1:30; 6:11—which contain traditional baptismal statements—the condition of being "washed," "sanctified," and "justified" is a new description of being, which has ontological validity because church members no longer *are* in the old being (1 Cor. 6:11a) but "in Christ Jesus," who has become "righteousness and sanctification and redemption" (1 Cor. 1:30). We will come back to these statements later (cf. 11.3 below).

In Christ and the *Spirit* are the focal points of an ellipse, which, understood both anthropologically and ecclesiologically, coincide with the new creation. The ellipse is, moreover, the central assertion within a larger context, which we would like to designate early-Pauline election theology. First Thessalonians is profoundly and comprehensively shaped by it. This is to be presented in a special section (cf. 6.2 below). According to 1 Thessalonians, this election theology is, for Paul as well as for the Christians in Thessalonica, the natural language of faith. That is a sign that the conception—documented by 1 Thessalonians very soon after his departure from Antioch—originated during the apostle's Antiochene period. This assumption is plausible if we note one decisive mark of this doctrine of election, namely, the fact that its point is the eschatological election of the nations through the gospel. If it is indeed the programmatic devotion to non-Jews that characterizes this election teaching, then we must ask: Where else but in Antioch was this step first taken? Where else could such a program find a home in this early period? This leads us to the thesis that the Pauline election theology of 1 Thessalonians is deeply rooted in the apostle's Antiochene period and well suited to provide the theological foundation for Antioch's Gentile mission.

As indicated by the context in 1 Thessalonians 1, this election theology includes the homiletical schema of a Gentile mission sermon as sketched by Paul in 1 Thess. 1:9–10. In this passage the apostle reminds his readers "what a welcome we had" among the Thessalonians: how they "turned to God from idols, to serve a living and true God, and to wait for his Son from heaven, whom he raised from the dead, Jesus who delivers us from the wrath to come." Because in this early period only Antioch programmatically carried on a mission to the Gentiles, this church was the first to face the task of designing a concept for such a mission that might expect general recognition in the Christian world. Here out of inner conviction it *wanted* to link up with the proselyte solicitation of the Hellenistic synagogue, at the same time it *could* do so on the basis of its heritage from the synagogue, and finally it also *had to,* naturally, for the sake of the Jewish-Christian brethren. This means, more concretely, that they reworked the monotheistic preaching of diaspora Judaism, as is visible in the first part of the sermon summary. Through the synagogue the uncompromising rejection of the polytheistic divine world was predetermined: the God of Israel and Father of Jesus Christ was alone creator and Lord of the world. The peoples worship only "dumb idols" (1 Cor. 12:2), who "by nature are no gods" (Gal. 4:8), for the whole polytheism of the Hellenistic-Roman world is due only to disobedience to the one God (Rom. 1:18ff.). The gods are, nevertheless, not without numinous power, for they are not simply in an enlightening way declared nonexistent but only reevaluated in their significance (1 Cor. 8:5): for humankind they are not healthy but demonic (1 Cor. 10:20) and a stabilizing factor in the depravity of the pagan life-style (Rom. 1:21–24). They are witnesses to how people suppress the truth of God in unrighteousness (Rom. 1:18). By contrast, it is true of the Father of Jesus Christ that "from him and through him and to him are all things" (Rom. 11:36), and while "an idol has no real existence," "there is no God but one" (1 Cor. 8:4). This idea is stated most impressively in the pre-Corinthian confession of 1 Cor. 8:6:

> There is one God, the Father,
>> from whom are all things and for whom we exist,
> and one Lord, Jesus Christ,
>> through whom are all things and through whom we exist.

For the Hellenists, this necessarily dethroned Zeus/Jupiter as the father of the gods and father of the world. They faced the alternative of worshiping either Zeus or the Father of Jesus Christ. Up against precisely the monotheistic tendency of the Hellenists, as indicated by the figure of Zeus, Christianity placed the demand to renounce the world of the gods in favor of the Father of Jesus Christ.

From this the synagogue had drawn the conclusion that the pagan cult and everything connected with it, even indirectly, was strictly to be avoided. The Jewish Christians in Antioch, who followed Peter (cf. 5.3 above), show how much the separation from all pagan uncleanness still played a hidden role even in Antioch. Yet things seemed different there at first, for the church practiced full table fellowship between Gentile and Jewish Christians (cf. 5.2 and 5.3 above), without holding to the Jewish ritual law. The Antiochenes had drawn from their creation faith the conclusion that "nothing is unclean in itself" (Rom. 14:14); rather, "everything is indeed clean" (Rom. 14:20); thus one can "eat or drink" everything as it is, when it happens with "thankfulness" and "to the glory of God" (1 Cor. 10:30–31; Rom. 14:6). For was it not true, according to Ps. 24:1, that "the earth is the Lord's, and everything in it" (1 Cor. 10:26)? Unfortunately, we can no longer verify whether the Jesus tradition, such as Mark 7:15, also played a role in this fundamental decision. This cannot be absolutely excluded, because such an innovation would surely need an unambiguous legitimation. Yet now we can only know that the Spirit also given precisely to the Gentiles provides a motivation for such freedom (cf. 5.1 above).

In the Hellenistic synagogue the Creator-God was at the same time already the eschatological judge. Thus the preaching schema in 1 Thess. 1:9–10 could also in its second part connect with the solicitation of proselytes. But as surely as divine judgment came to the whole world (1 Cor. 3:13–15; Rom. 14:10), Christians now talked about it differently. They placed Christ in the foreground as Savior from such wrath (1 Thess. 1:10). They energetically focused not on the threat of judgment for all pagan depravity (Rom. 1:18ff.) but on the salvation brought by God in Christ. To those "who have no hope" (1 Thess. 4:13) Christians could offer faith, love, and hope (1 Thess. 1:3; 5:8; 1 Cor. 13:13). Since Paul in 1 Thessalonians employs this now classic Christian triad as a matter of course, it must have already been an expression of Christian self-understanding in his Antiochene years. In all probability this is the way the Antiochene church had brought its new understanding of Christianity to a common denominator. That happened perhaps also through another concept: that of the *gospel*. If Antiochene missionary preaching accentuated salvation and not judgment, then such language is suggested. Moreover, through the Antiochene catchwords from Gal. 2:4, 5, 14, the use of the concept in Antioch with an antilaw accent is attested, and it is also supported by 1 Thessalonians, in which Paul uses this concept quite naturally in a Gentile-Christian orientation.

This new soteriological version of the judgment declaration, based on Christology, was naturally connected with the idea of the end of the world—familiar to Christians since Jesus—as an imminent expectation (1 Thess. 1:10; 4:15; etc.). This must again be mentioned here because through it the newly understood faith in creation received a second theme. To the judgment of all creation as "clean" is now added the eschatological trait of "passing away": "The form of this world is passing away" (1 Cor. 7:31). The positive attitude was the open door to missions, yet there was only a little time left for missionizing. Hence, ridding the world of taboos was not the forerunner of using creation instrumentally for the development of human possibilities. Rather, it was the elimination of theological boundaries, in order to be able to devote oneself to the lost world, shortly before its end, for the purpose of its salvation.

In this devotion to the nations, naturally, we must not forget that the Antiochene church came out of the synagogue and continued to live in its immediate physical and spiritual proximity. Not least of all the hard anti-Jewish polemic in 1 Thess. 2:15–16, which flows easily from Paul's pen so soon after his departure from Antioch, leads us to suspect that this relationship was not free of tension (cf. 15.2 below). Perhaps we may transpose the three great exegeses from 1 Cor. 10:1–21; 2 Cor. 3:7–18; Gal. 4:21–31 back to this Antiochene period with respect to their theological disposition. Interpreters today are largely in agreement that these passages were hardly newly conceived for their epistolary contexts and in general, with regard to the typological-allegorical method and the theological opposition of old and new covenant, cannot be smoothly accommodated in Pauline thinking. The place of experience for these three exegeses is the new creative Spirit, who has achieved in Christians what the "law" could never do: people are changed from the ground up. In each of these three texts Israel's time of origin and election (Abraham, Moses, exodus) is linked and at the same time contrasted with the eschatological election time in which the church is convinced it is living. The scripture preserved Israel's election and difficulties so that the eschatological Christian church could find its own situation indicated therein (1 Cor. 10:5–6, 11). Just as God was not pleased with the many Israelites of the exodus generation, so surely is he in a quite different way a faithful God vis-à-vis the Christian church (1 Cor. 10:5, 12–13). Yet the judgment of the wilderness generation because of its fall into idolatry and cancellation of election can be repeated in individual cases in a Gentile-Christian church as backsliding into the old world of the gods. This says indirectly that the holy scripture of Israel applies to the independent Gentile-Christian church but no longer to contemporary Judaism. In 2 Corinthians 3 the judgment on Judaism is harsher: Moses shows the inferiority of the old covenant. In contrast to the Christian eschatological church (2 Cor. 3:17–18), Israel today is still bound in service to the death-bringing letter and to death. Only its conversion to the Christian church (2 Cor. 3:15–16) can bring it salvation also. The polemical antithesis is similarly harsh in Galatians 4, where Israel is associated with Abraham's slave and its divine covenant is defined as slavery. The Christian church is linked with Sarah and interpreted as freedom and fulfillment of the promise to Abraham. As in those days Ishmael contested the inheritance with Isaac, so today the synagogue with the Christian church (Gal. 4:29). Here we see the nearness to 1 Thess. 2:15–16. This language could not have been used by Jewish Christians bound to the synagogue.

We have already seen how much the experience of the Spirit directed the church. Statements about the Spirit of the end time were certainly not merely theoretical means of interpretation. Rather, the Spirit directly shaped church reality. Quite naturally Paul urges the Thessalonians: "Do not quench the Spirit, do not despise prophesying" (1 Thess. 5:19–20). From Antioch he was accustomed to such association with the Spirit. His ecstatic transport into the third heaven during his Antiochene period caused him to hear "things that cannot be told"—no doubt the language of the angels (2 Cor. 12:1–5). To the Corinthians he attests that he is accustomed to speaking in tongues and does it more than they (1 Cor. 14:18). The Antiochene delegation goes to the council in Jerusalem because of a "revelation," that is, a Spirit-effected utterance from the church (assembly) or a personal revelation to Paul (Gal. 2:2). Similarly, Acts describes the prophet Agabus appearing in Antioch (Acts 11:27–28) and the sending out of Barnabas and Paul on the so-called first missionary journey, resulting from an utterance of the Spirit during a worship service (Acts 13:2). After returning from the mission, they had to report back to the church (Acts 14:27). The Spirit-led worshiping church assembly is apparently the basic decision-making administrative organ of the church (Gal. 2:14; Acts 13:2; 14:27). The setting up of five "prophets and teachers" (Acts 13:1) and the sending out of missionaries in the case of Barnabas and Paul (Acts 13:2), as well as the determination of the delegation to Jerusalem (Gal. 2:1–2), are certainly unthinkable without the consensus of the whole church. The church understands itself as a Spirit-led brotherhood that deals with commissioning and approval of all of this.

In closing this section we can perhaps now also go into Antiochene Christology. Here there are special difficulties because all the churches from Gaza to Cyprus must have been interested in it together. The immense dynamic with which Christology developed in these years is explainable only if (almost) all Christian churches of the time took part in this process, surely including the Antiochene. Yet it is naturally hard to make an individual church responsible for this or that statement. Here also we certainly cannot render hasty judgments of exclusivity and priority in favor of one church. There is, however, one viewpoint that can substantiate the Antiochene contribution to the development of Christology: it is the viewpoint of universalization, which is typical in general for Antiochene theology and doubtless also influenced Christology in various respects, namely, in regard to the eschatological salvific function of the Son, the universal lordship in missions, the mediation of all creation reality, and the comprehensive salvific death of Jesus.

In the schema of Gentile-Christian preaching in 1 Thess. 1:9–10, the Son of God is accorded the eschatological function of saving all who give credence to that preaching. Gentile-Christian preaching thus universalizes the eschatological redemptive activity of Christ to humankind, for the preaching is directed "without borders" to all peoples. A similar broadening is achieved by the mission formula in Rom. 1:3b–4, though here Jewish messianism (cf. Psalm 2) is used in order to interpret Jesus on the basis of his resurrection to become the world-wide sovereign as Son of God: his henceforth perceived spiritual lordship is accomplished as mission among the nations.

The borderless Antiochene missionary concept included the universal Creator statement: The reality that the mission finds present everywhere comes from the one Creator and sustainer and finds its ultimate meaning in him. To this (already Jewish) horizon Christology is now also added: The Lord is mediator of creation, as the mythologized wisdom was for Judaism (1 Cor. 8:6). As the church owes its redemption to him, so the whole world owes its existence to his mediation. From here then, the next step is to remember the mission formula of Gal. 4:4–5: "God sent forth his Son, born of woman, . . . so that we might receive adoption as sons." Even here the preexistence of the Son seems to be indicated casually and indirectly, and the sonship of Christians, as in the

Antiochene church formula of Gal. 3:26–28, is understood as the new being, the gift of the sent Son. Perhaps we can add: As Jesus lost his earthly limitation to Israel through resurrection and installation as Son of God on a world scale in Rom. 1:3b–4, so also can the key word "woman" be generalized: He is born for everyone who belongs to humankind.

There is disagreement as to the source of the formulaic and varied expression of Christ's salvific death "for us/for our sins." The oldest literary evidence is 1 Thess. 5:10, where the statement appears quite naturally and familiarly. There is no sure evidence from early Jerusalem Christianity or Jesus' proclamation. The next religious-historical parallels point to a Hellenistic-Jewish milieu (2 and 4 Maccabees; cf. *T. Benj.* 3:8). In them the death of the Maccabean martyrs is interpreted in such a way that the Old Testament–Jewish idea of expiatory sacrifice and the Greek conception of the vicarious existential sacrifice for another person or fellowship were shaped into a new semantic relationship in order to understand the innocent death of the martyrs as vicarious sacrifice for the transgressions of Israel. The salvific death statement about Jesus' death on the cross most likely stands in this tradition. It may possibly have arisen in Antioch. Yet at the same time, the Antiochene church universalized the Hellenistic-Jewish conception in favor of humanity, for the Son was the Savior of all Christians (1 Thess. 1:10), and his lordship, because of the resurrection, was given in the worldwide mission directed toward all people (Rom. 1:3b–4).

In closing we emphasize again what was stated at the beginning: in describing Antiochene theology, substantiated assumptions are possible, but nothing more. Basic traits that agree with each other are describable, but much must remain open. What was assumed hypothetically here (and yet is capable of expansion) justifies the judgment that during the Pauline stay in Antioch, the city apparently accomplished for early Christianity something substantial and pioneering in the history of theology.

5.6 Paul and Jesus

In the apostle's Antiochene period his relationship to the Jesus tradition also must have assumed a firm structure. To describe this relationship appropriately has long been a difficult research problem. When we compare the theological content of the Pauline letters with the Jesus tradition as it is preserved in the Synoptic Gospels, we find a striking state of affairs: in Christology and soteriology—that is, in the heart of

Pauline theology—there are no direct references to the Jesus tradition. Individual attempts to ferret out hidden relationships here are so hypothetical that they effect the opposite of what they seek to achieve. Namely, we cannot explain away the fact that Paul cites confessional traditions in crucial passages on these themes (Rom. 1:1–7; 3:21–31; 1 Cor. 15:1–11; 2 Cor. 5:11–6:2; Gal. 1:1–5; etc.) and also goes to great pains in a detailed scriptural proof (Romans 4; Galatians 3; etc.), but nowhere does he apply the authority of the Jesus tradition. Nowhere, for example, does it occur to him to say that because Jesus, according to Mark 10:45, spoke of his death as a ransom for many and, according to Mark 14:24, on the occasion of the Last Supper interpreted his death as expiation, his death must therefore be understood as an expiatory death. For Paul, Jesus' death is linked rather to the aspect "for us," because with this the meaning of Jesus' death is given as a divine salvific measure. What Jesus' own attitude was toward his death means nothing to Paul. By analogy the same would have to be true if we were to begin with the idea that Paul knew that some statements of eschatological expectation were formerly rooted in the Son of man tradition (e.g., 1 Thess. 1:10; 4:17; 1 Cor. 16:22) and he would draw on them, for instance, because Jesus understood himself as the Son of man. Quite apart from all the questionableness of such a multilayered hypothesis, the decisive observation is that Paul does not indicate at all that he has any theological or historical interest in the attitude of Jesus toward the Son of man tradition. He is completely indifferent to this issue. Crucial for him is not what Jesus himself advocated but in what way he is God's manifestation to human beings.

Also, in his creation statements Paul never makes an effort to use the Jesus tradition, which is not exactly lacking in such content. He forms creation statements on the basis of general Hellenistic-Jewish creation faith (1 Thess. 1:9; 1 Cor. 8:1–6; Rom. 1:18ff.; etc.), including the use of the Septuagint (cf., e.g., 1 Cor. 10:26). In the conception of the Spirit and in the understanding of the church it was from the beginning generally difficult, indeed impossible, to continue writing the Jesus tradition. For here the post-Easter experience of the Spirit and the formation of the church are too far removed from the situation of Jesus. That leaves only the expectation of the end and the exhortation of the Christian conduct of life, in which the conditions are more complex. Even here, however, before all differentiation we must ascertain that the starting point and material content of the Pauline ethic are developed without basic reference to the Jesus tradition. Paul bases his ethic on the new being (Rom. 12:1–2; Gal. 5:25; etc.) and describes its material content in manifold ways; and the Jesus materials and Jesus' authority appear only seldom and among other things. Passages such as Romans 8; 1 Corinthians 15 demonstrate further how Paul can develop his end expectation without reference to Jesus' hope. It is clear that Pauline theology cannot be understood as the direct continuation of Jesus' message of the kingdom of God. By its nature it is not the tradition-oriented actualization of Jesus' proclamation (Jesus said . . ., therefore . . .) but follows its own linguistic and conceptual model. If we want to formulate it with a modern concept, between Jesus and Paul a "change of paradigm" took place. Only if we begin with this and keep this in mind can we come to an appropriate definition of the relationship between Paul and Jesus.

For this it is important, further, to exclude 2 Cor. 5:16 completely from the discussion. This passage reads: "From now on, therefore, we regard no one from a human point of view [lit., according to flesh]; even though we once regarded Christ from a human point of view, we regard him thus no longer." This statement, which depreciates a knowledge of Christ "according to flesh," is often used to serve as Paul's judgment about the earthly Jesus in general, as if Paul intended in the sense of a conscious theological program to let the life of Jesus shrivel to the mere fact that Jesus lived. But only by disregarding the context can such a program be read out of this verse. It does not speak of the earthly or historical Jesus in contrast to the exalted Christ but judges a certain way of knowing. The object of that knowing is the unified Christ as the earthly and exalted One. The condemned way of knowing is the merely human and unbelieving versus the spiritual, according to which faith also understands precisely the earthly One as the Christ, in whom "God was," in that "for our sake he made him to be sin who knew no sin" (2 Cor. 5:19, 21). Yet even if 2 Cor. 5:16 were to be understood differently than indicated, it would still remain methodologically precarious to loose a single remark from its contextual fabric and load it with an entire program that one should first, and on sounder methodological ground, derive from the whole Pauline epistolary corpus.

In a similar way the use of Gal. 1:18 is also to be criticized if this mention of Paul's visit with Peter in Jerusalem is supposed to serve, conversely, to demonstrate the apostle's fundamental knowledge and dependence on the Jesus tradition. We could then expand this: since his calling, Paul in general had constant contact with the chief witnesses to the Jesus tradition at that time. Also, the churches continually cultivated so many relations with each other that we can count on a rich knowledge of the Jesus tradition everywhere. With this hint we will easily be inclined to regard such rare echoes of the synoptists in

Paul as indications of the intentional adoption of the synoptic tradition. In that way the Pauline letters will quickly and stealthily become readers that show how abundantly the Jesus tradition was interpreted. This, however, attributes too much (or does violence—cf. ch. 2 above) to the personal relations between Paul and Peter, and to church contacts, and to the Pauline letters. Such construction runs aground simply on the Pauline texts themselves, which on the contrary show no reflection of such an assumption.

Naturally we can assume that Paul knows more Jesus tradition than he demonstrably quotes. General knowledge is always to be estimated as more extensive than its actual application. An explanation is needed, however, as to why Paul nowhere appeals to the synoptic narrative material (miracle stories, legendary tales) or to the passion report (1 Cor. 11:23–26 is a worship-related individual tradition!), why he nowhere draws on teaching and quarreling dialogues, biographical apothegms, parables, blessings, and self-assertions of Jesus, but essentially only admonitions for the regulation of community life and statements of the expectation of the end. In addition, it remains conspicuous that this application, which is limited to certain genres, also on the whole plays a subordinate role, if we disregard the vague and disputed echoes suggested here and there, for it is methodologically advisable to start with the minimum of the relatively assured and not from the maximum of the perhaps still probable. This sharply restricted role of the Jesus tradition is clearly also distinguished from other areas of early Christian tradition and literature, since the Pauline reserve vis-à-vis the Jesus tradition is by no means the rule outside the synoptists.

Furthermore, we must also be careful in dealing with the term "Jesus tradition." In this early period the concept cannot simply be regarded as synonymous with the synoptists' complete stock of tradition (including the sayings source). Without a separation—however admittedly hypothetical—of tradition and redaction in the Gospels, we should not compare directly with Paul. A look at the special material or a comparison between Mark and the sayings source teaches us further that it is not advisable to assume that the same Jesus tradition was known or actively used everywhere. Even the Johannine church cultivated the Jesus tradition in a quite characteristic way. In these transmitting and adapting processes the theological positions of the transmitters in each case played a crucial role, but not they alone: nontheological factors have also affected these processes. The rural world of Galilean villages, as reflected in Jesus' parables, may have had little or no meaning in urban Christianity. Here, conversely, the image of competition in the gymnasiums (1 Cor. 9:24–27) may have attracted much more attention but again may have been foreign to the Jesus tradition. Was there a need in Corinth to deal with Pharisaism in the sense of Matthew 23? Can we imagine that in Thessalonica Jesus' violations of the Sabbath were of current concern? Yet this means that everywhere theological as well as nontheological factors must have contributed to the knowledge of Jesus being rewritten or repressed. Thus even at the beginning there may well have been a difference between the Lord's brother James and the Hellenists in regard to the active use and extent of their Jesus tradition. At first this differentiation must have continued with the ongoing development of Christianity. Not until the postapostolic period did a compiling of the various materials take place in the form of the great Gospels.

Finally, we must make a basic comment on the methodological problem of comparison. One should distinguish a general competence in the tradition (variable in the individual case) as passive knowledge about a particular area of tradition from the individual active use of tradition with its conscious adoption and interpretation. Passive competence in the tradition is naturally in each case more extensive than the active use of the same. On the former we can only speculate in regard to ancient authors and associations. In the last analysis, however, for the understanding of Pauline theology it is unimportant how extensive Paul's passive knowledge of the Jesus tradition was. Peter may have informed him of, among other things, Jesus tradition; the Hellenists may have done the same in their mission, including in Damascus; Antioch may have learned such things directly from Peter, James, and Barnabas; but the crucial point is how Paul, Antioch, or others actively dealt with it and in which theological coordinate system and what general life contexts they did or did not make use of that tradition.

The proof of active use of the Jesus tradition turns out to be more complicated than we at first would assume. Simple is the case where Paul demonstrably claims to cite Jesus tradition and this is attested in the synoptic realm in relatively analogous form (e.g., 1 Cor. 7:10–11; Mark 10:2–12; Matt. 5:31–32). The situation becomes more complicated already when, as in the case of 1 Thess. 4:15–17, Paul claims to be using a saying of the Lord but such cannot be found in the tradition of Jesus known to us. Is the apostle thinking of a saying of the earthly One at all? Does he not mean a saying of the exalted One? Then come cases in which synoptic Jesus material is employed anonymously in Paul (e.g., Rom. 12:14; Luke 6:28a). Apparently for Paul such tradition has its own jurisdiction and does not need the authority of Jesus. Even that is a theologically significant observation. Is one supposed to remember at all that such a saying is in agreement with the Jesus tradition? But is it really? We always presuppose in familiar fashion that the

Jesus sayings of the synoptists are older than (anonymous) Pauline statements in his paraenesis. But is this presupposition correct? At any rate, the opposite case cannot be excluded: anonymous early Christian admonition, which Paul also used, is, in the course of time, accorded the authority of Jesus within the synoptic tradition (an example, perhaps, is 1 Thess. 5:13c; Mark 9:50c). Certainly one can further refine the scale of possibilities, but that is not the point now. Decisive is the assertion that the person who keeps such manifold possibilities in mind and grants insight into historical reality only to a procedure that begins with them naturally has a much more difficult time than someone who simply compares the text level of the synoptists with the text level of Pauline letters and statistically gathers all more or less clear and scanty convergences. Yet what is sought is not the quantitatively achieved sum but the qualitative judgment.

For this it is, above all, necessary to take into account the overall theological conception under whose presupposition the Jesus tradition belongs and is processed. Thus it makes an essential difference whether we, like Matthew, understand Jesus as a messianic teacher in word and deed, whose rejection by Israel brought him death, but whom God raised, so that now as the exalted One he can bind missions to the teachings presented by him as the earthly One (Matt. 28:19–20), who, moreover, as the earthly One expressly warned against the post-Easter prophets who in his name would say and do more and different things from what he as the earthly One commanded (Matt. 7:13–27). Or whether we, like Paul, comprehend Jesus on the basis of his destiny, which as the eschatological action of God is basic for the salvation of humankind, and let the person of salvation described by his history be experienced in the Spirit of the church, understand the power of the Spirit reshaping humanity as the starting point for ethics, and would like expressly not to see this Spirit of the Lord extinguished in the church. In the first conception, everything must depend on the tradition of the sayings of the earthly One and on the inculcation of their validity, as surely as one can at the same time be actively involved in shaping them. In the second position, words of the earthly One are basically dispensable. Naturally they can also be used, since the earthly One and the exalted One are indeed identical, but they have no fundamental systematic function as in the first program. Thus, for example, a saying of Jesus can be employed authoritatively to substantiate strict monogamy (1 Cor. 7:10–11)—when it is used, naturally, it always has authority—yet the same theme can also be treated in the same way in terms of content without Jesus' saying (1 Thess. 4:3–5). The second possibility is, from the beginning, one that conforms to the system; the first is an additional possibility. If Antioch and Paul indeed represent this second position, then for them it has basically determined the status and function of the Jesus tradition.

We can describe the status of the Jesus tradition in Paul's letters in this general way but claim that in his missionary preaching Paul presented the earthly Jesus in a more comprehensive way and taught the traditions of the earthly One as basic information. He could then forgo doing this in his letters, which are directed to long-standing churches, since he did not need to repeat familiar common knowledge. Possible evidence for this assumption could be provided by Luke, since he apparently has the Pauline missionary preaching determined by Jesus tradition, among other things (cf., e.g., Acts 13:23–25, 28–29; 17:3; 28:23, 31). Yet we should only listen to Luke when there are at least related points of contact in Paul, but here the situation is not promising. In the schema of Gentile mission preaching in 1 Thess. 1:9–10 (cf. 1 Cor. 1:4–9) there is no indication of such detailed basic knowledge of Jesus of Nazareth. Also, when Paul in other places recalls his initial preaching, such as 1 Cor. 2:1–5; 11:2, 23–26; 15:1–11; Gal. 1:9; 3:1–5; 4:13–14; 5:21; Phil. 4:9; 1 Thess. 1:5–10; 4:1, 6, 11, there is no perceptible hint that he proceeded in that way. On the contrary, the passages show that Paul calls to mind exactly what is also to be found elsewhere in the letters. Thus, in the sense mentioned, missionary message and epistolary content cannot be distinguished, and the thesis that claims to distinguish between the two on that basis proves to be unfounded. Then it clearly speaks for itself that pointing to passages such as 1 Cor. 6:2–9; 1 Thess. 5:2, which relate quite generally to community knowledge, naturally also produces little evidence of instruction in the Jesus tradition.

Thus it is appropriate that we inquire more exactly into the overall Pauline conception and discuss first of all what significance the historical Jesus has in general in the theology of the apostle. Paul did not know Jesus of Nazareth. This is an important difference from Peter and other Jewish Christians, but it agrees with the situation of, say, Barnabas, Timothy, and Titus and the church in Damascus and Antioch. Anyone wanting to assert the opposite for Paul will fall into the realm of fantastic speculation. Therefore it is also historically unfounded to presuppose for Paul an overall impression of Jesus' piety and personality in order to explain on this basis the development of Pauline Christology. Even if Peter, for example, perhaps later transmitted such things to him, we can know nothing of it from Paul. That alone carries decisive weight. Even such a statement as Heb. 5:7–10 (cf. 2:17–18; 4:15) about the temptability of Jesus and his withstanding temptation would be basically contrary to the style of the Pauline Christology.

Paul's experience of Jesus Christ begins with his calling. He feels himself called into service by God, who declares the resurrected One to him as God's deed, and consequently orients himself toward this exalted Lord. From the present position of the Lord, Paul looks to the history of the earthly One, especially to Jesus' salvific death, and perceives even this as an act of God that reveals Jesus as the redeemer of humanity. Therefore the earthly One is not presented as a personage, not as the agent of the approaching dominion of God, not as a miracle worker. What is interesting is not his preaching in Galilee and Jerusalem but God's accessibility through the basic dates of Jesus' history, that is, Jesus as divine activity or as a God-obeying person through whom God has become active for the benefit of humanity. Thus Pauline Christology with respect to the earthly One can be very well expressed in this brief statement in 2 Cor. 5:19: "God was in Christ reconciling the world to himself, not counting their trespasses against them, and entrusting to us the message of reconciliation." Paul can also express this with Christ as subject instead of God, for example, in Gal. 1:3–4: "Jesus Christ, who gave himself for our sins to deliver us from the present evil age, according to the will of our God and Father." The two expressions are two sides of the same historical reality, which is interpreted: Christ's destiny is God's will and eschatological deed, which happens for the benefit of humankind.

This basic beginning of Pauline Christology can be filled with contents that are few in number but crucial for Paul. This is more than the mere fact that Jesus lived as a statement about the earthly One, but by no means enough to write, for example, a Gospel of Mark, and certainly not enough to form a text genre such as the sayings source Q. From their post-Easter viewpoint the Gospels are highly kerygmatic, yet they begin with the premise that the individual and the particular—be it a word or a deed of Jesus—fixes forever a piece of the reality of Jesus. Paul, on the other hand, forgoes this way on principle, completely and without exception. While only looking back over the life of Jesus as a whole, Paul makes a clarifying comment or interprets the meaning for salvation of the "boundary situations," such as entrance into the world, death, and resurrection. Correspondingly, Jesus is Christ from two lineages; he is, namely, preexistent (1 Cor. 8:6; Phil. 2:6–7) and at the same time from Israel (Rom. 9:5) or of Davidic descent (Rom. 1:3). He was born of a woman and placed under the law (Gal. 4:4). For the sake of God's truthfulness he became the servant of the circumcised, so that the promises to the patriarchs would be confirmed as valid (Rom. 15:8). Thus he lived not to please himself, but, in accordance with Ps. 69:10, he took the reproaches of others on himself (Rom. 15:3). He emptied himself, took the form of a servant, became like human beings, and was obedient unto death on the cross (Phil. 2:7–8). Although rich, he became poor, so that through such poverty he might make us rich (2 Cor. 8:9). He who knew no sin was made sin for us, so that in him we might become the righteousness of God (2 Cor. 5:21). He was crucified in weakness, but now he lives by the power of God (2 Cor. 13:4). His death was achieved by the Jews (1 Thess. 2:15) and occurred for human beings (1 Cor. 15:3b). Before he suffered death on the cross and is therefore considered simply "the crucified One" (1 Cor. 1:23)—hence, in general Paul intends to know only Jesus Christ and him crucified (1 Cor. 2:2)—Jesus founded the Lord's Supper as a memorial, so that through the celebration of the meal his death is proclaimed until his imminent eschatological coming (1 Cor. 11:23–26). Because his earthly existence until death was an existence only for humankind, God raised him (1 Cor. 15:3b–4) and exalted him to godlike Lordship (Phil. 2:9–11). This concrete historical Jesus is the "likeness of God," so that the gospel shines from this "glory of Christ" (2 Cor. 4:6). At the same time the overall significance of the earthly One as existence for others is the archetype with obligatory consequences for the Christian transformation (Rom. 15:1ff.; Phil. 2:1ff.). His crucifixion and his resurrection are present in a characteristic way when they are "repeated" in the believers through their dying with him and being raised with him (Rom. 6:1ff.; Gal. 2:19–20; 6:14; Phil. 3:10, 21).

Immediately conspicuous in this characterization of the earthly One is the extreme concentration on the basic meaning of Jesus' life. Gone are the villages of Galilee, the Lake of Gennesaret, and Jerusalem, including temple and priesthood. Jesus does not speak as a teacher, nor does he accomplish individual deeds. He is not baptized by John and calls no disciples into discipleship. There are no synagogues and no Passover, no Pharisees and no opponents, neither a Herod nor a Pilate. Jesus has no "biography" and does not belong in a particular Palestinian environment. We see only God's soteriological plan for him, his appearance "when the time had fully come" (Gal. 4:4), the basic structure of Jesus' life as a life for people, the burdening of the unburdened and the unburdening of the burdened, and the present Lordship of Jesus Christ. The Pauline churches are not supposed to memorize and actualize Jesus' sayings but practice being crucified with him. That alone is sufficient for salvation, because that is enough to validate the fact that Jesus' history is an event of God's love (Rom. 5:5–6). Therefore this alone is the content of the gospel. If we ask where the apostle got these assertions, the answer is clear: primarily from the confessional tradition but also from the Old Testament (e.g., Rom. 15:3–8). Otherwise we have judgments that the apostle himself formed in accordance with his christological way of thinking. In any case, he does not draw on synoptic or other Jesus tradition. Who Christ is is given by his history, which is staged by God, and by its characterization. These form a unity and constitute God's eschatological salvation event.

Based on these considerations, there is no need, in my opinion, for further reflections on why, for example, Paul should have avoided the Jesus tradition. It is futile and all too hypothetical to grant him presumed knowledge of certain elements of the Jesus tradition in order then—say, in connection with his opponents' postulated and un-Pauline use of the same Jesus tradition—to seek reasons why it was impossible for Paul himself to make use of such tradition. Rather, insight into the christological initiative is to be evaluated hermeneutically: because Paul in the described way typified the earthly One into a basic idea and thereby completely asserted his relevance in general for all people (in his sense), everything has been said for the founding of Christian existence and for its achievement. Through such typification Paul reached his solution to the problem of how Jesus Christ could be related to all peoples. Precisely this was, (for Antioch and) for him, a new and urgent problem, because the Gentiles as new addressees were supposed to receive the preached Christ (cf. 5.5 above). This reduction to a basic idea immediately understandable everywhere was appropriate to the new aim of calling all peoples to the gospel. Because of this initiative, which in a humanity-oriented way typified the story of Jesus Christ into a terse, yet unambiguous and general basic meaning (say: Jesus Christ is God's love for all), there was the possibility within the resulting framework to develop Christology with statements and materials that were understandable and close to the Gentile-Christian churches in terms of their heritage. The christologically oriented gospel is expressible with Gentile-Christian concepts.

Let us look at these basic remarks again in terms of the individual use of Jesus tradition in Paul. As already indicated, the apostle preserved the tradition of Jesus in relatively concentrated form in two thematic areas: in the expectation of the end and in the exhortation to change. Certainly, in Paul's expectation of the end, the kingdom of God is removed entirely from the center of the proclamation. But 1 Thessalonians gives hints that the hope for a final fulfillment in God's dominion was still alive in Antioch's early preaching (1 Thess. 2:12) but was then reshaped by the expectation of the Parousia of the Lord (2:19; 3:13; 4:15; 5:23) and of the following everlasting being with him (4:17; 5:10). Because since Easter the salvation figure Jesus Christ has been considered the decisive content of the kingdom of God, this change is comprehensible. Yet in the language of mission and baptism, talk of the dominion of God remains in fixed linguistic form (e.g., 1 Cor. 6:9–10), without it ever being indicated, though, that this had once been the characteristic language of Jesus. Such direct linguistic continuity is without fundamental importance, because the substantiation and significance of the new language of hope results basically from the above-described typical christological scheme. In Paul's overall interpretation of Jesus Christ there is indeed continuity with the earthly One.

Within the Pauline expectation of the end we still find the "word of the Lord" in 1 Thess. 4:15–17, whose core inventory contains Antiochene church tradition, which stands under the authority of the Lord. Did the church and Paul have Jesus tradition before them (as in, e.g., 1 Cor. 7:10–11)? The answer must be no: the tradition speaks in first person style of the church and in third person of the Lord. No Antioch Christian would accord such linguistic structure to Jesus. Everyone knew that this is the way the prophetically gifted church talks. Thus it is a saying of the exalted Lord. Paul also knew of this when he used it. This also shows clearly what is really self-evident already from the christological scheme, namely, that Paul does not distinguish between the authority of the exalted One (1 Thess. 4:15–17) and the earthly One (1 Cor. 7:10–11; 9:14): the earthly and the exalted are one and the same person. Naturally Paul can nevertheless tell here and there whether the exalted One spoke to him directly (2 Cor. 12:9) or whether he stands in a chain of tradition that reaches from the earthly One to him (1 Cor. 11:23–25). But this has no influence on the importance of the word.

Finally, also included in the eschatological proclamation of the apostle is the comparison according to which "the day of the Lord will come like a thief in the night" (1 Thess. 5:2). It is well possible that between 1 Thessalonians 5 and Matt. 24:43 (cf. Luke 12:39) there is an (indirect) dependence. For one thing, however, Paul does not cite this metaphor as Jesus tradition but as general church knowledge. For another, the image is also used in 2 Peter 3:10; Rev. 3:3; 16:15. Moreover, the contexts are in all cases rather variable. Should we let all passages be dependent on an earlier unique tradition from Matthew 24 or reckon with a typical, in each case independent, use of an image from apocalyptic admonition? What course did the tradition history of Matt. 24:42–44 par. take? There are only hypothetical answers to these questions, so that in 1 Thessalonians 5 the use of Jesus material is not unambiguous.

The Pauline exhortation to the Christian way of life has long been the place where most of the references to the Jesus tradition have been made. It will pay us to consider first the commandment to love and related statements. Here it is clear that Paul never treats this theme with an indication that this was a teaching of Jesus. If in Jesus the basic statement is love, made more pointed by applying it to the enemy and substantiated with the actions of the Creator (Matt. 5:44–45 par.), then in Paul the basic statement is brotherly love, urged by the Spirit of Christ (e.g., 1 Thess. 4:8–9), though, naturally, the thematic treatment of love of enemy is not missing in Paul (Rom. 12:14, 20). The double commandment of love in Mark 12:28–34 par. is often compared with the Pauline passages in Rom. 13:8–10; Gal. 5:14, but here, nonetheless, the differences are great. Paul sums up the law only as love of neighbor, while in Mark love of God and neighbor are treated as equal. Besides, there is much to be said for the assumption that Mark 12 does not belong to the old Jesus tradition but is a variation of the early Christian love theme, which was subsequently—and that also means after Paul—placed under the authority of the earthly One. The parable of the Good Samaritan (Luke 10:29–37) is not used by Paul, but in its place—for example, in the triad faith-love-hope (1 Thess. 1:3; 5:8; 1 Cor. 13:13) and the so-called hymn of love (1 Corinthians 13)—he has comments on the theme that are unknown to the Jesus tradition. Such distinctions could be multiplied. In any case, for Paul the important thing is not Jesus' sayings on the theme but the overall meaning of his destiny, which makes Jesus the binding archetype of all love (Rom. 15:1ff.; Phil. 2:1ff.). This archetype with its obligatory character is present in the church's experience of the Spirit (1 Thess. 4:8–9).

In spite of this general state of affairs, we may of course in individual cases attribute a saying such as Rom. 12:14, "Bless those who persecute you; bless and do not curse them," to the Jesus tradition contained in Luke 6:28. But 1 Cor. 4:12; 1 Thess. 5:15 warn against proceeding too quickly with such theses. Can it not also be that Luke 6:28 is later than the Pauline paraenesis? A look in the same context at the thematically related urging not to repay evil for evil (Rom. 12:17) perhaps gives additional help. It has respectable variations in Hellenistic-Jewish wisdom (cf. *Joseph and Aseneth* 23:9; 28:5, 14; 29:3; *Apoc. Sedr.* 7:7; etc.). Might this anonymous wisdom teaching have found its way into Romans 12, because in this case it could describe the archetype of Christ so well? Then Paul was not even thinking indirectly of Jesus' words in Romans 12. We might also note, incidentally, that in the so-called hymn of love in 1 Corinthians 13 there is a smaller but conspicuous connection between 1 Cor. 13:2 and Matt. 17:20 par. Luke 17:6. The catchword of the faith that moves mountains is so striking that here Paul is no doubt using Jesus tradition. But whether he did it consciously and knew that the motif stood under Jesus' authority is a different question.

Even if in connection with the Pauline paraenesis we may still observe here and there analogous loose parallels between Jesus tradition and Paul, it is in any case clear that in the context of ethical norms Paul consciously cites the Jesus tradition only twice: 1 Cor. 7:10–11; 9:14. Paul does not feel himself obliged by the second instruction. In the first case, 1 Thess. 4:2–5 shows that the apostle can also treat the norm of monogamy without reference to Jesus, as already mentioned above. In addition, Paul stresses in the cultic realm that the Lord's Supper tradition goes back to Jesus (1 Cor. 11:23–25). Further indications of conscious references back to the words of the earthly One are, to say the least, uncertain. On the whole, this is—especially for those who want to make Paul the tradition bearer of authoritative Jesus material—a meager output. It receives its profile not least of all through the fact that Paul conversely makes very rich use of the Old Testament, whether in the form of direct quotations or in loose reminiscences.

All the more urgent, then, in view of the far-reaching "paradigm leap" and the acute lack of tradition-historically demonstrable relations of Paul back to Jesus, is the real question, To what extent can we talk of a continuity between the two? If we do not approach this question so as to answer it with individual items, such as the expectation of the imminent end, but rather grasp it as fundamentally as possible, then for us the question boils down to the problem of whether the Pauline understanding of the earthly One can be an appropriate interpretation of the historical reality of Jesus as a whole. Whoever answers this question affirmatively will see a gain in the Antiochene-Pauline reshaping of the Christian message, because it is an attempt, while preserving the basic idea of Jesus Christ, to speak the gospel of him in a historically new way. Whoever follows such a result will then, however, also have no problem when Paul does not allow himself to be understood as the tradition bearer of Jesus material.

6

The Beginning
of Independent Missionary Activity

6.1 The Road from Antioch to Corinth

We have presented (in 5.3 above) the thesis that Paul left the Antiochene church soon after his quarrel with Peter and began independent missionary work. Within two or three years—from his departure from Antioch to the writing from Corinth to the Thessalonians (cf. 1 Thess. 3:1–6 together with 1:7–8 and Acts 18:1, 5)—churches arose in Galatia, Philippi, Thessalonica, and Corinth.

This dating of the apostle's first European journey is not completely undisputed. For there have been attempts to place it in Paul's Antiochene period so that at the Apostolic Council he could look back at considerable Gentile-Christian missionary success. This early dating, however, leads to insurmountable problems. Above all, the Antiochene Barnabas would then have had to accompany Paul, but there is no trace of him during the whole trip. Also, Acts, 1 Thessalonians, and 1 Corinthians agree so well on a travel time after Paul's exit from Antioch that it is hardly advisable to disturb this unity. Through the so-called first missionary journey (Acts 13–14), moreover, there is already sufficient documented success for the Antiochene mission (cf. ch. 2 and 5.1 above). Finally, this would lead to difficulties with Galatians 1: if Paul had indeed wanted to trot out his independence and geographical distance from Jerusalem during the time before the council, he would not have failed to use his first European journey as an argument; he could scarcely have staged himself more independently or at a greater distance from Jerusalem.

Regarding evaluation of the journey, it must be said that, based on the number of churches, the trip was astonishingly fruitful (some missionaries have had to wait years for the first Christian in a region!). Also, the geographical spread is unexpected, no matter how accustomed we are to these facts. The already considerable spread of Christianity through the Hellenists and Antiochenes is again decisively surpassed. Paul must have intentionally begun to missionize where Christ had previously not been proclaimed (Rom. 15:20). He leaves the Antiochene mission field and thinks from now on in terms of Roman provinces and, above all, visits their capitals and centers. We cannot exclude the possibility that soon he already had Rome in mind as an ultimate goal (Rom. 15:22) as well as the western boundary of the Roman Empire (Rom. 15:24). Only later, however, did he realize this in modified form. All this demonstrates yet again the obvious independence and vastness of Paul's orientation after his calling. For he could have simply sought out a neighboring church from the missionary successes in Acts 13–14 and then worked there.

Acts takes into account the significance of Paul for the Gentile mission, in that after the Apostolic Council it gives the reader in two large sections, Acts 16:36–19:21 and 19:22–28:31, the impression that Paul now dominates the epoch of worldwide mission all by himself. As surely as missions other than Paul's should not be underestimated, even if they lie in the darkness of history, a prominent discussion of the Pauline mission and an emphasis on the inner dynamic of his activity are, beyond doubt, justified. Yet Acts describes the beginning of this Pauline mission rather unprogrammatically and in detail also differently from Paul himself (Acts 15:36–41). Luke says nothing of the Antiochene quarrel, although he indicates a "sharp contention" between Barnabas and Paul (Acts 15:39). This takes place immediately after the Apostolic Council, but it has as its object a personal problem rather than a problem of substance: Paul, in contrast to Barnabas, does not want to let John Mark come along as a helper. So Mark and Barnabas move into the latter's Syrian homeland to visit churches. Paul and Silas/Silvanus choose a route through Syria and Cilicia, Paul's home province, in order likewise to strengthen contacts with existing churches. There is no talk of opening up new mission fields.

Of course, we will have to judge Acts 15:36–41 to be Lukan composition. Luke probably harmonized the outcome of the Antiochene quarrel (Acts 15:13ff.) directly with the Apostolic Council (cf. 5.2 and 5.3 above). Also, with the "sharp contention" in Acts 15:39 he is probably indicating that there was more that was separating Paul and Barnabas than Mark, whose problem is not even mentioned. Conversely, the Lukan itinerary of the apostle according to Acts 16:1ff., which toward the beginning (15:36–41) shows missionary extent, is essentially confirmed by Paul: the route leads directly from Syria via Cilicia and Phrygia to Galatia, then to Troas and from there to Macedonia and thus for the first time on European soil—more exactly via the island of Samothrace to the port of Neapolis (today Kavalla) to Philippi. Here Paul founded his first European church. The journey leads farther on the Via Egnatia through Amphipolis and Appolonia to Thessalonica. From there, turning southward toward Berea and leaving the Via Egnatia, Paul travels via Athens to Corinth.

This itinerary shows how Paul crossed the Antiochene mission area by the quickest route; he did not spend time visiting churches here but had something new in mind. Why he did not choose the way via the coastal cities of Asia Minor must remain a mystery. We could presume hypothetically that in Asia there were meanwhile individual Jewish-Christian churches that Paul wanted to avoid, because he had in mind missionizing with a Gentile-Christian goal and holding to Rom. 15:20. On this journey we can confirm the company of Silas/Silvanus (1 Thess. 1:1; 2 Cor. 1:19). When according to Acts 16:1 Paul, while under way in Lystra, likewise wins Timothy for his plans, this also corresponds in effect to 1 Thess. 1:1; 3:2. Silas, a Jewish Christian with Gentile-Christian theology like Paul's, doubtless stood on the Pauline side already in Antioch (versus Acts 15:22–35), otherwise Paul would not have taken him along (Acts 15:40). Timothy, son of a Jewess and a Hellenist, is the first coworker that Paul wins on his independent missionary journeys. The idea that Paul should have him circumcised (Acts 16:3) contradicts so blatantly the Pauline conception (Gal. 2:3; 1 Cor. 7:18–19) that this note deserves no credence. Indeed, Paul had just left Antioch in order to found law-free missionary churches upon whom not even Leviticus 17–18 should be imposed, to say nothing of circumcision! More likely he chooses Timothy so that the trio will contain an uncircumcised man as a sign of freedom from the law (analogy: Gal. 2:3)!

Through Gal. 4:13 it is further confirmed that on the journey Paul founded churches in Galatian territory—that is, in the region of Ancyra (today Ankara), Tavium, and Pessinus—to whom he later wrote Galatians. Yet Gal. 4:12–20, in contrast to Acts, also shows that the mission did not operate completely without problems. Paul became severely ill (cf. 2 Cor. 4:10–11; 12:7), and the churches of Galatia lovingly took him in. The itinerary Troas-Samothrace-Neapolis was typical in those days: one sailed along the coast from port to port. The sequence from Philippi to Thessalonica is confirmed by 1 Thess. 2:1–2. The passage also makes it certain that Paul—as Acts 16:11–40 relates anecdotally—had to flee from Philippi. Likewise 1 Thessalonians 1–2; 1 Cor. 3:6, 10–11; 4:15; Phil. 4:15 reinforce the fact that the apostle founded new churches in the cities of Philippi, Thessalonica, and Corinth. Again, this did not happen without conflict even in Thessalonica (1 Thess. 2:14ff.; 3:1ff.; Acts 17:5ff.) and Corinth (Acts 18:1ff.).

Paul himself notes incidentally that he visited Athens on the way to Corinth (1 Thess. 3:1), but the extensive Areopagus speech (Acts 17:22ff.) is a Lukan concept. Naturally Luke has his now independently missionizing apostle preach his decisive and broadly executed Gentile-Christian sermon in the classical city of antiquity, which during the apostle's time had nevertheless become a modest provincial city without political and economic significance, above all because, since Sulla's time, Athens had almost always taken the wrong side politically. Also in terms of content the speech contradicts Pauline theology so strongly that even in its basic traits we cannot credit it to the apostle to the Gentiles. From ancient history writing, Luke had learned how, through speeches inserted at crucial turning points, to make clear to the reader an event's sense of direction. An analogous concern is served also by the dream that Paul has in Troas, which is supposed to give the reason for the crucial step from Asia Minor to Europe (Acts 16:9–10). Of course, we cannot deny the apostle visionary and ecstatic experiences (2 Cor. 12:1–10; cf. 1 Cor. 2:10; 14:18), but Acts 16:9–10 must be seen together with Acts 18:9–10; 22:17–21; 23:11; 27:23–24: typical form, linguistic style, and contextual function show the passages to be Lukan. In religious-historical terms, Luke is in good company with such narrated events.

Also not untypical for Acts is the observation that the Pauline mission was accompanied by miraculous deeds—here by the exorcism of the slave girl in Philippi (Acts 16:16–18) and the liberation miracle in 16:25–34. Here too, such miracles, in the legendary episodic style of Luke, belong to the means of presenting the powerful expansion of the gospel. On the other hand, Paul also stresses that his mission was accompanied by miraculous signs (Rom. 15:18–19; 2 Cor. 12:12), but he mentions this only incidentally and summarily. Nowhere is there the possibility of using the Pauline letters to verify an individual case described by Luke. In each case Luke may know these stories from local tradition. He and his tradition, however, tell them in supraindividual form, which makes it practically impossible to apply successfully the criteria of historical verification. Thus the situation corresponds roughly to the synoptic tradition: that Jesus worked miracles may remain beyond doubt, but the narrated miracles are so typically stylized that we cannot get a concrete grasp of history in the individual case.

In Luke this is related to yet another circumstance. The miracle traditions are, among other things, means by which Luke characterizes the Pauline mission in general. In each case he combines several individual traditions of various kinds episodically into an overall impression and sketches this apparently for Paul's first stay in a city. For the ordering of such episodes he makes use of a dramatic schema that shows roughly the following structural elements, which do not all have to be found in every case (cf. on the text material Acts 13:13–52; 14:1–7; 16:11–40; 17:1–15; 18:1–17; etc.). Paul and his coworkers visit a new place. They find an opportunity to participate in the synagogal worship service in order to direct the preaching of Christ to the Jews. Miracles may take place. The first Christians are won in the city, and a small church comes into being. Out of jealousy, however, the Jews mobilize the citizens. Paul is persecuted or hauled into court. He and his coworkers are driven out of the city or, yielding to authority, they voluntarily move on. In Corinth, by exception, the Jews have all their trouble for nothing, and Paul can visit longer than usual in the city; in all other places, however, because of this typical course of events, he remains only a short time.

Now and then it is possible to verify elements of the Lukan schema with Paul, such as which coworkers accompany him, the names of the first Christians in the cities, the general travel route, and the persecutions. We have already seen examples of this at the beginning of this section. Yet traditions that are not concretely verifiable, such as the conversion of Lydia, the seller of purple goods (Acts 16:14–15), are also hardly free inventions, for it is generally true that churches preserved the memory of their first converts (Rom. 16:5; 1 Cor. 16:15). In addition, we must remember that on the whole Paul shares only a little of his biography and the history of his churches. Some of what he indicates, moreover, cannot be historically and geographically defined with precision, such as the many persecutions in 2 Cor. 11:23–29. Yet the beating in Philippi in Acts 16:22, for example, may be contained in 2 Cor. 11:25 (cf. 1 Thess. 2:2). Thus, in spite of his schematism, Luke did not necessarily construct everything. Nevertheless this mode of presentation raises uncomfortable questions for the historian, such as: To which stay in a city does an episode belong? Which legend is a nomadic legend without a solid local tradition? How long was Paul really in a city? How are typology and history intertwined in a particular case? Here, naturally, much has to remain open. Yet we have also seen in the path of the Pauline mission from Antioch to Corinth that some information about that can still be made relatively certain.

The literary testimony that Paul left behind for us from these beginnings of his independent mission is the First Letter to the Thessalonians. In Thessalonica—at that time the capital of Macedonia, seat of a proconsul, and one of the most important trading centers, with its own court system—Paul is said to have worked not even a month, according to Acts 17:2. That is only conditionally probable; an established church that could get along well without Paul is hardly to be formed so quickly. If the Philippians supported Paul financially in Thessalonica and sent a delegation to him apparently twice for this purpose (Phil. 4:15–16), this presupposes an appropriate period of time, since the distance between the two cities amounts to about a hundred miles. Besides, Paul himself worked in Thessalonica in order not to be a burden on the church (1 Thess. 2:9). This also suggests more than a short stay. Yet however long we might extend the work of the apostle in Thessalonica beyond one month, it must have been rather brief, because Paul had to leave the city (1 Thess. 2:17). Even after the departure of the apostle the church was subject to tribulations (1 Thess. 1:6; 2:2, 14). Concerned about the well-being of the young church, Paul tried twice to return shortly after his flight, but was unsuccessful (1 Thess. 2:18). This may have been planned from Berea. In any case, Paul then sent Timothy from Athens to Thessalonica (1 Thess. 3:1–2) and—in the meantime having moved on to Corinth—received through him good news from the young church (1 Thess. 3:6–7). Now he himself writes to the church, thus making this second Pauline church on European soil the addressee of the oldest Pauline letter and this letter—not the Areopagus speech—the most important testimony of Pauline theology of this period.

Founded in, say, A.D. 49/50 and presented with the letter in 50/51, the church should be imagined, according to Acts 17:2ff., as of Jewish-Christian origin with a sizable number of former God-fearers. Also, "leading women" are expressly mentioned. But this agrees only very conditionally with 1 Thessalonians, which in any case lifts up the prominence of the Gentile-Christian element (1 Thess. 1:9–10; 2:14; 4:3ff.) and does not mention Jewish Christians. Also, the church may have been rather poor (2 Cor. 8:2; cf. 1 Thess. 2:9). The synagogue remains (hostilely) distant (1 Thess. 2:15–16), yet the church experiences tribulation from its own countrymen (1 Thess. 2:14), that is, from Macedonian society.

6.2 First Thessalonians as Testimony of Antiochene Mission Theology

Although in the meantime Paul had become an independently active apostle, he wrote 1 Thessalonians so soon after his departure from Antioch that we can consider his statements to be still Antiochene. The letter contains its own theological concept, namely, a theology of election that comes into view when 1 Thessalonians is not regarded from the standpoint of Romans but read for itself alone; that is, when we endeavor to understand it with the original recipients, who did not yet know the other Pauline letters. The young church in Thessalonica, in any case, did not fit the letter addressed to them into the message of justification known from Romans but rather interpreted the letter for itself without such a transposition.

Before taking this road, we must discuss another preliminary question, namely, whether 1 Thessalonians is not the later artificial product of several Pauline letters. The answer should be negative. The letter has no harsh breaks like those, for example, in 2 Corinthians. The doublets and repetitions that are mostly the reason for literary-critical operations on 1 Thessalonians are retained in part even after dissection. The newly constituted letters presuppose complicated operations and sometimes lack inner coherence. If we try to grasp the structure of the present letter, we perceive as dominant stylistic means threefold word groups, doublets, repetitions, and eschatologically oriented conclusions. These structural elements are found in this form in no other Pauline letter. Above all, the triad faith-love-hope (1 Thess. 1:3; 5:8) seems to provide the key words for the letter's structure: in each case there are two sections ordered under one of these key words (faith: 1:2–2:16; 2:17–3:13; love: 4:1–12; 5:12–24; and hope: 4:13–18; 5:1–11). Thus it is advisable to proceed on the basis of the unity of the letter and not remove any parts as non-Pauline.

If we ask about the main ideas of the letter, we encounter the relationship between gospel and election. Right away in 1:4–5 the apostle asserts: "For we know, brethren beloved by God, that he has chosen you; for our gospel came to you not only in word, but also in power and in the Holy Spirit and with full conviction." This primary fact about the church, characterized by the key word "election," not only stands right at the beginning of the letter as the heart of the thanksgiving typical of the epistolary formula but is likewise lifted up at the end (5:23–24): "May the God of peace himself sanctify you wholly; and may your spirit and soul and body be kept sound and blameless at the coming of our Lord Jesus Christ. He who calls you is faithful, and he will do it." About evenly spread through the short letter are three more pertinent assertions on the theme. Paul closes the description of his "entrance" (1:9; 2:1) to the church with the admonition in 2:11–12: "For you know . . . we exhorted each one of you . . . to lead a life worthy of God, who calls you into his own kingdom and glory." Just as clear are the two like-formed basic statements in 4:7 and 5:9, which in each case substantiate the paraenesis or the presence of hope with a passage that is analogous in form and as important in its content: "For God has not called us [to a life in] uncleanness, but in holiness." "For God has not destined us for wrath, but to obtain salvation."

Cognizance of these five central passages leads to the assertion that 1 Thessalonians is marked by a theology of election that provides the organizing coordinate system in which all other statements of the letter have their place. In order to take a closer look at this, the concept of election should be described in more detail. Without exception the one who calls is God (never Christ). Therefore the participial construction translated "who calls you" (2:12) can serve not only as a characterization of God but also as an independent designation for God ("he who calls you"—5:24). The distinguishing formulations in 4:7 and 5:9 make clear that election happens through removal from a general state of unholiness. Positively, the calling has as its aim "to obtain [eschatological] salvation" (5:9). God calls "into his own kingdom and glory" (2:12). These statements are interpreted in that the final state is described as the church's being with its Lord (4:17; 5:10), who is the deliverer from wrath (1:10). Here the divine wrath is the reaction of God to the condition of humanity (2:16; 5:9), which thereby becomes a state that has "no hope" (4:13).

From these observations we may draw the following conclusion: God's call comes right before the end of history. It is the eschatological election of grace. The called will not be subjected with humanity to the wrath but will immediately experience final deliverance. As those called in the end time, they are the church, the *ekklēsia* (1:1), that is, the eschatological community, which with the exception of a few dead will almost all be alive and present at the Parousia of the Lord (4:15–17). The church is the humanity gathered right before the end who are to escape the wrath and who, beginning with the imminent Parousia, will always be together with the Lord (4:17; 5:10). In the short time span until the end, the life of the church stands under the protective sanctification by the God who is faithful to his elective act (5:23–24); every member of the same stands under the demand to match his or her calling through holiness in conduct of life (4:7).

The calling is accomplished by the "gospel" (1:4–5). This term is the fixed expression for the characterization of the Christian message. Prominent is the phrase "gospel of God" (2:2, 8, 9), because in it the God who calls is at work. Paul is entrusted with this message (2:4), so that he can speak of "our [i.e., my] gospel" (1:5). Thus he characterizes it as the gospel preached by him (cf. Gal. 1:8–9). Alongside "gospel" he speaks without a distinction of the "word of God" (twice in 2:13) and the "word of the Lord" (1:8). We also find here the absolute use of "the word" (1:6). Thus God's election through the gospel is verbal. Just as crucial is the observation that the use of "gospel" and "word" is encountered only in 1 Thess. 1:2–2:16; 3:2, that is, in the thematic milieu of the missionary origins of faith. Therefore we propose the thesis that "gospel" is a missionary language term.

The addressees of this gospel are the Gentiles, who until now did not know the one and only true God (4:5), yet who through this message are supposed to turn to him and away from the gods (1:9). As acceptance of the gospel, their conversion is faith in God (1:8). They are thereby transferred from being determined by the eschatological wrath (1:10; 5:9; cf. 5:3) into the new determination by the eschatological expectation of salvation (1:10; 5:9). Those who did not know God before (cf. 4:5) know him now. Therefore they are prepared for the day of the Lord. They put no stock in current words of peace and security that are spoken in ignorance of the imminent end (5:2–3); they are awake and sober, having put on the breastplate of faith and love and the helmet of hope and salvation (5:6–8).

By this time at the latest, it will be clear what basic question is answered by this theology: In view of the lostness of humanity and the imminence of final judgment, how can a person be saved? The final answer always concerns the eschatological destiny of the individual, whose disastrous prospect is overcome by the granting of a new destiny through the gospel. This is based on Christ's death and resurrection (1 Thess. 4:14; 5:9–10), that is, on the eschatological history of Christ, which destines humanity, provided that there is faith in the God revealed in that history. In this way election through the gospel becomes the eschatological act of God.

The connection between election and gospel would not be completely described if we did not discuss the apostle's existence, which is interwoven with it. If Paul forgoes the apostolic title in the opening of the letter, and in 2:7, 11 selects metaphors from the parental relationship with children to characterize his relationship with the church, he nevertheless knows himself to be fundamentally empowered "with weight to be as [one of the] apostles of Christ" (2:6 [literal]; cf. 2 Cor. 11:13). This empowerment rests on the fact that he was "approved by God to be entrusted with the gospel" (2:4), so that now this gospel is his gospel (1:5). This approval is, naturally, no determination of his qualities but is divine approbation, the call into apostolic service (1 Cor. 15:9–10; Gal. 1:15), which, according to its content, is the entrusting with the gospel for the peoples. As God once entrusted Israel with his oracles (Rom. 3:2), so he entrusts Paul with this special service.

Now, the recipients of the gospel do not simply acknowledge a new teaching about God but rather are overcome by the message through the Holy Spirit: "For our gospel came to you not only in word, but also in power and in the Holy Spirit" (1 Thess. 1:5). In the word the Holy

Spirit works toward the acceptance of the message in joy (1:6). One who accepts the gospel does not accept a human word but the word of God, which has proved itself to be at work in believers (2:13). This effectiveness is related to the convincing power of the content of the word itself (1:6–7; 2:13), but it would be premature to limit it to this viewpoint. We should be warned against this already by such statements of the apostle as 2 Cor. 12:12; Gal. 3:5; Rom. 15:18–19, which speak of signs, wonders, and mighty works and accompany the Pauline gospel. With this background we must interpret the exhortation of the apostle in 1 Thess. 5:19–21 ("Do not quench the Spirit, do not despise prophesying, but test everything; hold fast what is good") to mean that he wants to see such pneumatic phenomena consciously developed. The eschatological church is a Spirit-led communion.

Even with these points, however, what is crucial about the Spirit has yet to come into view. It will not be seen until election is comprehended as the new eschatological constitution of believing persons. Thus the "brethren beloved by God" (1:4) through the giving of the Spirit are "taught by God" to achieve their "holiness" as brotherly love (4:4, 7–9). The event that changes the inner nature of the believers and enables and calls them to love is here described as redemption of the eschatological giving of the Spirit, which was promised by Ezekiel (Ezek. 36:26–27). Hence, through election on the basis of the gospel, in which the Spirit works, God, at the end of days, accomplishes the creative change in a person's nature that was expected through the prophets. There is no doubt that this context, which Paul describes here along the lines of gospel and gift of the Spirit, is found in Antiochene Christianity in the context of baptism, Spirit, and new creation (5.5 above). That Paul in 1 Thessalonians is thinking in terms of the missionary message may be related to the fact that he expressly knew himself to be called to preach the gospel and not to baptize (1 Cor. 1:17; indirectly 1 Thess. 2:1–12). In regard to the strong emphasis on the new constitution of believers, however, we must also remember that Paul himself had experienced a deeply transforming call (cf. 4.4 above). To a certain extent this provides the hidden horizon within which Paul now understands the acceptance of the gospel and the working of the Spirit. Paul will remain true to this emphasis on the movement from gospel to faith in the subordination of the baptism statements, for he not only begins thus the presentation of larger developments of his understanding of Christianity, say, in Gal. 3:1ff. and Rom. 1:14ff., but also reshapes baptismal traditions expressly in this sense (cf., e.g., Gal. 3:26–28; Philippians 3).

On the basis of this sketch we can now better appreciate that in 1 Thessalonians Paul presupposes that at the imminent arrival of the Lord, the elect who are still alive will always be together with him, just as they are (4:17; 5:10). In addition, we must first observe that Paul speaks nowhere—although the opportunity was there in 4:13ff.—of the idea that Christians will have to undergo a change for the final salvation (thus later in 1 Cor. 15:51). Viewpoints such as that expressed in 1 Cor. 15:50, "Flesh and blood cannot inherit the kingdom of God," still lie far away from Paul in 1 Thessalonians. The never-ending ("always"—4:17) communion with the Lord is already prepared by election, so that the fundamental transformation of the individual has already occurred. Or, in other words, in the gospel God makes the definitive gift of his new-creating Spirit. And precisely in this sense, the *ekklēsia* is the eschatological church, the elect are counted as raised above judgment, and the short time between election and Parousia is seen under the double aspect of divine faithfulness (5:24) and human preservation in holiness (4:1ff.).

As surely as the new being includes a fundamental change of the individual, so unambiguously does Paul make clear that personal viewpoints stand in the foreground here. For him, it is not without reason that the new being is inserted into the movement from gospel to faith (1:4–9), so that Christians are designated "the believers" (1:7; 2:10, 13) and hope is grounded in the state of faith (4:14). The creative power of the Spirit, who works in the gospel, changes a person through faith. It is also not coincidental that the Spirit addresses people as those who act by teaching brotherly love and creating the willingness to love (4:9–10). With the believing acceptance of the gospel the new constitution is not given without obligation. It is, rather, obligating presence. Here Paul knows of a double aspect of Christian existence, the aspect of the initial "entrance" (1:9; 2:1) and that of the ever valid exhortation "to please God" and "to do so more and more" (4:1, 10). Thus he knows faith as acceptance of the message (1:8–9) and also as faithfulness to the faith (3:2, 5–7). He knows that faith, love, and hope have to be ongoing destinies in the fulfillment of existence (1:3; 5:8). Holiness is the destiny (4:7; cf. 3:13) and the fulfillment of the call (4:3–4). For those called to the eschatological church, the state of salvation is indeed assured by the power of the faithfulness of God (5:23–24), but just as naturally the normative demands of human existence belong to the essence of election (4:1–12).

With this we have brought the rudiments of the paraenesis in 1 Thessalonians into view. It is the fulfillment of the newly determined existence in faith. Chosen by the gospel (1:4–5) and—as Paul can say a few years later in old traditional language—sanctified in the onetime act of baptism (1 Cor. 6:11), we have thereby fulfilled our belonging to God in the eschatological church and our separation from the world. This fundamental precondition for the attainment of salvation (1 Thess. 5:9) is the work of God's Spirit, whose instruction gives normative guidance to the believers and urges them to love (4:8–9). Therefore exhortation is no longer a law brought to human beings from the outside to be adopted by internalization, but explication of the Spirit experience of every Christian, and it serves the common, progressive practice of the love that all feel within themselves (4:1–2, 8–9, 10); having become holy, they fulfill the holiness with which the crucial key word is named under which the transformation stands (3:13; 4:3, 4, 7). Therefore in this context the Old Testament law and also the word of the Lord are not independent norms. The requirement of monogamy (4:4) may correspond in content to the old Jesus tradition, and the egoistic taking advantage of the comrade (4:6) may also be faulted in the Old Testament; nevertheless it remains crucial that "God has not called us [through his eschatological election of grace in the gospel] for uncleanness, but [to life] in holiness" (4:7). Spirit-led holiness must live in a holy manner.

Above all, the exhortation orders the relationship of the members of the eschatological church to each other: not general responsibility for the world but brotherly love (4:9) is the basic rule. Not society as a whole but the fellowship is supposed to live in the new way of life. External relations are ordered as conflict avoidance and described as inconspicuousness and decency (4:12). The world is the object of mission. What matters for it is the gospel (1:9–10) but not the immediate challenge of aligning itself with particular norms. When an eschatological church knows itself alone to be removed from the general divine wrath and is only waiting for the imminent coming of its Lord, in order to be together with him always, should it orient itself any other way?

The content of the gospel is soteriologically structured, concerns the salvation of the Gentiles (2:16a), and above all must be definable in concentrated form by Christology inasmuch as the gospel is designated "gospel of Christ" (3:2). More is to be learned through the thanksgiving in 1:2–10. It states that the Thessalonians have "received" the Pauline gospel as word (1:5–6). This acceptance is their faith (1:7), more exactly, "your faith in God" (1:8), so that Paul can indicate his "entrance" to them (1:9) through a summary of the Gentile mission preaching (1:9–10; cf. also 5.5 above). It describes devotion to God, the only creator and judge, who raised Jesus from the dead, so that Jesus can be awaited as his Son, who will deliver from the coming wrath. Thus through the gospel God elects the Gentiles, in that in the gospel he makes himself heard as the living and true God and judge of the world, who before the last judgment raised his Son from the dead, so that the Son can now be deliverance in the otherwise inescapable judgment.

This way of defining the gospel through fixed tradition is also frequent elsewhere in Paul, so that we may assume that Paul was familiar with such definition very early after his calling. The biographically special calling of the apostle is a calling under the same gospel that is common to all Christians. Paul himself understands it this way when in 1 Cor. 15:1ff. he confirms not only this but in general the observations on the catchwords in 1 Thess. 1:2–10. For here he speaks of the gospel, which he preached to the Corinthians, which they accepted, through which they are saved, and which he himself received, in order then to describe its content with a fixed double formula on the salvific significance of the destiny of Jesus Christ. He proceeds quite analogously at the beginning of Romans (Rom. 1:1–7). Thus we may begin on the basis that 1 Thess. 1:9–10 is well suited in the apostle's sense to grasp the core content of the gospel.

This preaching of the Gentile mission stresses the future Savior function of Jesus. This harmonizes with the future calling statements in 1 Thessalonians. That this future-christological statement is primary for the christological concept of 1 Thessalonians is also evidenced elsewhere in the letter: no literary testimony of early Christianity is as concentrated on the eschatological coming of the Lord as 1 Thessalonians. It not only dominates the two sections 4:13–18 and 5:1–11, which expressly have the imminent coming (Parousia) of the Lord as content; rather, this hope shines forth right at the beginning of the thanksgiving (1:3, 10) as well as in the closing blessing (5:23–24). In between are further references to it, which serve as illuminating pointers (2:19; 3:13). The texts demonstrate how much the proclamation is defined by this hope and how the phrase "coming of the Lord" has in the meantime become a fixed expression. That in this function it has taken the place of the expectation of God's kingdom can be studied in 2:12: according to this text formulated with such typical obviousness, God calls "into his own kingdom and glory." As surely as this statement cannot be declared without the basis of Jesus' message of the kingdom of God, it is also clear that talk of the coming of the Lord has replaced this terminology (cf., e.g., 2:12 with 3:13).

The concentration of Christology on the soteriological function vis-à-vis the eschatological church elected by the gospel is intentional. Christ is the personification of the offer of salvation in the gospel, which is for all nations (2:16a). This function of the Lord is accentuated in a particular way: Christology is found primarily as expectation of the coming Lord. Jesus' death (4:14; 5:10) and resurrection (1:10; 4:14) are seen this way. They do not have the independent meaning that they have later— for example, as early as 1 Corinthians. Jesus' destiny serves, rather, as an aid in describing aspects of the final salvation. Finally, this destiny is mentioned far less often than the fact that the eschatological church lives by the acceptance of the gospel "in the Lord" (1:1; 3:8; 4:1; 5:12) or "in Christ" (2:14; 5:18; cf. 4:16) and experiences exhortation "through the Lord" (4:2); that is, it lives already in the salvific realm of the coming One and is related to him.

Thus far the theological concept of 1 Thessalonians has been described without considering Jews and Greeks. Yet the synagogue hindered the gospel (2:14–16), and so did the Greeks (2:14). The latter cannot understand the uncompromising monotheism without cult (1:9; 4:5), have hardly any understanding for the close connection between adoration of God and ethical attitude (4:1ff.), and also can comprehend the eschatological expectation only with great effort. Even election, in spite of all openness to the Gentiles, is a Jewish theme. To the Greeks these offensive oddities were a foreign world. Things were different for the synagogue. It could actually rejoice about the monotheism and the ethical seriousness. Yet these Christians had replaced the God of the patriarchs, the covenant, and the law with the gospel, and in it exalted Jesus Christ as the central soteriological figure. A choice between an ethic of the Spirit and an ethic of the law was not difficult for the Jews. The new version of the election idea was for them an evil plagiarism that struck them hard as the people of salvation. They wanted to make proselytes, but to have even themselves chosen only through the gospel, so that law and circumcision became meaningless—this was too much for them! For them, Christianity was an illegitimate offshoot of their religion.

Both positions can sharpen our look at the peculiarity of 1 Thessalonians. Quite naturally it is Gentile Christian in orientation and no longer constantly refers back to its onetime Jewish origin; the discussion of the law and its validity is not a topic for consideration. The compulsion to understand itself as the continuation of Israel's salvation-historical election is nowhere to be found. This assertion cannot be limited by a reference to the brevity and coincidental nature of the letter, for it is not a question of whether Paul in 1 Thessalonians completely developed his theological ideas (answer: of course not) but of the observation that he is in a position to develop the theological independence of Gentile Christianity through a self-contained theology, whose outlines are easily recognizable.

Yet the election theology of 1 Thessalonians carries hidden within it a peculiar relationship of nearness and distance to Judaism. Election (1:4), according to information from Rom. 9:11; 11:5, 7, 28, is for Paul a genuine Israelite concept. That God's election is described with the verb "call" (1 Thess. 2:12; cf. 5:24) is familiar to Israel above all through Deutero-Isaiah (cf., e.g., Isa. 45:3). Also "entrust with" (1 Thess. 2:4), according to Paul himself (Rom. 3:2), belongs to the description of Israelite election. The elect are called those "beloved by God" (1 Thess. 1:4; cf. Rom. 11:28; *'Abot* 3:14) and are "brethren" to each other (thus, e.g., *Testaments of the Twelve Patriarchs*). Their elected status is based on the faithfulness of God, which is brought to bear in the formulaic phrase, "Faithful is he that . . ." (1 Thess. 5:24 [KJV]; cf. also 1 Cor. 1:9; 10:13; 2 Cor. 1:18), and has Old Testament–Jewish precursors (Deut. 32:4; Isa. 49:7; *Pss. Sol.* 14:1; 17:10). That it is a question of pleasing God (1 Thess. 2:4, 15; 4:1), or serving him and worthily living for him (2:12), of turning to him (1:9) and thus escaping his wrath (1:9), does not have to be demonstrated again as Jewish language.

Positionally, the connections between Pauline election theology and the Hellenistic-Jewish synagogue are also easily recognizable. There are above all three basic positions: (1) the preaching of the one God, who has chosen Israel and allows the Gentiles to come as proselytes but who in the others sees the lost (for the diaspora Pharisee Paul, cf. Rom. 2:17–20; 3:2; 9:4); (2) the understanding of election as covenant for life and at the same time as obedience (ibid.) in contrast to the disobedience of the Gentiles in idolatry and wickedness (Rom. 1:18–32); and (3) the responsibility of all before God in his coming judgment, which no one escapes (Rom. 2:1–11) but in which the chosen people cannot be lost (Rom. 9:6a; 11:1–2, 26).

At the same time, concealed within these three basic positions are the differences. Crucial at this point, naturally, is the orientation toward the coming Lord, who is defined by his destiny of death and resurrection. Since this is a divine production, God himself is given a new interpretation. The God of the patriarchs becomes the God in Christ. Then, the new understanding of history is significant: those addressed by the gospel are not inserted into a long history of salvation but orient themselves toward the imminent judgment, the coming Lord, the Spirit of the end time. The most remote past event of significance is the fate of Jesus, yet that is not at all the past but rather the present through the present certainty of "in the Lord." The judge of the world gathers the elect right before the final judgment; this is decisive. Also important is the new option for the addressees of election. The gospel goes out directly to all peoples: the particular election of Israel is no longer the point of orientation. One does not have to join the covenant of Abraham but is chosen directly by the Spirit—independently of the law, which is no longer mentioned. Finally, the ethics of the elect are conceived anew: we love others not by bringing them to the Torah and thus to the first of the three things on which the world stands ('*Abot* 1:2, 12). We are no longer created to practice the Torah and thereby obtain for ourselves life in the world to come ('*Abot* 2:7–8). Rather, the Spirit creates us anew, so that our actions consist in brotherly love, and with the Parousia of the Lord we can live together forever with him. The self-understanding of Judaism rests on the relationship between patriarchal covenant, law, and life; that of Christianity, according to 1 Thessalonians, on the triad faith-love-hope.

6.3 Hope in Crisis

Paul writes 1 Thessalonians not least of all because of an inquiry from the church he had to leave after a short founding visit. Between the first mission and the sending of the letter lies less than a year (cf. 6.1 above). Timothy had probably communicated to Paul the problem in Thessalonica, namely, that Christians had died (cf. 1 Thess. 4:13). In order to understand how the grief (4:13) of the Christians in Thessalonica came about, we must remember the concept of election theology (cf. 6.2 above). Election through the gospel constituted the eschatological church, which in its hope (cf. 1:3; 2:19; 5:8) concentrated not on the resurrection but on the imminent coming of the Lord (2:19; 3:13; 4:15; 5:23), about which the church had absolutely no need for instruction, for it no doubt associated itself directly with this day (5:1–11).

The whole first generation of early Christianity had generally lived with a similar intense imminent expectation: it was part of Jesus' message and is evidenced even in the latest testimony from this period (Rom. 13:11–14). Not until after the death of the apostle, say, in the middle sixties, is hope transferred out of the stage of intensive near expectation and into more extended concepts of time. Imminent expectation always comes—as is often observed in church history—in a decisive crisis when death comes to the protagonists of the original generation, who were themselves supposed to experience the end, and the fellowship they leave behind enters as such into a new age. They understand themselves now as the second generation, which looks back on the closed history of its beginnings and must make the deceased fathers the reason for linking hope with patience and perseverance. Intense imminent expectation is a sign of the intensity of hope, but this must be transformed into a different quality when the end is delayed. Now the passage of time must be qualified as the possibility of preserving hope under the forbearance of God.

Even before this decisive crisis of hope, however, intense near expectation already had to be flexible, for it could be called into question by unexpected events. In this regard, the history of Paul and his churches shows a typical disrupting factor, namely, the death of a few Christians. This was precisely the cause of grief in the church in Thessalonica after Paul's departure. Thus Paul's task is not to tell them how they are to think in general about the fate of those who have passed away. Rather, he is supposed to explain whether it is now a question of a fateful race between individual death and the coming of the Lord. For the operative assumption was that the church now living will be present at the Parousia: Are the dead thus outside this near future?

Paul gives a two–stage answer (cf. the double "for" in 4:14, 15), declares at the close a result (end of v. 17), and ends with a typical exhortation (v. 18; cf. 5:11). The answer in general aims at incorporating the exceptional cases of death into the eschatological church through the hope of resurrection. Thus in 1 Thessalonians 4 Paul teaches neither a general resurrection of the dead nor a resurrection of deceased Christians linked with a transformation of living Christians (1 Corinthians 15) but uses the concept of resurrection only within the framework of the intense near expectation in order not to exclude exceptional cases from participation in the final salvation. Afterward he can then in 1 Thess. 5:1ff. again interpret the coming of the Lord as an event in the immediate future, without touching again on this special problem. In contrast to the special case of a few deceased Christians, which put the church in a difficult situation, Paul expressly emphasizes that it is actually not necessary to instruct the church on its new being as the eschatological church and on its eschatological reception of salvation, which is imminent (5:1). These observations lead to the conclusion that Paul, in fact, did not touch on the theme of resurrection in his missionary preaching in Thessalonica. It is not found in any of the Parousia statements of 1 Thessalonians. The dominance of the Parousia expectation was thus total, and after the writing of 1 Thessalonians, because of a special ruling for deceased Christians, it is confirmed again as the dominant hope.

It is certainly believable that in Thessalonica there were dead Christians to mourn within the short history of the church. But it is questionable whether, for example, the Antiochene church, which in the meantime looked back on a history of about fifteen years, had lasted that long without any deaths. Yet the church in Thessalonica probably still had no contact with this church, especially since Paul had recently left it in disagreement. Thus, despite possible analogous experience in older churches, for the Thessalonians the problem of death was new.

But was it also new for Paul? From the first substantiation of the resurrection hope, which Paul delivers in 4:14, it has been said that the apostle had difficulties with the argumentation, and this indicates that the problem was also new for Paul himself. Apart from the fact that this judgment on v. 14 is by no means assured, with such an interpretation one falls into chronological problems. That within a half generation Christianity had no natural deaths of members to grieve is hardly imaginable, even if we make the special assumption for Christian martyrs (e.g., Stephen) that they, according to the current view, were transposed directly into heaven (cf. Acts 7:59; Rev. 6:9ff.; 7:9ff.; 2 and 4 Maccabees).

Since a prior dating of 1 Thessalonians and the first European trip in the early Antiochene period is excluded (cf. ch. 2 and 6.1 above), we will consider whether the solution that Paul offers comes from this period in terms of content. That would mean that dead Christians are not a new problem for the apostle but only a secondary aspect of the expectation of the Parousia. For this reason he did not talk about it during his brief founding stay in Thessalonica. For the same reason he can also now offer the Thessalonians a solution already thought through in Antioch. Whether this recommended solution makes sense is decided by evaluation of the Pauline argumentation in 4:14.

This verse reads: "For since we believe that Jesus died and rose again, even so, through Jesus, God will bring with him those who have fallen asleep." For Paul, this argument has unrestricted priority over the second in vs. 15–17. Here he infers hope on the basis of belief. Thus faith also takes first place in the traditional triad faith-love-hope; faith is fundamental, the basis of love and hope. Faith, moreover, is related to God's action in the destiny of Jesus Christ: because God raised Jesus after death, there is substantiated hope that the same God will also raise the sleeping Christians, in order not to let election through the gospel come to naught because of such deaths. Yet this conclusion, as surely as it is intended factually, is described somewhat differently. Paul says God will "bring" the Christians. Jesus' destiny is, of course, a demonstration of God's power over death, which God will also verify with the deceased Christians, but the text says nothing explicitly about the resurrection of Christians. According to Heb. 2:10, however, Christ is the "pioneer of their salvation," "bringing many sons to glory." Also Heb. 13:20 (cf. Isa. 63:11) speaks of the God "who brought again from the dead." Paul employs the same expression also in Rom. 10:7. Thus "bring" seems to belong to resurrection language. Yet the context also calls attention to another connection: What is described in 1 Thess. 4:16–17 under the double aspect of resurrection and rapture is apparently supposed to be summed up in the "bring" of v. 14. Thus v. 14 is no doubt reflectively formulated. The special use of language makes sure that the dominance of the Parousia aspect is maintained and at the same time the resurrecting activity is indicated. Paul wants to say: In the Parousia, God brings the dead from the graves and to the coming Christ (cf. 2 Cor. 4:14). Thus v. 14 is doubtless not a first tentative effort to infer the resurrection of all Christians on the basis of Christ but a purposeful formulation that puts the necessary answer to the question in its proper contextual place. Paul's later typical deduction from Christ's resurrection to that of the believers (1 Cor. 6:14; Rom. 8:11; etc.) is not conceived better linguistically than in 1 Thess. 4:14, but only differently in its content: The assertion of the resurrection has freed itself from the framework of the Parousia announcement, as have the statements in the resurrection chapter, 1 Corinthians 15, in general.

First Thessalonians 4:14 has yet another linguistic oddity that must be treated briefly. This is the phrase according to which God will bring the Christians to him "through Jesus." Here too we hardly have a tentative and uncertain formulation, but one that is usual for Pauline-Antiochene language, as 1 Thess. 5:9; 1 Cor. 15:21, 57 (as assertion of the Spirit: Rom. 8:11) can attest. It means that the basis of salvation is thereby given: on the basis of the Christ event, God will raise the dead Christians.

After this christological argument Paul adds a second one, which reaches back into pre-Christian apocalyptic views. After the christological confirmation has occurred, he can now talk of the apocalyptic worldview in such a way that it is made serviceable to the christological gain in knowledge. We can make a formal comparison: just as Paul the Pharisee placed the apocalyptic assertion of the last judgment under the interpretation of the law (cf. 3.2 above), so now he interprets in apocalyptic language the hope that resides in faith in Christ. It is not that the Pharisaic apocalyptist became a Christian one and in the process only exchanged law and Christ; rather, the interpreter of the law became preacher of the gospel and could now as then place even the apocalyptic view under his own theological standpoint. This did not happen without the adaptation of apocalyptic views on the basis of the pregiven norms—whether of the law or of the gospel of Christ—determining the different ways in which Paul treated apocalypticism. As a Jew he was concerned about poetic justice in the world (cf. 3.2 above); as a Christian he looks exclusively to the God who remains faithful in Christ and who through the gospel will bring the elect to the election goal (1 Thess. 4:10–11; 5:7–10, 23–24; etc.). Thus 1 Thess. 4:13–17 is revealed as a first illustrative example of how Paul rethinks and reevaluates everything in view of the central figure of Christ (cf. 2 Cor. 10:5; Phil. 3:8).

Central to the second argumentation is the saying of the Lord that Paul first summarizes in his own words (1 Thess. 4:15) and then quotes (v. 16). We have already seen (cf. 5.6 above) that this is a prophetic saying of the church. It is older than 1 Thessalonians, is equivalent in content to the Antiochene solution found in v. 14, and must therefore come from Antioch, especially since its vocabulary and individual motifs do not otherwise flow freely from Paul's pen. The saying that stands under the authority of the exalted One is not unified. The core content probably reads: "The Lord himself will descend from heaven with a cry of command, [that is,] with the archangel's call, and with [actually: on] the trumpet of God. And . . . we . . . shall be caught up . . . in the clouds to meet the Lord in the air." This corresponds to the Parousia expectation of the church that still has no dead Christians to mourn. When in Antioch, in the sense of the apostle's first argumentation in v. 14, the first deaths in the church provided the occasion to bring in the resurrection hope as salvation for those asleep, vs. 16–17 were also expanded to their present content, so that now the dead Christians will also be resurrected by divine action and, united with the living ones, be able to meet the Lord, so that the eschatological church will forever be joined together with the Lord, as the gospel promised.

Thus Paul now makes known in Thessalonica this saying that is familiar to him from Antioch and helps the church understand anew the element of hope from the schema of Gentile-mission preaching (1 Thess. 1:10), with which the Thessalonians were also won to the faith. If this interpretation of Christian hope (like the Aramaic *marana tha,* "Our Lord, come!"—1 Cor. 16:22) was formulated with the Jewish-apocalyptic concept of the son of man, so also was the saying in 1 Thess. 4:16–17. The church can thus make clear within the same concept how the elective action of God in the gospel is valid, even if a few of the elect die before the Parousia. They are to know that there is nothing, not even death, that can thwart divine election, and thus it is further true that God remains faithful (1 Thess. 5:24); he will preserve the final communion with Christ (cf. *1 Enoch* 71:15–16).

If this is the basic idea, then it is not surprising that in view of later Pauline statements the contents of 1 Thess. 4:16–17 seem variable. According to these verses the relationship of the few who have died to the many living is defined differently from that in 1 Cor. 15:51. In vs. 16–17 the church, to whom the resurrected ones are added, takes in the Lord like an honored guest, in order to be together with him on earth "always." In 1 Cor. 15:50ff. death as the last enemy is not conquered until all are resurrected or transformed, that is, when mortality is overcome. This is so important that neither the taking in nor the Parousia nor the place of final salvation plays a role. We could continue and also compare with yet other texts, but the basic result would remain the same. In 1 Corinthians 15 faith (15:1–11) does also open up hope (15:12ff.), yet the development of hope varies in content except for the constant basic idea, which is that the God grasped in faith will not withhold from believers the promised everlasting nearness of Christ.

With this we can summarize in closing the fruits of this interpretation of 1 Thess. 4:13–17. It is obviously again the Antiochene church of the Pauline period that developed and set the course of inferring hope from faith—also in regard to experience with deceased church members (which still has to be worked out in Thessalonica). It is clear that these early churches, as well as Paul himself, are not apocalyptic groups, but can paint the newfound Christian hope with apocalyptic colors (v. 14), whereby not only the basis of the hope (v. 14) but also the actual goal of the hope (end of v. 17) is expressed christologically. The basis of salvation and the goal of salvation is the God who is near in Christ. Beyond this nearness in the gospel and the promise to be redeemed in the future, people need nothing, for only in this way do they reach the destiny appropriate for them, which saves them from the hopelessness that otherwise applies without exception (v. 13b).

6.4 The Founding Visit in Corinth

According to Acts 18:11, the first Pauline visit in Corinth lasted about eighteen months. This was likely the period from fall A.D. 50 to spring A.D. 52 (cf. ch. 2 above). Paul probably arrives in this city together with Silas/Silvanus, who is coming from Athens. Soon Timothy reaches them from Thessalonica (1 Thess. 3:6). Possibly speaking against this view is 1 Thess. 3:1–2, according to which Paul remains "alone" in Athens. Then Silas would have come with Timothy (cf. Acts 17:14–15; 18:5). In 1 Thessalonians 3, however, Paul has only himself and Timothy in mind and means to say that he remained behind in Athens without this coworker. Silas is nowhere to be seen. Therefore 1 Thess. 3:1–2 cannot serve as an objection to the proposed reconstruction. Both coworkers are mentioned in 1 Thess. 1:1 in the opening of this writing composed in Corinth and probably worked with Paul most or all of the time in Achaia's harbor city (cf. 2 Cor. 1:19; Acts 18:5). Titus, who later from Ephesus maintains contact between Paul and the church, is not present during the founding visit. The last trace we have of Silas in Paul and Acts (1 Thess. 1:1; Acts 18:5) is his presence in Corinth; after the Corinthian stay we have only the fictitious account in 1 Peter 5:12 that he is employed as the conveyer of this letter. Was there a tradition in early Christianity that Silas changed over to the Petrine mission?

We know that Corinth looked back on a splendid history. Its favorable location contributed not inconsiderably to the fact that for a time the city could boast the largest number of inhabitants in Greece and was famous on account of its riches, acquired through trade and handiwork. But the city—Roman in Paul's time—could not look back on this past without interruption. Rome had punished its permanent anti-Roman politics and in 146 B.C. annihilated the city—also in the interest of its own unrestricted expansion of trade. This happened so radically that the rubble piles of Corinth remained uninhabited for about a hundred years. In 44 B.C. Caesar ordered the reconstruction, so that beginning in 27 B.C. new Corinth could serve as the seat of the Roman proconsul for the province of Achaia. The large portion of Italic settlers is evident in the Roman names that are known in the Corinthian church. Soon the outstanding Corinthian characteristic was again its trade, and riches and enjoyment of life increased. Corinth was considered a sinful city and alongside the relative prosperity of its citizens possessed a colorfully mixed harbor proletariat.

Since Paul needs to tell the church nothing about its own history, he gives us only incidental information about the year and a half he was with the Corinthians. As an overall impression we learn two things: apparent amazing missionary success and a conflict over the apostle's support. First, regarding the conflict, Paul has to defend himself in 1 and 2 Corinthians because he did not become a "burden" to the church, although, left to his own resources in Corinth, he in part suffered want. The Corinthians would have gladly supported him, but, as in Thessalonica, Paul wanted no one to take from him his boast of having preached the gospel for free also in Achaia. Of course, brothers from Macedonia had brought congregational gifts to him in Corinth. This probably means donations from Philippi, since this church also supported him in Thessalonica. The poor Thessalonian church had accepted this procedure, but not Corinth. It continued to offend the Corinthian church (1 Cor. 9:1ff.; 2 Cor. 11:5–15) that Philippi was allowed to support the needy apostle, but the certainly not poverty-stricken Corinthian church could not provide for its guest—that is, that Paul deceived the Corinthians concerning the honor-bound duty to care for guests, which was especially highly esteemed in antiquity. This became a lasting conflict, because the church soon learned that other missionaries quite naturally let themselves be supported by the church (2 Cor. 11:20). Therefore they never completely forgave Paul his willfulness.

On the other hand, Paul soon has considerable success in his mission. Stephanas of Corinth becomes the first convert in Achaia (1 Cor. 16:15). Paul can baptize him and his house (1:16), which in the writing of 1 Corinthians 1 he at first passes over and adds later, no doubt because Stephanas is now staying with him in Ephesus, accompanied by (two of his dependents or slaves?) Fortunatus and Achaicus (16:17). Then Paul baptizes Crispus the ruler of the synagogue (so called only in Acts 18:8) and Gaius (1 Cor. 1:14). The latter's especially large house serves—at the latest on Paul's third visit—as the meeting place for the whole church (Rom. 16:23). Paul himself lives here during this collection visit and dictates to Tertius the Letter to the Romans (16:22). It is obvious also to include Phoebe, who plays a leading role in the church at Cenchreae, among those who came very early to faith, for over a lengthy period of time she must have had the opportunity to distinguish herself through outstanding work for Paul and the church (Rom. 16:1–2). The remaining names from Rom. 16:21–23 are hardly to be included with certainty in the founding visit.

Yet one thing is clear: Paul is not sure whether he has named all of those baptized by him, and he presupposes that in Corinth there are clearly still more Christians whom he did not baptize, because only exceptionally did he himself undertake baptism (1 Cor. 1:16–17). Also the groups in Corinth that arose soon after the apostle's departure presuppose enough Christians to form groups (1 Cor. 1:10–11). Did this all begin quite harmlessly because only with difficulty could they come together in one house and they therefore went to celebrating the services of worship in various houses? In any case, Paul succeeded in a short time in founding a large and active church. Unfortunately, it is not possible to express the size of the church in numbers. Nonetheless, for Corinth we know seventeen names in all and also a few Christian families. Most of these apparently belong to the better off, yet they form the smaller part of the church (1 Cor. 1:26). They were the tone-setting minority. Incidentally, on the size of the Corinthian church, Acts speaks of "many people" (Acts 18:10). Can we reckon with fifty to a hundred Christians for the time when Paul left Corinth in A.D. 52? Could such a number perhaps even be compared to the number in the local synagogue?

In any case, for no other Pauline church founding is it reported that a synagogue showed such insurmountable losses as in Corinth. With this we are in Acts 18, where Luke reports the following details regarding Paul's founding visit. At the beginning of his stay, Paul immediately finds the Jewish-Christian couple Aquila and Priscilla. They take Paul in, and he is able to work with them in his trade (Acts 18:1–3). Every

Sabbath Paul speaks in the synagogue (Acts 18:4). When Silas and Timothy arrive, he stops working and intensifies the mission at the synagogue. The unavoidable conflict there causes Paul to go over to the Gentiles (Acts 18:5–6). He changes his residence, going into the house of Titius Justus, a God-fearer whose house is next to the synagogue (Acts 18:7). The crossover of the synagogue ruler Crispus precipitates a great missionary success. A vision confirms to Paul that he should continue, and so he remains eighteen months in the city (Acts 18:8–11). The end result on the part of the synagogue, represented by the (new) synagogue ruler Sosthenes, is a complaint before Gallio (Acts 18:12–17). Paul soon leaves the city with Priscilla and Aquila (Acts 18:18).

In order to be able to evaluate this bundle of details, it will be helpful to recall what has already been mentioned (cf. ch. 2 above), namely, that Luke's presentation rests on two arrangements at work here. (1) Luke likes to place all the tradition on Paul's first visit in a city. (2) He likes to position a striking fact at the beginning and the end. The chronology of the trial before Gallio was discussed earlier (cf. ch. 2 above). Among its details we are sure of the names of the actors (Gallio, Sosthenes, and Paul) and presumably also the good outcome for Paul. Luke, however, constructs the scene according to the way he believes a representative of Roman state power should deal with Christians: they are not evildoers, and thus the Roman state can release them unmolested, but it should keep a sharp eye on possible plaintiffs. Since in this case the synagogue has problems with the Christians only on religious issues, the state takes care to keep itself out of such a quarrel. Thus Gallio behaves in model fashion. Therefore we must practice discretion in the historical evaluation of literary details in the text and in reference to the temporal placement of the event at the end of the Pauline visit in Corinth.

We can move a little bit farther in our assumptions if we look at the Lukan note on Crispus. His name is the first to occur to Paul in 1 Cor. 1:14 when he thinks of those baptized by him. That suggests that his crossover to Christianity raised a stir. This would be the case if he was really, as Luke states, ruler of the synagogue and perhaps also provoked further crossovers. Thus Paul missionizes at the synagogue and through his success causes considerable unrest. Certainly it is not every day that a synagogue ruler becomes a Christian. If this is granted as a logical reconstruction, the synagogue had to select a successor for Crispus. Without competition, Sosthenes is available for the position, which is probably what Luke logically intends to say. Then soon after taking office, Sosthenes may have lodged the complaint with Gallio on behalf of the synagogue. Of course, we will have to set aside speculations that would identify the Sosthenes from the list of greetings in 1 Corinthians 1 with the one in Acts 18. The name occurs often. It is hardly imaginable that two synagogue rulers would, one after the other, become Christians. Or would a synagogue ruler who is publicly beaten by his own people (Acts 18:17) be ready to emulate his predecessor? If Acts 18:17 is historical, he at least must have understood that he was thrashed out of his office.

Now the Lukan depiction of the Pauline beginnings in Corinth can be discussed. That Paul met Priscilla and Aquila in Corinth and went with them to Ephesus may be regarded as historical on the basis of the greeting in 1 Cor. 16:19. Also Paul's activity in his trade is attested for Thessalonica (1 Thess. 2:9) and Corinth (1 Cor. 9:15, 18; 2 Cor. 11:9). If, however, Paul suffered want in Corinth, then it was most likely while he was still a stranger in the city and had no work. But if he had work right at the beginning of the Corinthian period, as Luke describes, his nourishment was doubtless assured. If he met the couple so early, his nourishment—in view of his good relations also in Ephesus—should have been sufficiently regular. Thus we must doubt that Paul came across Priscilla and Aquila so quickly after his arrival in Corinth. If they had been there before Paul, incidentally, there would have already been Christians there before Paul. He stresses, however, that he began the founding of a church in Corinth (1 Cor. 3:6–8). Thus many things suggest that the couple did not make their stop in Corinth until during the course of the Pauline visit.

These considerations raise the question whether the information—certainly not freely invented by Luke—that Paul lived next to the synagogue with the God-fearer Titius Justus is an indication of where Paul made his home in Corinth. Luke cannot motivate Paul's move away from Priscilla and Aquila. Also, in terms of tradition history, Acts 18:1–3 and 18:7 are separate traditions that were later combined, whether in the itinerary on which Luke bases his presentation or by Luke himself. It is known that especially the God-fearers were a special target group of the early Christian mission, and among them Christianity attracted many "fringe participants" from the synagogue. Thus it makes good sense to assume that right at the beginning of his stay in Corinth Paul—with the synagogue in mind—took his lodgings with a God-fearer and synagogal neighbor.

Two basic traits of Acts 18:1–17 must still be set forth. As so often, Luke embraces his typical schema: first comes the mission in the synagogue, then strife and rejection, and then the way is free to the Gentiles. This is one reason for the fact that Luke speaks only generally about the Gentile Christians in Corinth. By name he mentions Jews and God-fearers who become or are Christians. This suggests a false picture of the makeup of the church. It not only lives in a Gentile-Christian fashion but is also largely determined by former Gentiles (1 Cor. 7:12ff.; 8:10; 12:2). The Jewish-Christian component is small. Most of the problems that Paul discusses in 1 Corinthians are understandable only if we presuppose a prior Hellenistic socialization of the church. Thus here the impression of Acts 18 must be modified. If we overlook this information on the first visit in Corinth, we will decide that Paul experienced a good and rather successful time there. The reason why he left the city lies in the dark.

7
Paul in Ephesus and Asia

7.1 The Ephesian Events

After his stay of about eighteen months Paul leaves Corinth, probably accompanied by Timothy (and Silas?—cf. 6.4 above), and sails together with the husband and wife Aquila and Priscilla/Prisca to Ephesus (cf. ch. 2 above; Acts 18:18–19; 1 Cor. 16:19b). The years that Paul then spends in Asia are among the most fruitful and at the same time most critical of his life. After his richly successful time in Macedonia and Achaia and untroubled relations with his churches, now come years of enormous creative power and very difficult problems with his churches. Nowhere after his departure from Antioch did Paul have as long an uninterrupted period of activity as in Ephesus and in Asia. Only Acts, however, provides information on the length of stay. Acts 19:10 states two years, based on the events in Acts 19. Yet we must also add the time for the trips in Acts 18:18–23. Even if it is in part a construction, sufficient time will have been included. Thus a time span of about three years is probably appropriate.

Ephesus is not a mission founded by Paul, as Acts 19:2ff. hints. Nor was this ever claimed by the apostle. The history of the Ephesian Christian church probably begins with a Jewish-Christian congregation (Acts 18:26ff.; 19:32–34). For a large part of Asia this is not untypical, since traditionally Jewry was strong here and could thus form Jewish-Christian churches. Later on, Revelation, for example, will provide clear evidence of a Jewish-Christian standpoint in Asia. Yet the Ephesian house of Priscilla and Aquila (1 Cor. 16:19) probably housed a Gentile-Christian church, as was later true of the couple's Roman house (Rom. 16:3–5). Also, the couple already lived in Corinth as Gentile Christians, since they were a part of the Corinthian Gentile-Christian church. Thus we can presume that it was not first through Paul that a Gentile-Christian church arose in Ephesus. Acts 18–19 gives two further indications of this. Also working in Ephesus was Apollos, known as a Gentile-Christian-oriented missionary from his activity in Corinth, even if according to his heritage he was a Hellenistic Jew from Alexandria (if we may trust Acts 18:24). Second, outside of the typified statements in Acts 19:8–9, Acts also knows nothing to report about a conflict between Paul or the Christian church and the synagogue. This presupposes the independence of the Ephesian church from the synagogue.

Ephesus fits in well with the places that Paul sought out for missions. The city lies on the west coast of Asia Minor and had originally been settled by Athens. In 133 B.C. it was integrated into the Roman Empire and was soon the capital of the Roman province of Asia with the seat of the Roman proconsul (who here at least always took up his duty) and the provincial administration. Since Augustus it has experienced a powerful upswing, indicated by bustling building activity. It has become unchallenged as the first city of Asia and, after Rome, Alexandria, and Antioch, the fourth largest city of the empire—to the regret of Pergamum, which was thereby displaced. This was favored by the good location: the city is a harbor city at the mouth of the Cayster. From there the old Persian royal road goes to Sardis and, in an eastward direction, leads via Philadelphia, Hierapolis, Apamea, and Antioch of Pisidia to the Euphrates. Somewhat more southerly the old caravan road runs through the Maeander valley and near Hierapolis joins the route just described. Another important road follows the coast toward the north and runs from Ephesus via Smyrna and Pergamum (with a spur toward Thyatira) to Troas. Those are all names of cities that were held in good repute in early Christendom (see below).

That alone, however, does not give sufficient reason why Ephesus was one of the most frequently named cities of antiquity. This lies, above all, in the most famous temple of antiquity, whose guardian was Ephesus, namely, the Artemision, the temple of Artemis/Diana, which stood not far from the city. Its size (four times as large as the Parthenon in Athens) and its beauty (among others, Apelles, Phidias, Praxiteles, and Polyclitus decorated it) gave it an unchallenged place among the seven wonders of the ancient world. As was typical of antiquity, it served at the same time as a treasure house and bank for Asia Minor and was a known place of asylum. The cult goes back to pre-Hellenistic times. In the Roman era Artemis was fused with Diana. She is the virgin goddess, daughter of Zeus and sister of Apollo, the promoter and protector of all life, goddess of the hunt, helper at birth, and goddess of death: "Great is Artemis of the Ephesians!" (Acts 19:28, 34).

Although Acts consciously describes especially lovingly and in detail Paul's stays in Athens and Ephesus and captures quite well the typical picture of the latter city, on closer examination it leaves a great many questions open. If we were dependent on it alone, Paul's effectiveness in Ephesus and Asia could hardly be given even a rough evaluation.

Hence, we must gather, above all from the Pauline letters and other early Christian writings, indications that shed a little more and better light on this Pauline period. We have already seen (in ch. 2 above) that the Lukan sketch of the apostle's Ephesian beginnings (Acts 18:18–23) does not stand up to examination. The only assured items seem to be the move to Ephesus and possibly the immediate mission in Phrygia and Galatia, but in no case the journey to Jerusalem.

While Luke has the apostle taking a trip to Jerusalem very soon after his arrival in Ephesus, the author passes the time until Paul's return with the help of a local Ephesian tradition about Apollos (Acts 18:24–28). The historical worth of its details is rather questionable. According to 1 Cor. 16:12, Paul and Apollos worked together in Ephesus, yet according to Luke the two never meet. As 1 Cor. 3:4–9 attests, Apollos arrives in Corinth after Paul and is with him in Ephesus at the time 1 Corinthians is written. Thus the sequence of Apollos's activity is first Corinth, then Ephesus. Acts assumes the reverse order: first Ephesus, then Corinth. Since in 1 Corinthians 1–4 Paul naturally recognizes Apollos as a Christian missionary who works in the Gentile-Christian manner in Corinth, the information in Acts that "he knew only the baptism of John" (Acts 18:25)—a good twenty years after the beginning of Christianity!—is absurd. Since Luke, finally, could also surmise from 18:26 the information that Apollos received remedial Christian instruction from Priscilla and Aquila, Acts 18:24–28 as a whole is hardly historically reliable.

For Luke, then, the actual beginning of Paul's Ephesian stay is in Acts 19:1. As the opening event (constructed in accordance with the Lukan typology), Paul conveys the Holy Spirit to about twelve disciples of John the Baptist through the laying on of hands and thereby inducts them into the Christian church (19:1–7). This episode, which is described in Lukan language, is not verifiable. We may proceed on the basis that there were churches of the Baptist that existed parallel to the beginnings of Christianity and that crossovers to Christianity also occurred (just as disciples of the Baptist came to Jesus, according to John 1), but neither is an Ephesian Baptist church demonstrable, nor an encounter of Paul with a Baptist group attested elsewhere.

Luke continues describing the Ephesian events with a schematically summary description of the Pauline activity (19:8–20). Again, in the light the historical worth melts away, for we are left basically with only the time indication for the Ephesian stay (see above), the local tradition that Paul preached in the classroom of Tyrannus to the Gentiles, and the general reference to the missionary success in Ephesus and Asia (cf. 1 Cor. 16:8–9, 19). Above all, the episode of the Jewish exorcists (19:13–17) recognizes Paul only as a marginal figure. It was probably once told without reference to him. Also, the victory over magic arts (19:18–20), which indeed bloomed especially well in Ephesus, is too summary and legendlike in its exaggeration to be judged historical.

After Luke then in 19:21–22 constructively prepares the post-Ephesian events, the reader again encounters pre-Lukan material in the legend of the uprising of the silversmiths in Ephesus (19:23–41). The enmity between pagan faith and Christian message, because the latter is detrimental to the commercial successes of the former, is also a Lukan theme elsewhere (Acts 16:16ff.). In the Lukan presentational concept, Acts 19:23–41 is the typical closing story of Paul's Ephesian stay. In this legend the pre-Lukan storyteller adeptly captures local color, and naturally Luke did not want to let an event with the Ephesians' world-famous Artemis get away. Of course, it is also true here that Paul is only a marginal figure, probably first brought into the story by Luke (cf. 19:26, 30–31). Furthermore, the opponents of the silversmiths are the Christians Gaius and Aristarchus (19:29), but a Jew named Alexander is also mentioned (19:33–34). The two oppositions are not related but competitive. The Jewish involvement in the uprising can probably be explained by the Lukan purpose. Especially the Jews of Asia (cf. 6:9; 21:27, 29) are for Luke the archenemies of the Christians. Now in this case the Jews could not support the pagan silversmiths, but they could still participate in the uprising against the Christians, so as to stress the Jews' innocence of the income reduction from the pagan devotional trade and to expose the Christians as the cause.

On the other hand, there is, in any case, an important note in Paul about one of the Christians: in Philemon 24, Aristarchus is connected with the incarcerated Paul in Ephesus. Thus we may perhaps conclude that the Pauline imprisonment at the end of the Ephesian stay can be related to an event that, now decorated in episodic and legendary fashion, is presented in Acts 19; here, however, it is more than doubtful whether a small Christian missionary church could have achieved as great a success over an established cult as Luke alleges. Thus the story is intended more to inspire Christians with courage as to what all may be possible for them than to recount Ephesian history directly. Nonetheless a collision with a pagan devotional trade is actually a possible reason why the Christian church in Ephesus, and in it especially Paul, could have fallen into an acute persecution situation. Anyone who will not infer this from the Lukan legend must still find a plausible explanation for the mention of Aristarchus.

If we look over the yield of the Lukan presentation, we find that it is in fact meager and rather vague. Of course, not even Paul will come close to answering all the questions about his effectiveness in Asia, but he places at our disposal the outlines of a qualitatively and quantitatively better picture, which, however, can only be assembled from many little observations and scattered references, and which in many respects must remain open. According to this picture, there is some probability that after his arrival in Ephesus (around spring or beginning of summer in A.D. 52), Paul first visited churches in Phrygia and Galatia (Acts 18:23; 19:1; Gal. 4:13). For this he could have used the royal road through Sardis or the road through the Maeander valley, on whose route lay Magnesia and Tralles, two places for which Ignatius attests Christian churches. This second route gains more probability if we remember that Paul could then have visited the Phrygian city of Laodicea south of the Maeander in the Lycus valley. In any case, it is not only Acts 3:14–22 that knows of a Christian church here. Also an apocryphal Laodicean letter, which is fictitiously attributed to Paul, bears testimony of the later information that Paul had something to do with this church. This information presumably goes back to Col. 4:16. Here a student of Paul encourages the church in Colossae to exchange their Pauline letter with that to Laodicea. This letter shows that very soon after the death of the apostle people in churches with Pauline tradition began to gather his letters and supports the assumption that Laodicea was Pauline missionary territory. The letter, nevertheless, has not survived. The suggestion that the Letter to Philemon be understood as the Laodicean letter is not a good one, for it is a letter not to a church but to an individual, whose residence in Laodicea, moreover, is not assured. Thus we must ascertain that the letter was lost, as was, for example, the first letter to Corinth (cf. 1 Cor. 5:9).

It would have been obvious that Paul visited the other two cities in the Lycus valley, namely, Colossae and Hierapolis. Yet Col. 1:3–9; 4:7–9, 12 prove with certainty that at least to the Colossians Paul was not known personally, and his coworker Epaphras missionized there. Did Paul take Epaphras with him from Ephesus and leave him to work in the Lycus valley, while going farther himself? At the end of the Ephesian stay Epaphras is a fellow prisoner of Paul's (Philemon 23). Yet still another trace of the Pauline mission can be recognized: Philemon—to whom Paul, to our knowledge, wrote the only letter to an individual—was apparently converted to Christianity by Paul (Philemon 19). His slave Onesimus comes from Colossae (Col. 4:9), and Archippus, who along with Philemon is addressed in Philemon 2, also lives there at the time of Colossians (Col. 4:17). Therefore we can assume that Paul converted Philemon on this trip in the Lycus valley. Yet this could have happened not in Colossae itself (Col. 1:3–4) but in the near vicinity. Did Paul then visit Antioch of Pisidia, a mission founding from his Antiochene period

(Acts 13:14ff.)? The farthest goal of this journey was apparently the Galatian churches, which Paul had founded soon after his departure from Antioch (cf. 6.1 above). The best indication (yet not completely certain) is Gal. 4:13. In contrast to the later problems between Paul and the Galatian churches, this stay must have passed harmoniously, for Paul was able, among other things, to take the opportunity to promote his collection for the benefit of the poor in Jerusalem and to make arrangements for it (cf. 1 Cor. 16:1–2; Gal. 2:10; cf. ch. 2 above).

After this the trail of the apostle is completely lost for a while. The next reconstructable events are determined through the letters that go back and forth between Paul in Ephesus and the Corinthians. This communication following the apostle's founding visit begins with a letter, now lost, from Paul to the church ("precanonical letter," Corinthians A; cf. 1 Cor. 5:9). We know about it only by accident, because the church misunderstood something Paul wrote. The attempt to reconstruct the outlines of this letter has been repeatedly undertaken, yet for one who advocates the integrity of 1 Corinthians (cf. 8.1 below), this is not an appropriate way to learn more details about the letter. Further presumptions about the overall content and character of the letter are thus impossible. Now, it is clear that Paul, among other things, addressed the young church's problems of relations with non-Christians. It goes without saying that this quickly becomes a problem for a young mission church in a pagan environment. In addition, 1 Corinthians attests that a little later this very thing also gave rise to special inquiries from the Corinthians. At some time during this period, Apollos, a missionary previously unknown to the church, must have appeared in Corinth and continued the Pauline work (1 Cor. 3:4–9). Since Paul nowhere makes Apollos himself directly responsible for the party spirit in Corinth and indeed, despite the strife that has broken out there, speaks of him in a good way in 1 Cor. 16:12, he can hardly have actively brought about the divisions himself. The divisions begin when Apollos is already with Paul in Ephesus.

The next events can also all be understood as preconditions and presuppositions of 1 Corinthians. There is first the danger of which the apostle speaks in 1 Cor. 15:32 (cf. ch. 2 above). Next, he meets with Chloe's people, who report on the Corinthian divisions (1 Cor. 1:11). Then Stephanas, Fortunatus, and Achaicus are with him (1 Cor. 16:15–17) and apparently bring a letter from the Corinthians (1 Cor. 7:1; 8:1; 12:1; 16:1; etc.), whose questions Paul answers in 1 Corinthians. Also, Paul himself has already sent Timothy to Corinth. He is announced in 1 Cor. 16:10–11 and probably takes the time-consuming land route through Asia Minor and Macedonia, while Stephanas and his traveling companions choose the faster sea route, with the First Letter to the Corinthians in their baggage. Paul certainly did not send Timothy without reason; he receives an express declaration of authority, and the church is exhorted to receive him in peace. For a church that Timothy has known well from Paul's founding visit, that is a clear comment. Because of the news from Chloe's people regarding the parties, is Timothy supposed to straighten things out? That would explain why he is already announced to the Corinthians in 1 Cor. 4:17. Then, unforeseen and surprising to Paul, Stephanas probably came in with the Corinthian letter after Timothy's departure, so that Paul himself now answers the written message with a letter and, among other things, explains in writing in 1 Corinthians 1–4 what Timothy was commissioned by Paul to deliver orally.

During this period, naturally, the apostle is not only concerned about the events in Corinth but, like Apollos, and maybe with him, is in Asia actively missionizing. Asia can be designated as the Roman province that has the most flourishing and widespread Christianity in the first century A.D. Paul was surely not uninvolved in this. He also has documented success in Asia, for he himself speaks of "a wide door for effective work" (1 Cor. 16:8–9) in regard to Ephesus and has "the churches in Asia" send greetings (16:19; cf. Acts 18:24; 19:1ff.). There are further indications: It is not by chance that a student of Paul later directs a pseudepigraphical Pauline letter, Ephesians, to the Ephesian church. Later the pastoral letters emphasize the "Paulinism" in Ephesus (1 Tim. 1:3; 2 Tim. 1:15, 18; 4:19). Revelation 2:1–7 indicates the central position of this church in Asia by putting the Ephesian missive in first place. Ignatius also seconds this and underlines with his letter to Ephesus the later importance of the Christian church there, which must have been quite large (Ignatius, *Eph.* 1.3). Thus the significant role of Ephesus in early Christianity is almost attested with one voice by Paul himself, Luke in Acts, Revelation, and Ignatius.

Beyond this we can ask whether one or another of the cities with a Christian church, to which the Revelation to John sent missives and Ignatius wrote letters, was a Pauline mission goal or at least was missionized by one of Paul's coworkers. Here a comparison between Revelation and Ignatius shows that both name only a portion of the Asian churches; for example, Revelation does not mention Magnesia, Tralles, Troas, and Colossae. Ignatius, *Trall.* 12.1, and Polycarp, *Phil.* 13, give evidence that there are more Christian churches in Asia than those for whom letters from Ignatius are preserved. In which of the churches did Paul work? Unfortunately there are, as a rule, no sure answers to such questions, but we can at least make a few assumptions. In the missives to Pergamum and Thyatira (Rev. 2:12–17, 18–29), the Jewish-Christian-oriented prophet John, who wrote the Apocalypse, is fighting against Gentile Christianity, which, in its contact with meat offered to idols and in marital questions, violates the Jewish Christians' minimal demands of Gentile Christianity in Acts 15:29 (cf. 5.2 and 5.3 above). If we look at the ecclesiastical landscape, there is actually only one conclusion: the Christianity in Pergamum and Thyatira is Pauline. Revelation campaigns against it from the Jewish-Christian position. Does Revelation also remind us that according to Acts 16:14–15, in Philippi Paul converted and baptized the seller of purple goods, Lydia of Thyatira? As a trader did she still have contact with the trade and handicraft city of Thyatira, for which dyeing with purple is well attested? Did she become acquainted with Pauline Christianity there? Going from Ephesus to Pergamum, one cannot avoid Smyrna. Here too there is a Christian church, according to Rev. 2:8ff. The addressees of James are unknown, but its author writes from a Hellenistic, Jewish-Christian standpoint against the Paulinism of his time (James 2:14ff.). Where else is such a dialogue situation more conceivable than in Asia! We are on sure ground in the case of Troas. At the close of the Ephesian stay, Paul worked here with definite success (2 Cor. 2:12; Acts 20:5–6; Ignatius, *Phld.* 11.2).

Paul's effectiveness in Ephesus and Asia is soon determined again by the Corinthian events. Timothy seems to have returned to Ephesus from Corinth and brought Paul news of the activity of unknown missionaries in Corinth. In any case, this situation seems to be presupposed in the present 2 Corinthians (3:1; 10:12–14; 11:4; etc.). This changes the whole picture in comparison to 1 Corinthians. Paul not only must deal with the living inner history of his church but must also find a way to give new impetus to the energies of the church, which he wants to be committed to his idea of a church. For in the newly arrived missionaries and their work the church has recognized spirit of its spirit and, setting itself apart from Paul, sees itself confirmed in the very views for which it brought on Paul's criticism. Paul promptly reacts with the letter Corinthians C (= 2 Cor. 2:14–7:4; cf. 8.3 below), which Titus no doubt conveys. The letter is written under the impression that Paul needs only to support the ultimately good way of the church in order to allow no great influence to the unknown missionaries.

Titus returns, however, with an unexpected failure. Paul must have been so disappointed over this vexing situation and at the same time so concerned about the church that, believing a further exchange of letters would offer little help, he reaches for the most powerful means he has left: an impromptu visit to Corinth that for the Corinthian church was surely a surprise. Yet what Titus encountered is now also the apostle's fate. A deep disagreement develops between him and the church, in which one member behaves especially insultingly toward Paul (2 Cor. 2:3–5, 9; 7:8–12). Details of this are not indicated by Paul. Only the result is clear. As surprisingly as he arrived, just as quickly and resolutely he leaves the city and returns to Ephesus. With all his personal resources he had gambled heavily and lost!

Should he now give up on the church? Should he, as once in Antioch, avoid further contact with it and leave it to the unknown missionaries? He decides on one more attempt to overcome the disagreement and writes again "out of much affliction and anguish of heart and with many tears" (2 Cor. 2:4) to the church (Corinthians D, the "letter of tears" = 2 Corinthians 10–13; cf. 8.3 below). This letter is stamped with great emotionalism, marked with hard polemical traits, and at the same time releases more of the apostle's passion and personal piety than any other Pauline letter. Titus (who perhaps also accompanied Paul on the interim visit) conveys the writing. He is apparently supposed to return to Ephesus and Paul afterward.

In the meantime, however, events in Ephesus take an unpleasant turn for Paul. Toward the end of A.D. 54 the Christian church in Ephesus comes under pressure. Acts describes this anecdotally with the help of the legend of the uprising of the silversmiths (Acts 19:23–41; cf. ch. 2 above). The imprisonment of the apostle in Ephesus is probably at least indirectly related to this (2 Cor. 1:8–9; Philemon; Phil. 1:12ff.; cf. Col. 4:10, 18). Thus Paul may have been in prison over the winter. Paul is cared for by Timothy (Philemon 1; Phil. 1:1) as well as by Aristarchus (Acts 19:29 = Philemon 24) and other coworkers from Asia (Philemon 24). Paul is not the only imprisoned Christian; at least Epaphras is in jail with him (Philemon 23). Here we can compare the details from the pseudepigraphical Colossians (Col. 4:7–14), which contains minor variations.

In this period of imprisonment belongs the "small" mission success that Paul records in regard to Philemon's slave. Onesimus, who has run away from his master—who was apparently once converted to Christianity by Paul (Philemon 19)—but comes into contact with Paul in Ephesus and, now as a Christian, is sent back to Philemon with a letter (Philemon). Also the faithful Philippians report to Paul again during this winter. They have heard of his imprisonment and send gifts to the apostle through Epaphroditus (Phil. 4:10–18). He expresses his thanks through Philippians A, the "imprisonment letter" (cf. 12.3 below). From it we learn that toward the end of his Ephesian imprisonment things were not going well for the apostle and that he even feared for his life (Phil. 1:21–24).

Nevertheless the situation turns again for the better. After his (unexpected?) release from prison, Paul is able to flee from Ephesus and head toward Troas, where he missionizes a short time and then departs for Macedonia (2 Cor. 2:12–13). In Troas the apostle apparently expects Titus, coming from Corinth, but does not find him. Therefore he goes to Macedonia to meet him (2 Cor. 2:13). Priscilla and Aquila probably helped Paul in his flight from Ephesus. In any case, it makes good sense to relate Rom. 16:3–4 to this last Ephesian imprisonment of Paul's. Here Paul says, in praise of the couple he knows so well, that they "risked their necks for my life." Perhaps Acts 20:16–17 also says something indirectly about this situation: since Paul, on the occasion of his collection journey, ceremoniously has the Ephesian church delegation come to Miletus, and thus himself avoids Ephesus, this may mean that danger still threatened him there.

Looking over the three Ephesian years, we see at the beginning and at the end the collisions with the polis and in between widespread missionary efforts and the great crisis with the Corinthian church. If we assume that now, around the close of this section, Paul also heard of the Judaizers who had penetrated Galatia and whom he would soon move against in a letter sent from Macedonia (cf. ch. 11 below), then we see how in these years glory and misery lie close together for Paul. Because in this period the wheel of history rolled rather hectically for him, we will summarize these events in tabular form (see pp. 161–163).

Probable Course of the Ephesian Events

Event	Comments	Approx. Date A.D.
1 Close of the founding visit in Corinth: sea voyage with Silas and Timothy, as well as with Priscilla and Aquila, to Ephesus	Acts 18:18–19; 1 Cor. 16:19b	Spring/ Summer 52
2 Visit to churches in Phrygia and Galatia (2nd Galatian visit); mission in Lycus valley, etc., also through Epaphras	Acts 18:23; 19:1; Gal. 4:13; Philemon 19, 23; happened before 1 Cor. 16:1–2	Summer 52
3 Letter A to Corinth: "precanonical letter"	1 Cor. 5:9; before no. 5	52
4 Apollos in Corinth	1 Cor. 3:4–9	52/53
5 Paul in danger in Ephesus	1 Cor. 15:32	52/53
6 Apollos with Paul in Ephesus; (joint?) mission in Asia	1 Cor. 16:12; Acts 18:24ff.; 19:1ff.; cf. no. 3	53
7 Chloe's people from Corinth with Paul	1 Cor. 1:11	Spring 54
8 Stephanas, Fortunatus, and Achaicus from Corinth with Paul. They bring letter from the Corinthians to Paul	1 Cor. 16:15–17 1 Cor. 7:1; 8:1; 12:1; 16:1; etc.	Spring 54
9 Timothy on his way to Corinth	1 Cor. 4:17; 16:10–11	Spring 54
10 Letter B to Corinth (conveyed by Stephanas et al.?)	= 1 Cor.; sometime after no. 5; before "Pentecost," 1 Cor. 16:8	Spring 54
11 Successful mission in Asia	1 Cor. 16:8–9; 19; Acts 19:10; Philemon; cf. Eph.; Col.; pastorals	52–54

(continued on next page)

Probable Course of the Ephesian Events *(continued)*

Event	Comments	Approx. Date A.D.
12 Unknown missionaries ("super-lative apostles") in Corinth	2 Cor. 3:1; 10:12–14; 11:4	Summer 54
13 Collection ends in Corinth	2 Cor. 8:10; 9:2	54/55
14 Timothy comes back and brings news about no. 12	News in no. 15 pre-supposed; cf. no. 20	Summer 54
15 Letter C to Corinth, brought by Titus	= 2 Cor. 2:14–7:4	Summer 54
16 Failure of Titus in Corinth; Titus returns to Paul	Presupposed in no. 17	Fall 54
17 Interim visit in Corinth (2nd visit); disagreement with church member; hasty departure	2 Cor. 2:3–4, 9; 7:8–12	Fall 54
18 Letter D to Corinth ("four-chapter letter," "letter of tears"), brought by Titus	= 2 Cor. 10–13; cf. 2 Cor. 2:4; 12:18; written soon after no. 17	Late fall 54
19 "Uprising" of the silversmith Demetrius	Acts 19:23–41; leads to no. 20 (Acts 19:29 = Philemon 24?)	End of 54
20 Lengthy imprisonment with mortal danger at the close Timothy with Paul	2 Cor. 1:8–9; Philemon; Phil. 1:12ff. Phil. 1:1; Philemon 1	Winter 54/55
21 Onesimus with imprisoned Paul; Philemon written, delivered by Onesimus	Philemon 10–13; Paul already in prison for some time: Philemon 9–13; hopes for freedom soon: Philemon 22	Winter 54/55
22 Philippi learns of Paul's imprisonment, sends Epaphroditus with gifts	Phil. 2:25; 4:10ff.; mortal danger for Paul: Phil. 1:21–24 (cf. 2 Cor. 1:8–9)	Winter 54/55

(continued on next page)

Probable Course of the Ephesian Events *(continued)*

Event	Comments	Approx. Date A.D.
Letter A to Philippi (= "imprisonment letter"); delivered by Epaphroditus	= Phil. 1:1–3:1; 4:1–7, 10–23	
23 Judaizers missionize in Galatia	Gal. 1:6–9; 3:1–5; 4:8–11, 17–20; 6:12–16	Winter 54/55
24 Release from prison, hasty departure for Troas, further journey to Macedonia	2 Cor. 2:12ff.	Spring 55

7.2 Paul's Polemic Against the Dangers of the Church

The apostle's Ephesian period and the following journey through Macedonia to Corinth are conditioned not least of all by Paul's "anxiety for all the churches" (2 Cor. 11:28). The fact that this does not simply mean rather generally his constant apostolic care for all missionary foundings but recalls for Paul acutely threatening problems in the churches is proven by the Corinthian correspondence, Galatians, and Philippians. These first literary testimonies of early Christian positions, polemically confronting each other, make it clear that we can in fact speak of a double crisis in the Pauline mission field. For, however we may describe the apostle's opponents in detail, two theological foci can be recognized. The one polemical situation arises from the quarrel over the law and its validity; the other, from the interpretation of the understanding of the Spirit and the self-representation of the missionaries. The former is the topic of Galatians and Philippians; the latter is the Corinthian problem. The first is the Judaizing front; the second, that of enthusiasm. In the apostle's judgment the two fronts pose a similar fatal threat to his work. After a rather winding and stormy history and after a dramatic breaking off of dialogue, he brought the Corinthian church to his side again. Most likely the Galatian churches were lost.

The Judaizing front (cf. in detail 10.2 below), recognizable in the demand that Gentile Christians be circumcised and in the resulting new legalism, is a betrayal of the Apostolic Council (cf. 5.2 above). Paul can argue here subjectively from a position of strength, which is founded on the consensus of the whole church, attempting to preserve the Gentile-Christian churches from the anachronism of falling back into existence as an intra-Jewish sect. Objectively, the situation for Paul is worse, for the Judaizers apparently have strong support in Jewish Christianity and not least of all in Jerusalem, the site of the Apostolic Council. In these circles there is little concern about the council's decision. Paul cannot simply ask the Jerusalemites of that time to call upon the Judaizers to uphold the council decree for the sake of church unity. There is church unity only in the synagogue, not otherwise—this is their thesis. Thus, in spite of the council decree, Paul still must ward off these opponents alone. This Judaizing danger does not arise in the Pauline mission field itself; it is an import. The Judaizing missionaries come from outside the Pauline fields of endeavor, seem to travel right behind Paul's law-free mission, and even cross over from Asia Minor to Europe (Philippians B).

The enthusiastic danger is, above all, an unwanted consequence of the Pauline mission itself (cf. more detailed 8.2 and 8.4 below). Paul wants the Spirit to be able to develop freely in his churches (1 Thess. 5:19; Gal. 3:1–5) and Christian freedom to thrive. Now, however, the former pagans of Corinth come and link this concern with views and attitudes that they knew from their religious-cultural background before baptism. They recognize spirit of their spirit when they then meet unknown missionaries who, in Paul's opinion, now make everything even worse. Thus Paul's situation is somewhat more delicate and more complicated. He must say, "Yes, but": Uphold Spirit and freedom, but, against the enthusiasts, redefine the nature and boundaries of Christian self-understanding through the theology of the cross and the binding of freedom to love.

Thus, on the one hand, Christian freedom threatens to be swallowed by the law; on the other, it seems to call forth symptoms of disintegration. Paul must fight against both fronts, one immediately after the another. The ways and means by which he takes up this double struggle are practically the same. How he does this is important not least of all because only thus can we observe the conditions under which Paul's opponents are known to us at all. At the same time, aspects of his personality and his interaction with the churches become visible. In contrast to this, the content of the dealings with the problems will be postponed until the relevant correspondence itself is treated (cf. 8.3; 8.4; 10.2, 11; and 12.4 below).

First, it is clear that Paul's firsthand knowledge of the missionaries who penetrated into Galatia or Corinth is probably nonexistent or only fleeting. He knows of the Judaizing front in relatively well defined ways by analogy with the council (cf. 5.2 above). There is no indication that the opponents then are the same ones in Galatia. He cannot have known the Corinthian opponents at the time of Corinthians C (cf. 8.4 below). He could have seen them briefly on the occasion of his interim visit (cf. 7.1 above) and been more immediately informed about them when he wrote Corinthians D (cf. 8.5 below). Apparently, however, he knows current and concrete things about all opponents only by hearsay, that is, through third parties, because, as he writes in Corinthians C and D and in Galatians, he is staying neither in Corinth nor in Galatia. Yet the information that reaches him through his coworkers or perhaps also through church members loyal to him has long been positionally colored and selective. This applies now all the more to Paul's dealing with this news. Also, he does not have to describe to the churches what is happening before their eyes. As a rule, they, naturally, know this better than Paul himself. Hence his letters presuppose more than they state explicitly. Yet even where Paul, as direct witness to a quarrel, himself later reports about the event to others, as in Gal. 2:11–21 about Peter's visit in Antioch, he immediately describes the opposing side in only a selective and authoritatively depreciating way. The other side gets to speak only in a very limited way, while his own standpoint is brought to bear broadly and discursively, and naturally stands uncontradicted at the close.

Thus it is apparent that Paul does not want to do justice to his opponent at all, for his discussion, quite understandably, is deeply rooted in fighting off the current opponents. It is very deeply conditioned by apologetic bias. That is, he does not court understanding of the various standpoints, discuss the pros and cons of the positions, and then from such a differentiated presentation draw conclusions. As surely as the other person can also cite his own positive aspects, Paul's own standpoint, despite certain possibilities for touching up, is the more solid. Therefore, out of insight, one should follow this better way. Thus, by no means carrying on even the rudiments of an open dialogue, Paul naturally holds his own view to be the only true one. The opponents' concern is naturally wrong (cf., e.g., 2 Cor. 10:12–13; Gal. 1:6–9; 3:1–5; 5:7–8). He himself does not have to make corrections but from the beginning has been on the right side (e.g., Galatians 1–2). His opponents, on the other hand, are supposed to abjure; the church must put itself again on the right side (e.g., 2 Cor. 2:9; 10:6; 13:9–10; Galatians 3–5). Thus in such a polemical quarrel there is only an either-or. Possibilities of settlement or compromise are excluded. Hence, in such an apologetically biased discussion there can be no listening to the other side or empathetic consideration of the actual motifs, substantiations, and backgrounds of the opponent. His self-understanding and deeper intentions are of no importance. A real objective evaluation of his standpoint remains unwanted. Because he has long since been condemned—before Paul reaches for his pen—it would be strategically foolish to allow him still to express himself in detail, to dignify him with an evaluation, or even to admit one's own weaknesses.

Furthermore, in such a polemic the person cannot be separated from his cause. Rather, anyone who stands outside the truth must also be personally a liar, a charlatan, a troublemaker, a pompous person, and so on; must act out of impure and dishonorable intentions; and can have only base motives. One can present "false" teachings only if one is "false" oneself (cf., e.g., 1 Cor. 4:18–19; 2 Cor. 11:3, 13–15; Gal. 2:11, 13; 4:17; 5:12–13; Phil. 3:15–19; etc.). Just as an enemy, on the one side, must have a bad character and way of life, so, on the other, must a representative of the truth naturally be a person of integrity who is innocent, honest, pure, and without blemish (cf. 1 Cor. 1:14–17; 4:1–5; 2 Cor. 1:12, 18; 4:2; 10:12, 15; etc.). At the same time, the opponent is denied future salvation through cursing (Gal. 1:6–9), or his doom is predicted (2 Cor. 2:15; 1 Thess. 2:16). Paul himself knows that he is in a good position in regard to the divine judgment (1 Cor. 3:10; 4:4). Similarly, the origin and provenance of the opponents are naturally defined by satanic powers (2 Cor. 11:14); Paul's own position, on the other hand, by God (2 Cor. 2:17). Such links between person and cause are naturally supposed to strike at the opponent, weaken his appeal to others, and from the beginning place him in a bad light. Positively, it is supposed to show the representative of truth in a white hat, so that his cause will be successful. Even this basic trait confirms that in the polemical situation there can be only victor and vanquished—and this antithesis extends into the last judgment (cf. 1 Thess. 2:16; Gal. 1:8–9; Phil. 3:19; Rom. 16:20).

The literary conquest of the conflict follows typical strategies. The opposing position is indicated by conscious selection and thus is presented only in atomized form, in that slogans, catchwords, indirect references, or short quotations are felt to be sufficient as characterization (e.g., 1 Cor. 1:12; 6:12; 8:1; Gal. 6:12–13; 1 Thess. 5:3; etc.). It is not enough that these are torn out of the context that gives them meaning and thus consciously neglected as exponents of a greater view; in addition, they are judged negatively right away, corrected in the same breath, or simply rejected. Thus they are reduced to the indicated dark background on which Paul's own true position is presented broadly and in detail. Favored in such a context of polemics are the means of irony (2 Corinthians 10–13) and of sarcasm (2 Cor. 11:16–21; Gal. 5:12). With suggestive rhetorical questions Paul promotes his own standpoint as if it were the most obvious thing in the world that he is right in everything (e.g., 1 Cor. 5:6; 6:2–3, 5, 15–16; 9:4ff.; 11:22; 2 Cor. 11:7; Gal. 4:8–9). He sets up clear alternatives, such as good and evil, wisdom and folly (Rom. 16:19; 1 Corinthians 1–2), truth and hypocrisy (Gal. 2:11–14). Or he disparagingly reshapes positive sayings, so that they now capture negatively what the opponents expound positively. Thus the missionaries in 2 Corinthians 10–13 probably understand themselves as apostles gifted with the Spirit. Paul reformulates swiftly—and not without rhetorical cleverness—so that they become "superlative apostles" (2 Cor. 11:5; 12:11), in order thus to make his value judgment immediately known. Naturally he cannot refrain from using this new term several times. Repeated judgments make a more solid impression. Likewise, the Judaizers have not convinced the Galatians; they "bewitched" them (Gal. 3:1). He fundamentally rejects the opponents' ways, even when he practices them himself in different form. Thus Paul presents himself as the enemy of rhetoric, because the opponents shine there (Rom. 16:18; 1 Cor. 2:1ff.), but he very intentionally employs such rhetorical means as elements of courtroom speech or the so-called diatribe in order to place his viewpoint in the proper light. Personal weaknesses are reinterpreted as strengths (1 Cor. 2; 2 Cor. 11:16ff.). Paul himself has the strengths of the opponent, such as familiarity with charismatic experiences, only he has not talked about it previously (2 Corinthians 10–13). He makes it clear to the church that he only wants their welfare, is preserving them from division and destruction, and thus represents their own well-understood interests (Rom. 16:17; 1 Cor. 1:10ff.; 11:18; 14:1ff.; etc.). In general, Paul believes his position always to be in accord with "higher interests," which he also now and then later names for the church, so that they, at least in retrospect, will understand the larger contexts and see which is the right side (cf. 1 Cor. 2:6ff.; 2 Cor. 2:9–10; 7:8–13). On the whole, in cases of conflict he represents the side of truth with relative authority, even if not always as crassly as in 1 Cor. 5:3–5.

We must observe, further, the literary-rhetorical means with which Paul works. Recently scholars have investigated from various angles how Paul in 1 Corinthians 1–4; 15; 2 Corinthians 10–13; and Galatians uses ancient rhetoric, at least in part in the form of a defense speech in court, in order to support his position. Today as then such an apologia is not a neutral instrument of presentation. On the contrary, here rhetorical means are intentionally placed in the service of a cause. Not the description of objective truth, but the promotion of a standpoint and its ultimate victory are the aim. The apologia is the teaching of the defense strategy transformed into speech; it aims with every means at only one thing: to have the expounded position win. It is not a dia-logue with the goal of seeking the truth but an instrument for forcing the opponent to his knees. Moreover, with Paul it is also always designed so that the apostle does not deign to speak directly to his opponent. He always speaks only to his churches about the oppo-nents. The struggle is thus always over the direct winning of the church by separating it from the opponents, about whom Paul no longer concerns himself. Hence he is never led by the general, com-prehensive question, How can we get all Christian movements to a dia-logue at the conference table? Rather, he asks the limited and special question, How do I keep the churches I founded under the gospel as I understand it?

Another literary means is the possibility of so generalizing the indi-viduality of the opponents or their position that they lend themselves to association with a supraindividual typology; that is, they can be characterized by typology and normal classification. As we can distin-guish between usual and topical paraenesis, so must we also separate traditional topoi from topical polemic in fighting other positions. At any rate, a polemic like that in Rom. 16:17–20 obviously is predominantly typical and thus usual, for the church itself is expressly praised (v. 19), and we can discover as the basis of Romans no immediately topical sit-uation that could give rise to these verses. The situation is different in 1 Cor. 11:18–19, for example; here the topical occasion is apparent from the context (abuses in the Lord's Supper), yet Paul nonetheless uses a tradition in order to point to the larger context, that is, to under-take a generalization. It is also notable that Paul distinguishes himself from the rhetoric of others (1 Cor. 2:4, 13) not only, for example, in the Corinthian party strife (1 Corinthians 1–4) but also elsewhere (e.g., 1 Thess. 2:4–6; 2 Cor. 10:10–11; 11:6; cf. also Rom. 16:18). Although in Corinth this aspect of the quarrel may also involve a bit of topicality, Paul is, in any case, obviously also expressing a typical basic position.

Finally, a little-considered field of the Pauline polemic is its emotional-ity. Deep inside, Paul is always jealous when strange workers appear in the churches founded by him, for these churches are one day supposed to be his glory when he steps before his Lord in the final judgment. Other people are not supposed to take this glory away from him (cf., e.g., 1 Cor. 3:1–17; Gal. 1:16; 3:1–5; 4:12–20; 1 Thess. 2:1, 9–12, 19–20). In the quarrel with the superlative apostles he sternly lectures the Corinthians: "I feel a divine jealousy for you" (2 Cor. 11:2). He imputes zealotry to the Judaizers in order to disqualify them (Gal. 4:17–18). Thus the tension between his mission and that of the strangers is also charac-terized by jealousy. By all the rights that should be granted to Paul, such a position must naturally lead to emotion-induced cuts, exaggerations, and difficulties of understanding. Is the uncompromising cursing of the opponents in Gal. 1:6–9 not also embedded in the emotional wooing of the church (4:12–20) and the equally emotion-laden judgment of the opponents (6:11–16)? As Paul can even directly name his emotion (e.g., joy: 2 Cor. 7:4, 9; love: 2:4; affection: 6:11–13; 7:3; confidence: 7:4; but also pride: 7:4; perplexity: Gal. 4:20; anguish of heart with tears: 2 Cor. 2:4), so he also promotes positive feelings in the church (e.g., 6:11–13; 7:5–16). Anyone who represents a false position, on the other hand, should be ashamed (1 Cor. 6:5) and ought to mourn (5:2). Thus here too the human dimension of feelings is clearly involved. It will color position and language. We can even say, the closer the opposing front stands to the apostle and the less the viewpoint of their represented cause is distinguished from the Pauline position, the more emotionally loaded becomes his polemic (2 Corinthians).

Finally, there is a kind of comment on the carrying out of such polemical feuds. They obviously include a phenomenon already noted in another context: in the course of a quarrel Paul never talks directly to the opponent. There is no section of a letter or special letter addressed to opponents. Paul talks about them only to the church. It is the church that is supposed to be convinced, not the opponents themselves. There is a second element of this comment. Where the either-or is so highly emphasized, where the gap between truth and falsehood is so extremely drawn—which naturally happens on both sides—there are, as a rule, only two outcomes for the quarrel: acquiescence or breaking off relations. In Corinth, Paul was ultimately able to prevail; the church acquiesced. In Antioch, vis-à-vis Peter, Barnabas, and the church, Paul had all his trouble for nothing (cf. 5.3 above). He left the church as a "loser"—conscious, nevertheless, of being the bearer of truth—and apparently broke off all further connections with it. Similarly, he apparently lost the churches in Galatia.

If we survey this panoramic sketch of the Pauline polemic, before making an assessment we must again state that in principle the means employed are not new. Anyone who reads, for example, Cicero's speeches against Catiline will find that they contain most of these means. Thus, here also Paul is clearly a child of his time. The first consequence then has to be that we must exercise restraint in the reconstruction of opponents and opposed positions. The filters through which the polemicist Paul allows us to see his opponents are hardly transparent; they color and they distort. Hence it is no wonder that as a basis for a reconstruction we have at our disposal only a little that is really certain about the position of the other side. In any case, the

Pauline polemic, on the whole, does a better job of revealing the accentuation of the Pauline opinion than making the opposing conceptions visible. Nevertheless, calculating the hypothetical carefully, we will not have to forgo entirely the representation of the opponents. Of course, much will simply have to be honestly left open where earlier reconstructing reason was more gripping. At the same time, Paul's polemic is also a mirror of himself. It shows a time-bound and rather human apostle, who with this kind of polemic no doubt also made things unintentionally difficult for himself, his churches, and his opponents.

7.3 Dangers to Life and Limb

For Paul the time in Ephesus is marked at the beginning and at the end by conflicts with the municipal authorities, which go as far as acute threats against his life. As a rule, Pauline interpretations acknowledge this and treat Paul's information on his sufferings as an aspect of how he sees his existence in the context of his theology of the cross. This may indeed be an important viewpoint of Pauline theology (cf. here also 8.5 below), but dangers to life and limb are qualitatively and quantitatively so great for Paul that we must first consider their historical factuality. Of course, the martyrdom of other persons in early Christianity is likewise attested (e.g., of Stephen, James, and Peter). Paul does not sit alone as a Christian in prison, as certainly shown by the imprisonment at the close of the Ephesian period (cf. 7.1 above) and as reported for the apostles legendarily, but typically, by Acts (4:2–3; 5:17–18; 12:1ff.). The Hellenists in Jerusalem were likewise persecuted (Acts 8:1; 11:19), and in Damascus, Paul himself sought to annihilate the Christian church (cf. 4.3 above). In 1 Thess. 2:13ff. Paul reports on the persecution of the original Jerusalem church and the church in Thessalonica. Yet whatever details we may quote, and however we may take into account the meagerness of our tradition from this period, there can be no doubt that the apostle was subjected to conspicuously frequent and especially severe persecutions. When in 2 Cor. 11:23 he also argues against his opponents, and is thus talking in a polemically pointed way, even then his remarks still speak a clear language: "with far greater labors, far more imprisonments, with countless beatings, and often near death"; in this way he distinguishes himself from the superlative apostles (cf. 2 Cor. 11:5). Indeed, he can talk of his powers being completely exhausted in the face of extreme peril, so that he even despaired of his earthly life (2 Cor. 1:8–10).

As a rule, Paul does not say much about the dire situations he survived. Just as he draws very little, and only in typical language, from his Pharisaic period and his persecution of Christians for the theological significance of his calling (cf. 4.3 above), so also for him there is no biographical interest in this suffering side of his missionary existence. He hides the concrete biography behind catalog-like and typical series (cf. Rom. 8:35; 1 Cor. 4:9–13; 2 Cor. 4:7–9; 6:4–10; 11:23–33; 12:10), which he, as a former Hellenistic Jew, knows in form and partly in conceptuality as a stylistic mixture from the realms of apocalypticism and popular philosophy. Still another comparison suggests itself. As Paul talks only incidentally of his great gift of glossolalia (1 Cor. 14:18) and only as a "fool in Christ" gives up his personal experiences of revelation (2 Cor. 12:1ff.), so also he can inscribe his personal experiences of suffering within a typically structured form, so that they are still relatively concrete and biographical. That happens within the same fool's speech in which he speaks of his revelations, namely, in 2 Cor. 11:23–33. On the basis of this text we can also examine the other catalogs of outside influences and individual data, such as 1 Cor. 15:30–31, for their biographical relevance.

The core of this listing in 2 Corinthians 11 reads as follows:

I

V. 23 . . . with far greater labors [than the superlative apostles],
   far more imprisonments,
   with countless beatings, and
   often near death.
V. 24 Five times I have received at the hands of the Jews the
   forty lashes less one.
V. 25 Three times I have been beaten with rods;
   once I was stoned.
   Three times I have been shipwrecked;
   a night and a day I have been adrift at sea.

II

V. 26 On frequent journeys [I proved myself as servant of Christ],
   in danger from rivers,
   danger from robbers,
   danger from my own people,
   danger from Gentiles,
   danger in the city,
   danger in the wilderness,
   danger at sea,
   danger from false brethren;

III

V. 27 in toil and hardship,
      through many a sleepless night,
      in hunger and thirst,
      in fastings often,
      in cold and exposure.

The text clearly has three parts. It begins with "labors" through synagogue and polis, then describes "journeys," and finally comes to speak about "toil" (the same key word in Greek as that behind "labors" in v. 23) because of disturbed vital living conditions. Of course, as clear as this outline is indicated in the linguistic structure, it is not completely carried through in the content. For example, Paul places under the key phrase "near death" those experienced on journeys in v. 25b, which actually belong in the second part. Likewise, here again is the contrast between his own people Israel and the Gentiles as an area of danger. Yet this is already talked about in v. 24. We would also imagine that the toil of the third part would already be contained at least in part in what was previously enumerated. Paul does not intend to gather statistically the sum of his sufferings but rather under various viewpoints to qualify his life as suffering. Thus individual experiences can generally serve more than once as examples.

Further, we see certain typical pairing principles such as rivers/robbers, city/wilderness, (the unpredictable, treacherous) sea/false brothers, cold/exposure. Likewise—only more seldom—there are typical triads: imprisonment/beatings/mortal danger, hunger/thirst/fasting. Even the sentence structure (e.g., beginnings, endings, arrangement and number of words) is kept consciously stereotypical. We see in this how Paul hides the biographical multiplicity behind the form. For on the basis of context and not least of all because of vs. 24–25, there can now be no doubt: Paul can bring all these troubles and dangers into congruence with his life up to this point. He is not exaggerating.

If we want to define this living reality closer, then we have to assume that in the catalog of outside influences Paul is describing his apostolic existence prior to the time of his writing 2 Corinthians 12; that is, the sufferings refer to the period from his calling (A.D. 32) until the writing of the apologia (ca. late fall A.D. 54), thus encompassing a good twenty years. After this time there is abundant opportunity to expand the list. The Ephesian imprisonment with its mortal danger follows immediately (cf. 7.1 above). Then comes the arrest in Jerusalem and the long road until Paul arrives as a prisoner in Rome, where his fate is decapitation (cf. 15.3 below). Thus it is no wonder that Paul also indicates elsewhere that constant nearness to death is his experience: "For I think that God has exhibited us apostles as last of all, like men sentenced to death; because we have become a spectacle to the world, to angels and to men" (1 Cor. 4:9). Or he speaks of himself in the apostolic plural, while using Ps. 118: 17–18, "as dying, and behold we live; as punished, and yet not killed" (2 Cor. 6:9). Also the catalog in Rom. 8:35–36 ends, after the enumeration of outside influences, with a quotation from Ps. 44:23: "As it is written, 'For thy sake we are being killed all the day long; we are regarded as sheep to be slaughtered.'" Finally, we find in 2 Cor. 4:10 the christological assertion, "always carrying in the body the death of Jesus," after the things that wear down earthly existence are described in catalog fashion.

Therefore we can no longer be astonished when 2 Cor. 11:23–27 quickly goes to mortal dangers in the narrower sense. For the enumeration—labors, imprisonments, beatings, near death (cf. 2 Cor. 6:5, 9: ". . . beatings, imprisonments . . . labors . . . as dying . . .")—climaxes not only in the mortal dangers in the narrower sense but is also the occasion to specify, appending in a biographically concrete way, the beatings (cf. 1 Cor. 4:11; also 2 Cor. 12:10: "insults") and other mortal dangers (cf. Rom. 8:35: "sword"). Paul begins with the Jewish punishment of whipping (Deut. 25:3), in which one is supposed to receive forty lashes on one's bare body. Yet since a counting error can slip in, the whipping stops with thirty-nine lashes in order not to transgress the law. The fivefold chastisement of this kind attests how often Paul fell into conflict with the synagogue. Neither Acts nor the apostle himself tells in even one case when or where this happened. Many people, incidentally, did not survive this punishment, and afterward all had a back that was torn to pieces and bleeding heavily. The later Mishna tractate *Makkot* gives exact instruction on how one was to proceed: while the synagogue attendant struck forcefully, the judge read aloud words from the Torah.

The threefold beating with which 2 Cor. 11:25 begins is the Roman punishment (cf. the order, "my own people . . . Gentiles," in v. 26). It was accomplished with rods, sticks, or whips, and the delinquent— usually bound firmly to a pillar—was beaten unclothed. There were no limitations on the beating (cf. Acts 16:23: "many blows"). In the provinces Roman soldiers usually performed the deed. Scourging was used as torture, chastisement, and means of death, and it was also carried out against Roman citizens (Acts 16:37). Acts locates one of the three Roman beatings in Philippi (16:22–23). On the others all sources are silent. Whether Jewish or Roman, beating was an especially cruel punishment and often led to the death of the one tormented. In any case, Paul's body must have also been covered with deep scars from these chastisements, because scourging left behind numerous and deep wounds. Even if all through antiquity there was a quick readiness to use punishment by beatings of this kind, we may still assume that for a person to tolerate eight beatings was surely a rarity.

The mention of stoning, which follows in 2 Cor. 11:25, is again a Jewish practice (cf. Lev. 24:10–14; Deut. 17:2–7; Acts 7:58–59). It is a synagogal capital punishment and is imposed, for example, in cases of blasphemy. The condemned person is led outside the city and pelted by the crowd with stones until dead (Acts 7:58; cf. John 8:5). According to Acts 14:19, Paul suffered this method of killing in Lystra while on the missionary journey he undertook from Antioch with Barnabas. When Acts 14:20 reports that immediately afterward Paul rose up and reentered the city, Luke must have imagined this as a miracle. As a rule, no one survived stoning—nor was one supposed to. Anyone who nonetheless as an exception came away with his life was so covered with manifold and severe injuries to head, trunk, and limbs, and had so many fractures, that he required a very long time to become relatively healthy again.

After mortal dangers from synagogue and Roman authorities—that is, from human beings—Paul names dangers of nature, concretely, the three shipwrecks, perhaps, but not necessarily including the twenty-four hours adrift on the open sea. From Homer's *Odyssey* into late antiquity there are abundant descriptions of sea voyages with all the dangers to ship, cargo, and people. The core material in Acts 27 is apparently also such a representation, which originally had nothing to do with Paul. Whether Paul suffered shipwreck at all on the journey to Rome as prisoner can be left open here. In any case, the event would be in accordance with the enumeration in 2 Corinthians 11. Unfortunately, neither with the help of Acts nor of Paul can we more closely define these three or four grave sea emergencies. We know of the following shipboard passages of the apostle that are before the composition of 2 Corinthians 11: (*a*) missionary journey with Barnabas (Acts 13:4, 13; 14:26), (*b*) first European journey (16:11–12), (*c*) trip from Corinth to Ephesus (18:18ff.), and (*d*) interim visit in Corinth (cf. 7.1 above). Thus on (almost) every journey on which he used a ship, Paul met with an emergency at sea. It is hard to determine whether that was unusually often. In any case, sea voyages were considered dangerous in antiquity, and freight rates and surcharges for ship transport were correspondingly high.

The four pairs of dangers (cf. the naming of "peril" in Rom. 8:35) on journeys (cf. all-inclusively: "homeless"—1 Cor. 4:11) cannot be determined sufficiently beyond what has been said. On the dangers of travel, the current literature also contains vivid descriptions of the difficulties and hazards, among which the robber nuisance often assumes a sad predominance. Probably in Paul's sense we will count among these dangers the hazard of which 1 Cor. 15:32 speaks and which lies at the beginning of the Ephesian period (cf. ch. 2 above). Also the flight from Damascus appended to the catalog type of enumeration (2 Cor. 11:32–33) fits here best. The vital detriments to life are also named by Paul elsewhere, namely, watchings (2 Cor. 6:5), hunger (Rom. 8:35; 1 Cor. 4:11), thirst (1 Cor. 4:11), fastings (2 Cor. 6:5), and inadequate clothing (Rom. 8:35; 1 Cor. 4:11). We may conclude that these phenomena were the uninvited but frequent guests of Paul. Above all, the prisons of the time were anything but humanitarian places. In them Paul must necessarily have had such experiences, without their being limited to this area.

If we look over these observations, we will ascertain that Paul was uncommonly robust but also led a life on the fringe of current society. His collisions with the Jews and city officials, as well as his unsettled life-style without a fixed home and family, allow the suspicion that, seen from the outside, Paul could indeed be easily regarded as "refuse of the world" and "offscouring of all things" (thus the self-designations in 1 Cor. 4:13 at the close of a catalog of outside influences).

In his sufferings, finally, the apostle also counts his ailment (cf. 2 Cor. 12:6ff.; Gal. 4:13ff.). Its diagnosis is almost completely impossible, for the patient is no longer alive and he described his bodily sufferings not as a doctor of his time—to say nothing of ours—and in general in only a limited way and with coincidental indications that lead especially to two interpretations: one that uses demonology for understanding and one that refers to a physical handicap. The two understandings are not antitheses for Paul but are ways of seeing that can be integrated. If we begin with the more certain one, we can ascertain that it is a chronic ailment (2 Cor. 12:7–8) that from time to time unpredictably afflicts the apostle (Gal. 4:13–14) and perhaps causes pain ("beatings" of Satan!). Where Paul got the malign condition remains ultimately open. Nevertheless Satan, who strikes Paul in the face, is otherwise still the very enemy of the gospel (2 Cor. 12:7; cf. 11:14; 1 Thess. 2:18). According to 2 Cor. 12:10, Paul also includes his ailment in the experiences of suffering that he must take upon himself for Christ's sake in the preaching of the gospel. This suggests that it is not a congenital illness or one from his pre-Christian period but perhaps one that is a consequence of his life-threatening persecutions, for example, the stoning in 2 Cor. 11:25. According to Acts 14:19, this happened before the first mission in Galatia—on which occasion Paul, for the first time that we know, suffered from his illness—and surely led to multiple severe injuries. Such anamnesis—although not certain—can lead to the assumption of internal brain injuries that cause the external symptoms to which Paul makes reference. In any case, an interpretation that tries to relate the calling

vision, the glossolalia, or Paul's ecstatic experiences to the symptoms of
the illness and view all of this as one and the same overall phenomenon is excluded by the texts. Not the tiniest indication in the Pauline
correspondence suggests such a conjecture. Acts 9:8; 22:11 match the
typology of such description and cannot be reminted as biography.

On the external symptoms of the illness there is only ambivalent
information. The interpretive means of Satan striking in the face can refer
to attacks of epilepsy or depression (2 Cor. 12:7), in which the face
becomes cramped or impassively dull; in ancient times such interpretation found application to a broad spectrum of illnesses, because antiquity used demonology generally to explain unhealthy phenomena. Yet it
remains noteworthy that Satan strikes precisely "in the face." If the Galatians would gladly have plucked out their eyes to give them to Paul
(Gal. 4:15), this could indicate symptoms that manifested themselves in
the area of the eyes. But this statement can also be well understood figuratively: the Galatians would have given him their most valuable thing,
so warmly devoted were they to him. Nevertheless the little restriction in
Gal. 4:15, "if possible" the Galatians would have done this, should perhaps indicate that it is a question of a direct and not only a figurative
statement, for in general the Galatians have indeed probably given their
best (Gal. 4:14b!). When the Galatians did not carry out the apotropaic
act of spitting in front of Paul (Gal. 4:14)—though it would nonetheless
have been understandable if they had—this means again that it was easy
to relate the ailment to demonic powers. Thus we see how ambiguous
the indications of the external symptoms already are. Even more, it must
be practically impossible to make a diagnosis. Yet we can still develop
the hypothesis of the stoning as cause and note that the possible disturbances in vision are only one aspect of the symptomatology, but not the
only one, because Gal. 4:13–14 and 2 Cor. 12:7ff. must be considered
together. If we proceed thus, all three indications of the external phenomena can fit together well. Epileptic cramps are especially recognizable in the face and eyes, were interpreted in ancient times as
possession, and are demonstrated as a consequence of brain injuries.
Also possible are severe migraine attacks with vision disturbances,
which, of course, the beatings of Satan do not fit as well. But again, conjectures and diagnoses are and remain of two kinds.

After the factuality of the suffering is established in its entire severity,
we must next ask how Paul dealt with this gall, of which he had to drink
a cup filled to the brim. We have already pointed out that he would
rather hide it than describe it broadly. He did not at all get into a mysti-
cism of suffering or a martyr ideology, nor did he heroicize his experiences, as did, for example, the Heracles saga, and as also happened in

Hellenistic Judaism, for example, with the image of Joseph (*Testament of Joseph*). Also established is the fact that Paul did not seek suffering himself. Suffering was not an achievement that he wanted to produce, something that he imposed additionally, like the earning of his bread (1 Cor. 9:15ff.). Rather, it is clear that he can ask for deliverance from the experience of suffering—more than once—(2 Cor. 12:8), and his gospel is identified by signs and wonders (Rom. 15:18–19; 2 Cor. 12:12), which for him surely include healing miracles. The sick in the church can be understood as the unhealthy consequence of perverse faith existence (1 Cor. 11:30). Thus suffering comes to the apostle when, and to the extent that, he stands in the service of Christ, because everywhere enemies of this service grow up and intentionally (e.g., the Jews and the civil authorities) hinder the Pauline proclamation of the gospel or unintentionally (e.g., the robbers in 2 Cor. 11:26) get in the way of Paul's missionary activity. The robbers are not interested in the fact that Paul must travel for the sake of the gospel. Suffering is a sign of the transient world (Rom. 8:18; 1 Cor. 4:11, 13) that the gospel encounters. When the Lordship of Christ finally prevails, suffering and death will come to an end (1 Cor. 15:26). Until then, of course, it will remain true for Paul that the messenger of the gospel will not be spared experiences of suffering in view of the nature of the world.

With this background Paul interprets his experiences of suffering on the basis of the one whose apostle he is: the crucified Christ. Here we can recognize several motifs. First, the sufferings can be understood as the other side of the apostolic service to whose gospel proclamation they are suited, for on the basis of his suffering the apostle is "the aroma of Christ . . . among those who are being saved and among those who are perishing, to one a fragrance from death to death, to the other a fragrance from life to life" (2 Cor. 2:15–16). Thus he serves the gospel—as he writes in the "we" style—"as unknown, and yet well known; as dying, and behold we live; as punished, and yet not killed; as sorrowful, yet also rejoicing; as poor, yet making many rich; as having nothing, and yet possessing everything" (2 Cor. 6:9–10). Far from revolting against suffering or complaining against God and humanity, Paul can integrate what has been forced upon him; it serves the exposition of the deeper meaning of the gospel itself. Thus Paul copes with suffering in precisely the opposite way from Job.

The second motif receives its most striking Pauline formulation in 2 Cor. 4:10: "always carrying in the body the death of Jesus, so that the life of Jesus may also be manifested in our bodies." Thus sharing his sufferings is becoming like him in his death (Phil. 3:10). This conformity with the cross of Christ is the qualifying proof of belonging to Christ;

therefore we can also hope to be glorified with him (Rom. 8:17). Just as the Christ who dies in weakness demonstrates the resurrecting power of God, so also, "we are weak in him, but . . . we shall live with him by the power of God" (2 Cor. 13:4). Hence suffering inducts us into communion with Christ. This encompasses not only suffering but also being resurrected by God.

A third motif asserts that the present experience of suffering is also, even now, at the same time the experience of the comforting God, the experience of his grace (2 Cor. 12:9–10). Suffering demonstrates that "the transcendent power belongs to God and not to us" (2 Cor. 4:7). Thus it is practice in the evangelical principle that we "rely not on ourselves but on God who raises the dead" (2 Cor. 1:9). Whoever carries the death of Jesus in his body also learns how the life of Jesus is now already manifested in him (2 Cor. 4:10). Daily wasting away and being killed bodily are paired with the renewal effected by God (2 Cor. 4:16). The new arises even now in the passing old as a daily process. The place of suffering is thus at the same time the place of divine nearness (2 Cor. 1:5). In the nearness of death we encounter divine life.

A fourth motif weighs earthly suffering against heavenly salvation and comes to the conclusion that "this slight momentary affliction is preparing for us an eternal weight of glory beyond all comparison, because we look not to the things that are seen but to the things that are unseen" (2 Cor. 4:17–18; cf. Rom. 8:18). Thus the Pauline hope asserts that suffering is in no proportion at all to eternal glory.

Finally, the last motif develops the idea that the apostolic suffering is exemplary. All Christians are fellow heirs with Christ; if they suffer with him, they will also be glorified with him (Rom. 8:17). Thus the Thessalonians are praised because they have followed the example of the apostle and under much tribulation have accepted the gospel with joy, so that they in turn became the model for the believers of Macedonia and Achaia (1 Thess. 1:6–7). Similarly, the church in Philippi is praised because they not only believed in Christ but also suffered for him, experiencing the same conflict that they have seen and heard to be the apostle's (Phil. 1:29–30). Apostolic existence, as the very signature of suffering, is also the model representation of Christian life. It calls for emulation.

7.4 The Infrastructure of the Pauline Mission Field

The apostle's Ephesian period directs our attention most conspicuously to a structural aspect of his mission. Neither before nor afterward did he have to maintain contact with so large a number of churches—as their apostle (1 Cor. 1:1; Gal. 1:1; etc.), father (1 Cor. 4:14ff.), and fundamental preacher of the gospel of Christ (1 Cor. 3:5ff.)—to solve the everyday problems of these young churches, to strengthen them in the gospel when they were exposed to the dangers of other missions, and so forth. The Pauline mission in Asia Minor, Macedonia, and Greece quite likely encompassed an area more extensive than that opened up and cared for by any other missionary in early Christianity. When Paul in 2 Cor. 11:28 points to "the daily pressure upon me of my anxiety for all the churches," that is no empty flourish but describes a situation that practically by itself grew out of his missionary successes.

Moreover, Paul did not found churches in order to have them live as monads. The local church concept of a congregation connected with a house and coming together in it (cf. 9.1 below) was not supposed to mean that there were many individual house churches, which each, for example, shaped into its own private club and limited its activities and relationships to living in its particular place and relating only to itself. Paul cultivated the consciousness of the general church and the feeling of belonging together, as even the greeting lists of the letters indicate or as shown by a reference to general-church custom such as 1 Cor. 11:16. This happened above all, naturally, when he passed on to all churches the same early Christian witness to Christ and introduced baptism and the Lord's Supper. Yet he wanted not only this but also the church as the bearer of responsibility to the general church. Thus Philippi supports the Pauline mission financially. The churches provide hospitality for other missionaries for a time. But, above all, the churches make coworkers available for the mission or gather a collection for Jerusalem. Thus there are sufficient concrete indications of how Paul expects the local church to participate actively in the building up of the worldwide eschatological church.

Such selected indications of how Paul stimulates an attitude favoring one general church are not surprising for him, because he was apparently the first early Christian theologian to develop any conception of church unity. It is based on the one salvific work of Christ (cf. 5.6 above), as it is expressed for instance in the traditional confession-like formulations on the destiny of Jesus Christ (e.g., 1 Cor. 15:3b–5) and has its uniting bond in the one gospel and the one Spirit, through which God calls us into the eschatological church (cf. 6.2 above). Thus through baptism we are received into the one "body of Christ" and share in the charismata of the one Spirit (1 Corinthians 12). It was Paul who, with his Antiochenes, learned by experience that the historically new way of the local church needs to be linked to the general church.

This is shown by the Apostolic Council in Jerusalem (cf. 5.2 above). Without this fundamental decision behind him, Paul would hardly have been able to go against Peter in Antioch (Gal. 2:11ff.). Only in the knowledge that in these cases others were placing unity at risk could he stand against Peter. Because the idea of unity is so basic for him, he must also step in immediately in the party divisions in Corinth (1 Corinthians 1–4) and hold such behavior to be incompatible with the nature of the church. If in his judgment the gospel and Christ are being adulterated, for the sake of the preservation of the foundation of church unity, he can exclude others from the church, such as the itinerant missionaries in 2 Corinthians (cf. esp. 2 Cor. 11:4, 13–15) and the Judaizers in Galatia (Gal. 1:6–9). He knows of the historical dangers to church unity and that the idea of unity will not prevail on its own but must have someone to champion its cause.

Did Paul succeed in creating structures that made feasible his responsibility for the churches and the responsibility of the churches for the whole of Christianity—structures that did not consist in individual spontaneous activities? In answering this question, we must first look at the conditions that underlie the erection of such a structure. In contrast to the mission from Antioch, Paul does not join into a "church network" newly founded churches that are relatively close geographically in the vicinity of a metropolis. Even if these new mission churches in the vicinity of Antioch were independent, as were Paul's later ones, from the beginning they still had as the precondition of mutual contact a natural union through the geographic, political, and economic relationships of the region. Also, the distances between them could be quickly overcome with a journey of a few days at most. Hence, it was relatively easy to maintain contacts. All of this changed fundamentally with Paul's independent and far-flung mission. Seldom did the congregations live as close together as in Corinth and in Cenchreae (Rom. 16:1). Worlds lay between Corinth and Galatia, and Philippi and the Lycus valley hardly had close natural relationships. Also, the Pauline churches in the Hellenistic cities lacked a place with a Christian church that served for them a central political function. Rather, they themselves were the central places of a region in which almost throughout they alone were at first the only Christians. In addition, they were oriented toward a missionary who, after a relatively short founding stay, left them alone, and as a rule they did not even know exactly where he was currently staying. Even if that was perhaps known, he might be far away and unreachable, especially in the winter rainy season.

Thus from the beginning, and as a part of the system, Paul demanded of his new foundings a great deal of independence and responsibility for their own development. We know of sufficient churches that could handle this—for example, those in Thessalonica and Philippi—or that, like Corinth, with Paul's help slowly learned to live in the spirit of Pauline Christianity. But how many churches were not equal to such demands and disbanded (cf. Pliny, *Letters* 10.96.6) or succumbed to a countermission (as the Galatian churches apparently did)? In addition to the internal problems that necessarily appear in all missionary churches, the Pauline mission field also had to deal with the fact that Paul's mission was not undisputed in the rest of Christianity. How was the church supposed to act here in the individual situation? What position was it supposed to take regarding strange missionaries who missionized in competition with Paul or even denied him the right to be a missionary?

How, then, did Paul keep in contact with his churches? How did he cultivate their consciousness of the general church? First, it is clear what he did not do. He did not create local or provincial offices and then hold them responsible. Of course, certain tasks in the church are looked after by particular individuals and are supposed to receive attention (Rom. 12:6–8; 1 Cor. 12:28–29; 1 Thess. 5:12–13). But these tasks belong to the church as a whole and can be performed individually or by many or alternately. They are defined charismatically and not as office. Thus Paul never calls "officeholders" of the church to account. It is always the entire church that he addresses, admonishes, challenges. Nor does Paul bind the individual churches to one another through councils or divisions of duty on different levels. Each church by itself is responsible for everything. It is not a part of the church but is the whole body of Christ.

Vis-à-vis the churches stands only the apostle himself. His authority is derived directly from Christ (cf. 4.5 above). Therefore it does not come from the church. For its part, that authority has its general-church signature through the apostle's belonging to the limited circle of Easter witnesses (1 Cor. 9:1; 15:8–11). Therefore it is not surprising that the general-church infrastructure of the Pauline mission field is practically and primarily organized around personal association with him as church founder. He knows what is happening in Galatia (Judaizers), Corinth (e.g., 2 Corinthians 10–13), Philippi (Philippians B), and Rome (cf. Romans 14–15). He knows which Christians known to him are currently staying in the imperial capital (Romans 16). He writes the letters and sends out coworkers. In a certain sense Paul is the personal nerve center of his mission—in spite of difficult conditions: he himself is on the road a lot, often in improvised fashion, and is often severely hindered in his freedom of movement (cf. 7.3 above).

If we inquire how with such a beginning Paul establishes contacts and interchurch connections, we find that he employs three instruments:

his personal visits to his churches, his letters, and his circle of coworkers. These are further expanded through the special collection for the poor in Jerusalem, to which Paul, even after his departure from Antioch, feels obligated and which makes clear especially to the Gentile-Christian churches the connection with Jewish Christianity. We have treated this elsewhere (cf. ch. 2 above; 15.1 below). Paul's visits are nothing new structurally, as we can see, for example, with Peter or James's people, even if Paul is especially well traveled. In general the itinerant preachers not bound to the churches—from the Judaizers through figures like Apollos to Paul's opponents in 2 Corinthians—were certainly not entirely rare. Their wandering from church to church doubtless strengthened general-church understanding. We must, however, also see that at the moment when Paul purposefully orients himself toward a mission in the western part of the Roman Empire, he effectively intends to leave his churches in the East alone.

In the first early Christian generation the apostle's written correspondence was quite unusual. There are, by our reconstruction, more than ten letters that Paul wrote, and they are (almost) all writings of theological significance. By comparison, within the Christianity of this period we know only one written inquiry from the Corinthians to Paul (1 Cor. 7:1), if the writing of the Jerusalemites to the church in Antioch in Acts 15:22–29 is a later construction (cf. 5.2 above). Even if in regard to the first early Christian generation we cautiously leave open whether here or there another letter was written, we can establish with relative certainty that the conscious employment of such correspondence was a specialty of Paul, who reacted with it to the demands of his broad mission field. After the death of the apostle the whole church learned to treasure this correspondence as a means of general-church unity. The Pauline letters were exchanged among the churches (cf. Col. 4:16), expanded through pseudepigraphical emulations, copied, and collected, so that they were able to become the core of the later canon (cf. 1.1 above).

Yet in this connection we must particularly remember the coworkers, because especially through them Paul also calls for the activity of the churches. We can distinguish two types of coworker, namely, those whom Paul himself selects independently of the churches and those sent by the churches, which the individual local churches place for a certain time at the disposal of Paul's missionary work.

Among the closest coworkers whom Paul himself selects we must name first of all Timothy. Paul calls him as a coworker at the beginning of his first independent European journey (cf. 6.1 above). Timothy must have been converted by Paul (1 Cor. 4:17) and accompanies the apostle without interruption from now on, as far as we can tell (cf.

1 Thess. 3:2 and Rom. 16:21). In four Pauline letters (1 Thess. 1:1; 2 Cor. 1:1; Philemon 1; Phil. 1:1), Timothy is named as fellow sender. This prominence of Timothy matches the esteem that is expressed for him here and there in the Pauline correspondence (1 Cor. 4:17; 16:10–11; Phil. 2:20–22) and the assignment of duties that Paul gives him (1 Cor. 16:10–11; 1 Thess. 3:2–3; Phil. 2:20–22). The post-Pauline period regarded Timothy as the successor of the apostle to the peoples in Ephesus and Asia (1 and 2 Timothy) and also established a monument to him as coauthor of 2 Thessalonians and Colossians.

Right after Timothy we must mention Titus. He was also won to Christianity by Paul in the Antiochene period, at least according to Titus 1:4. As a Gentile Christian and companion of Paul he took part in the Apostolic Council in Jerusalem (cf. 5.2 above and Gal. 2:1–3) and earned his special merit in the troubles with the Corinthian church, since as Paul's confidant he contributed decisively to the fact that this church was not lost to the apostle (cf. 7.1 above; 8.3 below). After Paul's departure from Antioch, Titus apparently does not run into the apostle again until Ephesus. Like Paul, he probably left Antioch soon after the Antiochene church oriented itself toward Peter and in the meantime missionized in Asia. Although Timothy is still named in Romans (Rom. 16:21), there is no mention of Titus here. If he had been with Paul in Corinth when the Letter to the Romans was written, the apostle would surely have mentioned him. Thus we may assume that after he helped reconcile Corinth and Paul, he and the apostle went their separate ways from Macedonia. A local tradition names Dalmatia (2 Tim. 4:10), and according to Titus 1:5 he was (later?) on Crete. The postapostolic period established a memorial honoring Titus in the pseudepigraphical Letter to Titus. The ancient church revered him as a missionary and the first bishop of Crete.

On Paul's first European journey he was accompanied by Silvanus/ Silas in addition to Timothy (cf. 6.1 above). In Antioch he stood on the Pauline side as a Jewish Christian with Gentile-Christian orientation (versus Acts 15:22–29). His collaboration on the first missionary journey is assured by 1 Thess. 1:1; 2 Cor. 1:19. Since in 1 Thess. 1:1 he is named in the opening of the letter before Timothy, he has apparently served Paul longer. After the founding stay in Corinth we lose his trail, if 2 Thess. 1:1 was indeed adopted from 1 Thess. 1:1, and if the mention in 1 Peter 5:12 permits no certain conclusions either. According to this last passage, Silvanus writes the First Letter of Peter from Rome under commission from Peter. This is perhaps an indication that he went over to the Petrine mission.

Without doubt these three persons are the most important in the Pauline mission. They have in common that they were selected directly by Paul as coworkers; like him, they are independent of a church and live without a family; they have no possessions or permanent residence; and they are apparently largely supported by the apostle himself (2 Cor. 12:18). They do not bear the apostolic title but are simply coworkers of Paul. They fulfill this task over a lengthy period of time. Paul initiates them into his way of doing mission (cf. 1 Corinthians 9), and through their involvement in his mission he is able to augment his work in an especially impressive way.

In addition to these three coworkers, there are some who are probably also not sent to Paul for a time by the churches but through Paul's initiative missionize in the Pauline spirit, such as Apollos in Ephesus and Epaphras in the Lycus valley (cf. 7.1 above). Also Onesimus (Philemon) is solicited by Paul for special duties. The mention of Sosthenes in the opening of 1 Corinthians likewise attests that he belongs to the inner circle of coworkers, especially since otherwise only Silvanus and Timothy have been thus distinguished. On the whole, we know very little about these four apparently rather close coworkers, because our information about them is very shadowy and limited to little snapshots.

In principle a common mission was not new in early Christianity. In addition to individual missions, for example, by Philip in Acts 8, Peter in Antioch, and Apollos in Corinth (1 Cor. 3:6ff.; Acts 18:24), the collegial mission in pairs had always existed (Mark 6:7 = Luke 10:1) and, independent of the church, understood itself to be sent into mission directly by the Lord or the Spirit. The number of superlative apostles is not given in 2 Corinthians, yet they also belong here by analogy, for they are not commissioned by a church but rather have their independent work attested by the visited churches ("letters of recommendation"). There had been mission work independent of the church ever since the post-Easter beginnings of the church in all of early Christianity and beyond. Thus in setting up his inner circle of coworkers, Paul was further developing a preexistent structure.

The situation with the coworkers sent to the apostle by the churches is more differentiated. The presupposition for this is the assignment of missionary activity to the responsibility of the church. Here it is not individual persons but the church as a whole that has the missionary obligation. Paul is familiar with this concept in principle from Antioch. There the church had sent, for example, Paul and Barnabas on a temporally and regionally limited mission (Acts 13–14). The two apostles lived within the community, were sent into the surrounding Antiochene area, and then returned to the community. Paul begins at this point, but he independently reshapes the theology and the organization. He holds that the churches, as administrative centers of a region or province, not only are responsible for the Christianization of their environs, as in general every Christian is supposed to win people for Christ in his surroundings (cf. 1 Cor. 7:16; 9:19ff.; 10:31–11:1; Phil. 2:14–16; etc.), but bear missionary responsibility for the Pauline mission field as a whole. Therefore Paul expects the churches to send him coworkers for the broad range of activities in his missionary service (1 Cor. 16:15–18; Phil. 2:29–30). These are selected by the church for a period of time (2 Cor. 8:19; 1 Cor. 16:3), so that the whole congregation is responsible for their sending—apparently including the necessities of life for these "messengers of the churches" (2 Cor. 8:23; Phil. 2:25). They do not become independent of the churches but return to them after their service.

Naturally this larger circle of coworkers is constantly changing. Its significance becomes clear already in the fact that Paul, Acts, and the letters of the Pauline school in all give the names of more than fifty of Paul's coworkers, even before we give consideration to summary information (e.g., 2 Cor. 8:18, 22–23; 9:3, 5; 12:18) and reflect on the local help from individuals (such as Priscilla and Aquila), who always stood at Paul's side when he visited the churches. That is without doubt a strikingly large number, which bears witness to the vitality of the churches as well as to Paul's organizational achievement. In this way the churches were directly bound to ecumenical missionary thought and action, and in this way Paul, thanks to their collaboration, could missionize over such a broad area and after a short time leave his churches without depriving them of contact with him. But it was important to the theologian Paul that these coworkers were not "his" helpers but were counted as coworkers in the work of the mission (1 Thess. 3:2; 1 Cor. 3:5–9; 2 Cor. 6:1–4). They are thus under the gospel, not subject to Paul. Also, he constantly kept the significance of the circle in mind (Rom. 16:3; 1 Cor. 3:9; 2 Cor. 1:24; 1 Thess. 3:2; etc.) and no doubt knew that with it he was creating a new structure. As we can see by the deutero-Pauline writings, the inner and the broader circles of coworkers survived Paul. And that, no doubt, was his intention, for in view of the many mortal dangers he escaped—and also in spite of every imminent expectation—he still had to worry about what would become of the churches when he was no longer alive. Even if the fate of these coworkers is as good as totally unknown, indeed often not even the names or just barely the names of such missionaries are known, this circle achieved something absolutely crucial for the spread of early Christianity.

Paul and the proclamation of the gospel form a classic theme of the literature on Paul. Not only could Paul handle words, but also in the organizational realm he shaped a part of the unity of Christianity. This should not be forgotten.

8
The Spirit of Freedom
and the Theology of the Cross

8.1 The First Letter to the Corinthians as a Literary Unit

Almost the entire Corinthian correspondence falls into the apostle's Ephesian period, beginning with the letter mentioned in 1 Cor. 5:9 and 1 Corinthians itself (cf. 7.1 above). There is disagreement, however, on the unity or multilayered nature of 1 Corinthians. Even and especially where there is agreement on literary-critical operations in 2 Corinthians and Philippians, for example, the literary judgment on 1 Corinthians is completely divided. Naturally one's position depends on how one traces the development in Corinth and Paul's attitude toward it. Previously we have presupposed the unity of 1 Corinthians and described the history of the Corinthian church accordingly. If we now want to trace the theological lines of this situation, we must first explain why 1 Corinthians can be better understood as a unified letter and why hypotheses that divide it up are problematic.

Anyone who examines Romans 1–8 in regard to implicit compositional information, unity of thematic concept, and ordering of ideas can quickly gather basic signs of coherence on the textual level. For the Pauline train of thought is here subordinated to a cohesive thematic area (cf. 13.2 below). Accordingly, Paul forms his presentational concept argumentatively in ordered conceptual steps. His method of presentation approaches that of the treatise. In 1 Corinthians, however, things are completely different and unique in the Pauline epistolary literature. Here various pieces tailored to an individual problem follow one after another, reflecting concrete church situations and treating current problems of various kinds in a loose order and in a way that is related to the situation. The party divisions in 1 Corinthians 1–4, marriage between relatives in 1 Corinthians 5, and the wearing of a veil in 1 Corinthians 11 at first have only one thing in common: they indicate the diverse nature of Corinthian church life. Such an abundance of the various aspects of church life is in fact no longer visible in any other early Christian source, and thus 1 Corinthians opens up invaluable insights into the community reality that stands behind the text. Yet on the textual level the question of literary coherence in this letter must be asked differently, for the epistolary concept, as indicated, is different from that in the example of Romans 1–8 given above.

This must be considered before one attempts to take 1 Corinthians apart. For in principle a dissection does not change this loose coherence, which is, in any case, nondeductively constructed. Of course, we can take the self-contained section on the party divisions in Corinth (1 Cor. 1:10–4:21) by itself and then maintain for it, as an exception, only one special thematic and literary context. Practically speaking, however, all of the more recent attempts to rearrange 1 Corinthians and divide it into various letters lead to the same result: the new epistolary constructs still have as a basic trait the kind of presentational method that is characteristic of 1 Corinthians as a whole. Therefore from the observation of the epistolary character for a literary-critical argumentation we must conclude that missing transitions between the individual sections or minor irregularities between one theme and another in the relatively uniform treatment still do not offer any grounds for proceeding with literary-critical operations.

This approach of looking first at the present overall impression of the letter is also to be recommended in the light of the other Pauline letters. We have already considered the special peculiarity of 1 Thessalonians (cf. 6.2 above). Again, quite differently structured are the letter in 2 Corinthians 10–13 (cf. 8.3 and 8.4 below) and Philippians B (cf. 12.4 below). This leads to the conclusion that Paul possessed a great capacity for conceptual change in the shaping of the letters. The written dialogue with his churches by no means follows structurally restricted paths.

Still another consideration makes caution advisable in literary-critical operations on 1 Corinthians. In the division of 2 Corinthians, for example (cf. 8.3 below), we can recognize in the reconstructed letters, alongside a particular theme and presentational concept, also a particular situation of the letter writer and the addressees. Here the situational difference is so large that the idea that the different situations belong to one and the same letter can be excluded on proven grounds. The discovery of such a situational difference is a crucial and indispensable aid in evaluating and supporting the literary-critical observations. Without such dissonance in the situations a letter should be taken apart only with the greatest discretion and preferably not at all. If there is no contrast or serious discord in the situational information, the results of literary-critical operations for the historian will be meager and the hypotheses of the literary-critical position unverifiable.

It appears that the situational information in 1 Corinthians is not absolutely homogeneous but certainly not contradictory. It is correct, for example, that in 1 Corinthians 1–4 and 11:18ff. Paul speaks with differing accentuation about party divisions. In the two cases, however, he is dealing with different problems; moreover, in the second passage in 11:18–19 he is obviously appealing to an early Christian tradition, and he places the two individual problems relatively far from each other in the letter. Further, it is also true that the Pauline travel plans in 4:19 read somewhat different from those in 16:3ff. Yet the perceivable nuances do not lead to the judgment that Paul contradicts himself or that he clearly changed his plans. These two examples may suffice to establish that until now no one has demonstrated with adequate certainty different situations for individual parts of 1 Corinthians. If, however, the situation presupposed in the letter as a whole is still understandable in a uniform way, then literary criticism has no substantial leg to stand on.

Some of the literary-critical operations on 1 Corinthians often lead to a general assumption that presupposes that earlier letters have now been incorporated piecemeal into the two canonical letters to Corinth, so that a redactor must have first taken the letters apart in order then to allocate the parts to different letters. Such an assumption raises fundamental doubts, for this hypothetically proposed process of origination of 1 and 2 Corinthians is too complex. Above all, however, it also overlooks the fact that 2 Corinthians—clearly different from the situation in 1 Corinthians—presupposes the same state of affairs as its parts in that strange missionaries have newly penetrated into Corinth. First Corinthians, on the other hand, possesses a bond of unity in the fact that problems have arisen from the internal history of the church and require an urgent solution according to Paul. This different bond of unity in the two letters should not be neglected without cogent reasons. Thus we will be quite able to advocate the unity of 1 Corinthians and the multilayered nature of 2 Corinthians and to employ for that the observation just made. This special reference to 1 and 2 Corinthians can also be generalized: the more complicated the interlocking and the piecemeal insertion on the present textual level and the more numerous the inferred letters, the more improbable is the thesis on the origin of the now extant letter. It is, for example, comparatively simpler to imagine 2 Corinthians 10–13 added as a block than to conceive of it as various small pieces of earlier letters now split up and spread over the new text levels of 1 and 2 Corinthians without holding to the old sequential order.

Yet these considerations alone cannot secure the assumption that 1 Corinthians is unitary. For that we need selected examples of coherence signals in the letter. Naturally it would be a strange assumption that Paul chose at random the order of the problems treated. So, even with all the looseness of the thematic sequence, there still must be connecting lines. Before the dictation the diversity of Corinthian problems went through Paul's own interpretive adaptation and arrangement. He wants to guide the history of the church; hence he must interpret the Corinthian diversity of life and bring in higher viewpoints, common backgrounds of individual behavior, unifying values, and so forth. As such work of the apostle is opened up and made transparent, literary-critical judgments can at the same time be implicitly questioned.

If we seek elements that further the overall impression of coherence in 1 Corinthians and at the same time reveal a bit of the particularity of the letter, we will certainly name the manifold sources of information, among them especially a letter from Corinth. We will have more to say about this. As the apostle reacts to such sources, he must be governed by ordering requirements, unless he arbitrarily goes back and forth among information and issues. Thus the situation in which Paul plays his part already has a certain structure, even if we no longer know it exactly today. The diversity of concrete problems has been singled out as a further peculiarity of 1 Corinthians. On closer inspection their arrangement also does not simply follow the throw of the dice. They are dependent on key-word sequences and thematic connections. Here we point as an example only to the theme of freedom, as it repeatedly echoes and is so thoroughly treated in 1 Corinthians (3:21–23; 4:6–8; 5:2; 6:12–13; 8:1, 9; 9:1, 4–5, 19; 10:12, 23–24; 14:9, 12, 23, 26). The diversity of life in Corinth receives thus topical and epistolary structure. A third observation leads to the thesis that, except for the short Philippians B, there is no longer a Pauline letter in which Paul repeatedly brings himself in so often and naturally as a model (cf. 1 Cor. 2:1–5; 4:14–16; 5:3–5; 7:7, 8, 40; 8:13; chs. 9; 10:33; 11:1, 2; 14:18–19; 15:32). In the situation presupposed in the present 2 Corinthians he could no longer do this, because there he himself is drawn in to the quarrel as apostle. His repeatedly making his conduct of life obligatory presupposes an intact authority relationship. Is this observation not also a good indication of the unity and literary coherence of 1 Corinthians?

These three observations show that it will definitely pay us to examine 1 Corinthians in regard to its structure and particularity. This examination will now be continued with a walk through the letter. After the opening of the letter (1 Cor. 1:1–3) and the thanksgiving (1:4–9), Paul begins with the long unitary section 1:10–4:21 on the "parties" in Corinth. These party divisions are an internal community problem that endangers the unity of the one eschatological church elected through the gospel (1:18–31). Paul does not yet see the church drifting apart into separate confessions, for he still addresses it throughout the whole of 1 Corinthians as one church. In the rivalries, however, he perceives a bit of egotistical self-representation that is in tension with the selfless seeking of the welfare of the whole church. This rivalry unfolds in connection with baptism and baptizers (1:10–17) and Spirit-effected wisdom (2:6–16) or the rhetorical representation thereof (2:1–5). Paul argues globally from an overall judgment against such ideas of spiritual competition by praising the richness of spiritual gifts (1:7)—and this also includes the secrets of wisdom conveyed by the Spirit (2:7, 10)—but through a refinement of his doctrine of election, known from 1 Thessalonians, he places gifts under a theology of the cross (cf., above all, 1:18–31), by which, according to him, all spiritual life must be ordered and judged.

This internal church problem is communicated to Paul by a special group of informants, Chloe's people (1:11). It may be that this theme also stands at the beginning of the letter, because for Paul it is chronologically the oldest news. Yet we can also advance another viewpoint. Basically the life of the church on the Pauline mission field can be conceived in two concentric circles, namely, the strongly emphasized inner circle of brotherly love and the outer circle of the citizens of the polis, which is treated subordinately. This is easy to see in the structure of the typical paraenesis in 1 Thess. 4:1–12; Gal. 5:13–6:10; Romans 12–13. This conceptual point of departure, which is at the same time an ordering principle, now also determines the sequence 1 Cor. 1:10–4:21 (internal relations) and 5:1–6:20 (external relations). For the individual cases that are treated in 5:1–6:20 can all be placed under the church's relations with the surrounding Gentile world.

The first case in 5:1–8—which is appended through a catchword (cf. "arrogant" in 4:18–19; 5:2) and thus uses a means that we are already familiar with from 1 Thessalonians (cf. 6.2 above)—deals with the situation of an illegitimate marriage into which a church member has entered. This falls under "immorality" as it is found not even "among the pagans" (5:1). The evildoer must therefore be driven out of the church (5:13). The catchword "immorality" then gives Paul the opportunity to clear up a misunderstanding that appeared because of his earlier letter (5:9–13); there he forbade them to "associate with immoral men" (5:9). For Paul, immorality generally includes all forms of sexual communion apart from strict monogamy. The church understood that it was not to associate with such immoral people, who generally lived in the polis; thus the Pauline statement referred to the external relationship. Paul makes it clear: he meant internal community relations. Then comes the treatment of a property matter before a pagan judge

(6:1–11). According to Paul, the external relations of the church should not be burdened with such judicial quarrels (beloved in Greece). Rather, the quarrel should be resolved within the community or by giving in. Here we should observe that the sequence of themes, immorality/monogamy and affairs of all kinds between the brethren (in commerce and law), also determines the paraenesis in 1 Thess. 4:4–5 and 4:6–7, which Paul writes from Corinth to Thessalonica (cf. also Heb. 13:4–6). The sequence of 1 Corinthians 6 after ch. 5 is thus structurally predetermined. Paul then comes back again to the theme of immorality (that is, for the third time), namely, in the general form of traffic with prostitutes (6:12–20), which was usual in that period of the cultural history of Greece. He begins his comments with the Corinthian slogan, "All things are lawful for me" (6:12), after he has already gone into the consciousness of freedom expressed therein at the end of the treatment of the parties (3:21–23).

All the problems in the section 5:1–6:20 have yet another constitutive commonality: Paul treats them from the perspective of the holiness of the church. This holiness—which was already a decisive catchword in 1 Thess. 4:1–12 and in 1 Corinthians had been heard twice in connection with the party strife in 1:30–31; 3:16–17—cannot be called into question by dealings with external relevance (5:6–8, 12–13; 6:2, 9–11, 17–20). Thus we can give the whole section the following title: church problems with external ramifications that affect the holiness of the church. We note finally that in distinction to the previous section, 1:10–4:21, Paul names no informants here. The first case was "reported" to him (5:1), and this may well apply also to the other problems within 5:1–6:20. In any case, he does not noticeably reply to the written inquiries of the Corinthians until 7:1. Does this perhaps correspond to the temporal sequence in which the news came to him—namely, first Chloe's people visited him, then unnamed informants come in 1 Corinthians 5–6, and finally he receives the letter from the Corinthian church? Unfortunately, this must remain an assumption.

First Corinthians 7 is an independent part on marriage and celibacy. It may have been the first question in the Corinthians' letter (7:1), yet it also follows well the main theme from 1 Corinthians 5–6 to the extent that the catchword "immorality" and the questions on legitimate Christian marriage are two sides of the same problem area (cf. 1 Thess. 4:3–5). Of course, we must observe that if it was a question of the abuse of sexuality in 1 Corinthians 5–6, the dispute now is over the question of the relationship between sexual asceticism and legitimate monogamy. Here Paul discusses the single case, "marriage and asceticism," in such a way that he fundamentally expands it by drawing in the other structures undisputed in Corinth, such as circumcision and uncircumcision, slavery and freedom, and indeed generally sketches the relationship of the Christian to the world. Moreover, it may also not be coincidental that 1 Corinthians 7—similar to the section 1:10–4:21—also makes a reference to thanksgiving, namely, the catchword "gift" (1:7; 7:7).

Then a further question from the Corinthians' letter is answered, beginning with 1 Cor. 8:1. The problem is the special relationship of the Christian church, which advocates an exclusive, monotheistic faith, to the pagan cult and to the gods of antiquity. The section ends with 11:1. Its attachment to 1 Corinthians 5–6 and 7 may be motivated by the connection—typical of the Old Testament and Judaism—between the cult of foreign gods and sexual sins (cf. Rom. 1:18ff.), or "mixed marriages" (1 Cor. 7:12–16) and idolatry. Here, naturally, Paul may also have simply followed the sequence of questions in the Corinthian letter. Scholars who divide 1 Corinthians into several letters also find in this section, 8:1–11:1, sufficient reason to uncover strata. Here too, however, there are enough observations to allow the section to be understood as a unit.

First, with clear appeal to the fundamental position of the Corinthians (8:1–6), Paul deals with a crucial disputed case of current urgency, namely, whether a Christian can accept a social invitation to an area that is part of the temple. Here it is not a question of a solemn cultic celebration but "only" of a celebration, for example, of a guild, an extended family, or business relations. Anyone who is "at table in an idol's temple" (8:10), as the temple district is referred to in typically disparaging Jewish language, comes indirectly into contact with the pagan cult at least in the enjoyment of meat—ancient slaughterings always have a sacral side (cf. 8:1a, 7, 13). The Pauline position is clear. From the standpoint of the Christian faith (8:4–6) acceptance of such an invitation is possible in principle. A Christian, however, is not oriented solely toward his faith and his knowledge of the same; he lives not from his strength but must be oriented toward the weak brother, for whom Christ also died (8:10–11). This brother may have doubts about such freedom, because he still cannot with assurance make the separation between cultic and social meal in the temple area and thus still accords numinous character to the social event.

Further individual cases are not treated until later, namely, in 10:12ff. These cases are discussed in such a brief and subordinate way that we get the impression that they are not the real examples in need of a rule. Paul discusses, in order, the total prohibition of participation by Christians in pagan cultic meals (10:14–22), permission to purchase meat at the municipal market (10:24–26), and the invitation to a pagan private home (10:27–30), at which, as a rule and under certain conditions, everything may be eaten. With this, Paul has addressed in 1 Corinthians 8 and 10 all the typical cases in which a Christian can normally come into contact with his pagan past and surroundings, when it is a question of eating. If we put all these cases in systematic order, the result is as follows: Purchase at the market is not a problem. The invitation to a pagan private home is almost always free of problems. Participation in a celebration (without cult) in the temple area is properly an issue in Corinth. For it is indeed possible but will be the rare exception because of orientation toward the weak brother. It goes without saying that participation in the pagan cult is forbidden. Anyone who understands and weighs the individual cases in this way—and thus, above all, does not find in 8:7ff. and 10:14–22 the same case treated differently—has no reason to divide pieces among various letters.

On the basis of this situation, the function of 1 Corinthians 9 can be defined. If knowledge makes the strong ones free in Corinth (8:1, 4), then Paul is also "free" as an apostle (9:1). His freedom is revealed, according to 1 Corinthians 9, especially in a matter in which people like to attack him: he is free to let himself be fed by the churches. He also has the right to be accompanied by a wife (9:4ff.). For the sake of the gospel, however, he renounces entirely this side of his freedom, just as he demands renunciation by the strong, whose "freedom" he does not deny (8:9–11). Especially as a free apostle he becomes a slave to all (9:19–23), to Jews and to non-Jews. It is not without reason, then, that in the series in 9:20–22, before the summary that forms a framework with v. 19, Paul states that he became weak for the weak (cf. 8:10–12!). This does not fit well into the organization of the list, but it shows all the more vehemently how Paul is targeting the case in 1 Corinthians 8. Like a competitor in the stadium, he puts all his effort into reaching his life goal with this voluntary service as a slave (9:24–27). Thus Paul presents himself to the strong as a model that is also supposed to define their course of action. As Paul thinks from the standpoint of others whom he wants to win for Christ, so also the strong should let their actions be determined from the standpoint of the brother. Yet this means that anyone who has to muster up as wordy a context as 1 Corinthians 9, in order to move the strong of 1 Corinthians 8 to renounce their freedom, knows that he has a difficult standpoint vis-à-vis those who lay claim to the living out of their freedom and thus demonstrate their strength. Have the strong not learned from Paul himself that actions are supposed to be based on the faith? Why should they not take this context into consideration and orient themselves toward the brother who is weak in the faith? The case treated by Paul in

1 Corinthians 8 is the real bone of contention in Corinth. After that ticklish problem comes 1 Cor. 10:14ff., because it gathers up (almost like a typical paraenesis) whatever else is related to the general topic.

This interpretation has a further consequence: at the time of 1 Corinthians the Pauline apostleship cannot have been contested in Corinth. For if Paul thematizes his apostolic freedom (9:1–2) and stresses his renunciation of this freedom as a model (9:3ff.), then he cannot have been currently under attack as an apostle, as is often deduced from the "defense" (9:3). This is also unlikely for other reasons: Paul is highly appreciated at least by the Paul party (1:12–17). In 1 Cor. 15:1–11 he can formulate the basis of his argumentation, which is subject to agreement, in such a way that he also includes his apostolic office in the formulation without any current polemical context appearing. Also speaking against a current polemic is the fact that not only Paul but also Barnabas lives in this same way. Both are thereby as a group quite generally placed over against another apostolic group (9:4–6). Also in 9:3, in his "defense," Paul is not at all addressing the Corinthian church. Rather, he writes very generally that he can answer quite well those who interpret his renunciation of right as weakness. Thus the apostle presupposes only a very general knowledge among the Corinthians, and Christendom in general, about such attacks against his apostleship, among other things. Paul turned this weakness, for which people here and there liked to reproach him and Barnabas, into his strength, and for the strong ones this carried the normative character of a model. This is the crucial point.

Yet another consideration supports this thesis. At the very end—namely, in 10:31–11:1—Paul again comes to speak expressly about his function as a model. Just as we can regard 8:1–6 as the programmatic entry into the problem area, so 10:31–11:1 is its consciously shaped conclusion. First, in a brief maxim he sums up the theme and its result (10:31), in order then to demand that the Corinthians should behave inoffensively vis-à-vis the Jews and Greeks as well as in regard to the church (v. 32)—that is, outwardly and inwardly—just as the apostle himself proceeds completely in the spirit of 1 Corinthians 9 (v. 33). The church is supposed to imitate him, as he imitates Christ (11:1; cf. Rom. 15:1ff.; Phil. 2:1ff.). Anyone who so emphatically presents himself again as model must not only have a relatively uncontested position in the church but also cannot have shaped 1 Corinthians 9 only—as often assumed—as an excursus in the middle of another theme. In view of the whole of 1 Corinthians we must add, as already indicated above, that in no other letter does Paul so often, and at the same time at so many central points, thematize his role as model as the solution to a problem.

Finally, with these insights into the structure of 1 Cor. 8:1–11:1 we can also define the function of the section 10:1–13. The strong are not only supposed to limit their freedom for the sake of the weak (1 Corinthians 9), but know that they themselves, like all Christians, are also still in danger. Thus Israel was indeed baptized into Moses and drank from the spiritual rock that was Christ, but this preparation did not preserve it from a whole catalog of sins, in particular from falling back into idolatry (10:7). That happened as a warning to Christians (10:11): Whoever, like the strong ones, thinks that he stands—and thus plays out Christian superiority over the world of the gods—should "take heed lest he fall" (10:12), that is, fall again into the power of the old gods! So we can see that Paul works up the topical problem of participation in a social meal in the temple district in such a way that he demands, above all, the limitation of freedom for the sake of the weak, but then also gives the strong pause to consider that their strength could quickly turn into weakness. It is probable that the typological exegesis of Israel's wilderness period is not newly conceived but is a relatively finished one which Paul employed here (cf. 5.5 above).

After the problems in the relationship to pagan worship, Paul now speaks of problems of Christian worship in Corinth (11:2–34). He discusses two particular cases, which were apparently brought to him orally: a woman's wearing of a veil (11:2–16) and the lack of love in the meal that occurs immediately before the Lord's Supper (11:17–34). The loose transition may have a bridge in the fact that the closing admonition from 8:1–11:1 to live inoffensively vis-à-vis Jews and Greeks and in the church also provides the theme for the treatment of the wearing of a veil. The section does not have to appear suspect within 1 Corinthians if its natural and unproblematic presupposition that women may also express themselves in worship (1 Cor. 11:5) is not contradicted by the commandment of silence in 14:33–36. Anyone who holds the commandment of silence to be a post-Pauline interpolation (cf. 1.1 above) has, therefore, no compelling reason to remove 11:2ff. from its context. Consideration for the weak as the main requirement in 8:1–11:1 is then topical in the abuses connected with the second case, namely, the behavior of some at the celebration of the Lord's Supper (10:17ff.).

In 1 Corinthians 12–14 Paul handles another inquiry—probably the third—from the church's letter (12:1). It concerns the charismata, the spiritual gifts, which come to lively expression in the church and have led to turbulence in the worship service (1 Corinthians 14). Paul chooses a long and basic approach to the qualification of the charismata as expressions of life in the body of Christ—which reaches a climax

(12:31b) in the description of love as the measure and content of gifts of the Spirit—in order then in 1 Corinthians 14 to discuss the concrete problems of the Spirit coming to expression in the worship service in a vehement and unbridled fashion.

In 1 Corinthians 15 Paul comes to the last great theme of the letter, namely, the hope of the resurrection. The fact that hope and eschatology stand at the close of the comments is generally known from speeches, paraeneses, and, for example, the triadic motto faith-love-hope. The subject hardly came to Paul from the church's letter but more likely orally (15:1, 12). Yet the letter probably receives another response in the closing chapter 16 in connection with the collection (16:1). For the rest, the final chapter exhibits the usual closing of a Pauline letter.

With this we can close the discussion of coherence on the text level. We have demonstrated that the letter can be well understood as a unit and that there are no really compelling reasons to divide it up. The following discussion proceeds on the basis of this unity of 1 Corinthians.

8.2 Enthusiasm and Cross

Between the end of the Pauline founding stay in the capital of Achaia and the writing of 1 Corinthians lie about two years. In so short a time it is relatively improbable that a young church would drift any considerable distance from its theological and ethical starting point. Rather, in its beginning phase a young missionary church is in general largely dependent on its founder. This lies in the nature of the matter: it hardly knows any other Christianity than that represented by the first missionary. Thus he is almost the unrivaled authority. Yet this mostly correct assumption is not necessarily valid always and everywhere. As a rule, nonetheless, it takes precedence over other assumptions.

Yet some have perceived that the differences between Paul and the Corinthians, as reflected in 1 Corinthians, are so great that they have assumed for Corinth a vigorous non-Pauline modifying thrust. They then speak, for example, of a profound gnosticization of Corinthian theology, against which Paul has to struggle. Yet there are no comparable Gnostic texts from such an early time. Therefore only in the form of a hypothetical inferential procedure do they succeed at all in reclaiming little indications and isolated sentences of 1 Corinthians as hidden allusions to a Gnostic theology. Then these allusions are used as the building blocks of a Gnostic system to which essential parts—above all, the systematic context—must be added.

In particular, no one has been able with adequate probability to reconstruct from 1 Corinthians a Gnostic Christology—certainly not one capable of consensus. Rather, such attempts have provoked vigorous criticism. Also, the desire to verify a dualistic, Gnostic picture of the world and history, including a corresponding cosmogony, has run aground on such clear monistic statements about creation as 1 Cor. 8:1–6. The perceivable differences between Corinth and Paul in anthropology, eschatology, and ethics are such that in no case can they be interpreted as only Gnostic; indeed, some observations on these topics resist such interpretation. (More will be said on this below.) If we now add to this state of affairs the unfavorable situation regarding sources for comparative religious-historical material and the observations on the typology of the Pauline polemic (cf. 7.2 above), then we will not be able to extract much of a Gnosticism in Corinth, especially since Paul expressly praises the church in basic questions of faith, as we will soon see.

Another attempt to evaluate the Corinthian situation begins with the idea that Apollos, who according to 1 Cor. 1:10ff.; 3:1ff. is to be counted among the so-called party leaders, initiated an innovative thrust toward Gnosticism after Paul's departure from Corinth. One can then connect the note in Acts 18:24—that Apollos was an Alexandrian and well versed in speaking and the scriptures—with the wisdom theology in 1 Corinthians 1–4 and see in Apollos an Alexandrian missionary who knew how to unite this thought with Christianity. With this basic theological position he would then have fundamentally altered the concepts of the Corinthian church.

This hypothesis also can hardly be maintained. We would then have to tear Acts 18:24 out of Acts' overall picture of Apollos and also neglect the general typology of such characterization of an early Christian person within the framework of Acts, and thus enter the field of unhistorical simplification. It is equally clear that a bridge from Acts 18:24 to the wisdom statements in 1 Corinthians 1–4 is a later construction, for the special statements about wisdom in 1 Corinthians 1–4 are absolutely nowhere mentioned in Acts 18:24. Moreover, Paul himself indicates no theological oppositions between Apollos and himself that could make these two rivals. On the contrary: according to 1 Cor. 16:12 he asks Apollos to return to Corinth! Finally, one should in general not select the striving for wisdom in the party factions of Corinth as an explanatory basis for all other Corinthian problems, since wisdom and parties disappear from the apostle's discussion after 1 Corinthians 4. One should, rather, ascribe individual Corinthian problems, including party strife, to a basic orientation toward guidance by the Spirit, which worked itself out in various expressions in life—including striving for wisdom.

Thus it apparently still makes the most sense not only to understand the Pauline answer to Corinth as a continuation of the apostolic theology but also to comprehend the theological development in Corinth itself as an intrachurch development on the basis of the first Pauline mission. Speaking for this thesis, in any case, is the dialogue structure in 1 Corinthians, which runs in such a way that Paul (1) employs his first preaching as the common and uncontested basis for winning a consensus (e.g., 1 Cor. 1:26ff.; 15:1ff.), (2) brings himself in play at the same time as valid model and respected authority (cf. 8.1 above), and (3) does not mention anyone who set up a countermission in Corinth. This Corinthian development took place under the conditions of a newly arisen Gentile-Christian church, which did not simply lay aside its former culture, understanding of religion, and interpretation of the world, nor did it adapt itself fully to the apostle's understanding during Paul's stay in Corinth. Thus the problem of the Corinthian church was, first, how the Paulinism known to it stood in contrast to the old ways or to what extent the old ways could also be a help in giving life to the new. Second, and even more important, in Corinth Paul did not simply leave behind a teaching, as a rabbi would his interpretation of the law; rather, the living work of the Spirit had its own important dynamic in the various gifts of the Spirit. This is basically also what Paul intended (1 Cor. 1:4–9).

With such an approach we can also appreciate that the Corinthians did not simply follow a new theological movement and thereby abandon an old one. It is naive to derive the church's every expression of life exclusively from a characteristic theological position. Our approach allows us, rather, also to consider nontheological factors and unprogrammatic behavior in the individual case. On the whole, the differences in socialization between Paul and the church also play a role, and in part the church produces expressions of life that could have appeared in any other Gentile-Christian church in Greece.

The Greeks, for example, loved going to court (cf. 1 Cor. 6:1ff.). If two Corinthian Christians went before a municipal court, they and the church perhaps thought nothing about it at all; it was a part of normal everyday life. This case looks different from Paul's perspective. In typical fashion he brings in, as the moderate solution, the way of the Hellenistic synagogue, which, as far as possible, had built up its own judicial system. Not in all nations was it forbidden (was Corinth also an exception?) for a son to marry the second wife of his deceased father, for whom, in any case, he had to provide (1 Cor. 5:1ff.). Yet for the former Jew Paul, this is quite naturally a scandal, based on the norms of the Old Testament legislation, and it was also prohibited, for example, in Rome. In Hellenism the covering of a woman's head (1 Cor. 11:2ff.) was a custom then undergoing change. In the East it was handled much more strictly than, say, in Greece. How it was practiced in Corinth during Paul's time is beyond our knowledge. Perhaps in the homes (where the worship service took place and all were brothers and sisters) the Corinthian women only wanted to do what was no doubt the common custom in many houses of the city, namely, to appear without a veil before familiar people in the household setting. Were church members not among the familiar ones after all? What Christian women did in public in the city, on the streets, and in the market is not at all under discussion. Paul, however, is thinking from the standpoint of the custom in the Hellenistic synagogue and in the eastern part of the empire, where also in Christian churches (1 Cor. 11:16) the covering of a woman's head apparently was (still) taken for granted and not an already changing practice.

These examples, which could be multiplied, illustrate how in fact not everything that happened in Corinth had to be, in the strict sense, a new theological program. They also show that this judgment can perhaps even be valid when Paul for his part wants to understand a case such as the forbidden marriage in 1 Cor. 5:1ff., among other things, as a case of enthusiastic attitude, as the reproach of arrogance in 5:2 indicates (cf. 4:6, 18–19; 8:1; 13:4). Do we know how Paul from his viewpoint modifies the case through diagnosis and evaluation? Also, there may be examples that Corinth itself places under the slogan of freedom for later justification, as it were. Secondary theologizing of everyday behavior is not entirely rare in church history. In any case, going to a prostitute is culturally so natural to the Greek that such an undertaking did not first have to be introduced or maintained by a new libertine program. Of course, one could even make this into a theological program in order thus to continue such a familiar pagan custom (6:12ff.). One can also, however, out of exaggeration turn emphatically away from the reigning culture. It is not unusual for young churches to incline toward such "overreactions." For example, in the world of the Greek gods and in the polis, sexuality played an especially prominent role. On the other hand, the God of the Christians was completely above this sphere: Christians were advocates of strict monogamy (1 Thess. 4:3–5), and Paul himself was even a sexual ascetic. Was that not for Christians the only logical—and thus the only possible—way of turning from the old world that is passing away (1 Corinthians 7)? That is, one can also understand the antithetical position in 6:12ff. and 7:1ff. as a problem of continuity and rejection of traditional culture. In any case, we cannot look at the problems between Paul and his church one-dimensionally. The web of conditions is many-layered and manifold. Unfortunately, however, we often cannot perceive which and how many factors play a role and which are dominant. That is because Paul completely forgoes such a multidimensional view. His view filters our understanding. The strength of the apostle, which lies in the fact that he immediately thinks through each individual concrete case theologically and extracts what is basic, is at the same time an aspect of his weakness as an informant, for the many-layered nature of a case is thereby lost for us.

Beyond these examples in the realm of actions, we may be able to make similar observations in the intellectual realm of the interpretation of the world, in which the different intellectual heritage of Paul and the church shines through, even if thereby the new Christian theological position also receives decisive significance. Thus the party divisions in 1 Cor. 1:11–17 allow the suspicion that for the Corinthians the religious understanding of the Hellenistic mystery religions—according to which a mystagogue (the person who initiates a new worshiper of the divinity) takes a special position vis-à-vis the neophyte (novice)—was transferred to the Christian baptizer of a believer. This is probably a background motif in 1 Corinthians 1–4, which was at best known to the former Jew Paul by hearsay and definitely not from his own experience. Much of what Paul perhaps attributed to the Corinthians' desire for freedom (6:12–13; 8:1; 10:23) also had something to do with, among other things, the fact that in the Greek world, in distinction to Judaism, religion and ethics were connected only loosely. Also, the fundamental orientation of the Corinthians to the exalted and victorious Lord (4:8; 12:3), who had overcome the cross, could correspond to a basic trait of Hellenistic hero worship, according to which the victorious hero is celebrated after surviving trials (*per aspera ad astra*). This basic trait is true of the Heracles saga that was flourishing particularly well at this time. Heracles was worshiped as hero and god after he took upon himself many burdens and sufferings and victoriously left them behind him. Could we not also interpret a Christian hymn like Phil. 2:6–11 (if it was known in Corinth) according to this pattern? The anthropology that shines through in 1 Cor. 6:12ff.; 15:1ff., with its division of a human being into ego/soul and body, is familiar in the Greek world in contrast to the Old Testament–Jewish holistic image of a person. Naturally these indications alone do not enable us to understand the Corinthian problems. In the interpretation of the Corinthian situation as one particular case it should be clear that such aspects of an interpretation of the world, typical for the Greeks, do not have to be newly introduced in Corinth with a theological program, as clearly as they also could appear within a theological concept.

At the same time and going beyond this, we can tell from Paul's reaction that the Corinthian situation also had a theological dynamic. This is indicated by the way Paul answers the Corinthians with theological argument; for his theological argumentation in his response to the Corinthians may in some cases disregard the secondary theological dimensions, but it cannot miss the general line of the Corinthian theology. Paul is too familiar with the Corinthian church for that. Yet precisely this polemical way of Paul's in dealing with his church also poses a clear limit to our insight into Corinthian theology. We have already spoken of this in detail (cf. 7.2 above). Keeping in mind such a limitation, we therefore have to look for those indications of Corinthian theology which in Paul's letters occur more frequently than in only one quarrel and which, without constructing hypothetical links, reveal aspects of an overall view. If these indications can then be understood as special accentuations and further developments of the theology advocated by Paul on his founding visit in Corinth, there is a large possibility that the reconstruction can, at least in broad outlines, be credited with historical probability.

Here we need to observe that in crucial basic views Paul ascertains agreement between himself and the church. This assertion is of fundamental significance because it makes visible the agreement between Pauline missionary preaching and Corinthian community reality, on the one hand, and the testimonies for Antioch and Thessalonica on the other (cf. 5.5 and 6.2 above). In fundamental characteristics, then, the initial basis of the Corinthian development corresponds to the message of election previously advocated by Paul. This becomes visible right at the beginning in the thanksgiving where Paul maintains (1 Cor. 1:4–9) "that in every way you were enriched in him [i.e., Jesus Christ] with all speech and all knowledge—even as the testimony to Christ was confirmed among you—so that you are not lacking in any spiritual gift, as you wait for the revealing of our Lord Jesus Christ." With this, Paul has not only formulated as praise what is at the same time the crucial danger for the church, namely, the riches of spiritual phenomena, but has also in principle ascertained agreement with the church in Christology (cf. by contrast Gal. 1:6–9!). This can be stated more explicitly. The Corinthians too understand themselves in the sense of the election theology of 1 Thessalonians as an eschatological church (Paul can often address this: 5:6ff.; 6:9ff., 19–20; etc.), which is elected (1:4–9; 1:26ff.; 7:17ff.) through Christ's saving deed (5:7; 6:20; 8:11; 11:24; 15:3b–4) proclaimed in the gospel (15:1–3; cf. 1:17a). The members of the church are constituted anew through the Spirit, quite in the sense of the statements on the spiritual transformation of the believers (cf. 5.5 and 6.2 above; 1 Cor. 1:30; 3:8; 6:11, 15, 19; 7:13–14; 12:12ff.; 15:29). They hope for the imminent coming (7:29ff.; 10:11; 15:51; 16:22) of their Lord (1:8–9; 3:11ff.; 11:26; 15:50ff.; 16:22). They have forsworn idols (8:1–6; cf. 1 Thess. 1:9) and hold the early Christian creation faith (1 Cor. 8:1–6; 10:26). The destiny of Jesus Christ, as it is drawn on in the confession in 1 Cor. 15:3b–4 for the definition of the salvific gospel, is also their confession (15:1–3), for Paul argues in 15:1–11 with the knowledge that to that extent he is in agreement with his church. Baptism (1:14–17; 15:29) and the Lord's Supper (11:23ff.), both understood as the decisive sacramental actions (10:1–6a), are in use with them and highly treasured. This corresponds to the Antiochene church in that here the value of baptism is completely analogous (cf. 5.5 above) and the Lord's Supper is the focus of church life (cf. Gal. 2:11–21; 5.3 above). Thus we can state that in Corinth Paul missionized with his election theology and toward this the church oriented its Christianity. To this extent there is no quarrel between Paul and the church but rather harmony.

As already stated in 1 Thessalonians, the chosen eschatological church lives in the Spirit, and Paul exhorts his readers not to extinguish this Spirit (cf. 6.2 above). Yet with the many gifts of the Spirit vehemently and vigorously pressing to speak and act, the Spirit presents new problems in Corinth. Paul recognizes the abundant gifts of the Spirit in the Corinthian church (1 Cor. 1:5–7), but in this he also sees deep theological problems and dangers for community life. Through the Spirit the Corinthians achieve quite directly identificational unity with the exalted Lord and thereby participate even now in his superiority over the world and in his final dominion (4:8); indeed, they understand the salvation event as the spiritual revelation of the deepest mysteries of God. This is interpreted as hidden wisdom, which is not accessible to the world (2:6–12). The possession of the same means a state of salvation that leaves the world behind.

Furthermore, baptism and the Lord's Supper, speaking in tongues, and ecstasy are sacramental actions and experiences that substantiate, or represent, the salvific state of being lifted up and carried away from the world. In baptism not only is the Spirit given (3:16–17), which was the general early Christian conception, but apparently the spiritual experiences and insights of the baptizer were also transmitted (1:12ff.). Moreover, baptism is a spiritual drink of Christ's immediacy (10:4) and lets one share in his state of immortality. Therefore unbaptized believers who have died must be subsequently baptized through the action of vicarious baptism, which is accomplished with believing and baptized relatives acting in their place. In no other way can they attain eternal life (15:29). Only baptism charms against earthly transitoriness. Here the quarrel over circumcision as a precondition of baptism is long forgotten; what the strict Jewish Christians formulated in Acts 15:1–5 is no longer topical. Nonetheless we can now advance a formally analogous statement of faith: One must be baptized; otherwise one cannot partake of transmortal salvation (cf. John 3:3, 5). This statement has fundamental significance for the problems in 1 Corinthians 15.

The Lord's Supper is numinous, Spirit-filled food (10:2–3); therefore it may in no case be withheld from a church member, whereas the love feast can begin even without the latecomers (11:20–22). This means an increase in orientation toward the sacrament, with a laying aside of general human problems such as satiation. The numinous participation in the Lord through the consumption of the sacramental elements spiritually feeds the individual. This alone is the point.

Ecstasy and glossolalia are signs of the overflowing Spirit in every service of worship. The more this becomes visible and experienceable, the better—even if the worship service threatens to turn into chaos (1 Corinthians 14). Only one thing is decisive: the more an individual church member acquires spiritual experience and achieves immediacy with the Christ who overcomes the world, the more essentially that member lives and the freer from the world he or she may feel even now.

As yet Paul has not criticized this ecstatically and sacramentally oriented Christianity as such—up to the vicarious baptism. That means he has not taken back the characterization of the eschatological church as life in the Spirit and as spiritually and sacramentally transmitted new creation in Christ, which he had already advocated in 1 Thess. 4:9–10; 5:4–10, 19–20. But he takes issue with the enthusiasm that the Corinthians developed from this. He criticizes this new early Christian theological position from the standpoint of his understanding of the gospel. Here we stand before the consequences of the high estimation of Spirit and sacrament in Corinth.

For Paul, these consequences are first evident in party divisions (1 Corinthians 1–4). A few groups gathering around the baptizers in individual houses (1:12ff.) compete among themselves for the best and highest insight into the divine wisdom as a sign of present participation in the heavenly place of redemption. Paul polemically calls this "dissensions" and "quarreling" (1:10–11), yet he addresses the church as a whole and thus still does not recognize real divisions. What bothers him, rather, is how, judging each other from house fellowship to house fellowship, they are "puffed up" (4:6); each claims to have a more perfect insight into wisdom than the others (2:6ff.). At the same time, through this Spirit-conveyed wisdom, which penetrates into the depths of the Divinity (2:10), they experience themselves already transported now into the heavenly perfection, for they are, in the judgment of the apostle, "filled" with heavenly gifts and "rich" in spiritual abundance, so that even now they "reign" with Christ (4:8). Though still earthly, through the power of the baptismal Spirit and his gifts, they are already "heavenly" and "perfected."

More pointedly, for Paul in his polemical exaggeration, the church seems to have turned into ecstatic individuals and groups, competing among themselves and quarreling back and forth over the deepest revelations. Paul indicates something of this also in 14:2, 23 and makes known in 2 Cor. 12:1–5 that ecstatic experiences as such are not foreign to him (cf. also 1 Cor. 14:18). But he puts such triumphalism of identificational unity with the exalted Lord and with the heavenly world back under the conditions of the eschatological church, which still lives in the middle of this world and before the end of all things. According to 1 Thess. 4:1ff., the Spirit leads into the concrete everyday life of a good marriage and occupational honesty, that is, into the middle of that immediate part of the world in which the believer lives. An ecstatic exit from the world was obviously not on the agenda. For Paul, this has now unpleasantly changed in Corinth. Therefore he emphasizes the Christian's confinement to the world by moving the focus from the exalted Christ to the crucified One. Election (1 Cor. 1:26ff.) and the gift of the Spirit (1:7–8) happen on the basis of that witness of Jesus Christ (1:6) which is the "word of the cross" (1:18ff.). Thus in all affairs it is not the exalted One but the crucified Christ who must be the divine wisdom of the church (1:30).

This emphatically sets forth the significance of the election message of 1 Thessalonians, which from now on is crucial for Paul. It is sharpened by the key word "cross." When Paul wrote 1 Corinthians, this word and its verbal relatives ("crucify," "be crucified with") were not at all to be found on the usual path of early Christian history. Naturally the passion report of the Gospels talks of the crucifixion of Jesus, and there is much evidence that this was also already the case in the oldest form of the report. But it tells only of the historically special means of Jesus' death (in distinction, say, to stoning), without giving the fact itself a theological significance. This suggests that Paul also knew the key word "cross" in a way that told how Jesus died. Other than this, however, we can find no linguistic proof before or contemporaneous with Paul of the use of the word stem "cross" with its derivations. At least nothing like this occurs in all of the early Christian confessional formulations that Paul somehow knew or could have known.

Here, the death of Jesus is, of course, mentioned and interpreted, but not death as crucifixion (cf., e.g., 1 Thess. 4:14; 5:10; 1 Cor. 15:3b–4; Rom. 1:3b–4; 3:24–25). Also, the old Jesus tradition can at best contribute the saying of taking up one's cross (Mark 8:34 par.), but this singular saying has its own language. For the Pauline theology of the cross we cannot establish the slightest traditional-historical connection, so that we do not even need to discuss the difficult question of the age of the tradition. On the basis of this finding we are close to the assumption that it is not mere coincidence that the still recognizable basic traits of Antiochene theology (cf. 5.5 above), including 1 Thessalonians (cf. 6.2 above), are also completely silent on language of the cross. This leads to the thesis that Paul did not take up this language and give it theological relevance until his dealings with Corinthian enthusiasm. The language and the theology are thus his new, personal achievement. He uses this new potential in order to state pointedly his counterposition in regard to Corinth.

This thesis is supported by a look at the Pauline letters written after 1 Corinthians and at the post-Pauline early Christian literature. After he composes 1 Corinthians 1–4 according to the theology of the cross, Paul himself continues to speak in this language—particularly with his justification message (Gal. 2:19; 3:1; 5:11, 24; 6:12, 14; Phil. 2:8; 3:18; Rom. 6:6). Above all, however, he will continue to follow the theological lines he first drew up in 1 Corinthians, even independently of the word "cross." In our consideration of the post-Pauline early Christian literature, it will reward us to make a distinction between those writings which preserve Pauline influence and those which speak independently of Paul and his theology. In addition, we should consider only those writings which not only sporadically come to speak of Jesus' cross but which offer a concept of the theology of the cross. Under these conditions it can be established that in the realm of Pauline influence we have Colossians and Ignatius with statements pertaining to the theology of the cross. Independent of Paul, such statements are presented in the post-Pauline period by Mark, John, and Hebrews. That means that in early Christianity Paul is the first witness to statements of the theology of the cross. Their special character shows the independence of the apostle, which clearly sets them apart from the other writings, even if that is not to be elaborated more closely at this time.

If it is true that in the light of the Corinthian problems the apostle transforms his election theology into a special theology of the cross peculiar to him, then there is good reason to follow the contours of such a new version of Pauline theology on the occasion of its first appearance. The apostle employs it first with the problem of the party divisions (1 Corinthians 1–4). Within this section, 1 Cor. 1:18–31 is a key text. It is not only the first text in 1 Corinthians that mentions the key word "cross" but also expressly reflects the connection between election and the cross of Christ. This happens in such a way that with intentional signal effect the gospel that elects humanity is interpreted as the "word of the cross" (1 Cor. 1:18–25). Then Paul looks to the yield of such a proclamation of the gospel, namely, to the called community (1:26–31). Here there is no doubt that the election described in the second passage under the guiding theological function of the "word of the cross" is now focused, beyond the statements of 1 Thessalonians, on a new characterization of the objects of divine election, in that they are defined analogously to the crucified One as objects that have nothing to display. Thus in 1 Cor. 1:18–31 Paul allows us a kind of workshop inspection of how he rewrites his election theology through a new variation of the same. Or, in other words, the apostle characterizes 1 Cor. 1:18–25 as the normative theme of theology that now imposes its conditions on the description of election theology that has developed up to this point. The theology of the cross now becomes the "canon" (or "rule"), as Paul will later designate it (Gal. 6:16), from which every theological assertion receives its contour and content.

Furthermore, through 1 Cor. 1:18–31 we can describe very nicely what Paul understood by his theology of the cross. In this passage he succeeds in calling up the essential features of this approach, so that there is clear continuity with it in his further writing in the Corinthian correspondence and in the letters with justification language. Therefore it makes good sense to spend a little more time with 1 Cor. 1:18–31 in order to see the outlines of the Pauline theology of the cross.

We must expressly emphasize that this theology is not an attempt to grasp anew the christological idea of substitution, that is, to give a new interpretation to the salvific death of Jesus as death for humankind. The interpretation of Jesus' death in such a sense remains of surprisingly little interest to the theology of the cross in the whole Corinthian correspondence. Jesus' death is connected in traditional fashion with the idea of substitution in 1 Cor. 1:13; 8:11; 11:24; 15:3; 2 Cor. 5:14–15; etc., without opening up what is formulaic and obvious in these statements. In general, for the apostle the theology of the cross is not an individual assertion within Christology, a special question of how Jesus' death is to be interpreted. It does not teach how to understand the key word of the cross more precisely as, say, a station in the life of Jesus along with the incarnation, exaltation, and his eschatological return.

Rather, the theology of the cross concerns the God who elects the church in the gospel and God's relationship with the world. The "word of the cross"—experienced as the "power of God" by those who are called and thereby elected (1 Cor. 1:18, 26) and with the crucified One as its content—reveals how God, contrary to human expectation, chooses what is weak and destroys what is strong. This gives lasting significance to this insight drawn from the crucified One, because God appears here finally and forever as the one who chooses that which counts as nothing, so that no one can boast before God about any aspect of greatness (1:28–29). Thus the theology of the cross says what the believer may believe of God and what one has to believe of oneself and all the world. It is thus a way of interpreting God and the world, in that it teaches one to understand everything from the standpoint of the God revealed in the crucified One, and at the same time it puts all reality in its place before God. In the theology of the cross, the cross is not the object of discussion, but through the cross everything simply comes up for a new discussion.

If the foregoing provides an initial sketch of the concern of Paul's theology of the cross, on taking a second look we can give attention to individual elements from 1 Corinthians 1–4. We begin again with the concept of God. Important here, namely, is the Pauline refinement that God proves to be God only by always and without exception choosing what is nothing. Therefore Paul wants to "know nothing . . . except Jesus Christ and him crucified" (2:2). There is thus no divine action with and for humankind that is not defined solely by the principle made known in the cross of Christ: God's power proves its strength where weakness, as the cross, is great. Through this approach the theology of the cross is also always determined by a polemical basic tone: human evaluations as to what is wisdom or folly and classifications according to education, political power, and family heritage (cf. 1 Cor. 1:22–23, 26) are thwarted. God's electing action does not allow human beings to prescribe the common criteria according to which this is to take place but rather has its own criterion in the cross. In Corinth this applies to the Corinthians who seek wisdom. In Philippians 3 it applies to Paul's seeking his own righteousness. Thus in the cross there is a revaluation of all things in this reality in a lasting and binding way, because the crucified One makes known once and for all only the God who in the depths, in deathly misery, in lostness and nothingness intends to be God and Savior. Only because he wants to be God in this way, and never in any other way, is the gospel salvation for all who believe—without exception.

In 1 Corinthians 1–2, with the help of the theology of the cross, Paul especially appraises the wisdom of the Corinthian ecstatics. By criticizing their world-surpassing way, and thus wanting to bring them back from the exalted One to the crucified One, he shifts the accent within Christology. If the prominent connection with the coming Lord was typical for 1 Thessalonians, and the Corinthians sought to overcome the world through reigning together with the exalted One (1 Cor. 4:8), then now, on the basis of the new experience with Corinth, Paul binds the faith to the crucified One. It is not the place of Christians to be already with the reigning Christ (1 Cor. 15:23) but to be in the middle of the world, where God is present for them and their lostness. Thus Paul directs them to experience God where God himself brings Christ and human misery together. It is not the time to anticipate perfection; rather, the crucified Christ is to be grasped as gift to humanity (1 Cor. 2:2, 12). This new emphasis within Christology will continue right into Romans.

Finally, Paul exhorts the Corinthians to reflect on their understanding of themselves and the world from this point of view. They have nothing of which they can boast before God; they can only boast of the Lord (1 Cor. 1:28, 31). Their mutual depreciation (4:1–5) is exposed as being "puffed up" (4:6). What is required is to follow the Spirit of God and to see thankfully what Christians are given (2:12). Therefore it must be important for the apostle that worldly standards (1:22–23, 26) not gain entrance into community behavior again through the back door in spiritual clothing, as obviously happens in Corinth through competition over spiritual gifts. Instead, an attitude is demanded that Paul later describes as the world being crucified to him and he to the world (Gal. 6:14). This has to be valid because the believer is crucified together with Christ (Gal. 2:19; Rom. 6:6; cf. Phil. 3:10).

Now, finally, an idea of the theology of the cross that was already heard in 1 Thess. 2:5ff. can also be put into its proper place. Since an impressive presentation of the gospel is not consistent with the cross, it is quite logical when the gospel in its rhetorical way of presentation (1 Cor. 2:1ff.) and in the personal life-style of the apostle as the proclaimer of the same (4:9ff.) is offered in such a way that in the eyes of the world it is weak, in order to bring to bear all the more clearly the divine power at work in it.

It may be that Paul placed the Corinthian partisan strife at the beginning because, among other reasons, he thought that this would be an exemplary demonstration field for assessing the Corinthian development as a whole. It may be that with the argumentation against the heaven-storming spirit in 1 Corinthians 1–4 he intended to bring together and judge the variety of Corinthian life expressions. In any case, in all his correspondence with Corinth Paul repeatedly works out basic traits of his theology of the cross as the decisive way to understand Christianity in general (cf. 8.4 and 8.5 below). How he does that in detail in 1 Corinthians—even without speaking directly of the cross—will now be sketched with a few basic outlines.

If we look over the apostle's comments following 1 Corinthians 1–4, it becomes clear, first, that in many ways he submits the sacramental concept and the ecstatic experience to the same critique. In 1 Corinthians 1–4 he brings the baptismal Spirit from the heights of heaven into the depths of the cross. In 10:1ff. he presupposes that the Corinthians believe themselves so surely united with the heavenly Christ on the basis of baptism and the Lord's Supper that they imagine they are secure against any earthly, historical temptation to fall from faith, and he reminds them of the wilderness generation, which disowned God in spite of such gifts. In 11:17ff. the high value placed on the Lord's Supper leads to the lack of love in concrete dealings with the brethren within earthly living conditions. In 1 Corinthians 14 the apostle struggles against the priority of heavenly rapture and in favor of historical order in the celebration of worship. The vicarious baptism in 15:29 marks a conception according to which baptism makes one already immortal on earth and declares death, as a still valid historical reality, to be unimportant. Yet, for Paul, death, as the last enemy, will not be conquered until the end of history (15:54ff.).

These signals can be reduced to a common denominator. The Corinthians have certainly not yet given up the horizontal, historically oriented expectation of the coming Lord, but for them, in accordance with the Greek worldview, vertical, up-and-down thinking repeatedly shows through. Participation in the perfected One residing above is crucial. Everything that points above and grants a share therein is right and is eagerly adopted. In view of this fundamental concern, everything historical and earthly can be neglected, that is, one's own temptation-filled existence, the brethren, the fellowship, and death. Here Paul must provide a counterbalance with his theology of the cross: Until the end of history Christ alone will rule. Until then the church still stands where the crucified One was, namely, on this side of death (1 Cor. 15:20ff.). Until then the consummation as immortality is given only as the pledge of the faithful God (1:9; 15:51ff.). If seeing face-to-face is thus in the future (13:12) and not already a present condition (2:10), then imperfection includes not only limited knowledge (13:12) and only momentary ecstasy but also sin (15:3b, 56) and temptation (10:11ff.). Then it is also important to have consideration for the weak brother (8:9–11), the church (14:1ff.), and the stranger who comes to worship (14:23ff.).

A second basic characteristic is the critique of the Corinthians' consciousness of freedom. Here too there is at first agreement between Paul and the church. Paul maintained in 1 Thess. 4:8–9 that God gave the Spirit to the entire church and thus to each individual; therefore, all are directly "taught by God"; that is, they are pneumatics (those gifted by the Spirit). Consequently, if one is to place no limitation on pneumatic activity in the church (1 Thess. 5:19–20), then that means concretely that every pneumatic is free in the unfolding of his spiritual gift. In 1 Cor. 2:15 Paul can even, in agreement with the Corinthians, pointedly coin the proud saying, "The spiritual man [pneumatic] judges all things, but is himself to be judged by no one."

In 1 Thessalonians, however, Paul defined the freedom that comes from such immediacy to God as holiness and brotherly love, for, according to him, the Spirit itself inducts a person into both (1 Thess. 4:3–10). Thus freedom was being free from the old life-style, being bound to the will of God, and being concerned with the welfare of the community. One was dressed in the "breastplate of faith and love" (1 Thess. 5:8) and at the same time a member among all "sons of light" (1 Thess. 5:5). In Corinth this connection, according to the apostle's diagnosis, is now certainly at least loosened, if not in many cases broken. Being "puffed up" (1 Cor. 4:6–7) contradicts the commandment of love. Therefore in Corinth the admonition is appropriate: "Let no one boast of men. For all things are yours, whether Paul or Apollos or Cephas or the world or life or death or the present or the future"; up to this point Christian freedom is described, completely in agreement with the Corinthians, as the new world-surpassing being, in order then to receive the crucial continuation: "[But] you are Christ's; and Christ is God's" (1 Cor. 3:21–23). Who Christ is was just explained by Paul (1 Cor. 1:18ff.), namely, the crucified One.

With the same intention Paul takes up the Corinthian slogan, "All things are lawful (for me)" (1 Cor. 6:12; 10:23). It is an expression of pneumatic self-understanding, as attested by 2 Cor. 3:17b ("Where the Spirit of the Lord is, there is freedom"), and the context 2 Cor. 3:4ff. at the same time makes it clear where the statement has its roots, namely, in the discussion of freedom from the law. "All things are lawful" is thus the Corinthian description of freedom in Christ (Gal. 2:4), as it was understood on the basis of the work of the Spirit in Antioch and interpreted against the law (cf. 5.2 and 5.3 above). Here it is first clear that Corinth did not simply subsume all norms under the "all things" that were lawful and thus in effect dissolve all ethics through licentiousness. Concretely, a look into 1 Corinthians leads only to the conclusion that in Corinth taboos regarding dietary precepts (eating meat) and extramarital sexual contacts with courtesans or prostitutes were apparently discussed. That is attested by the Corinthian slogan from 1 Cor. 6:13: "'Food is meant for the stomach and the stomach for food'—and God will destroy both one and the other," and by the discussion of meat offered to idols in 1 Corinthians, chs. 8; 10, as well as the comments on immorality in 6:13bff.

With the treatment of these themes, of course, the accents have now also changed. The abrogation of Old Testament ritual law, for example, no longer has to be substantiated vis-à-vis a Jewish-Christian front but was tacitly regarded as an undisputed and self-evident decision that now belongs to church history. A discussion of the basic Antiochene decision in opposition to the synagogue has become meaningless. For they had applied this "freedom in Christ" anew in the context of the current problems of contact with the old paganism, and here, in terms of cultural history, the world of the gods and sexuality are, not coincidentally, the two crucial foci. From divine creative activity (1 Cor. 8:1–6) and from God's expected eschatological interaction with a person's earthly body (6:13) it was concluded that in these cases freedom can reign.

Paul rejected this interpretation of Christian freedom especially clearly through three aspects. In 1 Cor. 6:12a; 10:23 he urgently stresses usefulness for the community. Freedom is not an individual Christian right that can be set apart from the church or even used against it, but, like the Spirit and its charismatic ways of appearing, it is related to the upbuilding of a body of Christ (1 Corinthians, chs. 12; 14). Second, the sequence faith-knowledge-action is therefore to be questioned. Even when knowledge is great and correct, the right to turn it into immediate action is not yet given; for love, which builds up the church, will have to be given priority, because, for example, the weak brother, for whom Christ also died, must not fall back into paganism (1 Corinthians 8). Third, freedom is always endangered by temptation and human backsliding into the old life. Thus freedom has its boundary where it turns into new imprisonment (1 Cor. 6:12b; 10:1ff.). We can probably assert, without fear of contradiction, that this dialogue between the Corinthians and Paul on the Christian concept of freedom is in general the most profound discussion of this theme that early Christianity has to offer. This is due in no small part to the fact that Paul does not simply legally bind and thereby nullify the Corinthian urge for freedom and the pneumatic consciousness of freedom; rather, he thinks from the standpoint of the nature of Christian freedom and gives it plenty of room.

A third fundamental point in the apostle's critique of the Corinthians, and one especially difficult to delineate, is their anthropology. Here the concrete concern is whether and to what extent Paul must reject the Corinthians' dualism. As a rule, in this discussion the term "dualism" is used rather generally, that is, in the sense that Paul has a unified anthropology, according to which a person is a "body" (*sōma*), while the Corinthians divide a person into body and soul and grant redemption only to the better part, the soul or self. Yet it is important to clarify to what extent the Corinthians are thinking only in a generally Hellenistic or in a pointedly Gnostic fashion. The distinction can be seen in that in the first case we have only dichotomous thinking; that is, within a splitting of the individual, the body is not already a negative power and as such also a prison for the soul; rather, it only remains excluded from the eschatological redemption, because it is earthly and transitory, and thus belongs only to this passing creation. In the second case the body is a phenomenon of an evil world that can no longer be regarded as good creation. It is the prison warden of the self and at the same time a power hostile to God.

According to everything still discernible in the Corinthian correspondence, Paul may only be turning against a dichotomous anthropology. For this assumption we have, first of all, the fact that the Corinthians share with Paul faith in the creation (1 Cor. 8:1–6)—that is, "the earth is the Lord's, and everything in it" (10:26)—and thus also hold the earthly existence of humanity to be good creation. Further, we may take 1 Cor. 6:13a and 15:50 as the point of departure for an outline of Corinthian anthropology. Both statements agree that the body will be annihilated by God and cannot inherit immortality. Yet neither statement asserts anything about a new spiritual corporeality, as described by Paul himself (15:35ff.). They presuppose that after death the self/soul will be unclothed and thus "naked" (2 Cor. 5:3). Here both statements distinguish tacitly and typically hellenistically two parts of a person: the invisible self/soul and the visible body. By its nature the self/soul is, for the Corinthians, suitable for reshaping into immortality, yet it is initially mortal; it needs baptism in order to become immune to death through the Spirit (2 Cor. 5:5!). Hence for the Corinthians vicarious baptism is absolutely necessary (1 Cor. 15:29) when an unbaptized person has died. In death the self wanders "away from the body" (2 Cor. 5:8), and the "earthly tent . . . is destroyed" (5:1), that is, decomposes. The point is precisely that the body is for a time the earthly dwelling, not a prison against God's intentions. Self and body are not qualified and distinguished as good and evil but only separated eschatologically and historically and thus characterized respectively as becoming eternal and remaining mortal.

Because, however, the body is only the earthly housing, which does not share in salvation, the Corinthians could declare it ethically irrelevant (1 Cor. 6:13bff.) or abandon it even now in terms of behavior; one could, for example, practice marital asceticism (1 Corinthians 7). Going to a prostitute is thus not demonstrative contempt for the evil body;

rather, the corporeal has become an ethically nonobligatory affair, because the body has no constitutive significance for the final salvation. The Corinthians who advocate sexual asceticism are not enemies of an unholy body; rather, in view of the transitory nature of the body, which means it will soon pass away, they want even now to be free from it and to concentrate entirely on their self/soul, which in baptism has become immune to death. Thus the Corinthian anthropology is the product of a customary dichotomous anthropology already present in pre-Christian cultural history, of a new conception of Christian baptism, and of an eschatological expectation that assigns the antithesis transitory—eternal to body—soul.

Paul corrects such a conception in several ways. For him, it is true throughout that the body is not a part of a person; rather, an individual *is* a body. Therefore a person cannot distance the self from the body. This means that he or she is as a whole a creature of God and stands in wholeness before God. For Paul, naturally, baptism also relates to the whole person: the old self is crucified with Christ, so that the "sinful body" is destroyed and the Christian is no longer enslaved to sin (Rom. 6:6; cf. 1 Cor. 6:9–11). Thus the body—that is, the whole person as bodily existence—belongs to the Lord (1 Cor. 6:13b) and must offer itself as a living sacrifice (Rom. 12:1). It is the temple of the Holy Spirit, and thus it is with our bodies that we are supposed to glorify God (1 Cor. 6:19–20). At the last judgment the focus will be on this bodily existence of a person (2 Cor. 5:10). Finally, the ultimate human condition of salvation is not regarded as a bodiless self but as a new spiritual corporeality (1 Cor. 15:35ff.; 2 Cor. 5:1ff.). Thus Paul argues for the obligatory nature of bodily existence and permits a dichotomy of the individual neither now nor later. A person is always a whole self and stands as such before God, the creator and judge, and beside the neighbor.

A fourth aspect of the Pauline polemic vis-à-vis Corinth is his disagreement with tendencies toward the premature termination of relations with the world. The ecstatic who soars up to the exalted Christ overemphasizes his freedom from the world and exercises a relatively uncompromising distance from the world. This misunderstanding is based first on the apostle's precanonical letter (1 Cor. 5:9ff.). In Corinth they like to understand Paul in the sense that he advises them to break off contact with all evildoers outside the church. Perhaps there are spouses who would like to get out of their marriage with a pagan partner (7:12ff.). In the worship service ecstatic confusion dominates to such an extent that a stranger, in whom the church really should be interested, must get the impression that the people have lost their minds (14:23ff.). Preserved in 2 Cor. 6:14–7:1 is an un-Pauline passage—but perhaps not entirely untypical for Corinth—which, for the sake of the church's holiness, practically terminates fellowship with the world. But it is a rejection not only of the world as encountered in other people but also as something we belong to and are a part of. Through asceticism, marriage is left behind (1 Corinthians 7). Through the sacraments, death and temptation are out of the way (10:1ff.; 15:29).

In all such cases Paul leaves the Christian in the middle of the reality of the world. It is not abandonment and rejection of the world that are Christian according to him, but faithfulness and patience in the middle of the world. Thus for a Christian wife living with a pagan husband, it is much harder to hold fast to that marriage than to break it up and move into a Christian home. Marital asceticism may indeed remove part of the concern for this world, but Paul advises one not to terminate marital vows and marriages on one's own and to give priority to mutual partnership. Finally, it is folly to overlook one's own temptation as a part of the world. The Christian approach is to include it in one's calculations, without abandoning trust in God (1 Cor. 10:12–13).

A fifth and final viewpoint can be treated briefly, since it is already contained in the other themes, namely, the disagreement on the expectation of the end. Corinth had structured the early Christian expectation of the imminent end and the eschatological election, including the gift of the Spirit, in such a way that even now the ecstatics share in the dominion of Christ. Anthropologically, moreover, the Corinthian church had taught the immunization of the self/soul against death and its ultimate salvation but consigned the body to transience. Paul maintains that the creature as a whole will be redeemed by the Creator (1 Cor. 15:35ff.) and lets stand until the end the subordination of even the elect to the destiny of death in this world. Only Christ has already overcome death; a coregnancy with him is not given until the end, when death will be conquered in general (15:20ff., 52ff.). The Christian knows about the passing world but practices distance from it, not in ecstasy, but in the middle of the world in concrete interaction with all worldly concerns (7:29ff.). The tension with the passing world is not interrupted by a pneumatic withdrawal for good but is maintained ethically in the everyday world.

We can summarize as follows. Paul attempts throughout to call the Corinthians from the heaven of ecstasy and premature perfection back into the middle of this world. His theology of the cross serves here as a reminder to the believer not to confuse faith with premature vision, not to let love grow cold through spiritual self-representation, and to understand hope as the certainty of a redemption still to come (1 Cor. 13:13). The Corinthians at this time seem to have had open ears for Paul. At any rate, 1 Corinthians gives the impression that Paul looked with relative confidence to success in steering them away from enthusiasm. For he writes, on the whole, from a position of calmness and strength; as founder of the church he knows that it must be led, yet it also listens to him. Nevertheless things then changed: Corinth received the unexpected visit of itinerant missionaries who were sympathetic to Corinthian enthusiasm and strengthened the church in the very Christianity that was criticized by Paul. He was far away in Ephesus; the new missionaries were on the scene. They stiffened the backs of the Corinthians; 1 Corinthians, on the other hand, demanded a rethinking and a less comfortable way. Thus there came what had to come: the Spirit bubbled over in Corinth once again. Paul has to renew the struggle for his church but now in a way that is much more dramatic than the problems of 1 Corinthians.

8.3 The Collection of Letters in Second Corinthians

The presentation of the Ephesian events (cf. 7.1 above) already gave us the opportunity to go into the apostle's correspondence with the Corinthian church as it continues after 1 Corinthians and is preserved in 2 Corinthians. There it was presupposed that the canonical 2 Corinthians is an epistolary collection that contains several apostolic letters. This assumption must now be substantiated, so that the development of the dialogue between Paul and the church can be evaluated. Today there is fortunately broad agreement in the basic points of such a literary-critical analysis, even if warnings against a division of the letters have not died out and details of the analysis are disputed.

Probably the most striking reason for literary criticism in 2 Corinthians is the fact that in two amply composed chapters (2 Corinthians 8 and 9) Paul, having a good relationship with the church, promotes the collection for the Jerusalemites, and then in 2 Corinthians 10–13 writes what constitutes, along with Galatians, the sharpest and most polemical utterances of Paul that we know. This profound dissonance cannot be simply explained, for example, by new information that Paul received during dictation or by a sleepless night. Anyone who writes 2 Corinthians 10–13 in such a harsh, ironic, and even in part sarcastic tone and pulls out all the apologetic stops in order to wrench the church free from the foreign missionaries, with whom at the time it largely agreed, cannot immediately beforehand solicit gifts of love and still expect success. Rather, anyone who places 2 Corinthians 10–13 after the solicitation of the collection must know that he is torpedoing this solicitation. Presupposed in 2

Corinthians 10–13 is a climate between Paul and the church in which anything in the nature of a request for a freewill offering is useless.

Second Corinthians 10–13 not only has simply no connection with 2 Corinthians 8–9, which it abruptly follows with no transition, but is also independent of all other statements in 2 Corinthians. From the standpoint of text genre (apologia) and content, 2 Corinthians 10–13 is independent; it shows a threefold, well thought out structure, in whose center is the fool's speech (11:16–12:13), as the corresponding text signals in 11:1, 16–17, 19, 21; 12:6, 11 attest; and it has a closing in 13:11–13, which is similar to the typology of 1 Thess. 5:16ff.; Phil. 4:4ff. and takes up key words from 2 Cor. 13:9. The apologia perhaps lacks only an epistolary opening. It was probably deleted when joined to 2 Corinthians 9 and was lost. That leads to the following thesis: A redactor deprived 2 Corinthians 10–13 of its independence as a letter and placed the four-chapter letter as a block without introduction at the close of the present 2 Corinthians.

This literary-critical operation, of course, is still not sufficient to explain the changing situations and inconsistencies in 2 Corinthians. On closer examination we can observe in the letter three different and unharmonizable relationships between Paul and the church. In the first situation Paul must defend himself against reproaches put forward especially by the foreign missionaries. The topic here is his apostolic conduct of life and his kind of preaching (2 Cor. 2:17; 3:1–2; 4:2–3; 6:3). These reproaches are not treated as excessively as in 2 Corinthians 10–13; rather, Paul centers his comments on a long presentation on the Spirit-effected freedom of the gospel, on Christian hope, and on the apostolic ministry of reconciliation (3:4–6:2). Thus he wants to describe his standpoint primarily through positive discussion. He does this in the knowledge that the church is basically devoted to him and a relationship of mutual trust still exists, so that he can speak in a warm, fatherly, solicitous tone (6:11–13; 7:2–4). Accordingly, Paul is suspicious of recent events in Corinth, takes the foreign missionaries' criticism of himself seriously but reckons that his earlier good relationship with the church has suffered no damage and that, by building on it with a moderately polemical yet largely objective presentation of his understanding of the gospel, he can overcome the outside danger.

The second situation can be understood as an aggravation of the one just described. It is the one that comes to light in the apologia of 2 Corinthians 10–13. Paul now takes the reproaches of the foreign missionaries so seriously that he devotes himself exclusively to them. He attacks relentlessly, even turning the opponents into devils (cf., e.g., 10:2, 12; 11:5–6, 12–14). He feels so deeply struck by their reproaches that he resorts to a quite extraordinary means of defending himself against their reproaches: he gives a fool's speech (11:16–12:13). He realizes that it is not only a simple question of individual reproaches against his person—which are surely there—but of the general understanding of the gospel (11:4). As he later hurls curses at the Judaizers (Gal. 1:6–9), now he calls the superlative apostles disguised servants of Satan (11:13–15) and predicts their terrible end (11:15b). Even his relationship to the church is overburdened and deeply disturbed. He sees an acute danger of losing the church entirely, for it largely agrees with the missionaries and has an anti-Pauline orientation (10:2, 6, 9–11; 11:2–5, 18; 12:11–13, 16). Paul threatens the church and repeatedly announces drastic measures on his next visit (13:2–3, 10): "For I fear that perhaps I may come and find you not what I wish, and that you may find me not what you wish; that perhaps there may be quarreling, jealousy, anger, selfishness, slander, gossip, conceit, and disorder" (12:20). Is this the writing of one who still fancies himself as the master of the situation? Of course, Paul still hopes for the complete renewal of the church and demands its return to order (13:9, 11), but the solemn enumeration of eight descriptions of dissension and misguided dialogue demonstrate how conflict-laden the mutual relationship between Paul and the church has become.

The third situation is found at the beginning of 2 Corinthians (1: 1–2:13) and in the section 7:5–16. Its basic attitude is joy over reconciliation (1:7, 13–14): "I rejoice, because I have perfect confidence in you" (7:16)—this is the way the comments end. Paul tells the church that he wants to "work with you for your joy" and that "you stand firm in your faith" (1:24). The conflicts of the past echo only in the margins (1:12; 3:1). They are no longer current but are considered overcome. Even the special case of an offense by a church member is to be forgiven (2:5–8). A harsh letter written earlier is now likewise interpreted in a more conciliatory way, so that some of its harshness is removed after the settlement of the conflict (2:4, 9; 7:8–9). The present reconciliation requires a touching up, so to speak, in regard to his understanding.

Since the first situation hardly had to be overcome in a way so demonstratively conciliatory as happened in the third situation, a comparison of situations leads to a historical sequence in the presented order. This can be supported by further observations. According to 13:1, Paul has a third visit in mind after a second went badly for the apostle, since Paul was humbled by many who had not decided on repentance, and he was not able to prevail with them (12:21; 13:2). This second visit must be after the happy time of the longer first stay. It is also mentioned in 1:15–2:11: Paul must justify his changed travel plans, and he makes it clear that he was avoiding another visit with a grievous outcome and instead wrote a letter "out of much affliction and anguish of heart and with many tears" (2:4), which Titus conveyed (2:13). The letter saddened the church, but with Titus's help it also led to a change of heart among the Corinthians (7:6–16).

These text statements lead to the probable sequence. After the second, unsuccessful visit Paul wrote the harsh letter, which Titus conveyed, and then later the letter of reconciliation. It is clear, further, that 2 Cor. 2:14–7:4 must have been written before the hard struggle with the church itself and thus before the second visit, for here the relationship between Paul and the church is still good and the danger from the missionaries is judged to be limited. Now, furthermore, since Paul does not speak until the letter of reconciliation of his mortal danger in Ephesus, which he escaped through flight (1:8–10), everything that happens earlier in the Ephesian period must be placed before the last imprisonment there (cf. 7.1 above). Moreover, the first, still calmly written letter must have been a failure. Afterward Paul decides on the impromptu visit in Corinth and experiences a disaster as complete as any he ever had, as far as we know, during a visit to any of his churches. Then, with the apologia of 2 Corinthians 10–13, written soon thereafter—that is, with the letter of tears, according to 2:4—he is successful.

In this evaluation of the situation, however, a few problems still remain and must be briefly considered. If we make the obvious identification of the harsh letter with the so-called letter of tears (2:4), then we must ask where in these four chapters (2 Corinthians 10–13) Paul is talking about tears. We read about aggression, polemic, irony, and other things, but not really about tears. This problem is resolved, however, if we see that in the letter of reconciliation (i.e., the apologia) there is no objective reasoning. The letter gives no exact table of contents for the annals of history; rather, it intends to put in a better light the burden of the past, which has now fortunately been overcome. Paul wants to say this: The letter written "out of much affliction and anguish of heart"—this characterization is also in the first part of 2:4— is one I wrote at the time out of anxiety about you Corinthians and not really in anger, but with deep sadness ("with many tears").

A further problem is the church member who offended Paul on his interim visit (2:5–11; 7:12). This member is mentioned only in the letter of reconciliation, not in the letter of tears (2 Corinthians 10–13). Does this not speak against the identification of 2 Corinthians 10–13 as the letter of tears? We can also argue the opposite: it may have been the topic earlier in the opening of the letter. Yet this is less likely, because Paul would hardly have jumped right in with this personal affair. It may be, rather, that Paul intentionally disregarded the personal situation in the apologia and that this affair lies hidden in 12:20–21; 13:2; he was primarily concerned with eliminating the influence of the foreign missionaries, since otherwise Corinth was entirely lost for him. This could also be brought into congruence with the remark in 7:12. After the foreign missionaries had departed—which is presupposed in the letter of reconciliation—Paul and the church only had to bring this internal case to a close. Finally, we have to assume that Titus traveled to Corinth with the apologia. It is quite imaginable that in case the church could be won for Paul, Titus had instructions to address this personal situation. For the rest, it is totally unclear why the church member took an offensive position against Paul. If we knew that, we could better evaluate the whole situation. If a little imagination is allowed, we can present the following supposition: The foreign missionaries were staying with this church member. On his interim visit Paul demanded their departure, which this church member resisted out of theological sympathy for the missionaries and also because of the right of guests. This occurred in a way that was very insulting to Paul. Then it would be clear that the missionaries would have to be gone before this case could be settled. Thus the apologia would not yet have been suitable for handling the situation.

In this reconstruction of events from 2 Corinthians, furthermore, we have not made a decision about 2 Corinthians 8–9. Both chapters presuppose that Paul is in Macedonia, writing to a church that is devoted to him and that he has just praised highly in Macedonia because of its enthusiasm for the collection (cf. ch. 2 above). It should be self-evident that this situation only fits that of the letter of reconciliation, but this does not mean that both chapters must belong to it. For many exegetes the two have, at first glance, made an independent impression and, because of their parallelism, aroused the suspicion that they belong to two different occasions. Thus far, however, no one has succeeded in defining a really different situation in the two. Also, there is little sense in assuming two (almost) identical writings sent one shortly after the other to the same church or in provisionally distinguishing the addressees between Corinth and Achaia. Earlier we attempted (cf. ch. 2 above) to explain why Paul possibly spoke in such detail about the collection. Also, it is still simplest to explain 2 Corinthians 8–9 not as a special writing but as the closing of the letter of reconciliation, because otherwise at the end of the apostle's Macedonian stay, Titus would have to have commuted back and forth rather often between Corinth and Paul. Whoever, nonetheless, prefers a complicated solution for 2 Corinthians 8–9 actually gains no real advantage in understanding the events of 2 Corinthians.

Finally, we must again recall that we have already classified 2 Cor. 6:14–7:1 as post-Pauline (cf. 1.1 above) and that we previously became acquainted with two Pauline letters to Corinth: Corinthians A (1 Cor. 5:9) and Corinthians B (= 1 Corinthians). Thus the results of the literary-critical considerations on 2 Corinthians can now be summarized:

1. Foreign missionaries arrive in Corinth (2 Cor. 2:17; 3:1; 5:12; and throughout the apologia).
2. Paul still reacts relatively calmly with letter C (= 2 Cor. 2:14–7:4 without 6:14–7:1), which Titus apparently delivers.
3. The failure of letter C leads to Paul's interim visit, which ends in sharp disagreement.
4. Titus delivers the apologia (= letter D = 2 Corinthians 10–13—the letter of tears or the four-chapter letter).
5. The church sides with Paul. The missionaries depart.
6. Paul escapes Ephesian imprisonment and on the way to Macedonia writes the letter of reconciliation (= letter E = 2 Cor. 1:1–2:13; 7:5–16; chs. 8–9).

If we look at the redactional work of the combining of three letters into the present 2 Corinthians, we may assume that the editor probably did not leave much out—except for a few openings and closings here and there, which were considered unnecessary—because in letters C, D, and E, at any rate, we can observe no large gaps. That does not, however, necessarily lead to the conclusion that he deleted nothing from the formerly independent letters. Nevertheless it is purely speculative to form a judgment about missing sections. We will judge the correspondence on the basis of the texts we have and presuppose that in this way we can describe the situation adequately.

The redactor's viewpoints regarding content can only be surmised. It may be that at first letter E was used as a framework for letter C, so that the conciliatory basic tone could dominate and the plea for the collection would stand at the end. Letter D was later added because in other places also the warning against false teachers, divisions, and dangers for the churches often stands at the close of speeches, letters, and testaments (Matt. 7:21ff.; Rom. 16:17ff.; etc.). The redactor no longer had to be concerned with the success of the collection. Indeed, the letters that the redaction combined in 2 Corinthians were no longer interesting because of the historical problems, but rather as general upbuilding and exhortation for the church. In its own way it could make 2 Corinthians relevant, without taking the concrete Corinthian problems into consideration.

8.4 Ecstasy or Ministry of Reconciliation

The collection of letters in 2 Corinthians shows a lengthy and rather controversial discussion of the foreign missionaries who had come to Corinth. What are the theological points of the dispute? What is the outcome for Pauline theology and Paul's self-understanding? If we view the correspondence from these standpoints, we learn that in comparison with 1 Corinthians the colorful variety of living reality has disappeared. There is no treatment of individual themes that determine life within the church (e.g., party divisions, celebration of the Lord's Supper, worship) or discussion of ethical problems in internal relations (e.g., marital issues, brotherly love) or external relations (e.g., a quarrel before the court, eating meat offered to idols). There is no controversial discussion of aspects and individual themes of the triad faith-love-hope. From this abundance in 1 Corinthians we get an overall picture of the enthusiasm only through repeated reading and reflection, a picture that must be taken into account as the basic attitude regarding many of the named phenomena. By contrast, in 2 Corinthians everything is characterized exclusively by the uncompromising tension between the spiritual self-understanding and corresponding self-representation of the foreign missionaries on the one hand and the analogous Pauline position on the other. Thus the itinerant missionaries who have recently entered the church are the decisive cause of 2 Corinthians. The controversy is characterized not by individual dogmatic or ethical problems but by the fundamental question of the true understanding of an apostle and his proclamation: Who can lay claim to apostolic self-consciousness, and how should he express himself when service to the gospel of Jesus Christ is the appropriate standard?

The posing and the exploration of these questions also point immediately to the difference from the problems in Galatians (cf. ch. 11 below). The foreign missionaries in Corinth are, of course, also former Jews (2 Cor. 11:22) like the Judaizers in Galatia, but their Christian self-understanding does not allow them to advocate circumcision and the law. Therefore their Jewish heritage no longer plays a role. They are not Judaizers, have no relation to the original Jerusalem church, and do not appeal to a prominent Jewish-Christian figure (e.g., Peter). Rather, like Paul and many other Christians of the first generation of early Christianity, they have laid aside their Judaism. Similar to Paul, they would reject the requirement of circumcision as a return to the observance of the law overcome by Christ. They no doubt agree with Paul's formulation: "Where the Spirit of the Lord is, there is freedom" (2 Cor. 3:17). They also harmonize so well with the Corinthian church precisely because they live as Gentile Christians and see Christianity as realized in certain experiences of the Spirit. They are enthusiasts who support the Corinthians against Paul and his theology of the cross; for a time the Corinthians readily listened to them, because they experienced mutual enthusiastic sympathy.

Then did the new missionaries advocate doctrine no different from Paul, for example, in Christology, eschatology, and anthropology? They may have, but this can no longer be determined with sufficient clarity from 2 Corinthians, because Paul concentrated his efforts on describing the differences as two mutually exclusive ways of understanding Christian apostleship and its commission. Naturally Paul also sees that the enthusiastic theology of experience implies its own understanding of religion and theology (2 Cor. 11:4). Thus he develops his understanding of the gospel and apostleship expressly in terms of content (2 Cor. 3:4–6:2). He polemicizes, however, not against individual details of another theology but against its point of departure. He wants to show how and why an understanding of apostleship on the basis of the theology of the cross excludes in principle an interpretation of apostleship on the basis of certain present experiences of the Spirit.

To this extent Paul seems to have correctly struck the fundamental concern of the foreign missionaries. Those who make the experience of ecstatically belonging to the heavenly world the starting point of Christian understanding and consider the demonstration of superiority over everything earthly to be the direct consequence of such enthusiastic immediacy with the exalted Lord will, of course, see all Christian tradition in this light; but they do not necessarily have to design a theology that one can condemn as heresy, like, for example, the docetism in 1 John. The spiritual experience can take absolute precedence over all development of a theology. The greater one regards the immediacy with Christ on the basis of that experience, the less a detailed doctrinal development will be the focus of attention or necessary. Ecstatic experience translates into heavenly being. That is always more important than later reflection about what can be worked out subsequently as doctrine. The missionaries' thoughts may have been along such lines. Their missionary aim may have consisted only in lighting the fire of the Spirit everywhere and promoting ecstatic experience. Those who want to credit Paul's opponents with a fully developed heresy must ask themselves whether they are perhaps seeking something that historically did not exist. And even if we suppose it did, there still remains the limitation of a reconstruction through the manner in which Paul deals with the missionaries. That limitation consists in two things: in his decision to go into a discussion of principles concentrated only on the understanding of the term "apostle" and on his commission to preach, and in the typically polemical structure of the argument (cf. 7.2 above).

This concentration on a crucial point in a polemical situation is also common in Paul's other writings; indeed, it plainly characterizes his way of leading a discussion. Thus we know so little about the party divisions in Corinth from 1 Corinthians 1–4, because Paul, pushing aside the individual phenomena, discusses fundamentally why rivalry within the church contradicts the nature of the gospel (cf. 8.2 above). Or, in another example, in the speech against Peter, according to Gal. 2:14–21 (cf. 5.3 above; 11.2 below), Paul focuses the problem on the closing assertion: If righteousness can be attained through the law, then Christ died in vain. These examples, which could be multiplied, show that this way of discussing is often chosen by Paul.

Of course, there have been repeated attempts to reconstruct a theology of the opponents. The question of their Christology has naturally stood at the center of interest. At this point there are suggestions ranging from a docetic and thus Gnostic Christology to a Jewish-Hellenistic Christology of the God-man (*theios anēr*), linked with the cultivation of a corresponding Jesus tradition, to a conception of Jesus as the second Moses and eschatological prophet (which can be well related to the God-man Christology). It almost gives the appearance that, faced with the meager indications in 2 Corinthians itself, one wants to try out the broad religious-historical palette of the time. In any case, the richness of variations shows how ambiguous the evidence is and how hypothetical the reconstructive effort. This will be elucidated with two examples.

The antithesis of old and new covenant in 2 Cor. 3:4–18 has been used to reconstruct an earlier version from the difficult text. Based on Exodus 34, the earlier text is supposed to deal positively with Moses and with Jesus as the perfecter of Moses. Paul, on the other hand, in his comments is thought to depreciate the concept antithetically in the light of the new covenant. The earlier text is supposed to reflect the theology of the foreign missionaries, so that Paul attempts to overcome their position by reinterpreting the biblical text and the opponents' position and by adding his own antithetically. Quite apart from the doubtfulness of such exact reconstruction of an earlier text that is so contrary (!) to Paul, the attribution of the same to the opponents is pure speculation. The mere indication of the missionaries' Jewish origins (2 Cor. 11:22) naturally cannot assure such an assumption. Above all, however, through this procedure Paul casts such a reflection on himself that we can hardly believe him capable of it: How does the apostle intend to convince anyone whose holy text and whose own understanding of the same is completely turned back by the opponent? We must assume, rather, that because Paul agrees with Corinth and the missionaries in the corresponding depreciation of the old covenant, he can use this—certainly not newly conceived—exegesis of Exodus 34 (cf. 5.5 above) to present his understanding of the gospel and his own commission.

In addition to 2 Cor. 5:16 (cf. here 5.6 above), interest in the search for the opponents' Christology is also focused in 2 Cor. 11:4, where from the formulation that the opponent "preaches another Jesus" the conclusion has been drawn that the opponents have a docetic doctrine about the earthly Jesus or a God-man (*theios anēr*) understanding of the earthly One. Now, from time to time, of course, Paul can use *Jesus* absolutely (without saying, e.g., *Jesus Christ*) to express the idea of the earthly Jesus (2 Cor. 4:10–11; Gal. 6:17), but he also uses a simple *Jesus* as *Jesus Christ* or *Jesus the Lord* (cf. only Rom. 3:26; 8:11; 2 Cor. 4:14; 1 Thess. 1:10; 4:14). Thus from this standpoint the formulation in 2 Cor. 11:4 is not unambiguous, especially since in the immediate context (11:2–3) Paul has just used the *Christ* title. Yet we must, above all, voice the criticism that the context of the statement has been entirely neglected. In its full wording it reads: "For if some one comes and preaches another Jesus than the one we preached, or if you receive a different spirit from the one you received [from us], or if you accept a different gospel from the one you accepted [from us], you submit to it readily enough." Here we cannot tear apart the triad of Christology, pneumatology, and proclamation. Rather, the statement as a whole and in its contextual function is intended to emphasize that these three basic elements, which stand for a description of all of Christianity, are understood by the opponents in a way that is different from Paul. He is not speaking of a different teaching about the earthly One, but an altogether different understanding of Christianity. Theology of the cross and enthusiasm stand in opposition to each other.

If the search for a Christology contrary to Paul makes little sense in view of the source situation, then we can pay even more concentrated attention to the description of the broadly discussed antithesis regarding the understanding of apostleship. Within the Corinthian correspondence this discussion occurs first in letter C, which has its center almost entirely—namely, in 2 Cor. 2:14–6:10—in a presentation of Paul's apostolic service that in detail is often especially hard to understand, yet is clear in broad outlines. Paul looks at his preaching ministry from two viewpoints: first from that of the divine glory (2 Cor. 2:14–4:6 = part 1) and then under the leitmotiv of the earthly nothingness and weakness of apostolic existence (2 Cor. 4:7–6:10 = part 2). Part 1 begins the great intellectual arch with the image of the triumph of Christian proclamation. God arranges it; Paul is the means by which God accomplishes it

(2:14–16). We find the end of the arch in 4:5–6. Here Paul describes how the victorious triumph of Christ (2:14) comes to its goal: The power of the Creator-God is at work in the gospel. It lights up the hearts, so that in them the knowledge of the glory of Christ spreads, which changes the believers from glory to glory (cf. 3:18).

Under this arch of the glorification of the power and the content of the gospel stands the basic question, Who is competent for service to this gospel (2:16c)? The first answer is given in 2:17–3:3: Paul is demonstrably competent, because through him, as apostle, the Corinthians have experienced in their hearts the power of the gospel, that is, the Spirit of the living God as the power that changes them and creates salvation, for they are a Pauline missionary success. The second answer (3:4–11) says that God himself enabled Paul to be the servant of the new covenant and thus of the life-giving Spirit. A third answer follows in 3:12–18: Paul can practice his service in such a way that without having to hide anything he can proclaim with great openness the glory of the Lord. Finally in 4:1–6 comes a last answer, in which is integrated the end of the arch in 4:5–6: The open proclamation of the truth does not always lead to the desired goal but brings about a separation between believers and nonbelievers. The success of the gospel is ambivalent.

Great is the power and glory of the gospel of Jesus Christ! This is the title we could give to part 1. The opponents of the apostle certainly liked to hear the triumphal statements as such. In particular the triumph over death and the immediate inner illumination and transformation, as it is expressed at the beginning and at the end of the arch, no doubt were met with willing agreement. Those are words and content which the missionaries and the Corinthians liked to hear. Paul probably knew that and considered it as he conceived his letter. The quarrel would therefore be about whether the competence that Paul claimed for this service is applauded by the missionaries. This is apparently the way that Paul himself also sees the dialogue situation, for the question in 2:16c, "Who is sufficient for these things?" (e.g., service to the gospel), is not answered generally but is discussed as if it read, "Am I, perchance, not sufficient for these things?"

Now particularly in part 2 this uncertainty with the personal aspect receives full attention. If Paul suddenly abandoned the theology of the glory of the gospel by turning his attention away from himself—he is only an instrument in the triumph (2:14); the church is the work of Christ (3:2–3); his competence for service comes from God (3:5); he does not preach himself but Christ (4:5)—he now pointedly describes his apostolic existence with predicates of humility and nothingness, knowing that this is not what his opponents want to hear as criteria for apostleship. They would rather take the immediacy of divine knowledge and transformation into the glory of Christ as the occasion to present themselves as already perfected. Was this not the old Corinthian spirit that Paul had already addressed in 1 Corinthians (cf. 1 Cor. 2:10ff.; 3:7–8; and 8.2 above)?

We pause here for two incidental comments, one on form and one on content. In terms of form we must note that Paul in other places as well can formulate a section describing or creating a consensus, in order then to bring out the controversy. In 1 Corinthians 15, for example, concerning the quarrel over the understanding of the resurrection, Paul first describes the common, undisputed basis (1 Cor. 15:1–11) in order then to discuss the controversy and lead to his solution. Or: in Gal. 3:1–5 Paul exhorts the Galatians to remember the common first mission between him and them, in order subsequently to go into the quarrel over law and gospel. As a last, randomly chosen example, 1 Corinthians 8 should serve. Again Paul introduces the discussion about meat offered to idols (8:1–6) with a consensus. Then he takes up his position in the current dispute.

Regarding the observation on content, it is astonishing how persistently the apostle maintains from 1 Corinthians to letter C the sole effectiveness and power of the word of God and the theology of the cross with its important aspects for Corinth (cross of Christ as content of the gospel, suffering of the apostle, weakness of Pauline speech). It is also striking how in both places he brings this theological position to bear with such different linguistic means, available traditions, and varied conceptual shaping of the epistolary segments. For the penetration of a problem area and its creative presentation, Paul without doubt had strikingly great talent—even and precisely in relation to early Christianity.

We can describe part 2 in detail as follows. The beginning in 2 Cor. 4:7 marks the new viewpoint: "We have this treasure [namely, the heart-transforming gospel that was just so highly glorified] in [fragile] earthen vessels, to show that the transcendent power belongs to God [alone] and not to us." Formally, here too, as in part 1, the arch is drawn from this beginning to the conclusion: "as poor, yet making many rich; as having nothing, and yet possessing everything" (6:10). Everything that is said in between serves this dialectic. Four intellectual steps can be recognized. In the first section (4:7–15) the apostle's "carrying in the body the death of Jesus" is described in four diastases, so that the "life of Jesus" can also become visible (4:7–10). Such sufferings of the apostle, in which he has the experience of not being abandoned by God, have the missionary goal of winning people on the basis of the sole effectiveness of the gospel and nourishing the hope that Paul and his churches will together take part in Jesus' resurrection (4:11–15). The second section (4:16–5:10) begins in a style analogous to the first (4:16–18). It places the destruction of the outer person in dialectical tension with the simultaneous renewal of the inner person in order then (again completely analogous to the first section) to continue with reasons (cf. 4:11) why this tension will one day be resolved in confidently expected heavenly dwelling with the Lord (5:1–10). The third section is formally also structured in a way similar to the first two (5:11–6:2: [a] 5:11–13; [b] 5:14–6:2). It shows how Paul, under the conditions discussed in the two preceding sections, now proclaims the content of the gospel that contains the message of reconciliation, as substantiated by the cross of Christ. In the last section (6:3–10) Paul summarizes in closing the description of his apostolic existence: he gives no one offense and proves himself as God's servant in tribulations, in dealing with the Christian gifts of the gospel, and in the contradictions of being misunderstood and being recognized.

In retrospect, the short trip through letter C makes two things clear: 2 Cor. 2:14–6:10 is not fragmentary in content. Whatever may have fallen by the wayside in the redaction, the part that has been retained is thematically and formally well rounded. In content letter C shows how Paul is personally attacked in his service and therefore must describe his service. The designation *service* for missionary activity is general in early Christianity (Rom. 12:7; 1 Cor. 12:5; cf. Rom. 16:1; 1 Cor. 3:5), but apparently an especially beloved characterization of the foreign missionaries for their activity, for nowhere does this word stem occur as often as in 2 Corinthians. According to 2 Cor. 11:23, the missionaries expressly call themselves "servants of Christ" (cf. 11:15). Thus Paul uses their language without being guided by an expression completely foreign to him. In the process he designed his argumentation chiefly so as to make his position clear to the church. Only now and then does he make it clear in a direct way that he is now talking about the foreign missionaries. In these cases the style and train of thought are both marked by the opposition of two standpoints (e.g., 2:17; 3:1, 5; 4:2–3, 5; 5:12–13; 6:3–4); he rejects the one (first clause with negation), and the second he sets positively against the first (style: "but . . ."). Beyond that, there may also be indirect or hidden allusions to the opponents' understanding, but they are uncertain. Therefore we will discuss especially the open and thus unambiguous indications.

The organization of the letter, as we said, makes it clear that the issue of personal suitability for apostolic service (2:16; 3:5–6; 5:5) is controversial. In Paul's judgment, the opponents "claim" something "as coming from [themselves]," whereas Paul bases his competence on God alone (3:5). The opponents "pride themselves" by pointing to themselves and their abilities (5:12). The continuation in 5:13 makes it clear that the abilities are ecstatic experiences. As already in 1 Cor. 14:13–19, however, Paul wants to do this only in the private presence of God and have missions and congregational preaching presented as understandable speech. Therefore, in 2 Cor. 2:14–6:10, Paul remains entirely silent about his own ecstasy and develops—in the spirit of 1 Corinthians 14—his apostolic understanding of the gospel as understandable speech by interpreting the reconciliation from God that is spread through Christ (5:14ff.). Later, in letter D—and only out of necessity—he will, as a fool in Christ, go into the special pneumatic experiences (12:1ff.). There Paul will paradoxically describe his ecstatic heavenly trip without mentioning to the church a revelation, yet he will let everyone know the answer to his request to be freed from his illness, because it is relevant to the church; and from the standpoint of the theology of the cross, it divinely authorizes his understanding of his apostleship.

From these observations we may conclude that the opponents were, so to speak, virtuosos of ecstatic experience. Their "boasting" consists in the description of what they have experienced, for example, as heavenly trips and in the demonstrative presentation of their ecstasies in the worship of the church, so that the believers are carried along with it. In this way the disturbances in the Corinthian worship service (cf. 1 Corinthians 14) are continued by other persons, who credit themselves with such abilities: We can transport ourselves and the church ecstatically into heaven and thus share—and cause others to share—in perfection! Since they are itinerant missionaries, they are pleased when the church they are leaving gives them written accounts of everything they have accomplished ecstatically in that church. These are probably the "letters of recommendation" that Paul so energetically rejects in 3:1 and because of which he generally detests a self-recommendation so strongly (5:13).

Paul permits only one possible recommendation. The preaching of the cross and the Spirit working in it grasp the hearts of people, who in this way are overcome from within by the love of Christ (5:14). Thus, in contrast to the Corinthian opponents, Paul does not point to his calling. In his understanding his conversion is not an initial ecstatic experience after which it is possible to attach others permanently through this ecstasy. It is, rather, a onetime authorization for the understandable interpretation of the gospel, through which alone God works. Where such sole effectiveness of the divine word creates the church, there the apostle is recommended (3:1–3). It also becomes clear how Paul can call the activity of the missionaries indirectly a self-proclamation (3:5; 5:12): in them he misses the historical reference to the idea that "God was in Christ"

(5:19) and diagnoses that their ecstatic experiences have become the content of their proclamation. Where the present experience of faith loses contact with the cross of Christ, the word of God is falsified (4:2–3). The present immediacy of ecstatic fusion with eternity eclipses the divine act of salvation in Christ. The latter must be made known to the conscience (5:11), and this includes apostolic existence as similar to the death of Christ (4:9–10). In this way Paul contrasts the ecstasy, which is contagious and leads to overcoming the world, with the gospel message, which is understandable to everyone (5:14ff.), which speaks to conscience and heart (3:3; 5:11), leads to faith (4:13–14); and through the faith experience of how God saves in lostness and nothingness (4:16ff.) nourishes the hope of final salvation beyond the last judgment (5:1–10).

Paul has one last objection to the missionaries, which irks him so much that he comments on it right at the beginning: "We are not, like so many, peddlers of God's word" (2:17). These new missionaries let themselves be paid for the application of their pneumatic power. Paul had already written to the Corinthians once before on this matter (1 Cor. 9:13ff.), so he does not go into it again. He states his clear dissent only briefly. This part of the problem is not worth more to him here. It is clear even in 1 Corinthians 9 that Paul's refusal of support by the church is the exception. The usual and generally practiced rule was that missionaries are fed by the churches. Thus when Paul attacks the missionaries on this point, he will not meet with immediate understanding.

Perhaps for a moment we can ignore this picture of the foreign missionaries in the mirror of the Pauline polemic in order to describe at least the rudiments of the ecstatics' self-understanding. Perhaps they will say against Paul that simply from speaking about the Spirit and about Christ, he never gets around to leading the church into the Spirit and to Christ. That is, he above all ties the church retroactively to the history of Jesus Christ and not to the exalted One. Did Christ not overcome the cross? Why, then, should we cling to what is overcome? Christologically this is old-fashioned and out-of-date, for Christ is now the exalted One, whose Spirit is supposed to blow through the church in order to bind it to himself. According to the Pauline standpoint, as they see it, Christianity is therefore given only indirectly. The important thing, however, is to live it as the immediate experience of the Spirit and the direct relationship to the exalted One. Because Paul does not do this—and apparently cannot do it at all, since he does not offer proof of the Spirit and of power—he is not a true apostle. The church has too little when it follows him. Therefore Paul's initial work in Corinth must be completed in the Spirit. They have come for this purpose. Gospel and faith are good; Spirit and ecstasy as heavenly release from the world are better.

The apostle hoped that with letter C he would win the church again for himself. It did not work out this way. The conflict intensified, particularly through his interim visit (cf. 7.1 above). Afterward Paul again reached for his pen and wrote letter D, the apologia of his apostleship (cf. 8.3 above). A look back to letter C shows how Paul continues his theme of the theology of the cross from 1 Corinthians. A look forward to letter D shows how in this letter the apostle uses the theology of the cross even more pointedly against his opponents.

8.5 Paul as a Fool in Christ

Behind Paul is the visit in Corinth that led to disaster, humiliation, and sadness (2 Cor. 10:1, 10; 12:20–21). Ahead of him are plans for another visit, which can be announced only with threatening gestures and the pledge of harsh and drastic measures (10:6, 11; 12:20–21; 13:2). And the present is burdened with the struggle against the "superlative apostles" (11:5; 12:11) and a severely strained relationship with the church (11:7, 12, 19–20; 12:20–21; 13:9), which he still jealously loves (11:2; 12:14–15). These are hardly good conditions for successful communication. Also, the letter itself (2 Corinthians 10–13 = letter D—cf. 8.3 above), which Paul, deeply wounded, writes aggressively and harshly, begins right away with a discussion of reproaches against the apostle (10:1, 7, 10) and ends with a demand for subjection (13:9, 11a). Certainly, this did not promote a good outcome of the dialogue, which seems more like an exchange of blows. And yet, without wanting to diminish the role that Titus may have played in the reconciliation, we must say that it was this letter, not letter C, which led the church back again to Paul.

Moreover, the astonishment expressed regarding letter C (cf. 8.4 above) increases again with the reading of this apologia of the Pauline apostleship, if we consider how in a brief time Paul can concretize his theology of the cross again in such an intellectually rich and independent way. The imaginative stratagem of doing this with a fool's talk (11:16–12:13) is a strong sign of the apostle's rhetorical and conceptual abilities. This judgment is valid, whatever the opponents may have thought about Paul's rhetoric. It is also rewarding to compare, say, 1 Corinthians 1–4, letter C, and letter D as the essential representatives of the Pauline theology of the cross and thus make discoveries about the flexibility and creativity of the apostle, in order to understand how great were Paul's opportunities to continue his theological initiative, to give it new linguistic form, and within limits to modify it.

In the center of the apologia is the fool's talk (11:16–12:13), which culminates in the revealed statement in 12:9a. This has fundamental and normative significance for the whole speech. If the superlative apostles boast of ecstatically belonging to the heavenly world, then Paul can also base his theology of the cross—which boasts its weakness and thus makes room for God's power—on his special revelation, which he experienced in regard to his illness: "My grace is sufficient for you, for my power is made perfect [especially] in weakness." This is the only personal revelation whose content Paul shares with the church, whereas the superlative apostles probably have many to report. With this one he devalues all others and opens the way to understanding apostolic existence in the sense of the theology of the cross. Thus around the fool's talk he frames two parts, with the beginning and closing parts often corresponding in their themes (cf. 2 Cor. 10:2a with 12:14; 13:1—2 Cor. 11: 7ff. with 12:14–18—2 Cor. 10:2 with 12:20ff.; 13:2b—2 Cor. 10:8 with 12: 19b—2 Cor. 10:7 with 13:3—2 Cor. 10:9–11 with 13:10), because in each case the disputed apostle sees himself faced with the same problems.

In the opening part (10:1–11:15) the apostle purposefully goes right into three reproaches that are raised against him. In 10:1–11 Paul argues against the reproach that he is personally weak in appearance though "his letters are weighty and strong" (10:1, 11). Then 10:12–18 revolves around comparison, boasting, and self-commendation (10:12, 13, 18), in which the opponents are great and make Paul small. Finally, in 11:1–15 Paul devotes himself to the reproach that because he is clumsy in speech, he does not have the courage to let himself be fed by the church (11:6–7). The three passages increase in aggression and denigration of the opponents. In 10:2, 7, Paul refers to the opponents in a way that is still relatively mild; in 10:12–13 they are given a thorough scolding. In 11:13–15, finally, they become decidedly satanic. The apostle deals with the three reproaches in different ways. The first will be refuted on his third visit, if necessary (10:2, 6, 8, 11). He admits to a certain weakness that he has shown in his previous visits (11:21; 13:3–4, 9). Regarding the third reproach, he begs the church for forgiveness (12:13b), so that only the middle one requires a thorough epistolary treatment. This happens in the fool's talk. With this, Paul has once again focused a complex discussion on a single point that for him is theologically crucial.

The fool's talk in the middle of the letter likewise conceals within its framework (11:16–21a; 12:11–13) three sections. In 11:21b–33 the focus is on the great catalog of outside influences, with whose help Paul boasts his weaknesses. It is followed by descriptions of the two revelations (12:1–6, 7–10). The closing section (12:14–13:10) revolves around the preparation of the church for the apostle's third coming; even then he will not become a burden for the church (12:14–18), but he will take harsh and drastic measures (12:19–21) and act in God's power (13:1–4), if the church does not examine itself beforehand on the basis of his stern letter (13:5–10). In the closing section Paul no longer talks about the opponents. He presupposes that when he comes he will have to deal only with the congregation. This probably means that he will come only if the church has already made the foreign missionaries move on. In fact, this is how the church reacted, for the letter of reconciliation presupposes this situation (cf. 8.3 above): in it Paul only has to clear up his relationship with the church completely; the interloping missionaries have disappeared.

Based on the insight that for Paul the fool's talk addresses the crucial point of controversy, it makes sense to use it as a standpoint for interpreting letter D. Its framework makes clear where the lines are drawn. The church is to let him have his own way as a fool. It is to tolerate his boasting. After all, the Corinthians bear it even when the superlative apostles make slaves of them, prey upon them, take advantage of them, put on airs, and strike them in the face (11:20): five harsh judgments of the opponents' appearance and at the same time descriptions of the bondage and humiliation of the church. For such modes of behavior, of course, Paul is "too weak," but here already he sounds the key word of what he wants to boast about, namely, his weaknesses (11:16–21a). At the close he summarizes: Of necessity he has become a fool, even if the church would have to boast about him before the superlative apostles. In nothing is he inferior to them, although he is nothing, for the signs of the apostle have been accomplished by him among the church members. They have not been shortchanged in his mission (12:11–13).

Paul then holds up to the church his boasting talk first by recounting especially his apostolic sufferings. In this way he is the servant of Christ. Here he seems to strive for a certain completeness. Thus, after the close in 11:30–31, he apparently adds the flight from Damascus (11:32–33; cf. formally 1 Cor. 1:16), in order not to leave out anything he can now remember. Also, he does not want this section of the letter on his sufferings to come out shorter than the description of the "visions and revelations" (2 Cor. 12:1). In this way 11:21b–33 contains the longest catalog of outside influences Paul ever wrote. If he as a servant of Christ boasts in this way of his weaknesses, the foreign missionaries presumably boasted of their strengths. They understand themselves as servants of Christ because of their ecstatic experiences. With these they enslave the church and exploit it, manifest an arrogant self-confidence, and reflect themselves in their revelations. Because Paul knows this, he himself has to speak of such experiences (12:1ff.).

In order to achieve a literary balance with his description of weakness, he now becomes taciturn. With two like-structured and typified sentences (12:2 and 12:3–4) he describes in detached fashion a rapture into the third heaven, that is, into paradise. Something like this could actually come from the material from which the ecstasies of the superlative apostles came. They rise above their earthly existence through ecstatic heavenly trips. What did Paul experience on such a journey that would be analogous to the self-proclamations of the superlative apostles? Can he also proclaim special revelations to the church? The result of the rapture is captured in the short, supplementary final clause of 12:4b. His eyes have seen no heavenly typography; only his ears have perceived anything at all, yet his tongue is incapable of uttering the sounds.

That there is a heavenly home (paradise) prepared for believers was already known to the faith (1 Corinthians 15; 2 Cor. 5:1ff.; Phil 3:20–21). Yet this eternal home now remained invisible even in ecstasy (cf. 2 Cor. 4:18). The Spirit attests that all Christians are fellow heirs with Christ (Rom. 8:16–17). Yet under the conditions of the sufferings of the present time (Rom. 8:18; cf. analogously 2 Cor. 11:23ff.) there is only the hope for what Christians still do not see but patiently expect (Rom. 8:24–25). It is also futile to seek Christ in heaven or in the underworld; rather, he is near in the gospel (Rom. 10:5–8). Therefore in the rapture Paul experienced nothing more that he could communicate. Thus the "fruitlessness" of Paul's heavenly trip—even if it prompts the disapproval of the superlative apostles—is for Paul precisely the result for whose sake he now discusses the matter. It is good enough to show that except for the gospel there is no revelation with its own content. Thus the situation can remain the same as it was when Paul wrote to the church earlier: Christians as well as apostles have the treasure of the gospel—there is no other revelation—only in fragile earthen vessels (2 Cor. 4:7; cf. 11:23ff.).

The church does not have to conclude this with difficulty indirectly from the result of the rapture, which lacks a result of its own. Paul can perform this for the church directly in connection with a further revelation and thereby also provide the hermeneutical key to the understanding of 12:4b (12:6–10). Namely, if Paul wanted to behave differently and, just like the superlative apostles in the church, boast of his heavenly experiences, he would be prevented by his affliction. This is described by Paul again in more eloquent fashion, because he has now turned once more to his weaknesses. Here he uses the typical language of the recounting of healing miracles (stylized description of the illness, petition for healing, and authoritative answer) and also shapes the two-part denial of healing (authoritative divine decision and substantiation) in the form of typological language. Thus Paul presents the revelation in a superindividual linguistic model. To this extent the experienced world and the recounted world are surely to be distinguished. In terms of content the description asserts that an angel of Satan pushed a thorn into his body. Satan is the tempter (1 Cor. 7:5; 2 Cor. 2:11), who is also a hindrance for Paul elsewhere (1 Thess. 2:18); he will be annihilated by God in the end (Rom. 16:20) but now allies himself with the superlative apostles (2 Cor. 11:13–15). Paul is burdened by an affliction (cf. 7.3 above) that prevents him from becoming arrogant. Thus ends the description of the affliction; now follows the petition for healing. He besought God for recovery three times—this indicates that any further petition is pointless. The heavenly authoritative answer is a final and recountable speech like the gospel, because it corresponds to the gospel's basic meaning. Then Paul turns again to the theme of the catalog of outside influences in 11:23ff. The "visions and revelations" (12:1) lead to no other result than the sufferings added from the outside to the apostle in his apostolic office. He is to be the weak apostle, so that the grace of God that is near in the gospel can demonstrate its power visibly as the only effective power. Therefore Paul wants to boast of his weakness and not of some strength, as do the superlative apostles, who fancy themselves to be something because of their ecstasies. He wants to accept his miserable experiences of all kinds with affirmation, because then he does not have to ascend into the heaven of ecstasy like the missionaries; rather, the power of Christ then descends to him as the power of the gospel that is near (Rom. 10:8–9). Therefore he is paradoxically strong when he is weak.

This shows how, in a way that is analogous in content to letter C (cf. 8.4 above), Paul understands his existence from the standpoint of the theology of the cross and in this perspective sees the real antithesis to the opponents, who try to overcome the destiny of death in this world (1 Cor. 15:26, 54–55) even now by crossing over into heaven. Instead of such a rising above earthly limitation, threat of death, weakness, and pain, Paul pleads for their acceptance, so that in, with, and through them one can experience the now (2 Cor. 6:2) near (12:9b) divine word of reconciliation (5:20–21). With this he challenges his opponents and the church by being basically in agreement with the latter that his apostolic existence—like all Christian existence—must present itself believably. Credibility is substantiated only in a way quite contrary to that of the missionaries. They offer the unusual, the experience of ecstasy, which leaves earthly conditions behind. Then, logically, they reproach Paul, saying that he still lives in these earthly circumstances, and precisely this is suspect (10:2). Paul insists on a proof of experience right in the middle of the most adverse conditions of the world, so that therein the power that is divine and thus superior to the world can be perceived (10:3; 12:7–9). The other Jesus, the other Spirit, the other gospel (11:4)—in short, the other understanding of Christianity—are thus exposed.

This systematic pervasiveness of an initially diffuse problem and the examination of its inherent principles are without doubt also a strength of the apostle elsewhere. Yet in the process he never failed to omit from consideration the concrete individual phenomena. This occurs in 2 Corinthians 10–13 before the fool's talk. The apostles (inference from 11:5; 12:11) and servants of Christ (11:15, 23), as they no doubt call themselves, not only live in their ecstasies; they also translate the resulting feeling of superiority into action. They appear in a personally imposing fashion and prepare themselves for competition in that they extol their ecstatic advantages as signs of apostolic legitimation, they do this in a rhetorically well versed manner, and they let themselves be fed by the church as a matter of course (inferences from 10:1–11, 15; cf. also 12:11–13). Since Paul is and does the opposite, he is considered disqualified, because he consistently avoids providing such a legitimation (cf. 13:3). All of this corresponds almost exactly to the situation in letter C, except that in the apologia the letters of recommendation are not expressly named, and in letter C, on the other hand, the question of the appropriate rhetoric of the gospel still stands in the background. Especially strident also is the way Paul at the beginning of the apologia slings out the reproaches against him in a concentrated charge, as it were, and dismisses them or goes on a counteroffensive. It is conceivable that 2 Cor. 10:1–11, 15 reflects the state of the discussion as Paul remembers it from his interim visit.

If we want to do historical justice to the foreign missionaries, we must make clear that their phenotype was not unusual in the Hellenism of the early Christian period but occurred rather often. It is Paul who sets himself apart from it from the very beginning. Thus the Corinthian church was well acquainted with the type of such "superlative apostles"; it was Paul's understanding of his apostleship that was at first foreign to them. For what Acts reports about the Athenians—that they were always eager to hear something new (Acts 17:18–21)—applies equally well to the Corinthians and all the other Hellenistic cities of the time. The marketplaces and schools of rhetoric and philosophy, as well as the junctions of trade routes, had always been the meeting places of wandering heralds of salvation such as Sophists, rhetoricians, magicians, and miracle workers. Itinerant preachers with teachings of salvation were plentiful enough; why should Christianity not also make use of such promotional possibilities? Naturally people did not always regard them as "gods . . . in the likeness of men" and want to make sacrifices to them, as in the case of Paul and Barnabas at Lystra (Acts 14:11–13). But they were quite often believed capable of extraordinary contacts and relations with the world of the gods and their special powers (cf. Acts 8:9–11). And the teachers of salvation themselves, naturally, played out their mastery of superhuman powers and abilities, their sovereignty over merely human and normal everyday things, gained through their divine power, their secret, profound knowledge of the powers of nature. They extolled their abilities, through which, they claimed, people were strengthened in the face of an evil fate and could be freed from serious illness and trouble and become friends of the gods, who would have mercy on them in Hades after their death. They provided a bit of superiority over fate and the world; they could not make the lot of humans like that of the gods but could still grant the human race a limited share in divine power and perfection and at least moderate misery and hopelessness. They could let people experience the nearness of the gods and teach them that human beings also come from the divine race (cf. Acts 17:28). As divine humans distinguished from the people, they were mediators of divine powers and teachings.

They advocated this and combined it with a demonstratively distinct way of living. In personal appearance they tried to stand out through particular beauty or through an offensive, unkempt look. The competition was stiff, and for effective advertisement they had to resort to special signal colors. Also in their demeanor they liked to cultivate a particular distance from the people; they made a special point of showing off, understood situations and individuals immediately, and played the superior role to the hilt. Also in their life-style they distinguished themselves from the usual. They often lived without a family, made a show of poverty and moderation, and lived from begging and payment for talks, miracles, and so forth (cf. Acts 8:18–19); they got themselves invited into homes, but also they often slept in holy groves, in temple districts, and in the open. They lived in an unsettled, restless fashion—on principle and also because after a short time they were all too often revealed as charlatans, were chased out of town, or had to flee before the wrath of duped citizens. Since none of these people could work miracles daily or perform demonstrative deeds (e.g., ecstasies, divination), they were especially dependent on making themselves prominent rhetorically. Speaking and debating skills were highly valued. Anyone who could not shine here and persuade the people with blinding rhetoric was soon left behind in this hard, competitive business. Naturally, however, they also had to demonstrate their charismatic power through deeds: miracles, prophecies, interpretation of dreams, and ecstatic events were the favorite means. On the whole, the times were quite addicted to miracles and expected supernatural demonstrations.

The foreign missionaries in Corinth also roughly fit this phenotype. They move around, appear in a demonstrative and imposing way, have better than average rhetorical training and make use of it, boast a special nearness to the heavenly world, and are ecstatics; they let the church clearly sense their prominent special nature and, of course, take it for granted that they will be fed and paid. Thus they are an acute hellenization of Christian mission.

With this background the difference from Paul again becomes clear. Paul appears in weakness; that is, he avoids showing off and presumably was also little suited for cultivating this style. In addition, however, he does not want a prominent separation from the church, for instead of demonstrating power and preserving distance, he personally wants to be close to the church like a father or a mother (cf. 1 Thess. 2:7ff.; also 2 Cor. 6:11–12; 7:3–4). Of course, his preaching is also accompanied by "signs and wonders" (2 Cor. 12:12; Rom. 15:19), but these are not the content of his teaching, nor do they have the purpose of making Paul himself stand out. For him, the real miracle is the gospel, which succeeds on its own. Where churches arise from the proclamation of the gospel, there, in his view, God is at work. For such divine activity Paul will accept no money, although he knows that missionaries are supposed to be supported by the churches. He falls into ecstasy more than the Corinthians, who are richly gifted in that way (1 Cor. 14:18), but that happens in private. He does not ignite mass ecstasy in the church or demonstrate through rapture his superiority to the world. He wants only one thing, to proclaim the gospel as understandable speech, and he relies on the Spirit present in the word to convince people. It is the crucified and not the triumphant Christ that he wants to paint before their eyes (Gal. 3:1; 1 Cor. 1:18ff.), and therefore even his weaknesses and sufferings belong to his apostolic service. Therefore he does not want to wheedle and persuade through purposeful rhetorical means (1 Thess. 2:4–5; 1 Cor. 2:3–4), as taught, say, by Sophist rhetoric, but to missionize convincingly on the basis of the issue and related to the issue. He follows thereby a Ciceronian concern, for example, and yet hardly intends to advocate orthodox Ciceronian rhetoric. For this position is, for him, based on his understanding of the gospel. Since he already indicates his fundamental difference from his Hellenist competitors in 1 Thessalonians 2, and here more generally, we may assume that he consciously dissociated himself from them from the beginning and presented himself as an antitype.

To him, his behavior was in accordance with the gospel alone, for even so he could demonstrate most clearly that he was no deceiver or missionary on the lookout for personal gain. He faces up to the competition by defeating the weaknesses of these missionaries (arrogant appearance, payment, and often deception) through the opposite in his conduct of life (cf. 2 Cor. 1:12; 2:17; 5:11–12; 7:2). We may presume that the Corinthians—in spite of the harsh letter D—understood this and perhaps therefore got rid of the superlative apostles and became reconciled again with the apostle of the crucified Christ. Also, we will be somewhat better able to understand Paul's verdict on his opponents (e.g., 2 Cor. 11:13, 20) if we place ourselves in the opposite position, as practiced by Paul.

We have already spoken of the further events between Paul and Corinth (cf. 7.1 and 8.3 above). Paul is obviously overjoyed when he has won his beloved church back and can write the letter of reconciliation (Corinthians E) from Macedonia: the great polemicist has now become the Paul who is moved by joy and reconciliation.

9
Missionary Churches as House Churches

9.1 The Social Situation of the Churches

The Corinthian correspondence, especially 1 Corinthians, offers the clearest information regarding the nature of the general social structure of the churches. Moreover, from the Corinthian letters in connection with other letters, we can derive clear contours of house churches as the form of social organization in the young churches. These two are interrelated and will therefore be discussed together.

In order to come to a sound judgment in regard to the general social structure, we must begin with a look at general social conditions in antiquity. It is not appropriate to use ideal or modern social orders as a lens for observing early primitive Christianity; rather, the early churches of the Hellenistic cities must be described on the basis of the contemporary fabric of their social conditions. For the characterization of the social stratification in the Roman Empire in the post-Augustan period, we can best orient ourselves with a trisection of a pyramid. The highest level is occupied by the Roman class of senators, immediately followed by the nobility. The two groups could be regarded together as the especially small point of the pyramid. This small number was inversely proportional to the privileges that were theirs by birth and heritage. They amassed, namely, riches, power, and education. Into this stratum Pauline Christianity had not yet penetrated at all. Conversely, the broad base of the pyramid was formed by the especially large mass of the have-nots, slaves, wage earners, craftsmen, peasants, and others. It included the rural population and the urban proletariat. Between the top level and the bottom we find the middle stratum, which, supported by imperial measures, is to be met, above all, in the urban environment and achieved relative affluence through trade, production, or service. When Paul missionized in the cities, he dealt primarily with this propertied class and with the lower urban level. He left out the rural population in his missionary efforts, because he concentrated on the Hellenistic cities.

On the basis of these observations we can now look at the Corinthian data. It is clear that a church that gathers in a house can survive only if well-to-do citizens make their houses available for that purpose. This was done, for example, by Priscilla and Aquila (1 Cor. 16:19; Acts 18:18–19; Rom. 16:3), Crispus (Acts 18:8; 1 Cor. 1:14), Stephanas (1 Cor. 1:16; 16:15–16), and Gaius (Rom. 16:23; 1 Cor. 1:14), and apparently also Phoebe (Rom. 16:1–2). We may also think of church meetings in the houses of Titius Justus (Acts 18:7) and Erastus (Rom. 16:23). The greeting list in Romans 16 mentions several house churches. Again, other persons (or perhaps the same ones) care for the reception of the apostles and emissaries in their houses, travel themselves, or finance the trips of others (cf. Rom. 16:23; Acts 18:7). When Apollos and foreign missionaries, for example, stayed in Corinth after Paul, they were supported (e.g., 2 Cor. 11:7ff.; 1 Corinthians 9; cf. also Acts 19:1; 1 Cor. 1:12; 3:4–6). Except for Paul himself, all itinerant preachers apparently let their expenses be paid as guests during their visits in Corinth. The groupings in parties (1 Corinthians 1–4) presuppose various meeting places centered in houses. Regarding abuses in the celebration of the Lord's Supper, it was probably the rich who brought gifts for the general supper and then began the meal before the others gathered; the others could not spend their time as they pleased and had to settle for leftovers (1 Cor. 11:17ff.). Judging by their occupation alone, a synagogue ruler like Crispus (Acts 18:8), the ranking city administrative official Erastus (Rom. 16:23), and the God-fearer Titius Justus (Acts 18:7) must have belonged to the upper class. From the ruler of a synagogue one expects generous contributions to the support of a synagogue. No poor man gets an office like that of Erastus, nor does anyone in it become poor. The majority of God-fearers belong to the upper class; therefore, because of social pressures, they in particular shy away from total involvement in the synagogue. When Paul asks the churches to send out coworkers in larger numbers and rather regularly and to make them available for service with Paul, for example, this also indicates that the churches must have been financially capable of doing so (cf. 7.4 above). Even Paul accepts support from the "rich" churches in Philippi, and Corinth is a little jealous that Paul does not allow it to support him (cf. 8.2 above). Finally, the collection from Macedonia and Achaia for the original church in Jerusalem turns out very well (cf. ch. 2 above). All this does not exactly indicate the meagerest social conditions.

Above all, however, the apostle himself unintentionally attests in 1 Cor. 1:26–29 that the well-to-do class of the provincial capitals was represented in the churches. Following his train of thought, Paul would have to assert that the educated, the politically or financially powerful, and those of noble birth were lacking in the Corinthian church, because God chose the foolish, the weak, the low and despised. In contradiction to the theological assertion of election, however, Paul says that there are "not many" of the well-to-do in the church. Yet that means that the church is a mixture of upper and lower urban strata. In accordance with the general sociological situation the representatives of the "rich" are fewer in number, and the lower levels are more strongly represented. Closer knowledge of individual Corinthian names, however, leads us to presume that the well-to-do in Corinth were proportionally somewhat better represented in the church than was their class in the city itself. However that may be, one thing is clear: the Christian church did not belong to a certain class, nor was it marked by specific occupations or ethnic selection; it was devoted to "all." Thus it faced the problem of integration within the church but not the problems that normally emerge through restriction to particular circles.

Our sketch of general social conditions has already made reference to the way in which the churches were constituted, namely, as house churches. It is striking that the religious communions that spread from east to west, as early Christianity also began to spread, made their way essentially in independence of family structures. Only diaspora Judaism depended for centuries on the home and that means on the family. Early Christianity then adopted this from the Hellenistic synagogue, yet with three crucial differences. Early Christianity had no counterpart to the temple, Judaism's symbol of unity, to which it paid a worldwide yearly tax and to which one also made a pilgrimage, if possible, during one of the pilgrim feasts. Second, as a rule, where it was somehow possible to arrange it in a city, diaspora Judaism had one or more synagogues, in which a part of the cultic activities and, naturally, the Torah instruction took place. Here again, there was no counterpart at all in the beginning period of Christianity. Finally, Judaism depended on the genealogical relation to the Jewish people. Again, there was nothing analogous in primitive Christianity. Thus, in an even clearer way, early Christianity in the Hellenistic cities was dependent on the home. The house of antiquity, in the sense of a house as living space and a place for family life, generally became the founding center of a local church, the locus of gathering for worship, an inn for missionaries and emissaries, a base for going out in mission, and the framework for a new Christian way of life.

In the Roman Empire the ancient home, with the position of the father at the head, was the cornerstone of the city and the empire, and the family was not simply the only social network that antiquity knew.

As a rule the home was also basic for the economy, in that the things on which the family lived were produced there. Naturally the home was of great significance also for ancient religion. Accordingly, it was provided with many rights for the development and shaping of life. Thus the fact that Christianity spread from home to home must be considered an especially fortunate decision on the mission field, for it made use of an already present structure that also offered especially to religious minorities sufficient room to develop.

This room for development was used so as outwardly not to attract the attention of pagan society, city councils, and Roman provincial officials; rather, civil normality was practiced and no offense given (cf. 1 Thess. 4:12; 1 Corinthians 5–6). Accordingly, this early Christianity had no program for changing the world. It did not set out to solve antiquity's slave problem, to build a society with social justice, to recommend the redistribution of political power, to improve the lot of oppressed groups, or to kindle general discussions of human rights. The hope for the very near end of the world alone would not have permitted this. Also, in early Christianity there is nowhere an indication that differences in power, possession, and position in the world were held to be sociopolitically damaging. We must not be too hasty in transposing into antiquity the sociopolitical topics of, say, the period since the Enlightenment. Yet this is only the one side of the coin.

On the other hand, especially while holding to the general structure of society, in the home itself one could lead the Christian life as the eschatological church. Thus the home, as the place used for worship as well as the place of daily life, became the place where faith, love, and hope were practiced without separating Sunday worship and daily life. Since Christianity now addressed all the residents of the city, this meant that everyone came together in a Christian home—even many who formerly had few or no relations with each other: poor and well-to-do, slave and free, women and men, Greeks and orientals, people of various occupations. Here we stand before the crucial task of the house churches, namely, the question of how they could bind these members into one communion. In antiquity this was not really a problem for any other large community of faith, since others usually practiced social and occupational selectivity. Thus here Christianity, by the nature of its orientation, had a singular and particularly difficult task, without being able to appeal to previous models.

9.2 The Integrating Power of the Churches

Churches arise because messengers of the gospel know themselves to be sent by God, the message is heard, faith arises from that hearing, and faith leads to the worship of the Lord. Thus is the missionary process described by Paul in Rom. 10:14–15. Immediately before is a statement that, in our context, is crucial for the overall result of the mission: "For there is no distinction between Jew and Greek; the same Lord is Lord of all and bestows his riches upon all who call upon him" (Rom. 10:12). Thus participation without distinction in the gospel, which is open to all and in which all are treated alike, is the first and fundamental aspect in our consideration of the integrative effort of the churches.

The second follows immediately. Certainly, Christianity demands of the individual much courage and the ability to distance oneself from one's old life, one's social connections, and one's former religion. But in their place there is something new for all members of the Christian church, which Paul describes in Philippians in set, pre-Pauline language:

> Our commonwealth is in heaven,
> and from it we await a Savior, the Lord Jesus Christ,
> who will change our lowly body
> to be like his glorious body,
> by the power which enables him
> even to subject all things to himself.
>
> (Phil. 3:20-21)

Thus Christianity understood itself as the bearer of the hope of a world-overcoming power, which pledged to all who accept the message a home beyond all transitoriness, and this meant a tremendous superiority over the world.

None of this was limited to verbal assertions. This common canon of conviction was borne by a life tailored on communality, a life in which there was on principle equality of all members. This was already stated by an old, probably Antiochene, baptismal tradition (cf. 5.5 above):

> In Christ Jesus you are all sons of God. . . .
> For as many of you as were baptized into Christ have put on Christ.
> There is neither Jew nor Greek,
> there is neither slave nor free,
> there is neither male nor female;
> for you are all one in Christ Jesus.
>
> (Gal. 3:26-28)

The commonality of baptism makes everyone brothers and sisters of equal status; in their fellowship the privileges, differences, and disadvantages that matter in the transitory world no longer matter. Anyone who comes from baptism is clothed in Christ, shares in the abundance of gifts (1 Corinthians 12–14), and may speak in worship, even if a woman (1 Cor. 11:5), and, as a slave, for example, can also render service as a coworker with Paul (Philemon). At the Lord's Supper all take part, and it is expressly an abuse when at the preceding regular meal one does not wait for workers and slaves (1 Cor. 11:17ff.).

This equality, however, is not connected only with the worship service, nor would we expect it to be. First, worship and the daily life of the Christian are bound together in the household. In a Christian home both spouses are obligated to mutual consideration and yielding love through the reciprocal orientation of the one toward the well-being of the other (1 Cor. 7:3–4). Likewise, in a house operated in a Christian way, the relationship between master and slave changes. The slaves belonging to a household neither are forced to be baptized, nor can they demand freedom from their master through conversion to Christianity, but both are reminded that the content of social relationships now stands on an entirely new basis, and that has consequences for the development of these relationships (Philemon; 1 Cor. 7:21–24).

Added to this practical equality in Christ is Paul's central concern of preserving the unity of the church. Competing groups are not only foreign to the gospel but also an abuse that stands in opposition to the integrative task of the church (1 Corinthians 1–4). The church is supposed, rather, to glorify God "with one mind and one mouth" (Rom. 15:6, KJV). In worship one cannot bring one's gift to bear whenever one will. Such chaos disturbs the common service of worship. There is centrifugal force that must yield to integrative respect and order (1 Corinthians 14). The "upbuilding" of the church as a whole remains the highest aim and concern (Rom. 14:19; 15:2; 1 Cor. 8:1). Thus a high value is placed on inner peace (Rom. 15:33) and the agreement of all (1 Cor. 1:10). This concept of the unity of the church also is expressed very nicely in the idea that the coming Lord will, at the end of days, unite the church as a whole with himself (1 Thess. 4:17; 5:10).

Integration is experienced and practiced when individual responsibility and the ability to compromise gain importance. Just the fact that after a first missionary visit Paul left his newly formed churches—under compulsion or with the intention of missionizing elsewhere—calls attention to how quickly and naturally he expected them to be independent. Even to so young a church as that in Thessalonica he wrote, without ifs, ands, or buts, that they did not need exhortation to brotherly love, because they have been taught this by God (1 Thess. 4:9–10). The Corinthians certainly make it difficult for him to continue to speak the word of freedom without restriction, but each time Paul strictly and consistently takes care not to impose a ruling, without argumentation or seeking a consensus. In spite of the Corinthian experiences, in regard to the Philippians he holds fast to the line of freedom (Phil. 4:8).

Likewise, the apostle himself can suggest compromises within the limits of what is possible for him. For example, quarrels over property are unchristian for him, because a Christian would rather bear injustice than inflict it on others. When, nevertheless, such a dispute is necessary, one should not go to the pagan courts, yet a wise brother may pass judgment (1 Cor. 6:1ff.). In a second example, in view of the end time, it would be good for all to remain single. Since the majority do not possess this gift, however, the apostle can suggest quite a number of flexible solutions concerning getting married, being married, and getting divorced (1 Corinthians 7). Also, on the eating of meat offered to idols he rejects the radical solution, which Jewish Christianity has apparently taken for granted (cf. Rev. 2:14): he does not simply forbid such eating but suggests various solutions that stress understanding and consideration (1 Corinthians 8; 10:14ff.).

Certainly, this way requires of the church much inner strength, and we cannot emphasize enough how little practiced these young house churches were in the Christian conduct of life. Paul may also have still had his Antiochene experiences in mind. There the way to independence of the synagogue was achieved through congregational consensus. It is notable, furthermore, that outside the genuine Pauline letters the catchword "freedom" hardly played a role in later primitive Christianity.

9.3 Heavenly Citizenship and the Transitory World

In addition to the fundamental problem of new community formation, the young missionary churches naturally also had to reorder their external relations. The limiting conditions for this are provided by the self-consciousness of the churches. These churches had been called by the electing gospel to be the eschatological church (cf. 6.2 above). This did not mean only that temporally they expected the imminent end of the world; rather, it meant that they were the eschatological church in a more qualified sense: the Spirit had already been given to them as a sign of the end time. Through the gospel and baptism they were so transformed that they only had to wait for the final, everlasting being together with the Lord. Their citizenship was no longer bound to an earthly city but was in heaven (Phil. 3:20).

Therefore they had a new attitude toward the world. The transitory nature of the world (1 Cor. 7:31) will soon be made apparent by the day of the Lord, which will come like a thief in the night (1 Thess. 5:2). This will be experienced by the church now alive (1 Thess. 4:15; Rom. 13:11), for the time is compressed, that is, very short (1 Cor. 7:29). In addition to this temporal aspect, there are theological limitations. Humankind has no hope outside the gospel (1 Thess. 4:13); it stands under the wrath of God (Rom. 1:18–3:20). Accordingly, conversion to Christianity through baptism was interpreted as a break with the transitory, evil world: at one time the believer belonged to sinful humanity but now was holy (1 Cor. 6:9–11).

This sketch makes it clear that conversion to Christianity must have been felt as a revolutionary step—all the more so since the gospel required of Gentiles an uncompromising turning away from the gods. Gentiles were normally familiar with something different. They took part in the festivals of various deities, were initiated into several mysteries, and could venerate, along with Zeus, a whole host of very different numina. The Greco-Roman religious world was tolerant and syncretistic. Exclusive monotheism was known only in Judaism. But now Christianity—with all the flexibility that Paul can exhibit in 1 Corinthians 8–10—also demanded the strict renunciation of the old world of the gods, for it was a sign of human godlessness and contempt for the true Creator and Savior. Because in antiquity religion, culture, politics, and everyday life formed a close symbiotic union, at this point we can hardly draw deep enough the break required by the gospel. Was it not a danger for the polis when Christians scorned the official gods, who guaranteed the well-being of the city? If someone no longer wanted to swear to a business contract by recognized gods, was that person still a reliable contractual partner? If a Christian woman and wife of a pagan man no longer wanted to pay homage to the household gods with the whole family, could she still be trusted with household affairs? If a family no longer responded to invitations to go to the temple, could one in the long run maintain social relations with that family? Questions upon questions! They make clear how profoundly becoming a Christian reached into people's lives.

If Christian relations with ancient religions meant only confrontation and separation, it was neither possible nor desirable to carry out such constant conflict in all other areas of culture, politics, and society. There were indeed such tendencies. According to 1 Cor. 5:9–10, Paul has to guard himself expressly against being wrongly understood to say that one must stay away from every sinner. Also, the foreign text in 2 Cor. 6:14–7:1 demands the breaking of all ties with the world, but Paul and his churches probably did not think this way. One had to make distinctions. Naturally every Christian has to preserve an inner freedom in regard to everything worldly (1 Cor. 7:29–31), but separation from the sinful world must be strictly maintained only within the fellowship (1 Corinthians 6). It is true that the holiness of the church is to be achieved through sanctification (1 Corinthians 5–6; 1 Thess. 4:1ff.), but this is still a long way from advocating a premature exit from the world.

First, there is the political order of the state with its various authorities. Here Christians do not scorn the state, for they basically recognize in these worldly structures a system of order coming from divine creative power (Rom. 13:1–7). With the advice of Jeremiah (Jer. 29:5–7), Hellenistic diaspora Judaism had already practiced a pragmatically conforming and basically loyal relationship to foreign state powers. Since the religious separation was uncompromising, there was a desire to show the Gentiles an essentially cooperative attitude toward foreign governments. Was the foreign king, Cyrus, not also an instrument of the one God of Israel, the ruler of all history (Isa. 45:1–7)? This tradition now also became the orientation of the young Christian churches in the Hellenistic cities. Thus Paul, as a bearer of the Spirit, refuses to be judged (1 Cor. 4:1ff.), but as a Roman citizen he did not simply withdraw from the Roman courts. Especially since the churches—presumably more often than the diaspora synagogue of this period—repeatedly fell into unintentional conflict with the governments (cf. 1 Thess. 1:6; 2:14; 1 Cor. 15:32; 2 Cor. 11:23–33; Acts 13–14; chs. 15–18), one had to try to ward off trouble: Christians were not disloyal or rebellious citizens on principle and thus did not want to be publicly regarded as subversive. Naturally they could not participate in the official state cult. Yet for this very reason they wanted, for example, to be all the more particular about paying their taxes (Rom. 13:6–7), so that it would be clear to all where the only conflict lay.

For the rest, external social relations were such that Christians knew themselves to be "blameless . . . children of God" living "in the midst of a crooked and perverse generation" (Phil. 2:15), that they might command respect (1 Thess. 4:12; cf. Phil. 4:8), "do good to all" people (Gal. 6:10), adopt the concerns of others (Rom. 12:15), and "repay no one evil for evil" (Rom. 12:17). If possible, they were to "live peaceably with all" (Rom. 12:18). Thus external ethics were oriented toward the good life of the individual in the individual case. There was as yet no word of the church to the world. Programs of social change were beyond its field of vision. The intent was to missionize and in that way change people, but there was no reflection on what a state and its society would basically need to look like.

In one case, however, things went a little bit farther, namely, in the case of the common ethics of the time. Certainly, the concrete life-style of non-Christians was considered negative through and through (Rom. 1:18ff.; 1 Cor. 6:9–11; Phil. 2:15; etc.). Gentiles were simply sin-ners, and they stood under divine wrath. But were the norms in cus-tom, usage, and law also to be rejected totally and in wholesale fashion as part of the old, transitory world? No. Christians had the obligation to reflect on whatever is true, honorable, just, pure, lovable, and of good report, indeed on every virtue and every deed worthy of praise (Phil. 4:8). Paul attaches great importance—above all, vis-à-vis the Jews—to the idea that the commandment of love, understood in a Christian way, fulfills the law of the old covenant (Rom. 13:8ff.; Gal. 5:14). Yes, the apostle can even take a fundamental idea of Hel-lenistic Judaism farther when he ascribes to all people a basic knowl-edge of the divine will in regard to the shaping of life, even if, practically speaking, they do not always intend to do that will (Rom. 1:19; 2:12–16). Thus in the middle of a world headed toward the end, there are still flashes of a Creator's will. This means, however, that vis-à-vis Greeks and Jews one does not claim to advocate an absolute, special ethics but to aim at what is held in common in the develop-ment of true humanity. In spite of the lostness of the world, in its ethi-cal discussion there is truth and goodness, which Christians know how to appreciate in such a way that this truth and goodness receive their due, as ordained by God.

This appreciation had two sides. On the one hand, if Christianity wanted to take part in the common discussion of ethics, it had to decide how it intended to evaluate and select. On the other hand, where it ascertained the weakness of all non-Christians, namely, that norms and deeds did not always coincide, it had to offer something better. In the second case, we can doubtless begin with the fact that young churches rigorously and consistently placed high ethical demands on themselves (cf. Rom. 12:1–2; etc.), and outsiders observed this also. In the first case, Paul succeeded from his christological starting point in introducing a standard for selection and evaluation that had a clear shape in the love discernible in the destiny of Christ (Rom. 15:1ff.; Phil. 2:1ff.).

The overview of the relationship of Christians to the transitory world would be incomplete if we did not call to mind that these churches had worldly structures present even in the midst of their houses. We have already indicated (cf. 9.2 above) how the churches reshaped from inside out the tensions between poor and rich, slave and free, and the relationship between husband and wife. Thus, as surely as structures were not a topic in external relations, in internal relations they were filled with the Christian Spirit.

9.4 Worship in the House Churches

With the help of the Corinthian correspondence—especially 1 Corinthians—we not only learn through the Corinthian church the most concrete information about the social structure of an early Christian church but also can gain exceptional insights into its worship life. Naturally there were still no fixed forms for worship services (let alone orders of worship). Yet Paul made sure that the basic elements were similar in all the churches (1 Cor. 11:16; 14:33). To this extent we can probably no doubt generalize from Corinth to the Gentile-Christian mission field in general, once we have set aside the special problems of Corinth in regard to the abuse of the regular meal (1 Cor. 11:17ff.), the confusion of utterances of the Spirit (1 Corinthians 14), and the conspicuously high estimation of the sacraments and their theological interpretation (1 Corinthians 1; 11:17ff.; 15:29).

Paul distinguishes several forms and occasions for the gathering of the church. Yet verbally they all bear the common designation of assembling or coming together (1 Cor. 5:4; 11:17, 20, 33–34; 14:23, 26). This mode of expression, borrowed from the language of Hellenistic societies, indicates the avoidance of typically cultic ways of thinking. Theologically, it is used figuratively to describe the existence of the believers and their transformation (Rom. 12:1–2; 15:16; 1 Cor. 1:30; 5:6–8; 6:11; 7:14; etc.). Corresponding to this is the fact that the Christian churches were probably the only communion in antiquity that had no special place of worship but rather came together in the places of daily life, in private homes (Rom. 16:5; 1 Cor. 16:19; Philemon 2). Accordingly, they lacked cultic accessories, vestments, symbols, and ritual preparations (washings and purification laws). Christian existence and its ethics became worship in the world; services of worship in the narrower sense took place at the family table and in the rooms of houses—that is, in the midst of the world. Christians gathered in the same room and at the same table for the regular supper and the Lord's Supper, which followed one another without a break (1 Cor. 11:17ff.).

In particular, we can recognize various acts of worship. When Paul treats the problems of the Lord's Supper and the problems of the overflowing of the Spirit in the service of the word in two widely separated places in 1 Corinthians (1 Corinthians 11; ch. 14), that indicates two institutionally different gatherings. This conclusion is supported by the fact that in 1 Cor. 10:1ff., on the other hand, Paul places together baptism and the Lord's Supper, the two acts later designated sacraments. We must also ask whether special problems, such as those named in Acts 15; 1 Cor. 5:1ff.; Gal. 2:11ff., were not treated in actual assemblies of the whole church. Then we would be dealing with sacramental acts, services of the word, and special meetings.

Let us first gather observations on the sacramental acts. Baptism occurred "in the name of the Lord Jesus Christ" (1 Cor. 1:13; 6:11). Through baptism, believers were placed under the Lord (1 Cor. 12:3) and shared in the salvific work of Christ (1 Cor. 1:13). They became full members of the Christian church (not only of an individual house church), that is, they were received into the "body of Christ" or "in Christ" (1 Cor. 12:4ff.; Gal. 3:26–28), so that their previous existence no longer counted; indeed, they belonged to a new creation (1 Cor. 6:9–11; 7:19; 2 Cor. 5:17). They received the Spirit (1 Cor. 6:19) and shared in the gifts (1 Corinthians 12–14). They were washed, sanctified, and justified (1 Cor. 6:11; 1:30) and had to live in a manner befitting this state of sanctification (1 Cor. 5:1ff.; 6:1ff.; 1 Thess. 4:1ff.). In the act of baptism the one to be baptized apparently had to make a public confession of Christ (similar to Rom. 10:9–10) in the presence of the church and received a baptismal exhortation, which naturally always applied to the whole church as well (Rom. 6:1ff.; 1 Cor. 6:9–11, 15–20; etc.). Now they could participate in the Lord's Supper (cf. the sequence baptism-Lord's Supper in 1 Cor. 10:1ff.). The service of the word, on the other hand, was also celebrated by the unbaptized (1 Cor. 14:22–25). New converts apparently first had to participate in the service of the word for a certain period before they were baptized. Surely, however, there were still no firm rules for a catechumenate. The baptisms were performed by church members and missionaries (1:11ff.). The fact that Paul as an apostle only rarely baptized is apparently an exception (1:16). The first baptized enjoyed special respect in the church (Rom. 16:5; 1 Cor. 16:15). In Corinth, baptism was especially connected with immunization against transitoriness, so that relatives (or friends) who were already baptized had themselves baptized as representatives of believers who had died unbaptized (vicarious baptism: 1 Cor. 15:29). We do not know the extent to which this was a more widespread practice. There is no evidence from other churches in this period.

The Lord's Supper (the set expression in 1 Cor. 11:20) was celebrated in Corinth together with a preceding regular meal (11:20ff.). This was not the only early Christian form (cf. 11:25). In the center are the words of institution, which bring to mind and convey the salvific death of Jesus but also direct attention to the Parousia of the Lord (11:26). We can infer from 1 Cor. 10:1ff.; 11:27ff. that a distinction was made between the offerings of the regular meal and the sacramental offerings; the latter are spiritual, numinous food and drink and in a special way contain Christ (10:3–4). Therefore they have their own designation ("breaking bread," "blessing the cup"—10:16) and can be consumed to judgment (11:27ff.) for the church (and this may not be calculated individually). They grant "fellowship" with the exalted Lord (10:16; cf. 1:9) and actualize the "fellowship of the Spirit" (2 Cor. 13:14; Phil. 2:1). The fellowship of the believers with each other occurred in the common meal that took place beforehand. This deeply sacramental understanding of the Lord's Supper does correspond to the Corinthian concept of baptism, yet it was certainly not the only one current in primitive Christianity. Even if Paul's words in 1 Cor. 16:20–23 are not a liturgical formula, he has nonetheless probably adopted elements and echoes from a widespread Lord's Supper liturgy. These may include the fraternal kiss, the curse on those who have falsely slipped in, and the invocation, "Our Lord, come!"

Individual elements of the service of the word are also apparent. There is as yet no obligatory order. The Corinthian disturbances (1 Corinthians 14) could have occurred only under the condition of a relative openness in the individual formation of the service. Naturally there were genre-specific utterances that defined every service of worship; to that extent there was a fixed component of forms of worship. In 14:6, 15–16, Paul names singing, teaching, and spiritual phenomena such as prophecy, revelation, speaking in tongues, and the translation of speaking in tongues. In 14:1ff. he also mentions prayer, praise, and the church's saying amen, as well as the acclaiming confession in 12:1–3. A certain ordering of these utterances seems to have been usual (11:34; 14:33, 40), yet our knowledge is not sufficient for details or an exact reconstruction.

We have examples of some of the forms, which are not always precisely distinguished from each other. In 8:1–6 Paul refers to the confession familiar to the church. In Phil. 2:6–11 he cites a hymn of the church. For praise we could also refer to sections such as 1 Cor. 1:3–7 and for thanksgiving, say, Phil. 1:3ff. The request that the church pray regularly, especially for the apostle, occurs several times (Rom. 12:12; 15:30; Phil. 4:6; 1 Thess. 5:17; etc.). Teaching and prophecy no doubt have to do with preaching Christ and exhorting change, as these are promoted by the Pauline letters themselves. The latter are also supposed to be read aloud in the worship service (1 Thess. 5:27). When Paul in 1 Corinthians 15, for example, explicates the gospel, expressed as a kerygmatic formula, or interprets longer passages in 1 Corinthians 10; 2 Corinthians 3; Galatians 3–4; Romans 4, or records typical paraenesis (Romans 12–13; Galatians 5–6; 1 Thess. 4:1–12), these no doubt reflect corresponding worship practices. Yet the express reading aloud of the Old Testament is not attested until later (1 Tim. 4:13). Did the churches already have a Septuagint, or at least parts of it, so soon after their founding? That is not always likely. On the other hand, Paul often presupposes knowledge of the Septuagint (cf., e.g., 1 Cor. 9:9, 14:21; Rom. 7:1). Can he do this without its being read in the worship service? The Spirit-effected exclamations certainly include "Abba!" (Rom. 8:15; Gal. 4:6), the invocation, "Our Lord, come!" (1 Cor. 16:22; Phil. 4:5; Rev. 22:20; *Did.* 10:6), and the acclamation, "Jesus is Lord" (1 Cor. 12:3). We can see by this that the Spirit, among other things, also uses set forms and fixed contents. The Spirit does not express himself only in random spontaneity with unpredictable content. Yet in view of passages such as 1 Thess. 5:19–20; 1 Corinthians 14; Gal. 3:1–5; Rom. 12:11, we must take into account an indeed intentionally Spirit-led and thus open format for the worship service. The mood is set for joy and jubilation (Phil. 4:4). According to the overall impression of the Pauline letters, the preaching of Christ and paraenesis must have taken a central position. Here apostles and missionaries probably spoke as guests. In this way, for example, the "superlative apostles" in 2 Corinthians were able to impress the church.

It is unclear to the historian when various worship services took place. In any case, prominence was probably given to Sunday as the day of the Lord's resurrection (1 Cor. 16:1–2; Acts 20:7; Rev. 1:10; *Did.* 14:1) and especially to Sunday evening, when the main meal of the day was usually consumed (1 Cor. 11:21–22). Yet the other days of the week cannot be simply excluded (Ignatius, *Ephesians* 13). Granted the prominence of Sunday, there were probably various practices in the churches. As yet there were no offices for the direction of worship. Naturally obvious duty assignments arose. Worship in houses in each case gave prominence to the man and woman of the house (Rom. 16:1–2; 1 Cor. 16:15–16; 1 Thess. 5:12–13—especially, of course, at the meal. In general, women could express themselves on an equal basis in the worship service (Gal. 3:26–28; 1 Cor. 11:5; on the other hand, 1 Cor. 14:33–36 is an addendum in the spirit of 1 Tim. 2:11–12). The confusion in the Corinthian service of the word exhibits an order that has little direction and is built rather on common consensus. Corinth accorded a certain prominence to those speaking in tongues. Paul wants to have this reduced in favor of understandable speech and also to see the number of utterances reduced. This is apparently a new rule for the Corinthians. Certainly the general practice was the predominance of understandable speech (1 Cor. 14:15–16). This also had to be the case not least of all because of the fundamental missionary orientation of the service of the word (14:22ff.). Thus Paul is guiding the Corinthians back to what is usual. As a greeting and farewell, the holy kiss soon became common as a Christian custom (Rom. 16:16; 1 Cor. 16:20; 2 Cor. 13:12; 1 Thess. 5:26). The participation of the Christian in the service of worship, especially in the Lord's Supper, excluded any participation in a pagan cultic act (1 Cor. 10:14–22) and naturally made no allowances for the Jewish ceremonial law.

On the assemblies of the whole church there is not much to say. They no doubt took place on important occasions as needed (cf. Acts 15; 1 Cor. 5:1ff.; Gal. 2:11ff.), that is, when it was a matter of consulting on something that had to be clarified by all the individual churches together in a city or region, which would otherwise gather house by house. For example, an expulsion from the Christian church could not be implemented by one house church alone with a simple prohibition from the house, and a blatant sinner, naturally, should not immediately gain admission to a neighboring house church. Also, a single house church on its own should not and would not want to take care of the collection for Jerusalem, for this was the task of a city or province through common planning (cf. ch. 2 above). Thus at irregular intervals there was again and again a reason for the whole church to come together. Whether at that time a common service of worship was held is beyond our knowledge.

Anyone who looks over the early Christian utterances on Christian worship must conclude that Christians were creating something of their own that was new. Certainly, they borrowed elements of synagogal worship (e.g., confession of faith, prayer, scripture reading and interpretation) and among other things adopted a Hellenistic understanding for the interpretation of the Lord's Supper in Corinth, but they made the message of Christ and its understanding the foundation and goal of worshipful acts and in the process also assimilated what they had received.

10

The Last Visit in Macedonia and Achaia

10.1 The So-called Collection Journey

For a long time Paul had planned another trip to Europe (1 Cor. 16:2, 5–9), but in the winter of A.D. 54/55 things went so badly for him in Ephesus (cf. 7.1 above) that for the time being his mind was not on travel plans. Paul landed in prison and his life was in danger, but he was narrowly able to escape in the spring of A.D. 55— probably through the courageous and dangerous actions of Priscilla and Aquila. So Paul apparently leaves Ephesus in flight. He will not visit this central location of his work again and must now begin his previously planned European journey under quite different conditions.

The first city that Paul visits after fleeing is Troas (2 Cor. 2:12). This place in northwestern Asia Minor is dominated by the Ida mountains and is the natural point of departure for a crossing to European Macedonia. According to Acts 16:8, it served this purpose at the beginning of the first Pauline journey to Europe. Conversely, the Greeks saw this location as an important foothold for the colonization and conquest of Asia Minor. Alexander the Great, for example, had won his first great battle very near the city on the Granicus when he set out to conquer Persia. This time it does not appear that the apostle used Troas only for transit. It seems, rather, that a missionary effort was planned. Paul also reports success in his preaching of the gospel (2 Cor. 2:12). Yet this church has retreated into the darkness of history. Timothy may have been with Paul (cf. 2 Cor. 1:19) and accompanied him at least to Corinth (Rom. 16:21), even if Acts 19:21–22 presents this somewhat differently. Paul, on the other hand, waited for Titus, who was finally supposed to bring him the desired good news from Corinth (2 Cor. 2:13).

Yet Paul apparently has to wait too long for Titus. After longing in vain for his coworker's return to Ephesus, the apostle now starts on his way from Troas without having seen Titus. The inner unrest in the Corinthian church continues to gnaw at him. He crosses over to Macedonia and writes about the bad times he experienced; he finds no rest and is plagued by every affliction possible, "fighting without and fear within" (2 Cor. 7:5). If the latter refers to Corinth, the fighting without possibly means the Galatian situation. The Letter to the Galatians is Paul's reaction to the entry of Judaizers, of whom he had recently heard just before departing from Ephesus.

We can no longer determine when Titus finally saw Paul. The apostle expressed himself all the more clearly concerning the good news that his faithful coworker brought: "But God, who comforts the downcast, comforted us by the coming of Titus, and not only by his coming but also [and especially] by the comfort with which he was comforted in you [Corinthians], as he told us of your longing, your mourning, your zeal for me, so that I rejoiced still more" (2 Cor. 7:6–7). Thus Titus was successful with his mission, which was as delicate as it was difficult. The apostle was overjoyed to have regained his beloved Corinth.

Naturally Paul told of the reconciliation with Corinth in Philippi and Thessalonica, for he almost certainly visited the two cities on his journey through Macedonia. It was his last stay in these churches. Overjoyed about the Corinthians, he then reported also in Macedonia on the collection that had been going on for a year in the capital city of Achaia. The Macedonian churches spontaneously join in this activity (cf. ch. 2 above). Such a gathering of funds in an entire province takes somewhat longer. Thus Paul probably spends the winter in Macedonia (A.D. 55/56). Also during this time he is completing his plans for taking the collection from all of Greece to Jerusalem himself, in order then to leave the eastern part of the Roman Empire entirely and set out finally (cf. 6.1 above) for Rome and Spain (2 Cor. 8:18–24; Rom. 1:15; 15:22–29). Titus is again sent to Corinth, accompanied by two Macedonians. Naturally Paul also wants to accept the Corinthians' offer of reconciliation and at the same time now energetically promote the collection by telling of the Macedonian participation (letter E to Corinth: 2 Cor. 1:1–2:13; 7:5–16; chs. 8–9).

There has been much discussion on the significance of this collection. We have already made some observations on it (cf. ch. 2 above), which give important indications of the appreciation of the gifts for Jerusalem. From Gal. 2:10 we learn that the two Antiochenes Paul and Barnabas accepted for Antioch the obligation of financial support for Jerusalem. The historical situation and the framework of the council in no way permit the conclusion that Gentile Christianity in general was thereby committed to this service. Against this idea is the fact that the missions founded by the followers of Stephen had no part in the discussions, and Paul's independent mission was still to come. Nevertheless, as an individual who had given his word, Paul felt committed for life to this agreement. Yet he always made a point of stressing the free decision of the churches that he asked for collection (e.g., 2 Cor. 8:3–4; 9:2, 7).

The obligation that Paul accepted in Jerusalem is, moreover, not a part of the actual council decision. The apostle emphasized this expressly in Gal. 2:10. The decision is completely independent of this additional agreement. After his departure from Antioch, Paul understands the latter as a personal obligation to Jerusalem and avoids all legal terms in its designation. There is, therefore, absolutely no analogy to the temple tax of all Jews. It is not the idea of tax or law that is appropriate but the description as gift and contribution. Of course, the contributory character also must not lead us to place the collection in the larger context of alms for Israel from outsiders and proselytes. Paul himself nowhere indicates this general framework, and his churches certainly did not understand it thus. In any case, as a former Pharisee, Paul knew of the synagogue's self-understanding expressed here, namely, its self-estimation as preeminent over all other peoples. Since Paul, however, advocated the equality of Gentile Christianity, this understanding of the collection was out of the question for him. He would have accepted it neither at that time in Jerusalem nor at any later time. Furthermore, alms for Israel are by nature contributions of individuals, but in the Pauline collection, it is a matter of gifts from church provinces.

The collection is for the socially poor Christians in Jerusalem, for that is the only way to interpret "the poor among the saints" (Rom. 15:26). The Jerusalem Christians as a whole are "the saints" (Rom. 15:25, 31). Among them is an unquantified proportion of materially impoverished Christians who can be fed by the Jerusalem church only with difficulty. The collection of money is expressly designated for them. The extent to which we can draw conclusions from Acts 2:44–45; 4:32–37; 5:1–11; 6:1–6 about the background of the impoverishment is disputed. Luke, who largely speaks for himself here, wants to describe a normative early Christian time from a later standpoint, while borrowing from the Pythagorean social utopia. Historically, however, the situation in Jerusalem is caused rather by the near expectation and eschatological position of Jerusalem as the place of salvation of the coming Son of man. We can assume, say, that Galilean Christians wanted to wait with the Jerusalemites in the city of Zion for the resurrected One as the eschatological figure of salvation; thus they gave up their middle-class existence in Galilee, grew poor in Jerusalem, and became dependent on the assistance of Christians there. There was, in any case, probably no "communism of love" (voluntary sharing of all means of production) or voluntary sharing of all products as the life-style of the entire church. Yet, however one might decide here, Paul is nowhere interested in research into the causes of the partial impoverization of the early Jerusalem church. For him, the fact of its poverty alone is the reason that in this case also one should bear the burdens of another (Gal. 6:2) and that it is important to do good to everyone, but especially to the believers (Gal. 6:10).

Beginning on this basis, Paul can now name theological motifs that point to the value and significance of the collection. Thus in 2 Cor. 8:8–9 he writes: "I say this not as a command, but to prove . . . that your love also is genuine. For you know the grace of our Lord Jesus Christ, that though he was rich, yet for your sake he became poor, so that by his poverty you might become rich." Thus here the Corinthians are supposed to see themselves placed under the "law of Christ," which applies in like manner to all Christians (cf. Gal. 6:2). A little later (2 Cor. 8:13–14), the apostle mentions a second viewpoint when he speaks of an equality between want and abundance; that is, he points to the self-evident Christian duty of sharing (2 Cor. 9:13). Finally in Rom. 15:26–27 he comments: "For Macedonia and Achaia have been pleased to make some contribution for the poor among the saints at Jerusalem; . . . they are in debt to them, for if the Gentiles have come to share in their spiritual blessings, they ought also to be of service to them in material blessings." Thus as the peoples received a share in the gospel emanating from Jerusalem (cf. Rom. 15:19), so now they are also to give to the Jerusalemites a share of their gifts. Hence Paul wants to emphasize mutual give-and-take in the one church of Jesus Christ. In this way the collection becomes a bond of fellowship between Jewish and Gentile Christians. Thus for Paul it is "service" (2 Cor. 8:4; 9:1, 12–13) and "fellowship" (8:4; 9:13). For the sake of this idea of fellowship, Paul does not forgo the delivery of the gift (cf. 15.1 below), even in the face of threatening problems in Jerusalem (Rom. 15:30–32). Indeed, Paul plainly challenges the Judaizing forces—which will soon be our focus of attention—to see the collection as a test of whether Jewish Christianity still recognizes the equality of Gentile Christianity or really wants to terminate fellowship despite the council decision.

If we pursue further the events of the so-called collection journey, we must report some more bad news, which reaches Paul after he has left Philippi and probably also Macedonia: the Judaizers are following his tracks to Europe. His church in Philippi is threatened. Once again Paul has to defend himself against the anti-Gentile-Christian forces in Jewish Christianity. He writes Philippians B (cf. 10.2 and 12.4 below). Now, at the latest, he must have finally realized that his trip to Jewish-Christian Jerusalem with the collection of the Gentile-Christian churches involved serious problems (Rom. 15:30–31). Now the love gift becomes at the same time a crucial test of Jerusalem's attitude toward Gentile Christianity.

Corinth is the last stop on this journey (A.D. 56). On the occasion of the collection visit, Paul stays here about three months, if we can trust Acts (20:2–3), and from Corinth—after the successful completion of the collection in Achaia—he writes the Letter to the Romans (Rom. 15:25–32; 16:21–23). This letter becomes the last sign of life from Paul's hand and, not for that reason alone, his testament. This is especially true because in Romans he presents his theology uniquely in systematic maturity (cf. 13.3 below). According to Romans, Paul is on the verge of setting out for Jerusalem. Acts confirms that he indeed reached this destination (Acts 21). With this, however, Paul begins a new chapter in his life, for which we no longer have any information by Paul.

When we review the so-called collection journey through Europe, we find that for the apostle it contains the longed-for reconciliation with Corinth and the great success of the collection in Macedonia and Achaia. At the same time, however, heavy storms are gathering over the mission field that Paul now finally plans to leave (Rom. 15:23–24). The Judaizers are endangering his Gentile-Christian missionary work not only in Asia but also in Europe. Also, Paul must sincerely fear that in Jerusalem he will have problems when delivering the collection. Is the unity of the church of Jewish and Gentile Christians again at risk— in spite of the Apostolic Council? When Paul sets his sights on the western half of the Roman Empire, he leaves behind in the East anything but a stable situation. In addition, he is coming directly from mortal danger in Ephesus and already faces a new threat in Jerusalem. It appears that Paul himself and his churches cannot get out of trouble.

Yet we have to render another account for this period. If we disregard the conciliatory writing to Corinth, which somewhat belatedly, as it were, closes the Corinthian correspondence, then the literary yield of these two years consists in the letters that contain the apostle's message of justification. That is, during this time Paul formed the theology through which he influenced church history, not immediately after his time, yet, seen over the whole course of that history, at its crucial turning points. Paul himself, of course, could not have anticipated this, because his hope was determined by the expectation of the imminent end of all things.

In closing, we summarize the order of events of this period in tabular form as a continuation of the chronology at the end of section 7.1.

Paul's Journey from Ephesus to Corinth

Event	Comments	Approx. Date A.D.
1 From Ephesus to Troas; stay in Troas: missionary success, Timothy with Paul to Corinth	2 Cor. 2:12; 1:1; Rom. 16:21 (vs. Acts 19:22)	55
2 Journey from Troas to Macedonia; Galatians	2 Cor. 7:5; Gal. 4:13	55
3 Titus comes from Corinth with good news and reaches Paul in Macedonia	2 Cor. 2:13; 7:13–16; long break after 2nd visit (2 Cor. 1:23)	55
4 Paul in Macedonia (over winter); Macedonians take in Achaia's collection	2 Cor. 8:3–4; 9:2–3	Winter 55/56
5 Paul finally sets Corinth-Jerusalem journey, in order then to go on to Rome, Spain	2 Cor. 8:18–24; Rom. 1:15; 15:22–29 . (cf. Acts 19:21–22)	55/56
6 Letter E to Corinth: "letter of reconciliation"	= 2 Cor. 1:1–2:13; 7:5–16; chs. 8–9. Situation: 2:13; 7:5ff.; 8:6, 16–19	55/56
7 Letter B to Philippi	= Phil. 3:2–21; 4:8–9; written after 2nd visit in Philippi (Phil. 3:18), which is at the time of event no. 4	56
8 Stay in Corinth (3rd visit): "collection visit"	3 months: Acts 20:2–3; Rom. 15:25–26; 16:22	Summer 56
9 The Letter to the Romans as Paul's testament	from Corinth: Rom. 15:25–32; 16:21–23	56

10.2 Anti-Gentile-Christian Jewish Christianity

The last winter that Paul spends in Ephesus is characterized by, among other things, the fact that he learns of the intrusion of an unknown Judaizing mission into his Galatian churches (cf. 7.1 above). His hasty departure in the direction of Macedonia in the spring of A.D. 55 does not allow him personally to look after things in Galatia. Thus he apparently writes the Letter to the Galatians while he is on the road through Macedonia. The so-called collection journey now requires his whole attention. Therefore the new danger at this time in the northeastern part of his former mission territory doubtless strikes him as totally inopportune. It catches him off balance, so to speak, especially since for him the emerging disagreement had long been essentially decided by the Apostolic Council (cf. 5.2 above) and thus in his view was a completely superfluous quarrel.

Much to the annoyance of the apostle, it did not stop with the Galatian quarrel. For after Paul stops in Philippi on his journey through Macedonia and has already left the church there, he hears that the Judaizers also plan to visit Philippi and thus cross over from Asia to Europe and follow the tracks of the apostle. Paul acts in a way analogous to the Galatian situation: he follows through with his travel plans and writes to the church Philippians B (cf. 12.2 and 12.4 below). In this way the so-called collection journey is not ultimately characterized by the apostle's disagreement with this opposing mission.

It is, moreover, quite conceivable that Paul is likewise aiming at Judaizers with the warning in Rom. 16:17–20. For Romans not only belongs in the period of the collection journey (cf. 13.2 below) but suggests problems with the Judaizing Jewish Christians in Jerusalem during the trip to deliver the collection (Rom. 15:31; cf. 15.1 below). In addition, by all usual typology of the characterization of the opponents, in Rom. 16:17–18 the similarity to Phil. 3:18–19 is very striking. Thus if we consider this warning against false teachers addressed to Rome (cf. here 13.2 below), then we can ascertain that the imperial capital is not yet afflicted by these opponents, but Paul is expecting future threats against the Roman church also (Rom. 16:19). He pledges the church to a fight against the common enemy, whom he associates with Satan (Rom. 16:20a), just as he excluded the Judaizers from salvation in Galatians and in Philippians B.

How can these Judaizing forces be described in more detail? Certainly this kind of Pauline polemic (cf. 7.2 above) advises caution against wanting to know too much. Also, when Paul was in Galatia and on the way to Philippi, he probably did not know these opponents personally (cf. Gal. 1:7; 5:7, 12; 6:12–13; Phil. 3:2, 4; Rom. 16:17–18). But in addition to the news from Galatia itself (how else does Paul know such special facts as those in Gal. 4:9–10?), he knows the opponents' position firsthand from the Apostolic Council (cf. 5.2 above) and has good access to it on the basis of his pre-Christian existence as a strict Pharisee in regard to the law (cf. 3.2 above). Moreover, with the help of the central focus of the Judaizers' program, that is, the demand of circumcision (Gal. 5:2–3, 12; 6:12–13; Phil. 3:2–5), the historian can characterize their Jewish homeland and understand it against this background. Thus, although these opponents are exclusively attacked depreciatingly and polemically, Paul cannot have essentially misrepresented them, nor can a present-day reconstruction go completely astray in describing their basic characteristics.

The Judaizers are an extreme faction within Jewish Christianity. The term "Jewish Christians" here is a coinage of modern historians; no early Christian church ever gave itself that designation. This collective term refers to all believers who are of Jewish heritage, circumcised, and at the same time Christian. If Christians in Galatia, for example, let themselves be circumcised and thereby became proselytes, if they held to the Jewish law and at the same time remained Christians, they too belong to this group.

According to this general definition, the Jewish Christians include the early Palestinian church, the Galilean churches, the circle of Stephen, and the beginnings of his missionary foundings, and probably also the beginnings of the missionary churches in Alexandria, Ephesus, and Rome, and Paul's opponents at the Apostolic Council, in Galatia, and in Philippi, as well as those in 2 Corinthians 10–13 (cf. 11:21ff.). In general, early Christianity begins as Jewish Christianity. The Antiochene and then the independent Pauline missions are the first decisive exceptions of Gentile-Christian missionary foundings. The initially unexpected success of the Gentile mission makes the tensions between Jewish and Gentile Christians a decisive characteristic of the first early Christian generation.

If we look into the post-Pauline period, churches such as those of the sayings source Q, of Matthew, of the Fourth Evangelist, of James, and of the Revelation to John clearly show Jewish-Christian character, even if they slowly outgrew the synagogue with more or less harsh conflicts (cf. Matthew with John). The fate of Jewish Christianity in this period was determined by two events: the anti-Roman rebellion of A.D. 66–71/72 and the constitution of Pharisaic orthodoxy with the synod at Javneh/Jamnia under Gamaliel II around A.D. 80.

In general, toward A.D. 66, Jewish Christians had apparently already taken flight to Pella in the land east of the Jordan because of their antizealot attitude (Eusebius, *Church History* 3.5.3). They thereby lost their center, the holy city of Jerusalem, as did Judaism as a whole later on. There were other reasons for this flight. The head of the Jewish Christians at the time, James, the brother of the Lord, was killed at the instigation of the high priest Annas II between the departure of the procurator Festus and the installation of Albinus (A.D. 62; cf. Josephus, *Antiquities* 20.197–200; Hegesippus in Eusebius, *Church History* 2.23.11–18). This can be considered persecution of the Jewish Christians in Jerusalem: one kills the leader as a warning to all his followers. Thus James died in Jerusalem, the city of Zion, at about the same time as Paul in the metropolis Rome. In any case, the flight to Pella was also a flight from the tribulation indicated by the death of James.

After the lost war of zealotism—from the beginning it was hopeless and insane to engage in battle against Roman military might—the moderate powers, the Pharisees, assumed the leading role in Judaism and immediately excluded all "heretical" and disagreeable groups from Judaism; that is, the Pharisees molted into early rabbinic orthodoxy, so that the variety in Judaism that had existed before A.D. 70 died out. The visible sign of this new age was the damning of all kinds of "heretics," which around A.D. 90 was taken up in the Eighteen Benedictions. Even if this official prayer of the synagogue did not refer to the Jewish Christians alone or with special emphasis, they still could not damn themselves in the synagogal worship service. Therefore they could no longer remain in the synagogue, in which, for theological reasons, they wanted to be at home.

Thus, in the first century after Christ, Jewish Christianity had two difficult crises to work through: the blossoming of Gentile Christianity as competition and a questioning of its own (i.e., Jewish-Christian) position and, second, the years of the anti-Roman rebellion, which were dark for Judaism as a whole. It is clear—not least of all in view of such questioning—that attempts to make a place for itself were manifold, especially since even before A.D. 70 Judaism was also characterized by the pluralism of various currents. Within this search for identity, the anti-Gentile-oriented Jewish Christians held the extreme position, on the one hand, and, on the other, the Gentile-Christian-assimilating Jewish Christians in 2 Corinthians 10–13, for example, held the opposite position. In between, standing about in the middle, were those who shared the council decision (cf. 5.2 above) as well as those who later placed limitations on it, such as the people of James in Antioch (cf. 5.3 above), or who, like Paul, especially advocated a consistently Gentile-Christian theology when in his missionary foundings he required of Jewish Christians integration into the church on a Gentile-Christian basis (cf. the reproach in Acts 21:21). If the situation is largely described correctly, then two things are clear. Since there was hardly any possibility of dialogue between Paul's opponents in Galatia and those in 2 Corinthians 10–13, he had to become the central opponent for those who denied legitimation to the Gentile-Christian church. It is notable here that after the council they no longer take Paul to task directly but want to force his mission churches under the law, that is, into the synagogue. Thus these programmatically anti-Gentile-Christian-oriented Jewish Christians—that is, Judaizers—are carrying on a countermission in the Pauline mission field, because, for them, Gentile-Christian churches have no right at all to exist. This is expressed by their requirement of circumcision.

There can be no Judaizers before the Gentile-Christian churches are founded in Antioch. After this decision they begin to appear. Hence their first mention in Acts 15:1, 5; Gal. 2:4 in the events leading up to the council in Jerusalem and at the council itself is probably historically correct. From these references we can perceive that the Judaizers' center is the early Jerusalem church (cf. Gal. 6:12–13). Their originally Pharisaic attitude likewise fits in well, even if we should not overrate this information given only by Luke. Was it not the Pharisees who wanted to establish the law of Moses, including the purity laws, in the whole people? Had not even Paul earlier as a Pharisee persecuted the Damascus Christians—out of zeal for the law? Thus the first opponents of the Judaizers are the Antiochenes. In spite of the Judaizers' backing in Judean Jewish Christianity, they are defeated at the council. Their program for Christian unity says, "It is necessary [for salvation] to circumcise them [i.e., the Gentile Christians of Antioch], and to charge them to keep the law of Moses" (Acts 15:5; on the style, cf., e.g., John 3:3, 5; 3:27; 5:19; 6:44, 65; 9:33), but it does not prevail. Unity in Christ is defined not through the law but through gospel, Spirit, and baptism (cf. 5.2 above). The Judaizers apparently never reconciled themselves to this defeat in Jerusalem, and now they have become a group working against the council decision. For them, not even the stipulations of James (cf. 5.3 above) are a possible compromise, because for them Christianity cannot sanction such a far-reaching release from the law. Their center remains Jerusalem, which is supported by the fact that they appear as outsiders in Galatia and Philippi.

The Antiochene incident is not a major part of the history of the Judaizers, for here, with the recognition in principle of Gentile-Christian churches, it is a matter of the preservation of Jewish-Christian parts of the church (cf. 5.3 above). The requirement of circumcision does not appear. In general, it seems that the Judaizers at first held back with their activities, for they had lost out to a broad and respectable majority. They had no well-known spokesman but were strong only as a group; for the time being they could do little against the great Christian figures of this period. In any case, they do not reactivate their efforts in a way visible to historians until the middle fifties. In the meantime, Paul has carried on his independent mission very successfully with the two great centers in Corinth and Ephesus. Not until now, toward A.D. 55, do the Judaizers try again to guide the course of history solely down a Jewish-Christian path.

The time is strategically favorable for them. They begin off to the side in distant Galatia, and meanwhile Paul is completely occupied with the so-called collection journey and much more extensive later plans (Rom. 15:22–24). The council already lies several years in the past. Yet more detailed background can at best only be surmised. Was James, who later died as a martyr in A.D. 62, no longer strong enough in Jerusalem? Was zealot activity and thinking—which with nationalism and Torah strictness fought everything foreign—already so strong that the Judaizers' position received a boost from the general development of Judaism? After all, open rebellion against Rome begins about ten years later. Did the Judaic Christians have so much trouble with Judaism in general that for them Gentile Christianity became a serious burden? Did the collection delivered from Galatia play a role here? Gentile-Christian money is unclean and would be a topical and welcome reason for the Judaizers to carry on a countermission in Galatia. In any case, a short time later they also travel behind Paul, who had apparently just gathered up the collection for Jerusalem in Philippi. Paul also feared that the unclean Gentile collection could cause serious problems in Jerusalem (Rom. 15:25, 31–32; cf. Acts 21:20–26). Perhaps it would not be accepted there at all (cf. 15.1 below).

The aspects that resonate in these questions are hardly mutually exclusive; they are not alternatives. Moreover, they are all quite conceivable, but not all attested with certainty. In any case, there is also the obvious supposition that on Paul's last visit in Jerusalem the Judaizers interfered directly. What Acts 21:20–26 reports is, of course, rather legendary, but Rom. 15:31 seems to speak clearly for such a view (cf. 15.1 below). If they assumed the role of Paul's opponents, then this was the last known act in this continuous conflict between the two. In this way the intimate enemies of his mission made life difficult for the apostle to the Gentiles and perhaps even gave him a painful defeat in Galatia and Jerusalem. But they could not ultimately hinder the development of Gentile Christianity, because they could not seriously endanger the inner dynamic of this mission.

Because of the Jewish rebellion and the normative Jewish line that prevailed afterward, the Judaizers as a group apparently got lost in the whirlpool of history. Since they themselves no longer had a place in Judaism, their missionary goal of integrating all Christians into Judaism no longer had any basis, for they themselves were refused what they strove toward as a goal for all Christians: to live as a group in association with the synagogue. Thus they remain an episode of about twenty-five years in the history of early Christianity.

This sketch of the Judaizers' history has already brought echoes of important aspects of their theology, which we shall now discuss further. At this point it is quite clear that they can think of themselves only as a grouping within Judaism. Did Jesus and the beginnings of the post-Easter churches not also belong in Judaism? Thus they can understand themselves as the conservative preservers of this origin. Therein lies their strength. At the same time, however, this means that genealogical filiation from Abraham—belonging bodily to the twelve-tribed people—is basic for them. (Hence in Phil. 3:5 Paul polemically emphasizes his heritage as a genuine Jew.) For this reason, for Judaizers non-Jews can participate in Israel's history of election only if they are belatedly incorporated into Judaism through circumcision. When Paul makes a polemical and concentrated attack on the Judaizers' requirement of circumcision, he hits the crucial point of their concern. For in the view of the Judaizers, Gentile Christians are to be addressed as Christians only if they are regarded as a special case of the general Jewish solicitation of proselytes (cf. Matt. 23:15). For them, a Gentile-Christian church with its own legitimation is a theological impossibility, but this is exactly what Paul advocates in confrontation with them, for example, in Gal. 1:11–2:21. Hence the Judaizers are in the good Jewish sense representatives of the fundamental distinction between Israel and the nations, between the elected people and Gentile sinners (cf. Rom. 9:3–5; Gal. 2:15; etc.).

Circumcision is to be interpreted on this basis: it is the sign of covenant election and the mark that distinguishes Jews from uncircumcised Gentiles (cf. in Paul: Gal. 2:7; Rom. 4:10–12). Without circumcision there is no participation in the salvation that God promised when he elected Abraham. The uncircumcised can have no share in the blessing of Abraham (contrast Gal. 3:6–14). It is likewise true that Jewish Christians like Paul who decide for a Gentile-Christian life and no longer fulfill the circumcision of born Jews (cf. Acts 21:21) place themselves and their children outside salvation.

If election is concentrated on Abraham and his offspring, and the nations receive a share of this only by way of circumcision, then it is

understandable why Paul teaches a new, Gentile–Christian understanding precisely of Abraham (Gal. 3:6ff.; Romans 4), thereby setting aside
the natural lineage from him in order to substantiate in a figurative
sense a belonging to him that is bound to faith. In Phil. 3:5, 7, Paul can
describe his natural Jewish ancestry as worthless. At the same time, it is
clear that, for Paul, God's election did not happen only once with
Abraham; rather, the Gentiles are now newly and independently
elected in the gospel (cf. Gal. 3:1–5 and 6.2 above on 1 Thessalonians).
With this, Paul razes the boundary between Jews and Gentiles, which
is repeatedly erected by the Judaizers. They probably regard Antiochene theology, expressed in formulas such as those in Gal. 3:26–28; 5:6;
1 Cor. 12:13; etc., as blasphemy and heresy.

The requirement of circumcision is not an individual or formal concern of the Judaizers. It is an expression of the adoption of the whole
law (Acts 15:5). In agreement with statements such as those in Matt.
5:17–19; 7:21–23 (the Pauline antithesis: Gal. 3:19–22), for them there
can be no opposition between the law and Christology or the concept
of the Spirit. Exactly this, however, is what Paul vehemently advocates
in Gal. 3:1–4:31. If he insists on the antithesis of law and gospel, they
persist in equating these two entities. For only the law promises life for
them (cf. Gal. 3:12). Whoever does not adopt it stands under its curse
(cf. Gal. 3:10). Therefore, from their side there is also validity in the
reproach that Paul degrades Christ to an "agent of sin" (Gal. 2:17; cf.
Rom. 6:1, 15), because he abolishes the law (Rom. 3:31a). In their view
Paul lowers the divinely set price of election when he concedes to the
Gentiles an unlawful life, that is, sinful behavior with no obligation to
the revealed divine will. Therefore Paul must expressly describe the
newly established task of Christians in their conduct of life without the
law (Gal. 5:13–6:10; Phil. 3:12ff.). If the Judaizers measure Christ and
all of Christianity by the law, Paul measures the law and Christianity by
Christ alone (Gal. 2:21 as antithesis to 2:17; Phil. 3:7–11).

For Paul, the leading of the Galatians completely back under the
jurisdiction of the law is, of course, the way of the "flesh" (Gal. 3:3) and
is even comparable to the attitude of former pagans toward the cult of
the gods (Gal. 4:8–9), but for the Judaizers it is concrete reality—including the festival calendar (Gal. 4:9–10). This calendar is connected with a
particular teaching on "elemental spirits" (4:3, 9–10), which apparently
in some no longer knowable way was conceived in relation to the basic
elements of earth, water, fire, and air. This has led to assuming for the
Judaizers influences of a syncretistic kind. Yet caution is in order here.
Not only is the whole of Judaism a syncretistic phenomenon since the
empire of Alexander's successors, and thus also in New Testament

times, but it is also true that with such demands the Judaizers imagined themselves in harmony with the law. Certainly not everyone in Judea advocated a teaching on elemental spirits, but it can be used by a Hellenistic Jew such as Philo to promote honor and understanding of the law. Indeed, the law was not at all merely a fixed, written codex. It governed the cosmos and was the means through which God created the world. Thus the Torah also contained that which held the world together and, among other things, the order of the heavenly bodies and their orbits. The heavenly bodies, in turn, determined the festival calendar, which, naturally, was also fixed in the written Torah (cf. *1 Enoch; Jubilees;* Qumran). Thus the Judaizers must have also emphasized the harmony of creation and Torah, along with the teaching on elemental spirits and the festival calendar. It goes without saying that the festival calendar is necessary for salvation because it is in accordance with the Torah. Following it carries the promise of blessing. Feasts are not simply social achievements but are special times for the working of the divine blessing. Thus in this view the Torah is portrayed especially well as the mediator of salvation. Yet for Paul the mediator of salvation is Christ alone.

It is conspicuous that from Galatians and Philippians B we actually learn nothing unambiguous about the Christology of the Judaizers. Rather, Paul places his Christology against the opponent's conception of the law. If we take into account the Judaizers' starting point with the law, it should be clear that for them Christ continues election and the law, and he supports and extends their functions. But further attempts to concretize lead into speculation.

It is one of the ironies of history that the Judaizers indirectly and unintentionally became assistants in the development of the Pauline message of justification and thus of its history of influence to the present time. For if they had not challenged Paul to battle, we would not possess the first two testimonies of the apostle's formulated message of justification: Galatians and Philippians B. Romans is based on both letters. Thus they failed to achieve what they really wanted and against their will promoted what they had set out to fight.

11
Paul and the Galatian Churches

11.1 The Unknown Galatians

The Letter to the Galatians is the apostle's only circular. He names no places, but only the "Galatians" as addressees (Gal. 1:2; 3:1). Hence Paul is dealing with several local churches in the same region. If we did not possess the Letter to the Galatians and the short notice in 1 Cor. 16:1–2, we would attach no value to the few insubstantial and incidental allusions in Acts. Indeed, we would doubt whether the Christianity of this period of the first early Christian generation had even reached so far. Apart from the testimonies named above, historians know absolutely nothing about the further history of these churches. What is one supposed to know about an area of the Roman Empire that is located so far to the northeast and into which a Roman governor went only reluctantly? This province most certainly did not belong to the top diplomatic posts of the Roman Empire. The region was rough and inhospitable; to the Romans and the Greeks, the tribes were foreign and barbaric. At the beginning of the first century people remembered quite well that the notorious robber nuisance here could be kept under control only by the strong hand of the Romans. It is doubtful that anyone in the Roman senate was willing to guarantee that the area's political subordination under the Romans was assured in the long run.

Who are the Galatians? Linguistically the word "Galatian" is related to the word "Celt." This connection is no coincidence. The Galatians are Celts of Asia Minor who are ethnic relatives of the Celts that Caesar fought in Gaul. In the third century B.C. the Celts who lived in the Danube basin pushed into Asia Minor and for a good century overran the region with their militant hordes. Their pugnacity also commended them as mercenary troops of this or that ruler. They were still not very settled during this period. In 186 B.C. the Roman consul Vulso forced upon them a settled life and a fixed political structure. In the course of time the tetrarch (later: king), who now ruled by the grace of Rome, was able—not least of all because of fortunate wars against restless neighboring peoples—to suppress the native population, pacify and even incorporate the neighboring peoples into his kingdom, and attract benevolent attention in Rome. Thus, after the last Galatian king died, Augustus, the rearranger of the Roman Empire, turned the region into a Roman province (25 B.C.), which received the name Galatia and stretched much farther to the south than the old Celtic settlement area.

Now we can ask: Is Paul writing to the places in the Celtic settlement area or to churches in the Roman province of Galatia? Today it is generally and rightly assumed that in Gal. 3:1 Paul is addressing the Celts. Non-Celtic tribes in the province of Galatia would have refused to be included. Thus we must look for the Galatian churches above all on the Halys, with Ancyra (now Ankara) as the central city, as well as in Tavium and Pessinus. This is often called the regional or North Galatian hypothesis in distinction to the provincial or South Galatian hypothesis.

Yet we must be aware that this identification of the letter's addressees does not yield much information: we know very little about the cultural and religious history of this whole northeastern region of the Roman Empire. As everywhere else in Asia Minor at this time, the religion of the old tribes has been hellenized. Greek gods and Hellenistic cults have made their entrance and have in part joined with the old cults, in part replaced them. If there were Jews in the region, it is not attested, but this does not say a great deal. We might ask whether Judaizers would go where there is no synagogue but only a Gentile-Christian church. Yet one can, of course, also reshape a Gentile-Christian church into a synagogue church. Since even Paul communicates in his letter nothing on the background of the church, except that its present members were once Gentiles (Gal. 4:8–9), the letter's addressees remain practically unknown to us.

The history of the Christian churches on the Halys is knowable only to the extent that it involves contact with Paul. The founding visit around A.D. 49/50 probably occurred with Timothy and Silas (cf. 6.1 above). It was overshadowed by Paul's illness (Gal. 4:12–20). At the beginning of the Ephesian period (A.D. 52) Paul visits the churches a second time (cf. 7.1 above) and initiates the collection for Jerusalem (1 Cor. 16:1–2; cf. ch. 2 above). Around A.D. 54/55 the anti-Pauline Judaizers come into the area (cf. 7.1 and 10.2 above), and Paul, who has in the meantime fled from Ephesus, reacts to their countermission with the Letter to the Galatians (ca. A.D. 56; cf. 10.1 above). Who delivered the letter and what success or failure it met, we do not know. But we must reckon with Paul's defeat. The Letter to the Galatians is the oldest and most detailed witness to the anti-Judaistic struggle of the apostle to the Gentiles. At the same time it contains the most important information for Paul's biography after his calling (cf. ch. 2 above).

Finally, it is the oldest testimony of Paul's message of justification. The Letter to the Galatians can be considered the forerunner of the Letter to the Romans and is therefore often called the little letter to the Romans.

11.2 The Letter to the Galatians and Ancient Rhetoric

The circumstances under which Paul wrote Galatians (or rather, dictated it; cf. Gal. 6:11 and also 1 Cor. 16:21; Rom. 16:22) are already known to us (cf. 7.1 and 10.1 above). Likewise its readers have already been introduced as well as possible (cf. 11.1 above). Finally, the Judaistic opponents have been sketched (cf. 10.2 above). Now it is a question of the means with which Paul seeks through the letter to resolve the Galatian situation in his favor. Recent investigations have made it clear that Galatians in particular offers an especially good example for such observations. On this issue more general comments have already been undertaken (cf. 3.3 above). We have not only characterized the higher level of the apostle's general education, which conveyed to him the application of elementary rhetorical rules, but we have especially gone into the fact that in polemical situations such as in some parts of the Corinthian correspondence and particularly in Galatians, Paul has used rhetorical elements from courtroom language. Galatians is the only letter that as a whole—even if in broken form— follows the basic model of a courtroom speech and thus offers a peculiar interweaving of letter formula, letter style, and defense speech.

If this thesis is correct, then the value of such investigation is obvious. If the structural and functional arrangement of the letter can really be illuminated in this way, it will have fundamental significance for the understanding of Paul's argumentation. For then all the details of the letter can be understood from the standpoint of an overall concept. The contingencies in picking out statements and determining that they are essential or polemical, and so forth, will largely be avoided.

As the only circular from Paul's hand, Galatians is supposed to make the rounds of various churches and be read aloud in the worship service (cf. 1 Thess. 5:27; Col. 4:16). In being read aloud, the letter is supposed to replace the presence and preaching of the apostle, as was the common practice in this period. Thus it is intended to have a direct effect and create personal presence. To this end Paul uses various means, such as frequent address (cf. 1:11, 13; 3:1, 15; 4:12, 28; etc.), questions (cf. 1:10; 3:1–5; 4:9, 15–16, 21; etc.), personal judgments (e.g., 1:6; 3:1; 4:11, 20), reminders of common history (e.g., 3:1–5;

4:12–20; 5:7), and in general a discussion style (analogous to the so-called diatribe of the Cynics and Stoics) that imitates live dialogue situations (cf. 3:1–5, 12).

In the formula of the letter—as in his other writings—Paul draws on oriental epistolary style and shapes it according to his own ideas. This is especially true of the opening of the letter (*praescriptio*). While the Greeks write the epistolary opening as a usually short, impersonal sentence (e.g., 1 Macc. 10:18: "King Alexander to his brother Jonathan, greetings"; cf. Acts 15:23; 23:26; James 1:1), the oriental letter opening consists of two sentences; an impersonal one gives the sender (*superscriptio*) and the addressee (*adscriptio*) and is sometimes characterized by appositional and relative expansions, and a personal one contains the greeting (*salutatio*). Daniel 4:1 (Aramaic 3:31) will serve as an example: "King Nebuchadnezzar to all peoples, nations, and languages, that dwell in all the earth: Peace be multiplied to you!" Paul uses this oriental opening mostly to insert the first signals of the letter's content, and this is true in Gal. 1:1–5.

Galatians is the only letter in which the apostle brings in polemic right at the beginning (Gal. 1:1b: "not from men nor through man, but through Jesus Christ and God the Father"). With this he wards off a reproach which he will soon take up again in 1:10–12, 16b–20. It is more usual for Paul to weave into the opening fixed confessional formulas. In this case there are two: "God . . ., who raised him from the dead" (1:1c) and "Jesus Christ, who gave himself for our sins to deliver us from the present evil age, according to the will of our God and Father" (1:4). A beautiful formal analogy for the same content of the letter opening with confession-like formulations occurs in Rom. 1:1–7. Naturally it is no coincidence when Gal. 1:1–5 reveals two confessional traditions that together describe Jesus' cross and resurrection, that is, his salvation-constituting history. Likewise it is no accident when Paul immediately designates this destiny contained in the confession as "gospel" (1:6ff., 11ff.). For precisely this defines for Paul the content of the gospel (cf. 1 Cor. 15:1ff.; Rom. 1:1–7, 16–17). In Galatians, however, there is an additional aspect. It is precisely this gospel in its Pauline refinement as Gentile-Christian gospel that is disputed in the Galatian situation. Therefore Paul must substantiate that its heritage and authority are direct from God in 1:6ff., 11ff., in contrast to the reproach that they are only human. That means, however, that in his *praescriptio* Paul not only distinguishes himself polemically from his opponents (1:1b) but at the same time lays the foundation for his own viewpoint (1:1c, 4). Thus Paul—intentionally, as it seems—immediately gets down to business by getting into the dispute as he understands it.

Also associated with such planning is the doxology at the end of the letter's opening (Gal. 1:5). Its position here is unusual. The following observation is a possible explanation. Normally, after the preface Paul thanks God for the church (cf., e.g., 1 Cor. 1:4–9; Rom. 1:8–15). In the Galatian case he cannot do that. Thus he closes his preface with the doxology and then begins in vs. 6–9 to follow the structure of a court speech. Paul does not return to the typology of the epistolary formula until the closing of the letter (6:11–18), which lacks greetings and travel plans, for example, just as 1:1–2 names no fellow senders.

Galatians 1:6–9 can be understood as the entrance or beginning, according to the structure of the court speech (introduction: *exordium, prooemium*). Here it is a matter of trying to take the most direct possible approach to the case to be decided as well as a first urgent appraisal. The opponent is attacked and a clear signal given as judgment in the case. Right and wrong are alternatively accorded to the speaker and his opponent. Without doubt 1:6–9 is also alternatively and uncompromisingly judgmental when Paul's gospel is placed here in opposition to the other one, which is not one—when the opposing side is even cursed. The quarrel over the key word "gospel," as the Galatians received it from Paul, and the indication that the opponents' proclamation is no gospel are also to the point. The cursing of the opponents, which stands in the Old Testament-Jewish tradition, has its counterpart at the close of the letter (6:11–18) in the conditional blessing of the Galatians. This bridge also has a center pier, 5:1–12, which forms the close of the crucial argumentation section. Thus in three especially emphasized places Paul achieves a separation between the church and the unknown missionaries, and this is heavily weighted theologically through the alternatives of salvation and damnation.

A brief transition (Gal. 1:10), which also in the court speech is supposed to mediate between the hard initial tone and the historical exposition of the case, is followed, in accordance with ancient rhetoric, by the one-sided presentation of the history of the present quarrel (*narratio*): 1:11–2:21. Paul's own standpoint is to be supported by describing and evaluating, in careful selection and mostly in historical sequence, the decisive historical junctures that can be brought to bear in favor of his own thesis. Paul mentions three sets of circumstances: his calling and beginning period (1:11–24), the Apostolic Council (2:1–10), and the Antiochene quarrel with Peter (2:11–21).

Here the Pauline gospel, which the Galatians know from the initial preaching (1:9), remains the actual theme and, of course, is honed as law-free, hence Gentile-Christian-oriented gospel (1:11, 16; 2:2, 5, 14). Paul, who for the sake of the law had sought to destroy the church of

God, is called directly by God to the law-free gospel for the Gentiles. This divine origin and Paul's independence as an apostle are recognized by the Jewish Christians of Judea to the extent that they, not knowing Paul personally, praise God for acting thus with Paul (1:11–24). At the Apostolic Council the "pillars" and the Antiochene delegation with Paul as spokesman then agreed that as Peter had to be considered the divinely called apostle for the upbuilding of the Jewish-Christian churches, so Paul for the Gentile-Christian churches. Hence the Gentile-Christian gospel of Paul was fully recognized by the church (2:1–10). The Judaizers not only incorrectly denied the divine origin of the Pauline mission but also set themselves against the official ecclesiastical consensus. Of course, this consensus was again called into question as a result of Peter's visit in Antioch (2:11–21). Paul, however, did not give one inch on the truth of the gospel here, either (and, naturally, was even less inclined to do so now with the Judaizers).

Yet if we view the historical presentation in its rhetorical aspect, Gal. 1:11–2:21 is only in a limited way a historical exposition of the case at hand. For Paul devotes himself to his own life only as it relates to the problem and seeks in it only elements that belong here. He does not examine at all the history of the Galatian churches and the Judaizers. His procedure is not quite that orthodox.

After the historical part in the court speech, there is usually a small section that summarizes the results of the preceding comments and names the points that are then treated in the argumentation and discussion part (*propositio*, presentation of the crucial discussion points). This function is covered in Paul by the speech against Peter (2:14b–21), which really forms the closing of the historical part. Therefore it cannot be understood as a section in itself apart from the historical presentation. Rather, it is the closing of this section and at the same time introduction to 3:1ff. Thus, for a second time we can see that Paul does not proceed in a completely orthodox fashion. If we want to describe the speech against Peter structurally, it appears to be a short court speech within the letter as a long court speech and as such replaces the usual presentation. Thus we can interpret 2:14b as opening (*exordium*), 2:15–16 as historical defense (*narratio*), 2:17 as presentation (*propositio*), 2:18–20 as the marshaling of evidence (*probatio*), and finally 2:21 as the closing argument (*peroratio*). It may be appreciated as the apostle's personal knack when he avails himself of the rhetorical possibilities in this form.

Now in Gal. 3:1–5:12, following the structure of a court speech, Paul comes to the core of the presentation, that is, to the marshaling of evidence (*probatio* or *argumentatio* and *confirmatio*). Now he must put to the test the things that substantiate his thesis. It must become clear why his own and not the opponent's position is right. The introduction and the historical part only lead up to this point; now comes the decision. If the speaker cannot be convincing here, he has lost his chance. The argumentative chain should be presented in a lively fashion (as dialogue spiced with quotations, discerning with illuminating examples, broken up by rhetorical questions). The argumentative strategy is in principle open. Paul's strategy follows two lines of argumentation, with the second, according to the subject, repeating and strengthening what the first has established. The two lines are thus, so to speak, parallel (3:1–4:7; 4:8–31). Then follows a two-part closing section (5:1–6, 7–12), whose association with 1:6–9 and 6:11–16 has already been indicated. These doublings are, again, not quite orthodox.

The first line of argumentation in the marshaling of evidence begins with the questioning of the witnesses (*interrogatio*). Paul takes the Galatians to the beginning of their becoming Christians (3:1–5). Had they not been made free from the "law" by the law-free gospel, which now comes to expression through its effect, that is, as the giving of the Spirit to the Galatians? (Cf. the same argumentation in 2:7–9!) Do they now want to complete with the flesh what they began with the Spirit? Then in the second and third parts (3:6–9; 3:10–14), through interpretation of scripture (six quotations in all, with the focus on the figure of Abraham) and of Christian confessions (3:13–14) Paul explains the antithetical character of "works of the law" and "hearing with faith" in the reverse order from that in 3:5, in order to present a new evaluation of the law in view of the gospel in two further sections (3:15–18; 3:19–22) according to this antithesis conceived as confrontation and as alternatives. For historical reasons the law cannot change the gospel as the promise to Abraham nor compete with it in content and function. Now the tone changes: the descriptive and definitional style changes into "we" and "you." In two parallel sections (3:23–29; 4:1–7) Paul makes clear to the Galatians how through baptism and the Spirit they were transposed from the law as custodian and from the condition of being under age into the status of sons and adult heirs. With this, Paul interprets the gift of the Spirit through the gospel (3:1–5) and makes clear to the Galatians that their new service to the law means a falling back into a state that they have long overcome. The first line of argumentation is characterized by these sections—seven in all. The impressive structuring of the sections is recognizable not least of all by the fact that all the closings correspond and vary the main thesis (3:5, 9, 14, 18, 22, 29; 4:7).

The second line of argumentation (4:8–31) begins once again with an interrogation, but now in two steps (4:8–11; 4:12–20). Again Paul begins with the history of the churches, namely, with the problem of falling back and with the first reception of the apostle in the churches. The closing verses (vs. 11, 20) convey the helplessness into which Paul has fallen in regard to the present behavior of the Galatians. Then he begins again (cf. 3:6ff.) with scriptural proof (4:21–31), which ends with the basic thesis that is already substantially known from the closings of the first line of argumentation.

In 5:1–6; 5:6–12 the close of the marshaling of evidence urgently implores the Galatians and sarcastically passes final judgment on the opponents. Cursing (1:9), sarcasm (5:12), and exposure of the opponents (6:12–13) are consistent, as is, conversely, the apostle's wish, expressed in various ways, that the church might return to the way of the law-free gospel.

With these last comments Paul, for the time being, leaves the structure of the court speech entirely. Normally a rejection of the opposing arguments (*refutatio*) would now follow. Paul, however, does not have such a section in mind, so he deviates again from the orthodox opinion of the rhetoricians. Here and there in the marshaling of evidence for his position, he has rejected the opposing positions and thus, if you will, built the refutation into the marshaling of evidence. Moreover, the following section also contains a hidden refutation of the opponents' attack, as will now be shown.

The promotion of the law-free gospel was the crucial aim of the argumentation in 3:1–5:12. If, however, freedom from the law is not supposed to release the Christian without obligation, but rather life in the Spirit is supposed to bring with it spiritual change (5:25), then Paul must now invalidate the old reproach—long familiar to him—that a law-free gospel makes Christ the agent of sin (2:17; cf. Rom. 5:1, 15). He undertakes this by turning to paraenesis at the close of the letter— typical of other Pauline and early Christian letters (Romans; Ephesians; Colossians; etc.)—and thus describes the normative character of Christian change (5:13–6:10). He urges the church to comprehend freedom as opportunity and commission to love.

After Paul has done this in detail, he comes to the closing of the letter (6:11–18). Here we have a strange mixture of epistolary style and imploring repetition of the crucial difficulty, together with its solution, so that, among other things, the court speech is again present with its closing (*peroratio* or *recapitulatio*), guiding the structure. We have already mentioned the connection with 1:6–9.

Thus Galatians can be understood as an apologetic letter that varies the basic structures of the court speech. This understanding of the epistolary structure naturally affects the interpretation. Later we will take a special look at this understanding of the content of the letter (cf. 11.4 below).

11.3 The Roots of the Pauline Statements on Justification

Galatians is the oldest testimony on the apostle's elaborated message of justification in that in its center, the marshaling of evidence (*argumentatio* or *probatio*) in 3:15–5:12, the statements on justification receive predominant significance (cf. 11.2 above). Neither in 1 Thessalonians nor in the Corinthian correspondence is such a central position occupied by statements on the word stem "just/righteous." [In contrast to Greek and German, English Bibles use more than one stem.—Trans.] Though they are not entirely lacking there, they occur more incidentally and play no guiding and shaping role in the overall train of thought comparable to the dominant function of the language of election (1 Thessalonians) or the language of the theology of the cross (1 and 2 Corinthians). This changes with Galatians. Anyone who sees how Paul possesses the ability to present in a short space, say, the theology of the cross with as many rich variations as in the Corinthian correspondence (cf. ch. 8 above) cannot be overly amazed that the apostle can now once again reorient himself linguistically in Galatians.

But does he really do that? Or is the message of justification in 1 Thessalonians and 1 and 2 Corinthians only temporarily somewhat in the background? Was Paul, in other words, the apostle of the message of justification from the beginning? Where are the roots of this theological language? In any case, it has already become clear that Paul developed his theology of election and theology of the cross, and no one can or must maintain that these two linguistic expressions of his theology are incomplete in their content. It is notable, further, that in its typical Pauline expression the language of justification presupposes statements on the theologies of election and cross and in central places is developed from them. On the other hand, nonetheless, prior to Galatians the word stem "just/righteous" appears only in typical places with traditional statements, and then only rather sporadically.

On the question of the origin of the message of justification, furthermore, we must not ignore the fact that Paul first introduces it in highly polemical circumstances against the Judaizers—namely, in Galatians and Philippians B (cf. 12.4 below)—before he then develops it in Romans in the style of a more objectively oriented presentation. Does this enmity have anything to do with the use of theological language? This should not be excluded from the outset. We need only to recall that in the Corinthian correspondence the apostle goes at his opponents in a flexible and dialogical fashion. If we reckon with this possibility, we will then, however, also think about the fact that Paul has already—namely, in his Antiochene period—experienced a situation or a nature very similar to Galatians, when the question was what is the uniting bond of Christianity, and the question was answered in such a way that the law, in any case, was excluded from the defining standard (cf. 5.2–5.5 above). Did the language of justification already in some way or other have a special significance in this period? We cannot give this question a negative answer right away.

May we even go farther and recall the Damascus situation with the persecution activities and the calling to be apostle to the Gentiles (cf. ch. 4 above)? When we consider our sources here, however, inferences become extremely hypothetical. Even if the antithesis between law and gospel may have been established here, and the fundamental decisions of Pauline theology made, it is unlikely that in this early period Paul was already using the language of justification in the same way as in Galatians and Philippians B, because from the Antiochene period until Galatians it can be demonstrated only in quite limited formulaic contexts; conversely, Galatians and Philippians B contain the apostle's Antiochene and Corinthian theology as a constituent. Thus we must give preference to an explanatory model in which basic decisions (still independent of the language of justification) are made in Damascus, in which statements with the word stem "just/righteous" can be fixed at first in typical and formulaic language and in which, finally, Paul chooses this language in a specific way so that it can express the points of his theology.

Hence we must first ask: In what typical contexts do statements with the word stem "just/righteous" occur in the Pauline letters? We want to designate these groups of statements as semantic word fields, because from the standpoint of the presentation and statement they are complete contexts in themselves, which serve as meaning-constituting fields of vision, and because in them a typical but limited language is used. The first typical word field of this kind occurs in traditional statements on the last judgment. In order to appreciate this observation properly, we must recall that early Christianity as a whole (practically since John the Baptist) was fundamentally determined by the expectation of an immediate, imminent final judgment. God's justified wrath over the desolate condition of humanity will soon come forth, and only the eschatological church now already gathering will be able to be justified before God, for Christ will be their savior (1 Thess. 1:10; cf. 6.2 above). Here the final events are not described as final battle and divine victory or as cosmic conflagration or annihilation of the world. Rather, the presentation concentrates on the relationship of God and Christ to human beings. Thus in Paul we only rarely find an indication of a horizon with a view of reality in general and as a whole (cf.

1 Cor. 15:20–28; Rom. 8:18–22). The great majority of his statements describe only the crucial relationship between God and humankind—more precisely, between God or Christ and the eschatological church.

Exactly at this point we now find statements that more closely define the divine sovereign right of judgment (Rom. 14:10–11; cf. also 1 Cor. 4:4; etc.). These include the following typical formulations: "We shall all stand before the judgment seat of God" (Rom. 14:10; cf. 2 Cor. 5:10), and everyone must "give account of himself" (Rom. 14:12). It is important here that every individual without exception will stand thus before the judge (1 Cor. 3:13–14; 2 Cor. 5:10), so that his or her work can be tested (1 Cor. 3:13). Everyone's work "will become manifest" (ibid.) in that the Lord "will bring to light the things now hidden in darkness and will disclose the purposes of the heart" (1 Cor. 4:5). Everyone will then "receive good or evil, according to what he has done" (2 Cor. 5:10). This means, positively, that everyone "will receive his commendation from God" (1 Cor. 4:5). In this way he or she can stand in God's presence (cf. 1 Cor. 8:8). These themes, gathered from scattered textual statements of Paul, not only form a closed context but also can be very nicely tested by the detailed picture of judgment in Romans 2. This was already used to describe Paul as a former Pharisee (cf. 3.2 above). So we can propose the thesis that in the presentation of the last judgment as an eschatological, forensic court scene, there is continuity from the Pharisee Paul to the apostle to the Gentiles. The presentation is based on a graphic image that everyone in antiquity could experience in the courtroom and audience scenes of rulers, generals, and provincial governors. There are also examples of this in the New Testament (Mark 15:1ff. par.; John 18:19ff.; Acts 18:12ff.). Such everyday reality is used as an artist's palette to paint the scenes of final judgment (cf. Matt. 25:31ff.; Romans 2; Revelation 4; *Barn.* 21.1–6).

In close connection with such statements we now also find formulations with the word stem "just/righteous." Thus in 1 Cor. 4:4 we have the passive verb form for "be justified" (RSV: "acquitted"). Paul writes there that he is not aware of any wrong behavior, but he is not thereby justified, and he continues that this will be done by the Lord through his judging at the final day of judgment. According to Phil. 1:10–11, on the day of the Lord Christians are supposed to be pure and blameless, filled with the fruits of righteousness to the glory and praise of God (cf. also 2 Cor. 9:8–9). Or according to Gal. 5:5, Christians expect to see the hope of righteousness through redemption. In the words of Rom. 2:12–13, the doers of the law will stand "righteous before God," because they "will be justified." The day of wrath will in general be the day of "God's righteous judgment" (Rom. 2:5; cf. 12:19). With Rom. 4:4

we can say in summary: To the one who performs works, "wages" are awarded in the last judgment—"as his due"—and such a positive reaction of God can be comprehended as a "reckoning of righteousness."

It is important to see that even these statements on the word stem "just/righteous" still do not in any way contain Paul's special message of justification. In their unspecific and early Jewish-Christian commonality, however (cf. *1 Enoch* 1–5; chs. 48; 61; *Lib. Ant.* 3:10; *Jub.* 5:10–19; *Barn.* 21.1–6; etc.), they give a portion of the wood from which Paul carved parts of his message of justification. Of special significance here are the categories with which the apostle conceives God's judgment, which are marked by linguistic signals. First, he can use the language borrowed from the old concept of the action-consequence connection, that is the concept according to which the action of a community member strikes back directly at him and his community. Paul can describe this, for example, with the metaphor of the seed and the harvest: "Do not be deceived; God is not mocked, for whatever a man sows, that he will also reap" (Gal. 6:7). As the seeds and the resulting harvest are organically connected—one the immediate cause of the other—so also will the deed as seed produce consequences. In the analysis of Romans 2 (cf. 3.2 above) we came upon further examples, but at the same time we made observations that cast doubt on the heuristic function of this view.

Occurring much more often is a concept that we can generally describe as the authoritative expression of power. Such ideas are also a natural characteristic of throne and tribunal scenes. Now, misfortune does not, so to speak, automatically strike the evildoer, if he is only given free reign; rather, the deed stands there isolated. The case must be debated before the court as to how it will be decided. A special act of a ruler or judge is necessary. He decides mostly according to the current norms and thereby substantiates the verdict, which contains punishment or reward. The punishment is carried out by bailiff, soldiers, or prison guards, who receive an order as to how they are to proceed with a delinquent (cf. Mark 15:15; John 19:16); or the innocent defendant is set free with a pronouncement of the verdict (Acts 18:14–16). In these examples we see at the same time how isolated and alone is the one to be judged. Like his deed, he is individualized; his association with a community is, as a rule, unimportant. The predominant concept is the court over the individual perpetrator, who must justify his personal behavior. Finally, such authoritative expressions of power always not only serve the cultivation of generally recognized principles of justice but also implement power, stabilize victorious authority, and are thus instruments of political power.

Thereby the person doing the judging gains a quite different position from that of a mere administrator of a trial situation that basically runs by itself from the deed to its consequence. He is the sovereign, often not without arbitrariness and in any case characterized by mighty weight in his decisions. His judicial word creates new facts. The texts assembled above attest that Paul formulates out of such a view in aspect and in selection when he describes the last judgment. We can make this even more precise. In the framework of the divine authoritative judicial verdict, we find strikingly often in Paul expressions from the commercial and working world, such as receiving a wage, receiving wages pledged according to what is due, rendering an account, inspecting work, and so forth. We have already seen that such metaphors of his for the reality of the last judgment are probably of Pharisaic origin (cf. 3.2 above).

If this describes the first semantic word field that has significance for the Pauline message of justification, then we enter a quite different world when we turn to the next word field. It is the concept and language of baptism as shaped by the Antiochene church (cf. 5.5 above) and used by Paul, for example, in his theology of election (cf. 6.2 above). Now it is no longer a question of eschatological forensic verdicts but rather a Spirit-effected, present being in the new Christian existence as it was created in a unique act in baptism. Thus with the help of old baptismal tradition in 1 Cor. 6:9–11, Paul can speak of the Gentile Christians of Corinth once being "the unrighteous" (by nature). Now, however, they are no longer identical with this past, for "you were washed, you were sanctified, you were justified in the name of the Lord Jesus Christ and in the Spirit of our God." Baptism in the name of Jesus Christ was the act of conveying the Spirit. This event brought about an effective transformation of human existence, so that it is now washed of all sinful stain (cf. Acts 22:16; Col. 1:14; Eph. 1:7, 14), is subject to the sanctifying effect of the Spirit (cf. 1 Thess. 4:3–4 with 4:7–8 and Rom. 6:22; 2 Thess. 2:13), and, in contrast to the existential state of being as "unrighteous," is now "justified." Thus baptism is understood here as a unique action that fundamentally changes a person through the working of the Holy Spirit, which makes a new person from the old. The passive "being justified," which is linked with the baptismal act, is a description of the radical turning point from which the Christian now lives. A look at 1 Cor. 1:30 confirms that the triad of verbs (in reverse order) also occurs as an order of nouns in fixed baptismal language. For Christians, Christ has been made "righteousness and sanctification and redemption." Thus the Spirit-effected change has a christological origin, so that the Spirit lets salvation through Christ take effect in baptism. The

key words "righteousness" and "sanctification" likewise define the comments on baptism in Rom. 6:1ff. (cf. vs. 13, 16, 18–20, and 19, 22),
where the profound existential change is understood as dying with
Christ in baptism and as a new way of life; indeed, having died to sin
(Rom. 6:2, 6–7, 11) or having been set free from sin (Rom. 6:18) apparently takes the place of the "washing." There is, to be sure, no mention
of the Spirit in Romans 6. Instead, righteousness is understood as the
power that determines human beings (Romans 6:13, 18–20), that is, so
to speak, as the creative power of the Spirit and its resulting righteousness seen as one. Also, 1 Cor. 1:30 throws light on 2 Cor. 5:21, where in
traditional fashion the exchange between Christ and humanity is
described thus: "For our sake [taking our place] he made him to be sin
who knew no sin [as experience and as perpetrator], so that in him we
might [be able to] become the righteousness of God" (cf. "in Christ,"
Gal. 3:26, 28). Romans 4:25 is rather fitting here, when Paul formu-
laically closes the comments on Abraham by describing Christ as the
one who was given by God "for our trespasses and raised [by him] for
our justification." The last two cited traditions again show how the
Christians' new state of salvation conveyed through Christ is of essential
nature. Even if baptism is not expressly mentioned as the action that
conveys the new being, in view of the other passages it may still be
named as background. On the cited texts with baptismal statements on
the word stem "just/righteous" we close with the observation that
according to 1 Cor. 1:30; 6:11; 2 Cor. 5:21; Rom. 4:25, no special distinction in meaning is perceivable between a verbal formulation and a
noun formation used absolutely or with the genitive.

With this we have grasped the heart of the second semantic word
field, which is the starting point for discussing this context. Yet there
are, beyond this, further statements that under certain circumstances
should be placed close to these passages. This is true, first, for the formula in Rom. 3:24–26 if we choose the good possibility of shaping the
beginning of the formula thus: "They are justified . . . as a gift, through
the redemption which is in Christ Jesus." Moreover, we find a set chain
of salvific verbs in Rom. 8:29–30, when Paul joins together "predestined," "called," "justified," and "glorified," with God as subject and
human beings as objects. Finally, in the context of the un-Pauline section 2 Cor. 6:14–7:1, the new being of the church is described as the
temple of God. Therefore just as, in a certain way, the church by its
nature belongs with the light, for example, so also with righteousness.

We now pause to summarize. In addition to the statements in Paul
on righteousness, as they appear bound to the eschatological, forensic
judging act of God, there is an impressive number of statements on the

word stem "just/righteous" that belong to a quite different, independent semantic word field. There are baptismal statements concerning the present, which describe the new being of the Christian as initiated by Christ and conveyed by the Spirit. The two fields also are distinguished from each other in regard to the religious-historical roots. The judgment statements came from Jewish apocalypticism and also gained entrance into the Hellenistic Judaism of the Diaspora (cf. 3.2 above). The baptismal statements are of Hellenistic-Antiochene heritage (cf. 5.5 above). It will be shown later that the apostle's elaborated message of justification draws on both word fields and that in the same great train of thought Paul can integrate both kinds of statement into his presentation. This is especially true of Romans.

This thesis now reads that beside these two semantic word fields—except for an area to be regarded separately—there are no occurrences of the word stem "just/righteous" in Paul that are of decisive significance for his elaborated message of justification. For we can forgo regarding, for example, general, catalog-like enumerations on ethics (Phil. 4:8), qualifications of righteousness in polemical situations (2 Cor. 11:15; Phil. 3:6; 1 Thess. 2:10), and general predications of God (Rom. 3:5, 26) as essential components of the Pauline message of justification. That leaves only the one indicated exception, which is, however, not another semantic word field but a whole book, namely, the Septuagint. It is clear that Paul could not have formulated his message of justification without his Holy Scripture. If in Philippians B (cf. 12.4 below) a scriptural reference is missing, then it certainly was not intentional. For right from the first formulation of the message of justification in Galatians, Paul works intensively with scriptural proof.

Here we can show that there were certain core passages in which Paul found his views confirmed. These are references that are used by him not only once and that do not appear only incidentally. They include Hab. 2:4: "He who through faith is righteous shall live" (Rom. 1:17; Gal. 3:11); Ps. 143:2: "No man living is righteous before thee" (echoed in Rom. 3:20; Gal. 2:16); and naturally Gen. 15:6: "Abraham believed God, and it was reckoned to him as righteousness" (Rom 4:3, 9, 22; Gal. 3:6). To these three cardinal references, which contain direct statements of righteousness, one more reference is above all to be added, which—even without using the word stem "just/righteous"—gained crucial significance for Paul himself, namely, Jer. 9:24: "Let him who glories glory in . . . the LORD." As a central passage in the Pauline theology of the cross (1 Cor. 1:31; 2 Cor. 10:17), the essence of this text is taken up into the message of justification (cf. Gal. 6:14a; Rom. 3:27–31).

Can we now conclude that with these three supports (statements on the last judgment, baptismal tradition, and Septuagint) Paul developed his message of justification for the first time in Galatians? In a certain way this may be correct. Of course, we must again recall the as yet unanswered question: What part in this was played by Antioch or by Paul while he was still in Antioch? On this we offer the following reflection. Naturally, in Antioch they would have also been familiar with statements on the last judgment corresponding to those gathered above. Without doubt the baptismal statements quoted above point to Antioch as their place of origin. At crucial points, however, the Pauline message of justification always contains a polemical edge regarding the law. But in both semantic word fields that is missing. Are there traces of such a polemic in the statements on righteousness that reach back to Antioch?

This, at any rate, is the case when we regard a passage such as Rom. 14:17 as fixed. The text reads: "For the kingdom of God is not food and drink but righteousness and peace and joy in the Holy Spirit." The thesis that the verse comes from the period before the composition of Romans can be substantiated in the following ways. Talk of the kingdom of God—otherwise missing in all of Romans—is certainly older than Paul. It often occurs in Paul in definitional sentences (cf. 1 Cor. 4:20; 15:50; Gal. 5:21; etc.), which from the beginning maintain in thesis fashion a consensus of the church, as also in Rom. 14:17. The linking of "food and drink" does not fit into the context in Romans 14–15. The two key words will be sought there in vain. In terms of content, the problem of eating and the keeping of special days is prominent (Rom. 14:2–6); only quite incidentally is there also a special mention of drinking wine (14:21). All of that coincides with "food and drink" only in a limited way. The triad "righteousness and peace and joy" likewise has only limited roots in the context. The word stem "just/righteous" is completely absent, and peace or peace and joy is mentioned only in 14:19; 15:13, apparently in dependence on 14:17. Also, there is actually nothing of the Holy Spirit in the context, for in the closing blessing (15:13) he appears as much according to common style as unexpected on the basis of the foregoing problem development. Thus we can advance the thesis that 14:17 contains old tradition.

Its interpretation must now proceed in independence of the context. In that case, however, the following understanding is the most likely: The kingdom of God as the presence of the Spirit in the church does not consist in keeping ritual precepts at mealtime. According to its nature it exists as righteousness in the sense of baptismal righteousness, of which we have already spoken, as peace, that is, as the harmonious

unity of the whole church (1 Thess. 4:9–10; 5:13; Rom. 12:10; the opposite: 1 Cor. 3:3), and as the joyful basic mood of the church in view of
the salvific nearness of the Lord (cf. 1 Thess. 1:10; Phil. 4:4–5; Rom.
13:11–14). Was it not at mealtime that the quarrel was once ignited in
Antioch over the validity of the law (cf. 5.3 above)? Thus Rom. 14:17
can be understood as a fossil of the Antiochene situation, in which,
from the standpoint of the new understanding of the Spirit and the
church, the law was declared null and void. Hence we come to the verdict that while Antioch did not exactly know the Pauline message of
justification of Galatians, there are indications that in the Antiochene
church baptismal righteousness was interpreted in a directly antilaw
fashion.

This observation encourages us to seek further traces of such an
Antiochene attitude. Now, in the analysis of Paul's speech in Antioch
on the occasion of Peter's visit, we have already directed attention to
the monstrous sentence in Gal. 2:16 (cf. 5.3 above). In contrast to the
context, it contains an impersonally formulated sentence that dogmati-
cally maintains a consensus of the church: "A person is justified not by
the works of the law but [only] through faith in Jesus Christ" (NRSV).
This thesis is introduced as knowledge of the church ("we know
that . . ."), has a clear counterpart in Rom. 3:28 with an analogous
introduction, and breathes Antiochene air. This is shown by the generalizing term "person," which in the spirit of the old baptismal tradition
in Gal. 3:26–28 places every person, without precondition, under the
message of Christ and thus, for example, tacitly abolishes the distinction between Jews faithful to the law and Gentiles without the law.
Equally significant is the observation that in this sentence the works of
the law (e.g., circumcision and the ritual law) are deprived of their
salvific meaning, and the acceptance of the missionary message of
Christ (i.e., "faith"—cf. 1 Thessalonians 1–2; 1 Cor. 15:1–2; Rom. 13:11;
etc.) leads to baptism, which "justifies." Thus the church's basic tenet
formulates in its way what is contained in the Antiochene slogan "freedom in Christ" (Gal. 2:4; cf. 5.2 above).

A further passage that will reward discussion in this connection is
Gal. 5:5–6: "For through the Spirit, by faith, we wait for the hope of
righteousness. For in Christ Jesus neither circumcision nor uncircumcision is of any avail, but faith working through love." Even if we have
here no independent, fixed formula, the statement still contains typical
traditional elements. Among them is the talk of a future righteousness,
which Paul as a Christian makes a present definition of Christians
through baptism and faith but which corresponds to the Jewish understanding of salvation, which is defined through the law (cf. Rom. 2:13,

20; 3.2 above). Then there is the connection between "in Christ" and "neither circumcision nor uncircumcision" (cf. Gal. 3:26–28). Also, the three key words "Spirit," "faith," and "love" fit very well into the early Gentile-Christian self-understanding (cf. 6.2 above). Can we thus assume that also behind Gal. 5:5–6 is the shimmer of the Antiochene difficulty and decision? Then we can say that in Gal. 5:5–6 the Jewish way to salvation with its expectation is rejected by the new position "in Christ." Christians define their own understanding of salvation by delineating it from the Jewish one.

Thus our search for pre-Galatians statements on the word stem "just/righteous" with an opposition to the law has produced a positive result. There are remnants of tradition that can be understood to indicate that Paul in Antioch and the Antiochene church at the time of Paul still, of course, possessed no message of justification in the sense of Galatians, Philippians B, or Romans, yet could formulate justification statements in two typical semantic word fields and, beyond that, also made firm statements on the basic problem of the law and on the gospel that is oriented toward freedom from the law. Now that the roots of the Pauline message of justification have been uncovered, the interpretation of that message in Galatians can follow.

11.4 Galatians as the Oldest Testimony of Justification

An overview of Galatians shows that its justification language is restricted to the speech against Peter in 2:14b–21 and the argumentative middle section 3:1–5:12. For the word stem "just/righteous" occurs in Galatians in a verb only in 2:16–17; 3:8, 11, 24; 5:4, in a noun only in 2:21; 3:6, 21; 5:5, and in an adjective only in a quotation from Hab. 2:4 in Gal. 3:11. The speech against Peter assumes the task of an introduction and presentation of the crucial viewpoints. The large middle section of Galatians delivers the central argumentative settlement of accounts with the opponents (cf. 11.2 above). While the former lays out the key words and basic assertions in dogmatic and concentrated form, the latter develops them in comprehensive detail. Therefore it makes good sense to focus the following comments on 3:1–5:12 and, naturally, in the process to keep in mind Paul's speech against Peter.

Of course, it is not advisable immediately to approach 3:1–5:12 as if we had here an independent block of text. The section fits, rather, into an overall plan for the letter. As the rhetorical analysis indicated (cf. 11.2 above), in addition to 2:14b–21 we have above all 1:6–9 and

6:11–16, which, together with the closing section of the argumentation (5:1–12), offer particular aids to insight into the function and theme of the letter. At this point we are primarily interested in the assertion that without exception these pieces are characterized by election language honed by the theology of the cross; that is to say, they breathe the spirit of the Corinthian correspondence. God "called" the Galatians through the gospel of Christ into the new state of salvation (1:6–7; 5:8), namely, that of the "grace of Christ" or "of God" (1:6; 2:21; 5:4). This state is based only (6:14a!) on the "cross of our Lord Jesus Christ" (6:14). Now, however, comes the threatening possibility that the Galatians have perhaps already fallen away from this grace (1:6; 5:4), because they, led astray by the Judaizers (1:7; 3:1; 5:10), eliminate the scandal of the cross (5:11) by saying that the gospel advocated by Paul needs a supplement in the case of the Galatians (5:3; 6:12). It must be supplemented because the election of Gentile Christians through the gospel cannot become effective for salvation until it puts them under the law through circumcision. Even Israel, which was elected in the covenant of Abraham, is dependent on the law. Yet, Paul counters, in this way the gospel becomes a nongospel (1:6–9); that is, the very essence of gospel is eliminated, because the offense of the cross of Christ is nullified, and Christ then died in vain (2:21b; 5:11). Thus it is the graceful aspect of the gospel that is destroyed (cf. 1:6; 2:21; 5:4). Why? According to Paul, anyone who regards the law as an integral part of the covenant, so that the graceful election of God receives its subsequent counterpart in the human fulfillment of the law, grants the law an undue importance. This unity of covenant and law as the salvific way to life gives the "works of the law" a significance that, according to the apostle, they cannot have. Anyone who proceeds thus wants—as Paul judges—"to be justified by the law" (2:21; 5:4–5). He wants to support himself with his legal achievements and not grant to Christ alone the glory of redemption (Gal. 6:13–14). It is not enough for him "to be justified in Christ" (2:17). He does not depend on the grace of the cross alone but gives his doing of the law a share in his eschatological redemption.

From this we learn that the justification terminology emerges when Paul uses it in the coordinate system of election and the cross of Christ for sounding out the particular Galatian situation. Thus the Corinthian theology of the cross is a precondition of the apostle's Galatian position. Hence we can say that the message of justification is used in Galatians to actualize the concern of the theology of the cross by clothing it in new linguistic dress. The signals of the theology of the cross, which frame especially the argumentative middle section 3:1–5:12 at the beginning and the end (3:1; 5:11!), are thereby set as programmatic pointers, on the basis of which the language of justification is meant to be understood. In other words, the theology of the Corinthian correspondence has the most important guiding function for the understanding of Galatians next to the letter's internal structure, as indicated by the structure of the letter itself. We must note here, incidentally, that the fundamental reproach against the Corinthians (1 Corinthians 1–2) reappears in Galatians against the Judaizers (Gal. 2:21; 5:11): in both cases the salvific significance of the cross of Christ is minimized. Thus Paul reduces two so different theologies to the same common denominator: they are joined in the same opposition to the cross of Christ. They trust increasingly in what they themselves are and can exhibit (2 Corinthians 12; Gal. 6:13–14), where one must boast only on the Lord (1 Cor. 1:31), that is, glory exclusively in the "cross of Christ" (Gal. 6:14). In 1 Cor. 1:18–31 we have seen that the most profound basis of this judgment lies in the image of God revealed in the cross of Christ.

Paul's judgment of his opponents in Galatians leads us to ask what position the Judaizers were holding. From their characterization in 10.2 above, the following aspects are now significant. The Judaizers apparently understood the election of the Gentiles only as a continuation of the special election of Israel, and indeed in a particular way: it is based on the understanding of the divine election of Abraham. He and his seed, that is, the twelve-tribed nation as the genealogical continuation of the patriarch, are the ones chosen by God. Gentiles can be incorporated as exceptions into this context through circumcision, that is, as (Christian) proselytes. Therefore, in his argumentation in Gal. 3:6ff. Paul goes immediately to a new interpretation of Abraham. Now circumcision, furthermore, is not to be seen by itself as a requirement of the law but is to be understood only as a signal of the overall relationship of covenant and law. Thus by following the law the partner in the covenant responds to God's covenant and commits himself to the principle of the Torah that whoever follows the precepts of the law gains life on the basis of such deeds (Gal. 3:12). In this connection the Judaizers could indeed have formulated directly: One can "be justified" only through the law. For the Judaizers, naturally, also read Gen. 15:6 (cf. Rom. 4:3), for example, and interpreted the faith of Abraham that justifies as faithfulness to the law, which leads to life, in that God acknowledges it by justifying. The language of justification—as we saw already (cf. 11.3 above)—was quite generally known to Judaism, for example, in descriptions of the last judgment. Thus it is quite possible that Paul knows that his opponents talk in this language. Yet even if he did not have direct knowledge of this, it remains true that Paul, who was naturally familiar with the Jewish connection of Torah, righteousness, and life, engaged his opponents on his own in the knowledge that he could strike them well with the language of justification.

Paul's initiative with the theology of the cross can now be described more exactly at another important point. The Corinthian correspondence showed that Paul's theology of the cross did not aim at using Jesus' particular kind of death in order to present a certain view of the meaning of Jesus' death but that it was a matter of the experience of the gospel as the "word of the cross"; the gospel was thus grasped in its concrete effect on believers. According to the presentation of election theology (cf. 6.2 above), which is refined in the theology of the cross, it would now be downright unusual if nothing was said of the Spirit. And he is indeed mentioned in Gal. 3:2–5, 14; 4:6; 5:5 in such a way that he appears as the power of the gospel that reconstitutes human beings. This work of the Spirit is now interpreted in terms of the theology of the cross. The gospel, namely, places one in the grace of Christ (1:6–7) by having one die to the law so that one can live to God (2:19). That is later explained (4:1ff.) as freedom from slavery to the law and elevation to the status of free sonship and immediacy to God, yet in the speech of Paul just cited, it is first stated as having been "crucified with Christ" (2:20a). Thus life in the new divine relationship effected by the Spirit is described through the condition of being crucified with Christ. Through this a person no longer lives for himself, but Christ lives in him (2:20). Therefore the world is crucified to the Christian, and the Christian to the world (6:14), for through his spiritual crucifixion the believer is lifted up from the world, which does not call this signature of the cross its own. When this radical change of the Spirit-effected dying is then also brought into relation with the key phrase "new creation" (6:15), one thing becomes clear: the description, in terms of the theology of the cross, of the salvific working method of the Spirit in the gospel—which, nonetheless, leads through the dying of the individual—corresponds in content to Paul's view in the Corinthian letters (cf. ch. 8 above) and is a new edition of the interpretation of the working of the Spirit that fundamentally changes people, which comes from the theology of election (cf. 6.2 above). For the understanding of justification it means that it is spiritual dying, because at work in it is the God who calls into life exclusively that which is nothing (1 Cor. 1:28).

Based on this insight, a further viewpoint now becomes relevant. In 4:12ff. Paul reminds his Galatians that he once missionized among them as a sick apostle. In spite of that, they did not turn away from him;

rather, they accepted him as a messenger from God, indeed, as Jesus Christ. Now, however, for their sake he is again lying in the pangs of birth until Christ takes shape in them, naturally as the crucified One (4:19). Indeed, his weakness was also revealed to be in conformity with the cross, since the missionary success in Galatia must be credited solely to the power of the gospel, which springs from the cross. It should have long been clear that even these statements are a reflection of the Corinthian correspondence; they recall Paul's "weak" way of speaking, understood in terms of the theology of the cross (1 Cor. 2:1ff.), and are at home especially in the "letter of tears" (cf. 8.5 above). We can also support this judgment with the fact that the relatively unexpected talk of "glorying" in the cross of Christ, which does not determine the polemic until right at the end—a glorying that, paradoxically, occurs as a dying process for the individual (Gal. 6:14)—is naturally to be understood as an echo of the fool's speech in 2 Corinthians (cf. 8.5 above). Here it is actualized, for the glorying of Paul stands in contrast to the glorying of the opponents, who glory in the circumcision of the Galatians (6:13), while in the fool's speech the glorying of the superlative apostles stands over against Paul's glorying of his weakness.

This opens up for us a meaning-constituting foundation that at a deep level underlies the whole presentation of the theme in 3:1–5:12. Paul had to make clear to the Corinthians that in the gospel a God is at work who chooses the weak of the world, so that one cannot boast before God, whether of the gifts of Christ or of one's own weaknesses (1 Cor. 1:26–31; 2 Cor. 11:30; 12:5). The Pauline God does not confirm the strengths of humanity (1 Cor. 1:26–27) but is always occupied only with saving what counts as nothing (1 Cor. 1:18) and thus with saving all, because before him all are as nothing and sinful. This creative sole-effectiveness of God, which alone reaches into the depth of human lostness, through which, further, the gospel can exist comprehensively for all, and which, in short, offers the gospel as grace, with no ifs, ands, or buts—this is what Paul sees in danger of being betrayed when the Judaizers in Galatia preach circumcision. Since, for them, grace alone is apparently not enough because and inasmuch as they additionally require observance of the law, in Paul's judgment they are saying something like this: God's sole creativity is not sufficient to save people. They themselves must do something in addition: works of the law. Only the two together make up righteousness. This is the way the same God acted with Israel. He chose Israel and gave it the law. God cannot now choose the Gentiles without also imposing the law on them. Thus the Judaizers measure the new and Christian against the old, while Paul measures the old against the new, that is, against Christ

(Gal. 2:21; 6:14–16). They take Israel's covenant and its law as the original event for understanding God, whereas Paul makes a new statement of who God is by looking to the Christ event and seeing in it both the misery and the redemption of all people. Thus in the Pauline sense we can see something in common between the fiery virtuosos of ecstasy in 2 Corinthians and the sober preachers of the law in Galatians: neither lets God be only God, because both in their different ways want to correct God as interpreted by the cross of Christ. The ecstatics think very little of the idea that the cross is an abiding earthly description of the human situation. They overcome the sinful misery of humanity already on earth through ecstasy. The people of the law belittle the redemptive aspect of the cross. To the grace of the cross they add the demand of the law as necessary for salvation. They cannot warm up to the idea of grace alone.

On the basis of these observations we can now consider Gal. 3:1–5:12 itself. Paul begins his first line of argumentation in seven steps (cf. 11.2 above) with questions about the Galatian Christians' experience with the gospel during the first mission (3:1–5). The Galatians' answers, Paul tacitly assumes, will have to be what he expects, for he was indeed himself the first missionary and knows the early history of the Galatian churches. Thus it is a question of interpreting these experiences again by placing them on the broad horizon of a newly understood history of salvation; namely, the election of Abraham and the Mosaic legislation are newly defined on the basis of the message of faith with its center in the Christ event and so qualified that it becomes clear to the Galatians that with the gifts of gospel and Spirit, believing Galatians have enough for salvation. Indeed, the salvation effected by the Spirit cannot be augmented at all, for anyone who in the sign of sonship cries, "Abba," has the God of salvation in Christ in such an immediate way that it cannot be surpassed. Any expansion through the demand of circumcision would even destroy all of this.

Now in Galatia, Paul had carried on a law-free mission in the sense of the eschatological election of the Gentiles through the gospel. If our reconstruction is correct, he did this soon after his departure from Antioch and before the composition of 1 Thessalonians (cf. 6.1 above). Thus we may assume that Paul missionized in Galatia with the theological understanding of 1 Thessalonians (cf. 6.2 above). Then with the interrogation of the churches in Galatians 3:1–5 about six years later, Paul takes a path that is demonstrably in agreement with this mission. The church's original experience is in fact identical with the answers that Paul expects to his questions. The Galatians did not receive the Spirit from "works of the law" but from "hearing with faith" (Gal. 3:2).

And as Paul in his letter to the church in Thessalonica can address the fact that they accepted a gospel that came to them "in power and in the Holy Spirit" (1 Thess. 1:5) and that as "the word of God . . . is at work in you believers" (2:13), so he can also expect of the Galatians that they will confirm that the Spirit worked powerfully among them on the basis of Paul's preaching, not on the basis of "works of the law" (Gal. 3:5). Indeed, a comparison between 1 Thessalonians 1–2 and Gal. 3:1–5 shows how Paul in general often draws on the theological interpretaion of the first mission as a basis for his comments, whether for the strengthening of the church or for the winning back of a church that has already been almost lost to a foreign mission. Was the reference to the work of the Spirit not also a reason for the Apostolic Council to pay tribute to Antioch's mission to the Gentiles (cf. 5.2 above)? With the Corinthian party strife (1 Corinthians 1–4) or with the resurrection problem in 1 Corinthians 15 or with the struggle against the superlative apostles, had Paul not also started from the preached gospel, its content, and its consequences, for example, for church life, for hope, for the understanding of apostleship? Thus we will have to give great weight to this entrance into the topic in Gal. 3:1–5. Concretely, Paul does not begin, for example, with the question, what happened on the cross (cf., e.g., Gal. 3:13)? How would the question of the law be decided here? He orients himself, rather, toward the effect created by the law-free preaching of the gospel on the strength of its Spirit and draws from it his conclusions.

Thus if the preaching of the gospel makes an impression as the power of the Spirit, then in his further argumentation Paul has made every effort to distinguish the Judaizing preaching of the law—that is, the law itself—from his preaching of the gospel, so that the former stands there stripped of the Spirit and the latter is characterized by the God-willed working of the Spirit in it. Since Paul in no way wants to permit even one result that makes the gospel and the law compatible in some way or other (Gal. 1:6–9; 6:11–16), he cannot simply emphasize the disqualification of the individual as sinner, in regard to whom the law is then merely too weak, but otherwise leave the law touched. In such a case it might be possible for the gospel to change sinners in order for them now to do the law, as in Qumran the divine grace regenerated the fleshly, sinful existence of people in order for them to live for the law. Paul, however, on principle will not stand for any additive to the gospel, because it would falsify the gospel itself. Thus he must criticize even the law itself. In fact, Paul will say of the law that it had duties completely restricted by the Spirit and divine immediacy and surpassed by the Spirit of the gospel, and he will say of the preaching of the faith that the Spirit working in it counts as the fulfillment of the promise to Abraham and leads into eschatological sonship. In terms of the history of theology, this means nothing other than that Paul raises the law-free Gentile-Christian gospel as the standard of what Christianity has to be. Anyone who, like Paul, replaces the bodily offspring of Abraham with the offspring of faith (Gal. 3:9), who declares circumcision as the sign of election of the bodily offspring of Abraham to be unimportant for salvation (3:28), who even places circumcision under divine judgment (1:8–9; 5:10–12) when it is demanded from the Gentiles, is no longer grateful that Jewish Christianity now also recognizes Gentile Christianity as equal (cf. the situation at the time of the Apostolic Council in 5.2 above); rather, that person measures Christianity in general by the Gentile-Christian gospel. This is also theologically consistent for Paul, for one has no other choice if one classifies paganism and Judaism under the "old age" (Gal. 1:4; 3:26–28), under the time before faith came (3:23–25) and the Spirit worked (3:1–5; 4:6; 5:5), and declares this time before the Spirit as still the time of slavery for Gentiles and Jews (3:23; 4:3, 8–10, 24–25).

After the interrogation of the church in the first section, Paul moves on to Abraham (Gal. 3:6–9), with no preparation for today's reader. This surprising appearance is best explained on the basis of the background situation known at the time. The opponents—like Judaism as a whole—probably firmly connected Israel's history of election with Abraham. Paul also speaks of an electing action of God by which the eschatological church is now gathered in the gospel (cf. 6.2 above). If Paul cannot bring his mission and Abraham together, the Judaizers have the stronger position at this point, for Paul, naturally, wants to hold fast to the selfsameness of the Father of Jesus Christ and the God of Israel, just as surely as he employs the Christ event in a new definition of God. Therefore God's earlier devotion to humankind in the old covenant must be described in such a way that it can be recognized as analogous to Christ. To show this, the apostle paints a highly individual picture of the Torah's statements about Abraham. The promise of God refers not to a bodily son and bodily offspring; rather, Abraham's posterity is understood ungenealogically and in a spiritually figurative sense. The offspring are not Isaac and Jacob, together with the latter's sons, but whoever, like Abraham, bases relationship with God on faith alone (3:6–7). This bypasses the people of Israel as the people of the promise. All people—under the condition of faith—are the immediate objects of the promise. Even the promise of blessing itself is stripped of the concreteness of the promise of land and offspring, which are to be as numerous as sand of the sea. At first, in Gal. 3:8–9, the blessing remains formal and open, but then later it is defined by the gift of the Spirit to the Christian church (3:26–4:7). It is clear that here Paul intentionally creates preconditions in order to be able to interpret his gospel as the direct consequence of this estimation of the patriarch. For it is the gospel that calls all people to faith and blesses the believers, that is, endows them with the Spirit (3:9, 14).

This also reveals why Abraham comes into the picture only in two respects: as the recipient of the promise on account of God's address (Gal. 3:8 = Gen. 12:3; 18:18) and as the one who believes the God who turns to him in the promise and has this reckoned to him as righteousness (Gal. 3:6 = Gen. 15:6). That, according to Paul, is the present situation of every person under the gospel! Paul places the quotation from Gen. 15:6 at the beginning in order to achieve a signal effect through the two key words "faith" and "righteousness," because for him they are particularly suited to grasp the experience of the Galatians with the Pauline gospel. For the fact that Abraham believed and God reckoned his faith to him as righteousness (Gal. 3:6) is not simply a historical judgment about Abraham but a "foreseeing" of the scripture (3:8a), which through the eschatological sending of Christ (4:4) is the description of the nature of divine action in general. Thus Paul is not sketching a historically oriented picture of Abraham but rediscovering in Abraham what he has long known from Christ. In other words, what happened with Abraham has eschatological significance, just as in 1 Cor. 10:1ff. (cf. esp. 1 Cor. 10:6, 11; 5.5 above) Israel's time in the wilderness has relevance for the eschatological church of Jesus Christ. In the Christians' spiritual experiences with the gospel, such as Paul and the Galatians had according to Gal. 3:1–5, this meaning of the scripture is revealed to them as the meaning originally intended by God. Thus we can say that the Torah, from which the scriptural quotation on Abraham is taken, is no longer the representative of Israel and its history but is the announcement of the end time, which now with the preaching of faith (Gal. 3:23–25) is the present time. Hence Paul can conclude, "Those who are men of faith are blessed with Abraham who had faith" (3:9), and a little later fill the content of the promised blessing with the reception of the eschatological Spirit (in the gospel; 3:14b). Thus the experience of the Galatians in their first mission has become a redemption of the Abrahamic promise, and being blessed with the Spirit becomes identical with "being reckoned as righteousness," for both rest expressly on the faith that accepts the gospel (3:2, 6, 14).

From the thematic field baptism-Spirit-righteousness (cf. 11.3 above) Paul knows that the Spirit justifies. This language is probably also familiar to the Galatians from the same environment, for Paul does not have to introduce it anew. That means that his statements on the word stem "just/righteous" in Gal. 3:1–5:12 come, as a rule, from the baptismal tradition and this view: those gifted by the Spirit are the justified. This has its indirect confirmation in the fact that in general in Gal. 3:1–5:12 attention is given to the soteriological side of justification, that is, to the side oriented toward the patriarch (cf. 3:18b, 22, 29; 4:7). The aspect of the last judgment, which would condition the other semantic word field on the word stem "just/righteous" (cf. 11.2 above), is missing in this Pauline conception. But although the Spirit-effected righteousness is dominant, sometimes a juridical formulation or one dependent on the language of commerce comes in (cf., e.g., 2:17; 3:6, 13, 15–18; 4:1–2). For Paul, this is no antithesis; both means of expression are closely joined in 2:17–21.

Nonetheless we must still see that Paul has replaced part of the basis of this baptism-oriented statement of the Spirit. He does not say that the baptized person as one gifted by the Spirit is made righteous, or justified, in the act of baptism but that the gospel, under the working of the Spirit, lets the believer be counted as righteous, or justified, before God. Accordingly, we can distinguish Paul as follows. Faith is righteousness, or faith as life under the gospel is that relationship of humanity to God which God regards as righteous. Thus from the baptismal act with its onetime justification comes the individual's continuous being-in-relationship with God, and this relationship of faith is the state of righteousness.

If Paul has made clear in this way how he brings the preaching of faith and the Spirit working in it into relationship with righteousness, and at the same time has correspondingly demonstrated this line as the real self-testimony of the law by citing the law with Gen. 15:6, as well as 12:3; 18:18, now he can place in opposition to this the "works of the law," as quoted by the Judaizers. This occurs in various groups of statements in Gal. 3:10–29. We have already mentioned briefly that Paul is thinking here of a mutually exclusive opposition of gospel and law. Those who want to be justified by the law have fallen away from Christ and his grace (Gal. 5:4). That is the Pauline position. Concretely this means that the doing of the law—here in Galatia consisting materially of circumcision and the calendar of feasts—is detrimental. Thus, far from a concept of sin as merely a deficit in fulfilling the law, here the very fulfillment of the law is itself forbidden (just as clearly as in other contexts not doing it can, of course, be a sin). The Judaizers—correctly from the standpoint of the law—demand circumcision and with it the keeping of all commandments. Paul does not argue with them about this. His quarrel with them is over the fact that this contradicts the gospel. Thus Paul exhorts the Christians not to keep the law, and he sees their chance for salvation precisely and only in their having faith apart from the law. Indeed, service to the law even produces a detriment to salvation that can be considered analogous to the cult of the gods (Gal. 4:8–9). Therefore the closing statement in Gal. 2:16, for example, "By works of the law shall no one be justified [by God]," cannot be only a resigned description of the condition of human perversity but also contains a judgment in principle about the intention God himself has in regard to the law. God did not give the law so that it might give life and righteousness (3:21–22).

This means that the Father of Jesus Christ does not want to be active in giving the Spirit apart from Christ. Therefore in Galatians 3–4 Paul strictly avoids relating Spirit and law in any way whatsoever. This silence is eloquent for contemporary Judaism, for it was the very identification of wisdom/Spirit and Torah that establishes the life-giving power of the Torah, which came to bear through internalization of the law's precepts. If Paul breaks this connection, he abolishes the salvific aspect of the Torah and turns the law into "letters" that can then only "kill," because people are sinners (2 Cor. 3:6). Those who keep in mind statements written before Galatians, such as 2 Cor. 3:4–18, when they read Galatians 3–4 will recognize that it is no accident that Paul is silent about the Spirit in the law, especially since in 2 Cor. 3:15–17 he expressly attests to such an absence in the law.

The Pauline understanding of the law in Galatians 3 is similarly influenced by the fact that Paul abolishes the connection between covenant and law. It must have made the Judaizers and all Jews suspicious that Paul says nothing about the circumcision of Abraham. Here, of course, the theme of the law would come to bear. Paul's struggle with this issue later in Rom. 4:11–12 shows that he probably learned to understand this intentional silence as a weakness of his own position. Yet it is true that Paul wants to break up the close relationship of covenant and law in Judaism. If in 2 Corinthians 3 he built up for this purpose the contrast between old and new covenant (as bound to tradition), then now he uses a still more radical means: the relationship of God to Abraham is constituted beyond the law. The promise to Abraham runs straight to Christ and the believers. This promise counts as the final, no longer revisable testament of God. Paul expressly maintains (Gal. 3:17–18) that nothing can be done about this by the law given 430 years later (an early Jewish calculation that does have a point in that in the Old Testament narrative sequence the law was promulgated quite some time after Abraham lived). If the law is thus deprived of its reference to the grace of the covenant, which is fundamental for Judaism, then Paul must necessarily raise anew the question of the meaning and function of the law (3:19).

The answer we can expect is clear, namely, an understanding of the law that in any case includes the weakness of the law itself. Consequently, Gal. 3:19–20 probably has to be interpreted this way: Far from being the bearer of Spirit and life, the law is decreed only because of transgressions. It is the disciplinarian of sinners and is supposed to keep a close watch on them and forcibly drive them to obedience (3:22, 24; 4:1–3), so that at least a relatively regulated living together of the sinners is possible (cf. Rom. 13:3–4). Again, it is notable that Paul interprets in this way and does not relate the phrase "because of transgressions" to the cultic law. For that would be very Jewish: the law has a means of salvation to offer against sin, because in it God foresaw worship and atonement for offenses. But Paul will have absolutely nothing to do with this salvific institution of the law. He ignores it, although, naturally, he is familiar with it and knows that his opponents—as indicated by the calendar of feasts—make the most of this very side of the law. Paul counters polemically that from the beginning the law was given by God as a disciplinarian and as nothing more.

A second statement in Gal. 3:19–20 limits the time in which the law is supposed to work, namely, until Christ comes. If we again assume for the opponents a typical Jewish understanding of the law, then their position would perhaps be: The law was there before the world and is valid for all time without limitation (cf. 3.2 above). But according to Paul the law was "added" later and was in no case intended to be permanent. God wants it to implement his sinner-imprisoning nature only from Moses until the preaching of faith. It has no other purpose and has this one only for this limited period.

Now come two further statements that are best seen together. The law is ordained by angels and through the hand of an intermediary, namely, Moses, whose name is not mentioned. One could certainly not substantiate the idea that this characterization is supposed to do justice to the law within the scope of the argumentation. Of course, the angels are probably not hostile powers, for then Paul could not find in the law the promises of God (such as those in Gal. 3:6–9), nor could he later in Gal. 5:14 regard love in a special sense also as the fulfillment of the law. But the angels (close to God) do attest that the law consequently lacks immediacy to God. The law cannot have this, since God as the direct testator of the promise could otherwise expand his first testament (the old covenant) through the law. If God is not the direct giver of the Torah, it cannot complement the Abrahamic promise. Because of the plurality of the angels, the one intermediary is, naturally, now also required (3:20). Here, too, the opposing position is clear: the angels are considered the heavenly radiance of the revelation, and God, naturally, talks directly to Moses (cf., e.g., Exodus 34).

This assumption of a lack of immediacy, however, must be maintained by Paul for still another reason. For him, God speaks directly to Abraham (Gal. 3:6–9), and through the Spirit Christians have immediacy to God (Gal. 4:6). This Spirit-effected filiation to God, which no longer requires a disciplinarian, comes to the believer solely from the Spirit of Christ, which was promised to Abraham. In view of this direct relationship to God, the law simply offers Christians too little. It is not accidental that Paul hits this theme of evangelical immediacy at the beginning in 3:1–5 and at the end in 4:1–7. It is now clear that gospel and Spirit are transformed into sonship; this is the state of salvation of the righteous. The law comes to a person from the outside as a foreign demand (3:23–24; 4:1–3). The gospel as bearer of the Spirit leads from inside outward and immediately to the Father of Jesus Christ. Moreover, the basic idea of this opposition of gospel and law is already contained in 2 Corinthians 3.

These statements make clear a final statement on the law, and it structures the entire pericope: Paul divides the whole of human history into a long first period as the time of as yet unrealized promise and a second period of the gospel, which sets in with the coming of the preaching of Christ (Gal. 3:23–25; 4:4). It turns the present time into the end time (4:4; cf. 2 Cor. 6:1–2). It is the time in which Christ delivers us from the "evil age" (Gal. 1:4), and the Spirit makes the "Abba!" possible (4:6). In this contrast schema the law is placed in the old period now overcome; it still cannot even lead to Christ. Rather, it is restricted by Christ and set aside (Gal. 3:24–25; 4:2, 4). This contrast schema— extended to history as a whole—naturally recalls the contrast in baptismal statements when they talk of the one being baptized so as to say what he once was and now has newly become (e.g., 1 Cor. 6:9–11). The statements on righteousness in Galatians 3–4 have already directed our attention to the baptismal tradition. The formulaic traditions that Paul employs in Gal. 3:26–28; 4:3–6 come from the same *Sitz im Leben* (real-life situation). Thus it becomes obvious again and again how Paul formulates his ideas in Galatians 3–4 on the basis of statements from the understanding of baptism.

This understanding of the law can be checked by the way in which Paul substantiates and describes the Christian conduct of life in Gal. 5:13ff. As Paul first maintains in Gal. 4:21–31, the Christian church lives in the spirit of freedom and not in slavery. Thus Christians are called to freedom from the law (5:13). Because they live in the Spirit, they are also supposed to walk in the Spirit (5:25). For as people gifted by the Spirit they stand in such immediacy to God (4:6–7) that they are directly taught by God and can test what his will is (Rom. 12:1–2; Phil. 4:8; 1 Thess. 4:8–9). Naturally, in the clarification of norms for living, the Christian also runs into statements of the law. Thus Paul can maintain that the Christians' commandment of love is a summary of the basic norm of the law (Gal. 5:14). But according to its nature and in regard to its obligation, the commandment of love is first the "law of Christ" (Gal. 6:2), that is, a norm that comes from and corresponds to the basic meaning of Christ's destiny (Rom. 15:1ff.; Phil. 2:1ff.). Therefore it is obligatory, for it comes not as the letter of the law from the outside as demand on people but is the inner Christ presence of the Spirit in the believer.

Thus far we have considered the Gal. 3:1–4:7 passage without going into 3:10–14 in detail. Here, at the beginning, the people of faith are opposed to the people of the law, and in regard to the latter it is said that all who build their lives on works of the law stand under a curse, that is, death (3:13; 1 Cor. 15:56), because they can never fulfill all the works of the law (Gal. 3:10). Behind this we can see first an acute consciousness of the human duty of obedience to God, as it was advocated at the time by Jews and Christians (*Jubilees;* Qumran; *'Abot;* the older materials of the Sermon on the Mount). The law cannot be divided into lesser and greater commandments. All are of equal rank because all come from God himself. The question, however, is whether Paul thinks of it this way; that is, whether sin is indeed to be found everywhere, yet counts only as a deficit in following the law. In any case, this is opposed by the observation that Paul is then indeed driving the Christians to sin when he requires them not to do the law (circumcision, calendar of feasts). Also, the experience of the creative Spirit, who transforms a person from the ground up (Gal. 3:1–5; 3:26–4:7), is a signal that the person can be in accordance with God's will only when he conducts himself faithfully in the gospel's field of force. Then, however, the people of faith cannot even bring in the still lacking observance of the law as a quantitative addition; rather, people of the law and people of faith face each other as two alternatives, as two fundamentally different ways of life. Also, the quantifying thinking in Gal. 3:10 occurs only in the quotation from Deut. 27:26. Whether Paul himself understands it thus must be tested separately in the context. In any case, he wants neither to define sin with this quotation nor to stress the assertion of the possibility in principle of keeping the law, but to provide proof of the cursing, that is, condemnation to death, as the condition long since valid for human beings. In the context he does not say that those who do not accomplish all the works stand under the curse but that those whose lives are based on the law are burdened with the curse. They are different from those who live by faith and stand under the blessing of Abraham (3:9). Thus Paul does not mean to say that there is too little law done but stresses, rather, that instead of living by the law, one must believe! Paul does not demand of the Galatians: Do more law! Rather, he torments himself with the worry as to whether the Galatians have not finally abandoned the law completely, because they are not permitted to observe it for the sake of the promise of blessing. Thus an alternative understanding fits wonderfully, and alone, the overall intention of 3:1–5:12, as we have already sketched it.

For Paul, this statement must be immediately followed by a second: People of the law are not only sinners; they also expect the wrong thing from the law. For in the scripture God himself established that only those who are righteous through faith will attain life (3:11). Thus this quotation from Hab. 2:4 agrees with the word of God to Abraham in Gen. 15:6 (= Gal. 3:6). So the law itself points to the attainment of salvation beyond itself and apart from itself. The Judaizers expect something from the law that it, according to its own self-understanding, has no intention of giving. With this the way is open for Paul to understand the offspring of Abraham, for whom the divine promise is valid, exclusively christologically (Gal. 3:16), and to find the way to salvation outside the law in the Christian faith community.

Previously we have spoken only peripherally of the salvific act of Christ and his destiny. It appears in Gal. 3:1–4:7 in two traditional statements (3:13a, 14; 4:4), which are constructed according to the same "teleological schema" (structure: Christ . . . for us . . . so that we . . .), which we also can find elsewhere in early Christianity (cf., e.g., Rom. 8:3; 14:9; 2 Cor. 8:9; John 3:16; Titus 2:11–13; 3:4–7; 1 Peter 2:21, 24; 3:18; 1 John 4:9). In one statement Jesus' death is regarded as his destiny; in the other, his mission is. In both, what Christ did is described with the metaphor of redemption (cf. also 1 Cor. 6:20; 7:23), which belongs to the language of business (cf. for Paul 1 Cor. 7:30). It is no accident that these two passages have only now come into the discussion. For Paul's basic idea starts with the gospel and the reception of the Spirit and leads to the description of the spiritual situation of the church. In it the salvific act of Christ serves only the end of describing the source of the sonship established by the Spirit (4:5–6) or the reception of the Spirit through faith (3:14b). Thus the two statements are not made to clarify for themselves fundamentally and separately how Christ through his destiny set aside sin and its consequences. Paul does not speak on this topic apart from the inheritance of Abraham (4:5–7), entered upon in faith (3:14b), that is, independent of present church reality. This corresponds to the observation about Paul's previous writings, in which for the same reason Paul goes only briefly and as a matter of course, often within a fixed tradition, for example, into Christ's death for us. At no point does he feel compelled to explain for us Christ's act as such. He discusses no Christology detached from acknowledging faith. He asks, On what basis may the believer understand himself as redeemed? He does not ask, How do I describe Christ's preparation for salvation most clearly? Rather, his language fields and indications of conceptual contexts change, because they are concentrated in their identical function, namely, to clarify to the believer the gift that comes to him.

Now we must still cast a brief glance at the second line of argumentation in Gal. 4:8–5:12. Since it serves to solidify the position previously developed, we should expect very little that is new. Above all, Paul apparently wants to substantiate again his hard statements on the law. For this he employs the probably older Hagar-Sarah allegory in Gal. 4:21–31 (cf. also 5.5 above). Certainly, it is now aimed at the Judaizers. They, however, represent an intra-Jewish standpoint, and Paul also argues in such a way that the intended characterization of Judaism as the religion of the law becomes the fundamental assertion. For whoever places Hagar, slavery, Sinai covenant, and present Jerusalem in one group and, antithetical to this, builds up the series Sarah, freedom, and (Gentile-)Christian church has judged Israel as a whole. In content this judgment is as harsh as the statements in Gal. 3:6–9, 19, 25. The heirs of the Abrahamic promise are the (Gentile) Christians. Israel, however, with its law, stands in salvationless slavery even today.

Let us pause here and attempt a closing evaluation of Paul's argumentation. In so doing, we must ascertain that Gal. 3:1–5:12 is not a theologically balanced treatise on law and faith but a highly polemical text. As was expected in antiquity in a courtroom speech, all the stops are pulled out. Cicero and Philo can offer impressive examples of this. Thus with Paul one may also inquire whether the good intentions he pursues are not in part carried out with means that are open to criticism. Naturally it may be allowable for Paul to trim his picture of Abraham the way he does in Gal. 3:6–9. In 4:21–31, however, he probably goes too far: What Jews would allow themselves to be so plainly separated from Sarah? Do they not, from their standpoint, have the scripture completely on their side? Does the separation of the law from God in Gal. 3:19 not even contradict other Pauline statements (e.g., Rom. 7:12) and the Sinai tradition in the Torah? Where does the christological narrowing of Abraham's offspring (Gal. 3:16)—which, incidentally, Paul does not repeat in Romans 4—have a basis in the Old Testament text? Naturally the Judaizers can point to the current collective interpretation of the scripture. And, finally, is the sarcasm necessary that the circumcision people should castrate themselves (Gal. 5:12), when Paul knows all too well that the law declares eunuchs unfit for worship? So there is reason to ask how Paul would have represented his position in a less emotionally loaded situation. Thus whoever wants to understand Paul must distinguish between his serious concerns and his polemical attacks.

12
The Church in Philippi

12.1 The History of the Church in Philippi

When Paul writes to the church in Philippi for the first time (Philippians A, cf. 12.3 below), it has already existed for about five years, for the apostle had crossed over with Silas and Timothy on his first independent missionary journey, coming from Galatia, and in Philippi had founded his first Christian church on European soil (cf. 6.1 above). In fact, at that time Philippi had a strong Roman—and thus European—character, in contrast to the cities that Paul had previously known, which certainly could not and did not want to deny their oriental setting.

Naturally, in Paul's time no one knew that Philippi would be bound forever in this significant way to the spread of Christianity. For even if there had already been Christians in Rome earlier (cf. 13.1 below), at this time they were Jewish Christians still connected with the synagogue and not typical of the later history of Christianity in Europe. Philippi is thus the first Gentile-Christian church on European soil. This is not the only crossroad of history that is connected with the city, for it was known in antiquity that not far from there Mark Antony and Octavian had defeated Caesar's murderers. That was in 42 B.C. when Philippi was a small Macedonian village.

Philippi was originally called Krenides, that is, (the place of the) small springs, for it was marshland that Philip of Macedon first had to drain in order to turn the place into his bulwark against the Thracians. Also at this time the city received its new name. Later Philippi lost its importance to Amphipolis. Only after the famous Battle of Philippi—and the Romans' plans to secure the eastern boundary of their empire and the road from Rome to Byzantium—did Philippi become a well-fortified Roman military colony; the previous population was not driven out. Thus the city was founded twice, so to speak: by Philip of Macedon and by Augustus, who renamed it Colonia Julia Augusta Philippensium. The city not only lies on the Via Egnatia but in antiquity also possessed in its vicinity a double advantage highly valued.

The forest riches served shipbuilding, and the fruitful plain was known for its good agriculture. Also, the precious metal mines (gold and silver) in the Pangaion mountains had at one time multiplied the riches of the city substantially, but in Roman times they were probably exhausted. The citizens had the right of self-government, were freed from paying tribute to Rome, and had attained Roman citizenship. These privileges were normal for settlements of Roman army veterans.

When Paul comes to Philippi, he finds there, according to Acts 16:13, a Jewish place of prayer (not a synagogue) outside the city, but it is improbable that he met only women there. There was probably only a small Jewish congregation in the city, which had not yet acquired the right to build a synagogue within the walls or was financially unable to do so. This agrees with the sparse information from Philippians on the composition of the church; Epaphroditus (Phil. 2:25ff.; 4:18), Euodia, Syntyche, and Clement (4:2–3) are Roman-Hellenistic names. Also, Paul (3:2ff.) reports on his Jewish background in the way he has to for Gentile Christians. He says not a word indicating that in the church there were a notably large number of former Jews. Yet against this one could ask: Do Judaizers visit churches without any Jewish-Christian support in the congregation (Philippians 3)? Or was Philippi only on the way and not the real goal of their journey? In any case, Acts confirms the overall impression of Philippians (Acts 16:11ff.): it names the God-fearing Lydia of Thyatira, a businesswoman, independent and well situated, in whose house a Christian church gathers (Acts 16:14–15); the slave girl, who is a pagan soothsayer (Acts 16:16, 19–20); and finally the Roman official who was responsible for the prison (Acts 16:27, 31–32). Whatever may be the historicity of these data individually in Acts, they seem in each case to be correct in the typical sense. Thus in Philippi there existed a Christian church that was composed, above all, of former Gentiles. Lydia of Thyatira is hardly a pure invention of Acts; there was a biographical interest in new converts. Also, that she was an immigrant would be too clumsy for an invention. Of course, her not being mentioned in Philippians is conspicuous. Did Luke fashion the name Lydia from the Lydian, so that she is thus identical with one of the two women in Phil. 4:2? Or was she not in Philippi when Paul wrote Philippians A?

The apostle did not have only good memories of his short stay in Philippi. His sudden, forced departure from the city (cf. 1 Thess. 2:1–2) was probably connected with an official arrest and beating (Acts 16:22; 1 Thess. 2:2; 2 Cor. 11:25). Yet afterward there was lively contact between Paul and the church, although Paul passed a few weeks at best during the founding visit in the city (Acts 16:18). This presupposes friendly terms between him and the church. Philippians confirms this assumption, for the letter—apart from Philippians 3—has an especially friendly basic mood. The contacts that are still recognizable can be summarized. Right away the little church sends Paul financial support twice to Thessalonica (Phil. 4:15–16), as well as once a little later to Corinth (2 Cor. 11:9), so that on his first European journey Paul can work without additional help from other churches (1 Thess. 2:9; 1 Cor. 9:12). Then Timothy probably also visits Philippi on his way to Corinth before the writing of 1 Corinthians (cf. 1 Cor. 16:10–11). Titus, as the conveyor of Corinthians C and D, probably likewise made a stop there (cf. 7.1 above). During his interim journey to Corinth, Paul himself may have visited the church again. These possible visits of Paul and his coworkers are quite probable because anyone who chooses the land route from Ephesus via Macedonia to Corinth can hardly avoid Philippi. Attested with certainty is the presence in Ephesus of Epaphroditus from Philippi when Paul is arrested. Again his coworker brings him financial support (Phil. 4:10ff.). Naturally the apostle then visits his beloved Philippi on the occasion of the so-called collection journey. The gifts from Philippi probably helped assure a magnificent collection (cf. ch. 2 above). The collection stay is at the same time Paul's farewell visit in this church. A short time later, however, Philippians B arrives (cf. 12.2 below) with a warning against the Judaizers.

In distinction to the Galatian situation, there is probably a witness who can confirm how Paul, with Philippians B, could save the church for Gentile Christianity. Polycarp of Smyrna, in his letter to the Philippians about two generations later, reminds the Christians of that city of the firm rooting of their faith, which people have talked about for ages and which still persists today (Polycarp, *Phil.* 1.2); and in his remembrance he presupposes an untroubled relationship between Paul and the church. This would certainly be different if the Judaizers had won the church for themselves; it would then have become anti-Pauline.

12.2 Philippians as a Collection of Letters

Next to 2 Corinthians, it is, above all, Philippians that is difficult for the reader to understand as a unified letter. This is due mostly to Phil. 3:2–21, which does not seem to fit into the rest of the letter. Fundamental here is the indisputable observation that Philippians 1–2 and 4 have a joyful and friendly basic tone of an intensity and abundance not found in any other Pauline letter. Not only is Paul very warmly devoted to the church but also, aside from a danger from non-Christian outsiders (1:27–30) and a smaller, personal disagreement between two church members (4:2–3), he sees no problems that could disturb the church's relationship with him. Yet this changes abruptly and out of the blue in 3:2–21. In view of foreign Christian missionaries (3:2, 18–19) who are becoming a threat to the church, it must now bind itself to the theology and life-style of the apostle (3:15, 17). There is a polemical atmosphere and tense anticipation of what the church will do. It no longer receives the least bit of praise. Instead of loving and heartfelt agreement, there is a cold and strict dominant tone that makes clear what Paul's position is and what he expects of the church. Also, there are statements of self-justification (3:12–13), which naturally were not at all necessary in Philippians 1–2; 4. Even if the church itself receives no direct reprimand as did the Galatians, the difference between Philippians 3 and Philippians 1–2; 4 remains obvious.

Once we become aware of these contrasts, other observations can be added. It is striking that the phrase "Rejoice in the Lord" (3:1) stands immediately before this polemical section, is well connected through 2:18 with Philippians 1–2, and very soon after Philippians 3 appears again (4:4), as if there had been no problems at all in between. Also, the still recognizable church situations are different. According to Phil. 1:5, Paul praises the Philippians' fellowship in the gospel, which from the first day until the present moment continues undisturbed. In 2:12 the apostle confirms to the church that it has always been so loyally devoted to him that he can hopefully expect to learn how things are with the church (2:19). One who speaks to the church in such a clear language of praise and confidence cannot suddenly plunge into harsh polemics against foreign missionaries in order to save the church from imminent great danger. The anxiety about the church in 3:2ff. is not compatible with the relaxed and problem-free mood in which Paul views the future of the church in the rest of the letter. These observations lead to the conclusion that Philippians 3 stands as an isolated block in an unfortunate place.

Further observations are less powerful, yet not entirely without significance. Only in Philippians 1–2 does the apostle speak of his imprisonment and mortal danger. In Philippians 3, on the other hand, Paul's current life situation does not come up at all; as in Galatians, he keeps such personal statements to a minimum. Now he has no problems of his own, but he worries a lot about the church. Would not the content of, for example, Phil. 3:10–11 be an excellent occasion for perhaps mentioning the apostle's continuing mortal danger? Only in the polemics of Philippians 3 does Paul's language of justification come to bear (3:6, 9). In the rest of the letter the word field around the verb "justify" is present only in a limited, incidental, and unspecific way (1:7, 11; 4:8). Finally, it can be shown that Philippians 1–2; 4 and Philippians 3 each have good organization in themselves, that is, an appropriate smoothness and structure of their own. We will speak more of this individually.

Even with concerted effort, this whole state of affairs can hardly be explained with reference to a pause in dictation, a mood swing, a temperamental break in style, or new information that has arrived in the meantime. Another interpretation is much more apparent: two originally independent letters were later combined. Then we can assume, for example, that with repeated reading aloud in the churches, the harsh polemical tone alone was not suitable in a known and traditionally good relationship between Paul and this church. And could one really continue to generalize such weighty polemic against heretics? Was the letter not also somewhat short? Thus it was enclosed in another letter in order to soften its harshness. Somewhat boldly, we can even speculate that because the Judaizers could not get a foothold in Philippi, Philippians 4 signalizes that the relationship between Paul and his church is undisturbed afterward as before (cf. 12.1 above).

It is clear that if we use literary-critical means to decide on two letters, one now inserted in the other, then one of these is a complete letter and the other, namely, Philippians 3, is a fragment. In Philippians 1–2, of course, there is no possibility of finding a beginning for the fragment, but Philippians 4 is so long that we can look there for a conclusion to Philippians 3. It is especially difficult to take relatively loosely formed epistolary endings, such as 1 Thess. 5:12–28; 1 Cor. 16:1–24, and now Philippians 4, and ask of them literary-critical questions. Certainly a comparison of these in many ways very similar closings yields indications of a related structure and many of the same themes, sequences, and key words. Paul, however, does not mechanically follow a fixed paradigm but varies a typology with a certain breadth of modification. Thus Paul could, in fact, have dictated Philippians 4 entirely as a closing for Philippians 1–2. That is also true of Phil. 4:10–20 (–23). In this section one could see a separate thank-you for received gifts of money, as many scholars have suggested. Yet this not only destroys the connection between the two references to Epaphroditus (2:25–30; 4:18), including Paul's troubles (1:12ff.; 4:14), and the mention of the imperial house (1:13; 4:22); but also the motif "in the Lord," for example, as it appears in 3:1; 4:1, 2, 4, 10, each time in stressed position, is assigned to two different levels without sufficient reason. The especially friendly tone (cf., e.g., 4:14–15), moreover, goes extremely well with Philippians 1–2. Is the church collection not also mentioned at the end of the letter in 1 Cor. 16:1–4?

Nevertheless, in Philippians 4 we can probably still recognize a piece of the letter in Philippians 3, namely, in 4:8–9. The two peace greetings that follow each other immediately (4:7, 9c) stand curiously close together. Paul's role as model (4:9a) corresponds to the statement in 3:15, 17. Also, the generally held exhortation to good behavior (4:8) connects with 3:15–16. Thus we may assume that we are on the trail of the now hidden literary bridges between Philippians 3 and 4:8–9. We may add that 4:8–9 goes with the style and tone of the polemical letter; this view is supported by the simple brotherly salutation (cf. 3:13, 17) and a terse conciliatory greeting (4:9c), which also comes right after a sharp polemic in Rom. 16:20; 2 Cor. 13:11; Gal. 6:16.

That Phil. 4:1 or 4:1–3 is also often placed with the polemical letter creates problems. The friendly, harmonious salutation in v. 1 has counterparts in Phil. 1:9, 25; 2:1–2, 12, 24, but not in Philippians 3. The warm tone in v. 3 also fits here. The phrase "in the Lord" has already been recognized as a unifying motif in the context. Finally, the salutation "brethren" (4:8) would surely be superfluous immediately after the wordy salutation in v. 1. The discord between the two women in v. 2 (cf. 2.2 above) has nothing to do with the foreign missionaries. To construe from this discord that therein lies the hidden point of entry for the foreign missionaries is pure fantasy.

With this we can determine the following results. Philippians B (= 3:2–21; 4:8–9) was inserted into Philippians A (= 1:1–3:1; 4:1–7, 10–23), losing its opening in the process. Since 4:8–9 contains a final admonition and a closing peace greeting, the ending can be considered practically complete if we disregard possible personal greetings. Thus the redactor dealt very carefully with the letters. Conservative and respectful of the Pauline legacy, he only avoided the impossibility of a double opening for the letter.

The cross-check on this literary-critical result is the demonstration that both reconstructed letters are meaningfully structured units. This is generally conceded in the case of Philippians A, which is divided as follows: After the epistolary opening and the thanksgiving (1:1–2, 3–11) comes the description of Paul's needful situation, about which the church apparently would urgently like to receive reliable news (1:12–26). Then follows a section, 1:27–2:18, that describes the life of the Philippian church as claimed by the gospel and marked by the typical triad of faith (1:27–30), love (2:1–11), and hope (2:12–18). Finally comes the long closing section of the letter, which begins with travel plans (2:19–30), then with the leitmotiv of joy gathers admonitions to inner unity, outward relationship, and the future (3:1; 4:1–7), develops in detail the thanks for support received (4:10–20), and ends with closing greetings and benediction (4:21–23). The idea that this is not a complete letter would occur to no one, if 3:2–21 were not in the middle.

There is much more disagreement on the division of Philippians B, but only as long as one does not see that it is structured on the basis of an ancient court speech. For what Paul undertakes rhetorically in the comparable situation in Galatians (cf. 11.2 above) he also has in mind now in the dictation of Philippians B. He begins (introduction or *exordium*) with a sharp condemnation of the opponents. The church is supposed to know that they are disqualified (three times: "Look out . . ." at the beginning of clauses). Then, using words for mutilation (i.e., castration) and (spiritual) circumcision, Paul contrasts these opponents to the new being of the church (Phil. 3:2–3: "For we . . ."). In this way, as in Gal. 1:6–9, he creates strategically the same separation of church and opponents, who because of the demand of circumcision, which is mentioned right away in v. 2 (cf. also v. 5) as in Gal. 5:2; 6:12, are recognized right away as Judaizers. After this the style changes. The biographical "I" of the apostle appears in the foreground stylistically emphasized. Paul describes his former Jewish life in 3:4–6 and his new view of it on the basis of his experience of Christ (v. 7), in order to make clear that the Judaizers advocate a position that is long past and to be condemned (3:4–7). Here it is clear that Paul is speaking in the style of the historical diagnosis of the problem (historical presentation or *narratio*), as also found in Gal. 1:11–21, except that Paul goes exclusively into the events described in Gal. 1:11–24 in abridged form; that is, he restricts himself to his calling as an exemplary historical experience in which the wrong position of the opponents can be indicated. Between the beginning of the speech and the historical diagnosis, keyword connection reigns (Phil. 3:3, 4: "confidence in the flesh"). The same is true for the transition from Phil. 3:7 to 3:8 ("count as loss").

Now, beginning with v. 8, the "I" is retained, yet, while in 3:4–7 it is unmistakably biographical, here it is exemplary and thus capable of generalization. In 3:4–7 it is a matter of the historically individual in Paul's life; here, through the new measurement by Christ, the result of this Pauline turning point becomes a development of Christian existence in general. From the past measuring of Paul's life on the basis of Christ (3:7) comes the present judgment (v. 8), a judgment that has validity for all Christians. For this reason verbs in the present tense now predominate; subordinate to them are aorist forms characterizing the salvific act of Christ as the precondition of such judgment, and

future tense statements are added in order to indicate the consequences of the new understanding. Now, therefore, not only the individual Pauline way of life is measured (as in v. 7) but "everything" and
thus simply all knowable reality (v. 8, twice). That is, in contrast to v.
7, v. 8 begins a double generalization. In general and always, the
world will be measured from the standpoint of Christ, and Christ is the
measure of all things. Thus it becomes clear enough that with v. 8 Paul
is moving into the argumentative part of his comments (marshaling of
evidence, or *probatio*). As in the analogous section Gal. 3:1–5:12, here
we run into the polemically formed message of justification. Again Paul
abridges this part compared to Galatians in that he uses, in modified
form, only what he feels is the crucial argumentation, in terms of content, from Gal. 3:1–4:7, namely, the polemical message of justification.
As he begins with the church's experience in Galatians (3:1–5), so now
his argumentation is reflected in his own experience. Missing, therefore, is recourse to Abraham as well as any scriptural reference. The
new understanding of reality given with Christ is fully demonstrable in
Paul's calling. Also conditioned by this, the thinking in two historical
epochs, the time before Christ and the present newly defined through
him, is replaced by the description of the existential change from pre-
Christian to Christian existence. This new approach in Phil. 3:8 is the
beginning of a section that goes through v. 16. This central part of the
court speech divides into three subsections. In vs. 8–11 the gift character of the new life in Christ dominates the train of thought. In vs. 12–14
this gift is comprehended as the shaping power of life. It is the answer
of faith that knows itself grasped by Christ and now reaches out for the
heavenly calling. If the "I" of the apostle, which is open to generalization, dominates in these two subsections, then in the following
vs. 15–16 the described double aspect of Christian existence, represented in the apostle himself, is given to the church as a model of discipleship. Thus we can compare: just as in Galatians, at the conclusion
of the first round of argumentation in 3:23–29 and 4:1–7 after the basic
parts in 3:6–22, the new spiritual life of the church becomes the normative theme, so likewise in Philippians B the exemplary description
of Christian existence (3:8–11, 12–14) ends with the direct application
to the church (3:15–16). Thus 3:8–16 contains the argumentative part of
the court speech, in which v. 16 as the closing recalls the content of
3:3 as well as the comments in vs. 8–11.

Finally, Phil. 3:17–21 is easy to judge as a section comparable to
Gal. 6:11ff. (closing argument, or *peroratio*). We can recognize a last,
sharp contrasting of the opposing and Pauline positions and a final,
urgent courting of the church. The admonition in 3:15a to think like

Paul is taken up in the exhortation to imitate the apostle (3:17). The opponents are similarly condemned in 3:18–19, as in Gal. 6:12–13. Their demise is contrasted with the salvation of the church if it lives in the Pauline spirit (Phil. 3:17), as in Gal. 6:14–16 the conditioned blessing of the church stands after the condemnation of the opponents. The transition from the opponents' condemnation to the exhortation to the church reminds us linguistically of the transition from Phil. 3:2 to 3:3.

Thus none of the basic rhetorical elements of the court speech, as used by Paul in Galatians, is missing in Philippians 3. The course of the presentation is complete. Yet if Philippians 3 is a letter, Philippians B must also have had an epistolary closing like the one that occurs in Galatians 6 and is connected with the *peroratio*. This has already been found in Phil. 4:8–9. Indicated by "finally" (cf. Gal. 6:17) and the salutation "brethren," 4:8 begins with a last imperative, which in content is an abbreviated form of a paraenesis like that in Gal. 5:13–6:10, yet stands functionally in the place of Gal. 6:17. Likewise Phil. 4:9 corresponds to Gal. 6:18 as an epistolary closing. Of importance for the internal relationships within Philippians B is the indication that in 4:9 the special exhortation to follow the model of the apostle, which is known from 3:15, 17 and oriented toward polemical intensification, is now generalized: the church is supposed to hold completely to Paul's model.

The foregoing analyses of Philippians A and B show how a cross-check can confirm literary-critical work. In the eyes of some interpreters, a further confirmation is offered a good half century later than Paul by Polycarp in his letter to the church in Philippi, when he talks of several Pauline letters to the Philippians (Polycarp, *Phil.* 3.2). But since later in the same letter (*Phil.* 11.3) Polycarp speaks of only one letter to the Philippians, this additional support is lost. Beyond this the cross-check produces even more: It also allows us to describe the situations of the two letters. Philippians A is a prison letter, which presupposes the same precarious condition of the apostle as in Philemon and 2 Cor. 1:8–9 (cf. 7.1 above). Paul must reckon with his death (Phil. 1:21–24). The unexpected freedom and opportunity for the so-called collection journey is not yet tangibly imminent, for the description of the coming of the apostle to Philippi, held in prospect in Phil. 2:24, turned out rather poorly in view of the promises of travel plans regarding Timothy and Epaphroditus. Conversely, Paul has already been in prison for some time, since the church in Philippi has supported him with financial means from Philippi by way of Epaphroditus (4:10–20). Thus Philippians A is temporally near the Corinthian correspondence. We can even be somewhat more precise: The imprisonment that is still going on in

Philippians 1 has just passed in 2 Corinthians 1. Thus we would do well to put Philippians A before 2 Corinthians 1 and place it in the winter of A.D. 54/55. It was therefore written before Paul's great struggle with the Judaizers.

Matters are different in Philippians B. There is no more talk of an imprisonment. The struggle against the Judaizers dominates the whole scene. Here, it is unlikely that Paul wrote this letter before his meeting in Philippi on the occasion of the so-called collection journey, begun surprisingly in the spring of A.D. 55. Before the letter reached there by menas of envoys, Paul himself would have been there. Also, in Macedonia and Achaia there were originally no Judaizers. They must have migrated to Europe from Judea/Syria and Asia Minor. That makes it probable that, for example, they appeared first in Galatia before they moved on to Europe. Thus the Galatian struggle is to be set before Philippians B. And if Paul wrote Galatians at the beginning of the so-called collection journey (cf. ch. 2 and 10.1 above), then Philippians B would have been composed later.

This sequence is supported by a small indication in Phil. 3:18. There Paul writes that he has often warned the church against "enemies of the cross." Certainly, this does not fit the founding situation, because such a danger is not recognizable on Paul's first European journey. Before the hasty departure from Ephesus, however, Paul had learned of the Galatian Judaizers and written to Galatia on the way through Macedonia. This is an especially good reason for Paul, present in Philippi on the so-called collection journey, to warn the church against the Judaizers. But that would mean that Philippians B was written during the rest of the collection journey after the departure of the apostle from Philippi. The Judaizers are following Paul. He cannot and will not go back again to Philippi, because he wants to bring the collection to a close, and he still plans to visit Rome and Spain (Rom. 15:25–29). Thus the Judaizers are again threatening his church in Philippi at an inopportune time. Here, too, the Galatian situation is repeated.

If we draw this kind of picture of the events, it also clarifies the relationship of Philippians B to Romans, which was written in A.D. 56 from Corinth shortly before the departure to Jerusalem to deliver the collection, as can be inferred from Rom. 16:21–23 (cf. 13.2 below). Galatians and Philippians B are alike in that they are both polemically oriented. After the comments above, it seems obvious to understand Philippians B as a subsequently written "little Galatians." Conversely, Romans develops the apostle's message of justification for the first time without direct polemics against an actual opponent and as a systematic framework for Pauline theology as a whole. Then we may assume that Philippians B was written before Romans, so that the battle that Paul had to fight in Galatians and Philippians B is a precondition for Romans. Thus Philippians B was directed from Greece toward the church in Philippi also, say, in A.D. 56 shortly before Romans and after Paul's departure from Philippi. Hence three letters that contain the Pauline message of justification originate from the so-called collection journey, namely, Galatians, Philippians B, and Romans. This brings into view the third group of scriptures as the sign of the last phase of Pauline theology. It connects with the Ephesian group—the Corinthian correspondence, Philemon, and Philippians A—and takes up the pointed theology of the cross, which in turn continues the Antiochene, theology-of-election phase, including the first missionary journey to Europe.

12.3 The Letter from Prison

We can divide the letters of Paul into two groups by asking in each case where the real problem is that determines the letter: with the writer or with the addressee. First Thessalonians (cf. 6.3 above), the Corinthian correspondence (cf. ch. 8 above), and Philippians B (cf. 12.2 above) are each an impressive example of Paul dealing not with his own problems but with those of one of his churches. Thus he is solving the problems of others. In the short Letter to Philemon, on the other hand, the problem lies with Paul. The runaway slave Onesimus has come to him, and Paul must now see how he can solicit from Philemon an agreeable resolution of the case. The weighty Letter to the Romans also belongs to this group. Paul wants to visit Rome, a city still unknown to him, to introduce himself theologically and receive support for his Spanish mission. The church may have its own problems (Rom. 14:1–15:13), but they cause no real problems for Paul, for it is not a church of his that requires his concern (cf. 13.2 below). The third letter that belongs here is Philippians A (cf. 12.2 above). Through Epaphroditus the church supported the incarcerated Paul; therefore it is now up to Paul to express his gratitude (Phil. 4:10–20) and to describe his situation (1:12–26). Yet because everything is going so well in the church and Paul would like to give an apostolic "sermon" in order not to talk only of himself but to fulfill his apostolic duties to the church, we owe to this letter a brief but most impressive presentation of how Paul conceives the life of a church theologically. Here it is fascinating to compare the Ephesian Paul (Philippians A) with the Antiochene (1 Thessalonians, cf. 6.2 above).

The thanksgiving in Phil. 1:3–6 shows right away how the beginnings of the theology of election from 1 Thessalonians have been retained. Paul thanks God for the "partnership [of the church] in the gospel" as it has persisted "from the first day until now" (1:5). He is "sure that he who began a good work in you will bring it to completion at the day of Jesus Christ" (1:6). Of course, this immediately recalls passages such as 1 Thess. 1:2–7; 3:11–13; 5:23–24. The short time span between eschatological election through the gospel and the imminent day of the Lord (cf. Phil. 4:5) is characterized on the one hand by the faithfulness of God (2:13; 4:6–7) and on the other by the request "that your love may abound more and more, with knowledge and all discernment, so that you may approve what is excellent, and may be pure and blameless for the day of Christ, filled with the fruits of righteousness which come through Jesus Christ, to the glory and praise of God" (1:9–11). Election to salvation is thus not without obligatory consequences for the life of the church in the time between election and the day of the Lord. The key word "love" exercises a guiding function. It is named quite naturally and is a "fruit" of Christ's act for humanity, yet it is never oriented toward the law, which is not mentioned at all in Philippians A. This, of course, also has its basic counterpart in 1 Thessalonians. In distinction to the latter, however, the guiding term "sanctification" is not used in Philippians A.

Yet agreement with 1 Thessalonians goes even farther when we recognize that the three parts of the large main section Phil. 1:27–2:18 correspond to the triad—so familiar from 1 Thessalonians—of faith (1:27–30; cf. esp. vs. 27c, 29), love (2:1–11; cf. esp. vs. 1–2), and hope (2:12–18), although only the idea of hope occurs, not the word itself (cf. "salvation" in v. 12 and "day of Christ" in v. 16 with 1 Thess. 5:8–9 or 5:2, 4). Naturally it is also no wonder that faith is related to the gospel and associated with the request to "stand firm in one spirit" (Phil. 1:27), or indeed that love also comes before the "participation in the Spirit" in a series (2:1). Here the same Spirit-effected community life appears as in 1 Thessalonians.

Consequently, the apostle's intention is then directed toward unity and integration of the church (2:1ff.). This is broadly developed. By contrast, external relations are marked, on the one hand, by the consciousness of superiority (2:15) and, on the other, by the experience of suffering (1:29–30) and are only alluded to. Their active formation by the church is requested in the short sentence in 4:5: "Let all men know your forbearance." It is obvious that these accents and contents are in continuity with 1 Thessalonians.

Then what has changed since 1 Thessalonians? The crucial signal of an answer is given by the key word "cross" in 2:8. If indeed—as attested since 1 Corinthians—the Corinthian church's spiritual experience of drifting off and storming heaven is bound by Paul to the gospel, the content of which is in essence the crucified One (cf. 8.2, 8.4, and 8.5 above), then in 2:8 this key word helps us see exactly what has changed. Important here, first of all, is the observation that in Phil. 2:6–11, in substantiation of his exhortation (2:1–4), Paul quotes an early Christian hymn: the oldest one we know from primitive Christianity. It describes in informative praise the Christian bearer of salvation in two stanzas, namely, as a heavenly figure who humbles himself (2:6–8) and as a humbled, dead person exalted by God above the masses (2:9–11). Where the hymn speaks of the deepest humiliation ("he humbled himself and became obedient unto death," v. 8), Paul adds: "even death on a cross." We know it is an addendum simply because assertions of the theology of the cross do not occur in the first early Christian generation except in Paul (cf. 8.2 above).

There is no doubt that the Philippians would have to have noticed this addendum, which is conspicuous in the parallel line division of the hymn, even if they themselves had not already sung the hymn earlier in a service of worship. Then, however, in the same context they could observe that the motif of the humility of Christ used in v. 8 appears again in v. 3 as an exhortation to the church: "In humility [i.e., with a humble attitude] count others better than yourselves."

When this request is followed in v. 4 with the exhortation, "Let each of you look not only to his own interests, but also to the interests of others," then we are reminded of the beginning of the hymn, which tells how Christ did not eagerly hang on to being like God but emptied himself, taking the form of a servant (2:6–7). Thus beyond the theology-of-the-cross addendum in v. 6, there are two bridges that Paul has constructed between the exhortation to love and the hymn. All three text signals are closely related to the first verse of the hymn; that is, they have settled in the theme of christological self-humiliation. The second verse of the song has no links with the context and receives no Pauline addendum either.

In other words, since the church still lives this side of death, and only Christ has ruled thus far as the exalted one (cf. 1 Cor. 15:20–28, 53–57), for Paul the church, as it lives through the gospel and by virtue of baptism "in Christ" (Phil. 2:5), is dependent on the crucified One. For Christians the exaltation of Christ by God according to Phil. 2:9–11 makes Christ's self-humiliation phase the obligatory basic attitude toward their conduct of life. Love, to which the church of God, taught by the Spirit, is called (as 1 Thess. 4:8–9 has already said), is comprehended as the way of humility, as is appropriate to a theology of the cross. Hence, in Philippians A, Paul has now traveled farther—now unpolemically—down the theological path of the Corinthian correspondence. Taught by the Corinthian turbulences with the Spirit, he has concretized the general and therefore also misusable connection of Spirit and love by binding it to the cross of Christ. It is not Spirit and a (new) legalism that are coupled. Rather, the crucial point from the constituent original christological event of the Christian faith is bound together with Spirit and love, as they govern the church. Thus a historically open, creative dynamic remains characteristic of love, but through concretization with the help of the cross it also receives a fixed shape that, normative in terms of content, binds it to its origin.

This way of binding the Christian understanding of life and shaping of life in a basic fashion to the Christ event is also found elsewhere in Paul. In 2 Cor. 8:9 Paul solicits gifts for the collection as a test of love: "You know the grace of our Lord Jesus Christ, that though he was rich, yet for your sake he became poor, so that by his poverty you might become rich." Romans 6:9–11 reads: "Christ being raised from the dead will never die again; death no longer has dominion over him. The death he died he died to sin, once for all, but the life he lives he lives to God. So you also must consider yourselves dead to sin and alive to God in Christ Jesus [our Lord]." Closest to Philippians 2 are two passages in Romans 15. First, Paul formulates in 15:1–3: "We who are strong ought to bear with the failings of the weak, and not to please ourselves; let each of us please his neighbor for his good, to edify him. For Christ did not please himself; but, as it is written, 'The reproaches of those who reproached thee fell on me.'" (Ps. 69:10 is thus understood as a first person speech of Christ, who addresses each person as "thee.") A little later Paul writes in Rom. 15:7: "Welcome one another, therefore, as Christ has welcomed you, for the glory of God."

For the understanding of these statements it is important to see that nowhere is, say, a virtue or attitude of the earthly Jesus recommended for imitation. Jesus is not understood as a prophet or teacher who lives as a model for his students and whose virtuous model nature becomes the standard of life for his followers. This is contradicted by the crucial circumstance that Jesus' activity is not related at all to a mood or attitude of the earthly One; rather, the topic is the preexistent One who humbles himself into earthly existence. Thus the unique position of Jesus remains irreversible and is indeed the basis of the above assertion: Christ is described as the eschatological person of salvation, who calls his own a special, inimitable destiny. What Christian dies for humanity? What Christian can become poor in such a way that he gives up a heavenly way of life? What Christian can give up equality with

God and receive a position of dominion over all reality? If we are not to imitate a model human life, then how are these passages to be interpreted?

In order to know this, let us make clear that Christ is always described through a history that is the original soteriological event for all believers. Through it Christ becomes the eschatological central figure of salvation. His whole destiny happened "for us." Precisely this— not his subjective humility—is described with statements on the fundamental and objective overall meaning of this event and this person of salvation. Christ as the person of salvation lived not to please himself. As the preexistent One he humbled himself. That means that such statements describe what is salvific for humanity in the form of an overall judgment of the whole process of the sending of Christ. As the eschatological central figure of salvation Christ is so defined that in a fundamental way, judging by his entire destiny, he was there "for us." For this interpretation there is an indirect confirmation when we consider that in Paul there is always only one and the same basic trait of the christological event that is in view. That is, it is not various virtues or ways of behavior that are discovered in Jesus; rather, what is emphasized is always the one thing that turns the Christ event into the salvation event "for us," namely, the giving of himself through which Christ seeks what is lost and accepts it.

Believers live on the basis of this meaning of salvation. They are received into it. Through Christ—through gospel and Spirit—they are made rich; they are redeemed. This Christ has accepted them, that is, saved them. Thus they are transformed by the precursor of their salvation. The Spirit of the prevenient love of God in Christ has reached them (Rom. 5:5, 8). They live "in Christ" (Phil. 2:5). They have "put on" Christ (Gal. 3:27). In short, they have become new. They themselves have become a part of this reality of Christ. The significance of the Christ event—namely, "for us"—has reached them and reshaped them. Hence Christians do not establish a relationship with the model, Christ, through imitation. Their relationship with Christ is not at all based on an imitative doing but in a being, that is, in life in the new state of salvation.

Only now can we say that the Christians' understanding of life and living of life must be Christlike. Their understanding and actions must be appropriate to the new reality. Shaped by Christ, the life of Christians must radiate conformity with the original event, that is, with the destiny of Christ. The fundamental structure of the Christ event, to which the new being of Christians is indebted, was humiliation in the sense of existence for what is lost. Therefore, whoever is "in Christ" must bear this same signature. In this sense Paul can speak of being an apostle living "under the law" (1 Cor. 9:21). Or he can admonish the Galatians that they, the ones gifted by the Spirit, should, in the spirit of gentleness, restore the brother who has committed a trespass and even bear the burdens of others, for in this way the "law of Christ" would be fulfilled (Gal. 6:1–2). In these cases it is not a question of the continued validity of the Torah, which through Christ is supposed to receive new authority for Christians, but of the inner core, the "essence" of the Christ event as obligatory "rule" (cf. Gal. 6:16). Thus the law is mentioned in the figurative sense. It is a matter of the normative side of the Christ event itself as the other side of salvific meaning of this event. This meaning, in turn, can also be designated "the law of the Spirit of life" (Rom. 8:2; cf. also 3:27), that is, as defined by the life-giving Spirit.

Now we can observe further that along with normative molding by the reality of Christ, Paul himself can also appear as a model for the church. To the extent that Paul himself is an apostle molded by Christ, he represents the reality of Christ. The church, itself defined by Christ, should perceive this reality and recognize the apostle's actions as exemplary and therefore emulate them. Thus Paul as apostle becomes his churches' model for conduct of life. This is already mentioned in the oldest Pauline document (cf. 1 Thess. 2:1–12) and continues through the heavy usage in 1 Corinthians (cf. 8.1 above) to almost all letters. For example, Paul not only ends Galatians with this theme (Gal. 6:14–16; cf. also 4:12) but also turns his becoming a Christian and his being a Christian in Philippians B (cf. 12.4 below) into a paradigm for every Christian's understanding of life and shaping of life. As Paul himself is a piece of embodied reality of Christ (cf., e.g., 2 Cor. 2:15; 4:7–10), so also in his conduct of life he consciously places primary importance on being a Christian model as an apostle of his Lord (1 Cor. 9:19–27). This model is supposed to help the church itself to shape Christian life.

On the basis of these observations an idea that was already suggested in the discussion of Philippians 2 can be reexamined somewhat more fundamentally. It involves the question of ethical decision making in the churches. When, on the one hand, Paul takes for granted the obligatory nature of the Christian conduct of life because, for him, God's will may not be neglected (cf. Gal. 6:7–8; Rom. 13:1, 5) but, on the other hand, cannot and will not allow an ethic for Christians based on the Torah (cf. Gal. 2:19–20; 5:13; Phil. 3:8–10; Romans 7–8), then he faces the problem of how to structure the will of God normatively as sanctification (1 Thess. 4:3, 7–8) and describe its content, without falling into a new legalism. Is it really sufficient only to demand, "Test everything; hold fast what is good" (1 Thess. 5:21)? Is it enough to link the testing of the divine will with transformation through the renewal of one's own mind (Rom. 12:2)? With such basic statements the young churches were no doubt overtaxed in an emergency! That certainly did not apply only to Corinth. A way appropriate to the gospel to make a complex decision through a sensible and acceptable orientation without doubt now consists in describing the normative content of the Christ event or appraising the Christlikeness of one's own conduct of life. This is exactly what Paul does so richly in regard to Christ at this central place in Philippians and in regard to his model, for example, in 1 Corinthians.

Thus individual ethical questions are directed through the model of the apostolic life-style toward general determining factors. Decisions about problems are also affected by decisions about people. The live model allows the experience of a normative shaping of life and helps to reduce the complexity of life, so that one's own decisions become possible. There is probably a rather graphic example behind which reflection on this problem field is perceivable. It is in the letter to be discussed next, Philippians B. Here, after he had earlier emphasized his model in general, at the end Paul formulates in this way (Phil. 4:8): "Finally, brethren, whatever is true, whatever is honorable, whatever is just, whatever is pure, whatever is lovely, whatever is gracious, if there is any excellence, if there is anything worthy of praise, think about these things." One is tempted to say that the ethical decision can hardly be described more openly! But then Paul continues (4:9): "What you have learned and received and heard and seen in me, do." Thus the complex decision about a problem is guided through personalization.

Philippians A was described as a letter whose main purpose was to express thanks for support from Philippi. Yet at the same time Paul used this occasion to strengthen the church in Philippi in its conduct of life. The development of these themes was just traced. In closing, we must still say a special word about the exceptional situation consisting in the fact that only Philippi (cf. Phil. 4:15–16) was permitted to send gifts to Paul (cf. 6.4 and 8.5 above). First, regarding the apostle, Paul emphasizes that generally he has the right to be supported by the churches. He forgoes this aid voluntarily (1 Cor. 9:4–6, 9, 11). This right is not tied to his person but to his office: all apostles in general may have themselves and their wives provided for by the churches (1 Cor. 9:4–5). Paul names only the Antiochene Barnabas as one who, like Paul, personally refuses this provision (1 Cor. 9:6). Only from Paul do we have indications of why he proceeds thus. The main reason is that Paul would not like to put any hindrance in the way of the gospel

(1 Cor. 9:12). An outstretched hand too often closes the ear. Therefore he separates proclamation of the gospel and maintenance of life. He missionizes without pay and does occasional work to earn his bread (1 Thess. 2:9; 1 Cor. 4:12). Since competitors of all kinds in the mission field live from their talking, in this way Paul at the same time distinguishes himself from all of them (2 Cor. 11:12). With this background Paul can then also stress as an additional argument that the well-known wisdom that parents are not fed by their children also applies in his case: because he is father of the churches, he will not draw upon his children for life support (2 Cor. 12:14–15). Finally, two personal motives are involved in the decision. He would like to be able to boast that he has done more for the gospel than duty requires (1 Cor. 9:15). Moreover, he lives a life-style that is even a little bit ascetic (1 Cor. 9:24ff.; Phil. 4:11–13). But why, with this Pauline attitude, is it the Philippians who are an exception? This much is clear: If only one church is an exception, there can be no competition among the churches in regard to the apostle. Further, Paul himself never asks for gifts from Philippi but accepts voluntary help. In this way he remains independent. The exception is not provoked by him; he is only the recipient, not the initiator. But this, of course, is not a sufficient explanation. Yet in a case where Paul believed the church to be relatively well off and to enjoy giving (for indications, cf. ch. 2 and 12.1 above), all of this together could possibly help us understand.

12.4 The Letter Against the Judaizers

After Galatians (cf. 11.4 above), Philippians B (cf. 12.2 above) is Paul's second, and hardly less vehement, reaction to the Judaizers (cf. 10.2 above). This harshly drawn polemic is explainable because the Judaizers denied the Gentile-Christian—and thus Paul's—churches their justification for existence and thereby called the whole Pauline mission into question. In form Paul reacted with the same means of ancient rhetoric as in Galatians (cf. 11.2 and 12.2 above). Yet just as in the Corinthian confusion he had already proven himself resourceful in argumentation and the art of presentation, so also in this case he is not satisfied with simply repeating the content of Galatians. Although this repetition procedure is more likely here than in the Corinthian correspondence, since Paul is not writing to the same church but to two churches living far apart from each other, Paul nonetheless chooses the path of discussing again in a new way his basic position regarding the

Judaizers. With requisite caution we can make a comparison. The letters of Ignatius of Antioch, for example, which arose two generations later, without doubt do not have such riches in variation to offer. If we take the letters against the Corinthian enthusiasts and the Judaizers together, they all originated, say, within four years. Once more, this throws a clear light on the creative power of the apostle.

In the past Paul and the Judaizers shared a common position heart and soul: they strictly adhered to the law. But in the present the only thing they share is something on which they are opposed like fire and water: their current attitudes toward the law. If Paul succeeds in showing on the basis of his own history how his present position and the rejection of his old position are consistently Christian, he should be able to make clear to the Philippians where they too must stand.

Thus in Philippians, Paul chooses a clearly different plan from that in Galatians. If the latter was dominated by a division of epochs into the age of the law and the age of faith, now the apostle defines on the basis of his individual transformation what is old and what is new. This results in further differences. The soteriological arch from justification by faith to Abraham is missing, as well as any scriptural reference. The argumentation is no longer based on the Torah as guided by Christ; rather, on the basis of Christ, the law as a whole is judged from outside. Also, there is no starting with the spiritual experience of the church, since the experience—even at the beginning—is that of the person of Paul. In general, Gal. 3:1–5:12 had indeed discussed the difficulties "objectively," as it were, and in view of the church as a whole; the focus was not on the faith of the individual but on the general preaching of faith; not on the subjective attitude of the believer but on the state of salvation of the church, which was to be developed on the basis of faith. Now, however, in Philippians B the focus is on a view of Christian existence that is emphatically designed from the standpoint of the subject. Paul makes observations about his own existence as a Christian and generalizes these statements about himself. Thus at the same time the whole layout of the chapter has an open-endedness. Galatians 3:1–5:12 stresses that the aim of all divine promises is fulfilled in Christ and in the church's spiritual experiences, and in the process the future of the Christian faith recedes to the edge of the presentation (cf. Gal. 5:5 as a marginal remark). Now, however, the future dimension of Christian existence is moved into prominence: being a Christian means being grasped by Christ and therefore reaching out with Christ toward heavenly citizenship. When in this way the subjectivity of an individual becomes the place of experience for generally valid knowledge—that is, when subjectivity and understanding of Christianity are married—it shows what great significance was given to the individual and his subjectivity in early Christianity (cf. also 1 Cor. 8:11).

In the current strife, such paradigmatization of Paul's biography presupposes that his authority is (still) unchallenged in the church. In fact, a difference between the Galatians and the Philippians seems to become apparent here. For the former, the authority of Paul is probably no longer valid without any limitation (cf. Gal. 1:1, 10–12; 4:12–20). To the latter the apostle can present himself directly as the central model for a Christian life (Phil. 3:17; 4:9). In Galatians this is to be observed only incidentally (Gal. 4:12; 6:14–16). Closely interwoven with this is a further difference. In Galatians the church itself falls into the twilight and is almost conquered by the opponents (Gal. 1:6–7; 3:1; 4:16–20, 21; 5:7). In Philippians B, Paul has a more relaxed attitude toward the church, because it is probably still intact (Phil. 3:15–16, 18; 4:8–9). Paul warns against the coming infiltrators, but they have probably not yet arrived in the church. The Judaistic danger is present and serious, but its bacillus has probably not yet established itself in the Philippian church.

Whatever the opening of the letter may have looked like, its actual body, which has been preserved, begins with the *exordium* (opening of the court speech; Phil. 3:2–3). With a threefold anaphora of "look out" Paul begins furiously and militantly to disqualify the opponents, just as in the closing argument he again characterizes them loudly in a series of condemnatory statements (3:18–19). Here we find much that is known from Galatians. The circumcision people become the "mutilators" (cf. Gal. 5:12). Their thus signalized position on the law as constitutive of salvation makes them "enemies of the cross of Christ" (Gal. 6:12–13). That their end can only be destruction has also already been stressed by the apostle through his curse in Galatians (1:6–9; cf. 5:10). If their minds are now set (only) on earthly things, that fits with Gal. 6:12 (cf. 4:29).

If this characterization of the opponents as Judaizers is generally undisputed (cf. 10.2 above), the question still arises as to whether Paul, apart from the beginning and the closing argument, also polemicizes covertly in Philippians B. That is often presumed especially in the perfection statements in Phil. 3:12, 15. Does he emphatically defend himself against being "already perfect" and designate a part of the church as "perfect" because its own claim goes in this direction and with 3:13–14 Paul expressly wants to make a correction? It is theoretically conceivable that the idea of becoming "perfect" through the works of faith could be a reasonable standpoint of the Judaizers, as Jewish-Christian statements attest (cf. James 2:22 and 1:4; 3:2; also Matt. 5:48;

19:21). Or does the dispute go in the opposite direction? Paul is reproached for thinking in an unchristian way that he is already perfect, but does he first have to keep the law before he can say this? Paul would reject this for himself and ironically turn the reproach back on a part of the church. This view of the discussion is indeed basically possible; it is certain that some in Corinth, for example, valued the possession of the Spirit and participation in the sacraments in such a way that they considered themselves perfect and already complete, because Paul expressly polemicizes against this (1 Cor. 4:8) and thereby apparently adopts the language of Corinth, in which statements about perfection do appear (1 Cor. 2:6).

These two interpretive attempts, however, also create problems. They presuppose that the opponents have already gained a foothold in the church (Phil. 3:15). But there are no other signs of this in the text. On the contrary, the many who live as enemies of the cross of Christ are not at all identical with the church (3:18a). Would Paul not then also, as in Galatians, have to attack the church itself? We have, moreover, repeatedly been able to observe how Paul takes a crucial point of controversy and attacks its foundations. He probably also proceeded in this way in Philippians B. The substantive argumentation is in fact brought to one point in the historical presentation (*narratio*) and in the argumentative section (*probatio*): the antithesis of righteousness from the law and righteousness based on faith in Christ. Other polemics in Philippians B are then reserved for the framework of the letter (3:2–3, 17–19), where they are set out not argumentatively but in loud, condemnatory fashion.

How, then, are the statements on perfection to be understood? For 3:12, the context, which is always the best adviser in such cases, gives sufficient information. Paul wants to repeat unpolemically what he said in v. 11: He has not yet been resurrected but is still pursuing this goal. It is well attested that this final completion can be called perfection (cf. 1 Cor. 13:10; John 17:23; Heb. 5:9; 7:28). Again, in v. 15 Paul wants as many as possible in the church to accept his concept of Christianity, so he says that they are true Christians if they think as he does. Also for such common usage of "perfect" there are linguistic analogies (cf. 1 Cor. 14:20; 1 John 4:12, 17–18). Yet another interpretation is also conceivable. In Phil. 3:16 Paul probably has the state of the baptized and their way of life in mind: the church has "attained" spiritual circumcision (3:3). Then the perfected can quite simply refer to the baptized (cf. here Heb. 5:13–6:3). This means that whoever is baptized should think like Paul (3:15a); if he wants to deviate from that (v. 15b), he should take care not to leave the state of salvation as a baptized person (v. 16). Thus as a result we can maintain that it makes good sense not to burden the statements on perfection in 3:12, 15 with polemics. They can be well understood otherwise and are then in harmony with the letter as a whole.

When we turn to the direction of the statements in 3:4–16 (*narratio* and *probatio*), we see that Paul interprets his change of mind as a new orientation that is exemplary when people become Christians. Thus it is understood as conversion, not as calling (cf. 4.4 above). It is not his earlier Jewishness itself that is exemplary; what is paradigmatic, rather, is how Paul lays aside his old life and reinterprets everything on the basis of Christ. Naturally his "righteousness under the law" is welcome to him biographically, especially in dealing with the Judaizers. But it is replaceable by any other possible advantage a person can have (cf. 1 Cor. 1:21–31; Gal. 3:26–28). Paul's biographically unique "I" in 3:3–7 becomes in 3:8ff. a general "I" that in like fashion rejects "everything," whatever it may be, as old and worthless. The unique judging in the conversion of the apostle, which now already lies in the past, becomes the judging of a Christian that is expected of everyone and must be done again and again. Only in this way can the Gentile Christians in Philippi live according to the understanding presented by Paul. This is the aim of Philippians B.

That they are supposed to do this in this way is not only very obvious from the content but also very beautifully demonstrated by Paul through the design of the letter. He does not begin with himself but frames his exemplarily understood history with "we" statements, which are generally valid for the church and Paul, as for all Christians: "We are the true circumcision, who worship God in spirit, and glory in Christ Jesus, and put no confidence in the flesh" (3:3). At the conclusion his comments end in the same way (3:20–21): "Our commonwealth is in heaven, and from it we await a Savior, the Lord Jesus Christ." Does this not mean that because all Christians have received the Spirit of God (cf. Gal. 3:1–5) and thus the circumcision of the heart (cf. Rom. 2:28–29), the basic attitude of their lives is such that they do not set their hearts on what is found on earth (e.g., 1 Cor. 1:26–28; Gal. 6:13) and build their salvation on it, but boast exclusively of the people-changing gifts of the Spirit in the salvific realm of Jesus Christ and base their salvation on these alone? If so, it is only logical when Christians understand themselves on the basis of their heavenly citizenship, and their fulfillment of life is directed toward this goal. What Paul then does is nothing other than to comprehend his life as the exemplary interpretation of such a general understanding and thus at the same time to reject the Judaizers.

Paul's interpretation of his existence is now profoundly defined by the totality statement in 3:8: "Indeed I count everything [!] as loss because of the surpassing worth of knowing Christ Jesus my Lord. For his sake I have suffered the loss of all things [!], and count them as refuse, in order that I may gain Christ." It is no accident that this recalls passages such as 2 Cor. 10:4–5, according to which Paul, in obedience to Christ, takes captive every thought and destroys every stronghold that rises against the knowledge of God (cf. also 14.1 and 14.4 below). How can the apostle's individual experience in his conversion (3:6–7) make available a meaning of Christ that without exception redefines all reality? This is possible only under the condition that the Christ who appears to the apostle in his conversion establishes with his fundamental destiny the divinity of God in such a binding way that God's relationship to the world as a whole is thereby defined in a no longer revisable way, and thus everyone and everything must adopt it.

For Paul, this is in fact the case. Even as a Jew, Paul knew, naturally, that God as creator, sustainer, and judge of all reality is the all-surrounding and all-conditioning One (cf. 3.2 above and 1 Cor. 8:6; Rom. 14:10). Godlessness and human sin are impotent counterplots in the face of this all-surmounting God. In any case, God "be all in all" in the end (1 Cor. 15:28). Thus when we speak of God, we must speak with such totality in mind. Yet this understanding of reality, according to which the world is conceived as creation by God and for God, is now again raised by God himself into a new dimension in that in the eschatological salvation event of Jesus Christ, God makes himself the all-inclusive creator of the eschatological and salvific determination of lost humanity: "God was in Christ" (2 Cor. 5:19).

Because of this, Jesus Christ is not an Adamite like all other people but the numinous founder of a new humanity, which now no longer has to orient itself from the standpoint of Adam. Thus the God of creation also wants to be the God of salvation in a universal, exceptionless way. He shares his deity with no one. It consists in creation out of nothing and in raising from the dead (Rom. 4:17): As in Adam all must die, so now in Christ are all made alive by God (1 Cor. 15:22). Therefore the christological primer reads: "One has died for all; therefore all have died. . . . All this is from God, who through Christ reconciled us to himself." (2 Cor. 5:14, 18). Thus the eschatological destiny of Jesus Christ—that is, his mission, his death, and his resurrection—becomes the final determination of humanity. Jesus Christ, himself determined by the destiny allotted to him by God, becomes the exclusively predestined eschatological bearer of redemption for all. He is the redeeming wisdom, through which what counts for nothing is chosen and what claims to count for something becomes nothing, in order thus to be redeemed (1 Cor. 1:28, 30). Hence before God no one can boast, but only receive and then boast of the Lord (1 Cor. 1:29, 31): "What have you that you did not receive? If then you received it, why do you boast as if it were not a gift?" (1 Cor. 4:7).

Thus the totality statement in Phil. 3:8 is no accidental statement; it is deeply rooted in the fundamental christological concept that becomes recognizable above all in the theology of the cross of the Corinthian correspondence—and the cited evidence demonstrates this. Here the apostle only tersely notes the all-governing centrality of Christ, in order to develop from this center all the statements in Philippians B. This produces the following inventory of the human situation: the advantages that Paul as a Jew inherited from his parents or at one time acquired himself (Phil. 3:5–6) have become worthless. It is important that "from now on . . . we regard no one from a human point of view," that is, according to sinful Adamite humanity (2 Cor. 5:16). For Paul, "from now on" means, biographically, since his calling; for the Philippians, from baptism on (Phil. 3:3, 7). Afterward they are, of course, bound to Christ.

As the result of the inventory, however, Paul speaks not only of worthlessness. Much more, his judgment is that righteousness under the law is "refuse" (3:8). This recalls what was written shortly before in Galatians: The law was not at all added to give righteousness (Gal. 3:21). It is not the bearer of life but humanity's temporary fate of slavery. Hence the advantages of the experience of Christ do not merely cause the law to fade somewhat or make the old, legally blameless conduct of life only comparatively less valuable than Christ. Much more, righteousness under the law has a negative value. The metaphor of the (stinking) refuse in Phil. 3:8 is even an extremely negative term that belongs to the dogs that the Judaizers are supposed to be (3:2). The Jews call the godless and Gentiles "dogs." Thus whoever judges on the basis of Christ does not merely lower values but disqualifies fundamentally. This should also give the aim of Paul's discussion: Judaizers do not simply have an inferior theology; their theology of the law is a wrong way. The better (Paul's theology) is not only the foe of the also still good (the Judaizers' position), but the Pauline understanding of Christ decisively sweeps away the mixture of Christ and law. Therefore the righteousness of the law is "confidence in the flesh" instead of "worship[ing] God in [Christ's] spirit" (Phil. 3:3). It is revealed as a distorted relationship to God, and thus it is sin. It is not sin in the obvious sense that no one can ultimately keep the whole law, so that Paul's positive judgment of himself and his righteousness under the law is a false conclusion. It is sin because it profoundly ignores God's salvific will; that is, it has an understanding of life that in a fundamental way fails to appreciate the significance of Christ.

On the basis of Christ, however, not only is the past rejected but the future is opened in a particular way. To "know" Christ, namely, means to experience "the power of his resurrection" and the fellowship of "his sufferings, becoming like him in his death," and even, like him, to attain "the resurrection from the dead" (Phil. 3:10–11). Of course, this immediately recalls the pointed statements in 2 Corinthians 10–13. Yet Paul succeeds in describing this passive being shaped through the "repeating" experience of Christ's destiny at the same time as concentrated activity, when—again picking up a theme from 1 Cor. 3:24–27—he understands the life of the Christian as a goal-oriented pressing on toward the victory of the heavenly call of God in Jesus Christ (Phil. 3:13–15). But this is not enough: The goal of the ultimate call is also made understandable in a special way as mediated by Christ (Phil. 3:20–21). For the heavenly "citizenship" of the Christian is not a heavenly naturalization document on deposit but a person whom Christians expect: Being like him now in his death (Phil. 3:10) corresponds to the later transformation into the glory of Christ, the Savior and Lord. Thus the basic position of election theology, according to which gospel, baptism, and Spirit call one to eschatological salvation (cf. 6.2 above), is more profoundly explained through reinterpretation in the light of the theology of the cross. Dying with Christ as orientation toward the heavenly call begins with the gift of baptism and Spirit (Phil. 3:3). This call is to be like Christ in his glory. Sketched here is a general understanding of Christian life in which the original event of Jesus Christ is "repeated" with the individual believer. Because Paul does this, moreover, in such a small space—indeed perhaps even ending with a formerly independent hymn in Phil. 3:20–21—it gives the impression of being especially dense and compact.

The statements on righteousness are also within this explanation of Christian existence on the basis of the central figure of Christ. Paul wants to "be found in [Christ], not having a righteousness of my own, based on law, but that which is through faith in Christ, the righteousness from God that depends on faith" (Phil. 3:9). Here Paul apparently talks of righteousness in such a way that in this context it means salvation, which begins with the gift of the Spirit (v. 3) and ends with the transformation (v. 21). For this is what Paul would like: in all respects, on all sides, and always to be found "in Christ," that is, never to fall away from the completion of the eschatological original event of Christ. "Be found" (cf. Rom. 4:1; 1 Cor. 4:2; Gal. 2:17; also *Barn.* 21.6) means God's judgment of whether things are like this. The "righteous-ness" that comes "from God" is, of course, the salvation mediated through the destiny of Christ. It is opposed to "righteousness of my own, based on law." Thus righteousness that is a human product based on the law stands opposed to righteousness that comes from God, is transmitted through Christ, and is thus a gift of God. This recalls the interpretation of Abraham in Galatians 3 (cf. 11.4 above) and corre-sponds to the picture of God that was just sketched in connection with the interpretation of Phil. 3:8. Even if the typical Pauline key word "faith" occurs twice (Phil. 3:9), and the verb "do" never appears in direct opposition, the antithesis is made clear enough through the for-mulation "a righteousness of my own."

The text signal that is given with the expression "be found" leads to the question of how things stand in our text regarding the word fields (cf. 11.3 above) in which statements on righteousness occurred in Paul before Galatians and Philippians B. There is no doubt that Paul begins with the baptismal tradition and in part continues in this vein: the state-ment of essence (v. 3: "We are the true circumcision"), the figurative meaning of circumcision, the talk of the Spirit of God (both in v. 3), Paul's personal antithesis of past and present as spelled out in vs. 4–7 and 13, the way in which the destinies of Christ and Christians are linked by the word "like" (vs. 10, 21), and perhaps the designation of Christians as "perfect" (v. 15) can be listed here without arousing con-tradiction. Yet the baptismal act itself is never mentioned; the state-ments rooted in baptismal language are used to characterize Christian life as a whole. Not the sacrament but the whole conduct of life is described. This fits quite well the assertion that this way of describing Christian existence is in analogous form associated with the language of election and conversion, which only needs to be noted at this point.

Nevertheless it is also noteworthy that in addition, and in a fully inte-grated way, Paul uses yet another language, namely, the language of commerce; for example, he speaks of *gain* and *loss* (3:7–8), of *counting* (that is, valuing; 3:7–8), of the results of judgment as *blameless* (v. 6) or *refuse* (v. 8), of *having* (as one's own; v. 9), of *considering* (v. 13), and of *being found* (v. 9). It is precisely the statements of righteousness in vs. 6 and 9 that are embedded in this language. This recalls the use of the word stem "just/righteous" in the context of the eschatological description (cf. 11.3 above). Yet here also it is true that Paul removed these statements from their original place in that he is not trying to describe the future end time but has a present happening in mind. Thus, as in the baptismal statements, the apostle is describing the pre-sent life of Christians. But if the eschatological gift of righteousness is already present in faith (v. 9), then it is no wonder that in Philippians B, Paul no longer speaks of a future last judgment; rather, in correspondence with a basic idea of Romans 5 and 8, he infers the eschatological hope and completion directly from the exhortation to righteousness or from the gift of the Spirit.

A final comment on Philippians B is in order; it concerns the law. It is striking in Philippians B that Paul restricts the immediate polemic against the law to one basic statement. In Galatians he was much more extensive (cf. 11.4 above). Nevertheless there is full agreement in the basic position. Not only does the Torah no longer have any place at all in the description of the Christian life; it is also not even considered in the closing exhortation in 4:8–9. The will of God is not researched through study of the Torah but through looking at all ethical norms advocated all over the world—among them also the Torah. In the evaluation of the plethora of norms, the Torah again has no special place; this is held by Paul as model, since he lives in the spirit of Christian existence of 3:8ff. Consequently, the criterion of norms is the new life of the Christian: Ethics unfolds as the fruit of the Spirit of Christ.

13
The Letter to the Romans as Paul's Testament

13.1 The Origins of the Roman Church

The Christian church in Rome was no more founded by Paul than, for example, the church in Ephesus (cf. 7.1 above). Just as Paul carries on missionary work in Asia from a base in Ephesus, so also he wants to go to Spain (Rom. 15:24) supported personally (and financially?) by the Roman church. Not in Rome but in Spain he sees a land that does not yet know Christ (cf. Rom. 15:20). This does not preclude Paul's preaching the gospel in Rome himself, as in Ephesus (Rom. 1:13–15), yet—as he expressly emphasizes—as a mutual strengthening of faith (Rom. 1:11–12), not as a first mission. Indeed, he confirms to the Roman church that their faith has been known in Christendom long before his coming (Rom. 1:8; cf. 1 Thess. 1:8) and that he has wanted to visit them for many years now (Rom. 1:13; 15:22) and thus long before the writing of Romans. If we can assume Paul knew that in Italy there was at this point only the Roman church (Acts 18:1–2; 28:15), or at most Christians also in the port city of Puteoli (Acts 28:13–14; but cf. 15.3 below), then it was clear that his intention to missionize in the western part of the Roman Empire would find its best point of departure in Rome. Thus, how and when did Rome's Christian church arise?

Christianity spread quite generally from the eastern to the western part of the Roman Empire. Accordingly, west of Greece in Paul's time we know with certainty only of a Christian church in Rome. This Roman church must have already existed before Paul carried on his first missions in Macedonia and Greece, for about A.D. 50 in Corinth he makes the acquaintance of the Christian married couple from Rome, Priscilla and Aquila. The church in the city of Rome is thus probably the first demonstrable church on European soil, although Paul certainly missionized for the first time in a consciously programmatic way on European soil in Macedonia and Greece. Since before A.D. 50 there were practically no Christians outside Palestine, Syria, and Asia Minor (cf. 5.5 above),

Rome must have come into contact with Christianity directly from these areas. One more thing is certain: the Roman Christians understood themselves at first as Jewish Christians bound to the synagogue. Thus in distinction to the Gentile-Christian mission of Paul, it was a Jewish-Christian mission that was active in Rome. Therefore we must look to the synagogues of Rome to shed light on the beginnings of Christianity there.

Palestinian Jews apparently came into official contact with the growing power of Rome for the first time about 160 B.C.: Judas Maccabeus concluded a treaty with the Roman senate in order to have a better political position vis-à-vis the Seleucids (1 Maccabees 8). About two decades later Jews, along with Chaldeans and followers of Sabazios, were expelled from Rome by the praetor responsible for the city, because the authorities would not tolerate in the capital of the empire what was foreign and probably also the missionary activity of these eastern religions. Thus at this time there was already an officially known Jewry in Rome, apparently artisans and traders. At that time such expulsions seldom had lasting effect and were mostly aimed at those foreigners (peregrini) who became known and conspicuous. Thus it is no wonder that in 139 B.C. Jews were again expelled from the city. Then after Pompey conquered Syria and Palestine in 63 B.C., the number of Jews in Rome (prisoners as slaves) clearly grew. Under Caesar the Jews, who were already permitted to join together in societies, were then granted further rights throughout the empire, for example, keeping the Sabbath, a limited judicial system of their own, and exemption from military service (Josephus, Antiquities 14.190–264). Augustus confirmed these rights (ibid., 16.162–173), which under Tiberius were considerably reduced by senatorial decree (A.D. 19; Tacitus, Annals 2.85.4; Suetonius, Tiberius 36). At this time, yet another expulsion from Rome was decreed, which apparently was again caused by the solicitation of proselytes but at the same time also affected the Egyptian cult of Isis.

Even after this measure the Jews in Rome must have gathered again rather soon, since, probably in A.D. 49, Claudius decreed a new expulsion of Jews from the city of Rome, which for the first time apparently included Jewish Christians. For the historian this is the first insight into the history of Rome's Christians. Suetonius (Claudius 25) reports in connection with a whole series of imperial decrees: "Since the Jews, urged on by Chrestos, continually caused unrest, he expelled them from Rome." The name "Chrestos" was popular then. Suetonius means that a Chrestos living at the time of the expulsion had fomented the disturbances as ringleader. Suetonius, however, is not writing until two generations after the event, and he slips into the confusion of Chrestos with Christus, which was common among the Romans (cf. Tacitus, Annals

15.44; Tertullian, *Apologia* 39). Thus we may assume from this that the followers of "Christ"—that is, Christians—were causally involved in the disturbances. This judgment is supported by Luke in Acts 18:1–2, where he connects the expulsion of the couple Priscilla and Aquila from Rome directly with the edict of Claudius. If we interpret Suetonius and Luke together in this way, we also gain relative certainty in the dating of the expulsion. We have to reckon back from Paul's trial before Gallio (cf. ch. 2 above) and consider the chronological information given in Acts 18:2, 11. We arrive thereby at the most likely date of A.D. 49. This date is confirmed by Orosius (*Historia* 7.6.15–16).

Now we can ask when or where did Priscilla and Aquila become Christians: in Rome or in Corinth? The answer is in Rome. When Luke characterizes them as Jewish (Acts 18:1–2), he means that they are Jewish Christians (so also his manner of speaking in, e.g., Acts 16:1, 20; 22:12). Paul did not baptize the couple (cf. 1 Cor. 1:14–16) but worked and stayed with them in Corinth (Acts 18:2–3). It is inconceivable that Paul could or would carry on a Gentile-Christian-oriented mission in competition with the synagogue (e.g., 1 Cor. 1:14 = Acts 18:8!) from the house of a strict Jewish couple. This would be especially true if this couple had recently taken the Jewish side in the quarrel between Jews and Jewish Christians in Rome. Then they would have to react against Paul in Corinth! Rather, Priscilla and Aquila's house is well suited for Paul, because this couple, baptized long ago in Rome, experienced the quarrel between synagogue and Christianity from the Christian side and had already approved at least the tendency toward a separation from the synagogue, so that the Gentile-Christian mission could go on unhindered.

This, however, also names the probable reason for the Roman disturbances. The Jewish Christians of Rome are quarreling with the synagogue over the question of whether God-fearers in particular may be baptized without receiving circumcision, that is, whether the Jewish-Christian part of the synagogue may carry on their mission in such a way that Gentiles (as God-fearers) are fully accepted into the Christian communion, thereby wiping out the separation between the synagogue and the Gentile world. This problem has long been familiar to us from the mission to the Hellenists. Paul fought against it as a Pharisee in Damascus, and it led, among other things, to separation from the synagogue in Antioch (cf. 4.2, 4.3, and 5.1 above). This assumption also fits very well with the observation that the Roman church came into being when the development of Christianity under the Hellenists was still tied to the synagogue but intentionally violated synagogal boundaries without detaching itself from the synagogue. Thus Priscilla and Aquila were expelled from Rome with other Jewish Christians and Jews (Luke's "all the Jews" in Acts 18:2 is certainly a popular exaggeration), because from the Christian side they gave especially active support to the opening of the mission. Perhaps a Christian church was already gathering at that time in their house in Rome, as later also in other places (Rom. 16:3–5; 1 Cor. 16:19; cf. Acts 18:1–3).

If this correctly characterizes the theological orientation of the first Christians in Rome, it gives an indication of how Christianity came to Rome so early and with this propensity. The Christians who brought the gospel to Rome must have been those who were reached by the mission of Stephen. They must have come from the geographical area that— before the beginning of the independent Pauline mission—had Christian churches through the mission of the Hellenists yet were still tied to the synagogue. This rules out the Jerusalem Jewish Christians and a possible Galilean Christianity; in this early period and even for the most part later on, these Jewish Christians baptized only Christians who were already circumcised as Jews. Thus they did not provoke conflict with the synagogue by baptizing God-fearers. The Antiochenes, however, are also ruled out, because they—led by Barnabas and Paul—soon ventured directly into the Gentile mission and attained independence from the synagogue. This did not happen in Rome, however, until after the edict of Claudius, as we will see. Finally, the circle of Stephen in the narrow sense is also excluded as the founder of Roman Christianity. The geographical extent of the Hellenists' mission seems to be given correctly in Acts 6:5–6, 8–9; 8:4ff.; 9:1ff.; 11:19–20: it is appropriately described as the eastern edge of the Mediterranean Sea with modest extension to the south and north. Luke, whose intention is to describe the spread of the gospel from Jerusalem to Rome, would surely never have missed the opportunity to mention a so notable founding of the Roman church if it had been known to him. So Luke plainly must conceal the church in Rome that existed before Paul (Acts 18:1–2; 28:15): Paul begins, as it were, a new mission in Rome (28:17ff.). Even Roman Christianity, which often boasts of the martyrs Peter and Paul (*1 Clement* 5), has no prominent figure or date for the beginning of the mission in Rome. All of this indicates that unknown Christians, who were won by the mission of Stephen, were the first to promote Christ in Rome. They were Jews who, as seafarers, traders, or artisans originally resident in the eastern Mediterranean area, came to Rome and brought Christianity with them. As they were accustomed in their homeland, so also in Rome they oriented themselves toward the synagogue but brought with them the seeds of the quarrel that allowed Claudius to intervene.

This also fits with what we know about the Jews in Rome. At the time of Augustus we can demonstrate with certainty four synagogues in the city, with the predominance *trans tiberim* (i.e., on the other side of the Tiber), that is, approximately in the present district of Trastevere. Among those Jews are many emancipated persons, probably former slaves from the Pompey campaign, and resident aliens (*peregrini*), who had the right to live and work but no rights of citizenship. Of course, those who can negotiate with the city on the building of a synagogue must be a legally recognized group, have strength in numbers, and have the means to buy and build on a piece of property. This probably applies, among others, to many freed slaves, most of whom in addition received imperial Roman citizenship with their emancipation. In the post-Augustan period of the first century A.D. the Jewish population of Rome must have sharply increased, favored by the good conditions for trade and crafts created for the empire by Augustus and by the administrative connections between the provinces and Rome. The number of synagogues, demonstrable through inscriptions, clearly increases. These inscriptions are written predominantly in Greek and thus in the language in which Paul also addressed the Christian church. These synagogues also include ones named after places on the eastern edge of the Mediterranean, which thus give the hometowns of those who emigrated to Rome from the East. Among such Greek-speaking diaspora Jews coming out of the East and streaming toward Rome we will also find the first Jewish Christians who proclaimed Christ in Rome.

How did the development of the Christian church in Rome proceed after the edict of Claudius? Paul (Romans) and Luke (Acts 18:1) presuppose a Christian church also in the period after the edict. Tacitus (*Annals* 15.44.4) and Clement (*1 Clem.* 6.1) report a rather large number of Christians dying a few years later under Nero (A.D. 64). Thus, on the Jewish-Christian (and Jewish) side Claudius's edict apparently affected only the leaders of the strife who were well known and conspicuous to the authorities. These two bits of information even seem to allow the conclusion that right after this expulsion the Christian church experienced a rather large increase. To this we may add a second certain viewpoint: In Nero's time the Christians are already a group that is well known, yet distinct from the synagogue and thus independent. Nero can tie them into the overall political scene as conspicuous, suspicious adherents of religion and give them the blame for the burning of Rome in the face of general indignation over his deed, while the Jews go unharmed.

This development between Claudius's edict and Nero's persecution is concretely understandable only if we assume that the Jewish Christians who—unlike Priscilla and Aquila—were not expelled soon separated from the synagogue in Rome and became Gentile Christian in orientation. This is what the expelled couple also did right away in Corinth.

That was probably also the best solution to the quarrel over the mission to the God-fearers, which allowed Claudius to step in. That is presupposed by Paul in Romans about seven or eight years after Claudius's expulsion edict in Rome, when Paul asks the Roman church for support of his Gentile-Christian mission (Rom. 15:24), even in view of his fears of having problems with the synagogue and the Jewish Christians of Jerusalem (cf. 15.1 below). The demonstrably Gentile-Christian-oriented Christians, who like Priscilla and Aquila returned again to Rome before Paul, also have no problems in the Roman church; Paul greets the couple right at the beginning of a greetings list that is not lacking in prominent names (Rom. 16:3ff.) and knows that they have again gathered a house church around them. Thus around the middle of the century—that is, after the Apostolic Council (cf. 5.2 above)—the Roman church has taken the same road that Antioch traveled a few years earlier and that has probably been taken since then by many churches that, for example, originated from the mission of the Hellenists or inclined toward Paul's mission. Thus soon after the council the Pauline mission to the Gentiles went hand in hand with the transformation of Jewish-Christian churches in the Jewish Diaspora to churches that were independent of the synagogue and lived free of the law and in a Gentile-Christian way. Rome is a beautiful example of this and in no way an exception.

If very soon after the edict of Claudius the Christendom of Rome lived as an independent Gentile-Christian church, then we must ask how, in view of the background of this church, Jewish Christians and Gentile Christians related to each other in it. At this point it is important to remember that the Jews of Rome possessed numerous synagogues, which each had a certain organizational independence of its own. Jewish homes were, of course, concentrated in Trastevere but certainly not there alone. They were organized according to certain social or national commonalities as independent synagogues, as we can infer from the synagogue names in inscriptions. Hence there is a synagogue for the Hebrews, the Augustans (these were the imperially emancipated), and the Herodians, and there are synagogues that bear city names such as Tripoli. The Acts of the Apostles mentions a synagogue of the "Freedmen" (Acts 6:9) and has "Jews and proselytes" from Rome present in Jerusalem at Pentecost (Acts 2:10). Thus, if the Christian church came out of such Jewish infrastructure, it must have had an analogous form.

This is also confirmed by the greetings list in Romans 16, which mentions a house church that meets in Priscilla and Aquila's house (Rom. 16:3–5). In vs. 14 and 15 two additional circles of people are named and are recognizable as house churches. This can be assumed with other names in 16:3ff. but is not certain. This means that the

Christians of Rome have organized themselves in several house churches. From the data we can even marshal relatively reasonable evidence that at so early a time we are encountering such churches above all in Trastevere and along the end of the Appian Way near Rome. They probably met in a way similar to the synagogues or grew out of them. Thus the quarrel between the strong and the weak in Romans 14–15 over certain food and festival regulations probably reflects differences in the customs of the house churches.

We cannot, of course, stress these distinctions so much that we fragment Roman Christianity into various islands and cells living in isolation. Paul writes his letter to the whole Roman church (Rom. 1:7). He addresses Roman Christians in such a way that he makes no distinction between house churches except in the greetings list. The same picture is provided for the end of the first century by 1 Peter 5:13 and *1 Clement* (opening). This is not contradicted by the fact that at the beginning of the letter Paul does not designate the Roman Christians as an *ekklēsia* (church). "God's beloved" and "called to be saints" (Rom. 1:7) mean belonging to the eschatological church that is elected through the gospel (cf. 6.2 above). For Paul and early Christianity, there is nothing higher. Also, in our present Philippians the designation *ekklēsia* occurs only one time and incidentally (Phil. 4:15). In Galatians and 1 Thessalonians it occurs only once, in the opening of each letter. Paul is taking nothing away from the Roman church when he does not use the term to designate that church. He has opportunities enough to address these Christians as the church.

More conclusive are the inferences for the organization of the church from its synagogal origins. In the early years a substantial portion was probably provided by God-fearers as fringe participants in the synagogue. After all, they were the real cause of the quarrel between the Jewish Christians and the Jews. In addition, of course, the church probably included former Jews like Priscilla and Aquila. Paul names other former Jews in the greetings list (Rom. 16:7, 11). After the independence of the church the number of Gentiles is likely to have increased. In any case, Paul assumes in Rom. 1:5–8; 11:11–25; 15:15–24 that they had the leading positions and determined church life. Also, in Romans 14–15 the strong ones who do not keep the dietary commandments and festivals are dominant. We should not underestimate the proportion of Gentile-Christians among these. It is notable that by looking at their names we can establish oriental origins for over half of all the people named in the greetings list. This corresponds to the way in which the synagogue grew in the first century, so that we may take this information to mean that Roman Christianity consisted to a large extent of newcomers from the eastern end of the Mediterranean. And Rome generally did attract such people because of trade, crafts, and administration. Thus the composition of the Christian church was no exception. Conversely, this means that at this time Christendom had generally not penetrated the old residential society of Rome.

13.2 The Letter to the Romans as a Literary Unit

Regarding the circumstances surrounding the writing of Romans, we are quite well informed. Paul dictates the letter to Tertius, who is otherwise unknown (Rom. 16:22). Because of the length of the letter, the writing is probably spread over several days. Tertius lives with Gaius, who must be identical with the Corinthian Gaius once baptized by Paul (1 Cor. 1:14), because according to Rom. 15:26–27 the apostle considers the collection gathered from Macedonia and Achaia to be complete and is about to depart for Jerusalem. This situation fits only Corinth, Paul's last stop in Achaia on the so-called collection journey, immediately before the departure to Jerusalem (cf. ch. 2 above). Thus the frequent name Gaius (cf., e.g., Acts 19:29; 20:4) cannot make us doubt that Paul is lodging with his old acquaintance in Corinth. When Paul, moreover, recommends Phoebe from the Corinthian suburb of Cenchreae (Rom. 16:1–2) to the Roman church (not the Ephesian—see below), that also fits the geography in excellent fashion. Phoebe is probably the bearer of the letter. The fact that Timothy is with Paul (Rom. 16:21a) also fits into this mosaic. Of the three other persons whose presence is attested by name (16:21b), two probably come from Macedonia (cf. Acts 17:5ff.; 20:4), and thus it is reasonable to connect their presence with the collection completed in Macedonia. That is, they are accompanying Paul to Jerusalem as envoys of the Macedonian churches. This situation then also allows us to assume A.D. 56 as the approximate date of origin of the letter. In any case, the letter was written after 2 Corinthians 8–9, the two collection chapters that we have placed in "the letter of reconciliation" (cf. ch. 2 and 8.3 above). For in them Achaia's collection is not yet complete. Also the important relationship to Galatians (cf. 10.1 and 11.4 above) and to Philippians B (cf. 12.2 and 12.4 above) is thereby determined: Romans stands at the end of this series of letters with justification language and is, moreover, the last letter of Paul that we know.

Yet can we speak at all of only one letter? Must we not on internal, literary-critical grounds divide this longest of all Pauline letters and consider it a collection of letters? The most frequent impetus to such reflections has come from the greetings list in Rom. 16:1–20 (23). How can Paul know so many Christians from a church still unfamiliar to him? Why is it that the list includes numerous persons who point to Ephesus and Asia in general? Why did Paul add such a long greetings list to no other letter or indeed greet individual Christians in a church barely once? How can we explain the stern warning against false teachers addressed to the Romans in 16:17–20, when the church is practically unknown to Paul and otherwise he says nothing more about it? For many scholars, in any case, such questions are best answered if one sees in this section of Romans a letter of recommendation to Ephesus for Phoebe.

The observations that speak for a division of Romans, however, are anything but clear. The counterargument looks something like the following. Precisely because Paul is writing to an unfamiliar church, he greets the people he knows in order to show that he is not speaking as a total stranger. He wants to say: I have not been with you yet, but many of you have long been known to me from my journeys; I am coming to an unfamiliar church in which I, nonetheless, have many good friends. Perhaps Paul also puts Priscilla and Aquila at the head of the list because they are especially familiar people who had already helped him in Corinth (cf. 6.4 above), who gave him a place to stay in Ephesus (cf. 7.1 above), and who can now prepare for his coming in Rome (Rom. 16:3). If the mention that the couple risked their lives for the apostle refers to the last time in Ephesus (Rom. 16:4; cf. 7.1 above), it makes sense for Paul to apprise the Roman church of this. It would certainly be superfluous to write such information to Ephesus, because the people there at the scene of the event of course know about it. These events in Ephesus may also be connected with the fact that Priscilla and Aquila are again in Rome. Also, they may have returned there simply because the Claudian edict of expulsion was no longer enforced (cf. ch. 2 and 13.1 above). The other Asian Christians on the greetings list could also have come to Rome, to which all the roads of the empire lead, after Paul got to know them in his old mission territory. If the list consisted of Roman Christians, it would be much more conspicuous. Finally, in regard to the warning against false teachers, we must consider that Paul expressly praises the church (Rom. 16:19) and singles out the false teachers as common enemies (Rom. 16:20). The church is not yet in danger of falling away; the opponents against whom Paul warns the church have not yet even reached it. In addition, if reference to the Judaizers makes good sense (cf. 10.2 above), then the apostle's warning can be easily connected with the situation in which Romans was written. Had Paul not just offered resistance to these opponents as invaders in his mission field in Asia Minor and Europe (Galatians; Philippians B)? Did he not, because of them, have to expect trouble in the delivery of the collection, a fear that he also expressly communicates to the Romans (Rom. 15:30–32)?

In this way we can probably solve all the problems that Romans 16 seems to offer at first glance. Conversely, the Ephesus assumption raises new questions. At this point it still remains totally unexplained how a letter to Ephesus should have found its way into the letter to Rome. Only letters to the same church are contained in 2 Corinthians and Philippians. That makes a significant difference. Further, an epistolary form that consisted almost entirely of a greetings list would not be absolutely unique in antiquity, but it is not otherwise attested in Paul. Should one reconstruct through literary-critical operations an epistolary form that the apostle probably did not otherwise use? Or is it better then to place additional parts of Romans with Romans 16? To that end, Rom. 14:1–15:13, the passage on the strong and weak in Rome, presents itself right away, because here Paul shows—uniquely in Romans—that he has internal knowledge of the Roman church and, also unique in Romans, even becomes involved in the internal matters of Roman Christians. (That he also does this in Rom. 13:1–7 regarding a dispute in the church over the payment of tax, as some interpreters assume, is quite improbable.) But such an observation alone is hardly sufficient to remove the passage from Romans, especially since it is very probable that the apostle could have received news from Rome by way of the Christians on the greetings list or other people. The many Christians in Rome from Asia Minor are themselves an indication that there were active contacts between the Roman church and other churches.

Finally, we can compare Rom. 1:11–13 and 15:15–24, the two passages that talk of Paul's journey to Rome. The assertion that descriptions of the situations in the two texts do not completely coincide is correct. The first text, for example, talks in the spirit of an intention to visit Rome; the second speaks already more concretely of a departure. Yet these mild variations in the situational information should not be immediately exploited in a literary-critical way, because there are no real contradictions between the two texts. If Romans was indeed dictated over a longer period of several days, such minor inconsistencies were bound to slip in by themselves. Also the question must be raised whether Paul intentionally included these specifications at the end of the letter (see below). In any case, this observation does not serve to construct two distinctly different situations for two different letters to the Romans. A comparison with the situational differences in 2 Corinthians shows how insignificant these are in Romans.

Thus all in all we will maintain that Romans offers no clear signals for literary criticism. We might quarrel over this or that minor gloss and of course set aside the un-Pauline closing doxology (Rom. 16:25–27). But otherwise it is appropriate to regard Romans as a literary whole. Thus the next task consists in understanding the letter as a structured message to Rome. This task has two sides: clarifying the literary design of the letter and Paul's intention in regard to content.

Concerning the first area of observation, we must remember that Romans is Paul's longest letter. If we divide 2 Corinthians (cf. 8.3 above), we have only 1 Corinthians left if we want to place beside Romans a letter almost as long. In 1 Corinthians the structural problems are not the same: Paul had several sources of information and above all followed a letter with queries from the church (cf. 8.1 above). In it he was given crucial prior information for the choice and sequence of topics. Paul was reacting and did not have to start with setting aims or themes for the correspondence. In Romans, however, the situation is different. For a church not personally known to him, Paul must provide a kind of business card, so the members can see who they are getting involved with when he comes to them. Moreover, the Roman letter turned out to be so long that one can hardly imagine the apostle having all the details in mind when he began to dictate and then reproducing from memory, over a period of days, what he had already completely formulated in detail. Thus we will proceed with caution when we look for a detailed network of structure and content, consciously arranged right down to the filigree, which is supposed to make up the coherence of the whole letter.

Thus the larger blocks—as they are now seen surrounded by a framework of typical epistolary form—all leave an essentially independent look. The internal coherence in Romans 1–8 or 9–11 or 12–13 or 14:1–15:13 is doubtless of a much higher grade than that between the blocks, which ultimately can be regarded as self-sufficient and complete, but this is not to say that all bridges between them should be completely denied. Paul apparently oriented himself within the epistolary framework in such a way that in dictation he undertook relatively closed blocks.

Naturally the sequence of the sections is not determined arbitrarily. It is clear, for example, that the part presenting the Pauline doctrine of salvation, Romans 1–8, had to come before the paraenesis of Romans 12–13. On theological grounds alone this sequence was obvious to Paul, yet it had also been worked out as an epistolary arrangement in Galatians. Despite this typical structure—according to which the assertion of salvation precedes the exhortation to the appropriate shaping of Christian life because the exhortation follows from the nature of the new Christian state of salvation—we must see in particular that the introduction to the exhortation and subsequent themes of Romans 12–13 delve only rather generally into the previous content of the letter. In comparison to Gal. 5:13ff. and the relationship of this section to the previous content of Galatians, the connection in Romans is much less specific. Naturally the Israel chapters 9–11 come best after ch. 8 in Romans, for chs. 9–11 work through a particular problem that results from Romans 1–4 (Jews and Gentiles are sinners; the gospel of Jesus Christ alone saves and is there for all), just as the chapters immediately before chs. 9–11 also deal with particular issues of the message of justification. Does the eschatological horizon of Romans 8 not also go well with the following question about Israel's eschatological salvation? Likewise, the placing of Rom. 14:1–15:13 after the general paraenesis leads to a good assumption: Paul writes in order to introduce himself and in no case wants to get involved right away in the affairs of the Roman church. Therefore he places this section at the very end of the actual letter. Incidentally, like Romans 12–13, for example, this section is so self-sufficient that the language and problems of Romans 1–8 are absent.

Thus, using the building-block principle, Paul assembles prestructured parts whose content and syntactic inner relationships do not have to be constructed from scratch but are largely prefabricated. Hence, for the arrangement of material in the traditional paraenesis of Romans 12–13, Paul can fall back on the established order: internal relations, external relations, eschatological conclusion (cf. Gal. 5:13–6:12). Even the idea of the body of Christ (Rom. 12:6ff.) is not new to him, for in 1 Corinthians 12 he had already employed it similarly as the basic concept in regulating behavior within the church. A look into the next block in Romans reveals something similar. The problem between the strong and the weak in Rome, which is somewhat different in details from that in 1 Corinthians 8–10, is treated by Paul in Rom. 14:1–15:13 with quite related arguments, but of course he cannot, as in Corinth, bring himself in as a model for the church still unknown to him. Thus 1 Corinthians 9 is dropped, and in its place Paul develops Christ as the eschatological central figure with normative consequences, as he had already done, for example, in Philippians A (cf. 12.3 above).

Paraenesis is always a good example for demonstrating prestructured texts. Yet they can also be illustrated with such a complex corpus as Romans 1–8. After 1 Thessalonians it no longer astonishes anyone that Paul begins with the preached gospel (Rom. 1:1–17) and ends with the realization of eschatological salvation as the redemption of Christian hope (8:12ff.). The contrasting of sinful humanity with justified believers (1:18–3:20 and 3:21–4:25) corresponds to traditional baptismal statements, when they distinguish the former condition from the present state of salvation (cf., e.g., 1 Cor. 6:9–11). That from attained salvation (Rom. 3:21–4:25) consequences are drawn for Christian existence (5:1ff.)

is likewise as old as the oldest Pauline letter. If the argumentative and descriptive style with the predominant third person singular, as appears in 3:21–4:25, is detached from the ecclesiastically oriented "we" style (5:1ff.), there is also a parallel for this in Gal. 3:6ff. and 3:22ff. If in 1 Thess. 1:9–10 we see the two themes of the old Gentile-mission preaching (turning from the world of the gods and the Christian offer of salvation), then this sequence is likewise revealed in Romans (1:19ff.; 3:21ff.). This is not astonishing either, for according to Rom. 1:1–18 Paul appears as the apostle to the Gentiles, even if in 1:19–3:20 he associates the Jews' unsaved condition with the Gentiles' idolatry and wickedness as symptoms of their unsaved state.

Naturally the special contents of individual sections are also familiar to Paul before the composition of Romans. The presentation of the unsaved condition of the Gentiles, for example—as well as of the Jews—is too typical for Paul to have formulated it completely new for the first time. For the negative description of the Gentiles in Rom. 1:18ff. or the picture of the last judgment in 2:1ff., there are also counterparts from the Hellenistic synagogue. The treatment of circumcision in 2:25ff. has intellectual precedents in Phil. 3:3 and 2 Cor. 3:4ff. The conception of baptism in 6:1ff. has already left tracks in Gal. 2:19–20; 6:14; Phil. 3:10, so that we can assume that basic statements in Romans 6 were familiar to Paul before the dictation of this chapter.

Yet to this still incomplete and only exemplary enumeration we must add another more fundamental observation—as indicated in an initial overview by the following table—according to which Paul has Galatians in particular, but also Philippians B and Corinthians B and C, as background in the formulation of Romans.

Romans	Galatians		Philippians B	Corinthians B and C
3:21–31	2:16–21		3:9	
4:1–25	3:6–18			
5:1–11				2 Cor. 5:14–21
5:12–21				1 Cor. 15:21–22, 44–49
6:1–15		2:19–20; 6:14	3:10	
6:16–23				
7:1–25	3:19–25			
8:1–11	3:1–5; 4:4–5	5:16ff.	(3:10b–14)	
8:12–17	4:6–7			
8:18–30			3:20–21	

From the table we can draw conclusions. Romans 3:21–8:17 follows rather closely the middle part of Galatians in the realm of content as well as in the sequence of themes. That cannot be coincidental, especially since Galatians was written shortly before Romans. Yet Paul does not follow the presentational concept of Galatians at all but designs a new one for Romans, while making use of Galatians (cf. 13.3 below). If in Philippians 3, furthermore, Paul can present Christian existence in one sweep from becoming a Christian through Christian life to the final glorification, and in Galatians the future of the Christian has at best a quite subordinate importance, the given parallels in Philippians B become significant because Paul, precisely in Romans 5–8, arranges the material in a way that draws the line from the salvific status of the justified to their glorification. Finally, it is obvious that Romans 5 stands without analogies when compared with Galatians and Philippians B. Yet there are antecedents in the Corinthian correspondence.

Thus Paul has already plowed the fields of his presentation in Romans 1–8 at least once and indeed has probably, apart from the literary evidence available to us, given similar treatment in his letters and sermons. This may also explain in part the variations in vocabulary and linguistic peculiarities in the sections. Why is *flesh,* the term for sin, missing in Rom. 1:19–3:20, when it gains such central importance in Romans 7–8? Anyone who compares the picture of judgment in Rom. 2:1ff. with the end expectation in Romans 8 will have a hard time harmonizing the two texts. If we consider the antithesis between Adam and Christ in Rom. 5:12–21 in regard to its use of language, we observe, for example, a large number of noun formations with the ending *-ma.* These nouns occur elsewhere in Romans 1–8 only rarely. Without doubt the metaphorical personal use of "righteousness" in Rom. 6:13, 16, 18–20 is not to be found in Rom. 3:21–4:25, and in Romans 6 it is linked with the specific traditional understanding of baptism as a change of dominion. Why is the idea of freedom absent before Romans 6 and then so conspicuous (6:18, 20; 7:3; 8:2, 21)? How can one explain that two passages like 5:1ff. and 8:12ff. both develop the hope of the Christian but that in doing so each goes its own independent way? These observations, which could be multiplied, bring confirmation to our thesis. The individual Pauline trains of thought are also in part already roughly preshaped in terms of language with typical words and sequences of statements. Paul then varies more or less freely what he earlier has in part already thought out and clothed in words.

Yet the prestructuring in Romans 1–8 goes a little farther. In these chapters Paul naturally pursues his own theme, as expressly announced in 1:1–17. Yet it is also apparent that in the process he discusses opposing positions and objections, which he knows from previous discussions and for which he already has an answer. In 2:12–16, 25–29 Paul deals with law and circumcision from the angle of the deeds of Jews and Gentiles, and at the end he contrasts ritual circumcision with the spiritual circumcision of the heart. Behind this, obviously, is the Antiochene decision against the position of Jewish law (cf. 5.5 above). With this tradition Paul wards off the imaginary objection to his estimation that the Jew is a sinner before God; this objection maintains that before God the Jew is in a better position than the Gentile because the Jew has circumcision and the law. Also belonging here are the two objections that Paul treats in the same context, which, in view of his negative judgment of the Jews, come into Paul's mind automatically, as it were (Rom. 3:1–4, 5–8). The first involves a counterquestion directed at Paul: How can God's election still have validity when Paul so consistently puts Jews together with Gentiles. The second concerns the question whether the Pauline standpoint leads to simply taking God's righteousness to the point of absurdity. Also in these cases counterposition and Pauline answer have long since been thought out in principle by Paul. He was already practiced in dealing with them. Naturally this is also true of the differently phrased question whether Paul overthrows the law altogether (3:31), that is, invites the individual to remain in sin (i.e., lawlessness), so that grace can have an even greater effect (6:1, 15), or whether he even puts down the law as sin that is to be avoided (7:7, 13).

On the text level of the letter, of course, such inquiries appealing to the holiness of the law appear as aggressive counterquestions in the dialogue, but they are never raised in such a way that the Roman church now can be identified with them or should be. Nor is Paul attempting to mediate between two Roman positions in the church, that is, between a Jewish-Christian and a Gentile-Christian position. Otherwise the apostle would have to attack the church or parts of it directly in a way similar to Galatians. Furthermore, Paul talks to the church as a whole and as oriented in a Gentile-Christian way, as the beginning and the end of the letter demonstrate (1:1–17; 15:14–33) and Romans 9–11 confirms when it speaks to Gentile Christians about Israel and Jewish Christians. The Jewish-Christian element that is no doubt contained in the church (Rom. 4:1; 9:24; Jewish names in 16:3ff.; cf. 13.1 above) forms no special group. Also a reference to the weak in 14:1–15:13 does not help to fix an active Jewish-Christian position in the Roman church, because the catchword "law" does not appear here, asceticism of meat and wine (14:21) is not at all provided for by the Jewish law, and programmatic observance of the law would have to be fought by Paul as in Galatians. Nevertheless a comparison between this passage and Romans 1–8 is instructive in other ways. Anyone who compares the rhetorical means in the two texts will quickly recognize the differences. In 14:1–15:13 Paul has problems with the church itself and expresses this directly (cf., e.g., 14:1, 13, 19; 15:1–2, 7); in Romans 1–8 there is none of this way of speaking.

Nevertheless the situation remains that Paul involves the Romans in a controversy that he, apart from the highly topical occasions in Galatians and Philippians B, directly opened up in a letter for no other Gentile–Christian church. That means that with the help of the Letter to the Romans, the still echoing quarrel with the Judaizers (cf. 10.2 and 11.4 above) is also beating like waves against the gates of Rome. When Paul presents his Gentile-Christian gospel to Rome, he can do so, in view of his controversial position in Christendom, only by protecting it from objections represented especially by the Judaizers but also generally known elsewhere. Paul knows that he comes to Rome, of course, as the symbolic figure of Gentile Christianity, but his pointed theology is involved in a controversy that is also known in Rome. Thus Paul is not diagnosing a Jewish-Christian attitude against him in the Roman church but rather imagining a church while he describes his gospel as it lies under attack. The real quarrel that stands behind this was already fought out by Paul in Galatians and Philippians B.

Thus in this way there arises in Rome an imaginary literary quarrel, as in the so-called diatribe style. Yet it is a quarrel that has a real, non-Roman background and also provides the basis for understanding other things in Rome. When the apostle to the Gentiles places his gospel before Gentile Christians (Rom. 1:1-17), it is rather striking that he gives the sinful status of the Jews such a large amount of space. Is it not also striking, in contrast to Gal. 3:6ff., that in Romans 4 Paul again brings in the theme of Abraham's circumcision? Without doubt this strengthened his standpoint vis-à-vis the Jews. It was already observed long ago that Paul judges the law more positively in Romans 7 (cf. 7:12) than in 3:19ff. (cf. esp. 3:19, 24–25) but emphasizes human misery under the law more concretely than in Galatians. This shift in position apparently also strengthened his position in regard to the synagogue. Finally, Paul does not let it rest with his argument against Judaism. Rather, in Romans 9–11 he offers a self-sacrifice for Israel (Rom. 9:1ff.), gives it another chance for salvation (Rom. 11:25ff.), and warns the Gentiles against arrogance regarding Israel (11:11ff.). Thus these observations show that we will have to begin with the idea that the quarrel with the anti-Gentile-Christian oriented Jewish-Christian front had its fallout also in Romans 1–11. Is only the recent past really involved here or also a look into the future?

With these observations we probably also have at the same time a first indication of Paul's intention in writing Romans. What, then, is his purpose? The answers to this question are controversial not least of all because the reasons concretely named by the apostle could have easily been dealt with in a much shorter and less weighty letter. Do the visit to Rome and the journey to Spain (both announced by Paul in Rom. 1:11–13; 15:22–29) require such a thorough, comprehensive presentation of Paul's gospel—and this, moreover, in part with an internal dialogue partner that is really not the Roman church at all but rather, as we have just seen, the Jews or Jewish Christians? Why is it not enough for Paul to write a letter the size of 1 Thessalonians with a note that Priscilla and Aquila, who are sufficiently acquainted with Paul and at the same time well integrated into the Roman church, can say more about Paul if this is necessary? Were there not in general so many Christians in Rome acquainted with Paul (Romans 16) that the church was quite well informed about him even without such a thorough presentation of his message?

Nevertheless the directly named, outward reasons for the letter are now clear. Paul values the Roman church highly and has long had the intention of visiting it but has been repeatedly prevented from doing so. Now he wants to turn this visit into reality, not in order to missionize in Rome, but in order to strengthen the church, that is—as Paul immediately corrects himself—to be "mutually encouraged by each other's faith" (Rom. 1:12). Thus Paul begins in Rom. 1:11–13 carefully to introduce his concrete plans. He becomes clearer only at the end of the letter: he considers his mission in Asia Minor and Greece to be finished and has decided to devote himself entirely to the West, in order to remain true to his principle of appearing as the apostle to the Gentiles only where Christ has not yet been proclaimed. Hence he would indeed like very much to visit Rome, as noted in 1:11–13, but he really wants to go to Spain. Rome is not the goal of his journey but only a stop on the way; indeed, the Roman church is supposed to equip him for the mission to Spain (15:14–24). It is clear that Paul could not yet mention this plan in Romans 1. That would have been undiplomatic.

Thus at the end Paul put his concern regarding Rome into plain language. He could close the letter with it, but the problems he must get out of the way are not yet all out on the table for the Roman church. There is still, for example, the collection journey to Jerusalem, which affects the Roman visit and the Roman church (15:25–33). Certainly his plan remains to go via Rome to Spain, as he repeats once more (15:28–29). But he cannot move westward right away as Phoebe did (16:1–2). First he must go in exactly the opposite direction, eastward, to Jerusalem. Oh, if this were only a question of a few months delay! No, unfortunately this trip is as urgent as it is highly explosive. It even looks so bad that before his visit Paul already needs help from the Romans, namely, their prayers

(15:30–31). It may well be that as a result of this trip Paul will not be able to come to Rome at all and will thus be prevented again from making the trip, or that on account of the quarrel over the collection the bond between Gentile Christianity and Jewish Christianity will be cut, and thus the Romans could perhaps receive an apostle to the Gentiles who has been dismissed from fellowship with Jewish Christians. Paul hides all of this somewhat behind the words in 15:31 (cf. 15.1 below). The Romans can infer it for themselves or have Phoebe explain it. In the Jerusalem journey there is everything: fortunate success, for which Paul still hopes, and a many-sided, still incalculable disaster, which comes relentlessly into his mind when he analyzes the situation.

Now, finally, everything is out! Now the Romans can read the letter again, knowing what was preying on Paul's mind from the first dictated word, under the pressure of which he also wrote in such detail and in Romans 1–11 repeatedly thought of his position regarding the synagogue. Now they know: he not only wanted to go to Spain but in the face of all the threatening events that could come in Jerusalem he wanted to make the Romans witnesses to his theological testament; it shows why he must quarrel with Israel for the sake of the gospel (Romans 1–8) but, as a former member of this people, would personally offer himself for Israel's salvation, and still has not given up on Israel, because God's faithfulness to Israel has not been canceled (Romans 9–11). Is it so hard to imagine that for Paul himself Romans 1–11 also has the side effect of being preparation for the discussions coming up in Jerusalem, his next destination? Thus the external information on the situation at the sending of the letter puts us on the trail that leads to the internal situation: Before his Jerusalem journey, with which everything can be won or lost and where his life and his commission as apostle to the Gentiles in the one church of Jewish Christians and Gentile Christians are at stake, Paul lays his theological testament before the Romans, to whom he will come next if everything goes well. If he should no longer be able to come, they will have ahead of time, in writing, what he would have to say to them upon his coming.

Thus, because the success of the Jerusalem journey hangs by a thread, Paul composes the Letter to the Romans in a thorough, detailed way; as the apostle to the Gentiles, which he has been since his calling, he emphatically presents his Gentile-Christian gospel once again (Rom. 1:1–17). The guiding role for Romans 1–8; 9–11 is given to the language of justification, which Paul tested earlier in the struggle with the Judaizers and will probably also use in Jerusalem (cf. Rom. 3:21–5:21). Now, however, it is no longer presented in the language of battle but in the style of a theological treatise. Granted, this does not make Romans the first dogmatics of Christendom. Yet Romans 1–8 does present the last unfolding of the Pauline gospel; the apostle intended to live and die by this understanding of the gospel.

13.3 The Train of Thought in Romans 1–8

If we approach Romans 1–8 from Galatians and Philippians B on the basis of the comments in section 13.2 above, we see that Paul is faced with several problems. While adopting the justification language of these two previously written letters, the apostle must now speak so as to avoid a direct attack using the kind of polemic against the Judaizers and their countermission with which he put pressure on the churches in Galatia and Philippi. For Paul is now seeking contact with a church that has obviously not yet been exposed to such acute influence. Of course, at the very end of the letter he will warn the intact church against the possible Judaizing danger (Rom. 16:17–20), yet the internal community relations indicated in Rom. 14:1–15:13 show that the requirement of circumcision is not discussed in Rome and thus Judaizers are not yet at work. Furthermore, Paul can hardly draw on Philippians B any further and set up his calling directly as a model for the understanding of Christian existence. One could talk this way with a familiar church but hardly with the Romans, who still do not know him personally. Nor can he, as in Galatians, simply refer to the church's experience with the first Pauline mission, for he did not found the Roman church, which, especially in its first Jewish-Christian phase, did not give up its connection with the law immediately upon accepting the gospel (cf. 13.1 above). Finally, Paul must assume that the general knowledge of his person in Rome also identifies him as a controversial apostle, so that a clear, but at the same time careful and objective, presentation is appropriate. All of this presents Paul with the task of seeking a new way to organize his proclamation, which if possible will solve all these problems.

Up to this point, one result of our consideration of the Pauline letters is this: The apostle has the special ability to present his basic position in ever new ways and still remain true to the heart of the matter. For Romans, Paul chooses a way that also sets the Romans up as addressees of his apostolic commission and develops this gospel for them in a descriptive, treatiselike fashion (Rom. 1:1–17). Paul begins with his Gentile apostleship and the concomitant gospel for all nations with the Roman church as the addressee of this message; he maintains that this gospel of Jesus Christ rests on the common early Christian confession (Rom. 1:3b–4 is confessional tradition), and thus at this point Paul stands within the common early Christian consensus; then with the language of justification he interprets the content of the gospel with intentional signal effect for the following epistolary content—the theme of the controversial Paul is sounded: "For I am not ashamed of the gospel: it is the power of God for salvation to every one who has faith, to the Jew first and also to the Greek. For in it the righteousness of God is revealed through faith for faith; as it is written [Hab. 2:4], 'He who through faith is righteous shall live'" (Rom. 1:16–17).

This certainly well thought out beginning of the letter now gives structure to the following discussions. We will, of course, have to forgo the idea of finding in Rom. 1:17 a detailed plan for 1:18–8:39. But there is no doubt that 1:1–17 provides the viewpoint from which Romans 1–8 should be discussed. That means that irrespective of the internal relationships of the sections to each other, Romans 1–8 on the whole develops the gospel of Jesus Christ interpreted as the righteousness of faith that leads to life. Thus Paul orients himself toward the preached gospel as it works for the eschatological salvation of those who accept it in faith. This basically corresponds to the election theology of 1 Thessalonians (cf. 6.2 above). In principle Paul had also begun in just this way in Galatians (Gal. 1:6–9; 3:1–5). This correspondence becomes even clearer when in the "power of God" of Rom. 1:16 we recognize the Spirit of 1 Thess. 1:5–7; Gal. 3:1–5 (which then is later discussed in detail in Romans 8) and place it in the theology-of-election context of gospel-faith-called saints from Rom. 1:1–7. Thus Paul looks from the gospel entrusted to him to the addressees of this message and describes how under the gospel they become new people. Then this beginning with election theology is developed in the spirit of Galatians and Philippians B through the language of justification and with the special text signal of the quotation from Hab. 2:4, a key Old Testament text for Paul that we have already encountered in Gal. 3:11 (cf. 11.3 above). In this way he establishes agreement between his gospel of justification and the Old Testament, an aspect that will gain more importance especially in Rom. 3:21–4:25.

Naturally insight into this basic orientation of Romans 1–8 still does not solve all the problems of the structure, but it gives clear help in understanding the text. Now, however, we have to determine the function of the individual sections within this general aspect. That is, all sections in Rom. 1:18–8:39 must be comprehended as aspectual development of the series gospel of Jesus Christ-faith/righteousness-life. Only after this crucial ordering based on Rom. 1:1–17 do we then come in second place to observations on the arrangement of the sections among each other. The predominance of the first ordering principle already becomes clear in the fact, for example, that Paul writes no systematic treatise in which one conceptual step deductively and necessarily follows another. Nor does he choose, for example, a salvation-historical outline from Abraham (Romans 4) through the Mosaic giving of the law (cf. Romans 7), the coming of Christ (cf. 3:24–26; 4:24–25), the proclamation of the gospel, and its faithful acceptance, with the beginning of Christian churches (cf. 1:1–17), to the end of all things (Romans 2; 5; 8:18ff.). Instead, these themes appear quite unchronologically under various conditions in the text. Also, the contrast between the two epochs before Christ and after Christ, which characterizes Galatians 3–4, is not to be found.

The first test case for the discussion of the structure of Romans 1–8 is Rom. 1:18–3:20, the section that deals with the wrath of God over sinful humanity as a whole. The passage does not deduce the first partial aspect of the gospel, namely, the revelation of God's wrath, for the wrath of God does not come from the gospel but "from heaven" (1:18), and Paul described the gospel completely in 1:16–17 without mentioning the wrath. He asks rather: Whom does the gospel encounter? Answer: All of humanity, which has fallen into sin and stands under the general wrath of God. The election theology of 1 Thessalonians had already assumed that God does not choose people with special merits but those in the global unsaved state of all humanity and thus in the nations who previously scorned him (1 Thess. 1:9), and if necessary also Jews, as surely as they also live in sinful hostility to the gospel (1 Thess. 2:16). Thus the gospel redeems people from divine wrath and hopeless subjection to death (1 Thess. 1:10; 2:16; 4:13; 5:9). It removes them from this damnation by revealing the God who elects through Christ. Thus the gospel addresses the damnation that precedes it but does not carry out judgment on this damnation; the Jews who stand in the way of the gospel are not placed under the gospel as their judgment but under the wrath of God (1 Thess. 2:15–16), from which Christ himself saves (1 Thess. 1:10). This statement about the lost as addressees of the gospel was then refined in the Corinthian correspondence in the theology of the cross (cf., e.g., 1 Cor. 1:18–31).

If in Rom. 1:18–3:20 Paul answers the question, what does the gospel encounter, when he proclaims it worldwide (1:14–15), then he next asks: What is revealed in the gospel? (cf. on the verb 1:17; 3:21). He has already given the answer in 1:16–17 in the key term "righteousness of God" and maintained that the gospel as God's power creates righteous people under the condition of "faith." In this sense he discusses the justification of the godless in 3:21–4:25. Here the gospel must come to bear as the gospel of Jesus Christ, that is, be developed as the righteousness mediated through Christ. In Galatians 3 this happened in such a way that the promise of blessing to Abraham pointed first to Christ and through him came to the believer as the Spirit present in the gospel (cf. 11.4 above). Paul also thinks analogously in Rom. 3:21–4:25, but he employs other means for his explanation. Just as in Galatians, Christology is brought to bear in such a way that Paul sees only what God does for humankind through Christ. Hence Paul does not reflect, for example, on how Christ exercises an influence on divine wrath for the benefit of humanity, or whether Christ placed his righteousness before God for the benefit of the deficient righteousness of humanity. No, the apostle has God act through Christ for the benefit of sinners and describes this in Romans with two traditional confession-like formulations (3:24–26; 4:24–25).

With Rom. 5:1 the apostle starts again by looking at the accomplished justification—that is, at the condition of the faithful reached through 3:21–4:25—and sees the thereby initiated reversal of the sinner's relationship to God, which is determined by wrath (1:19; 5:8–9), transformed into a peaceful relationship of the justified. At the same time, death (1:32; 2:8–9) and life (5:10) are thereby exchanged. This aspect was also already indicated in 1:17, as righteousness and life are in general old twins. If we recall that election and eschatological salvation (cf. 6.2 above) have for Paul belonged together for a long time, it now becomes clear that the justified in Rom. 5:1 correspond to the elect in 1 Thessalonians.

How, then, are we to fit into this context the following opposition of the two humanity-defining figures Adam and Christ in Rom. 5:12–21? Certainly, 6:1 begins anew, just as the impersonal descriptive style of 5:12–21 has no real counterpart at all in Romans 6–8. Hence Rom. 5:12–21 does not belong to what follows. If Romans 6–8 with its predominant "we" style is oriented toward the present existence of the justified, then 5:12–21 formulates in the same fundamental way the opposition between sin and death, on the one hand, and righteousness and life, on the other, as it exists between the large sections 1:18–3:20 and 3:21–4:25. These sections are also marked by an object-related description and contain "we" and "you" only as the stylistic means of the so-called diatribe, but not as in 5:1ff. and chs. 6–8 as the "we" of the believing and justified church, the "we" that becomes the object of consideration after it, within the antithesis of death and life, is transferred to the side of life. Likewise in 5:12–21 (5:12, 18) we again find the linguistic usage typical of 1:18–4:25, as it looks beyond the church and speaks in a generalizing way of "all" people as sinners (Rom. 1:18; 2:1, 9–10; 3:4, 9, 12, 19–20, 23) and of "all" believers (1:16; 3:22; 4:11). Again, this way of speaking is missing in 5:1–12 and chs. 6–8 (8:32 is a justified exception). If we now think further about the statement, made in Philippians B in the context of justification language, about Christ as the figure of salvation who determines everything and from whom everything receives its judgment (cf. also 1 Cor. 1:23; 2 Cor. 10:5; Gal. 2:21), then we can assume that with Rom. 5:12–21 Paul wanted to confirm again this very Christology for everything that had been presented in Romans up to this point.

This then yields the following possibility: the two parts of Romans 5 have different functions. The first (5:1–11) is the immediate consequence of 3:21–4:25 and at the same time prepares for Romans 6–8, as indicated by the "we" style. The second (5:12–21) interrupts this procedure, in that Paul, again in terms of style as well as content, brings Rom. 1:18–4:25 to a conclusion. Thus in this context Romans 5 has a hinge function: it opens up for what follows and closes off what has been said. We can test this thesis by asking: Does 5:12–21 fit in with the question, What is revealed in the gospel? as this question defines 3:21–4:25? The answer is yes. It is now even more complete, because it can now read: In the gospel God reveals the righteousness of faith through the eschatological and humanity-determining figure of Jesus Christ. Also a good reference to Rom. 1:1–17 now becomes visible: in 5:12–21 as in 1:3–4, the gospel is described as the gospel of Jesus Christ.

Strictly speaking, Paul has developed the gospel completely with the discourse in 1:18–5:21. As already indicated through the "we" of the community of salvation in 5:1–11, with Romans 6–8 also the focus moves from the development of the gospel to the presentation of various aspects that concern the reality of the believing church. We can also look at it this way: The presentation of the gospel was accomplished through the contrast that arises from the fact that the gospel addresses sinners whose relationship to God is determined by wrath and death. The gospel itself constitutes a new relationship to God, in that through it the sinner is justified and offered the gift of life. Now Paul turns to this new result and describes the complex living reality of the believers between justification and final salvation.

This apparently occurs in five sections, of which the first three look at the present life of Christians and the last two at their hope. In particular we have the following division. The first two sections, Romans 6 and 7, are characterized by key words ("sin," "law") and divided by introductory questions (6:1, 15; 7:1, 7). Apparently Paul has to ward off typical attacks against him, which accuse him of lawlessness. In detail, in the first section (6:1–23, subdivided into 6:1–14 and 6:15–23) Paul discusses the state of grace treated in 5:1–12, which means liberation from sin (6:2, 11–12) and the service of righteousness for sanctification (6:18–19). This occurs with traditional baptismal statements, through which Paul received two models of interpretation: (1) the death of the old person and the enabling of a new way of life (6:1–14) and (2) the change of dominion from slavery under sin to the service of righteousness (6:15–23). The second section (7:1–6, 7–25) shows—as anticipated by 6:14–15—how Christians are dead not only to sin but also to the law. Here too an aspect from 5:1–12 is treated (cf. 5:6–9). Since the traditional baptismal statements do not treat the theme of the law, Paul must now select a new situation with which he can make clear the freedom of the law. He does this with the example of the legislation on marriage. The legal determinations on marriage are valid for the partners only as long as both are alive. Christians, however, have died (see 6:1ff.) and are thus free of the law (7:1–6). Moreover, their position under the law was anything but happy (7:7–25): they can be glad to be free from the disastrous triangle of sin, law, and death. Predominant in the third section, 8:1–11, 12–17 (note the new division signals in 8:1 and 8:12), is the antithesis of Spirit and flesh. The Spirit of Christ and the concomitant immediacy to God are a new quality of the Christian that makes the law superfluous and can defy the flesh as the power of sin. This train of thought is also anticipated in 5:5, as well as immediately prepared for by 7:6. With various linguistic means, all three sections revolve around the present reality of the Christian in contrast to his old nature. In each case they say nothing new but aim at the same complex reality of the justified person.

Directly prepared for by 8:11, 17 and based on 5:3–5, the fourth section, 8:18–21, 22–27, 28–30, then discusses hope amidst the adversities of the present, while broadening the view from Christ to all of creation, just as 1:18–3:20 had tacitly and naturally seen in the Judge of sinful humankind the Creator of all reality. Finally, 8:31–37, 38–39 as the fifth section, connecting directly with 8:27, forms the appropriate conclusion by formulating the certainty of hope right down to the concluding hymn. No one will fail to notice here the beautiful arch of the "love of God" in Christ between 5:5, 8 and 8:35, 39.

The presentational concept of Romans 1–8 can now be clarified again with the diagram on page 357.

13.4 The Justification of the Godless

Our look into the structural relationships of Romans 1–8 has provided important help in understanding the text. This is true first for Rom. 1:18–3:20. We saw that here Paul does not define sin but, using the attitude and conduct of Gentiles and Jews as an example, describes how the gospel encounters them as sinners (3:20). Thus this section

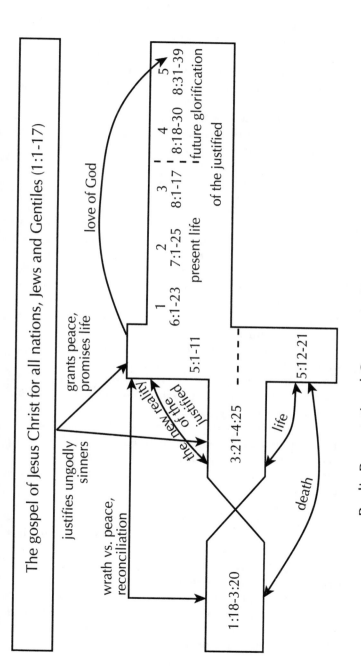

The gospel of Jesus Christ for all nations, Jews and Gentiles (1:1-17)

justifies ungodly sinners

grants peace, promises life

love of God

wrath vs. peace, reconciliation

the new reality of the justified

1:18-3:20

3:21-4:25

5:1-11

5:12-21

death

life

1
6:1-23

2
7:1-25

3
8:1-17

4
8:18-30

5
8:31-39

present life

future glorification
of the justified

Paul's Presentational Concept in Romans 1-8

asks: From what condition is humanity saved through the gospel of Jesus Christ? Hence the answer also contains aspects of Paul's understanding of sin. Yet it is especially striking that in the whole section the apostle does not employ the term "flesh" (cf. Romans 7–8), which is so typical of him as an expression of sin. That leads to the general observation that in Rom. 1:18–3:20 Paul is largely following traditional and typical statement contexts. For if we ignore the special Pauline thesis on the law, as it is woven into 3:20, Paul says hardly anything new to the Romans; they, like the first Christians, have long agreed with him that only the Christian message can save one from the general liability to judgment (cf. 1 Thess. 1:9–10; 1 Cor. 6:9–11 as traditional statements).

Upon closer examination, of course, the Romans will also observe that Paul organizes his discussion not—as would be appropriate for Rome—so that he is talking to a Gentile-Christian church about Gentiles and Jews (as, for example, in Romans 9–11). Rather, in 1:18ff. Paul speaks about Gentiles from a Jewish standpoint and expects unqualified agreement from the Jewish side, in order then, from the viewpoint of Hellenistic diaspora Judaism (2:17ff.), to include all of Judaism under the judgment of the general lapse into sin. Here he expects no unqualified agreement and expressly initiates a discussion (2:25–3:8). Thus Rom. 1:18–3:20 is actually a dialogue with Jewish Christians. The organization of the section has a structure that is older than Romans. It harmonizes with the dialogue between Paul and the Romans only because the closing judgment in Rom. 3:20 lies along this line.

In part it is even older than Christianity. For there can be no doubt that Paul borrowed the characterization of the Gentiles in Rom. 1:18ff. from his former Hellenistic synagogue. The compilation of Jewish transgressions in 2:17–24 is also not as new as it may seem at first glance. In terms of content, the contrast between the privileges and failure of Judaism is prevalent in the (in this case: Hellenistic synagogal) Jewish penitential sermon, especially since the compilations summarizing the points of indictment come from the history of Israel, are found in the Old Testament, and thus are known or available to every Jew. The fact that the Jewish apostate and Christian Paul says this is offensive to Jews, but not necessarily the statement as such; the Deuteronomic history, the Essenes, and John the Baptist have in their own way expressed analogous criticism of Israel by shining a harsh light on Israel's debit column. Incidentally, it must have been obvious even to Paul that his closing judgment in Rom. 3:20 was not substantiated by 2:17ff. alone. The polytheism of paganism was a fundamental flaw that characterized all Gentiles. For the Jews, however, Paul names no common basis of fundamental disqualification that is involved in each of their deeds. The jump from the individual misdeed to the defining universal judgment in 3:20 is thus applied to Judaism only through the authoritative judgment of scripture in the form of the collection of quotations in Rom. 3:10ff. Therefore, says Paul, the Jews can read in their own Bible about the divine judgment that concerns them all. Finally, also included in the compilation of traditional pre-Christian material in Rom. 1:18–3:20 is the picture of judgment in 2:1ff. (cf. 3.2 above), which likewise must be attributed to the Hellenistic synagogue.

If we take these observations seriously, in the interpretation of details we must constantly be aware that there are tensions between purpose and presentation. For example, if everyone is a sinner, can there be a good outcome of judgment at all, as Paul describes it in Rom. 2:1ff. in symmetry with the bad outcome? Likewise under the assumption of universal judgment in 3:20, can there be good Gentiles in the sense of 2:26–27? Is the sin of the Jews not worked out in a conceptually more insightful way in Rom. 10:1ff. than in 2:21ff.? We will put such questions aside and focus our attention on the apostle's pervasive expository themes.

When Paul asks whom the gospel encounters, he is asking at the same time: What is the status of all people before imminent divine judgment? In 1 Thess. 1:9–10 the purpose of the gospel was already to offer deliverance before imminent judgment. The imminent last judgment also remains the fundamental horizon in Romans (cf. 1:18; 2:1ff.; 13:11), so that 1:18–3:20 expresses the reality of humanity in the face of the imminent last judgment. If one looks at the history of all people, it promises nothing but divine wrath in the imminent judgment (1:18; 5:9). In 5:1, 8–10, according to Paul, the justified have peace with God and are saved from wrath through Christ, because God reconciled the enemies through the death of his Son. Thus the reconciliation brought about by God is deliverance from wrath, in that through his peacemaking act in Christ, God abolishes the enmity between himself and humanity. Thus what Paul wants to say about sin in Rom. 1:18–3:20 is clear. It is a concept that describes the relationship of people to God in its negative aspect in the face of the imminent last judgment. Sin is human contradiction in the sense of taking a position hostile to God, to which God reacts with wrath. Wrath and judgment express the fact that God cannot want people to appear in contradiction before him as creator and judge. He does not want such enmity; he wants peace.

This theological judgment of Paul's implies a previous general experience and understanding of aspects of sin. The apostle presupposes a human state of not being all right as a basic anthropological experience. Thus the idea that everyone experiences the difference between what should be and what is is the obvious assumption of Paul's discussion.

He can describe this with respect to two especially impressive phenomena. First, the apostle picks the conscience as the place in a person where human misbehavior reveals itself in that the self-accusation following the misdeed ("Actually I should have . . .") and the reacting defense ("They can't blame me for . . .") conflict with each other (Rom. 2:15). Alongside this internal experience Paul places the interpersonal experience according to which one creates hostile images, exalts oneself, and humbles the other person. This happens, for example, when we measure others by a norm but exempt ourselves from the same scrutiny (Rom. 2:17–24). Paul would be misunderstood if we credited him with the opinion that the first basic phenomenon is typically Gentile (against this cf., e.g., Rom. 13:5; 1 Cor. 8:7) and the second is typically Jewish (cf., e.g., Rom. 14:7–10; 1 Cor. 4:1–5). Both are human in general and remain themes of Christian admonition. Such experience of the dichotomy within oneself and perversity toward one's fellow human being always precedes the theological discussion of sin.

The apostle also speaks of the responsibility of the individual for his shortcomings. At this point the responsibility of Israel is no problem for Paul, for Israel was granted a special revelation of God (Rom. 2:17–18). The Gentiles are, in the apostle's eyes, also inexcusable before God, because they have denied themselves the truth of God as it is reflected in this world, for they "by their wickedness suppress the truth" (1:18–20). The "ungodliness" (1:18) of the Gentile is thus the creation—directed against the one God (1 Thess. 1:9)—of many gods out of the created world (1:21–23). It is the rebellious counterdesign of an interpretation of the world that makes itself the center of reality, which it comprehends only out of itself and for itself. It would be appropriate to interpret oneself and the whole world starting with the one true God. That the Gentile does not do this is his consciously chosen error. By expressly approving when others proceed this way (1:32), Gentiles reveal that they want such a corrupt shaping of life and the world, that is, that they are in it with all their heart.

Thus, for Paul, one's own knowledge of a failed design of life and the insight of bearing the responsibility for it are basic experiences of human life. But the knowledge that and how this is sin in the theological sense comes only when the gospel promises, in the sense of Rom. 5:6–10, that God through Christ offers peace to the sinner who is hostile to him. Only the experience of the peacemaking God (5:1), conveyed through God's Spirit (5:5), allows an appreciation of the depth of previous lostness. Only the knowledge of Christ allows a reevaluation of everything (Phil. 3:8–9). Therefore the gospel is also a topic in Rom. 1:16–17 before the general ungodliness is discussed (1:18–3:20).

The theological appraisal of the sinner as hostile to God (Rom. 8:7) and the sinner's being determined by inability to please God (8:8) has in principle been described by Paul also in 1:18–3:20. Sin is not merely a failure to fulfill commandments, that is, a falling short of the demands of God in all one's efforts regarding the law and the divine will. For the sinner not only lacks a large number of good deeds or has an over-abundance of violations of prohibitions. Sin, rather, is a position of the whole person against God. The description of the Gentiles' status as sinners begins with the naming of their consciously anti-God conception of life (1:19–21). Connected with this is a dishonoring of God, which is followed by the dishonoring of themselves (1:22–24, 28). The disqualification of the Jews ends with the point that the Jews dishonor God and nourish the Gentiles' blasphemy of God (2:23–24). The mixture of Old Testament quotations, which authoritatively announces God's judgment on humanity, ends in 3:18 with the statement, "There is no fear of God before their eyes." The fact that this is a basic concern of the apostle in the description of human lostness is shown by the antithetical description of Abraham in 4:20: he specifically honors God by placing his total reliance on the God who has promised him a son.

This observation helps us uncover a little more of the theological significance of the speech on sin. Abraham relies on the promises of God beyond his revelation in his deeds, for the patriarch is not responsible for his and his wife's advanced age. Rather, he relies on God in an onto-logical condition that makes apparent his creaturely dependence on God alone. In this situation he believes that God can give "life to the dead" (Rom. 4:17); that is, he will give the promised son to Abraham, who can-not beget, and Sarah, who cannot conceive. Because Abraham grew strong in this faith (4:20), he is righteous before God (4:3). Thus, expect-ing everything from God, a person should live before God. The opposite of this, then, must be sin: living from oneself and one's world, although one is a creature. Sin is planning one's life and understanding the world apart from God. This is hostility toward God, because it robs God of the honor of being what he is for all reality, for God is both life and the giver of successful life. Paul also expressed this in 1:18–3:20: the Gentile lives as one who has turned away from God in that he produces gods and does not let God be God (1:18ff.). His action is an ersatz creation according to his own possibilities and out of his own being. The world formed by him becomes a reflection of his isolation from the one true God. The Jew also dishonors God, because he teaches others but in his conduct removes himself from divine judgment (2:23–24). He creates for himself freedom from God at the same time that he believes himself superior to the Gentiles on the basis of God's gifts. Did Paul not con-

demn an analogous kind of Christian misbehavior in 1 Corinthians 1–4;
2 Corinthians 10–13? Hence we can summarize: Sin is being God's creature no more, that is, no longer wanting to expect everything good from
God. In this context the double question in 1 Cor. 4:7 is illuminating:
"What have you that you did not receive? If then you received it, why do
you boast as if it were not a gift?" Sin is rejecting or limiting this reception by overestimating human possibilities.

If indeed sin for Paul is perceived in its theological depth only when
a person has learned to think from the standpoint of having experienced the gospel, then the Pauline understanding of redemption has to
show how the Christian state of salvation overcomes one's sinful nature
and what takes its place. At this point we are ready for Rom. 3:21–5:21.

We can best gain access to this section if in appreciation of the special position of Romans 5 we develop our understanding from the
standpoint of this text. For this the inferential and summarizing character of the chapter is important. It is clear how Paul here emphasizes
the humanity-determining salvation figure of Christ (5:12ff.): in the face
of the imminent (13:11) last judgment (1:18; 5:9), which as the judgment of wrath is the fate of all humanity, and shortly before this catastrophe of humanity—the "now" in 3:21; 5:9 (cf. 2 Cor. 6:2) has an
eschatological ring—God has replaced Adam with the new central
eschatological figure of Christ. It is the act of salvation bound to his
person that establishes this meaning. In Rom. 5:1–11 it is described in
various aspects in that formerly independent groups of statements,
each with its special assertive power, are interwoven in a peculiar way.

More specifically, in 5:1–11 Paul arranges these statement groups in
such a way that a striking affinity to 2 Cor. 5:14–6:2 is recognizable. If
indeed in 2 Cor. 5:14–6:2 Paul's purpose is a very basic summary of the
early Christian proclamation in general, he pursues the same goal in
Rom. 5:1ff. Further, the two texts bring together (almost) the same salvation concepts under the sign of the love of God or Christ (Rom. 5:5,
8; 2 Cor. 5:14; cf. also Rom. 8:31–39), so that here we can see a phenomenon analogous to that of the majestic titles. The abundance of
titles, as Paul (and early Christianity) applies them to Jesus, corresponds
to the uniting of several interpretations of the salvation event in Romans
5 and 2 Corinthians 5. In both cases the same thing is attempted: the
originally independent ways of understanding, which are now united in
the characterization of the figure of Jesus, are, through this abundance,
supposed to paint his person as simply insurpassable. In each of the
textual transitions we can see indications that make it apparent for both
phenomena that at one time both the majestic titles and the salvation
concepts possessed linguistic and material independence. They were,

however, largely deprived of this in order to be integrated into a meta-context, which the person of Jesus Christ constitutes. For our train of thought it does not matter how the majestic titles and salvation concepts in part already underwent amalgamation processes before and beside Christianity. In any case we also still find them all independently, and nowhere has a figure magnetically attracted everything as basically and comprehensively as did the figure of Jesus Christ. Thus the christological process is certainly not completely without analogy, yet it is, at the same time, singular. In view of it we can say that no majestic title by itself is enough to say who Jesus is for the faith. Likewise no salvation concept is sufficient to comprehend the process of salvation. Thus it is true that no majestic title or salvation concept is preserved entirely with its specific content. They all become only limited means of expression. They each throw a certain light on the central figure of salvation, but even in this role are always serviceable in only a limited way.

On, now, to the statements in Rom. 5:1ff.! First we have the salvation concept that the ungodly (5:6; 4:5) and sinful person (5:8; 3:9; 4:7–8) will be justified (5:1, 9; 3:24; 4:5, 25; 5:16ff.) and thereby receive access to the divine grace (5:2; 3:24; 4:4, 16; 5:15ff.). God does not reckon a person's sins against him or her (4:8); he reckons faith as righteousness (4:3–5, 9, 22–23). He is thus gracious to the sinner. A second concept says that human beings are the enemies of God (5:10; 11:28). But God becomes reconciled with them. Such reconciliation (5:10–11; 11:15; 2 Cor. 5:18–20) leads from enmity to peace (Rom. 5:1; 3:17; 8:6; 15:33; Phil. 4:7, 9). Christians are pacified former enemies of God. The third concept is centered on substitution: people risk their lives for the "weak" (Rom. 5:6), whose lives are threatened, in order to save them (9:3; 16:4; cf. John 11:50). In Rom. 5:7 Paul reflects on the fundamental conditions of such a substitution. It is clear that Christ substitutes in a special way for "us" (5:8; 1 Thess. 5:10; 1 Cor. 1:13; 2 Cor. 5:14; etc.). Therefore Christians again have hope for life (Rom. 5:4, 10b). These three groups of statements are also to be found in 2 Cor. 5:14–6:2 in different variations and with different accents. In Romans 5, however, yet another salvation concept is indicated. We find it when we read of deliverance through Christ's "blood" (5:9) as a reminder of the cultic-oriented propitiation Christology in 3:24–25, which expressly states that Christ accomplished expiation "by his blood." Once our attention has been called to this accent in Romans 5, we find key words that fit this concept: expiation occurs for the "trespasses" (cf. 4:25; 5:15ff.) of sinners (5:8); expiation provides freedom from God's "wrath" (5:9) in the form of a suspension of the disastrous consequences of sinful acts.

Let us emphasize once more that these salvation concepts in Romans

5 do not simply stand side by side. They have been woven into a new tapestry and in the process have given up their separate lives. This has produced a new combined model that is more than the sum of its formerly individual parts. The all-determining structure of the tapestry is given in the key word of divine love (Rom. 5:5, 8). Here is the most profound reason for the salvation event. God does not will the death of his creatures, even if they live in ungodly sin. God does not want to be the judge who brings death (3:19), but the creative reshaper of human relationships. This self-definition as creative love was described by Paul earlier in 4:17. Then the act of love itself is first signalized as "justification" in 5:1 in summation of the comments in 3:21–4:25 and is taken up again at the end in 5:9. Yet this assertion is reinterpreted at the conclusion through the concept of reconciliation (5:10–11), which has the final, decisive word. Further, there should be no question that although the concept of propitiation is heard, general substitution takes the lead. These observations are in harmony with the comments on 1:18–3:20. If the sinner is depicted here above all as the one who despises and dishonors God, then this corresponds now to God's offer of reconciliation to his ungodly enemies. The destiny of Jesus Christ is, as it were, the hand of God reaching out to the ungodly and reestablishing the salvific divine nearness.

At this point we may take a look at the ungodly, who are now justified. They are justified on condition of faith (5:1) through the experience of the Spirit, who pours God's love into their hearts (5:5). Destined by this experience, they value God's act in Christ and their own future as well-founded hope. Therefore the typical "we" style of the believing church (cf. Gal. 3:23–4:7 after 3:6–22 with Rom. 5:1ff. after 3:21–4:25) is essential, for the redemption process is specified by the concept of reconciliation. Reconciliation is aimed at personal relationships and always involves two parties: someone who, like God, offers reconciliation and someone who accepts it—in this case, human beings. Therefore the following two statements stand closely linked in the "parallel text" of 2 Cor. 5:14–21, like two sides of the same coin: the statement that God reconciled us to himself through Christ (5:18), and the word of reconciliation with his request: Be reconciled to God! (5:20).

Armed with these insights from Romans 5, let us now look at 3:21–4:25. This section, in which Paul develops for the last time his conception of the justification of sinners, is given special weight by its extremely broad reception. Yet it doubtless also has a prominent significance in Romans itself. Its framing by 1:18–3:20 and 5:1ff., which we have just discussed, gives good indications of the orientation under which the section is formulated. Fundamental here is the assertion that in Rom. 3:21–4:25

Paul must clarify how sinners can escape—or have already escaped—the imminent judgment of wrath (5:1). Since Paul is speaking in the context of God's action in the last judgment (1:18; 2:1ff.; 5:1, 9), it is illuminating when he explains God's actions, which now already justify the ungodly, primarily with the juridical language of the last judgment (cf. 11.3 above). In particular it includes the talk of *reckoning* (as righteousness), which Paul borrows from Gen. 15:6 (= Rom. 4:3) and which, in distinction to Galatians 3 (where only Gal. 3:6 = Gen. 15:6), he now uses extensively—to be exact, another nine times in the text—and in addition supplements through Ps. 32:1–2 = Rom. 4:7–8. This is also striking in view of the prior indications in 2 Cor. 5:19; Rom. 2:26 and must be considered a peculiarity of Romans 4. This reveals a difference from Galatians 3: the perspective of the history of salvation, from the blessing promised Abraham to the Christian church's experience of the Spirit (cf. 11.4 above), conditions the baptism-oriented justification statements in Galatians 3–4, but it is no longer important in Rom. 3:21–4:25. Such a manner of speaking is (perhaps) present if we include the justification statement in 3:24 in the christological formula used in 3:24b–26a. Yet the juridical and commercial legal language dominates (cf. esp. 4:1–5).

The orientation toward the last judgment causes a further structural arrangement in Rom. 3:21–4:25: As all are sinners before God's judgment (3:19–20, 23), so all who believe attain God's righteousness (3:22). This levels the distinction between Jews and Gentiles (3:27–30; 4:10–12). Through the life-styles of all, this division of humanity had already, in ungodliness and under the wrath of God, become an undifferentiated fellowship sharing the same fate. Yet Paul expressly emphasizes that the judgment of the world by the one God (2:1ff.) belongs together with the worldwide and undifferentiated mercy of the one God (3:30) toward all sinners through the gospel. This worldwide horizon of humanity requires placing the accent on each individual who believes. Whereas in Galatians 3–4, through the statements of the Spirit, the Christian church as elected eschatological church formed the social framework of the statements, in Rom. 3:21–4:25 Abraham, before his becoming a Jew, is the prototype of every person who is related by faith to God's promise. This horizon, which spans all of humanity and at the same time is intended for each individual, is then taken up again programmatically in the opposition of Adam and Christ (5:12ff.), just as it was already expressed as a main idea in 1:16–17. In the face of the imminent judgment of the world, God's offer of the gospel, with which he wants to justify sinners, is intended for humanity, that is, for everyone who believes. Thus the justified, as children of God, are also precursors of a cosmic liberation, even if this is indicated in Romans 8 in only a barely understandable way. This horizon of the justification statements that is not limited to the church but encompasses humanity—indeed all reality—is particularly typical of Romans.

We must immediately add, however, that Paul does not explain to the salvationless present time its significance from the standpoint of this eschatological dimension. Rather, in typical continuity with election theology (cf. 6.2 above), Paul thinks from the standpoint of the gospel now being promulgated (1:16–17). It changes people and effects spiritual renewal (Romans 6–8). In this way the gospel of Christ, on condition of faith, creates righteous people (3:21–22). The Abraham story is correspondingly interpreted so that it is directed toward those who believe in Christ in the present (4:24). Abraham himself is characterized in such a way that his relationship to God corresponds in structure and content to the present relationship to God of the Christian who believes in Christ. This is possible because the Old Testament and especially Israel's history of origin describe the present eschatological situation in the sense of 1 Cor. 10:6, 11. Thus the whole passage begins with Rom. 3:21 in a way that speaks in the present of the righteousness that is received only in faith, as it has now "been manifested" in the gospel (the adoption of 1:16–17, in part word for word, is obvious). Also, the central assertion of the tradition in 3:25, which looks back to the expiatory death of Jesus Christ, is framed by statements that are oriented toward the gospel now being promulgated: "The redemption which is in Christ Jesus" (3:24b) is the same that is expressed in Gal. 3:26 as sonship "in Christ Jesus"; thus it refers to the present determination of Christians and does not describe historically what once happened through Christ as the redemptive work on the cross. Finally, at the point where Paul shifts from the use of the formula to his own train of thought (3:26) occurs the proof of God's righteousness pointedly "at the present [salvific] time" (cf. 2 Cor. 6:2; Rom. 5:1, 9), as it is determined by God's justifying and a person's faith. Thus here the topic is the "power" of the gospel, which saves those who have faith (Rom. 1:16) and which is now at work.

With this observation in mind, we will find it worthwhile to take another look at 1:18–3:20. Here, in the face of imminent judgment, Paul discusses the present state of sinful human beings before God. Then in 3:21–4:25 the apostle develops the eschatological possibility created by the gospel when it makes the sinner righteous before God, a possibility already announced in 1:16–17 and now described in detail. In other words, the two sections are different in content but correspond in their inner orientation. They treat the divine-human relationship negatively and positively. Thus we have exposed a third structure that Paul can apply to the message of justification. Just as in Galatians 3–4 he went from the blessing of Abraham to the Spirit that transforms the believer, or in Philippians B expanded his conversion to an understanding of Christian existence in general, so now he arranges his ideas through the contrast of the two possibilities of standing in a wholesome or disastrous relationship to God. In this sense we can say of Romans 1–4 that every statement about human beings is also a statement about God, and vice versa.

This is emphasized again by the fact that when the apostle speaks of faith in Rom. 3:21–4:25, he does not mean the acceptance of the gospel in the sense of the mission situation, that is, a coming to faith; rather, with the help of statements on faith he describes the fundamental and constant orientation of the individual toward the God who is near in the gospel. Faith is not simply a onetime act (cf., e.g., Gal. 2:16); it is characteristic and constitutive of one's relationship to God in general. Indeed, in Rom. 14:23 the apostle sees this understanding of faith as so fundamental that he can assert: "Whatever [a person] does not [do] from faith is sin." This statement is true because beyond the relationship to God initiated by faith the disastrous human situation described in 1:18–3:20 is taking over.

If, however, the relationship to God is on the apostle's mind, then this observation sheds light on the expression "righteousness of God," which occurs frequently especially in Romans. We must first state that this combination is already attested in Jewish sources (e.g., Deut. 33:21; 1QS 10:25–26; 11:5, 12; 1QM 4:6; *T. Dan.* 6:10; *1 Enoch* 71:14), yet it does not appear as a formulaic or fixed expression. Therefore we cannot begin with a formulaic content of the combination that transcends the particular context. In early Christianity, "righteousness of God" seldom occurs in non-Pauline texts (Matt. 6:33; James 1:20; 2 Peter 1:1). Here only very limited aids to Paul's understanding are recognizable, so that this comparison with Paul is not very helpful. Paul uses this combination perhaps twice in traditional contexts (Rom. 3:25–26; 2 Cor. 5:21); otherwise he formulates it independently only in Romans (1:17; 3:5; 3:21–22; 10:3). It is in no small measure the purpose contained in 1:16–17; 3:21–22 that makes the combination a new Pauline theme that the apostle has not used before, for in 2 Cor. 5:21 the formulation occurs unexpectedly without further development. Yet Philippians B, composed shortly before Romans, indicates that Paul uses this formulation with more than just 2 Cor. 5:21 and Rom. 3:25–26 as preparation. For in Phil. 3:9, at a significant and central point in the letter, Paul can oppose "a righteousness of my own, based on law" with "that which is through faith in Christ" and understand it more precisely as "righteousness from God that depends on faith." In a similar spirit he also offers formulations in Rom. 10:3–6. Thus for the context of

Romans we have two precedents: formulaic statements in 2 Cor. 5:21; Rom. 3:25–26 and the Pauline formulation in Philippians B.

We have already classified 2 Cor. 5:21 with the baptismal statements in 1 Cor. 1:30; 6:11 (cf. 11.3 above) and at the same time established that the word stem "just/righteous" occurs in various forms and means the same thing. When Christians "become the righteousness of God" through the substitution of Christ, this means they are made righteous (justified) through baptism; that is, God's righteousness is their new "being." Thus it is a question of the righteousness that comes from God and is bestowed on the individual. We must note that all the named baptismal statements speak of righteousness as fruit of the work of the Holy Spirit, are silent about faith, and are not pointedly against the law like Galatians, Philippians B, and Romans. Even with all its independence in details, Rom. 3:24–26, with its formulaic content, also fits into this finding at crucial points. Here, however, analyzing and determining the extent of tradition is especially difficult. In particular, what is the aim of the text? Is it intended to describe Jesus' death soteriologically as the eschatological great day of reconciliation, in order to expound, vis-à-vis Judaism, what is new and special about the central figure of Christ? Or is the aim to describe the new reality of the baptized and with it the expiatory act of Christ as presupposition? If we assume the latter (by analogy with the baptismal tradition in Galatians 3–4), we can begin the formula with v. 24 and interpret as follows. The baptized are the ones "justified . . . as a gift" (cf. 1 Cor. 6:11). This happens through the "redemption" appropriated in baptism (cf. 1 Cor. 1:30), as it is given for them with the new determination "in Christ Jesus" (cf., e.g., Gal. 3:26). With their baptism their pre-Christian sins (cf. the catalog in 1 Cor. 6:9–10) come under the "divine forbearance" (cf. Rom. 2:4; also Titus 3:4 implicitly), that is, forgiveness and grace that are determined by "his righteousness"—thus God's (covenant) loyalty; for this reason God put forward Christ as an expiation, and his "blood" abolished the sins of present Christians before they became Christians. Hence baptism is the conveyance of Christ's salvific work, which is described as expiation. All of this is the expression of divine righteousness as God's own gracious action on behalf of the sinner. In Rom. 3:26, however, Paul turns this divine righteousness into a righteousness that promotes a person into the ranks of the righteous and links with faith the righteousness of God appropriated to the individual (3:25a, 26b; cf. also the baptismal tradition adapted with the faith motif in Gal. 3:26).

If we want to consider Paul's statements on the righteousness of God, with this last indication we already have in our hands an important observation for Pauline interpretation. Yet in terms of method it is advisable to make central the places in Paul where the apostle expresses himself independently and forcefully. Following this line, we can ascertain that Rom. 1:16–17; 3:21–22; 10:3–6 share the same context with the precedent in Philippians 3. It is the saving gospel that grants the righteousness of God to the believers, and only to them, thereby negating righteousness from the works of the law as a possibility of salvation before God. This common level of statement makes it reasonable to connect the genitive combination "righteousness of God" with the "righteousness from God" (Philippians 3), especially since in Rom. 1:16–17; 3:21–22 the goal at which divine righteousness aims is expressly given as the believing individual. Thus the "righteousness of God" proves to be a relational concept indicating the gift of salvation that comes from God and is directed toward human beings. Romans 5:1ff., in closing, puts this very succinctly: The justified—that is, those who in faith have received the righteousness of God—"have peace with God."

What, in particular, is Paul asserting about the justification of the sinner? Standing emphatically at the beginning—and as no surprise for the reader of Galatians 3–4 and Philippians B—is the characterization that justification occurs "apart from law" (Rom. 3:21). This repeats the assertion in Rom. 3:20 that "by works of the law" no one will be justified before God (cf. 3:28). As in Galatians 3–4 and Philippians B, here too Paul makes it clear that he does not want only to pronounce a verdict on those who have fallen short of the law's demand and to let them be granted righteousness beyond the law's threat of disaster, and yet leave the law itself untouched and still valid. Rather, Paul pronounces a fundamental judgment on the law. This becomes clear when he speaks of the law itself and not only of one of its functions (namely, to react to violations of the law with disastrous consequences). In this way the apostle also expressly defends himself against the reproach that he is overthrowing the law itself through faith (Rom. 3:31). Therefore to the thesis in 3:21 that the righteousness of God is revealed "apart from law" he immediately hastens to add that this is in agreement with what the law itself says (3:21b), and thus through this assertion the law is upheld (3:31). He offers proof of this in Romans 4 when he contrasts works, glory, and wages with faith and granted righteousness, so that the person who defines himself through works is placed opposite Abraham and his trust in God; the person who works and expects wages is contrasted with the patriarch who relies on God's promise. Abraham cannot be helped at all by appealing to his powers of self-development. His problem is not one that can be solved through work. His only choice is to contemplate his inability to procreate or to believe in the divine promise (4:19). He grows strong in faith and honors the God who promises; that is, he has him "call into existence the things that do not exist" (4:17). Of this Abraham, the scripture (Gen. 15:6) says: "Abraham believed God, and it was reckoned to him as righteousness." Thus for Paul the relationship between God and Abraham, according to Romans 4, reflects the statement in 1 Cor. 1:26–31 about the God who chooses "things that are not" and other similar statements on the topic in the whole Corinthian correspondence (cf. 8.2, 8.4, and 8.5 above).

Therefore here as there we have the catchword "boast," which on the basis of the key Old Testament text in Jer. 9:23–24 ("Let him who boasts, boast of the Lord"—1 Cor. 1:31; 2 Cor. 10:17) became an essential characteristic of Paul's theology of the cross and, as attested by Gal. 6:13–14, had already found its way into the formulated message of justification before the apostle elaborated broadly on this theme in Romans. We must remember at this point that in the oldest evidence, namely, in 1 Cor. 1:26–31, the divine election to the eschatological church, which is directed toward the "things that are not," already contains the idea that "no human being might boast in the presence of God" and that the gift of Christ leaves room only for "boasting in Christ." This guarantees that the election that comes from God is and remains his work alone. We cannot boast of what we have received, as though it were not a gift (1 Cor. 4:7). In the presence of the salvific loving openness of God, we can only boast of our weaknesses, as Paul does in the fool's talk (2 Corinthians 10–13; cf. 8.5 above).

These basic ideas are also found in Philippians B without the catchword "boast," when the apostle counts the "gain" achieved through the law—the basis of his boasting—as loss for the sake of the surpassing worth of the knowledge of Christ. The "gain" corresponds expressly to a "righteousness of my own, based on law," which is contrasted with the "righteousness from God that depends on faith" (Phil. 3:7, 9). This same antithesis also occurs in Gal. 6:13–14: The glory, or pride, of the Judaizers in the circumcision of the Galatians—that is, their adoption of the way of the law—belongs, as in Phil. 3:3, to the "flesh" and is the opposite of glorying "in the cross of Christ." Thus in Galatians and Philippians B, Paul has extended the revaluation of all human values, known from 1 and 2 Corinthians, to righteousness under the law, so that now it too is included among the worthless things that give no reason to "boast."

The apostle can also express the "boasting" in other ways. In Phil. 3:3–4 he speaks of the "confidence" that one places in something. In Rom. 2:17 "rely upon" stands parallel to "boast." The glory that Abraham would have before God through his own work (Rom. 4:2) corresponds not only to the "gain" in Phil. 3:7 but also to the recognition that is accorded the good work in Rom. 2:10, 29 (cf. 1 Cor. 4:5). Hence it is clear where this language has its normal ambience, namely, in the language of the court (cf. 11.3 above). Anyone who must render an account before God asks on what can he rely for a good verdict and for what can he receive recognition (cf. Rom. 14:10–12; 2 Cor. 5:10).

This is also precisely what determines the statements in Rom. 3:27–28; 4:2–5; 5:1–5: Can the Jew before God rely on "works of the law"? Paul raises this question in Rom. 3:27–28 and clarifies his no with a reference to justification, which is possible only through faith in Christ. This is further explicated in the interpretation of Abraham's relationship to God. Anyone who achieved righteousness before God from works would have his (own) support apart from God, namely, his laudable way of life. But God's valuation of Abraham, on the one hand, is not based on such works. Rather, God reckons as righteousness Abraham's faith, that is, his adherence to the promise of God (4:20). On the other hand, Abraham does not do works in order to receive his due reward. Rather, he founds his relationship with God, apart from his works, solely on the God who justifies the ungodly (4:2–5). Thus neither from God's side nor from Abraham's standpoint is the relationship with God built on human works and their recognition. Abraham shows God nothing that comes from himself and thus produces no personal achievement as something to boast about before God, nor does God praise such a display of individual activity; rather, God only promises and gives, and Abraham only believes and receives. For this reason the basic sense of the question in 1 Cor. 4:7 (a person receives everything of value from God) has become the fundamental description of the divine relationship, which the message of justification sets forth as the only thing possible before God. Thus the righteous person "boasts" only in the hope of the eschatological granting of the last fulfillment and "sufferings," as the Pauline "weaknesses" are taken up from 2 Corinthians 10–13 (Rom. 5:1–5).

This makes it clear that God's gift and a person's faith are not merely the initial determination of the true divine relationship and are then expanded like the gift of the covenant through the law and obedience to it. Naturally Paul wants to say that basically God and human beings can stand in a relationship that is wholesome for the human beings only if faith is righteousness. This is not contradicted by the fact that in places such as 1 Thess. 2:19; 1 Cor. 9:15–16; 15:31; 2 Cor. 1:14; Phil. 2:16 the apostle would, nonetheless, like to lay claim to one boast before God. All of these texts refer to one and the same special case: the apostolic work of the mission, in the judgment of which Paul expects "praise" in order not to have run "in vain." He ascribes this work to divine grace (1 Cor. 15:10–11). It is a testing of whether Paul has faithfully fulfilled his special commission (1 Cor. 3:10–15). This test is not a part of the justification of sinners, for in the last judgment all Christians will be tested, without receiving life or being excluded from it on the basis of their works (cf. 14.8 below).

Thus far our look at Romans 3–4 has focused on several special features (the combination "righteousness of God," the talk of "reckoning," the logical incorporation of the boasting motif into the message of justification). Yet there is another assertion that can rightly be considered the key sentence of the text and is well suited to express succinctly the meaning of justification. That text is Rom. 4:5, according to which God is the one who justifies the ungodly. It is not by coincidence that this participial predication of God recalls an analogy from the language of election, according to which God is the one who calls into the grace of Christ (Gal. 1:6) and calls those who stand under his judgment as sinners (cf. 1 Thess. 1:9–10; 5:24). This makes the apostle's theology of the cross all the more pointed: God's call is aimed at bringing to nothing things that are and choosing things that are not (1 Cor. 1:26–31). There-fore "boasting" before God is impossible. This basic assertion remains consistent in Romans 4, though translated from the language of election into the language of justification: God now justifies as the one "who gives life to the dead and calls into existence the things that do not exist" (Rom. 4:17). Therefore before him none can boast of their privileges (3:27; 4:2). He justifies especially the "ungodly"—the connection with 1:18; 3:19; 5:6, 8 is now established. Anyone who takes seriously this conceptual context, attested in its main features since 1 Thessalonians, will in Rom. 4:5 put the divine statement into the context of God's offer of salvation now being spread in the gospel and thus, in reference to the addressees, have it go to the readers of the letter. The interest of the statement is not in a belated historical judgment about the yet uncircumcised Abraham (Rom. 4:10–11), for it speaks in a fundamental way not of Abraham's onetime self-evaluation but of God. In fact, for the readers the predication of God reduces Paul's message of justification to a terse statement: In the face of the thoroughly disastrous condition of humanity, which has brought this on itself with its ungodliness, God has revealed himself especially in Christ as the creative conqueror of ungodliness and its consequences, and he lets faith in his peacemaking action (Rom. 4:23–25; 5:1, 9–10) count as righteousness. He breaks a person's ungodliness by calling him or her into his presence (Rom. 5:2). So God lets his action be determined not by the wickedness of the people but by his love (Rom. 5:5). The justification of the ungodly is God's gracious triumph over sinners based on his love: God does not capitulate to the person who will not let him be God. He creates the possibility of a faith that gladly lets God be God again.

14
An Outline of Pauline Theology

14.1 The Starting Point and Structure of Pauline Thought

The dialogue of the apostle with his churches, documented by his correspondence, shows an apostle who is full of ideas and intellectually alive, who faces challenges and is himself also changed in the process. The letters reveal their own riches, especially if we first allow each one to stand on its own instead of using it right away to supply proof texts for particular themes in systematic theology. We have tried to safeguard these riches by evaluating each letter for itself. It is clear, however, that Paul did not give voice to a completely new theological starting point in every communication. With all the diversity of Pauline statements there are naturally elementary lines and basic decisions that prevail because they come from a common conceptual starting point. The apostle's ability to change rests on a persistently maintained theological starting point. This will now be our topic as we look back at the letters.

To begin with, we must guard against the expectation that in the end such an undertaking will lead to the derivation from Paul of a kind of standard dogmatics. The apostle's theological thought is not the early Christian counterpart of what the *loci communes* of Melanchthon provides for the Reformation period. Yet on a wide variety of occasions Paul brought to bear his theological starting point as his new understanding of reality gained from the gospel, in order to discuss and perhaps solve concrete problems in the church. This understanding will be sketched in its basic traits.

On what basis does Paul compose his theological statements? If we ask this, we can make an observation that is valid from 1 Thessalonians to Romans: Paul speaks out of the experience of his call and especially out of the experience gained by him and the churches through the effect of the gospel on the worldwide mission field. Thus the apostle expresses himself on the basis of the new being effected by the Spirit, the common experience of all Christians with the gospel that changes people. Right in 1 Thessalonians he begins by reminding the church of its original experience with the gospel (1 Thessalonians 1–2), in order then to discuss their being determined by that same gospel (1 Thessalonians 4–5). In Gal. 3:1–5 Paul begins in his argumentative discussion of the Galatian problem by reaching back to the first experience with Paul's missionary proclamation and everything else is discussed from this perspective. In Philippians B he takes the knowledge gained about Jesus Christ, as experienced in his call, to be the foundation of his presentation. Romans 1 begins with the order "called to be an apostle" and "gospel of Jesus Christ." These selected examples clearly attest that the movement of Paul's thinking is from experienced gospel and hence the work of the Spirit to faith and the new existence of the church, just as after the development of the gospel in Rom. 1:16–17; 3:21–5:21 the new determination of believers is presented in "we" style in Romans 6–8, and beginning in 3:23ff. the Abrahamic promise in Gal. 3:6ff. flows into the "we" of the church, whose new being is described. In this sense the theology of Paul is the theology of experience under the influence of the gospel and of the Spirit connected with it.

Pauline theology is therefore not to be described as, say, presentation of the kerygma and its interpretation in reference to the Christian understanding of existence. The kerygmatic tradition serves rather—within the context of the experience of the gospel and the response of faith to it—to interpret the Christ promised to humanity in the Christian message. Thus the early Christian traditional formulas are not primal data with which Christian existence understands itself but have a serving function in order to witness to the relationship between Christ and the Spirit active in the gospel.

Yet Pauline theology is also not to be comprehended as the attempt to understand the Christian perspective as an extension of the history of Old Testament–Jewish tradition, so that this history is carried forward and still written under the predominant viewpoint of continuity. An understanding of Paul oriented primarily toward the continuity of historical tradition misconstrues the new experience given with the gospel and its Christ Spirit and fails to appreciate the fundamentally new view of everything that came before. Paul's first concern is not how he might successfully extend Old Testament–Jewish religion into the Christian, or even whether he does justice to the Jewish self-understanding. His pressing concern is how he can let the Christ who is near in the gospel determine and value everything.

If Paul is a theologian who thinks and lives out of his experience of the gospel, then it is only logical that his presentation is predominantly concerned with the new determination of humanity by the gospel under the double aspect of God's electing action and the simultaneous human reaction as a life of faith, love, and hope. Thus Paul energetically moves the goal and the consequences of the experienced gospel into the center of interest: "God has not destined us for wrath, but to obtain salvation through our Lord Jesus Christ" (1 Thess. 5:9). "In Christ Jesus you are all sons of God, through faith" (Gal. 3:26). "Since we are justified by faith, we have peace with God through our Lord Jesus Christ" (Rom. 5:1). We do not need further Pauline statements to demonstrate that the treasury of quotations is in this case especially rich. The responding life of the believer in the fellowship of Christians is also easily set forth with central examples. Even in his first letter Paul comments that sanctification as brotherly love and hope as expectation of the coming Lord are basic determiners of Christian life (1 Thess. 4:1ff.; 4:13ff.). Seldom did Paul so urgently and repeatedly infer the community's conduct of life from the Spirit-effected state of salvation ("the temple of the Holy Spirit") as in 1 Corinthians 5–6. In Gal. 5:13ff., being called in the freedom of the children of God is the point of departure for the testing of freedom in the house churches and in the world. For this aspect also, the cited examples are but a meager selection.

If this context—that God calls through the gospel and human beings answer in faith, love, and hope—is the basic idea on which Paul concentrates, then it is no wonder that he discusses classical themes of later theology not as independent problems, but goes into them only indirectly and tangentially, or that other themes are discussed only from certain viewpoints. His theology is an attempt to interpret all of reality, but it has clear accents. In this sense Paul lacks, among other things, an independent interest in the history of the world and salvation from creation to the end. There is also no development of an independent doctrine of God and doctrine of creation. So central a theme as Christology comes to expression only as the soteriological basis of the preached gospel. Hope is described in such a way that the elected church may expect to be with its Lord always. The end of the present reality as a whole is considered at best by way of suggestion from the standpoint of the shared fate of the children of God (Romans 8). The experience of the gospel as the nearness of God, through which he makes peace with his godless enemies through Jesus Christ (Rom. 5:1ff.), is so overpowering that it simply dominates everything else.

For Paul, however, this gospel does not stand forever at the disposal of human beings, as if the whole of human history were determined by two different ways for God to rule, namely, (1) by leaving a God-hostile humanity to its perversity and self-centeredness (Rom. 1:18ff.), while maintaining a possibility of life—for example, through the order of the state (Rom. 13:1ff.)—and (2) by the divine offer of the gospel of Jesus Christ, through which God creatively changes his rebellious creation for the good through the Spirit working in that gospel. No, the gospel is the divine gracious election immediately before the end of history. The offer of the gospel goes out as the new call of God and in the last possible moment of history (2 Cor. 6:1–2; Gal. 4:4; Rom. 13:11; 1 Cor. 7:29, 31; etc.). Without it the whole of humanity would simply be delivered up to the divine eschatological wrath, which is imminent in the form of the last judgment (1 Thess. 1:9–10; Rom. 1:18; 3:20). With the gospel God does not abandon humanity to its imminent and certain death, which he must carry out in the last judgment, but intervenes creatively in history. He destines people for eternal life with himself, while changing them, and thereby calls them out of the general hopelessness. Thus the end time begins with the gospel of Christ. The coming of faith (i.e., the proclamation of faith) or the mission of Christ (Gal. 3:23; 4:4)—the two are the same for Paul—is the beginning of the eschatological event. Consequently, the gospel contains an interpreting grasp of the world and history in that it asserts what hour has struck and what qualification this means for all of creation.

This orientation toward the imminent end, which God as judge has set, also has the consequence that Paul does not raise the fundamental question, How does humanity stand before God? in this general way, but only in the special form, How does God in the imminent judgment stand with regard to humanity? Does he grant ultimate communion with Christ, through which he places people forever in the all-encompassing divine nearness (1 Thess. 4:17; 1 Cor. 15:28), or does he encounter them as wrath (Rom. 1:18; 2:1ff.), that is, keep them from an eternity of life hostile to God? The apostle's statements on election, reconciliation, and justification are misunderstood when they are not interpreted as answers to this special question.

The power of the gospel for the eschatological salvation of humanity and its ability to reinterpret the world and history rest on the message of Christ as the fundamental content of the gospel. If Paul designs his theological statements on the basis of his experience of the gospel, then the content of the gospel must consequently be the measure and criterion of everything—in short, for the interpretation of all of reality. So it is not surprising if Paul declares everything he previously counted as gain to be loss for the sake of Christ; indeed, he considers everything as loss in view of the surpassing worth of knowing Jesus Christ (Phil. 3:7–8). He absolutely wants "to take every thought captive to obey Christ" (2 Cor. 10:5). Thus the object of faith is made the criterion of faith and of the understanding of reality guided by faith. It is quite conceivable that this approach came to the apostle right away during his call. At least he locates it at this very point (Gal. 1:11–12, 15–16).

These are probably the oldest Christian statements that touch on the area of faith and thought. Certainly Paul does not (yet) discuss the conditions of thought itself by making the thought process an independent topic of discussion. But by prescribing the knowledge of Jesus Christ as the obligatory sole measure of faithful thought, Paul implicitly makes two fundamental assertions. First, faith is thereby banned from the realm of the irrational or arbitrarily subjective. There is, as it were, an internal thought process of faith, which can and should prove itself argumentatively. Second, for Paul the gospel does not bring partial knowledge within an otherwise untouched, persistent scheme of reality: it does not sing a variation of an already known song. Conversion to the gospel of Jesus Christ is not only a change of position within the same coordinate system. It is not simply the creation of new and different value judgments about the same things within a fixed whole. No, the gospel has within it the possibility of understanding absolutely everything in a new way. With the gospel nothing remains as it was, for the gospel brings a new content that guides knowledge and necessarily leads to a new view of everything.

In never tiring linguistic variations Paul carried out this thought process especially intensively in regard to Christology. For him, Christ is simply the central figure of the end time: God showed his love for us in that he sent his Son and made his destiny the salvation of humankind (1 Thess. 1:10; 2 Cor. 5:18; Gal. 4:4; Rom. 5:8). Since then he determines time and history as end time with its quite short duration until the final arrival of Christ (cf., e.g., 1 Thess. 4:13–5:11; Rom. 13:11–14). Since then, where the gospel of Jesus Christ is proclaimed, there is the eschatological day of salvation (2 Cor. 5:18–6:2); there eschatological election occurs as redemption from wrath and as the destiny of eternal life (1 Thess. 5:9–10). In Paul there is no timeless Christology of being but a christological thought process, which characterizes Christ both eschatologically and soteriologically and therefore makes him, as the central figure of the end time, the measure of all present and future reality (1 Thess. 4:17–18; 5:9–10; 1 Cor. 15:20–28, 54–57; Phil. 3:8–9, 20–21; Rom. 8:19–39). Hence it is no wonder that Paul knows only two humanity-determining figures: Adam and Christ (1 Cor. 15:20–22, 44–49; Rom. 5:12–21). It is also clear that this all-determining presence of Christ shapes the apostle's view of salvation. It leads to the statement of the sole effectiveness of divine grace and love (cf. 14.4 below) and also means that even now the apostle can lay

world, life and death, present and future at the feet of Christians if they
will only consider that "All are yours; and you are Christ's; and Christ is
God's" (1 Cor. 3:22–23; cf. Rom. 8:38–39).

It goes without saying that after the mission of Christ the One to
whom, according to the apostle, all reality is indebted must now also
be understood anew from the standpoint of Christ: "For it is the God
who said, 'Let light shine out of darkness,' who has shone in our hearts
to give the light of the knowledge of the glory of God in the face of
Christ" (2 Cor. 4:6). Thus Christ is determined by God himself as the
place where God can be known. So the "depths of God" (1 Cor. 2:10)
are known through the Spirit given to Christians, which is bound to the
"word of the cross" (1 Cor. 1:18). But what, according to Paul, does
faith know when it makes sure that the word of the cross is not deval-
ued (1 Cor. 1:17)? One of the precise Pauline answers is found in
Rom. 5:8: "But God shows his love for us in that while we were yet
sinners Christ died for us." Even before Paul early Christianity had, so
to speak, redescribed the God who led Israel out of Egypt as the God
who raised Jesus from the dead. This was the new, decisive statement
about God, now valid for Christians. Paul consistently pursues this
course already taken: in the destiny of Christ, God interprets himself to
humankind. Therefore in Paul there is no speculative transcendence of
world and history in order to comprehend God. Nor does Paul know
any mystical plunge or ecstatic ascent above the world as an independent way of experiencing God. Glossolalia and rapture (1 Cor. 14:18–19;
2 Cor. 12:1ff.) are emphatically pushed to the side. The God who is
near to people and who through his nearness makes this day the day
of salvation is the God who in Christ reconciled the world to himself
and provides for the passing on of his word of reconciliation (2 Cor.
5:19; 6:2).

This fundamental dependence of faith on Jesus Christ—especially
when it is necessary to comprehend God as the object of faith—is
plumbed again to a final depth when Paul molds God's activity into the
destiny of Jesus Christ in a way that makes God the one "who gives
life to the dead and calls into existence the things that do not exist"
(Rom. 4:17, 24–25). Through the folly of the preaching of the cross
God saves and elects "things that are not, to bring to nothing things
that are, so that no human being might boast in the presence of God"
(1 Cor. 1:21–31). Therefore Paul wants to boast only of his weaknesses,
for he stands under God's word: "My grace is sufficient for you, for my
power is made perfect [especially] in weakness" (2 Cor. 12:9). On the
basis of the Christ event Paul infers not only the depth of human lostness (in sheer classical form in Gal. 2:17, 21) but also the depth of

divine grace and love, which alone are efficacious in achieving the deliverance of humanity. God is not a bookkeeper, who on judgment day will be satisfied with reading the historical balances and deriving from them a final calculation. He does not wait until he can let the principle of poetic justice rule. Rather, according to Paul, his nature consists in re-creating the unlovely so that under his love they become lovely, in turning enemies into reconciled people, in giving worth to the worthless. This is the self-characterization of the Father of Jesus Christ. That people can live only on this basis is the meaning and purpose of Paul's message of election, reconciliation, and justification.

Finally, the person who answers the message of Christ with faith is now also understood on the basis of the christological thought process. Faith, love, and hope are the living expressions of one who is "crucified with Christ" (Gal. 2:19; Rom. 6:4–5), who has put on Christ like a piece of clothing (Gal. 3:27) and therefore has become united with faith, love, and hope, like a second skin (1 Thess. 5:8–9). Similarly, it is not he who lives but Christ who lives in him (Gal. 2:20). This also means that the theological conception of the church involves understanding it not as an independent institution but as an aspect of Christology. The church is the "body of Christ" (1 Cor. 12:4ff.; Rom. 12:4–5) and the realm of salvation "in Christ" (e.g., 2 Cor. 5:17; Gal. 3:26; Rom. 8:1). Finally, we do not need to demonstrate at length that the object of faith is Christ (e.g., Rom. 9:33; Gal. 2:16; 3:22), love has its norm in the model of Christ (Phil. 2:1ff.; Rom. 15:1ff.), and hope refers to the salvific function of the Son of God (1 Thess. 1:10), as its content includes being together with the Lord (1 Thess. 4:17; 5:10) and being made like him (Phil. 3:20–21). Indeed, Christ is in such a comprehensive way the crucial loving openness of God toward human beings that the faith that reflects on this event simply can leave nothing free from Christ. Thus if Paul wants to "take every thought captive to obey Christ" (2 Cor. 10:5), he himself is the best example of this endeavor.

14.2 The One God and His Creation

Anyone whose theological standpoint is oriented toward experience of the gospel (cf. 14.1 above) can hardly be expected to speak independently and in detail about what was later summarized in the first article of faith. Nevertheless statements about creation are not merely accidentally woven into Paul's various discussions. Also, we do not find only remnants of Hellenistic Judaism (cf. 3.2 above on this point) when we test the Pauline texts for this theme. Rather, the conception of reality as God's creation conditions Pauline thought in a constitutive way. Because the preaching of faith in Christ determines the present eschatological situation of the world (2 Cor. 6:2; Gal. 3:25; cf. 14.1 above), this preaching is so urgent that other things must recede into the background, although they still initiate basic decisions that guide the overall theological understanding.

We have already noted that Paul, led by Christ, describes the God of the gospel. Now we must observe that he extends this christological dominance to creation in only a rudimentary and very limited way (cf. 14.1 above). Christ's mediatorship of creation is mentioned as a fragment of tradition (1 Cor. 8:6) but is not evaluated in the context, which concentrates on treating Christ with respect to his substitutionary death (8:11). And such a statement as the one that the rock from which Moses struck water possesses a kind of spiritual identity with Christ (1 Cor. 10:4) is more of a onetime hermeneutical appeal to an Old Testament text than a systematically reasoned statement of Pauline Christology. Also, Christ's existence before his mission is otherwise as good as out of the picture (cf. also 2 Cor. 8:9; Gal. 4:4; Phil. 2:6–7; Rom. 8:3). Therefore we conclude that Paul understands the final determination of human beings and the God of salvation christologically but otherwise deals separately with God as creator and with God's relationship to creation.

God alone is "Father" of the world (1 Cor. 8:6; 15:24; Phil. 2:11) and "God who is over all" (Rom. 9:5). The Gentiles can know this Creator, so their turning from him is guilty behavior (Rom. 1:18ff.). God will also one day be "everything to every one" (1 Cor. 15:28). He is the One with power over being, the truly creative One, who created the world and who alone can raise the dead, as he also raised Christ (Rom. 4:17; 1 Thess. 4:14). Everything is simply from him, through him, and to him (Rom. 11:36). Everything is as it is because he is Creator. Therefore even where a syncretistic multiplicity of gods still reigns, the Hellenistic-Jewish mission theme of the one true God is taken up, and Christ as Savior in the last judgment comes in as a second theme (1 Thess. 1:9–10). If everything comes from God, is permanently related to him, and moves toward a final union with him, then such a fundamental determination of the relationship of God and reality expresses the unity of the same: there is nothing that is not and does not remain the creation of the Creator (1 Cor. 10:26).

Paul is so convinced of the self-evident nature of this statement that he has been correctly said to be incapable of a principled atheism. He cannot conceive of an alternative for understanding reality either on the basis of God or only in terms of oneself; he can only think in terms of the antithesis (from the Hellenistic synagogue) between the one God and the gods. Polytheism is not an intellectual deficiency in the pervasion of the appropriate idea of God, but guilty misbehavior, dishonoring God, so that the religious adoration of the Gentiles is godlessness, in spite of their many gods, and the concomitant wickedness is the other side of the same coin (Rom. 1:18ff.). Indeed, in view of this observation of Paul's complete inability to conceive the possibility of atheism, we must say that Paul would regard an explanation of the world based on its own nature as an expression of the original sin of humanity, because for him the whole of reality is never left to itself. Paul is deeply convinced that humanity and the world are not their own creators and therefore always remain dependent on relational determinations. And this is demonstrated not least of all by the Gentiles: they have relinquished the wholesome relationship to their Creator and built up ersatz relationships with their gods (Rom. 1:18ff.). Likewise, the Galatians who leave Christ fall back into their old relationships to the gods (Gal. 4:8–11).

The one Creator's creation is, incidentally, an interpretation of the presently experienced world. God is the permanent "Father" of the world, not just the onetime origin or procreator. There is no interest in when or how in the beginning God once created everything, or even in how the world looked before Adam's fall. Adam is the central figure of sinful and thus already fallen humanity (Rom. 5:12ff.), not the speculative object of the discussion of a good original state. So humanity is described with the loss of its original glory (Rom. 3:23; 5:12–13), but there is no asking how things were when this glory was still there. Thus Paul is trying to say that in spite of the inexplicable enmity of humankind toward God, the world, as we experience it in us and around us, is God's creation, even if now the nonhuman creation has, through human disobedience of God, been drawn into a (merely suggested) sharing of our suffering (Rom. 8:20–21).

From this present standpoint we can also see what Paul says on the world of the gods and on numinous beings hostile to or serving God. The world does not originate from a battle of the gods or fall of Satan, and although such beings are to be taken into account, reality is interpreted monistically and not dualistically. Especially in view of the problem of the gods in 1 Corinthians 8–10 it is true that "The earth is the Lord's, and everything in it" (1 Cor. 10:26). With the Stoic philosophical tradition it is polemically explained to the Galatians that their numina, which they are getting ready to worship again, "by nature are no gods" (Gal. 4:8). Yet restraint is advisable, should one want on this basis systematically to attribute to Paul the thesis that except for the one

God numinous powers do not exist—that is, they have no being and are perhaps only projections from the consciousness of people. Even with Satan that is not the case, for he must expressly be conquered (Rom. 16:20; cf. also 1 Cor. 15:24–25) and in the present is a negative force for the church (cf., e.g., 1 Cor. 2:6–9; 5:5; 7:5; 2 Cor. 2:11; 4:3–4; 11:14; 12:7; 1 Thess. 2:18). Also, the world of angels subordinated under God is, for Paul—even if mentioned only in passing—mythically "real" (Rom. 8:38; 1 Cor. 4:9; 13:1; Gal. 1:8; 3:19; etc.). Paul makes further use of the Hellenistic-Jewish tradition by reducing the gods to effective demons and belittling them (1 Cor. 10:20).

Anyone who at one time attacks the existence of the gods, at another only their quality, must have a special perspective in order not to regard the two as contradictory or unbalanced. This position is verified, for Paul, if one lets him deal with all the numina from the present meaning-perspectives that are related to the church and recognizes that it is not at all his intention to make broad, far-reaching statements. At this point 1 Cor. 8:1–6 is instructive. To the strong in Corinth, Paul concedes: "We know that 'an idol has no real existence,' and that 'there is no God but one.'" But Paul does not understand this as an abstract statement of being, for he immediately adds, "although there may be so-called gods in heaven or on earth—as indeed there are many 'gods' and many 'lords.'" This double assertion is to be resolved as follows: For the Christian church no idol still has meaning; only God alone is worthy of worship and trust, even if besides him there may be many worshiped numina. It is a question of the present conditions in which the Christian lives, or should live. Thus in this case also the Pauline principle holds good that a human being as a creature lives in relationships; the objects of these relationships, however, determine his salvation or damnation.

Up to this point we have spoken in relatively undifferentiated and general terms about the creation and must still add how Paul as a rule deals with the phenomenon. Here two observations are important. First, creation is not simply space that is already present and material that is at the disposal of humankind. Second, creation is then regarded above all anthropocentrically. The first statement means that heaven, earth, and the underworld belong to creation (Phil. 2:10–11), yet not only in the formal sense but in their present state. People do not make history; God guides it—for example, through the mission of Christ (cf. Gal. 4:4). Once Paul even designates God's power over history in terms of predestination (Rom. 9:14–29)—something not otherwise characteristic of the apostle.

Central for Paul, however, is the sheer superiority of God, with which he guides everything (Rom. 11:33–36). God also gives the world a social and political structure (Rom. 13:1ff.; 1 Cor. 7:17ff.). This includes, for example, a particular relationship between husband and wife (1 Cor. 11:6–9) as well as a general norm in human behavior (Rom. 1:18ff.). Of course, Christ causes some changes here in the church (1 Cor. 11:11–12; Gal. 3:26–28). First, however, it is taken for granted that the world has an "order" intended for it by God. By these examples we can see already that Paul is concerned primarily with humankind in creation, which he sees in a plainly anthropocentric way (cf., e.g., 1 Cor. 9:9–10). This viewpoint persists through the eschatological expectation (cf. 14.8 below). Paul tells nothing about the ordering of the stars or the seasons or the animals and plants (as wisdom and apocalypticism do), but he works hard as the first in early Christianity to indicate at least aspects of an anthropology and, for example in Romans 6–8, arrives at astonishingly complex statements, as seldom found in analogous differentiation at least in antiquity.

Yet in the sketching of Paul's conception of humanity we repeatedly have problems because the apostle uses no fixed terminology. Hence there is a great danger of subjecting him to a foreign system. Nonetheless a very important principle has worked especially well: All of Paul's statements come from a holistic view of human beings. The soul or reason, for example, is not a better part of a person than the body. According to Paul, a human being does not have a body, a soul, a heart, a mind, and a will, but is each of these from a special viewpoint. People cannot as "I" or "heart" distance themselves from their body; rather, when they say "I," they are at the same time "I" in their corporeality. Thus the characterization of a person as spirit, soul, and body in 1 Thess. 5:23 is not intended, for example, to express a threefold classification and rank order but to understand a human being as a unit. For terms like "heart," "spirit," and "body" we can often simply substitute the person as willing, thinking, and acting subject—in short, we can say "I."

The whole person, characterized in his rich variety, is now, like creation in general, seen in his relationships as his fundamental way of living and being determined. The modern concept of individuality as expression of the autonomous personality is totally foreign to the apostle. Paul does stress the responsibility of the individual in faith, love, and hope, and naturally as a sinner; he knows about the special worth of each "brother for whom Christ died" (1 Cor. 8:11). At the same time, however, for him a person as a part of creation is determined by his relationship to God or the gods (1 Thess. 1:9; Rom. 1:18ff.). It is precisely our relationship to Christ and God that is our decisive salvation (Rom. 14:8; 8:38–39). We are likewise members of a community (1 Corinthians 12). Our concrete relationship to our neighbor says more about us than our individual conviction (1 Corinthians 8). We are as God wants us when we live from others and for others but not seeking our own advantage (Philippians 2; 1 Corinthians 13). Anyone who describes the relationship of human beings to all of reality, including God's reality, has stated what a human being is (Rom. 8:38–39; 1 Cor. 3:21–23).

From yet another viewpoint a human being is not seen by Paul in the ideal of the autonomous person equipped with independence and strength of ego. Paul uses, for example, the metaphor of the temple in order to characterize a person as the residence of God's Spirit (1 Cor. 3:16–17; 6:19). The indwelling of the Spirit substantiates the resurrection hope (Rom. 8:11). Indeed, not only do Christians no longer live for themselves (Rom. 14:7–8); they have died altogether and Christ lives in their place (Gal. 2:19–20; Rom. 6:4–11). They are like Christ in his death, and Christ has made them his own (Phil. 3:10–12). Also, they can participate in the resurrection only by means of another break and new starting point (1 Cor. 15:35–57; 2 Cor. 5:1–10). Thus the identity of human beings is constituted not through stable internal conditions but through divine gifts like Spirit and Christ, which reconstitute his being (1 Thess. 5:4–10; Gal. 3:26–29) and demand breaks in the old creatureliness, without which the divine determination of a person cannot be achieved.

If we look at the holistic views from which human beings are interpreted, it is obvious that Paul places special emphasis on everything that has to do with the human will, with a person's aspirations and intentions, as well as with a person's corporeality. These are all aspects that contribute to a person's "works," whether they are good or evil. This makes clear how the apostle is to this extent molded by the Old Testament-Jewish picture of humanity. Above all, the term "body" (sōma) receives conspicuous attention in Paul (along with "flesh" as a term for sin—cf. 14.3 below). It is the basic anthropological term that seemed especially suited to him for the description of the concrete creatureliness of humans. Nowhere does Paul say that God is "body." God "incorporates" his love and grace in Christ, so that Christ is "corporeal" (Rom. 7:4; 1 Cor. 11:24, 27). As the resurrected One, Christ possesses transfigured corporeality (Phil. 3:21), into which Christians are changed (Phil. 3:21; 1 Cor. 15:35ff.). In general, all of the nonhuman world is corporeal (1 Cor. 15:35ff.). Thus a distinction is made between the Creator and his creatures. So in the eschatological kingdom Christ is in a concretely corporeal way together with his followers, as 1 Thess. 4:16–17 presupposes. It is said much more abstractly of God that in the end he will be "everything to every one" (1 Cor. 15:28). Paul knows nothing of an eschatological theophany of God. The judgment seat of God (Rom. 14:10) is occupied by Christ in 2 Cor. 5:10. In distinction to

Matt. 5:8, seeing face-to-face no longer has an object in 1 Cor. 13:10–12. Paul certainly did not intend to take a position theoretically on the distinction between God and everything created, yet he seems to indicate that human corporeality is a special expression of human creatureliness, because that means—if we sketch Rom. 5:12–21 a little bit—that in their corporeality human beings are bound into the antithesis of obedience and disobedience, of life and death. So one sins bodily (Rom. 1:24; 6:12; 8:13), has therefore a "body of death" (Rom. 7:24), and before Christ as judge must answer for deeds in the body (2 Cor. 5:10). One should give the body to God as an existential sacrifice in devotion to God's will (Rom. 12:1–2). Fornication is a false corporeal relationship, for this body belongs to the Lord (1 Cor. 6:15–18). God is faithful to his commitment (1 Cor. 1:9; 1 Thess. 5:24). But since he is accountable to no one (Rom. 9:21; 11:35), he cannot be obedient or disobedient. He also has in himself power over life (Rom. 4:17; 1 Cor. 8:6). Hence he does not have life as a gift and cannot die. Thus corporeality seems to be the sign of fundamental dependence (1 Cor. 4:7) and therefore of due responding obedience. Incidentally, Christ is also characterized not only by corporeality but also by obedience (Rom. 5:12ff.; Phil. 2:8).

There have been attempts to interpret human corporeality as the ability to have a relationship with oneself. But this not only presupposes a modern anthropology that Paul does not know but also seems to run into direct resistance in Paul (cf., e.g., 1 Cor. 4:4). A further concept takes as a basis for interpretation the communicative ability of human beings. Yet here too it is probably not accidental that this interpretation has contemporary roots, namely, in the rise of sociohistorical questions in the theology of recent times. Here, of course, Paul is somewhat more adaptable, but the approach is too unspecific: Paul's concern is not communication in general; rather, his theme is the status of the individual person before God.

Thus far we have spoken of the Creator and the one reality deriving from him and of human beings as creatures of God. Yet this section cannot end here, because, for Paul, the present creation—and, as we have already seen, this is what his thinking is based on—bears the imprint of the domination of sin. When the creature in opposition to the Creator attempts a contrary design for life (Rom. 1:18ff.; 5:12ff.), God reacts with wrath and judgment. This is an expression of the fact that God is the enemy of evil. Paul indicates that in death as the boundary of human life he sees an immediate consequence of sin (Rom. 5:12; 8:2; 1 Cor. 15:55) and that he also does not regard the futility of creation as a whole as one of its original characteristics (Rom. 8:20). Yet world and history do not simply somehow run their course on their own. Rather,

God sets his judgment as a limit and time of accounting for every life history. This judgment is so near that on that basis the Christian's relationship to the world is to be seen from the viewpoint of the transitory world (1 Cor. 7:29–31). Through the message of judgment, evil is qualified as sin in relation to the Creator, to whom his creature is responsible (1 Cor. 4:4–5; 2 Cor. 5:10; Rom. 14:10). So, faced with the human contradiction, God takes care that he is not mocked (Gal. 6:7) or dishonored (Rom. 2:23–24; 3:18). Therefore the basic human question for Paul is not: How should humanity fit into the order of the cosmos? Rather, the apostle asks: How should the creature live in view of the imminent judgment? The answer reads: The creature should believe in Christ.

14.3 The Sinner, the Law, and Death

As creatures of God, humans always find themselves to be in reality those who have personal experience with misguided and misspent life (cf. 13.3 above). The full seriousness and depth of their lostness, however, become clear only in the light of the gospel (Rom. 1:21; 5:8–9—Rom. 7:7ff. is described from the standpoint of 8:1ff.). Yet what is misspent human life? What is sin?

Anthropologically speaking, sin is a wrong basic attitude toward one's own life and toward reality in general (Rom. 7:10; 8:5). Such a basic attitude is revealed as "covetousness" (Rom. 7:7–8; 1 Cor. 10:6), namely, scooping up life first and foremost entirely for oneself as center of the universe (cf. the opposite in, e.g., 1 Cor. 10:31–11:1). This attitude is possible only when one no longer understands reality as created, ordered, and maintained by God, but as a world that is available for one's own shaping (Rom. 1:18–32; 5:12). And it changes an individual's relationships to God, fellow human beings, reality, and self, which are granted by God.

If the Creator and his purpose in creation are thereby denied, then close on the heels of "covetousness" follows idolatry among the Gentiles (Rom. 1:22ff.) and in Israel (1 Cor. 10:7). Covetousness includes the godless illusion of being able to create one's own gods. If they arise from human possibilities, then a person is free to form the world in his or her own spirit. In this way God is doubly "dishonored" (Rom. 1:21; 2:23–24; 3:18—the opposite, e.g., in 1 Cor. 10:31; Phil. 2:11): God himself is replaced and his creation misinterpreted and misused.

Because, however, all the world is God's creation (Rom. 1:25–26; 1 Cor. 8:6) and has its life from him, human beings, dependent on and oriented toward themselves, fall under the power of death. Being separated from God as the source of life necessarily and without fail brings with it death. Sinners miss life and face only death (1 Cor. 15:56; Rom. 5:12; 6:21; 7:24). But that is not all: even before their death they do not find true, abundant life, for their covetousness is never satisfied (Rom. 1:26; 7:7–8), they are controlled from outside (Rom. 7:15–17) and thus are not the master in their own house (Rom. 7:23), and they lose the standards for prosperous life in the community (Rom. 1:28ff.; 1 Cor. 6:9–10). They even become blind and unwise (Rom. 1:21; 2:5), so that because of darkness (1 Thess. 5:3–4; 2 Cor. 3:15–16) they no longer know where they have landed and how their hopelessness can be overcome. This lack of capacity for self-evaluation corresponds to the constant lack of capacity for true love and devotion to neighbor. Thus Paul characterizes the love of God, Christ, and Christians (Rom. 5:5; 2 Cor. 5:14; 1 Corinthians 13) as the opposite of covetousness. Covetousness thinks about itself and from its own standpoint; love thinks of the other person and is devotion to him or her (cf. Rom. 14:13, 19; 15:1–2; 1 Cor. 10:24; 13:5; Phil. 2:4).

Since God set the norm and aim of life for creation and in particular for the human creature, humanity's wrong attitude is enmity toward God (Rom. 5:10; 8:7). God reacts to it with wrath and judgment (Rom. 1:18; 2:1ff.) and with the law as disciplinarian (RSV: "custodian"—Gal. 3:23–25), which at the same time drives people still deeper into sinfulness (Rom. 7:7ff.). There is also, however, the unexpected possibility of the gospel. In the sovereignty of his love God does not let his actions be prescribed; he reconciles people to himself in Christ (Rom. 5:1ff.; 2 Cor. 5:14ff.) and creates them anew (Rom. 6:1ff.; 2 Cor. 5:14ff.). This is the content of the Pauline gospel, which turns sinners doomed to death into believers pardoned to life (Rom. 3:21–4:25).

At the present time, this Pauline understanding of sin and the law (indicated above in principle) is strongly contested in several respects. Yet the most profound question is: What understanding of reality underlies Paul's talk of the good or evil deed and its consequences? The real issue here is this: Does the apostle still live relatively without interruption in the schema of deed and consequence, found especially often in the Old Testament wisdom literature, according to which the deed independently and directly effects a sphere of salvation or damnation for the doer and his community, so that deed and consequence are two aspects of the same phenomenon? Or is Paul describing human action normatively from the standpoint of God's forensic judgment? Related to these alternatives is the question whether one should characterize sin in Paul—especially in view of the pointed statements in Romans 6–8—as (quasi-mythic) power or see in it, rather, a certain kind of personification. Should one understand these attempts to determine the ontological content of the sin statements at all as alternatives, or do they appear in Paul (at least in part) as aspects, so that it is a matter of seeing their serving function and the intended assertion? This bundle of problems must be discussed at least briefly.

We begin with the idea that the deed itself activates consequences, so that God's activity consists only in maintaining this process, or in accelerating or retarding the appearance of the consequences, but also in the abolishing of a context of damnation, especially through cultic expiation. This is the situation of Prov. 26:27: "A stone will come back upon him who starts it rolling." In this view, sin is not a moral judgment or norm but an inner-worldly, self-acting entity that destroys prosperous life. Anyone who commits wickedness lives "in" his or her wickedness. Therefore deed and consequence are referred to with the same expression, so that, for example, the term "sin" means the deed and its subsequent condemnation without any terminological distinction.

Such fundamental conceptions of reality are for the most part very stable. Yet they are still subject to changes and separation processes. It would be too much at this point to demonstrate this deed-consequence connection in detail. We must limit ourselves to a few suggestions. At least skeptical wisdom (Job) harbored deep doubts in this worldview, because for it the experience of a close connection between deed and consequence broke down, in that the good fate actually deserved by the righteous went to the evildoer, while the righteous had to suffer in this world. Thus the experience of reality itself eroded this understanding of reality without replacing it with a new one yet. Jewish apocalypticism let the consequences of deeds be fulfilled only through the last judgment. The lack of experience with immediate consequences of deeds is compensated here with the hope that God will execute poetic justice at the end of days; thus God, so to speak, suspends the deed-consequence connection until then. This, however, also partially changes the description of the judgment. When there is no longer only the turning back of consequences on the doer but also the pronouncement of a forensically normative final judgment (cf. 11.3 above), then obviously the view of the deed determining the fate has at least lost strength or even been abandoned. Much more fundamental, however, were the changes that came in under the influence of Hellenism and are especially to be observed in the Hellenistic Jewish Diaspora; evidence of this is found, among other places, in the Septuagint, Philo, Josephus, and 4 Maccabees. Now this old conception is in part no longer understood and misinterpreted as a legally normative retribution concept, or it is replaced by a virtue-and-vice teaching. Finally, the early rabbinic collection of sayings *'Abot* also shows how eschatological forensics and conceptions of labor legislation become dominant here. It remains to mention that the linguistic witnesses of the old deed-result connection also still occur within these literary witnesses, but the question is to what extent they are still understood in the traditional sense. In any case, there can be no doubt that Paul—especially as diaspora Jew—is to be placed in the middle of this historical change. Therefore we cannot simply ascribe this or that conception to him; rather, we must observe, above all, what help he gives for describing his conception of reality.

Clearly, Paul is still describing the immediate connection of deed and consequence when he uses it with the image of seed and harvest (Gal. 6:7–8; cf. Rom. 7:5). There are, for example, sick people even in the Corinthian church, because the church celebrates the Lord's Supper without love (1 Cor. 11:27ff.). Here too the deed already carries "judgment" within it, just as in the case of 1 Thess. 2:16, where Paul interprets the behavior of the Jews hostile to the gospel to mean that they always "fill up the measure of their sins" and therefore "wrath has come upon them completely." Apparently in this formulation also, sinful deeds and wrath as sin's consequence are two sides of the same coin. Conversely, Christ's atoning sacrifice can annihilate past sins, as it were, so that the consequences do not occur, as Paul says with the tradition in Rom. 3:24–26. Yet there are also significant observations in the Pauline scriptures that keep us from simply crediting Paul with thinking in the deed-consequence connection. So it is striking that Paul no longer really says a word about the double meaning of the words bound up in the deed-consequence connection (e.g., sin as single deed and unsaved condition; righteousness as deed and saved condition). Also, the language of human life "in" sin or righteousness (indicating a sphere of damnation or salvation with its own power) flows from Paul's pen only twice and tangentially (Rom. 6:2; 1 Cor. 15:17). Just these two linguistic patterns, however, where they occur, are decisive reasons for bringing up the deed-consequence connection, but four further basic observations must be added.

First, the language with which Paul describes the last judgment shows that he is thinking forensically of an authoritative judgment that is interpreted in categories of the world of trade and labor (cf. 11.3 above). This indicates that sin no longer produces its consequences by itself; rather, they are added on the basis of a divine initiative through an independent act of justice. Second, interest in the comprehension of sin has shifted. The focus is no longer on the self-acting sphere that is ominously unfolding before the doer and his community but on the individual internal relationships within the person himself or herself. Ungodliness leads to the inexplicable and inexcusable inclination to continue in this attitude (Rom. 1:18, 21–22). The law feeds desire and therefore leads continually and all the more intensively to the sinful deed (Rom. 7:7ff.). A person is "sold" under sin like a slave, and this metaphor is resolved by saying that the person is "carnal" (Rom. 7:14). Sin comes into the world through the doing of sin (Rom. 5:12); that means that a person becomes "flesh" (Rom. 8:3). So a person's living "in" sin (Rom. 6:2) is emphatically formulated: sin now dwells in the person (Rom. 7:17, 20). Thus the evil deed does not lead to the sphere of damnation that surrounds the doer and his community and, if the community is not to be destroyed, must be eliminated. Rather, the internal relationships of the person as sinner are of crucial importance. The experience that ungodly living is beautiful (Rom. 1:18, 32) and that satisfying insatiable covetousness releases new covetousness (Rom. 7:7–8) is now a fundamental part of the understanding of sin. The perception belongs all the more to the additional view of the redeemed individual that all of this is to be interpreted as the inner confusion of the sinner, as the unhealthy dichotomy within (Rom. 7:15ff.); for sin is like a second person at work within an individual (Rom. 6:6, 12–14; 7:23). Therefore Paul cannot be satisfied with the idea that Christ abolishes the consequences of sin, as in the tradition cited in Rom. 3:24–26, but rather describes in Romans 6–8 how the old person had to die and become a new being through gospel, Spirit, and baptism (Rom. 6:2, 6–7; 7:25–8:2). The transition from old to new person, described as dying and being raised (Rom. 6:1ff.), as a change of dominion (Rom. 6:14ff.), as a creation event (2 Cor. 4:3–6), as a new sonship that invalidates all former subordinate relationships (Gal. 3:24–26), or as a new being with new clothing (1 Thess. 5:4–8), makes it clear that a person is not simply a doer alternately of good or evil, and that this then has consequences lying outside the self, but rather that in an unfathomable way he or she is a sinner as a person and his or her sinful deed is the consequence of this being. Sin is not a deed and its consequence but an aspect of the person himself or herself. The nature of sin is therefore not a sphere but the unity of sin with the person.

Third, closely connected with the concentration on a person's internal relationships is a further theme. Sin is no longer qualified simply as the external actions of a person; rather, the judgment of what sin is depends crucially and primarily on the person of the doer and his or her inner attitude. The essential question is not whether one distinguishes foods or days but whether one does one or the other in thankfulness to God (Rom. 14:5–6). Without love no human action—even if otherwise

good—is worth anything (1 Corinthians 13). All deeds that do not proceed from faith are now sin (Rom. 14:23). The works commanded by the
law are not simply good as such; on the contrary, as the basis for one's
own righteousness before God they are particularly worthless (Phil.
3:7–8; Gal. 4:8–11). But the Spirit of God, which leads to the "striving of
the Spirit," helps to kill the "works of the flesh," so that it is pleasing to
God (Rom. 8:5–9, 14). Thus the objective view of deed, from which
comes the deed-consequence connection, has become doubtful. This is
why the apostle so often stresses that God probes the heart and knows a
person's hidden attitude (Rom. 8:27; 1 Cor. 4:5; 14:25; 1 Thess. 2:4) and
that the Christian, on the other hand, should willingly do what he or she
does (Rom. 12:8, 11; 2 Cor. 8:7–8; Phil. 2:14).

Fourth, to the description of sin within the individual we now add
the external normative evaluation, which is by nature foreign to the
deed-result connection. This appears where law and sin are related to
each other: the law is the reason why sin is "counted" (Rom. 5:13) and
is revealed as guilt before God (3:19), why the "judgment" on it is
"condemnation" (5:16; cf. 8:1) and its nature is determined as "disobedience" (5:19). The normative law lets sin be recognized as sin (7:7).
As with the conception of the last judgment, here too we see a concept
of normative law that comes to bear as an absolute factor based on the
Jewish tradition. These observations lead us to the conclusion that Paul
describes with various categories the phenomenon of sin, which is for
him complex and many-faceted, and it is only the insight into this variety that allows us to recognize where Paul places his accents.

We hope to gain this insight, for example, when we stress the power-
character in sin as interpreted by Paul or understand sin as a kind of
personification. There are traces of both interpretations in Paul: in his
independent formulation Paul always speaks in the singular of "sin"
(exceptions: Rom. 7:5; 1 Cor. 15:17), and he prefers the absolute usage.
Both have Jewish precedents, yet the emphatic concentration on this
way of speaking is a Pauline peculiarity even within early Christianity.
This language is particularly characteristic of Romans, especially since
here the absolute usage leads to statements that show sin acting and
human beings ruled by it. Thus the baptism chapter (on a traditional
background) pictures baptism as a change of dominion, with the aim
being to explain how Christians have been liberated from sin and no
longer have to be its slaves (Rom. 6:18). Once they lived for sin (6:12);
that is, they gave it obedience (6:16), served it as slaves (6:6), and
yielded their members in service to it (6:19). The view from the standpoint of sin corresponds to this view from the standpoint of human
beings: it reigns in their bodies (6:12) and appears as lord (6:14).

Yet we must note that sin reigns because and when a person gives in to desires (6:12), just as it comes into the world because and when a person sins (5:12–13). Romans 7 explains this further by saying that sin acts (7:17, 20), deceives a person (7:11), and uses the favorable opportunity of human covetousness to lead a person astray (7:8). Nevertheless all this happens within the person (7:8, 18), so that being sold under sin is the carnality of the person himself or herself (7:14). Sin is not external but dwells in the person (7:20). In the language of Romans 8 this means that to the extent that a person's striving is flesh, it is enmity, that is, sin against God (8:7). So the negative term "flesh," which characterizes a person as a whole as a sinner consigned to death (8:3, 6; cf. 7:24; 8:10), offers the best help in interpreting Paul's talk about sin in Romans 6–8. The personal statements on sin and its power seek to describe the inexplicable, even if experienceable, compulsion to sin and at the same time the human possibility of making oneself and one's actions the object of self-observation. The compulsion to give in to desire is one's own and at the same time is felt as foreign determination.

If we interpret this way, we can then ask whether this phenomenon is better described as a foreign force (an *it,* so to speak) or as a personalized entity (an *I*). The answer would more likely be the first possibility if we consider what all is involved for Paul in being a person, including corporeality, language, feelings, and relationships. Only in the last area does sin show attributes. Yet even the concept of force has its pitfalls and thus should be used with reserve, because the apostle always gives prominence to the active character of sin and would in no case allow human responsibility for deeds to be diminished by talk of the dominion of sin, just as he does not trace sin back to Satan either. For Paul, the human creature is not a tragic or possessed figure who could point to a foreign fate when it is a question of guilt before God and neighbor (1 Cor. 8:12; Rom. 1:21; 2:1). Furthermore, there is in Paul himself an analogy to the talk of sin as power, namely, death. Death is no mythic power but always the mortality characteristic of a human being as sinner (Rom. 6:23; 7:24; 8:6); nevertheless Paul can speak of it with verbs of motion (Rom. 5:12) and of dominion (5:14, 17; 6:9). Death is the last enemy that must still be destroyed (1 Cor. 15:26). And that is just what happens, when mortal human beings are transformed into the heavenly glory (1 Cor. 15:50–57).

The Pauline conception of what is an evil deed or a good deed—of when a person is a sinner and when he or she is righteous—and the significance of "works" for one's relationship to God are fundamentally determined by another question, namely, that of the significance of the law for Christians and non-Christians. Because, for Paul, the law functions only for the sinner, it belongs systematically to the Pauline conception of sin. It is due no special place as order of salvation. Paul describes his understanding of the law above all in Galatians, Philippians B, and Romans. Yet the basic decisions regarding his understanding of the law are made in connection with his calling (cf. 4.4 above). The one who understood the Torah as the covenant will of God that must be thoroughly fulfilled and who therefore persecuted the Christians in Damascus, who were lax with respect to the law, had to learn that God had placed himself on the side of the despisers of the law. He learned for Christ's sake to approve the very things the law forbade. That led to the task of correcting the Jewish understanding of the law and shaping a new one on the basis of Christ.

Traces of this rethinking are recognizable in Paul's Antiochene period (cf. 5.2 and 5.3 above). The Antiochene church, led by Barnabas and Paul, travels a fundamentally new road: Christian truth and freedom from the law now belong together like two sides of a coin. Gospel and Spirit establish what Christianity has to be and how it has to be lived. This has fundamental consequences for the understanding of the law. A sign of this is the observation that circumcision, although a requirement of the law, is now no longer the will of God. Circumcision is not just any commandment; it is the first step in the keeping of the whole law (Gal. 5:3). Has the law then lost its meaning altogether? Certainly this is true of the ritual law, which preserved Israel's identity through separation from the Gentiles. This very separation, however, is no longer desired. It is precisely such boundary drawing that the Christian mission makes obsolete (cf. Rom. 14:17 and 5.5 above; also Gal. 2:12 and 5.3 above). Then did Antioch distinguish between ritual law and other commandments? This could at least have been a possibility (cf. Rom. 14:17 and 1 Cor. 7:19). It is striking, however, that in Paul another view clearly prevailed as a result of the Antiochene discussions, namely, that such a distinction is not really helpful, because the obligation of a Christian conduct of life is no longer derived from the law at all but from the faith that becomes active in love (Gal. 5:6; cf. 1 Thess. 1:3). Or, as expressed in 1 Thessalonians, the Spirit drives us to holiness, teaches the will of God, and creates the willingness to do it (cf. Gal. 2:1ff.; 1 Thess. 4:8–9; and 5.2 and 6.2 above).

Therefore, as we can see in 1 Thessalonians and the Corinthian correspondence, Paul's proclamation no longer contains any interpretation of the law. This omission is by no means an indication of a still unclarified, potentially problematic understanding of the law. It can be clearly asserted from two standpoints. First, Paul makes several clear decisions against the Torah in 1 Corinthians. In this, however, he does not mention the Torah, but simply no longer considers it as a norm. Yet as a former Pharisee he must have known very well what he was doing. In 1 Cor. 6:1ff., for example, contrary to the Old Testament and Judaism, he demands the legal renunciation of property. In 1 Corinthians 7 he places the charisma of abstinence higher than marriage and describes the latter now as a partnership. Both of these go against the Torah and the way it was understood in contemporary Judaism. Moreover, for the Jewish marriage based on Gen. 1:28, the duty of marriage and the purpose of marriage are given by the commandment to produce offspring, but this plays no role in 1 Corinthians 7. Likewise, the freedom with which Paul approaches pagan worship in 1 Corinthians 8; 10 is in contradiction with the law and with Judaism. Furthermore, we can clearly observe in 1 Corinthians 5–10 that Paul orients himself toward the general ethos of the surrounding world (1 Cor. 5:1; 6:1–2; 10:32–33; 11:13) and that his regard for this general value has replaced appeal to the Torah.

Second, Paul expressly demands a testing of the "will of God" and as a former Pharisee naturally knows that in Judaism that will is defined by the Torah. But he bases the will of God for the sanctification of life on election (1 Thess. 4:3, 7) or on the "mercies of God" (Rom. 12:1–2) described in Romans 1–8, and then with the love commandment he provides the standard for the test (1 Thess. 4:8–9; 1 Cor. 10:33). In this testing he expressly includes the ethic of the entire world (Phil. 4:8; Rom. 12:2; cf. 1 Thess. 5:21–22), without favoring or even mentioning the Torah, although for better orientation he can offer himself as model (1 Cor. 10:33; Phil. 4:9). This finding does not exclude the possibility that Paul also tests the Torah—like everything else. In so doing, he can determine that the love commandment, as independently established in Christianity, is also found in the law (Gal. 5:13–15; Rom. 12:8–10). Yet we must also note that the love commandment is valid because of Christ (cf. 12.3 above) and would be valid even if the law read differently. It is also a criterion of selection that turns against the law, for in the one-sided option for it Paul says nothing, for example, of the Old Testament's requirements of revenge. Also the love commandment is thereby emphasized in a way that does not correspond to the Torah and its Jewish interpretation.

This finding means that the tangential consideration of the theme of the law in 1 Thessalonians and 1 and 2 Corinthians (1 Cor. 15:56) is by no means accidental; it is a theological program. Christians are absolutely no longer under the law, since for those who believe, Christ is the "end of the law" (Rom. 10:4). Therefore the "law of faith" (Rom. 3:27) or the "law of the Spirit [and] of life" (8:2) or the "law of

Christ" (Gal. 6:2) is not the Torah newly understood in a Christian way but the canon that corresponds to the nature of the gospel. This finding, finally, is also to be placed beside the three traditional exegeses in 1 Cor. 10:1–21; 2 Cor. 3:7–18; Gal. 4:21–31 (cf. 5.5 above). They indicate with particular acuity the distance and depreciation of the law in the Gentile-Christian church before Paul's quarrel with the Judaizers, when in them service to the law is described as slavery and the law as the killing letter. Gifts analogous to baptism and the Lord's Supper come to the Sinai generation expressly from the preexistent Christ (1 Cor. 10:1–4), but the law—speaking with 2 Corinthians 3—carries out its killing function (1 Cor. 10:6ff.).

Thus Paul did not first work up a basic critique of the law on the occasion of the Judaistic threat. Rather, we must see that the position that the apostle advocates in Galatians, Philippians B, and Romans was clarified before the quarrel erupted. Because immediately after his calling Paul saw himself faced with a fundamental decision regarding the law, we cannot assume a development in the apostle's understanding of the law. His position was essentially formed at the beginning of his years in Antioch. And we may add that there is little point in seeing further traces of a development between Galatians and Romans. The differences probably consist only of the polemical accents that mark Galatians and the deeper discussions contained in Romans.

The mention of Galatians brings into the discussion the scripture that for us today is the apostle's first detailed statement on the question of the law (cf. 11.4 above). Faced with a polemical dialogue situation, the apostle so fundamentally denied the law a relationship to the Abrahamic covenant and to the Spirit that according to his conception the law never had the task of imparting life (Gal. 3:21; cf. 11.4 above). From the beginning God equipped law and gospel differently. So in Galatians 3–4 the Abrahamic covenant, Christ, gospel, and Spirit form a unit, and the law has nothing to do with any of these entities. The law comes too late for this and must soon—namely, with Christ—give way to faith. From the beginning it was decreed by God's angels only to serve sinners as "disciplinarian." Thus Paul does not separate an original task (giving life to righteous doers) from a reduced function in view of the state of humanity (only revealing sin). The law never had any function other than this actual one. And it received this one function after humanity was already living sinfully. A further aspect connected with this function is the fact that for the way to salvation—for example, in the figure of Abraham—the law points away from itself to Christ and, since he and his gospel have become known, no longer has jurisdiction over Christians. Thus the law relates only to sinners before and outside Christianity.

Is this position, however, in accord with the statements in Romans? Is the giving of the law, according to this letter, not a precious possession of Israel (Rom. 9:4)? Is the law not a support on the basis of which one can distinguish good and evil (Rom. 2:17–18), so that one who follows the law can expect righteousness and life (2:7, 13)? Is the Torah not holy (7:12), spiritual (7:14), and good (7:13, 16)? Is it not given for "life" (7:10)? Before we interpret these positive statements about the Torah, which at first glance are in such close harmony with the Jewish view of the law (cf. 3.2 above), we should remember that similar judgments about the Torah are not to be found in Paul's other writings. So either the apostle revised his understanding of the law or the passages must be understood differently. There are indications supporting the latter assumption. Even in Romans the law still concerns the sinner (5:20), who is sold under the law (7:14) and cannot be obedient to the law, which is shaped by the mind's being "set on the flesh" (8:7–8). In distinction to this, for Judaism the life (and death) function of the Torah is linked to the human ability to choose freely between good and evil (Sir. 15:11–20; *Pss. Sol.* 9:4–5; *4 Ezra* 8:55–56). This coupling makes sense. Since Paul thinks more radically with regard to the sinner, the Torah's ability to give life is meaningless, unless Paul also allows the Torah to possess the power to break down the sinner's enmity toward God. But the apostle expressly denies this to the law (Rom. 8:3). In Romans also, only the gospel is equipped with "power" (1:16–17), while the law is weak. Has God, then, offered the sinner life in two stages, first in the law—not properly and, so to speak, only as if—and then effectively in the second attempt? Would God not be taking human beings for a ride with such a law, in that he would be attracting them with a gift of life and at the same time would provide that the attractive law is not at all capable of bringing this about? Or did Paul merely keep a lot of Jewish tradition? Both ways would lead, in any case, to our having to say Paul was inconsistent. Or in view of his Jerusalem trip, did Paul diplomatically accept such inconsistency in the bargain (cf. 13.2 above)? That too is difficult.

We can say one more thing, however, about the cited positive statements on the Torah. We have already seen how in Rom. 1:18–3:20 Paul brings in prestructured material that in many respects is in tension with 3:19–20. Also, Rom. 2:7, 13 cannot be balanced with this result. Indeed, Paul also uses the Torah in the whole section only so that it works as the "killing" letter. Furthermore, the positive evaluations of the Torah in 7:12, 13–14, 16 do not have to mean more than that the Torah comes from God and as such is not the enemy of humanity. Even in Gal. 3:19 Paul did not deny this but only weakened it polemically. Thus only

Rom. 7:10 remains as the core of the positive statements. This verse, which speaks of the unredeemed person under the law, does this with means that are taken from the fall of Adam in Gen. 2:16–17. In this situation the commandment not to eat from the tree of knowledge is not given in order to kill Adam from the start but to protect his life in paradise. So God's instruction reads: Do thus, so that death will not threaten you, but the life already given you before the instruction will remain protected! Hence this commandment serves about the same function that the law has in Gal. 3:23–24: it is for Adam's preservation. But it turns inexplicably into the impetus of covetousness, followed by trespass and death. Paul chooses his formulation in Rom. 7:10 so that God will not appear as the initiator of sin. Adam alone (e.g., in Rom. 5:12) is to bear the guilt for his fall. The passage says nothing, then, about a general function of the Torah in giving life to every doer. This interpretation has the advantage that Paul's thought remains unitary and without inconsistency.

Up to this point we have assumed that the law is valid only for sinners, Gentiles as well as Jews. This is in accord with the global perspective of Rom. 1:18–3:20. Naturally the law is first of all the Torah of Sinai (Gal. 3:17; Rom. 2:17, 23; 3:19; etc.), but every Gentile knows the requirement of the law (Rom. 2:14–15). Paul can include the Gentile Christians of Galatia in the statement, "Now before faith came, we were confined under the law" (Gal. 3:23). Thus the law is the Sinai Torah and at the same time an expression of world order (Gal. 3:24; 4:8–11) and of the human social constitution (Rom. 2:14–15; 13:3–5). Therefore in Rom. 5:20 the apostle regards the law as given to all descendants of Adam and in Rom. 7:7ff. describes the legal determination of all people. Thus the quarrel with the Judaizers over the law is not a special problem in history for Paul; it is a basic problem that emerges where the gospel is heard and old values are reevaluated. Hence Phil. 3:4ff. is for a Gentile-Christian church.

Thus we can turn to the question of what the law does for all people as sinners. Here in Romans, Paul remains within the lines of Galatians (cf. 11.4 above) yet becomes more differentiated. Fundamental in this is the idea that the law pronounces the judgment of God on sinners as a judgment of guilt and death and places all humanity under this judgment (Rom. 3:9–20). The law makes sure that humanity is recognized for what it already is: ungodly (5:12–13, 20). For it qualifies the deeds of people as trespass against the divine will (4:15) and makes sure that the deed is "reckoned" to the sinner (5:13). In persistent repetition, the law says that misspent creaturely life must face God as judge (1:18; 3:19). Therefore through the law a person gains "knowledge of sin" (3:20);

that is, knowledge of oneself as an errant being (2:14–15) is subjected to divine judgment, and the failure appears as sin before God.

Little developed in Romans is the function of the law as guardian and disciplinarian (Gal. 3:23–24; 4:1–3), that is, the protecting function of the law until Christ and faith come. It is probably implied in Rom. 7:10 and can be explained with 13:3–5: under the threat of wrath the law creates a relatively ordered togetherness. Thus, as written Torah or as law written in the heart (2:12–14), it rules human life in the time of "divine forbearance" (2:4; 3:25).

This understanding still does not adequately describe the relationship between law and sinner. In Rom. 7:7ff. Paul calls attention to the idea that the sinner—interpreted from the viewpoint of the redeemed—fatefully misuses the law. What began with Adam (Rom. 5:12) is repeated by all his descendants. The law does not affect the person who is open to God and neighbor but always—inexplicably and unfathomably—the egocentric person who "covets" (7:7–8). Though not its original intention, the law becomes an amplifier of covetousness. Desire grows precisely because the prohibition sets boundaries whose crossing is desirable. This situation is the elixir of life of sin, which now comes alive. Hence the law becomes the "power of sin" (1 Cor. 15:56). Thus human beings are already predisposed as sinners when the law comes to them. By revealing this, the law at the same time unintentionally becomes the means of nourishing sin. The law, which exposes sin as trespass and imposes sanctions, becomes the stabilizer of human beings as "flesh." It is too weak (Rom. 8:3) to defend against such misuse.

If sin is thereby revealed where a person becomes involved with the law in a certain dubious way, then we are not far from the passages in which Paul discloses that boasting before God as reliance on spiritual advantages (1 and 2 Corinthians) or as trust in fulfilling the law (Philippians B; Romans) is sin. In the latter case also the instrumentalization of the law occurs against its own intention. For in the sinner's reconciliation to God the law points to faith in Christ; Rom. 3:21, 31 is redeemed by the interpretation of the law in Romans 4 (cf. Gal. 3:6–12). This character of promise of the law is at the same time its inherent indication that for the believers "in Christ" (Rom. 8:1) there is no more need for the law. For the believer "in Christ" has died to the law (Rom. 7:3–4; Gal. 2:19). This not only breaks the condemnatory connection between law and sinner (Rom. 7:24–8:4) but the setting of one's mind on the flesh is replaced by setting one's mind on the Spirit (8:5ff.). If the former was enmity against God and its end was death, then the latter is "life and peace" (8:6).

14.4 The Gospel of Jesus Christ

The gospel is an address to humanity. It reads: "Be reconciled to God" (2 Cor. 5:20). Where this offer of grace finds a hearing, there is the eschatological day of salvation (2 Cor. 6:1–2), because people come out of sin and death to redemption with the hope of life. This offer is based on God's action in Christ and represents God: "God was in Christ" (2 Cor. 5:19)—this is the content of the gospel. God was in Christ in such a way that "for us" God ordained Christ to become "our righteousness and sanctification and redemption" (1 Cor. 1:30).

Everything that Paul draws on for a more exact description of Christ is based on this fundamental meaning of his overall destiny. Naturally this "for us" is centered in a special way on his giving of his life. But one can never take the interpretation of individual aspects of the story of Jesus Christ and separate them from this overall significance of his person. This is especially true of Jesus' death. Jesus does not, for example, as a martyr offer his death to God as expiation for others (cf. 4 Macc. 6:28–29); it is, rather, an event that God himself produces, through which God is there for humanity, just as he is in general there for humanity in Christ. Jesus' death is not our salvation because Christ dies "for us," but because Christ is "God for us," his death is salvation for people if they accept the word of reconciliation.

Thus the apostle's particular conception of the person of Jesus Christ presented in the gospel must first be considered. Only when it is appropriately described can, for example, Paul's interpretation of Jesus' death be meaningfully traced. Who, then, is Jesus Christ?

Jesus Christ or the Lord (the two most frequent titles for Christ in Paul) is presented in the Pauline correspondence as the eschatological central figure who shapes the destiny primarily of believers, yet also of all people (1 Cor. 15:20ff.; Rom. 5:12ff.) and all creatures (1 Cor. 3:21–23; 15:24ff.; Rom. 8:18ff., 38–39). With his story he is the personalized loving will of God (2 Cor. 5:14, 18; Rom. 5:8). His preexistence is mentioned as an indication of heavenly origin, yet not elaborated independently as being before all creation (1 Cor. 8:6 is tradition that Paul let stand unused). For Paul's efforts with Christology are focused on Christ as the sent One, the crucified One, and the resurrected One, as well as the coming Lord. It is thus the earthly One and his future that receive significance.

This is where Paul concentrates his attention, because in Christ God reinterprets his eschatological relationship to the world. Through Christ, namely, God wants to elect and change sinful human beings shortly before the end of all things, so that they can live with the Lord forever (1 Thess. 4:17; 5:9–10). With the coming of Christ, history is qualified through this action, so that the end time is beginning (Gal. 4:4). Unsuccessful and perverted life receives a determination toward the good as a new offer in that in Christ God remains bound to the world for its salvation, although the relationship of God to humanity would really have to be characterized by wrath and judgment.

Yet the apostle never describes all of this in the form of an independent christological theme, as occurs in the classical development of Christian dogmatics, where the person and work of Christ are independent topics of discussion. Rather, with the apostle Christology is always brought to bear as the content of the gospel that is now proclaimed in the power of the Spirit and therefore transforms into the new state of salvation, which can be described as standing in faith, love, and hope. Thus, quite analogous to the way in which Paul proceeds with his experience of being called (cf. 4.1 and 4.4 above), he does not begin with the question of what happened when Christ died and was raised, in order then to deduce what this means for believers in their present situation. He speaks, rather, of what is true and happening now, that is, of the gospel now at work and its consequences for the church. In order to speak of this appropriately, he reaches back to Christ and his work; indeed, we must actually say that he speaks of the Lord present in the gospel as he is characterized by the outcome of his destiny.

This conceptual and presentational direction of all Pauline letters has consequences for the way Paul describes christological salvation and weighs aspects of this salvation. If experience with the gospel is the approach to Christology, then in redemption we can disregard neither the Spirit at work in the gospel (and in baptism, the Lord's Supper, and worship) nor the faith of the individual. As a result of this approach the gospel does not simply report that reconciliation with God and judgment over sin have already occurred with the death of Jesus, and humanity only has to become cognizant of these things. Rather, the gospel solicits by proclaiming the crucified One: "Be reconciled to God" (2 Cor. 5:20). What happened for people when they were still sinners and nonbelievers never comes to them in any way other than by being themselves transformed, and only after their transformation can they comprehend what has happened for their benefit. Christ's death does not mean simply that people are released from or relieved of "something" (e.g., the consequences of sin, death, judgment), but because they are transformed by the Spirit of the gospel, they know in faith: Christ died for us.

There can also be no doubt that the apostle always writes a great deal about the human consequences of gospel, baptism, and Spirit, but practically speaks only with terse traditional statements about the death of Jesus. The oldest letter is already typical of this. The substitutionary death of Jesus is mentioned one time in traditional form naturally and unproblematically (1 Thess. 5:10), whereas Paul speaks untiringly of those who believe, hope, and love, as they live under the Spirit. On closer examination we find the same situation in all the letters, even in Romans, which at present is the main occasion for finding Christ's death interpreted in the categories of cultic expiatory death with great weight on Paul's understanding. Romans 3:24–26 is the chief evidence of this. Yet here Paul cites only tradition, as he often does in Romans in reference to understanding Jesus' death. These passages do not become the great occasion for Paul to comment on the understanding of expiation, the manner of substitution, and so forth. On the contrary, we must laboriously reconstruct the implicit elements of such a conceptual fabric. Conversely, Paul becomes very eloquent in Romans when he speaks in the "we" style of believers as of those who live under the transforming power of the gospel. For this we can no longer merely name verses; we have to refer to whole chapters.

These observations can be expanded. It can be no coincidence that many times when Paul cites traditional confessional statements about Jesus' death, he expressly adds the condition under which the death of Jesus is the salvific death for human beings, namely, the condition of faith (cf. Gal. 3:13–14; Rom. 3:24–26; 4:24–25). Likewise Paul can also formulate the same state of affairs as an assertion about the Spirit: Only in the Spirit can one appeal to Jesus as the eschatological central figure of one's salvation (1 Cor. 12:3). The reception of the Spirit and sonship lets one hope for eschatological deliverance (Rom. 8:23–24). Thus according to the experience of gospel and Spirit, faith considers what is to be said of the cross, since it should be interpreted in agreement with this experience.

Following this principle that there is no redemptive action without gospel and Spirit is yet another: The death of Jesus is not to be interpreted without his resurrection. Naturally the idea of substitution (for us, for our sins) depends on Jesus' death. That is the case from 1 Thess. 5:10 to Rom. 5:6–8; 8:32; 14:15; etc. The resurrection is not treated in the same way, but Paul can emphasize—for example, in 1 Cor. 15:12–19—that without the resurrection of Jesus the Christian message is empty and faith is in vain; indeed, in spite of Jesus' substitution in his death (1 Cor. 15:3) Christians are still in their sins. Thus Jesus' salvific death is not valid as such and in itself but depends on the person of Jesus and his overall destiny. Therefore in Rom. 10:9, for example, Paul can also name only the confession of Jesus' position as

Lord and faith in the resurrected One, without mentioning the cross, when he explicates who will be saved. Or he divides the salvific significance of Jesus between death and resurrection (Rom. 4:25). Thus we can state that it is not Jesus' death that makes him the Savior; rather, he is the eschatological Savior sent by God, and therefore his death is also a basis of salvation. The Jewish martyrs of 4 Maccabees ask their God to let their death count as expiation for the people, so that the suffering of the people may come to an end. Paul's Christology proceeds differently: God sends his Son; therefore everything that makes up his destiny—especially his cross—is from the beginning salvific action on behalf of human beings.

The central meaning of the person of Jesus Christ would still not be sufficiently grasped if we spoke only of his defining history as mission, death, and resurrection, as it is present as content of the gospel. This is fundamental but still does not say everything. Rather, it is Paul's concern to establish this reality of Christ fundamentally and comprehensively as the understanding of reality in general. If God was in Christ (2 Cor. 5:19) and with this the end time begins (Gal. 4:4), in that the old age is passing away (1 Cor. 7:29–31) and Christ delivers us from it (Gal. 1:4), then all understanding must be determined by the relationship to the world that God thus reshapes in Christ. So Paul can programmatically affirm that he wants to know absolutely nothing except Jesus Christ and him as the crucified One (1 Cor. 2:2). He wants to take every thought captive in obedience to Jesus Christ (2 Cor. 10:5). He counts everything as loss because of the surpassing worth of knowing Jesus Christ. For his sake Paul rejects everything, considers it refuse, and wants only one thing: to gain Christ (Phil. 3:7–8).

Paul also translated into action this accentuated goal setting for his understanding of the world. We can see this first in the expectation of the end. In 1 Thessalonians we can still recognize how the expectation of salvation in God's kingdom is replaced by hope for the Lord's coming (cf. 6.2 above). When the eschatological relationship of God to the world is set by the person of Jesus Christ, the kingdom of God naturally becomes the presence of Christ. The same is true in regard to the description of the final situation: the traditional expectation of seeing God (1 Cor. 13:12; cf. Matt. 5:8) now becomes being together with the Lord (1 Thess. 4:17; 5:10). Even the judgment that God carries out at the end (Rom. 2:1ff.; 14:10) and from which the Son originally delivers (1 Thess. 1:10) becomes occupied by Christ (2 Cor. 5:10). Making the dead alive is the eschatological majestic privilege of God (cf., e.g., 1 Corinthians 15; 1 Thess. 4:14), yet in Phil. 3:20–21 Christ has the power to transform mortal humans into a likeness of his heavenly resurrection body.

These are all scattered signs of how, for Paul, even at the end reality is not released from its Christ-dependent divine relationship. Since the sending of Christ, when God is named, his relationship to the world cannot be described apart from Christ.

That is also true of the present time. Naturally, when the end time begins with Christ's being sent by God (Gal. 4:4), the world must be regarded as coming to an end (1 Cor. 7:29–31); everything that already belongs to Christ must be counted in the "new creation," so that it is true that "the old has passed away, behold, the new has come" (2 Cor. 5:17). Christ now rules over all reality, transforming and reshaping it so that through him—in the sense of the relationship to the world initiated by God with him—"God may be all in all" (1 Cor. 15:28, KJV). Therefore there is simply no phenomenon of reality that can separate Christians anymore from the love of God in Christ (Rom. 8:39). The world, death, and life, the present and the future—indeed, simply all things—now belong to those who are Christ's (1 Cor. 3:22–23). It goes without saying that this is no plan of world conquest for Christians but rather a numinous weakening of these phenomena (cf. 1 Cor. 8:5–6; 15:25–26) and thus for Christians a participation in the victory that God has brought about through Christ: Christians know that "all things" are subordinated to Christ (1 Cor. 8:6). So they also know that they still belong to this dying world: "None of us lives to himself, and none of us dies to himself. If we live, we live to the Lord, and if we die, we die to the Lord; so then, whether we live or whether we die, we are the Lord's. For to this end Christ died and lived again, that he might be Lord both of the dead and of the living" (Rom. 14:7–9). Being Lord means having set with his destiny the conditions under which life before and after death is to be shaped according to God's will. Finally, these considerations naturally also include the antithesis of Adam and Christ formulated by Paul in 1 Cor. 15:20–22, 44–49 and Rom. 5:12–21. It is not Adam, the bearer of fate for sinful and mortal humanity, who has the last word on world history, but Christ, the antitypical central figure of the new humanity. World history does not remain the indefinite repetition of Adam in his descendants; it is a new beginning based on the grace personalized in Christ and hence the history of blessed sinners.

Finally, this also has consequences for the reality of the church. We must begin here by saying that the Spirit experienced by believers can be designated the Spirit of Christ (cf. Rom. 8:9; 2 Cor. 3:17–18; Phil. 1:19). Naturally he is, above all, God's Spirit. Yet he is the Spirit of the God who "was in Christ" (2 Cor. 5:19); hence on the basis of this self-binding of God he can now keep the reality of Christ present. As the gospel has Christ as its content, so the power of the gospel consists in that Spirit which brings Christ and humanity together in faith. The understanding of the church is shaped quite analogously in Paul: To the universal early Christian expression "church (of God)" is now added the understanding of the church as the "body of Christ" (1 Cor. 12:4ff.; Rom. 12:4ff.). We can formulate this more pointedly: In this way the church becomes an aspect of Christology (cf. 14.6 below). The discussion of Philippians A (cf. 12.3 above) showed how the Christian shaping of life is directly tied to the Christ event. Finally, in Philippians B (cf. 12.4 above) Paul showed how Christians' whole understanding of life, their dying with Christ as basic characteristic of earthly life, and their final transformation into the reality of Christ after death are formed by Christ. There is one formulaic expression of Paul's that can tersely summarize how Christ and his new reality incorporate all three realms of which we have just spoken. It is the expression "in (Jesus) Christ." If it is used prominently to characterize the church (cf., e.g., Rom. 8:1; 1 Cor. 1:2; Gal. 2:4; 3:26; 1 Thess. 1:1; 2:14), it also stands in eschatological contexts (e.g., 1 Cor. 15:22; Phil. 3:14) and indicates the qualification of the whole present (e.g., 2 Cor. 5:19). "In Christ" states how one day "all things" (cf. 1 Cor. 15:27–28; Phil. 3:21)—particularly the church—live or will live in a reality determined by Christ.

Thus, beginning with the programmatic intention of the apostle to take captive all thinking under Christ, we have demonstrated in three steps (from the eschatological hope through the present world to the believing church) how logically Paul himself masters this task. In fact, according to him there is no light for the world except for that which falls on it from the redemption in Christ. Thus Christ must receive such prominence everywhere. Then, however, it is all the more important how the apostle conceives of this redemption. Our attention must now be turned to the understanding of this question.

To talk of Christ's redemptive deed means to speak of his death for humanity. But according to everything we have said about the central figure of Christ, the death of Jesus cannot be seen in and for itself. It must be considered an essential aspect of the whole concept of salvation. This must always be kept in view. Now, in this case Paul did not make it easy for his present-day readers. The concept of expiation, for example, in which the sinful guilt is a communicable, "real" affair, seems to us to belong to a foreign world. But the apostle cannot be blamed for that. He is writing for his churches, not for us. What he does bear full responsibility for, however, is the variation-rich, mostly only suggestive way in which he treats Jesus' death "for us," how he incorporates such varied statements into his discussion, and what he emphasizes or only mentions as obvious. In order not immediately to place all of Paul's statements in simplified fashion under a particular view of redemption, we will begin with a sketch of the scope of the variations in the Pauline letters.

In 1 Thessalonians it is striking that Paul mentions Jesus' death as salvific act only once and in formulaic fashion (1 Thess. 5:10) but otherwise lets gospel and Spirit execute a person's calling and transformation. Conversely, in central texts such as 2 Cor. 5:14ff.; Rom. 5:1ff. he can accord prominent significance to the idea of substitution. On the one hand, he can make a special connection between Jesus' death and the concept of substitution (1 Thess. 5:10; 1 Cor. 15:3; Rom. 3:25; 5:6–8; etc.), yet, on the other hand, he can also comprehend Christ's destiny on the whole as the defining prototype of the new existence by faith (2 Cor 8:9; 13:4; Gal. 4:4; Phil. 3:8–21; Rom. 15:1–9)—which systematically, for example, fits in especially well with the theology of the cross. In the process the idea of substitution is at least suppressed, because it is not needed in this concept. Further, the apostle can think in rather different ways about substitution. Dominating at one point is the view that Christ intervenes vicariously "for us" or "for our sins" (1 Thess. 5:10; 1 Cor. 8:11; 15:3; etc.). Elsewhere Paul talks in the sense of inclusive substitution (e.g., 2 Cor. 5:14–15): Christ's death means that in it all have themselves died. The background of both conceptions of substitution is the intervention of one person for another, as can generally happen in life (e.g., Rom. 5:6–7; 9:3; 16:3–4). Again in other places we find the cultic substitutionary concept of expiation (especially clear in Rom. 3:24–25). What Christ achieves for us is also designated variously. In 1 Cor. 15:3 it is "sins" that are removed; in Rom. 3:24–25, transgressions that occurred before Christ's death. Speaking more basically are passages like 2 Cor. 5:21 and Gal. 3:13; here Christ became "sin" or "a curse." Thus the damnation that is loaded upon him is not limited to individual transgressions but is described in the form of a qualitative overall statement. The same is also true, naturally, when Christ dies "for us" (1 Thess. 5:10), "for all" (2 Cor. 5:14), and for the brother (1 Cor. 8:11). Going still farther are statements in which not only the negative and its consequences (death) are taken away by Christ but the new relationship to Christ and to God is itself established (2 Cor. 5:15; Rom. 14:7–9). In distinction to this, for example, Christ's death in Gal. 3:1–4:6 (cf. 3:13; 4:4) only wipes away the negative and thereby clears the way so that Spirit and gospel can come and work.

No one would want to deny that some of these variations are compatible. There remain, nevertheless, crucial ones that substantiate the thesis that Paul constructed no unified theoretical system for talking about the salvific significance of Jesus' death. It is all the more crucial to maintain this thesis, since in two passages that are prominently central to our theme, Paul integrated several conceptions of redemption (2 Cor. 5:14ff.; Rom. 5:1ff.) in order to use them for an overall meaning that is not simply equivalent to one of these conceptions. We now turn to this overall meaning, as we bring together common basic viewpoints of all the statements on the understanding of salvation.

Evil in Paul's sense should be understood throughout not only in the sense of a "something" that is taken away from people, but they themselves must be renewed from the ground up. Where a passage is linguistically only a witness for the abolition of a "something" (e.g., 1 Cor. 15:3b: "Christ died for our sins," which is repeated in v. 17), we mostly have tradition and, in the sense of the apostle's overall idea of redemption, always a falling short of the intended aim of the statement or incongruence with what is meant. God is always the subject of the salvific arrangement, Christ is the personal means, and his "obedience" to God (e.g., Rom. 5:11ff.) and his self-humiliation (classically in Phil. 2:6–8) may be named; sinners in their mortal misery are the ones to be saved. This movement from God to humanity is simply constitutive. Through it the sole effectiveness of God is to be emphasized. Paul knows no statement according to which a dichotomy in God between wrath and love, intended judgment and gracious decision would have to be resolved. Naturally God is angry with sinners (Rom. 1:18–3:20), but the mission of Christ rests solely on God's self-commitment to love (Rom. 5:8; 2 Cor. 5:14). It is the basic fact and presupposition of Christ's coming. It qualifies the entire redemptive process, and only through it does this process have the power to turn humanity. Because God as love "was in Christ" (2 Cor. 5:19), the Christ event is salvation that encompasses the world and history. Thus Christ's death aims at human slavery (under sin, death, law) but never intends to change anything with God. Nor is Christ's death a battle with the devil and his demons. Christ does not pay any kind of tribute to an antigod. God's salvific arrangement in Christ is in general so completely aligned with the direction from God to humanity that there is no place for a demonological component (1 Cor. 2:8–9 may be an arguable exception). Even if the Christ event is there for human beings, they still do not at first take part in the destiny of Jesus Christ (except in the external sense of 1 Thess. 2:15): Christ died "while we were yet sinners" (Rom. 5:8). In Christ all died (2 Cor. 5:14–15), without, as it were, being asked whether they wanted to have themselves represented by Christ. Again, this is emphasized in order to characterize the sole working of God in Christ. On the other side, through the Christ proclaimed in the gospel the faith of the individual comes into play immediately and without exception: Christ's death ends human damnation not automatically but only when sinners let themselves be renewed.

These basic statements just sketched can be systematized to some degree, in which case the following background ideas in Paul become important. God's love, in the sense of Rom. 4:17; 1 Cor. 1:28; 2 Cor. 1:9; 12:9, can be described as salvific deliverance from death and creation out of nothing. Thus Christ as the representative of this love (2 Cor. 5:14) has to "represent" this in his destiny. Therefore it consists of being sent in order to die obediently and of deliverance by God from death (1 Cor. 15:3–5, 12–19; Rom. 4:17, 24–25). In regard to human beings we can say that people are sinners ordained to die, who should live according to the intention of divine love. Thus Christ's destiny as the embodied love of God must represent how redemption from sin and death takes place and how this representation through Christ prevails in humanity as conformity to Christ, that is, how the shaping power of this central figure has its transforming effect on human beings.

Paul can fill out this basic framework in many ways. For this purpose he employs various semantic word fields (cf. 11.3 above). A word field, the reader will recall, is defined as a linguistic and subject context with a consistent overall view. It can be changed, and only some aspects of it may be used, yet it can be isolated because it can stand alone by reason of an original inner consistency. As already indicated, the apostle especially likes to mix such word fields, because none seems to him sufficient in itself to represent the entire way of salvation. Therefore we must first sort these mixtures. We can see, further, that although these word fields represent an overall view of redemption, they can be divided into two groups: those which focus on the relationship of God, through Christ, to human beings, and those which have their center in the anthropological changes of Christians. Briefly and simply stated, the latter are oriented toward the Spirit, the former toward Christ. Those connected with the work of the Spirit will be discussed (in 14.5 below); the others, now. Among these word fields we find five prominent ones, and thus our attention will be devoted to them alone. They are the word fields that describe redemption as reconciliation, liberation, substitution, atonement, and justification. Compared to these, other word fields, such as having mercy (Rom. 9:14–18; 11:30–32) and saving (e.g., Rom. 8:24; 10:9; 11:26), are definitely in the background.

Paul talks of *reconciliation* in 2 Cor. 5:14–6:2 and Rom. 5:1–11. Aspects of this word field are also found in Rom. 8:31–39. Thus it appears quite early in Paul in a striking position and still has a prominent place in his last letter—even in two passages; hence it has importance for Paul. Linked with this image field in an original way is the

key word "love" (Rom. 5:8; 8:39; 2 Cor. 5:14). Its opposite is enmity
(Rom. 5:10; 11:28). Reconciliation occurs when God, offering reconciliation, turns enmity into a condition of peace (Rom. 5:1), so that the
reconciled enemies can no longer be "separated" from the love of God
and of Christ (Rom. 8:35) and are given "all things" (8:32). In the background may be the behavior of a ruler who reconciles a rebellious
province and makes the reconciled state irreversible by striving for the
integration of the region with equal rights in his dominion. Instead of
achieving this through military subjugation of the enemies, he unexpectedly chooses the path of overcoming enmity through reconciliation. The offer of reconciliation can come in a wide variety of ways.
For Paul, in any case, this is an opportunity to introduce Christ. With
his sacrifice he is the unquestionable expression of divine love, which
at the same time is also the Son's love (Rom. 5:8; 8:35, 39; Gal. 2:20).
Thus God lets his Son die in order to affirm the seriousness of his love
in reconciliation. The word field is dominated by the inner dynamic of
surprise: Enemies expect war, yet they are offered peace. God does
not let human beings force him to react; instead, he overcomes enmity
with reconciliation.

The word field of *liberation* presupposes the oppression or enslave-
ment of the people to be liberated. They can be freed through defeat of
the oppressor or through ransom. The liberator must be stronger or
have more power than the enslaver. If the liberation is not to be only a
change from one dominion to another, then it must lead to a condition
of freedom and independence. In antiquity this was a familiar image
field in the context of the liberation of nations, the liberation of the
lower social groups, and the freeing of individual prisoners and slaves.
Also evidenced is the transference of the word field, for example, to liberation from demonic possession. Paul adopts this word field at some
points scattered through his correspondence. Functioning as the oppressor in these cases are sin (Rom. 5:21; 6:23; 7:7ff.), the law (Gal. 3:23–25;
4:1–3; Rom. 7:7ff.), and death (1 Cor. 15:25–26, 54–57; Rom. 5:14). One
is freed from slavery and into sonship (Rom. 8:15, 21; Gal. 4:3–5) or in
general into freedom (Gal. 4:31–5:1). If formally Rom. 6:15ff. only
describes a change from one dominion to another, Romans 7–8 quickly
makes it clear that this is only outwardly the case. Inwardly the new
arrangement has a quite different quality. Into this word field Christ
now steps as the liberator. He is, for example, the one who ransoms
(Gal. 3:13; 4:4–5); therefore Christians are "bought with a price" (1 Cor.
6:20; 7:23). Jesus' death is the unnamed price; the one who receives the
payment is also unnamed. Thus we are dealing with a faded image,
which probably still has only a general meaning of "liberation," as in,

for example, the "deliverance" in Gal. 1:4. In Gal. 3:13; 4:4–5 we find yet another statement linked with the liberator motif: Christ places himself under the law, or under the curse of the law. According to Phil. 2:6–8 he humbles himself unto death. When God exalts him (Phil. 2:9–11), he becomes ruler over all things. Eschatological central figure that he is, as liberator he becomes what people are: a slave. God exalts him, thereby once and for all shattering slavery, so that previously enslaved people can participate in his sonship, or lordship.

The word field of *substitution* with the consequence of death is known to Paul's Hellenistic readers in heroic examples from their classical literature. Heroes die for their homeland. The substitution of life for relatives and friends is not unusual. The Jewish tradition also has such examples (2 Sam. 20:20–22; Jonah 1:12–15; Josephus, *Antiquities* 13.5–6). The deed of a savior, who for the good of others vicariously substitutes his life, is caught in an often found fixed expression ("to die for"). Early Christianity also exhibits evidence of such an infusion of meaning into death (John 11:50; cf. Rom. 9:3; 16:4). Romans 5:7 shows that Paul can expressly reflect on this interpretation of a death. Here "die for" means "die in the place of." Someone dies in the place of another so that the other can keep on living. In addition, however, there is another interpretation of substitution. It rests not on the idea of replacement but on substantial union and identification. Thus Adam is humanity's bearer of fate: in him all of humankind is ontically represented and mythically present (1 Cor. 15:22), so that it can live its life only as a repetition of Adam (Rom. 5:12), because its bearer of fate "anticipates" its life. Adam "is" humankind. Where people live, Adam is there as shaping presence. Within this conception a vicarious death gains the character of inclusive substitution: in the numinous prototype, human beings bound with him die with him. It is no wonder that Jesus as the eschatological central figure attracts both ideas of substitution. Paul has good examples of the two understandings. The replacement idea is found, for example, in 1 Thess. 5:10; 1 Cor. 1:13; 8:11; Rom. 5:8; the numinous representative idea, for example, in 1 Cor. 15:22; 2 Cor. 5:15; Rom. 5:18–19.

The substitution idea is also essential in the word field of *atonement,* or atoning sacrifice. It can appear in both forms. Yet its home is not in the realm of social interaction but in cultic events. Cultic atonement through sacrifice provides for the removal of guilt or, better, for the removal or covering of the damnation that, because of a misdeed, burdens an individual or his or her community. Sin is, accordingly, not simply an individual act or an offense against a statute but bears or releases immediately from itself consequences of damnation, so that one talks of the deed-consequence connection (cf. 14.3 above). In the Old Testament, atonement is the means instituted by God to control or neutralize this process of damnation. Impressive testimony for this is offered by the representations of atoning sacrifice in Lev. 4:1–5:13; ch. 16. In all probability these sacrifice descriptions are supported by implicit concepts of substitution resting on identification. Things are different in Isaiah 53. This rather singular text in the Old Testament perhaps transfers cultically oriented atonement thinking to the suffering servant of God but follows the idea of replacement. Between the priestly authored texts of Leviticus (or the servant songs) and early Christianity, however, lie several centuries, in which culturally and religiously there was much change—some of it fundamental (cf. 14.3 above). Moreover, the particular Israelite conception of cult was not familiar at all to the Hellenes, and they are known to be the addressees of the Pauline letters. They too, however, hardly kept the same conception of cult and atonement from the pre-Homeric period until the time after Augustus. Finally, cultic atonement is shaped especially by the understanding of the damnation that is brought on by sin or connected with it. Here, too, we cannot simply assume invariability. Now, we are very poorly informed about the concept of cult in the Pauline period. Therefore we turn to texts such as those in Leviticus in order to discern semantic connections. Nevertheless we should exercise caution and not transfer the reconstructed understanding of sacrifice in Leviticus too facilely to Paul. Yet even in view of these cautionary measures we must see that Paul purposefully transfers the concept of atoning sacrifice to Christ, especially in significant passages in Romans such as 3:24–26; 5:9; 8:3. He did not, however, do this exclusively or without competition, as especially Rom. 5:1–11 shows. It is also certain that the apostle appeals to set tradition, so that we must always check how much he agrees with it, as evidenced by the context. In any case, it accomplishes, on the one hand, something that is close to Paul's heart: within the concept of atoning sacrifice he can show how Christ works through his death for the benefit of humankind, nullifying the consequences of sin. On the other hand, the word field does not cover the basic concerns of the apostle. Thus, for example, the inner systematic of the concept does not anticipate that sins other than those already committed can be expiated (cf. Rom. 3:25b). Therefore atonement is always necessarily dependent on repetition. Christ, however, died once and for all. His death includes sin that has not even happened. Furthermore, Paul says not only that earthly life is purified; Christ's destiny is also supposed to give eternal life after death.

Along with the word field of reconciliation, in the letters after 1 Thessalonians the word field with the language of *justification* belongs to the apostle's central ways of expression. We have already spoken in such detail of this in other places (cf. 11.3, 11.4, 12.4, and 13.4 above) that in spite of the importance of these statements, we will only go into them briefly. This language, as we saw, is indebted to two different image fields, the sacramental new constitution of humanity and the eschatological-forensic judgment scenes with authoritative expression of dominion, as they are entered into by ancient throne and tribunal scenes. In the first case the topic is the sacramental inclusion of the individual Christian in the determination by the central salvific figure of Christ, in which every way of understanding of Christ's salvific deed is possible, provided that it explains how Christ is now humanity's new bearer of fate. The second case speaks of the ruler's act of grace as the legally binding emancipation of the guilty, who according to the law should really be punished. In antiquity, incidentally, rulers often had the sovereign right of pardon regardless of laws promulgated by them. Romans 3:21–4:25 shows how Paul adapts himself to this view: everything is placed on the free commitment of God to grace (3:24; 4:4; 5:2) for the guilty ungodly person and on the person's "growing strong" (4:20) in this offer. Because this is such an inconceivable and overwhelming offer to those burdened with guilt, God demonstrates his covenant loyalty through the death of Jesus Christ ("to prove . . . that he himself is righteous," i.e., loyal to the covenant, 3:26; cf. also 5:8: "God shows his love for us"). Thus the death of Jesus is not placed primarily on the level dominated by the question of how satisfaction can be rendered to the law in such an act of grace. There is no talk of the law in Rom. 3:23–26 (or in 4:25; 5:1–11). It does speak, however, of the God who is righteous (i.e., in his devotion is and remains loyal to humankind, despite the latter's guilt) and who makes people righteous (3:26).

These word fields have demonstrated how rich are the Pauline possibilities for shaping the basic soteriological ideas of his christological proclamation. We also caught sight of the limits of individual word field applications. In Rom. 5:20–21 there is an attempt by Paul to express the basic ideas of this variety: "Where sin increased, grace abounded all the more, so that, as sin reigned in death, grace also might reign through righteousness to eternal life through Jesus Christ our Lord."

14.5 The Believer, the Spirit, and Life

Human beings learn that they are sinners, and in what way (cf. 14.3 above), on the basis of the early Christian missionary message, which, in the face of the eschatological wrath of God that threatens everyone, offers the gospel of Jesus Christ (cf. 14.4 above) as deliverance from this wrath (cf. 1 Thess. 1:9–10; Rom. 5:9). Anyone who accepts this message is said to have come to faith (Rom. 10:14; 13:11; 1 Cor. 15:11; Gal. 2:16; etc.). Indeed, this message itself can be called the faith, that is, the preaching of faith (Gal. 1:23; 3:5, 23, 25). Paul calls those who have come to faith simply "those who believe" or "believers" (Gal. 3:22; 1 Thess. 1:7; 2:10, 13). By that he means the whole church or Christians in general (cf. Gal. 6:10).

For Paul, the decisive roots of this language point to Antioch and can be well demonstrated in the election theology represented by 1 Thessalonians (cf. 6.2 above). It is certain that in Hellenistic diaspora Judaism, in a definite, if also limited form, we have the foundations of this language. Yet its central and frequent use in early Christianity is just as new as the christological determination of the faith. Early Christianity (Gal. 1:23) and Paul (Gal. 3:23) probably also saw it thus themselves, because they could designate Christian faith as "faith," without being more specific and without fear of confusion; also in the triadic formula faith-love-hope they saw no reason to describe faith more precisely (cf. 6.2 above). This corresponds to the evidence in Hellenism, where the religious use of faith and believing is not often to be observed and then is found especially concentrated in the realm of oracles: one trusts the saying of the gods and believes them. In any case, as a key word in self-presentation and promotion the word is nowhere to be found in the religious environment of Hellenism. The Christianity that was spreading over Palestine and beyond was first in turning faith into an essential statement. Without doubt, Paul had a special role in this development.

Thus if we want to characterize what faith is for Paul, it is advisable to observe its semantic surroundings in Paul himself. Faith, as we have already said, is the desired human response to the Christian missionary message. Proclaimed by the apostle, for example (2 Cor. 5:20), that message is God's eschatological elective action, through which, before the imminent last judgment, God places under Christ people who belong to the whole lost human race, so that they will attain salvation instead of wrath (cf. 6.2 above). Faith occurs on the basis of this preaching (Rom. 10:14), which is aimed at deliverance from wrath. Hence faith is salvific faith in the comprehensive sense. It lets one participate in ultimate salvation. Thus the believer does not, as with an oracle or a miracle, trust a numinous being in a particular case and for a limited time; rather, in faith one places oneself in an all-inclusive, lifelong relationship with God, which involves one's final and lasting determination: one's salvation.

The preaching of the gospel is interwoven with the Spirit (1 Thess. 1:5), and thus faith is the result of this power of the word (Rom. 1:16; 1 Cor. 2:5). The message is called the preaching of faith because it creates faith (Rom. 10:8, 14–15, 17). Faith is the fruit of the Spirit (Gal. 5:22; cf. 3:2, 14, 22). Of course, the Spirit also does signs and wonders (Rom. 15:19; 2 Cor. 12:12). But in such a context the apostle never gives faith a theologically significant place. He keeps linking faith with the gospel, because only the content of the gospel—that is, the eschatological central figure of Jesus Christ (cf. 14.4 above)—can grant the all-inclusive relationship with God, which is what faith is all about. If faith concerns all things and the ultimate things, then that to which faith refers must be capable of granting such a relationship. This context, then, is also the place to speak of "obedience to the faith" (Rom. 1:5; 16:19; cf. Rom. 10:3, 16; 15:18; 2 Cor. 9:13). It is a variation of the basic idea of 2 Cor. 10:5: that Paul wants to bring all thought under the obedience of Christ. Faith is accordingly obedience in the sense that it acknowledges for itself what Christ is for faith. Faith is obedience in that it corresponds to the appeal, "Be reconciled to God" (2 Cor. 5:20), and does not reject reconciliation. The obedient one is in this case not the recipient of a command but the one who answers out of insight into the salvific gift of God in Christ.

This leads to observations about the objects of faith. Faith is what it is because Christ exists. Therefore Christ is the new and crucial indication of the object of faith (Rom. 10:14; Gal. 2:16, 20; Phil. 1:29; 3:9; etc.). In addition, naturally, we also find God as the object to which faith relates (1 Thess. 1:8 etc.). For God is indeed the one who is at work in Christ for the benefit of human beings. It is noteworthy that traditional formulaic material that speaks of the Christ event is included in the content of faith (1 Thess. 4:14; 1 Cor. 15:1ff.; Rom. 10:9–10; etc.). Thus Christ is the object of faith as identified by his history. At the same time, we can see from this historical reference of faith that faith is not interpreted primarily psychologically (say, faith as feeling) but has its essence as "confession-bound" faith, as can also be seen in Rom. 10:9, where confessing and believing stand parallel. Yet faith is also not to be misunderstood as merely holding statements of faith to be true. Faith is, rather, a relying on God's deed and promises in Christ that involves the whole person (Rom. 4:20).

Therefore faith also possesses an existential and historical side, which can be made clear with three points. First, faith is strengthened through the exchange of spiritual gifts (Rom. 1:11–12). It can still lack something (1 Thess. 3:10). It can be weak faith (Rom. 4:19; 14:1; cf. 1 Cor. 8:7, 11). To each person is accorded a measure of faith

(Rom. 12:3). This is all true because faith is an affair of the "heart" (cf. Rom. 10:9–10), and the center of the person will not always hold on with the same intensity and strength (1 Thess. 3:13) to the truth of faith: that whoever believes in Christ will not be put to shame (Rom. 10:11). Second, this existential dimension of faith becomes visible in another way. It was probably not by accident that Antiochene Christianity had already coined the triadic formula faith-love-hope, which Paul often employed to characterize the Christian life (cf. 6.2 and 12.3 above). It makes clear that faith compels active love (cf. 14.7 below) and understands itself as the foundation of hope (cf. 14.8 below). Without love and hope, faith is "nothing" (1 Cor. 13:2; Rom. 8:38–39), as certainly as faith alone saves (Rom. 1:16–17; 4:2–5; etc.). It is true that "whatever [!] does not proceed from faith is sin" (Rom. 14:23). So it is the living principle of faith that it must become active (cf. Gal. 5:5–6). Finally, in 1 Cor. 13:8–13 Paul makes a remark that concerns the historical limitation of faith: The final completion leads from believing to seeing. Faith then loses its significance. Faith is the Christ relationship under the conditions of the present time.

The previous characterization of the Pauline understanding of faith can distinguish between early Christianity and Paul in only a very limited way. This immediately becomes different if we ask about the context in which by far most of the statements on faith are to be found in Paul. We find them in Rom. 3:21–5:11; 9:30–10:21; Gal. 3:1–4:7; and Philippians 3. These are the texts in which, in connection with the development of the Pauline message of justification, faith and righteousness are so closely related that faith and works appear in opposition. We have dealt with this in detail more than once (cf. 11.4, 12.4, and 13.4 above). The exclusion of works from the process of justification and the emphatic characterization of righteousness as righteousness of faith are without doubt the result of Paul's comprehension of the reception of salvation.

Thus if for early Christianity and for Paul, becoming a Christian and being a Christian are characterized by "faith," then when asked what distinguishes Christians from other people, Paul and the early Christian churches, while pointing to faith, would certainly at the same time have made reference to the experience of the Spirit. Historically we must also remember that after the original church-founding Easter event with its manifold ecstatic experiences, the early Christian missionary churches stood under the working of the Spirit through the preaching of the gospel (1 Thess. 1:4–7; Gal. 3:1–5), baptism and the Lord's Supper (1 Cor. 10:1–4; 12:13), and worship in general (1 Corinthians 12–14). Thus the churches as well as individual Christians are Spirit-led (1 Thess.

4:8–9; 1 Cor. 1:7; 3:16; 6:19–20). This is not only a subsequent theological expression of the Christian understanding that the inner religious experience is indebted to divine provenance and nearness, or that being inwardly conquered by the gospel comes from the convincing power of the word. Rather, there are clear signals that the Spirit was also experienced concretely as the gift of God. Paul is able to address the Galatians about this in a difficult situation (Gal. 3:1–5). He can refer to the power of the word (1 Thess. 1:5; 1 Cor. 2:5; Rom. 1:16) and to signs and wonders that accompany the word (2 Cor. 12:12; Rom. 15:19). He believes it possible that guests in the Corinthian worship service are getting the impression of madness (1 Cor. 14:23), and he knows that unpredictable spontaneous utterances of the Spirit (prophecy, speaking in tongues) should be regulated in the worship service but cannot and must not be completely quenched (1 Corinthians 14; 1 Thess. 5:19). Even if apparently not all churches had such overflowing experiences of the Spirit as did the Corinthians, it is still clear that the early Christian churches, including the Pauline missionary congregations, were charismatic churches.

Against the background of this field of experience we must now ask how this phenomenon of the Spirit was understood and interpreted. For Paul, no doubt, priority is given to the view that the Spirit is the present Christ in the gospel, which therefore has the power to persuade to faith (Rom. 1:16; 1 Cor. 15:45; 2 Cor. 3:17; Gal. 4:6). Hence Christ's message and the Spirit are signs of the end time (2 Cor. 5:5; 6:1–2; Rom. 8:23). With the coming of the Spirit the promise to Abraham is made good eschatologically (Galatians 3–4) and the prophetic word from Ezek. 36:27 is fulfilled (1 Thess. 4:8). The eschatological church is permeated with the Spirit, and the gifts of the Spirit coming alive in it are the presence of the coming salvation (Rom. 8:23; 2 Cor. 5:5; 1 Corinthians 12–14). The Spirit effects immediacy to God (Rom. 8:14–17; 1 Cor. 2:10–12; Gal. 4:6–7) and drives people to Christ again and again (1 Cor. 12:1–3). The Spirit effects the Christians' new concept of fellowship as unity among brothers and sisters (1 Corinthians 12). Last but not least, the Spirit leads to a transformation pleasing to God, in that the Spirit changes believers from within and instructs them in love (Gal. 5:25; 1 Thess. 4:8–9). It is clear that Paul pushed ecstatic spiritual phenomena to the periphery (cf. 1 Corinthians 14; 2 Corinthians 12) and interpreted theologically the experience of the Spirit by describing with it the presence of Christ as the people-transforming power that changes believers from inside out. The Spirit is the lasting determination of Christian life and not so much a special emotion in particular moments: "living by faith" (Gal. 2:20) and "living by the Spirit" (Gal. 5:25) are two descriptions of the same state of affairs. Thus the spiritual changes, as noted by Paul, have to interpret the Christian's standing in faith. The intensity with which the gospel grasps a person as a whole and leads him or her to faith has to be in accord with the statements with which Paul puts into words the spiritual transformation of the Christian.

These Pauline comments are not only helpful for getting an idea of his understanding of faith. They are also to be grasped as the positive counterpart of the negative characterization of human beings as sinners (cf. 14.3 above). Thus the statements form a cross-check, as it were, for the description of sinfulness. The radicality with which Paul declares all people to be sinners must receive a counterpart in the sketching of the new. At the same time, the description of a person's spiritual transformation is a welcome supplement to the Christ-centered description of salvation (cf. 14.4 above). Even at first glance Paul's statements show that in this case he can again speak in rich variation. This is no longer surprising to anyone who has made analogous observations elsewhere in the apostle. Paul not only makes use of a terminologically fixed language but can also exploit many linguistic possibilities, particularly in connection with central themes such as the interpretation of Jesus' death (cf. 13.4 and 14.4 above) and the description of God's gift of salvation to humanity (cf. 14.4 above). Again it is also striking in this regard that Paul not only applies linguistic means alternately or one after another but often intertwines them in the formation of the same context. What is discussed in two sections—specifically under the viewpoints of the new ordering of human relationships and the changes within an individual him- or herself—very often flows together in the apostle.

In regard to statements that emphasize the new ordering of relationships, one will doubtless recall first the language of election (cf. 6.2 above). One of its crucial statements is that those who once faced wrath and death have, with the attainment of salvation, now been promised a new destiny: they are called "to obtain salvation" (1 Thess. 5:9–10). With eschatological election the new goal is set. In the achievement of this promise, the Christian reaches toward this goal, which can be described with the image of a competition (1 Cor. 9:24–27; Phil. 3:12–16). Here the rejection of old goals as ordering entities for the overall understanding of life can be expressly noted (Phil. 3:13).

This already leads us close to the statements that capture in a contrast schema of "once" and "now" the Christians' situation of changes through which their whole lives are now determined; these statements speak disparagingly of the old and in contrast to it describe the new state of salvation. Under the sanctifying effect of the gospel and Spirit sinners become saints (1 Cor. 6:9–11), the unrighteous become righteous (1 Cor. 6:1, 11), drunks become sober (1 Thess. 5:7–8), sleepers awake (1 Thess. 5:6–7), and those oriented toward the flesh become spiritually oriented (1 Cor. 2:13–14; 3:1–3; Gal. 5:17; 6:1). One falls from the communion of the perishing to the saved (2 Cor. 2:15; 4:3), from impurity into sanctification (1 Thess. 4:7), from the darkness and night into the light and day (1 Thess. 5:4–5), from hopelessness into joy (1 Thess. 4:13; Rom. 14:17; 15:13), from a perverse generation into blameless children of God (Phil. 2:15). In these cases realms are set against each other, and general descriptions of the condition of groups of people are given. This is certainly typical of the situation of the first mission, when confirmation of the new is undertaken through such uncompromising contrasts. People do not grow up in a Christian world but must reorient themselves for the first time and with far-reaching consequences. One who comes to faith achieves such a change; the onetime unbeliever (1 Cor. 6:6; 7:12, 14; 10:27; 14:23–24) becomes a believer and experiences his or her new beginning as the contrast of "once" and "now."

This already borders in part on the statements that describe the change in lordship and ministry. Dominating here are statements that grasp human life as service (Rom. 6:6; 7:6, 25; 14:18; Gal. 4:8–9; 1 Thess. 1:9) and have one live under a power (Rom. 6:14–15) that rules over one (Rom. 6:12, 14). Here the old and the new state can be formally described as the same (e.g., Gal. 4:8–9; 1 Thess. 1:9). Yet as a rule the situation is qualified in such a way that the new relationship appears in a different light in terms of content. The new relationship is no longer slavery but freedom (Rom. 6:20–22; Gal. 4:3–7; 5:1, 13). Christians have not received the spirit of slavery but of sonship (Rom. 8:15). The ministry of death stands opposite the ministry of the Spirit (2 Cor. 3:7–8).

Old and new can be further characterized by the apostle through the language of relationship within a communion, and often in the background here as image fields are the communion of marriage and terms of kinship. The Corinthians once felt themselves drawn to the gods (1 Cor. 12:2). One can want to please the Lord and also a wife (1 Cor. 7:32–34; 1 Thess. 4:1), join with a prostitute as well as with the Lord (1 Cor. 6:16–17). As a man and wife become one (1 Cor. 6:16), so also the believers and Christ (Gal. 3:28), yet in a spiritual way (1 Cor. 6:17). The believer belongs to Christ as a wife belongs to her husband (Rom. 7:3–4). Moreover, being a Christian is sonship (Gal. 4:5–6; Rom. 8:14, 16). Christians are sons of light and of the day (1 Thess. 5:5); they are children of God (Rom. 8:16; Phil. 2:15). Therefore they are brothers and sisters (1 Thess. 1:4; 1 Cor. 6:5–8; etc.). The community relationship is expressed more generally when in the Greek text personal ordering is characterized through the genitive or dative of the person: "None of us lives to himself, and none of us dies to himself. If we live, we live to the Lord, and if we die, we die to the Lord" (Rom. 14:7–8). Everything belongs to the Corinthians, yet they "are Christ's; and Christ is God's" (1 Cor. 3:21–23). The Christian has died to the law in order to live to God (Gal. 2:19) or has died to sin in order to live to God in Jesus Christ (Rom. 6:10–11). It is clear that through this language Paul wants to emphasize the personal side of the new relationship to God and Christ.

Finally, the new is understood as a change of state or place. The Thessalonians are not in darkness (1 Thess. 5:4). Christians would be still in their sins if Christ had not been raised (1 Cor. 15:17); they were once in the flesh as sinful mode of existence (Rom. 7:5). Now, however, Christians live in the grace of Christ (Gal. 1:6), in faith (Gal. 2:20), above all in Christ (Gal. 3:28; 2 Cor. 5:17; etc.), and also in love (1 Cor. 16:14; cf. 4:21). Yet it must be noted regarding this evidence that with one exception such statements are used rather sparingly. Only the formulaic "in Christ" is prominently used.

Regarding the changes that occur with people themselves, the language of the clothing symbolism is a mode of expression that formally stands between the two groups of statements. Yet we must realize that the clothing in this case does not actually signalize one's status outwardly to others; rather, one is what one wears. Christians are dressed with the breastplate of faith and love, and the helmet of the hope of salvation; that is, they live as people whose nature is determined by faith, love, and hope (1 Thess. 5:8). In baptism they have put on Christ (Gal. 3:27), so that they are children of God (3:26) and can be expected in their way of life to put on the Lord Jesus and the armor of light (Rom. 13:12–14), that is, to accomplish what he has accomplished.

As Christians live in the Spirit and in Christ, so we can also say that Christ is in the believer (Gal. 2:20; Rom. 8:10) or the Spirit lives in the believer (Rom. 8:9, 11). As Christians are supposed to walk in love, so is God's love poured into their hearts (Rom. 5:5). Thus outside and inside, living space and inhabitant can be exchanged. This is possible because the Spirit is in the believer and at the same time works as determination of the whole church. Thus the Corinthians are told that they as the church are the temple of God and of God's Spirit (1 Cor. 3:16–17). It can likewise be said that the individual Christian is this (1 Cor. 6:19). This calls to mind that through the celebration of the Lord's Supper each individual church member shares in Christ as Spirit-filled food (1 Cor. 10:14–17; cf. 10:1–4) and at the same time through baptism has become a member of the body of Christ (Rom. 12:3ff.; 1 Corinthians 12).

It is also typical of Paul that he can comprehend becoming and being a Christian in a different way as a change of form. For example, Christ must be formed in the believer (Gal. 4:19), and believers, in view of the experienced mercy of God, are to be transformed by the renewal of their minds (Rom. 12:1–2). More strongly expressed is 2 Cor. 3:18–4:6: The glory of the Lord perceivable in the Spirit-filled gospel is reflected in Christians. They are transformed thereby from one glory (of the Lord) into another. Thus the reflected image of Christ's glory effects a transformation into that same nature. Paul can soon describe this process in a second treatment in this way: Christ is the image of God. Therefore he participates in God's glory. Christ's glory is present in the gospel. It shines forth from the gospel and its shining is seen. Thus it shines in the hearts of believers as the place of inner perception. By looking at the face of Christ, believers gain knowledge of God's glory. Hence God himself is revealed through Christ to the believers, who become new. For this entire revelation process is interpreted as the day of creation on which God let light shine out of darkness. These unusually triumphal statements, which on the basis of reflecting and looking—in good Greek-Hellenistic fashion—talk of a transformation into the seen, are not only put in their proper place through the letter's context of the theology of the cross (cf. 8.4 above) but also become more accessible in their intention if we look at them from 2 Cor. 5:14ff.; Rom. 5:5ff., that is, if we fill with love especially the statements about glory.

What is asserted through the image of Christ taking shape and effecting a transformation within an individual can also come to expression through the idea of conformity, concretely to being made like the destiny of Jesus Christ. The basic idea is this: A person must now become like the death of Christ and in the consummation like the glorification of the Lord. Paul borrowed this idea from a particular concept of baptism that lies behind Romans 6: Baptism is the sacramental repetition of the death and resurrection of Jesus. Thus in baptism there is a dying with and a being raised with Christ. Or: the old person dies, and a new one comes from baptism. Paul changes this in two ways. He does not let the repetition of death and life describe the unique baptismal act but indicates with it the life of a Christian as a whole. Further, he attributes dying to the phase of earthly life and resurrection to that of eternal life. Thus the Christian dies with Christ (Rom. 6:8), is made like him in his death, and is buried with him (Rom. 6:4–5). As Paul often says in his theology-of-the-cross language (cf. 8.2 above), Christians are crucified with Christ (Gal. 2:19). Therefore all their lives they "share his sufferings, becoming like him in his death" (Phil. 3:10; cf. in general 8.4 and 8.5 above). Likewise they hope in Christ, "who will change our lowly body to be like his glorious body" (Phil. 3:21; cf. Rom. 8:17). Thus the eschatological central figure of Christ is the shaping prototype, according to whose destiny of death and resurrection the lives of those who belong to Christ proceed then and now. Here Paul can in addition devote his special attention to that aspect of the change of form which shapes the transition from earthly to heavenly life (1 Cor. 15:35ff.; 2 Cor. 5:1–10).

Finally, Paul can talk simply of a Christian's new identity. Just as for Paul the transition from this life into the one to come passes through a new starting point and a break, in which continuity is only granted through God (1 Cor. 15:31ff.), so also he can describe the acceptance of the gospel as a break. Christians have died to sin, the law, and the world (Rom. 6:11; 7:6; Gal. 6:14). Yet Paul can refine these statements: As sin once ruled the person as "I" and not the sinner himself or herself (Rom. 7:20), so now he can say of the Christian: "It is no longer I who live, but Christ who lives in me" (Gal. 2:20). If the person once had in sin a competing "I," now he or she has Christ as a new "I." Here sin is a foreign, substitute "I"; Christ, on the other hand, is the one who lovingly offers himself and brings righteousness and life (Gal. 2:20–21).

If we survey these Pauline statements describing human spiritual transformation, we will see that apart from the students of Paul in Ephesians and Colossians, in the whole of early Christianity we can find no other such multifaceted and radical statements about human transformation under the influence of gospel and Spirit. This Pauline peculiarity obviously has its counterpart in the refined judgment (likewise not to be found elsewhere in early Christianity in this depth) about the sinner (cf. 14.3 above). In this way Paul translates the theme of the triumph of divine grace into anthropological reality.

14.6 The Eschatological Church

The gospel is directed toward the individual, and faith is the answer of the individual. In this way the former sinner becomes a righteous person. Paul does not have in mind a wholesale baptism of family clans as the goal of his mission; in a marriage it is quite possible for only one partner to be a Christian (1 Cor. 7:12–16). The family head Philemon has in his household non-Christians (e.g., Onesimus; cf. Philemon 10–11). Naturally the apostle expects the Christian spouse to persuade the other one with patience (1 Cor. 7:16). He rejoices when a household can be baptized (1 Cor. 1:16) and both partners of a marriage are won for Christ (Rom. 16:3, 7). Yet the gospel and the decision of each individual are closely bound. Those who come to faith on the basis of their personal decision should have themselves baptized. Baptism does not merely make a new person out of the old. It inducts one into the "body of Christ," the church (1 Cor. 12:12–13, 27). Paul does not recruit students; he founds missionary churches. He does not teach a philosophy or way of life that anyone at any time and in any place can adopt in self-realization. His gospel aims at sinners threatened by imminent judgment in order to incorporate them into the elected church, which the coming Lord will save as a whole (1 Thess. 4:17; 5:10).

The Spirit is given personally to every Christian, yet there is also the fellowship or sharing of the Spirit (Phil. 2:1). Each person must have his or her own faith, yet Paul also knows a sharing of faith (Philemon 6). We are called into the fellowship of the Son (1 Cor. 1:9), and this is realized in God's church concretely above all in the worship service (1 Corinthians 12–14) and in the church celebrating the Lord's Supper (1 Cor. 10:16), but also in all the church's other expressions of life. Christ lives in the individual believer, and the Christian together with all Christians lives in Christ, just as also the Spirit dwells in the individual and the individual in the Spirit. The Christian has a new identity, and he or she is one with all believers in Christ (cf. 14.5 above). The gifts allocated by the Spirit are individually different, but all together they serve the upbuilding of the church (Romans 12; 1 Corinthians 12). Paul looks forward to the mutual encouragement of faith when he reaches Rome (Rom. 1:12). Christian love is first directed to the church and its well-being (Gal. 6:10). The hope of Christians contains the redemption of the "children of God" (Rom. 8:16–17). It is the aim of Paul's upbuilding of the church that all Christians may praise God together (Rom. 15:6).

If the missionary message of Jesus Christ is thus aimed at the starting and promotion of churches, then the question is how does the apostle speak of this church. Nowhere does Paul develop his understanding of the church as an independent theme. Rather, he writes to the churches in such a way that he presupposes for them both the experience and the formation of fellowship under the working of gospel and Spirit, just as he assumes as a rule that between him and the churches there is a basic agreement in the concept of what a church is. He does not have to talk about this anew. It is not easy for us now to determine the details of this consensus, although even such a short letter as 1 Thessalonians gives crucial information about it (cf. 6.2 above). The Pauline position becomes somewhat more directly visible when he must polemically set straight a theological understanding that also touches on the concept of the church. This occurs especially in the Corinthian correspondence (cf. 8.2 above), in which Paul must employ his understanding of the church to confront enthusiasm because of its centrifugal forces. He points out the unity in the multiplicity of spiritual gifts and develops this by means of the "body of Christ" idea (1 Corinthians 12). This then emerges again later (Romans 12), without a current stimulus, as a theme that describes the nature and inner life of the church especially well. We find polemical encounter again in Galatians (cf. 11.4 above), where—faced with the Judaistic front with its genealogical concept of salvation—the apostle works out his special concept of the church, based on Spirit and faith, as the inheritance of Abraham.

It is clear, in any case, that in his understanding of the church the apostle begins with the individual congregation, that is, with its life and worship. Where gospel and Spirit are at work, where worship is held and brotherly love occurs, there is the church. Paul knows no semantic distinction between the local church and the universal church. Whether he talks of the saints or believers, of the church or the body of Christ, or of the descendants of Abraham, he always means concretely the local church addressed in the letter and often at the same time the church as a whole. Nowhere does he let the local church be a particular representation of the universal church. Nor does he regard the totality of all churches as the sum of all local congregations. This is not merely the accidental result of the fact that Paul addresses letters as needed to individual churches but is rather the consequence of his starting point in proclaiming the gospel: Where God calls through the gospel and the proclaimed Christ is accepted in faith, there is the church. Thus the universal element that is concretized in each congregation is not the church but the Christ at work in the gospel. Conversely, therefore, several local congregations cannot unite as a church. Naturally local churches do not each stand in isolation, but the overarching whole to which each local congregation owes its existence is the same gospel and the same Spirit who is at work in Jerusalem, Galatia, Corinth, and Rome. And where these are present, everything is there that constitutes the church. So Paul cannot distinguish terminologically between local congregation and universal church, as we are accustomed in our language tradition. Every congregation for itself and all congregations together are the church because—and to the extent that—the means of salvation are present in them.

Thus baptism is not reception into a local congregation. After their expulsion from Rome, Priscilla and Aquila are not baptized again in Corinth (cf. ch. 2 above). Baptism places one under Christ and "in

Christ"; it creates a unity of all Christians with Christ (Gal. 3:26–28). Thus from the beginning it is transcongregational. It is taken for granted that one who becomes a Christian in Asia can participate in church life in Rome, including the Lord's Supper (cf. Rom. 16:5). *In Christ* or *in the Lord* is not the designation of a local church but the determination of all Christians in general. Naturally, in all churches there are also common confessional traditions (cf., e.g., 1 Cor. 11:23ff.; 15:1ff.), hymns (cf. Phil. 2:6ff.), worship elements (cf. 9.4 above), and typical admonitions to change (e.g., 1 Thess. 4:1ff.; Romans 12–13). The ecclesiastical "we" that Paul uses—for example, in 1 Thess. 4:13ff.; Gal. 3:23ff.; Romans 6–8—refers to the particular church being addressed and yet is also valid for Christians in general. The hope of living together forever with the Lord (1 Thess. 5:10) and being changed into his glory (Phil. 3:21) is the bond uniting all Christians. Though now spread as individual churches over the whole Hellenistic-Roman world, together they are the elect for the day of the Lord. Thus each congregation is fully and completely the church and at the same time stands "in Christ" in the fellowship of all other congregations, who are in the same way also the church.

It has often been certified that the apostle has little interest in the structures of the local churches and of Christendom as a whole. There is justification for this verdict if we think concretely of fixed local offices (head of the church, say, as in a synagogue), of a Christian canon of scriptures beyond the Old Testament, of relatively fixed orders of worship, or of institutional entities of a transcongregational kind, such as synods and regional bishops. Yet if one tried to derive from this the thesis that these churches are only charismatically determined and that institutional structures did not come until later, one would form a false antithesis between Spirit and institution. For even if Paul does not think institutionally in the described sense, he still gave his churches a certain kind of structure and in the process also considered the transcongregational level.

In any case, Paul gives much importance to unity and to the consensus of concrete churches (cf. Rom. 15:6; 1 Cor. 3:1–5; 11:16; 14:1ff.). Also, in case of conflict there is a solemn process of exclusion from the church (1 Cor. 5:1ff.). For the life of the church he had in any case three emphases. First, he formed them organizationally as house churches (cf. 9.1 above). In this way an institutional framework was set up, which was already available in the ancient household and did not have to be newly organized. Beyond this Paul especially emphasized the common worship service as the assembly of house churches (cf. 9.4 above). Finally, he also strongly stressed communication with each other for the devotion and integration of all (cf. 9.2 above). For the solution of certain conflicts he used the means of the full assembly of the whole church (cf. 9.4 above).

Also, on the universal church level Paul was organizationally active. Here he even charted new territory with his formation of an infrastructure (cf. 7.4 above). Even when he no longer attempts supraregional consensus building as he once did between Antioch and Jerusalem (cf. 5.2 above), we cannot say that he practically lets his churches live as isolated units and presents the unity of Christendom only theoretically. Hence it is not meaningful to observe in Paul an antithesis of charismatic understanding of the Spirit and institutional structure. We should see, however, that the later institutional means of the church at large mostly became different from those which Paul initiated.

Naturally the apostle does not think in terms of the continuity of the church over the generations, as is attributed to him in Acts 20:17ff. He would still like, nonetheless, for his churches to hold to the gospel until the final arrival of the Lord and to be preserved in it, for they are also Paul's glory before God (cf. 1.1 above). This suggests the theology that decisively shaped the Pauline understanding of the church. The church does not move through the ages and generations; it comes into being through God's election at the end of all time and history. The church is the eschatological church in the strict sense that it lives for the imminent day of its Lord, in order to be gathered by Christ its Savior into his fellowship forever. Thus the church is not the people of God on earth in an ongoing history. It should not shape the world in the political and cultural sense. Rather, it knows that, according to Paul, it is already now torn out of this present evil age (Gal. 1:4) and given God's Spirit for the end time (Rom. 8:23). It lives in relative distance from the world (1 Cor. 7:29–31), because the end of the world is near (cf. 9.3 above). It looks forward to the Lord's coming in a short time (Phil. 4:4–5).

With this we have examined the theological environment in which Paul's understanding of the church becomes visible for the first time in a way that is fundamental to the whole Pauline corpus. It makes good sense to regard this eschatological election theology—as it was already developed in detail in 1 Thessalonians (cf. 6.2 above)—as the foundation of Paul's understanding of the church and therefore to make it the basis for discussion. Since this language and theology are found again in the theology of the cross and the message of justification, the material to which we can address our attention is sufficiently comprehensive. Considering the language and the content of Paul's understanding of the church on the basis of this theological approach is at any rate more promising than individually investigating Paul's typical designations for the church.

If we follow the recommended path, we will not—as most often occurs—begin with an examination of the term "church" (*ekklēsia*). For this expression is also used in pre-Pauline and extra-Pauline writing and is certainly not the sign of a particular theological concept (see below). Much more characteristic of the oldest Pauline theology is the language of election, which shapes the understanding of the church. It is of Old Testament-Jewish origin and is known to the Antiochene church as well as to Paul from the Hellenistic synagogue. Yet Antioch and Paul do not use it to assert soteriological continuity with the people of Abraham. For, first of all, the theology of election thrives on the very opposition to the synagogue and in competition with it. Second, this theology expresses the new eschatological election of all nations which receives its measure from the eschatological gospel and is not oriented toward God's loyalty to Israel (cf. 6.2 above). Above all, however, the special soteriological election terms of Israel and Judaism, such as "Abraham's offspring" and "people of Israel," are not used here, even in a figurative sense. They are set aside, and only those linguistic phenomena are employed which can be quite general signs of religious language for God's interaction with human beings. These include "God's elect" (Rom. 8:33; cf. Rom. 16:13; from the Pauline school: Col. 3:12; also 1 Peter 1:1), the "called" (Rom. 1:6–7; 1 Cor. 1:2, 24), "saints" (Rom. 1:7; 8:27; 16:15; 1 Cor. 1:2; 6:2; Phil. 1:1), and "God's beloved" (Rom. 1:7; 1 Thess. 1:4). In context these expressions can also be found bunched together and joined in typical ways. They characterize the status of the eschatological church, as they also did in part, for example, in Jewish literature (apocalyptic and wisdom literature, Qumran). They are an expression of the new self-understanding of the Christian churches and carry this message: Even now we Christians are called by the gospel to be the eschatological church, which will soon live together with its Lord forever. They also have this in common: They are often used as a form of address; therefore they are frequently found in the openings of letters.

We must also see that Paul does not speak only in this way. For one thing, he expands this series at least by one expression: the "believers" (Rom. 4:11; 10:4, 11; 1 Thess. 1:7; 2:10, 13). In this form this is a Christian neologism (cf. 14.5 above). Second, texts such as 1 Cor. 1:30; 6:11; 1 Thess. 4:3, 7–8 show that the understanding of the election terminology is also shaped by the early Christian concept of baptism, as it, with its ontological statements, was already recognized in 1 Thessalonians as a component of election theology (cf. 1 Thess. 5:4–10 and 6.2 above). Thus we must see how even the early Antiochene theology (cf. 5.5 above) in an emphatically Christian way reshaped the common election language borrowed from Judaism and filled it with its own life. Third, it is apparent that through the qualification "in the Lord" (Rom. 16:2; 1 Cor. 11:11; 1 Thess. 3:8; 4:1; 5:12) and "in Christ" (Rom. 8:1; 1 Thess. 1:1; 2:14; cf. 14.4 above) the apostle brings to light the christological mediation of the eschatological election. In most places "in Christ" becomes a mark of the church indicating its complete determination by Christ (cf. 14.5 above). Moreover, both expressions are neologisms, so that it again becomes clear how Christian election language not only reshapes traditional material but also contains new linguistic creations.

The ecclesiastical application of the formulaic usage of "in Christ" asserts that in this "domain" the Spirit of Christ is at work (Rom. 8:1–2, 9–10). So it is only natural that ecclesiastical reality can likewise be brought to bear through Spirit statements and that an analogous formation such as "in the Spirit" is indeed found (1 Cor. 12:3, 9; 2 Cor. 6:6; 1 Thess. 1:5). It is significant, further, that in the context of the transference of cultic terms to the church, the latter is regarded as the temple of the Holy Spirit (1 Cor. 3:16–17; cf. 2 Cor. 6:16; Eph. 2:21). The church's possession of the Spirit is the sign of its election. The Essenes already understood themselves as God's temple on the basis of their special consciousness of election (cf. 1QS 8:4–8; 9:3–6). Moreover, it is an appealing hypothesis that the metaphors of the church as God's building and as planting (cf. 1 Cor. 3:5ff.) had, in the tradition, already grown together for Paul with the temple metaphor. In any case, they already occur in Qumran in such a context (cf. 1QS 5:5–6; 8:5–11; 11:7–8).

Finally, within the context of election theology we also find the talk of God as Father of the church(es) (1 Thess. 1:1, 3; 3:11, 13; 1 Cor. 1:3; 2 Cor. 1:2; etc.) and of the church members as brothers (and sisters) to each other (cf. 1 Thess. 1:4; 5:26–27; 1 Cor. 16:11–12, 20; etc.). The terms of kinship are also interpreted in a special way in Gal. 4:6; Rom. 8:14–15.

In the linguistic manifestation of the understanding of the church within election theology statements we also find the term "church" (ekklēsia), not only for the Pauline churches (1 Thess. 1:1) but also, quite naturally, for the churches in Judea (1 Thess. 2:14; Gal. 1:22) and Damascus (1 Cor. 15:9; Gal. 1:13; Phil. 3:6). Paul can speak of the churches of the Gentiles (Rom. 16:4), of all the churches together (1 Cor. 7:17), and by this he means all his church foundings (cf. 1 Cor. 11:16); he can speak of the churches of a province (1 Cor. 16:1, 19; 2 Cor. 8:1) and of local churches (1 Cor. 1:2; 2 Cor. 1:1; 1 Thess. 1:1). He can talk of the church and the church of God without distinction (compare 1 Cor. 15:9 with Phil. 3:6; 1 Cor. 11:18 with 11:22; 1 Thess. 2:14 with Gal. 1:22). It is typical of the apostle to use the singular form to designate the local church and especially its gathering for worship (cf., e.g., 1 Cor. 14:12; 14:19, 23, 28). With the plural he includes several churches; the singular, in any case, very seldom serves to indicate the general church (cf., e.g., 1 Cor. 12:28).

Nowhere is the use of the word determined by a specific conceptual context. Nowhere can we make out an oldest usage that stands at the beginning of the development. This is also true particularly of the combination "church of God" (1 Cor. 1:2; 10:32; 15:9; 2 Cor. 1:1; Gal. 1:13). The attempt to relate it to Deut. 23:2ff. and the eschatological interpretation in 1QSa 2:4; 1QM 4:10 (eschatological actions of God) is difficult to substantiate, least of all by connecting it with the assumption that this had first been the self-designation of the original church in Jerusalem. For the Old Testament-Jewish witnesses know only the singular "church of God," whereas Paul also uses the plural "churches of God" and can talk without distinction of "church(es)" and "church(es) of God." Moreover, there is no demonstrable Pauline witness to a self-designation of the original church.

This perhaps suggests as a hypothesis that early Christendom took the term from everyday language as a common political word for all kinds of gatherings (cf. in the New Testament Acts 19:32, 39–40). At least this would best explain why theologically the term has no specific conceptual context. This is supported also by the verb meaning "come together, assemble," borrowed from social language (cf. 9.4 above), which in 1 Cor. 11:18; 14:23 is linked with the term "church." We may also recall that the talk, for example, of (heavenly) "citizenship" (Phil. 3:20) likewise comes from general political language. So it would not be unusual if the word "church" was also taken from the same context. In this case, then, the general use would be the starting point of Christian usage, and the combination "church(es) of God" a subsequent Christianization.

An analogous phenomenon is also found in the term "body of Christ." This expression for the church was probably first introduced by Paul himself into early Christian language as a description of his understanding of the church. When the inner harmony of the Corinthian church (cf. 8.2 above) is jeopardized by the spontaneous egoistic actions of individual bearers of the Spirit and by their valuations and devaluations of spiritual gifts (1 Corinthians 12), the apostle employs a linguistic means that was already frequently used before him in Hellenistic-Roman culture (not least of all in the middle Stoic period) in order to explain and substantiate the unity of a fellowship in all diversity—namely, the idea of the fellowship as a multifarious organism in which all individual members and organs must depend on each other if the organism is to have a healthy life. Especially with disturbances in community life, this means was often employed to convey the belief that the return to the old undisturbed order was best for all individuals and hence also for the welfare of the community. Agrippa M. Lanatus, for example, exhorted the plebeians not to break off fellowship with the city of Rome because, as in a human organism, all members need each other (Livy, *Ab urbe condita* 2.32–33). Plato also compares the state with an organism and, as in 1 Cor. 12:26, emphasizes the suffering and rejoicing of the members together (Plato, *Republic* 462C–D). Seneca can see the state as the body of the emperor, who is the soul of the body (Seneca, *De clementia* 1.5.1). This easily expandable evidence attests that in Paul's time such metaphorical usage was common, especially for political entities.

In 1 Corinthians 12 and Romans 12, Paul follows this tradition and assumes that the Corinthians and the Romans are culturally familiar with such argumentation. He was probably the first to transfer this idea to a religious communion. Yet he is breaking new ground in yet another way. In Paul the figurative and comparative use of the body idea as unity in diversity is still largely dominant. Yet because his theology is determined by the new christological being of the eschatological church, for him the comparison becomes a statement on the nature of the church. Now the church *is* the "body of Christ" (1 Cor. 12:27), not just comparable to a body. Through the one Spirit who expresses himself in the diversity of spiritual gifts, all are baptized into one body, which is Christ (1 Cor. 12:12–13). Romans 12:5 makes clear how this conception originated from the formula *in Christ:* "So we, though many, are one body in Christ." An old baptismal tradition like that in Gal. 3:26–28 (cf. 5.5 above) shows how this Pauline transformation of the comparative metaphor into a statement of nature is only an extension of long familiar positions. For those baptized not only receive the Spirit, whose gifts will now also work in and through them, but also become members of the Spirit-filled church. The Spirit is Christ's nearness ("put on Christ") for the individual, just as all are a spiritual unity "in Christ" ("you are all one in Christ Jesus"—Gal. 3:28). In general, as we saw (cf. 6.2 and 14.5 above), Paul describes the spiritual change of the believer as a change in nature and correspondingly the church as a reality shaped by Christ. This very understanding of the church now also changes the traditional body metaphor: The church is the body of Christ because the Spirit whose diversity can be experienced in the church is the one Spirit of Christ, which pervades and changes the church.

Beyond this new interpretation of the traditional image, which brings the apostle's christological understanding of the church to bear in an impressive way, we must see that Paul does not develop the concept of diversity in unity in a way that allows the maintenance of the Corinthian scale of values in the estimation of spiritual gifts. Paul does not follow, for example, the path of Lanatus, who wants to place the plebeians back under the domination of the Roman nobility and thus use the image of the organism to stabilize domination. Rather, for Paul the Spirit's expressions are not all meaningful in the same way; indeed, the ecstatic spiritual phenomena so highly prized in Corinth are questioned as to whether they are at all useful to the fellowship (1 Corinthians 14). In Romans 12, Paul takes this line of thought consistently farther by seeing the Spirit at work especially in everyday community duties.

In Rom. 12:1–13, furthermore, Paul succeeds in using the body of Christ idea for the description of the nature of the church and its life in such a way that he distinguishes the latter from public community formation, as it is then described with other options in Rom. 13:1–7. Even if today we might disdain this concept of the authoritarian state as undemocratic, Romans 12–13 remains the first early Christian witness to the effort to comprehend church and state through conceptionally different descriptions.

As already indicated, in the Galatian quarrel Paul again has to clarify his understanding of the church in regard to the standpoint of the Judaizers (cf. 10.2 and 11.4 above). In connection with the warning against the Judaizers we also find at the beginning of Philippians B (cf. 12.4 above) a statement relevant to the church that belongs here. Naturally, the problem of Israel in Romans 9–11 also leads to corresponding statements (cf. 15.2 below). Galatians makes it clear that the apostle sees himself faced with opponents who emphasize the continuity of the people of twelve tribes, impressively promoted through the demand of circumcision, and who try to understand Christianity within this people of salvation as the true Israel. Against this, Paul argues that being a child of Abraham can only be understood as something that is based on faith in Christ and on the promise fulfilled in Christ and that in the light of this the genealogical continuity of the people of Israel, as well as circumcision and the law, must be set aside for the sake of the gospel of Christ. In the process Paul practically ignores the history of salvation from Abraham to Christ and through statements about the Spirit and freedom emphasizes the special quality of Christianity in distinction to Israel. Paul thereby takes nothing away from his understanding of the church, as it can be perceived in 1 Thessalonians and the Corinthian letters. On the contrary, from it he deduces the relationship to the people of God.

Only once does the apostle relate the idea of God's people to the church, by quoting Hos. 1:10; 2:23 (= Rom. 9:25–26), just as he speaks only once of the church as the "Israel of God" (Gal. 6:16). In both places it is a question of a profound break with the history of salvation (Rom. 9:25: God calls a nonpeople to be his people; Gal. 6:15–16: circumcision counts for nothing in the new creation). Similarly, in Philippians 3 the apostle can count bodily circumcision among the nonvalues and is thus free to apply the term "circumcision" in a figurative sense to the church (Phil. 3:3). Otherwise the apostle also knows the key terms "Abraham's offspring" (Gal. 3:19, 29; Rom. 4:13–18; 9:7–8), "sons of Abraham" (Gal. 3:7; 4:22, 30), and "heirs (of Abraham)" (Gal. 3:29). They are used throughout in such a way that Abraham is placed with the church, while Israel is separated from the patriarch (most crassly in Gal. 4:25, 30).

Thus we will ascertain that the real trend in Paul's development of his understanding of the church is marked by the general language of election and by terms (like "church" and "body") not previously occupied by soteriology or religion. On the other hand, the soteriological continuity of the people of God is not prominent but rather is used with clear reserve.

14.7 The Obligation of Faith as Love

Being called by gospel and Spirit to the eschatological church does not happen unless the salvific will of God evident in this call is at the same time a will that demands a certain life-style of those who are called (Rom. 12:2; 1 Thess. 4:3; 5:18). The gospel changes sinners so that henceforth they no longer sin (1 Thess. 4:3, 7–9; Romans 6). In structure this approach corresponds entirely to Jewish thought: the calling of Israel to be the divine covenantal partner is coupled with the will of God in the covenantal law. Yet Paul's understanding of the law (cf. 11.4, 14.3, and also 12.3 above on the figurative use of the law) does not allow him to link calling and law in a similar way. Therefore Paul must expose himself to criticism that reproaches him for making Christ an agent of sin (Gal. 2:17) and with his doctrine of grace allowing the elect to continue in sin (Rom. 6:1, 15). On the other hand, in Greco-Roman antiquity a close relationship of religion and ethics like that propagated by Paul was foreign. This cultural connection of the Corinthians, for example, causes problems of a completely different kind for Paul (cf. 8.2 above). Thus he must substantiate the close connection between calling and life-style and describe its content so as to be able to prevail against both positions.

Paul does not set about this task in such a way that instead of interpreting the law he writes an ethic in the spirit of the Greek philosophical tradition. His aim is not the systematic penetration of an ethical problem but the concrete shaping of the church's living world. This world had to be discussed for some topical reason (e.g., in 1 Corinthians) or be made more generally relevant to the church through guidance toward "normal practice" (cf. 1 Thess. 4:1–12; 5:12–24; 1 Corinthians 13; Gal. 5:13–6:10; Romans 12–13). In the latter case Paul had in a conditional way a model in a certain synagogal form of instruction (cf., e.g., Sirach; *Testaments of the Twelve Patriarchs*), which was also employed in early Christianity in addition to Paul. Yet dependence on such admonition (paraenesis) did not occur blindly, for the new understanding of salvation naturally required a new effort toward a foundation of the ethic as well as weighing and selection in regard to the norms. Also, the particular contents of the ethics represented by Paul are, of course, deeply rooted in the structure of norms of his time, but that does not mean that the apostle approaches the norms uncritically and indiscriminately. What is special about him, rather, is that from his understanding of faith he describes in his own way the obligation of a Christian conduct of life in terms of form and content within the paraenetic tradition.

Turning to the Pauline approach to admonition, we find that its peculiarity lies in the fact that he advocates a characteristic relationship between the new salvific state and the conformity of believers to ethical norms; the state of salvation always determines the Christian's way of life, and at the same time what is granted to believers is demanded of them as the conduct of life to be achieved. Thus Gal. 5:25 says: "If we live by the Spirit, let us also walk by the Spirit." The baptized are sanctified (1 Cor. 1:30; 6:11), and they are urged to achieve their sanctification (1 Thess. 4:3, 7; Rom. 6:19–22). According to Gal. 3:27, Christians have "put on" Christ; according to Rom. 13:14, they are told to do so with an imperative. The Christian is clothed with faith, love, and hope (1 Thess. 5:8), yet at the same time is supposed to put on the armor of light (Rom. 13:12). Christians are not slaves but free people (Gal. 4:1–5); now they should live in freedom (5:13). They have died with Christ (Rom. 6:5; Gal. 6:14); now they should present themselves as a living sacrifice to God (Rom. 12:1). They have died to sin (Rom. 6:2); now they are not to let it reign over them (6:12). Through the gospel, Christians are called to ultimate salvation (1 Thess. 5:9; cf. 1:10); now they are to work out their salvation "with fear and trembling" (Phil. 2:12).

Today we have rightly abandoned the idea of regarding the assertion of salvation as the enthusiastic anticipation of the consummation and regarding admonition as the return to everyday life—that is, the salvific indicative as the ideal and the imperative as the correction of the actual. Also, it does not seem appropriate—above all, in view of the Spirit statements, as they, along with baptismal statements and justification language, characterize the saved state in our examples—to place the saved state only in God's judgment and place admonition only in the realm of experience. Furthermore, a refined formulation for the determination of relationship such as, "Become who you are," still sounds too covertly idealistic (for the Christians should live—not become—what they already are) and too individualistic (for baptism incorporates one into the "body of Christ"). This is avoided by a thesis formulated this way: "Remain with the Lord given to you and in his glory." The glory symbolism, however, falls far short of covering all of Paul's statements on salvation, and the saved state is not only the gift of a new Lord but also the transformation of the person. Finally, one cannot in any case connect the first justification through the gift of salvation with a further one still to be completed, which is then referred to by paraenesis. This does not agree with the way Paul talks of the last judgment of Christians (cf. 14.8 below). Yet this statement is correctly related to the eschatological dimension of election to salvation, in which the salvific will of the electing God is not to be separated from the will of God according to which human beings are to live: sanctified by the Spirit and thereby destined for ultimate salvation, the individual is supposed to fulfill that sanctification (cf. 6.2 above). Thus we can perhaps describe the relationship of the reception of salvation to the obligation of the recipient in this way: Fulfill the eschatological reality of Christ, which you have become through gospel, baptism, and Spirit, by proving yourself as a member of the body of Christ, that is, by recognizing the inner obligation of the new life, helping to shape it in the eschatological church, and not falling back into the old nature of the dying world.

This understanding of the obligatory conduct of life has the great advantage that the apostle bases the Christian ethic on the understanding of Christianity itself. He thereby demonstrates that there is no need for the law, because the Spirit urges one to good behavior from within (1 Thess. 4:8–9). At the same time, he shows the former Gentiles how the new faith implies a new conduct of life and that religion and ethics are thus closely connected.

Despite the predominance of the indicative-imperative relationship, we also find in the apostle, of course, a multitude of substantiations and motivations for the Christian shaping of life. Just this fact is in itself a sign that the apostle does not want to force obedience but seeks right behavior that comes from conviction. Almost all motifs seem to be traditional, because Paul desires the consensus of the whole church (cf. 1 Cor. 7:17; 11:16). Strikingly, often he uses the connection of behavior to the imminent end (Rom. 13:11–14 as the close of Romans 12–13; cf. also 1 Cor. 6:13; 7:29–31; Phil. 2:16). In doing this, Paul so clearly counts everything in existence as the dying world that the Christian is supposed to renounce foods for the rest of his or her life for love of a brother (Rom. 14:13–17) and no longer initiate change in the social order (1 Cor. 7:18–24). The reference to the last judgment, as it is borne by the majestic judicial right of God, forbids judging among one another (Rom. 12:19–20; 14:10–11; 1 Cor. 4:1–5; 5:12–13). Paul can emphasize, further, that Christian behavior always occurs before God and therefore must occur unhypocritically and willingly (Rom. 12:9; 13:5; Gal. 5:13; 1 Thess. 2:4; 4:1, 7–8). Thus it is never only a matter of the formal fulfillment of duty but of the integrity of deed and person. For this very reason Christian behavior is a question of human responsibility before God, which is realized through total and willing dedication to God's will.

We come into a quite different realm when we consider the statements in which Paul relates the inner meaning of the destiny of Jesus Christ and his own apostolic behavior as "model" in the churches of his readers. We have already treated this in detail (cf. 12.3 above). We saw how Paul can thereby guide concrete, person-related decisions and actions and especially impressively explain the anchoring of actions in received salvation.

Another group of motifs and substantiations involves the important and pressing task of the integration of the young churches (cf. 9.2 above). Again and again, for example, the behavior of the Christian toward a fellow Christian receives its measure and boundary, so that through consideration and self-limitation the eschatological church is built up (Romans 14; 1 Corinthians 8–10; 11:20ff.; ch. 13; Gal. 6:2; etc.). The peaceful upbuilding of the church is an often stressed high goal in the formation of community life (cf., e.g., Rom. 14:19; 1 Cor. 8:1; 10:23–24).

These substantiation contexts all involve the question of the general validity and obligation of the admonition. At this point it is clear that for Paul and his churches obligation first becomes evident within the community in Spirit-guided judgment and persuasion (1 Thess. 4:8–9). Here the Spirit is not seen individualistically but in the overall determination of the church. Therefore the church is addressed in its ability to judge, and then individuals as members of the church. Since this Spirit is the Spirit of Christ, Christ himself is the ultimate foundation in the realm of norms (Romans 15; Philippians 2). Yet with all of Paul's preference for an intrachurch orientation for ethics, he also considers the level of humanity in general. It is crucial for Paul not to overlook the general human context of Christian ethics. For him, there is no exclusively Christian ethics but rather an ethics oriented toward Christ, which at the same time is open to generalization. Christians have the general good in mind (Rom. 12:2; Phil. 4:8), and fundamentally Christian behavior must be something non-Christians can agree with (Rom. 13:3; 14:18; 1 Thess. 4:12).

For Paul, therefore, Christians cannot simply set their ethical standards prophetically; rather, the Spirit leads—with all the preeminence he possesses in the church—to patient argumentation, that is, to generally understandable substantiation and criticism of the practice. Basically, indeed, every person asks the question of the moral good; everybody knows about the qualification of morally good or evil actions (Rom. 1:18–2:29). So for Paul even non-Christian state authorities in the Roman Empire fulfill a duty that has them act completely in God's spirit as agents for the general welfare under the requirement of the good (Rom. 13:1ff.). A Christian can learn from an ethical discussion among pagans (Phil. 4:8), even if he or she lives in the consciousness of taking the conduct of life more seriously than non-Christians do (Phil. 2:14–15). Therefore the apostle does not simply discard the norms of the Torah, either. Through Christ, of course, the commandment of love is linked directly with Christian ethics (Romans 15; Philippians 2), yet Paul notes quite naturally that it is already to be read as divine will in the Old Testament (Rom. 13:8–10; Gal. 5:14). The Old Testament as such, to be sure, is nowhere the holy authority for ethical action anymore, but, removed from its self-evident obligatory character as life-shaping norm (Galatians 3; cf. 11.4 and 14.3 above), it can be used in the search for the generally human (in the sense of Phil. 4:8). And Paul hardly proceeds essentially differently with the Jesus tradition. Jesus is not a lawgiver who, for example, teaches the commandment of love. Its obligation rests on the overall meaning of God's salvific devotion in Christ, as we already saw, and not on Christ as teacher. So it is no longer amazing when long parts of the paraenesis refer nowhere to the Jesus tradition directly (cf., e.g., 1 Thess. 4:1ff.; Gal. 5:13–6:10; Romans 12–13). On the other hand, Paul can also apply Jesus' authority directly to the normatization of behavior (cf. 1 Cor. 7:10; 5.6 above).

Our characterization of Paul's ethics would be incomplete without pointing out a basic structural decision that thoroughly determines the apostolic admonition. According to Paul, the shaping of life is accomplished especially as brotherly community life, as this is influenced by the imminent expectation (cf. 9.3, above; 14.8 below) and by the contrast with non-Christians. Thus the basic ethical question might read: Until the imminent end of all things, how should the eschatological church prove itself in love, promote its own integration, not hinder missions through offensive behavior, and not fall back into worldly behavior? Thus was concrete life shaped in the house church (cf. 9.1 and 9.2 above). Therefore orderings, functions, and duties in this realm were prominent themes of the Pauline admonition, that is, the ordering of husband and wife, the relationship of master and slave, the occupational activity of Christians, the acceptance of guests in the household, and naturally the regulations for gatherings of worship. Outside the field of vision lie the responsibility for the shaping of politics, economics, and social institutions in general, general questions of human rights, schools and educational institutions, general administration of justice, questions of power structures, war and peace, and so on. Quite apart from the fact that some of these issues were not even current in the general consciousness of the time, Paul and his churches, like Christians of the first generations in general, look beyond the community only in that they want to carry on missions, live inoffensively (1 Thess. 4:11–12; Rom. 13:1ff.), not respond to aggression (Rom. 12:14ff.), and "do good" (Gal. 6:10). Thus again and again the Pauline admonition regulates, above all, the internal relations of the churches and only in a limited and subsequent way the external relations.

Another structural arrangement is also relatively unambiguous. In the relationship between individual and social ethics, the stress is predominantly on the second area. The statements in the realm of individual ethics can be quickly listed: Christians should achieve the inner renewal of their beings (Rom. 12:1–2), not let up in the struggle between Spirit and flesh (Rom. 8:1–11; Gal. 5:16ff.), and in general not make themselves available to sin (Romans 6). Like Paul himself, Christians should regard their conduct of life as, say, a "competition" in which they demand everything of themselves in order to reach the goal (1 Cor. 9:24–27; Philippians B). On close examination, we can paint the picture with only a few colors, but we reach the conclusion that none of these statements is made in order, for example, to achieve personal integrity or inner harmony, to promote the process of personal maturation, to achieve inner peace, and so forth, but for the sake of one's capability for fellowship in the spirit of the commandment to love and for the sake of harmony in the church. Throughout the immediate context of such statements are concretizations that have as their object the social relationship. The general admonition to keep a basic inner attitude, as given, for example, in Rom. 12:1–2, is a summary of the individual admonitions in 12:3ff., which have community life as their content. The motif of the struggle between Spirit and flesh in Galatians 5 is embedded in statements that have as their goal the formation of community.

Finally, the realm of social norms also exhibits a peculiarity that should be noted. Here Paul is not actually thinking structurally and institutionally but rather formulates the admonition in the spirit of personal relationships among individual members of the church. That this could also change the structures of life within the household is an effect that Paul does not prevent, although he also does not make it an independent theme. Thus he structures the Christian community by stressing the mutual dependence of the members and their basic equality "in Christ" (Gal. 3:26–28; 1 Corinthians 12) and in particular directs attention to weak brothers and sisters (1 Corinthians 8; 12:22ff.; Gal. 6:1–2; etc.). In other words, he turns the love commandment into the norm for personal relationships.

With that last sentence we have already addressed the commandment on which Paul preeminently sets his sights. For if we ask under what principle he orders ethics, we can, of course, also recall the key word "sanctification" (also "holiness" in RSV; cf. 1 Thess. 4:3–4, 7; 1 Cor. 1:30; Rom. 6:19, 22), yet the love commandment without doubt plays a much more prominent role. It appears in the triad faith-love-hope (cf. 6.2 and 12.3 above), is the activity compelled by the Spirit of Christ (cf. 1 Thess. 4:8–9; Gal. 5:22), is established as the behavior for the church on the basis of the fundamental meaning of the central figure of Christ (cf. 12.3 above), and often appears as the common denominator or summary of the Pauline admonition (cf. Rom. 13:8–10; 1 Corinthians 13; Gal. 5:14–15; Philippians 2; 1 Thess. 4:9). For Paul, it also proves its dominant position in current difficulties, when he tries to give meaning to freedom and the knowledge of faith, so that community will be promoted and weakness considered (Romans 14–15; 1 Corinthians 8–10). It should also not be overlooked that love, for Paul, like the structure of his ethics in general, is congregation-centered and thus occurs as brotherly love; nonetheless it is not limited to this (Rom. 12:14ff.; cf. also the general statements in 1 Cor. 13:4ff.). In any case, it always presses toward concretization and testing and does not persist in vague sentiment. Love is usually the inconvenient way that has the general welfare in view. Its frame of reference is not a person's own needs and interests (not even the religious ones; cf. 1 Cor. 13:1–3!) but sacrifice based on the prior sacrifice of Christ. It insists that people are themselves precisely in love, because this is what God wants them to be. Not faith and hope, but love is the greatest (1 Cor. 13:13), because relationships of love will also determine the final consummation, and without love simply nothing earthly has value, either (1 Cor. 13:1ff.).

The preeminence of love does not lead to love being the fundamental principle from which all other norms are derived, and yet every endeavor must be shaped by love (1 Corinthians 13). Since it is the nature of love to be patient and bear all things (13:4–7), it is also in the individual case the way that leads away from insisting on the truly required norm and toward compromise and the open solution that tolerates diversity (1 Cor. 6:1ff.; 7:1ff.; chs. 8–10). The permitted breadth of variation itself is then in turn limited by love (1 Cor. 8:11; Rom. 14:13–19). Finally, the preeminence of love also comes to bear in the weighing and collecting of Christian norms; so it is no wonder that the Roman virtues of bravery, manliness, equanimity in all of life's situations, self-control even in pain, and many other ideals are completely missing or decidedly deemphasized. This cannot be any other way when love as the guiding concept leads a series of norms (Gal. 5:22–23) that devalues harsh and aggressive ways of behaving (Rom. 12:9–21) and shapes community life through mutual interaction (Phil. 2:1ff.).

In particular, love was required where within Christian homes the churches had to ease concrete tensions, in order to do justice to the high demand of a fraternal eschatological church tailored for consensus and commonality (cf. 9.2 above). There were the great differences in heritage from the Jewish and Gentile worlds. Unity "in Christ" could thrive only if both sides were prepared for crucial sacrifices. The Jews had to give up the law as norm; the Gentiles, their gods and the culture determined by them. There were the differences between free and slave, which in antiquity were regarded as the (almost) natural order. Thus even the Christian Philemon kept (Gentile) slaves without any problem. Elsewhere slaves are attested in Christian and Gentile houses, when they belong to the church (1 Cor. 7:21–22; 12:13–14; Gal. 3:28). In general, the slavery question was not a current problem in the Pauline churches. Yet slaves are naturally and as a matter of course fully integrated into the church. No one denies them baptism, the Spirit, or participation in the Lord's Supper. How, then, should a Christian slaveholder treat his slaves in everyday life?

According to the Letter to Philemon he does not have to grant civil freedom to them, yet within current law he should at least cultivate a new, brotherly relationship with them. Also, for example, strict monogamy naturally prohibits the sexual misuse of slaves (cf. 1 Thess. 4:3–4). In the special case of Onesimus, Paul expects from Philemon a voluntary but benevolent compliance with the apostle's wishes. Thus the legal institution of slavery is in any case reshaped from within, and it is not surprising when Paul asks Philemon to entrust to him—under whatever legal form—the slave Onesimus. Yet in no case does Paul go so far as to decree that Christian homes may have no slaves. The context of the difficult text 1 Cor. 7:21 tells us, rather, that Paul advises slaves to remain in their status.

Paul orders more closely the relationship of husband and wife in Christian homes. Here too the principle applies that both sexes are addressed by the gospel in the same way. Without distinction, both receive the Spirit and are bearers of the charismata (Rom. 12:3ff.; 1 Cor. 11:5; chs. 12–14). In general, a sex-specific rank order does not appear. Indeed, in the Pauline churches, women sometimes occupy outstanding positions (cf. Rom. 16:1, 6). In Rom. 16:7 a woman apparently also receives the title of apostle. Since 1 Cor. 14:33–36 is an un-Pauline addition (cf. 1 Tim. 2:11–12), we can perhaps read only in 1 Cor. 11:2–16 a (limited) downgrading of women (cf. 8.2 above). In any case, it is true that the presupposition of the quarrel over wearing a veil is precisely the prophetic speaking of women in worship! Also, Paul seems to distinguish between the creaturely reasons for wearing a veil (1 Cor. 11:7–8) and equality "in the Lord" (11:11–12). Yet however one might interpret 1 Corinthians 11, it is the only Pauline text that could directly—here in regard to a custom—express a subordination of women. Marital communion is willed by the Creator (1 Thess. 4:4–5; 1 Corinthians 7). As clearly as Christianity accepts the weak, absolutely nowhere in Paul are women characterized as weak. Such devaluing typology is missing. Rather, the woman is fully accepted in both marriage and the church. Since a man may not have more than one wife and his access to harlots is denied (1 Thess. 4:4–5; 1 Cor. 6:12–20), the woman is thereby clearly valued highly. This judgment is all the more valid, since within Christian marriage the obligation to reciprocity between equals is fully represented (1 Cor. 7:3–5). Also, Paul does not allow sexuality or women to be downgraded or made the object of taboo through an ascetic demand. Celibacy is a special gift and is to be highly valued, especially in view of the end time. Marriage, however, remains the general rule and is in no way depreciated (1 Corinthians 7).

Finally, in the churches the difference between poverty and wealth plays an uncomfortable role (cf. 9.1 above) in attempts to further the integration of the church. Typically, however, this topic does not directly come to bear in the apostle, as it does, say, in the two Lukan books or in James. Yet there are "rich" churches like Philippi (conclusion from Phil. 4:10–20) and "poor" churches, for example, in Macedonia (cf. 2 Cor. 8:2–3). Paul does not strive for a social balance between the churches, as he himself also has freedom vis-à-vis situations of want and abundance (Phil. 4:11–12), which, nonetheless, leads neither to the devaluation of wealth nor to the ideal of poverty. Christians should be honorable trading partners (1 Thess. 4:6), and in a dispute over property they should preferably concede (1 Cor. 6:7–8). In principle, church members should all feed themselves and become no one's burden (1 Thess. 4:11). Yet the Christian is not permitted the vices related to property, such as greed, envy, deception, and robbery (Rom. 1:29–30; 1 Cor. 5:11; 6:9–10). Practices of the rich, such as revelry, intemperance, and gluttony (Rom. 13:13; Gal. 5:21), are not counted among Christian customs. By contrast, Christians should take care of the needs of the saints and cultivate hospitality (Rom. 12:13). Paul quite naturally expected homeowners to make their homes available for worship. However, mercy should also be practiced with joy (Rom. 12:8); the sharing of goods with the poor is worth nothing without love (1 Cor. 13:3).

We can see from this that Paul is aiming at a new, personal attitude toward poverty and wealth, and from such an inner attitude he expects that in individual cases, based on free will, social differences will be moderated. He knows no intrachurch social reform, nor does he organize care for the poor. This background makes it clear why Paul does not address directly the social tensions in the Corinthian church. Only inferences allow the insight that perhaps in the parties (1 Corinthians 1–4) or in the problem of celebrating the Lord's Supper (11:17ff.) the rich (cf. 9.1 above) demonstrated power and a lack of love. In these and other cases (e.g., 1 Corinthians 8) Paul practically does not treat the social dimension of the problem at all but argues on the basis of the gospel (thus, e.g., 1 Corinthians 1–4) or pleads quite generally for consideration (thus, e.g., 1 Corinthians chs. 8; 11).

The obligatory nature of the conduct of life also came to bear, finally, in the external relations of Christians. For Gentiles a radical change, as required by faith and baptism, was without analogy. The world of the gods, with its feasts, processions, and sacrifices, was definitively taboo. The general syncretism of the time was not valid for Christians (1 Thess. 1:9; 1 Cor. 8:4–6). Since religion, culture, occupation, and family life formed a symbiotic unit, this turning away from all foreign religion reached deep into the structure of a Christian's life. Nevertheless, Christians were supposed to remain where they had previously lived (1 Cor. 7:12ff., 17ff.) and there prove their Christian essence. Moving out of the world and withdrawing into Christian homes was not supposed to take place. Hence here Paul demanded from his church members a lot of courage, independence, and creativity in dealing with the many problems that now arose. For this task Paul does not set up special norms.

Somewhat different is the question of how Christians should deal with civil authorities. In this case Paul offers a lengthy comment in Rom. 13:1–7. There, in dependence on the synagogal heritage (cf. Jer. 29:5–7; Dan. 2:37; Wisd. Sol. 6:2–3), the authorities are considered divinely willed for the establishment of earthly welfare (Rom. 13:1–2). Therefore they may expect the citizens' duty of obedience (Rom. 13:5–7); as surely as Christians actually understood themselves as citizens of the coming world (Phil. 3:20–21), while all state institutions belonged to the world that was passing away (1 Cor. 7:29–31). This pragmatically conforming behavior showed that in spite of their striking and special way of life, Christians did not want to be despisers of the state. Romans 13, by the way, gives the rules for the normal situation. Possible conflicts are not addressed, although naturally Paul is also familiar with these (2 Cor. 11:23ff.).

14.8 The Future of Faith as Hope in the Lord

The early Christian conviction on which the Pauline statements about Christian hope are based can be described as follows. All of humanity stands under divine wrath, which in the immediate future, as God's act of final judgment on all sinners, will have the last word on the history of humanity gone astray. This unavoidable dark future is brightened only by the fact that now, immediately before the absolute end and already as the beginning of the end time, God, through the gospel of Christ, turns sinners into saints, into righteous ones. In this way he gathers an eschatological church, which through Christ as Savior from the wrath will, beyond judgment, always live together with him (1 Thess. 1:10; cf. 6.2 above). Therefore the faithful wait in tense, imminent expectation for the arrival of their Lord, in order through never-ending communion with him to achieve a salvific and ultimate determination, which the gospel promises and which the Spirit has already established through his influence on human beings. Thus Christ is the ground and goal of their hope and that hope is concentrated on the determination of the relationship of believers, as the eschatological church, to their Lord as the central figure of the end time.

If we look at Paul's letters in their historical order, we see that Paul does not abandon this orientation of the language of hope but that within it he undertook variations and reshapings. Remaining constant are the basic conviction of the lostness of humanity and the imminent revelation of this condition in the last judgment (even if there are slight postponements in the nearness of the end). Also remaining untouched is the basic viewpoint that can be described by the context of gospel, faith, eschatological church, and final communion with the Lord: according to Paul—from 1 Thessalonians through Romans—the faithful may hope that their relationship with Christ will move from one of faith and hope into one of ultimately seeing Christ. Only if we take this as the key to interpreting Paul's hope, will we be able to understand the crucial intention of the apostle's statements.

This basic viewpoint also remains thoroughly characterized by a certain understanding of time and history. Since the gospel of Christ makes the present the end time (Gal. 3:23, 25; 4:4; 2 Cor. 6:2), the present is neither merely the entrance hall and waiting room of the following end time, as in apocalypticism, nor a partial anticipation of the coming event; rather, it is the end time because the gathering of the eschatological church through the gospel is, in the strict sense, the eschatological event. With the coming of Christ it did not become five minutes till twelve on the world clock; it began to strike twelve o'clock. Related to this, for example, is the fact that Paul sets up no outlines of history, as did apocalypticism, in order to announce the position of the hands on the world clock and the reliability of the periodicity of world history (example: *1 Enoch* 85–90). Everything that happened before Christ's coming is interesting to Paul only in that it is a repetition of the sin of Adam (Rom. 5:12ff.). For Christians a positive orientation is no longer to be gained from this. Paul also rejected including the present Roman Empire in his judgment. For it is not the empire's age and condition that opens for believers the place of world history in God's plan of salvation; this is made apparent only by Christ. Through him past and present—to the extent that they are not determined by the gospel—become the "evil age" that is passing away (Gal. 1:4; 1 Cor. 2:6).

Furthermore, the described basic viewpoint causes Paul's final expectation not to be sketched as the outline of a drama in universal cosmic history. Paul is not describing the annihilation of the Roman Empire; he knows no world-historical periodicity of disaster that increases until finally redemption comes (as in Mark 13; Revelation). He knows no cosmic catastrophes. He does not relate primeval time and end time to each other. He knows of no Antichrist or thousand-year kingdom. He is not concerned about a final struggle as a cosmic world war, a world conflagration, a second flood, or all the other things (in part surely familiar to him) that Jewish apocalypticism had available in its repertoire for picturing the end time. Paul does not sketch the punishment and annihilation of evil ones, nor hell and its torments for the condemned. He paints no eschatological judgment theophany of God; even Christ's eschatological arrival remains, on the whole, pale (e.g., 1 Thess. 3:13; 4:16–17). He does not describe the creation of the new world, either, or how in detail things are to be in it. So the refusal to give a backward-oriented interpretation of history has its counterpart in a refusal to make an anticipatory utopian concretization of things to come before their appearance. Here too the reason is the same: faith that knows itself bound to Christ has in this eschatological central figure everything necessary for salvation. More is not needed; indeed, anything more would be less, because it would lead away from the ground of salvation.

This is not to overlook the fact that with minor, individual statements here and there in his comments on hope Paul goes beyond this basic viewpoint. Such marginal phenomena and fragments can be made out from time to time. In Rom. 16:20, for example, the eschatological annihilation of Satan stands out. According to 1 Cor. 6:3, Christians will one day judge angels. A heavenly household at Christ's coming at the end of the world is mentioned in 1 Thess. 3:13. For this series we can collect a few further examples. Yet these motifs produce no consistent total picture. They even hinder one, because they in part stand incoherently in opposition to each other and are accorded only limited, context-determined functions. Beyond these functions they are not pursued further by Paul. Thus, as apparent as it is that Paul does not always have his main viewpoint puristically in mind, so also it remains clear that Paul's final expectation is the unfolding of the future inherent in faith in Christ, a future that is Christ himself as the future of the believer.

Paul held fast to this basic assertion for the rest of his life. As already indicated, however, he varied it in some cases. The beginnings of the oldest variation on the theme of hope reach back into the early original church. In 1 Thessalonians we can still see how the announcement of the imminent kingdom of God and its coming (cf. 1 Thess. 2:12; 1 Cor. 6:9–10) as the legacy of Jesus' proclamation was reshaped into hope for the eschatological arrival of the Lord and for being together with him forever (cf. 1 Thess. 2:19; 3:13; 5:23–24 and 4:17; 5:10). This concentration of hope on the salvific person of Jesus Christ determined the old invocation of the Aramaic-speaking Jewish-Christian church: "Our Lord, come!" (1 Cor. 16:22; Rev. 22:20) and naturally was given new nourishment by Paul's Christology. We have already demonstrated that Paul presented Christ as Savior in the last judgment (1 Thess. 1:10), whose abilities include laying all reality at

God's feet and transforming believers into glorious immortals (1 Cor. 15:20–28; Phil. 3:20–21; cf. 14.4 above). Hence the dominant position of Christ in Pauline theology also prevails in the development of hope.

The second variation concerns the modification of the temporal conception of how long the present time will persist. The starting point of this series of statements is the assumption that the elected eschatological church as a whole, as it now exists, will experience the arrival of its Lord. Yet the first deaths—probably in Antioch and again later in Thessalonica—are, with the help of the expectation of the resurrection, the reason for giving a share in the expected future to those Christians who have by exception died prematurely (cf. 6.3 above). In 1 Corinthians 15 the relationship of Christians who have died or will die before the end to Christians who will see the Lord while they are still alive has so shifted that deceased Christians no longer represent an exception requiring explanation but rather are the rule (1 Cor. 15:51–52; cf. 15.5 below). In any case, the death of a large number of Christians before the arrival of the Lord is now no longer a problem. The modified concept of time is revealed all the more in Rom. 13:11 where Paul ascertains quite generally that ultimate salvation for Roman Christians is now already nearer than at the time when they became Christians. In view of the source situation (cf. 13.1 and 10.1 above), the amount of time can, unfortunately, only be figured approximately. Yet we can hardly go completely wrong with the assumption that Paul is thinking of a time span of, say, about ten years from the founding of the church until the sending of the Roman letter. On this assumption we can then assert that such a period is for the apostle a clear step toward the end (cf. as extreme opposite 2 Peter 3:8–9). The imminent expectation is thus still seen on the level of the present generation. Yet it is given only as a general expression of time, no longer accompanied by some kind of statement to the church of whether and how many will experience the end before their death. This corresponds to the observation that Paul—for example, in 2 Corinthians 5; Philippians 3; and Romans, chs. 5; 8—can discuss the future destiny of Christians in general, without mentioning the imminent expectation. That would not have been possible in 1 Thessalonians 4. Thus with the experience of ongoing time the imminent expectation is not abandoned (Rom. 13:11 is in the last Pauline letter!), yet the central problem in the statements on hope clearly shifts away from the time problem of 1 Thessalonians 4. Paul learns to grasp hope as only a statement of content, independent of a concept of time. This statement can now give certainty without being affected by the question of time. The reason for this shift in accentuation is the experience of a temporal extension before the end that is longer than was originally assumed.

Quite clearly, in the third place, the apostle also modifies the topic of death and resurrection. First Thessalonians still presupposes that gospel, baptism, and Spirit have so changed a person that on the basis of such change the eschatological church can participate in final salvation, without having to receive a further, supplementary qualification (transformation) (cf. 6.3 above). God's resurrection activity is only an aid to ultimately uniting the irregularly and prematurely deceased with the living, so that the whole church will be present at the arrival of the Lord. The next text, 1 Corinthians 15, already represents a different position. In a fundamental way, death is a curse on all humanity; it must be conquered, yet will not be set aside until the very end (1 Cor. 15:26, 54–56). So Christ becomes the "first fruits of those who have fallen asleep," who (like Adam with his death) anticipates with his resurrection the destiny of "all" and will "reign" until he has destroyed the last enemy, namely, death (1 Cor. 15:20–26). Because death and transitoriness are human problems, those who will be eyewitnesses to the arrival of the Lord must also be transformed. The equality of deceased and living can no longer occur through the resurrection of the deceased but is only reached when it is true for all that all transitoriness will be reclothed in immortality, which leads to the complete new constitution of human beings for immortality (1 Cor. 15:50–54). Thus in 1 Corinthians 15 Paul grasps for the first time the basic problem that ultimate life cannot be conceived at all under the conditions of historical transitoriness. He solves this problem also christologically. If, namely, in 1 Thessalonians 4 Christ's destiny is only useful as an analogy to God's resurrection activity for the deceased, then Christ himself as the resurrected One is now the humanity-determining, eschatological Adam.

This changed situation in 1 Corinthians 15 and its Pauline solution produce two different trains of thought. The first concerns the gap into which a person falls between death and resurrection; the second understands death not only as the break at the end of life but conceives of life as a whole as conformity to Christ's death. The apostle expresses himself on the first theme in 1 Cor. 15:35ff. and 2 Cor. 5:1ff. Here death is so closely bound to the historical existence of a person that the whole person must die, and only a new creative act of God can give that person the eternal mode of existence, and thus the individual's identity does not go beyond his or her soul but rests in the faithfulness of God. In this Paul probably has to defend against a Corinthian conception of the human being that grants to the soul permanence beyond death for the case that, conveyed through baptism, it is connected with the Holy Spirit (cf. 8.2 above). Paul wants to retain a holistic human picture and at the same time understand death as a break, so that the God who creates out of nothing also remains Lord of the transition from death into life. With this presupposition it is even sensible if the Christian longs to pass through this break into the resurrection body. Christians do not fear the nothingness but expect in death to experience the presence of their God in Christ (2 Cor. 5:1ff.).

The second train of thought comes from the theology of the cross. After Paul, in the dispute with the itinerant apostles of 2 Corinthians (cf. 8.4 and 8.5 above), had already related the power of the gospel to his suffering and death in such a way that the enduring apostolic weakness is the vessel of divine grace and sign of its victory, he succeeds particularly in the little Philippians B letter (cf. 12.4 above) not only in understanding death as the end of life (as, say, in 1 Thessalonians 4) but also in interpreting the whole of every Christian's life as a conformity to Jesus' death and the hoped-for resurrection as a conformity to the glory of the resurrected One. The destiny of Jesus Christ is thus seen as anticipation of the destiny of the believers, who through conformity participate in it. In Rom. 8:12ff., finally, a further aspect is included in this reasoning. The suffering of the present time, which is shared by the heirs of Christ, opens the view of the nothingness of the whole creation, which for its part also waits for liberation from such slavery.

A fourth variation is provided by the statements on the eschatological arrival of the Lord and on the judgment. In 1 Thess. 1:10 Christ has the task of saving the eschatological church; he preserves it from the wrath of God, which threatens all. Correspondingly, at the arrival of the Lord Christians will meet him in order to be united with him forever (1 Thess. 4:17). In this way the election whose aim is the reception of deliverance takes on final shape (1 Thess. 5:9–10). This concept does not speak of a judgment of Christians. With the Corinthian dispute Paul then again brings in the idea of judgment. The coming of the Lord to deliver his church turns into the eschatological judgment day, on which everyone will be held responsible (cf. 1 Cor. 3:10–17; 5:5; 2 Cor. 1:14; etc.). Yet 1 Cor. 3:15; 5:5; 11:31–32 show that the apostle cannot imagine that a Christian could be lost in the last judgment. That, of course, would not contradict the human situation, which under historical conditions is always dependent on forgiveness, but would be contrary to the promise of the electing God, who remains true to himself (1 Cor. 1:8–9; 10:13). To this extent, in the letters with justification language Paul also knows no double justification: now through faith and then through works. Rather, the present justification through faith is the only and final one on the basis of which one may hope for ultimate salvation (Rom. 5:1, 9). This does not exclude a final judging of Christians (Rom. 14:10). Still, ultimate salvation itself is not dependent on this judging (Rom. 8:11), for the whole church will one day be saved (8:23–25) because no one can separate it from the love of God in Christ (8:35–39). Moreover, nowhere does Paul indicate consequences for the final judging of Christians. He knows no graduated or temporally delayed participation in the final salvation and thus also no purgatory.

Some interpreters see another variation in the Pauline hope in the fact that the apostle changes his cosmic eschatological expectation of the arrival of the Lord (1 Thessalonians), or of a general eschatological resurrection of the dead, to a resurrection in the death of the individual Christian, because in Phil. 1:21–24 Paul longs to die in order to be immediately together with the Lord. In this variation he would have given up even the last shreds of the view of a great cosmic-historical catastrophe as the close of world history in favor of the assumption that each individual's death is immediately the gate to eternal life (cf. on such a view John 3:17–18; 5:24–25; 11:25–26; 12:31–32; 14:1ff.). Already speaking against such an understanding of the Pauline text in Philippians 1, however, are later statements formulated by Paul, such as Phil. 3:20–21; Rom. 14:10; 16:20, which all still contain a general cosmic expectation of the end. Also, the reference to paradise as the resting place of the dead, which Paul is supposed to have in mind in Philippians 1, hardly gives additional help, because Paul neither announces in 2 Cor. 12:4 that paradise, for him, is such a resting place, nor ever says Christ is there, nor mentions paradise in Philippians 1. Now, the particular character of Philippians 1 involves two things: Paul is talking exclusively of himself and especially of his possible death as a martyr. This recalls the Hellenistic-Jewish and early Christian tradition according to which martyrs, in distinction to the general rule, are immediately transposed into the state of final salvation (cf., e.g., 4 Macc. 6:29; 9:8; 16:25; Acts 7:59; Rev. 6:9ff.; 7:9–10; 1 Clem. 5.4, 7). It is true that in texts such as 1 Cor. 15:30–32; 2 Cor. 1:9; 4:7ff. Paul does not mention again such a special position, but in these cases he is speaking in terms of the destiny of all Christians. So in view of his special position we should interpret Philippians 1 in terms of possible martyrdom. This has the consequence that Philippians 1 is not evidence that on this point Paul changed the content of his hope. From the beginning he maintains his expectation of an eschatological arrival of Christ. Although he thus in a reduced fashion maintains the apocalyptic expectation of the appearance of a figure of salvation at the end of days (cf., e.g., *1 Enoch* 37–71), he remains bound to the apocalyptic worldview, which in spite of the *Sibylline Oracles* remained on the whole relatively foreign to the Roman-Hellenistic world (cf., e.g., Seneca, *Consolation to Polybius* 1.1–2).

Our glance at these variations indicated the variety of Paul's statements. At the same time, however, persistent themes became visible. These now deserve our attention. Fundamental and thoroughly demonstrable here is the way in which Paul integrated hope into his theology. It grows out of experience with the gospel, because the gospel itself aims at a final state of salvation. So in the theology of election the Christian is called into the eschatological church in order to take part in attaining final salvation (1 Thess. 5:9–10; cf. 6.2 above). In Corinthians C the gospel is capable of changing people from one glory into another (2 Cor. 3:18). Therefore for some it is a "fragrance from life to life" (2 Cor. 2:16), and they "know that if the earthly tent we live in is destroyed, we have a building from God, a house not made with hands, eternal in the heavens" (2 Cor. 5:1). In the language of justification the corresponding idea reads: "Since we are justified by faith, we have peace with God . . . , and we rejoice in our hope of sharing the glory of God" (Rom. 5:1–2).

Talking of the future determined by Christ, of course, simply means speaking of God as he has interpreted himself in the destiny of the eschatological central figure of Jesus Christ. That God is the one who makes the dead alive is shown, for believers, in Christ. Therefore believers can praise the God who makes the dead alive as they assert the destiny of Christ as the salvific ground of hope and regard for themselves God's resurrecting activity as their own hope. Thus the destination for ultimate life, which since 1 Corinthians has for Paul been realizable only through death and resurrection, or a transformation, is a certainty of faith. Conversely, "If for this life only we have hoped in Christ, we are of all [people] most to be pitied" (1 Cor. 15:19). Nowhere does Paul base the resurrection hope on Old Testament scriptural proof (as, e.g., in Mark 12:26) or simply develop it into a piece of the apocalyptic worldview; rather, from the center of the faith itself he introduces the resurrection theme (cf. 1 Thess. 4:13ff.; 6.3 above). This argumentation is predominant and fundamental right from the oldest evidence of this kind. It is then repeated with minor modulations through to Romans. A few examples will support this point: "Since we believe that Jesus died and rose again, even so, through Jesus, God will bring with him those who have fallen asleep" (1 Thess. 4:14). "And God raised the Lord and will also raise us up by his power" (1 Cor. 6:14). "If the Spirit of him who raised Jesus from the dead dwells in you, he who raised Christ Jesus from the dead will give life to your mortal bodies also through his Spirit which dwells in you" (Rom. 8:11). These easily expandable instances show that by speaking generally about Christ's death and resurrection rather than especially of Christ's crucifixion and exaltation, Christ's destiny is interpretable as God's self-determination, which is aimed at the resurrection of the believers. In these statements then lies, as it were, the nerve center of the Pauline hope.

The development of thought from faith to hope means for Paul that only believers can have hope for deliverance, because only faith is the righteousness that is valid before God (cf. 13.4 above). Nowhere does Paul deviate from this position, even faced with an Israel standing apart from the gospel (cf. 15.2 below). Nevertheless a look at the rest of humanity is instructive. There we notice first that the apostle does not raise the question of poetic justice at the close of world history. The great final reckoning, which permits the righteous to rejoice in the lot of the godless, does not take place in this way. For the world is in order, for Paul, not simply if all sinners are punished. It is in order, rather, because God's love rules over this world and its history. Hence Paul shows, for example, with Abraham in Romans 4, how the whole of humanity is the object of divine redemption (cf. 13.4 above). According to Rom. 5:1ff., God says to all people that he does not want to be the death–bringing judge of his enemies. His self-determination as love happens precisely in the face of his enemies (cf. 13.4 above). Above all, however, the apostle shows how for him God in Christ has established his eschatological relationship with the world—not only his relationship to the church. Christ is humanity's eschatological central figure of humanity, and thus the Christ event has an obviously more comprehensive horizon than that of the church. As Christ died for "all," so he is "Lord" over the living and the dead (Rom. 14:9). He will rule until "all things" are "in subjection under his feet" (1 Cor. 15:27). As in Adam "all" die, so in Christ are "all" made alive (1 Cor. 15:22). The grace of God in Christ is far more comprehensive than the Adamite destiny of humankind (Rom. 5:12ff.). As through Adam's disobedience "many" (i.e., all people) became sinners, so through the obedience of one "many" will become righteous (Rom. 5:19). To these observations we must add the reminder (cf. 14.4 above) that the formulaic term "in Christ" is not to be understood only in terms of the church but can assert the determination of present and end time through Christ. Finally, Paul can even look from the church and its expectation to reality as a whole and include it in the eschatological redemption, even if not in an entirely clear fashion

(Rom. 8:18ff.). Thus according to Paul faith knows that Christ is greater than the church and the gospel more comprehensive than church reality. Therefore hope grounded in faith knows that within this hope there is also more room than is presently taken in by the church. The church is the "body of Christ," but Christ includes more than the church. That is said, incidentally, in Romans 9–11 precisely to the Gentile-Christian church in a special case, namely, vis-à-vis unbelieving Israel.

If we have named the main points in the Pauline hope, then in closing we must still take a look at those passages in which Paul makes hope itself an object of reflection, namely, 1 Cor. 13:9–12; 2 Cor. 4:16–18; 5:6–8; and Rom. 8:23–25. In these texts the apostle attempts with Hellenistic-Jewish characterizations to describe hope per se: In the present time there is only a fragmentary knowledge of the perfect, because it can be perceived only as reflected reality in unclear form, and thus mediated, and not yet face-to-face, or immediate. So what is present is also visible and transitory; the eternal, on the other hand, is invisible and lasting. The light transitory burden of tribulation is balanced by the eternal weight of glory. These comments of the apostle show how Paul faces up to the discussion of how Christian hope is to be described within the understanding of reality of his time. He indicates thereby that, for him, Christian hope is not simply a matter of subjective arbitrariness but should be ready to render an account of the conditions and modalities of the knowledge belonging to faith and hope.

For the rest, such reflection also produces consequences in Paul for faith itself. He did not imagine "eternal life," for example, as a paradisiacal salvific meal (Matt. 8:11 par.) or concern himself with other "earthly" images. The apostle, rather, only approached the content of the concept of life under the conditions of perfection in such a way that he spoke negatively and in a delimiting way of overcoming and annihilating death (1 Cor. 15:26) and positively drew into the description the immediate nearness of God (1 Cor. 13:12; cf. also Rom. 5:2) as well as the lasting fellowship of Christ (1 Thess. 4:17; 5:10; Phil. 1:23). That is, Paul interpreted the love of God experienceable in the gospel (Rom. 5:8) as durable personal relationship, which by the faithfulness of God (1 Thess. 5:24; 1 Cor. 1:9) survives a person's death and remains his or her home (Phil. 3:20; 2 Cor. 5:8). Paul also intended such an assertion when in 1 Cor. 13:13 he characterized faith, hope, and love so that love alone will remain: if faith can see and hope does not come to nothing, then only love will be left as the bond of unity between God, Christ, and eschatological church. So love alone belongs to time and eternity. Therefore it is the greatest among the three that together determine the present time of Christians.

15
Paul as Martyr

15.1 The Delivery of the Collection

The collection visit in Corinth is the last event in the life of the apostle for which we have a self-testimony, namely, the Letter to the
Romans (Rom. 15:22–29). It mentions Paul's plan to deliver the gathered collection in Jerusalem: "At present, however, I am going to
Jerusalem with aid for the saints. For Macedonia and Achaia have been
pleased to make some contribution for the poor among the saints at
Jerusalem. . . . When therefore I have completed this . . . I shall go on
by way of you to Spain" (Rom. 15:25–26, 28). Paul is concerned about
the journey to Jerusalem, for he asks the Christians of Rome to pray for
him "that [1] I may be delivered from the unbelievers in Judea, and that
[2] my service for Jerusalem may be acceptable to the saints" (Rom.
15:31). Then the departure from Corinth begins the last phase of the
life of the apostle to the Gentiles, and we learn of it only through secondary testimonies, primarily through Acts. Since the evaluation of Acts
is not without problems (cf. 1.2 above), the historical presentation of
this journey is marked by serious uncertainties.

In order to arrive at verifiable statements, we must make clear the
viewpoints from which Luke describes the journey to Jerusalem. In this
regard it is immediately obvious that Luke—quite different from the
purpose of the journey given by Paul—carefully remains silent about
the delivery of the collection and mentions it only once quite incidentally, as if it were the most insignificant detail of this journey
(Acts 24:17). Likewise, giving this Gentile-Christian collection to Jewish
Christians can be no problem for Luke, for it is but a friendly present.
Naturally the envoys of the churches, who actually have come along
because of the collection, are now in the general sense traveling companions of Paul (Acts 20:4–6).

Why, then, does Paul travel to Jerusalem? First, it is his personal
decision (Acts 19:21) as a pious Jewish Christian to be in Jerusalem like
other diaspora Jews for the Festival of Weeks, the Jewish festival of the
spring harvest (20:16; cf. 2:1, 8–11). This pilgrimage then becomes the

triumphal march of the later martyr, for the journey is accompanied by prophetic announcements of deadly disaster (20:22–23; 21:4, 11), which Paul answers with the readiness to die and the composure of a martyr (20:24–25; 21:12–14). Also, right at the beginning there is the threat of an attack on Paul by the Jews (20:3). Because the future martyr is leaving for Jerusalem, the churches bid him farewell, and he instructs the elders of the church to guide the church after him (20:17–38; 21:5–6). Like holy martyrs, Paul also performs miracles on his way (20:7–12).

We can see in this that the biographical and anecdotal legends around Paul are becoming more elaborate. The interest is not in the historical and theological side of the journey but rather in weaving the gown of a great church martyr. Here the long since postapostolic church is not only looking back at this great Christian of the first early Christian generation but also knows itself in continuity with him through Paul's testament in Acts 20. At the same time, however, this distorts the historical Paul. Naturally, he is no pious Jewish Christian. His life-style is emphatically Gentile Christian. One who condemns the festal calendar, which the Judaizers in Galatia want to introduce, as a reversion to legalism (Gal. 4:8–11) cannot himself be governed by the Jewish festal calendar. One who lives in the immediate, imminent expectation of the end of all things (Rom. 13:11 was written directly before the journey!) and wants to complete his mission as the eschatological election of the Gentiles now also in the West of the Roman Empire (Rom. 15:23–24) and perhaps then still expects a last mission in Israel (Rom. 11:25–26; cf. 15.2 below) is not concerned before his death about the following generations of Christianity because he lacks such long-term perspective. One who, finally, regards the collection journey only as the last act before a new missionary task in the West does not shape his Jerusalem journey as the path of a martyr, as Ignatius, for example, did later with his journey to Rome. Thus the picture of Paul that Acts draws here makes clear how by the end of the second or already at the beginning of the third early Christian generation a very definite image of Paul was taking shape. But this gives no reliable presentation of the historical situation of this journey.

If a check on the Lukan representation against Paul was still on the whole possible for the previous part of the journey, such aid is entirely lacking for the events in Jerusalem. Acts divides these happenings into four sections. (1) It reports of the friendly reception by the Jerusalem church and stages the advice of James according to which Paul is supposed to redeem the vow of four men in order to demonstrate his faithfulness to the law (Acts 21:15–26). (2) This leads to Paul's apprehension in the temple a week later and to his mistreatment. It would have led to his death if the Romans had not intervened (21:27–36). (3) Paul declares himself to the Roman tribune, makes a speech to the Jews, and stands on his Roman citizenship (21:37–22:29). (4) He stands before the San-hedrin, in which, in connection with the proceedings against the apostle, Pharisees and Sadducees quarrel about the resurrection of the dead. Paul is again led away and learns in a dream that he will bear witness to Christ in Rome (22:30–23:22). With this we have the next important key word, namely, the indication of the prisoner Paul's journey to Rome.

The typical Lukan development of crucial turning points in the history of early Christianity through speeches—as can be impressively observed in these four sections—makes clear by itself how much the presentation is determined by Luke. The contrast between the unjust and mean treatment by the Jews on the one hand and the well-intended, always correct treatment by the Romans on the other is also of Lukan design. That even the Pharisees form a common front with Paul against the Sadducees in regard to the hope of the resurrection (23:6–9) is, naturally, already a glaring distortion of historical truth. In general, Paul is again described as a pious Jewish Christian (21:20, 26, 28–29; 22:3–5, 12–13, 17; 23:4–5, 6, 9), who is falsely accused of unfaithfulness to the law. Literarily, the dramaturgical strategy of the sequence of scenes is also deliberate: all of Jerusalem is in an uproar (21:31), and at the last moment the tribune personally keeps Paul from being lynched (21:31ff.). Yet the ill-treated Paul can immediately—with the unhesitating permission of the tribune—speak to the Jews and impressively repeat whole parts of Acts (21:37ff.). Naturally the chief priests must also sit in judgment over Paul, as over Jesus (Mark 14:53ff. par.); they are presented as the embodiment of disunity and make downright fools of themselves in front of the Romans, especially since they do not consult and pass judgment on the real accusation (Acts 22:30ff.). Well programmed in its timing, the Jerusalem journey then ends with the dream that opens the way to Rome (23:11). In short, the pen was guided here not by the desire to describe what had occurred but by dramatic direction.

Can we, nevertheless, make statements that are to some degree reliable about the journey to Jerusalem and the stay in this city? To a limited extent, this is the case. No one can seriously doubt that Paul wanted to realize his plan to deliver the collection in Jerusalem through a trip to that city. Paul confirms that envoys from the churches accompanied him on the journey—even if the list in Acts 20:4 does not agree with the Pauline information and therefore Acts must be corrected through Paul (cf. ch. 2 above). The two are also in agreement on the

time of the journey. Refiguring in absolute chronology, we can put
down A.D. 56/57. Since the travel route in Acts consists almost solely of
an itinerary, into which Luke then incorporates individual episodes,
generally without showing special interest in the route itself, we can
probably accept this information—at least in broad outline—as traditional. What is older than Luke, however, does not automatically have
to be historically reliable. Nonetheless, on the whole Paul may have
gone this way, since the result is a usual and sensible travel route. Of
course, anyone with a little bit of geographical knowledge can put
together the stops on the coast of Asia Minor and Syria, as given in
Acts 20:6, 13–15; 21:1–3, 7–8. In detail, Paul and his companions do
not travel from Corinth straight across the Aegean, for example, to
Samos or Miletus and then farther south along the coast. Instead, they
avoid the open sea and sail in a great arc along the coasts of Greece,
Macedonia, and Asia Minor, and the stops from Troas to Caesarea are
then named in quick succession. This route—laborious for today's seafarers—was in no way unusual in antiquity, since, for reasons of safety
and navigation, mariners liked to sail near the coast. Thus we do not
need the motivation of a Jewish plot (Acts 20:3), which also remains so
vague that one cannot imagine how Paul could avoid it simply by
changing his travel route.

Also instructive in Luke is the information about where Paul stayed
on his land route in the Roman province of Syria (cf. Acts 20:3; 21:7–8),
to which Judea and Jerusalem also belonged at the time. First, in Caesarea he stayed in the house of Philip, who belonged to the circle of
Stephen (Acts 6:5; 21:8), then in Jerusalem with Mnason of Cyprus
(21:16), but not with James, the brother of the Lord (21:18!). Both hosts
were apparently Hellenistic Jewish Christians who were at least open
to the Gentile mission. Earlier Paul would have had no trouble getting
a room with Peter in Jerusalem (Gal. 1:18); now that is obviously no
longer possible with James. Acts, which in connection with the persecution of Stephen's group in Acts 6–7; 11:13ff. had already glossed over
theological differences between the Hellenists and the apostles, may
have also kept silent here about the theological dynamite in this meager information. One can presume, namely, that under normal circumstances the universally known apostle to the Gentiles would, on the
basis of protocol, have enjoyed the hospitality of the most prominent
Christians in Jerusalem, who at this time certainly included James. This
expected observance of protocol, however, did not take place. James,
who in Acts 21:18ff. is by no means described as hostile to Paul, must
guard against being associated too closely with the suspect apostle to
the Gentiles!

This background focuses light on Paul's statement in Rom. 15:31. He had a double concern, namely, about the hostility of the synagogue and about the rejection of the collection by the Jewish Christians in Jerusalem. The two may be connected but are not simply the same thing. On the basis of the many Jewish persecutions that Paul himself suffered (cf. 7.3 above) it is understandable that he had to fear something bad from the Jews of Jerusalem. Yet the Jerusalem martyrdom of Stephen was probably also common knowledge in early Christendom and thus must have been known to Paul. Was not the Lord's brother James, in spite of his fundamental obedience of the law, executed a few years later—almost at the same time as Paul—on account of an accusation of violating the law (Josephus, *Antiquities* 20.200)? If indeed the intention was to get the Jewish-Christian church by striking its head, all Jewish Christians in Jerusalem stood under heavy pressure from the synagogue, in which in these years before the Jewish uprising of A.D. 66–72 the Zealot element was intensifying and therefore demarcation from and hostility against everything non-Jewish were flourishing. A scarce ten years later it was decided in Jerusalem no longer to accept gifts from non-Jews for temple and synagogue (Josephus, *Bellum* 2.408–409). Thus, since the Jewish Christians of Jerusalem were always in contact with non-Jewish Christians, they continually had to deal with synagogal criticism and hostility. This was all the more true of their visitor Paul, whose coming could endanger himself and the church. Therefore for Paul there had always been a clear risk in traveling to Jerusalem.

The Jerusalem church, however, of its own accord could have, nevertheless, somehow accepted the collection, especially since if need be it could have been concealed from the synagogue. Indeed, in delivering the collection, Paul is not afraid of the pressure of the Jews on the Jewish Christians; rather, he speaks of the possibility that it could be rejected by the Jerusalem Christians themselves. Thus there must have been people among the Jewish Christians in Jerusalem who favored a refusal of the collection.

In all probability these did not include James. Could he as the spokesman of the Jerusalem Christians not have signaled this when Paul was still in Macedonia and Achaia? Would propriety not have required it, at least on the arrival of the delegation in Caesarea? With shifting opinion, could he not, in any case, have already advised against Paul's journey and at most let the church envoys make the trip? Is it conceivable that through the official refusal of the Gentile-Christian collection, practically in the form of a public commotion, James could reverse his recognition of Gentile Christianity at the Apostolic Council

(Gal. 2:9; cf. 5.2 above)? Even his envoys in Antioch did not call into question Gentile Christianity as such (cf. 5.3 above). Therefore one will be more inclined to answer these questions in the negative the more one holds the picture that Acts draws of James in 21:17 to be historically correct in essence—not in detail. Naturally Paul did not reside with Mnason without the knowledge and approval of James. Thus James supports the Pauline presence in Jerusalem and hence, naturally, also the official visit of the church envoys with the collection. As head of the Jewish Christians, however, he cannot expose himself too much. According to Luke, he confirmed himself further as mediator in order to bring the journey to a satisfactory conclusion. So the recommendation that Paul should take over the vow of the four men is intended as a signal to the Jerusalemites to show how respectfully Paul regards the law. Even if we can ask whether historically Paul, with his understanding of the law, could go along with such a recommendation, the picture of James drawn by Luke remains.

Where, then, lie the dangers for the collection enterprise? Certainly no one knows exactly the possible tensions in the early Jerusalem church, but the assumption that it was a question of Judaizers and their sympathizers seems highly likely. Should those in Jerusalem not know that Paul had recently cursed the Judaizers in Galatia and had intervened in similar fashion in Philippi (cf. 10.2 above)? In this way Paul had suspended ecclesiastical fellowship with them. Should they now receive their archenemy and his entourage with open arms—the one who had years before, at the council here in Jerusalem, brought them public defeat (cf. 5.2 above)? Could they not finally now even the score? And was his very understanding of the law not the most radical far and wide (Gal. 3:19ff.) and for Judaizers and strict Jewish Christians simply undiscussable? And apart from Paul himself, their rejection of the Gentile-Christian church rested objectively on the lawlessness of these Christians. Thus they trusted the judgment that one may not accept impure Gentile money even if it comes from "brothers in the faith." Hence they agree here with the opinion of the synagogue. In addition, naturally, they could likewise adopt the argument that one has to show consideration to this synagogue, because in it one saw with good reason one's own theological home. Ultimately these Judaizers could make problems even for James, so that he dealt with Paul with them in mind, as described. Yet in spite of everything, there is one thing they cannot be accused of: they themselves did not deliver Paul to the Jews. From the standpoint of the general Christian ethos, this was not possible for them. They were against the collection but not for betraying Paul. Even Paul had probably excluded the Judaizers in Galatians from the church, yet not persecuted them or had them betrayed and accused to the local authorities.

If we review again this whole problem situation in Jerusalem, which was both fateful and critical, we can ponder whether the Jerusalemites ultimately accepted the collection. If the anti-Pauline forces prevailed, or if Paul was apprehended by the Jews before handing over the collection, then the rejection of the gift was probably unavoidable. Was Luke almost quiet about the collection because it became a failure? This question cannot really be answered. The situation regarding the arrest of Paul, however, is different. Even if the circumstances have disappeared into the shadows of history, it is still pointless to doubt that the apostle was seized by Jews and then in a likewise unclear way fell into Roman hands. In Acts 21:27–30 Luke describes the process: Jews from Asia take Paul to task in the temple, saying he took a Gentile Christian from Ephesus named Trophimus with him into the temple. That sounds very concrete and fits the temple law, according to which no non-Jew may enter the holy place. This prohibition, with the express threat of death, was also posted in writing at the entrance to the temple district. That Paul, however, who had just expressed to Rome his great concern about the threat of the Jerusalem Jews (Rom. 15:31), should have behaved in such an openly provocative manner is more than incredible. One simply cannot imagine that Paul would have so carelessly plunged himself, his delegation, and the early church into problems. Luke also hastens to free Paul from such an accusation (cf. Acts 21:29). Yet even so, all of this makes little historical sense: one then imputes to the Jews a consciously false accusation that at any time could collapse. It is equally difficult to regard 21:29 as a subsequent apologetic denial that at the same time is false. Probably Luke simply put into words an already present tradition. It is, nonetheless, hardly believable. Nor does the name of the Ephesian change anything, since the list of names in 20:4 also gives rise to criticism. So we are left with the scant information that this arrest—no longer clarifiable in detail—begins the period of Paul's imprisonment and his journey to Rome.

15.2 The Apostle to the Gentiles and His Jewish People

Immediately before his trip to Jerusalem, Paul writes in Romans 9–11 the most comprehensive, argumentative, and theologically substantial section in early Christian literature on the problem of Israel—indeed, the only early Christian text that does not simply condemn the Judaism

that stands apart from the gospel. Because of this tension we will discuss here Paul's evaluation of the synagogue. Owing to its positive attitude toward Israel, Romans 9–11 also plays a special role in the
present-day Jewish-Christian dialogue, especially since some interpreters
find in it a special way to salvation for Israel apart from Christ and, in
any case, a sympathetic discussion of Israel's incontestable election.
Opposed to this are views, for example, that accuse Paul of inconsistency because in Romans 9–11, after overcoming salvation-historical
thought (Romans 1–8), he now falls back again into a salvation-historical mode of argumentation. In Romans 1–8 he levels the special position of Israel (3:1–8) into the commonality of sinful humanity (2:17–29;
3:9–20) and sees all people, including Israel, standing sole before the
grace offered in the gospel (3:21–5:21), yet he again emphasizes this
special position in Romans 9–11. He succumbs, it is said, to speculative
imagination, or he makes contradictory statements here, so that one can
understand 9:1–11:10 and 11:11–36, for example, only as antitheses.
Thus Romans 9–11 is loved, criticized, and rejected. This illustrates, in
any case, how the text is one of the most disputed of Paul's writings.

A look at the Pauline letters reveals that from the oldest letter with its
harsh anti-Jewish polemic (1 Thess. 2:15–16) to the last letter, in which
Romans 9–11 stands, is also a long journey for Paul. The apostle clarified his relationship to the synagogue more than once, and the last
statement in Romans 9–11 is more of a surprise than the end of a logical path. This literary finding leads to the biography of Paul. It begins
with the Pharisaic Jew who persecutes the Christian church (cf. 4.3
above). It has its revolutionary continuation in the consistently Gentile-
Christian thinking apostle (cf. 4.4 above), who now, as seen from the
synagogue, represents missionary competition and who, indeed, so
keenly thinks through the tension between law and gospel that the synagogue becomes a salvation-historical anachronism. Nevertheless Paul
always mentioned his heritage from the people of salvation with pride
(Phil. 3:4–6; Rom. 9:1–5), but even so during his life he suffered greatly
under persecutions by the Jews (cf. 7.3 above). Even as he wrote
Romans 9–11, the fear of the Jerusalem Jews was present (15:30–31)
and, as the outcome shows, was not unfounded (cf. 15.1 above).

To this individual side we must add the perspective of religious and
cultural history. Paul not only knows from the Tarsus period the political privileges of the Jews and the social tensions between the Gentiles
and the synagogue; he is also a prominent figure in the history of early
Christianity. Thus we must take into consideration that history from
Jesus to the expulsion of Jewish Christianity from the synagogue (ca.
A.D. 70–90) when we read the Pauline texts. Between the principle of

Pharisaic Jewish Christians, "Unless you are circumcised according to the custom of Moses, you cannot be saved" (Acts 15:1, 5), and the judgment of Ignatius, "It is impossible to confess Jesus Christ and [nonetheless] live as a Jew" (Ignatius, *Magn.* 10.3; cf. 8.1–2), there is a broad spectrum within which the young Christianity placed itself with regard to Judaism.

We know Judaism's judgment on Christianity only through two direct texts and otherwise through indirect (i.e., Christian) texts. Josephus (*Antiquities* 20.200) reports the Lord's brother James being executed around A.D. 62 in Jerusalem because of breaking the law. The benediction on heretics, incorporated into the Jewish Eighteen Benedictions around A.D. 90, excludes all scorners of the law from the synagogue and thus all Christians, among others. Jewish Christians could not damn themselves in the synagogue service through prayer. In agreement with these two testimonies are Christian comments. Jesus dies because of his criticism of the law and the temple cult (e.g., Mark 2:1–3:6; 14:58). Stephen is charged with the same thing (Acts 6:8–14). As a strict law-abiding Pharisee, Paul persecutes the church. Thus the synagogue faulted Christians above all because they threatened the law as its central authority. In the Diaspora, naturally, it rightly feared the competition of the Christian mission, which found adherents in the very God-fearers who were connected with the synagogue. It was, of course, suspicious of the exit of many Jewish Christians from the synagogue, who, in the synagogal view, as assimilated Jews now lived a Gentile (Christian) life. Examples include Barnabas, Paul, Priscilla and Aquila, Apollos, and in effect also Peter. The nameless nomadic apostles of 2 Corinthians also belong here as well as whole churches (Antioch, Rome, part of the churches of the Hellenists, etc.). Where Paul and his coworkers missionized, the Jews who became Christians no longer oriented themselves toward the law (cf., e.g., Acts 18; 21:21). In addition, many nameless Jewish Christians probably attached themselves "lawlessly" to Gentile-Christian churches. All of this the Jews could not and did not want to accept, especially since the Christian mission probably led to the largest exodus from Judaism that we know about in antiquity. According to the way things were, the synagogues at that time naturally possessed the means of power vis-à-vis the underprivileged, powerless Christian minority. They exercised these means, and Paul's biography provides an impressive example of this (cf. 7.3 above).

The Jews, for their part, had no easy, comfortable position. Where military might decides order and justice, subjugated peoples are always and necessarily degraded. Moreover, because of their religion the Jews were among the especially despised oddities. Also, in the opinion of the Greeks and Romans they had contributed nothing of their own to the state, to culture, and to science, nor to general education. Rome had a few military conflicts with the Jews. In 63 B.C., Pompei rearranged conditions in Jerusalem in favor of Rome. Then there were two rebellions in Palestine (A.D. 66–72 and 132–135) and one in Egypt (A.D. 115–117). In all three cases the Romans were the reacting power, not the instigators, but they persistently let the Jews feel their victory. In religious matters Rome was tolerant and on many occasions stood by the Jews in the Hellenistic cities and indeed even supported them when they sought help in local conflicts of interest. There were special reasons for the edicts driving the Jews out of Rome: disturbances in the synagogues and the limitation of proselytizing.

We must make a distinction between these political conditions and judgments from the general cultural climate of the time. Cicero (*Pro Flacco*) and Tacitus (*Histories* 5.2–13), among others, give an impression of how the Jews were judged in Roman circles: Moses was regarded as a deceiver, and the Jews as godless because they rejected the world of the Roman gods. The Jews are enemies of the human race. They represent a barbaric superstition and are lazy because they do nothing every seventh day. Gentile Christians familiar with such statements used them occasionally to replenish their critique of the synagogue (e.g., 1 Thess. 2:15–16), but because of the same monotheism they inherited the anti-Jewish disqualification of godlessness and the characterization as enemies of the human race.

With this background, if we sketch in detail Paul's relationship to the synagogue, we will have to begin with his calling. For the Jews in Damascus this turning point in Paul's life was naturally a severe blow. It was discussed in the synagogue association, especially when a short time later Paul was involved in the move toward independence of the Jewish Christians, a group at first connected with the synagogue. The apostle's first extended missionary journey with Barnabas intensified the conflict, as attested by his stoning (cf. 5.2 above). If 1 Thessalonians still contains the mission theology of this period (cf. 6.2 above) and 2:15–16 in particular records a traditional Gentile-Christian anti-Jewish polemic, then the text reflects the theological reaction to this situation.

It is certainly not accidental that 1 Thess. 2:15–16 as word of judgment against the synagogue is placed in the missionary situation of 1 Thessalonians 1–2. From the Christian missionaries to Israel, analogous prophetic words of judgment are known, which are directed against Israel's rejecting attitude (e.g., Luke 11:49–51; 13:34–35). Transformed into a parable, the same speech form is also present in Mark 12:1–9 (parable of the wicked tenants). The Israel that disregards the sending of the messengers (12:1–8) gets the vineyard taken away from it (v. 9). According to Acts 13:10–11 Paul also speaks thus against a pagan competitor. All the named examples are in two parts. The immediate threat of judgment in a brief conclusion is preceded by the exhibition for the court in the form of a mostly generalized and broadly laid disqualification of the opponent. So 1 Thess. 2:15–16 also contains first the demonstration of guilt, verbose and comprehensive, then the almost monosyllabic announcement of judgment (v. 16c). The content can be stated simply: Because Israel is hindering the Gentile-Christian mission, it stands under divine judgment. For the Gentile-Christian mission is God's will; anyone who opposes it must necessarily face God's judgment.

The register of sins in 1 Thess. 2:15–16 begins with three Jewish-Christian ideas, which come from the Christianized Deuteronomic picture of history: (*a*) The Jews killed the Lord, (*b*) as well as the prophets, and (*c*) are persecuting Christian messengers (cf. Matt. 21:33ff. par.; 22:1ff. par.). Then follow three further points from the Gentile-Christian situation: (*d*) The Jews cannot please God; (*e*) they are enemies of all people and (*f*) are hindering the Gentile mission. The sequence of points d and e corresponds to the Hellenistic division of ethics into veneration of the gods and righteousness vis-à-vis human beings. In both basic commandments the Jews fail. With the reproach of enmity against the people, incidentally, the Romans are quickly ready (Pliny the Elder, *Natural History* 2.45.117; 7.7.46; 7.18.80)—also against the Jews (e.g., Tacitus, *Histories* 5.5.1). Jews (cf. Esth. 3:8; 3 Macc. 3:4, 7)—especially in the Diaspora—knew such accusations, as did, naturally, Gentile Christians. Added to the un-Pauline language of the two series is the observation that points c and f are parallel. The Jews hinder the mission to Israel and the Gentile mission. This lets us presume that a Jewish-Christian series was probably expanded in Antioch with a Gentile-Christian series and then closed with a final line ("so as always to fill up the measure of their sins"). The parable in Luke 14:1ff., incidentally, receives a similar expansion with the Gentile-Christian viewpoint in 14:23–24.

If Paul then probably has no immediate part in the formulation, he still adopts the text. It is an expression in a confrontation model between two religions in competition. With the general syncretistic tolerance of the time, the only one actually at home in such a confrontational, judgmental way of dealing with another religion was Judaism, which in this model judged the Gentiles and their world of the gods: The Gentiles are thus under the wrath of God, because they are totally lacking in the true worship of God, and therefore among themselves they are also an embodiment of wickedness. This judgment of the Gentiles was also adopted by early Christianity and Paul (Romans 1–2).

With regard to Judaism the Christian criticism begins at first within Judaism (so also 1 Thess. 2:15a). Such criticism is maintained and broadened (e.g., 1 Thess. 2:15–16) when Christianity becomes independent. Now the same confrontation arises between the Gentile-Christian mission and the Hellenistic synagogue as earlier between Judaism and paganism. Since both series in 1 Thess. 2:15–16 culminate in the hindering of missions, as signaled by c and f, then this problem situation forms the crucial point of the accusation. The other points are only "fellow travelers," even if none of their general importance and harshness may be explained away. In 1 Thess. 2:15 the placing of blame for the death of Jesus on the Jews is the oldest testimony of this kind. Behind 1 Thess. 2:15–16 theologically is the idea that by making itself the opponent of divine election, Judaism stood against God himself and thus had to draw divine justice upon itself. From the standpoint of Pauline theology, however, we must ask whether this Jewish opposition is to be placed under the power of the divine wrath or under the power of the gospel. We will also let this critical inquiry stand if we see that in those days—as attested, for example, by the cursing of heretics in the Eighteen Benedictions—Judaism did the same thing from the other side. Through this, then, it becomes clear that such a way of dealing with each other is also a problem of that time. Yet even with this comparison there remains a difference: the synagogue persecuted and expelled the Christians in parallel with divine judgment; at that time Christians left retribution up to God but otherwise suffered and did not strike back (cf. Rom. 12:14, 19–21). First Thessalonians 2:15–16 remains a verbal reaction of impotence vis-à-vis the harsh (cf. 2 Cor. 11:24–25), powerful synagogue. That Christians later, when they were in power, turned the tables, also using this text, is as true as it is bitter, but this has nothing to do with the historical truth of the first century.

Probably also belonging in essence to the Antiochene period are the three typological-allegorical exegeses of 1 Cor. 10:1–21; 2 Cor. 3:7–18; Gal. 4:21–31 (cf. 5.5 above), which Paul employs in various contexts. Israel's time of origin and election, interpreted in the scripture, is now applied to the chosen Christian eschatological church. All of that happened for its confirmation. Through election and Spirit it is free from the law—that is, it founded itself outside the synagogue—but took with it a heritage, the scriptures, which now, legitimated through the Spirit, are newly and for the first time correctly understood; so that they are at the same time torn from the synagogue and also turned against it. The Essenes also interpreted the scriptures for their community and time, which they declared to be eschatological (cf. 1QpHab; 4QpNah; 4QpPs 37). Here, of course, the scripture remained in intra-Jewish usage. Now, however, an independent new religious communion is laying claim to the Jewish canon for itself and represents itself as its only legitimate heir. It does this, for example, by having its Lord already present in Spirit in the time of Moses (1 Cor. 10:4), by denying that Israel is the legitimate offspring of Abraham (Gal. 4:24–25), and by declaring the revelation of Moses as service of the killing letter, and it replaces the old covenant with a new one (2 Cor. 3:6–7). This does not shed a favorable light on Israel and the synagogue. The Sinai generation was extremely sinful, so that God took no pleasure in it (1 Cor. 10:6–10). Even today Israel is still hardened, when the law is read (2 Cor. 3:13–14). Jewish religion is slavery and service to the law (Gal. 4:24–25). In the law (Gen. 21:10, 12 = Gal. 4:30) God himself demands that these offspring of Abraham be "cast out," in order to exclude them from the promise. Perhaps 2 Cor. 3:13 goes even farther: Moses even deceived Israel, for he hid the fact that his divine splendor on the occasion of the handing down of the law was fading. In that case the synagogue would be built on deception in regard to the revelation of the law as the central authority for Israel. Thus the priestly deception that Judaism imputed to other religions (cf. Bel and the Dragon; *Apoc. Abr.* 1–8) would fall back on Judaism itself.

Paul did not use this text directly against Israel: 1 Corinthians 10 is presented as an admonition to the Corinthian church; it should guard itself against falling from grace. In 2 Corinthians 3, Paul has to defend himself against attacks on his apostleship. The real aim is the description of the apostolic gospel that transforms hearts. In Galatians 4 he struggles against the Judaizers on behalf of the law-free gospel. Paul also leaves the way to the gospel open for the Jews (2 Cor. 3:14c). But the depreciatory confrontation with the synagogue is automatically woven into this text. It is part of the self-understanding of the Gentile-Christian churches and of Paul. The old covenant is dissolved by the new. The Spirit of the Lord has unmasked the law as the killing letter. The election of Abraham achieved its goal in the church, not in Judaism. Only Christians, not the synagogue, understand the scriptures correctly. Slavery under the law, the service of death, and condemnation are the traits of the Jews' state of damnation. This is not far from 1 Thess. 2:15–16. Yet if the catalog style of description of the present behavior of the Jews was in view in 1 Thess. 2:15, here the work is more fundamental, with theological and exegetical reasons. Since Paul uses these texts from 1 Corinthians to Galatians without objecting to the evaluation of Judaism, he betrays an anti-Jewish attitude until the time of the so-called collection journey.

Only Gal. 6:16 can speak against this assumption. Here in the closing of the letter the blessing is pronounced, namely, peace on those who live by this principle, that circumcision and uncircumcision mean nothing, but only the new creation. Then comes an addition to the recipients of the blessing: "Upon the Israel of God." To whom does this refer? Perhaps to still unbelieving Judaism, as it still stands under the promises of God? Then the terse statement would be a first signal that in Paul there is a new understanding of the problem of Israel, as will be developed a little later in Romans 9–11. But to have this understanding as the conclusion of Galatians creates problems. Such a statement would not only be surprising and unmotivated as appended at the close of the letter, but without the knowledge of Romans 9–11 it would also not be understood by any ancient or modern reader of Galatians. Anyone who has the promise to Abraham aimed exclusively at Christ and those who believe in him (Gal. 3:1–18), who declares that the time of the law has been replaced by the time of faith and who in the process massively devalues the law (3:19–4:7), who with the Hagar-Sarah allegory (4:21–31) sees the promise of Isaac fulfilled in the church and not in the present Israel, cannot expect that one will interpret 6:16 to mean (still unbelieving) Jews. Anyone who expropriates the blessing from the bodily offspring of Abraham, as it were, in favor of the Christians (3:16–17, 18, 29; 4:5, 7, 28, 31) cannot in closing and without preparation revoke this division of property.

Does it then perhaps mean the faithful remnant from Judaism, that is, the Jewish Christians? This is also impossible. Even if in Galatians Paul were not pulling out all the polemical stops against a Jewish-Christian group, namely, the Judaizers, he cannot place Jewish Christianity under the divine blessing here without separating from it the Judaizers. With such a blessing he would contradict the curse in 1:6–9. In addition, there is no other known Pauline text in which the Jewish Christians receive such a recognized, theologically significant, special position. If even the precondition of circumcision is irrelevant to salvation (2:15–16; 6:15), then Jewish Christians belong to the church on the strength of their faith, as do all other believers; more they may not claim, and more is not necessary for salvation.

Then ultimately the "Israel of God" can only designate the church as a whole. Even then the expression is not completely without its element of surprise, but as end product it allows us to understand the theology developed in the letter. If a writer draws a line from the promise of Abraham through Christ to believing Christians (Galatians 3–4), if he sees only these Christians under the covenant of the promise (Gal. 4:24, 26), if he talks of the difference between the earthly Israel and the church as "flesh" and "Spirit" (4:29) and designates Christians as "children . . . of the free woman" (i.e., Sarah; 4:30–31), he has tacitly made the church the spiritual Israel, even if he does not directly carry out the linguistic redefinition of the expression "Israel of God." Thus we will have to interpret Gal. 6:16 on the basis of the overall picture of the letter. As a result we can state that Paul adds linguistically what he has long represented theologically. The promise of Israel for him is fulfilled in the church. Therefore he can take a salvific term like "Israel of God" from Judaism and reclaim it for the church. Then the meaning of the blessing in Gal. 6:16 is that it is given to the Galatians if they, like the apostle, stand on the principle in 6:15 and do not follow the Judaizers (for then they would receive the curse of 1:6–9); and this blessing relates to the whole church in that it is founded on the promises of God to Abraham.

The Letter to the Galatians contains the last statements about Israel or Judaism before the Letter to the Romans. In conclusion, therefore, we must now discuss Romans 9–11. Yet a brief examination of these three chapters runs the risk of immediately focusing on the secret of Israel in Romans 11:25–26, of understanding the decidedly preliminary nature of the present judgment over Israel as the final suspension, for example, of 1 Thess. 2:16, and then only on the basis of this word determining the relationship of church and Israel for historical time until the end, with the consequence that Israel, according to Paul, does not need the message of Christ now. Such a hasty step, however, conceals problems. Can we reduce the long path in Romans 9–11 to this short statement? Can we neglect the context of Romans? Can we simply ignore the basic ideas of Pauline theology, especially his other comments on the end of the world and history? Is a prophetic word, as it is brought in by Paul in 11:25–26, automatically valid, or is it not also to be placed under the testing of the spirits (1 Cor. 12:10) because all prophecy contains only limited insight (13:9)? Questions like these and others have often been posed. They condition the manifold picture of the interpretation of this chapter in the same way as the theological positions of the exegetes, which influence the interpretation more directly than in hardly any other Pauline text.

Nowhere else in his letters does the apostle begin with so personal an introduction as here (Rom. 9:1–5). With its closing praise of God (v. 5) it is already preparing for the final hymn in 11:33–36, probably newly formulated by Paul for this purpose. The thus indicated unity of Romans 9–11, which can also be supported through the train of thought, the kind of argumentation, and the comprehensive and planned use of scripture, leaves us to inquire about the placement of the chapters in the Letter to the Romans. In any case, if Romans 9–11 were missing, it would never occur to a reader of the letter—especially judging from the

other Pauline letters—that something was omitted at this point. Romans
1–8 does not require such a continuation. Also the connecting links
from chs. 1–8 to chs. 9–11 are anything but obvious. There is no clear
preparation for the Israel chapters in the preceding part of Romans. The
clearest reference—namely, the comment on the special position of
Israel in Rom. 3:1–8—is a good touchstone. Israel's merits are treated in
such a way that they are suspended for the unbelieving Israel (v. 3)
through its being shown its place with sinful humanity (3:9–20), if
indeed the Israelites forfeit the covenant sign of circumcision through
their sinning (2:25). There is no trace of a special loyalty of God to the
still unbelieving Israel. Thus the way is prepared for Romans 9–11 at
best indirectly through the same basic theme but not directly through a
preliminary announcement of the special problem.

What is it, then, that connects Romans 9–11 with the Roman letter in
general? It lies in Paul's situation and his intention to visit the Roman
church after the Jerusalem journey. Paul is known for the fact that his
Gentile-Christian theology is emphatically critical of the law. As a result
he must defend against reproaches in this direction (cf. Gal. 2:17, 21;
Rom. 3:31; 6:1, 15; 7:7). From such pointedly Gentile-Christian theology
his opponents can quickly conclude that he is biased with regard to
Jewish Christians and against Israel and would not respect their priority
in the history of salvation. This nourishes distrust and hostility against
him. Therefore he not only looks forward uneasily to the turning over
of the Jerusalem collection (Rom. 15:31–32) but must also make clear
especially to the Gentile Christians of Rome addressed in Romans 9–11
(cf. 11:13, 17–21, 28–31) that—and how—he stands for the unity of the
church of Jews and Gentiles and in the history of Israel does not deny
the divine gifts to the people of God. He does not want to travel in the
western Roman Empire as the controversial missionary to the Gentiles,
but as a theologically accepted apostle, knowing that at the present
time his coming Jerusalem journey in the East places the problems of
his person and theology in the limelight of Christendom. Whatever
may happen in Jerusalem, he wants beforehand in black and white, as
it were, to make the Roman church witnesses to his personal, quite
honest lament for Israel (Rom. 9:1–5) and his hope (Rom. 11:11ff.) for
the people from whom he himself came. Against the background of
this entire situation we also understand why Paul in Romans stressed
so much Israel's priority in the history of salvation (Rom. 1:16; 3:1–2;
9:4–5), without disregarding Israel's lostness (Rom. 3:9). Paul wants to
show that his understanding of the gospel does include Israel.

It is important to see how the apostle sets about this task. He begins
with the guiding thought that God's promises (Rom. 9:4–5, 6a) cannot

fail. The substantiation for such an assertion is taken so much for granted by Paul and his readers that it does not have to be presented. Later it will be formulated thus: "The gifts and the call of God are irrevocable" (Rom. 11:29). On this faithfulness of God rests the calling of the Christian church (1 Cor. 1:9; 10:13; 1 Thess. 5:24). As God himself, even faced with the unfaithfulness of the church, remains faithful because he cannot deny himself (cf. 2 Tim. 2:13), so must this faithfulness of God also provide the basis for explaining the election of Israel. So the theme of God's faithfulness is not only a question concerning Israel but the foundation of the church of Jews and Gentiles (Rom. 9:24). The salvation of all people is basically founded on the faithfulness of God.

Paul answers this question about the divine faithfulness first by distinguishing between the people of Israel and Israel according to the promise, for in his view God's promises of salvation are not valid for every descendant of Abraham. They refer to the bearers of the promise (Rom. 9:6b–8). God determined these bearers by virtue of his own purpose in election, so that Jacob was the one who was loved but Esau the one hated (Rom. 9:9–13). At this point Paul, with his reflections about God, is pushing into the realm of double predestination (Rom. 9:14–21), toward which his theology does not otherwise really lean. Right afterward he is already following his basic theological line again when, on the basis of the sequence send-proclaim-hear-believe-be saved (Rom. 10:8–17), he sees the election process together with the God who calls in the gospel (cf. Gal. 1:6; 3:1–5). Yet for Paul the two statements are not antitheses. The description of the historical offer of grace and the grasping of the "depths of God" (1 Cor. 2:10) cannot be played out against each other. Paul needs the absolute free choice of God, because it must remain the choice of grace (Rom. 11:5). From this viewpoint Paul reaches a first conclusion: God's faithfulness has not failed, because the church of Jews and Gentiles is the bearer of the promise of Israel (Rom. 9:24), and here the Jewish Christians in particular, as the remnant of Israel, witness that God's concern for Abraham-Israel is fulfilled (Rom. 9:22–29).

But what can be said, then, about unbelieving Israel? In an especially tight chain of argumentation and with the means of his message of justification developed in Romans 3–4, Paul describes how Israel, persistently refusing the gospel because of its misdirected zeal about God himself, is now depriving itself of access to the gospel, which alone is God's gracious offer of deliverance (9:30–10:21). Thus unbelieving Israel itself bears the blame when it persists in unbelief, for the gospel does not fail to address it. Certainly deliverance does not lie in someone's will and exertion (9:16); in the gospel, however, the merciful God is also now close to Israel (9:16b; 10:12, 18), so that Israel's rejection of the gospel is its own responsibility. The Old Testament already witnesses that through Gentile Christians accepting the gospel God intends to make Israel "jealous" (10:19–20) but at the same time has not expelled Israel because, of course, Jewish Christians as Israel's remnant have come and are coming to the gospel (11:1–10).

If Paul had ended his presentation with this last thought, he would still have replaced the confrontational opposition between church and Israel with a new style. This is witnessed by the personal basis (9:1–5; 10:1) and the intensive search for reasons. Already judgment of Israel is no longer expressed as final. The hope that Israel might abandon its misdirected zeal for God and still come to the saving gospel shapes the presentation (10:1, 9–13). Here everything for Israel's repentence is historically still open. Naturally in this effort for Israel Paul brings in his own standpoint and his evaluation of all unbelief, including that of Israel. Anyone like Paul who on the basis of Christ so fundamentally devalues his positive past as an Israelite (Phil. 3:4–11) will not forget also to illuminate these same "privileges" of Israel on the basis of Christ. Paul is certainly not carrying out a neutral comparison of religions, nor does he assume an equal status of Israelite worship of God and Christian faith. His faith, which is determined by unambiguous positions, leaves no room for such possibilities. Anyone who sees God's election of all people as coming through Christ and faith, and understands precisely this as the content of the promise to Israel, cannot deny what he is moved by and what he hopes for. In relation to Romans, Paul has not forgotten what he presented in Romans 1–8.

Romans 11:11–32, nonetheless, goes beyond these statements. In the center of these verses, in 11:25–26, are concrete statements on Israel's future. These two verses should first be treated in terms of form and function, and only then in terms of content. Verse 25 presents itself as a prophetic word (*mystery*—cf. 1 Cor. 15:51). It is left open whether it is a revelation to Paul himself (cf. 2 Cor. 12:8–9) or a saying quoted from a (Jewish-Christian?) prophet (cf. 1 Thess. 2:15–16; 4:15–17). In any case, Paul agrees with the statement and probably understands it in connection with his petition to God for Israel's deliverance (Rom. 9:1–6; 10:1). A possible self-sacrifice by Paul on behalf of Israel remains impossible (9:3; cf. Ex. 32:32), yet an eschatological act of deliverance by the sovereign God himself, announced in a prophetic revelation, creates a way out of Israel's current hopelessness, so that the principle that God cannot revoke his means of grace (Rom. 11:29) is also honored in the fate of Israel.

The prophetic word in Rom. 11:25 is best comprehended as a three-part saying, whose emphasis and aim lie at the end:

> A hardening has come upon [only a] part of Israel,
> until the full number of the Gentiles come in,
> and so all Israel will be saved.

To this word Paul has added—as he does especially often in Romans 9–11—a scriptural quotation, which is recognizable as a mixture from Isa. 59:20–21; 27:9:

> As it is written,
> "The Deliverer will come from Zion,
> he will banish ungodliness from Jacob";
> "and this will be my covenant with them
> when I take away their sins."

It will be good first to consider prophetic word and scriptural quotation separately.

This inspired saying announces a revision of the widespread and tacitly assumed view that unbelieving Israel is lost. Hence it is clear that the saying also stands against the prophetic word of judgment in 1 Thess. 2:15–16. Romans 11:25 is a saying that, within the end time in which the election of the Gentiles is now being accomplished through the gospel (cf. 1 Thessalonians in 6.2 above; Rom. 13:11), expects something special to happen to Israel (cf. the analogous form in Mark 13:10). The Israel that has stood apart from the gospel being proclaimed to the world, which until now has only partially accepted this message—namely, in the form of the Jewish Christians—will only remain hardened until the full number of the Gentiles determined by God (and known to no one) have gone in (to the divine glory, or to life). Then immediately before the end of all things the hardening will yet be taken from Israel. In this way—namely, after the completed Gentile mission and before the end—"all Israel" (cf. *b. Sanh.* 10:1; Acts 2:36; 13:24) will be saved. "All Israel" does not mean simply the sum of all members of the Jewish people but is to be seen in connection with only the current partial hardening of Israel. Israel will go into life not only in the form of the few Jewish Christians who believe up to now but in a much more comprehensive and qualified way, so that an unknown, but representative number of Israelites will participate in the final salvation.

This eschatological event announced in advance in the word of the prophet, which is basically clear but less distinct in its details, is now, in the conception of many exegetes, determined more closely by the scriptural word. From Zion—that is, from the heavenly Jerusalem (Gal. 4:26)—Christ will come as deliverer (1 Thess. 1:10) and take away the sins of Israel. This Parousia-Christ is sent by God, who in this way forms the covenant between himself and Israel, in that he (through Christ) takes away the sins of Israel. This would then indeed be a special path, apart from the gospel, to the eschatological deliverance of Israel. It would be Christ-centered and purely gracious, though whether accepted in faith by Israel, the text does not say. Yet we probably must distinguish between, on the one hand, the concern of the text, the eschatological triumph of divine grace, which is stopped neither by the lostness of the Gentiles nor by the hardening of Israel, and, on the other, the textual concretion of especially this understanding of Rom. 11:26. It is one thing to say with Paul in Rom. 11:32, in contrast to 1 Thess. 2:15–16: "For God has consigned all men to disobedience, that he may have mercy upon all," and then to worship this theological perception in the praise of Rom. 11:33–36 (cf. 8:38–39); it is another to ask: Exactly what, in Paul's view, is concretely being asserted in Rom. 11:25–26?

If we examine this last question, it is clear that Paul inserted 11:25–27 not least of all in order to make clear to the Gentile Christians the gracious nature of their election (11:23, 25c): They have no reason to look down on Israel's remaining apart from the gospel. For it was Israel's holding back that brought the gospel to the Gentiles. Conversely, the apostle, precisely as apostle to the Gentiles, wants his missionary work to stimulate his own people to emulation (11:13–14). Thus he is far from withholding the gospel from them and not attracting them to it. Then, however, it requires effort to understand the quotation in 11:26–27 in the sense indicated above: Does a special eschatological act of God not make the present proclamation of the gospel to Israel superfluous? Where else does Paul have a statement that the salvific work of Christ also works apart from the proclaimed gospel? Is it not now the end time for him, because this very gospel is preached and it alone is the content of this time (2 Cor. 6:1–2)? Where is there the slightest hint in Paul that it is suspended as folly to the Gentiles and a scandal to the Jews (1 Cor. 1:18–24)? Does this not give rise to considerable tension with Romans 1–8 (cf., programmatically, 1:14) and not least of all with 9:1–11:10 (cf. 10:9, 12 and esp. 11:23)? We cannot prematurely systematize Paul. If without doubt he wants to be understood thus in Rom. 11:25–27, we must acknowledge this exegetically.

The interpretation reported above, however, conceals within it substantial problems. The difficulties begin with the fact that nowhere else does the Parousia-Christ come "from Zion." He comes "from heaven" (1 Thess. 1:10), and he "delivers" those who already believe in the gospel (1 Thess. 1:9–10), not the formerly unbelieving. Of course, Paul speaks once of the "Jerusalem above," but in antithesis to the present one (Gal. 4:25–26—in Rom. 15:19, 25–26, 31; 1 Cor. 16:3 the present one is intended) and, furthermore, in adoption of a traditional exegesis (Gal. 4:25–26). So it is very questionable whether one may infer from this text to Rom. 11:26. It is more sensible, rather, to consult the only other passage in which Paul talks about Zion, which, moreover, stands in a neighboring context, namely, in Rom. 9:33. There the present earthly Zion is intended. Once our attention is drawn to this relationship, we find the following connection: If Israel is presently stumbling over the preached Christ (9:32–33), then there will come a time (11:25–26) when the preaching of Christ will also effect the deliverance of Israel. It will do it because of its content, for it speaks of the Christ, whom God has put forward for redemption (3:24–26), and is therefore the "power of God" for the deliverance of all who believe (1:16). We may add that the confessional formula in 3:24–26 represents covenant theology and thus in this respect also agrees with 11:26–27. With this we also circumvent at the same time a further difficulty, namely, the singularity of a covenant statement that should relate to the end of all things. Otherwise for Paul only Christ's destiny and covenant reality go together (cf. 4:24–25; 1 Cor. 11:25; cf. 2 Cor. 3:1ff.; Gal. 3:6ff.).

We must see, further, that the interpretation in Rom. 11:26–27 in terms of the Parousia-Christ rests on two untested presuppositions: on the assumption that the introductory "as it is written" is to be understood as explaining and concretizing, and on the interpretation of the future verb forms in terms of the future still to come. Neither is compelling or absolutely obvious. The quotation formula has a substantiating task, for example, in Rom. 9:13, 33; 11:8; and elsewhere, and the prophetic future verb forms in 9:25–28, 33; 10:6, 13, 19; etc. refer to the present time. If we assume that these two statements are also true for 11:26–27, then the mixed quotation tells us why through the Christ event deliverance instead of offense (9:33) is possible for Israel—indeed, both were already long since attested in the scripture. If we now remember further that only through the scriptural quotation is the Parousia-Christ brought into the understanding of the prophetic word in 11:25, and that the latter itself speaks more generally, then we must interpret the Pauline understanding of the same in its context of 11:11–32 as a whole, and not base it only on 11:26–27. Now, this context gives no indication in 11:12, 15, 23–24, 31–32 that Israel would receive a last offering of salvation independent of the gospel. On the contrary, as the Gentiles were grafted onto the vine because of the gospel, so it can also happen again to Israel in the task of unbelief (v. 23), which now lives in enmity to God for the sake of the gospel (v. 28). According to 10:1ff., such delivering faith expressly comes only from the gospel. If Israel, according to 11:15, receives its renewed acceptance only as "life from the dead," then this recalls 4:17–18, that is, the justification by faith offered in the gospel, as it is given with the destiny of Jesus Christ (4:24–25). So Paul is talking in 11:25ff. about a last mission to Israel, which will take place before the end and after the proclamation to the Gentiles. Perhaps we can make it more concrete: When Paul wrote the Letter to the Romans, he had just closed his mission in the East and was now turning to the West (15:23–24). Following this mission and before the end of all things, he expected one last proclamation of the gospel to Israel which clearly has more success than the present one, which is already leading a few Jewish Christians to the church of God.

Now, however, we must add yet another line of thought. Whether for the sake of the context and in agreement with Pauline theology we interpret the questionable section as a last mission to Israel, or whether in tension with the rest of Pauline theology we find the assertion of a special granting of the Parousia-Christ to Israel, the prophetic saying must still undergo a fundamental discussion. It belongs to those few early Christian prophecies that announce details in the apocalyptic timetable, just as, for example, Mark 13:10 announces the missionizing of the world, 2 Thess. 2:3–8; 1 John 2:18, 22; etc. the "antichrist," and Revelation 20 the thousand-year reign. Such assertions were able to gain acceptance neither in early Christianity nor in Christian dogma. They belong in the conceptual context that from Daniel through *1 Enoch* and *Assumption of Moses* to *4 Ezra* and *2 Apocalypse of Baruch* (etc.) imagined the future historically and then was overtaken by history, as was the imminent expectation of early Christianity even in its own time. To the extent that Rom. 11:25–27 describes a bit of the future within the near expectation (13:12; 2 Cor. 6:1–2), the concept of the eschatological interweaving of Gentile and Jewish mission in Romans 11 falls in this category. To see these contexts and draw conclusions from them is a part of the testing of the prophetic spirit (1 Cor. 12:10). By its own self-evaluation early Christian prophecy is imperfect (1 Cor. 13:9), and even when it comes from Paul himself, or is favorably quoted, it must be tested as to whether it safeguards the function of establishing nearness to the salvific significance of the destiny of Jesus Christ and the hope to be based there.

15.3 The Martyr on the Road to Rome

In spite of the impressive presentation in Acts 23:12–28:31, there is an especially meager flow of historically usable information for this period in Paul's life. For, Luke, with the few traditions available to him here at the close of his work, again exploits all the creative means at his command. The result is an imposing, scenically structured course of events, which nonetheless bears little resemblance to what really happened. First, with the help of a nephew of Paul's, a Jewish plot against the imprisoned apostle is uncovered, which causes the Roman tribune of the Jerusalem garrison to take Paul, under exaggerated security measures, to Felix, the governor in Caesarea (23:12–35). A few days later the trial begins. The high priest Ananias, some elders, and a spokesman bring the accusation; Paul defends himself, but Felix postpones the decision (24:1–23). Indictment and defense are shaped by Luke as literary models of ancient courtroom speeches. In content both correspond to the typical Lukan conception of relations between Paul, the Jews, and the Romans.

For Luke, naturally, so famous a prisoner—as also attested in other ancient literature—must have been visited by high-ranking people. Hence Felix and his wife Drusilla come now (24:24–27), Agrippa with his wife Bernice later (25:23–26:32), in order to talk with Paul. These are welcome occasions for Luke to have Paul present his teachings—according to Luke's conception. In the process the author of Acts can describe for a third time Paul's life story, with his calling at its center (cf. 9:1ff.; 22:3ff.; 26:9–10). The reader will note how Luke clarifies here a special concern in his presentation. Then for no real reason Felix has Paul remain under arrest for two years pending trial. That an unconvicted Roman citizen could remain so long in prison without movement toward a trial is probably questionable from what we know of legal history. If one really believes of Felix that he perhaps hoped for a secret ransoming of Paul (24:26), this does not improve the legal situation. It is also the pure speculation of historians when they attempt on the grounds of the characterization of Felix by Josephus (*Antiquities* 20.8.9) to name Felix's poor and anti-Jewish administration as the reason for Paul's long imprisonment.

During the lengthening period of imprisonment the office of governor changes from Felix to Festus. It cannot be dated with certainty because of disagreements between Josephus (*Antiquities* 2.8.9) and Tacitus (*Annals* 13.2, 14), but probably occurred in A.D. 59 or 60. According to Luke, Festus turns his attention to Paul very soon and sits in judgment over him (25:1–12). There is no guilty verdict. Yet in response to Festus's suggestion to have Paul tried a second time in

Jerusalem, Paul appeals to the emperor in Rome. This is again problematic in terms of legal history. Either Paul is turned over to the Jews for judgment, and then Rome has no interest in the case and understands it as an internal affair of the Jewish religion; in such a procedure, however, an appeal to the imperial court of appeals in Rome is impossible. Or Festus sees Roman law involved, and then he must pass judgment. Only after a guilty verdict can Paul appeal to the emperor. Yet Luke has the unconvicted Paul appeal to Rome. So Paul comes to Rome as a prisoner awaiting trial who has appealed to the emperor. A remand of Paul's case to Jerusalem, however, is probably also difficult, for logically Paul would be released if Festus found the prisoner not guilty in terms of Roman law. So, was Paul nonetheless condemned by the governor? The next higher court could then come into play, with the consequence that Paul would be brought to Rome as a condemned prisoner. This course of events probably deserves serious consideration.

However one tries to make sense to this legal-historical thicket, Luke, in any case, achieves his aim: with increasing clarity the Jews are portrayed as those who desire Paul's death. The Romans on the whole are favorably inclined toward Paul. If they did not behave correctly in terms of the trial, no complaint is made, nor are popular stories disturbed at all. Paul himself is constantly in the middle of the action, is able to present his faith, and is not convicted. In this way he comes to Rome—and thus the gospel (cf. Acts 1:8; 2:39). It is important here that Paul be able to appear in Rome relatively unhindered and in part as a free man (28:1–10, 14, 16, 17ff.). This fits with the judgment unanimously given by Festus, Agrippa, his wife, and all who listened to Paul's lengthy comments in the municipal audience hall in Caesarea: "This man is doing nothing to deserve death or imprisonment. . . . This man could have been set free" (26:31–32). This is exactly what Luke wants to achieve: that Paul should be free in Rome and able to missionize without suspicion of state-threatening intrigues.

Luke takes this journey from Caesarea to Italy as an occasion to describe vividly the adventure of such a trip to the reader, in accordance with the taste of the time. At the beginning of the journey the Roman centurion and his group of prisoners took an ocean freighter, which sailed along the Asia Minor coast. In Myra they found an Alexandrian ship with plans to sail to Italy. They changed ships but made only slow progress until between Crete and southern Italy they ran into a severe storm. Shipwrecked, they saved themselves on Melita, which as a rule is identified with Malta, but by which the narrator perhaps means Cephalonia, an island west of Patras (27:1–44). It has long since been recognized that one can easily remove the Paul passages in this story (27:3b, 9–11, 21–26, 31, 33–36, 43a), thus eliminating some uneven places in the text and producing a general report of an ancient sea voyage, which Luke apparently used. Hence there is practically nothing historically usable in this chapter. The same must also be true of the Lukan description of the stay in Melita (28:1–10), where Paul appears as a holy man, whom a snakebite cannot affect, and a miracle worker for the benefit of the island residents. Miracles on the journeys of divinely graced men likewise belong to the repertoire of fictional literature about such figures. An example is provided by Apollonius of Tyana, a contemporary of Paul.

After wintering in Melita they then traveled via Syracuse (on the east coast of Sicily) and Rhegium (at the "boot tip" of southern Italy) to the harbor of Puteoli, which at that time had not yet been replaced by Ostia in its significance as Rome's seaport. On the contrary, at that time Puteoli was the largest harbor in the western half of the Roman Empire and had, among other things, a yearly turnover of more than 200,000 tons of Egyptian grain—above all for the provisioning of Rome. When Luke has Paul received by a Christian church in Puteoli, we may infer that at least in Luke's time Christians lived there. From Puteoli one can then walk the usual transportation routes via the Forum Appii and Tres Tabernae to Rome. On this road Paul meets Roman Christians. Then in Rome he is able to move about relatively freely (Acts 28:11–16). This whole travel route is also typical and familiar in antiquity. Thus Luke had all he needed in the knowledge of this trade route and a few decorative bits of information to honor Paul through two churches, who meet him in ways normal for the culture of the time. With good reason, therefore, the opinion has often been put forth that in 28:1–2, 7, 10b, 11–13 lies the rest of the ancient travel report that is recognizable in Acts 27. This makes 28:1–16 worthless for a historical reconstruction of the concrete conditions of Paul's journey.

Acts 28:17–31, the report on Paul's stay in Rome, is also shaped by Luke alone as the conclusion of Acts. Luke wants to describe the path of the gospel as divine plan. Therefore the death of Paul, with which Luke is familiar (19:21; 20:23–25; 21:11), is never mentioned. In Rome there is no trial, either, so that the reason for the long and arduous journey from Jerusalem to Rome has curiously disappeared from the narrative. Thus Luke again avoids a Roman condemnation of Paul, because he advocates a good relationship between the state and the Christian churches. Imprisonment and journey become merely the means for having Paul pursue his mission unhindered in Rome. So there is no meeting with the Christian churches in Rome, either—in spite of the reception by Roman Christians (28:15). Instead, Paul does in Rome what according to Acts he had always done in his mission, following the same schema. He first makes contact with the local synagogue. This meeting is developed here through, among other things, the discussion of the Jerusalem events. Since the Jews, however, then reject his gospel, Paul turns, as usual, to the Gentiles. This gives the impression that it was Paul who first founded a Christian church in Rome. Whether in view of this rather forced construction in 28:17ff. we can give historical credence to the note that Paul was able to missionize unhindered in Rome two whole years (28:30–31) is rather doubtful, especially since shortly before (24:27) Luke uses a similar length of time.

If in closing we again review Acts 23:12–28:31 as a whole, the historical yield is unfortunately extremely meager. We must conclude that Luke knew very little about Paul from the arrest in Jerusalem to the execution in Rome. Probably a general Paul legend about this period could not arise because there were no Christian eyewitnesses who could nourish its development. At best we can assume that fellow Christians had contact with the prisoner Paul in Caesarea and Rome. For the prisoner transfer itself, that can probably be excluded. It is likely that Paul was mostly left to himself and separated from his coworkers and Christian churches. The little bit of information that remains can be quickly summarized from Acts and little expanded: As a Roman prisoner Paul was brought from Jerusalem to Caesarea. There his trial dragged out so long that his imprisonment lasted beyond the change of governors from Felix to Festus. He appears to have been condemned by Festus. He appealed to the Roman imperial court and thus went as a prisoner to Rome. He probably lived yet some time in the imperial capital but was then executed—probably with the sword, because he was a Roman. This is also given in the late *Acts of Paul* as the kind of death, while Hippolytus in his Daniel commentary speaks of an animal fight. Thus his desire for judicial review was unsuccessful. We will not err if we place his death early in the sixth decade A.D., that is, under Nero but still before persecution of Christians in A.D. 64. The journey to Spain, which he was still planning as a free man in Corinth (Rom. 15:24, 28), was no doubt thwarted by these happenings, just as many of the apostle's earlier travel plans had to be given up because of new events. If Luke had known anything about the trip to Spain, he would probably have gladly reported the apostle's release and had Paul pursue his mission in Rome and from there to the western boundary of the then known world. The mention of the Spanish journey in *1 Clem.* 5:7 (cf. also *Canon Muratori* 38) is probably inferred from Rom. 15:24, 28 and thus is not historical evidence of a Pauline stay in Spain.

This brings up the second passage that deserves attention when we consider the end of Paul's life. For *1 Clement* was written from Rome to Corinth toward the end of the first Christian century and thus comes from about the same period as Acts. It could even be the oldest evidence for Paul's death. The text reads: "Because of jealousy and strife Paul showed the prize of patience: Seven times he wore chains, was driven out, stoned, became herald in the East and in the West, and received the genuine fame of his faith. He taught righteousness to the whole world and came to the boundaries of the West and witnessed before the holders of power. Thus he departed the world and reached the holy place and became the greatest model of patience" (*1 Clem.* 5.5–7).

The text follows a similar description of Peter and in the typical style of ancient athletics turns the lives of the two apostles into an exemplary life struggle, which is supposed to serve Christians for emulation. Both end this struggle as apostolic martyrs (*1 Clem.* 5.4, 7) and therefore after death directly attain the "holy place"; that is, they are taken up into heaven. Of course, the text does not say directly that Paul died specifically in Rome, but *1 Clem.* 6.1 seems tacitly to assume this for Peter and Paul. Since, moreover, in the whole ancient church there is no tradition contradicting Rome for both apostles, Acts is apparently correct in giving Rome as Paul's last place of residence.

This understanding of things excludes another assumption, according to which Paul became free again in Rome, visited Spain, returned to Rome, and landed in prison again. Only this second Roman imprisonment—first assumed by Eusebius (*Church History* 2.22.2) and then often repeated—is supposed to have ended with the death of the apostle. But this is a harmonizing construction that is borne by the intention to combine the Acts of the Apostles with the Letter to the Romans and above all to anchor the pastoral epistles (1 and 2 Timothy, Titus) in the life of Paul. For the various situations presupposed in the pastorals are claimed to have happened during the period Rome-Spain-Rome. These letters, however, nowhere presuppose such a sequence of events and are so un-Pauline in their theological stance that they cannot possibly have come from Paul.

Hence the historian can only give scant information about the final days of the apostle to the Gentiles. In contrast, say, to the death of Socrates, it is still true of numerous figures of antiquity that all traces of their death have disappeared. This makes Paul's epistolary testimonies shine all the brighter even today. They have not only made theological history but also influenced the history of the world.

Abbreviations

'Abot	'Abot Tractate
Apoc. Abr.	Apocalypse of Abraham
2 Apoc. Bar.	Syriac Apocalypse of Baruch
Apoc. Sedr.	Apocalypse of Sedrach
b.	(before title of tractate) Babylonian Talmud
Barn.	Letter of Barnabas
CD	Cairo (Genizah text of the) Damascus (Document)
1 Clem.	First Letter of Clement
Did.	Didache
1 Enoch	Ethiopic Enoch
Ignatius	
Eph.	Letter to the Ephesians
Magn.	Letter to the Magnesians
Phld.	Letter to the Philadelphians
Rom.	Letter to the Romans
Trall.	Letter to the Trallians
Jub.	Jubilees
Lib. Ant.	Liber Antiquitatum Biblicarum
Polycarp	
Phil.	Letter to the Philippians
Pss. Sol.	Psalms of Solomon
Qumran	
1QM	Milhamah (War Scroll)
4QpNah	Pesher on Nahum
1QpHab	Pesher on Habakkuk
4QpPs 37	Pesher on Psalm 37
1QS	Serek hayyahad (Rule of the Community, Manual of Discipline)
1QSa	Appendix A (Rule of the Congregation) to 1QS
Sanh.	Sanhedrin Tractate
Sir.	Sirach (Ecclesiasticus)
Sota	Sota Tractate
Testaments of the Twelve Patriarchs	
T. Levi	Testament of Levi
T. Dan	Testament of Dan
T. Benj.	Testament of Benjamin

Index of Passages Cited

Index of Places

Index of Persons